JOE ESZTERHAS

HOLLYWOOD ANIMAL

Joe Eszterhas is the author of *American Rhapsody* and *Charlie Simpson's Apocalypse*, which was nominated for the National Book Award. His fifteen films include *Basic Instinct, Flashdance, Jagged Edge, Telling Lies in America, Showgirls, Sliver, Jade, Music Box, Betrayed, F.I.S.T.,* and *An Alan Smithee Film: Burn Hollywood Burn.* He lives in Bainbridge Township, Ohio, with his wife and four sons. He is also the father of two grown children from his first marriage.

ALSO BY JOE ESZTERHAS

American Rhapsody

Charlie Simpson's Apocalypse

Nark

HOLLYWOOD
ANIMAL

HOLLYWOOD ANIMAL

A MEMOIR

JOE ESZTERHAS

VINTAGE BOOKS
A Division of Random House, Inc.
New York

FIRST VINTAGE BOOKS EDITION, MARCH 2005

Copyright © 2004 by Joe Eszterhas

All rights reserved under International and Pan-American Copyright
Conventions. Published in the United States by Vintage Books, a division
of Random House, Inc., New York. Originally published in hardcover in the
United States by Alfred A. Knopf, a division of Random House, Inc.,
New York, in 2004.

Vintage and colophon are registered trademarks of Random House, Inc.

The Library of Congress has cataloged the Knopf edition as follows:
Eszterhas, Joe.
Hollywood Animal / Joe Eszterhas.—1st ed.
p. cm.
1. Eszterhas, Joe. 2. Screenwriters—United States—Biography.
3. Hollywood (Los Angeles, Calif.)—Biography.
4. Motion picture industry—United States. I. Title.
PS355.S98Z467 2004
812'.54—dc22 2003060246

Vintage ISBN: 0-375-71895-8

Book design by Virginia Tan

www.vintagebooks.com

Printed in the United States of America
10 9 8 7 6 5 4 3 2 1

For Steve, Suzi, Joey,

Nick, John Law, Luke . . . Suzanne Perryman . . .

and Naomi, Sunlight

If freedom is truth and love,
then love is truth and freedom.

—István Eszterhás,
"The Last Poem"

CONTENTS

HOLLYWOOD ANIMAL

CHAPTER 1

The King of Point Doom

KARCHY

I wanna show off the car. I wanna show *you* off.

DINEY

Why do you have to show off all the time?

KARCHY

I ain't got that much to show.

Telling Lies in America

I

My great-grandfather grew up a poor kid in a tiny village in Hungary. He was about to be drafted into the Austro-Hungarian army and he fled to America. He worked as a miner in Pennsylvania for a while but didn't like the work. He went out to the American West and became a stage-coach robber. He became wealthy. He rode with Black Bart and Jesse James.

I grew up a poor kid in the refugee camps of Austria and on the West Side of Cleveland, Ohio. I worked as a furniture mover, a disc jockey, and a newspaper reporter, but I didn't like the work. I went out to the American West and became a screenwriter.

I rode with a whole lot of famous hombres.

I sold screenplays in Hollywood for record amounts of money.

My agent, Guy McElwaine, referred to these sales as "bank heists."

My wife, Naomi, wore a leather strap of silver bullets around one of her cowboy boots when I met her.

And when she knew she had fallen in love with me, she gave me the strap of silver bullets and tied them around one of *my* cowboy boots.

The day I married her, I wore her silver bullets.

. . .

My great-grandfather took his fortune and went back to the village in Hungary where he had grown up. Old crones wearing black babushkas said they saw him through the cellar windows of his castle playing cards by candlelight with the devil.

He had sold his soul to the devil in the American West and was trying to win it back now.

When I was a screenwriter in Hollywood, the *Los Angeles Free Press* wrote that I had sold *my* soul to the devil.

A columnist in South Dakota wrote that I was "in the devil's employ."

A Canadian magazine wrote that I was "a devil living in Malibu."

My hometown newspaper, the *Cleveland Plain Dealer,* wrote about me with a headline that said, "Eszterhas—Ordinary Joe or Satan's Agent?"

A cartoon in *Entertainment Weekly* showed the devil's hand on my shoulder and these words: "December 31, 1999—The Devil Takes Formal Possession of Joe Eszterhas' Soul."

A secretary at Paramount who liked to wear Blessed Virgin Mary T-shirts had a vision of me.

I was ascending from the putrid steam of a black-water pond.

And shortly after her vision, during the making of the movie *Sliver,* the actor Billy Baldwin and I were walking down Melrose Avenue in Los Angeles heading into a bar owned by the actor Tony Danza's brother.

A bag lady approached us, took one look at me, made the sign of the cross, and turned around and ran in the other direction.

"Wow!" Billy Baldwin said, "maybe you *are* the devil."

That secretary who liked to wear Blessed Virgin Mary T-shirts and said I was the devil worked for the producer Robert Evans.

My friend Robert Evans, as everyone in Hollywood knows, really *is* the devil.

Evans, the producer of *Sliver,* liked my *Sliver* script so much that he sent a voluptuous bimbo wearing only a mink coat over to my hotel. She pulled a note out of a certain intimate body part.

"Best first draft I've ever read," the note said. "Love, Evans."

The note smelled fantastic.

That mink coat she wore, I later discovered, belonged not to her but to Evans. He dressed all the girls in that same mink coat on the occasions when he was dispatching them as fragrant human telegrams.

11

Our house in the part of Malibu known as Point Dume overlooked the sea.

Wolfgang Puck's Granita, just down the road on the Pacific Coast Highway, catered our dinner parties. We bought our air-shipped white truffles at the Trancas Market, where Tom and Nicole shopped. We bought clothes for our four boys at Ninety-Nine Percent Angels, where Demi roamed with her team of nannies.

Sean Penn and Charlie Sheen and Emilio Estevez and Jan-Michael Vincent used to hang out at our neighborhood bar, the Dume Room. A few blocks south of us was a ramshackle little seafront house where William Saroyan once lived, collecting stones. So many stones that when he moved away, he needed *two* houses to store them.

Naomi and I and our little boys lived in our house by the sea. We had a swimming pool behind the house, a hot tub, a guesthouse.

We lived right across the street from Bob Dylan's house. Bob's roosters woke us each morning. His mastiffs left great heaping mountains of dog doo in front of our gate.

Buzz magazine picked Naomi and me as "two of the scariest people in Los Angeles" and as "the scariest couple in Los Angeles." Other "scariest people" were Michael Jackson, Barbra Streisand, Val Kilmer, Heidi Fleiss, John Tesh, and my producer pal Robert Evans. There were no other "scariest couples" nominated. Naomi and I won that category unanimously.

Naomi is part Polish and part Italian. She is the most beautiful woman I've ever met. She is also the smartest. She told me she will "hunt me down and kill me" if I ever cheat on her.

I will never cheat on her because she is my best friend and my wondrous lover. Also because I love her more than my children and I love my children more than anything in the world.

Naomi and I have four little boys: Joey, nine, Nick, six, John Law, four, and Luke, two.

"Dicks," Naomi said to me recently. "I wake up in the morning and all I see in every direction I look are dicks."

I have two grown children from my first marriage—Steve (also known as LaMon, also known as D. J. Rogue) is twenty-eight. He's a white African-American. He's the only white African-American member of the family, although Suzi, twenty-six (also known as Mo), spends a lot of time in Africa, photographing wildlife.

I think Suzi prefers wildlife to human beings.

I think she felt that way even before I left her mother, Gerri Javor, my first wife.

. . .

Even before we met, Naomi had spent months studying my face. She was a talented graphic artist and her boyfriend had given her a photograph of me and asked her to make a drawing of me as a Christmas present.

I thought her pencil portrait remarkable, especially my eyes. Naomi had drawn me with sad, wounded eyes.

You must understand why Naomi is the love of my life.

She grew up in Mansfield, Ohio, an hour away from Cleveland, where I grew up.

She was a cheerleader in high school, a Ramette—"a Ramit" is what they called them in Mansfield—who got straight As. She reads. She adores Edith Wharton and knows all of *Prufrock* by heart.

Her favorite meal in the world is McDonald's French fries.

She was voted "class tease" in high school.

Like me, she was a journalism major in college.

For many years she worked in public relations in New York for Time Warner and American Express.

Her specialty? *Damage control.*

An American friend of my father's drove me to Naomi's hometown, Mansfield, Ohio, from Cleveland when I was eleven years old. We visited the museum—home of a famous dead American writer named Louis Bromfield. The house was the biggest and most beautiful house I had ever seen in my life.

My father's American friend explained that if I, too, worked and studied like Looey Bromfield had worked and studied, I, too, could be a famous American writer one day and own a house as beautiful as this one.

After I met Naomi, I read a book about Looey Bromfield's life. Born in Mansfield, Looey left his hometown and spent many years in California and abroad, writing many best-selling books and Hollywood screenplays.

Approaching sixty, he then returned to Mansfield, Ohio, and bought the property that he called Malabar Farm. His friends Humphrey Bogart and Lauren Bacall got married there.

He never wrote any other best-selling books or big-buck screenplays and drank himself to death, dying in the ambulance on the way to the hospital in Cleveland.

There was a little hill on Malabar Farm called Oh Jesus Hill. Looey had named it that because he'd made love to the wealthy heiress Doris Duke on that hill and had said "Oh, Jesus!" at a certain moment.

Naomi's only visit to Malabar Farm was when she and her boyfriend visited it in high school.

Naomi claimed not to have visited Oh Jesus Hill but . . . *Oh, Jesus!* . . . I'm not sure I believed her.

I don't mean to sound insufferable, but . . .

I realized reading about Looey Bromfield that I'd written more successful screenplays than he and while he'd written many more best-selling books than I, I'd gotten a much bigger advance for *my* best-selling book than he'd gotten for any of his.

I also realized that my houses in Tiburon and Stinson Beach and Malibu were all bigger and more beautiful than the house I'd been so razzle-dazzled by as a child . . . Looey's relatively rinky-dink Malabar Farm in Mansfield, Ohio.

I had worked and studied like Looey Bromfield had worked and studied and had become a famous American writer like Looey . . . but I owned much bigger houses than Looey.

I was a Great American Success Story.

I had out-Looeyed Looey!

III

I was a militant, fanatical smoker. I smoked three to four packs of Salem Ultra Lites each day. I'd started smoking when I was twelve years old, thinking that those who smoked in the movies I liked so much—like *High School Confidential!*—with Jerry Lee Lewis—looked cool.

Now I was writing smoking into my movies, combining smoking with sex as in *Basic Instinct,* because I still thought smoking was cool.

Through the years, I'd smoked Marlboros and Gauloises and Luckies, even smoked a pipe for years, and then discovered menthol cigarettes, cool with a K. I'd worked my way down to Ultra Lites and didn't even have a smoker's cough in the morning.

My mother, a chain-smoker, died of cancer when she was fifty. Her mother, a chain-smoker, died of lung cancer at forty-five.

Naomi begged me to stop but her parents had been heavy smokers, too. Her father died when he was seventy-eight of complete respiratory arrest. Her mother's death was not smoking-related.

"Don't worry," I'd say to Naomi, "I'm going to be that little old guy you read the stories about, the one who's puffing away at a hundred and two."

A half hour before my mother died, she smoked her last cigarette. She was fifty years old.

I held it to her lips because her hands trembled so badly she couldn't hold it.

When she was finished smoking that cigarette, I left her room and went outside and smoked a couple of cigarettes myself.

Then I went back inside and held her hand.

She died holding my hand.

My hand was bleeding from how hard she had dug her fingernails into it.

My mother smoked Herbert Tareyton filters and then Viceroy filters, but only after she "purified" them.

She took each cigarette out of the pack and sliced the filter off it. Then she put the cigarettes back into the pack and took them out all day and smoked them that way.

I asked her why she didn't simply smoke unfiltered cigarettes but she said the unfiltered ones were too strong and filled with poisons.

She said the people at the cigarette factories purified their cigarettes in the process of putting filters on them and all she was doing was purifying them twice by slicing the filters.

That's why, my mother said, she didn't even have a smoker's cough in the morning.

Naomi's father, Barney Baka, smoked Viceroys, too, like my mother, but he didn't razor the filters off them.

After a lifetime of smoking, he never got cancer.

But he couldn't laugh. He coughed instead of laughing. He had a good sense of humor, so he coughed much of the time.

The morning my mother died, a hearse from the John J. Hriczo Funeral Home in Cleveland came to take her body away.

The two men from the funeral home had just gotten her body into the hearse and were ready to go . . . when the garbage truck came by for the weekly pickup.

The hearse had to stay in the driveway with my mother's body inside it as the garbagemen emptied out one garbage can after another.

For many years afterward, I dreamed about the hearse waiting for the garbagemen to empty the garbage cans.

The day my mother died, the roses she had so carefully cultivated at the back of our house in Cleveland Heights died as well. The roses in all of our neighbors' yards were alive and blooming.

After the worldwide success of *Basic Instinct*, a tobacco company released Basic cigarettes, no doubt inspired by the sex/smoking scenes in the movie.

Thanks to me, even more people in the world would be smoking.

Thanks to me, more people would die.

IV

Here are some other reasons Naomi is the perfect woman for me:

1. She rolls the best joints of any . . . of the very many . . . that I've toked.
2. She used to work pumping gas at the Sohio station on Crider Road in Mansfield.
3. She's hell on wheels on roller skates.
4. When she was a little girl, her mother addressed her as "The Little Devil."
5. In high school, she went to parties dressed as Marilyn Monroe.
6. She loves Madonna, and calls her "Madoo."
7. She keeps a journal.

Madonna almost played the part of Cristal in *Showgirls,* but Paul Verhoeven, the director, didn't like Madoo's script ideas.

Had Paul liked Madoo's ideas:

1. Then the critics would have liked *Showgirls* better because it would have been Madoo's script, not mine.
2. Then *Showgirls* may not have been one of the greatest clinkers of all time.

Besides Madoo, Paul Verhoeven nixed both Drew Barrymore and Sharon Stone for *Showgirls.*

He said Drew couldn't dance.

He said Sharon couldn't act.

I think he was lying about Sharon.

I think he was still angry that Sharon wouldn't have sex with him while they were shooting *Basic Instinct.*

Had *Showgirls* starred Madonna and Drew Barrymore instead of Gina Gershon and Elizabeth Berkley . . .

The script would have been very different, thanks to Madoo.

The acting would have been very different, thanks to Drew.

And it's just possible that *Showgirls* would have been a hit movie!

If the script had been Madonna's, then I probably wouldn't have called it "a deeply religious message."

Had I not called it "a deeply religious message," I probably wouldn't have issued a press release telling teenagers to bring their fake IDs to see it.

Had I not told teenagers to bring their fake IDs, I would have avoided making a colossal asshole of myself.

. . .

A hit movie! Showgirls! A hit movie!

You have no idea how happy that would have made me!

Because I had done something else tragically foolish, too.

I had named the lead character of *Showgirls* "Nomi" . . . *Nomi* . . . Naomi's childhood nickname . . . *Nomi* . . . the name I loved and was always going to call her in our most intimate moments.

Until the movie came out and disastered and turned my true love's childhood nickname into a national joke.

No more "Nomi"!

Now I never call the love of my life "Nomi" anymore!

For the record . . . what I was thinking by saying *Showgirls* has "a deeply religious message" was this:

At the end of the movie, Nomi Malone turns her back on stardom and leaves Vegas because of the amorality she has seen and experienced there.

She has become a star as the result of participating in that amorality . . . but rejects her stardom . . . and that amoral world . . . and gets back on the road, hitchhiking out of town . . . with her own billboard looming above her.

Whatever I was trying to do, I admit now that it was a dumb-ass thing to do.

For the record . . . what I was thinking by telling teenagers to bring their fake IDs to get into the theaters to see *Showgirls* was this:

1. There was nothing in the movie to harm them because I didn't believe that either four-letter words or naked body parts would do any harm to teenagers.
2. Since only those teenagers who look close to eighteen have fake IDs, I certainly wasn't calling for ten- or fourteen-year-olds to see it.
3. The movie, in my mind, for reasons I've explained above, has a moral message . . . it would be good for teenagers' values to see Nomi Malone rejecting stardom and money because of the amorality which was its cost.
4. It's impossible to show the rejection of an amoral world without showing the amoralities which make someone reject it.

Whatever I was thinking . . . I admit now that telling teenagers to bring their fake IDs to see *Showgirls* was a dumb-ass thing to say.

V

In the year 2000, I was fifty-six years old, a Hollywood screenwriter, the author of fifteen movies. Some of them (*Basic Instinct, Jagged Edge, Flashdance*) were some of the biggest box office hits of our time. Some (*Showgirls, Jade, Sliver*) were some of the biggest critical disasters in recent memory. Some were pretty good: *Music Box, F.I.S.T., Telling Lies in America, Betrayed.* Some were movies that I loved but few others did: *An Alan Smithee Film: Burn Hollywood Burn, Big Shots.* Some were movies that I hated: *Nowhere to Run, Hearts of Fire.*

My movies had grossed more than a billion dollars at the box office. I had made millions and millions of dollars writing them. I had sold one script for $3 million, another for $3.7 million, another for $4.7 million.

I was the only screenwriter in the history of Hollywood who had groupies.

I was one of the few screenwriters in the history of Hollywood who were paid more for writing their scripts than some directors were for directing them.

The *New York Times* headlined: "Big Bucks and Blondes—Joe Eszterhas Lives the American Dream."

ABC News called me "a living legend." And *Time* magazine asked this question: "If Shakespeare were alive today, would his name be Joe Eszterhas?"

I was "the Che Guevara of screenwriters" (*Variety*) and "the Andrew Dice Clay of screenwriters" (the *New York Times*).

Details magazine said, "He is a sexually transmitted disease."

Another *New York Times* article said, "In his own way, Mr. Eszterhas is as much an object of fantasy as Sharon Stone."

In a story about the rock group U2, the *Los Angeles Times* wrote: "Remember when people thought Bono just wanted to be God? Now he wants to be Joe Eszterhas."

I got two thousand fan letters a week.

The best fan letter I'd ever gotten came to me when I was a writer at *Rolling Stone* magazine in the seventies.

A young woman wrote: "Do you want to come to Mars with me and play?" It was addressed to "Ms. Esther Has."

When I knew I was falling in love with Naomi, twenty years later, I asked Naomi the same question: "Do you want to come to Mars with me and play?"

Fan letters and autographs and limos and groupies . . . I was in hog screenwriter heaven . . . I was insufferable!
How insufferable was I?
Well, I called one of my directors "a doddering old fuck."
How insufferable was I?
At a meeting with a group of studio executives, I said, "You guys better get your hands off my dick and stop diddling me."
I was wearing an International Brotherhood of Teamsters jacket as I said that. Underneath the jacket was a black T-shirt with the words: "My inner child is a mean little fuck."

How insufferable was I?

On my last movie, I wasn't content with screen credits for screenwriting and executive-producing. I insisted that the first credit to be shown on-screen say: "Joe Eszterhas presents."

How insufferable was I?

My hair was halfway down my back. I wore frayed jeans patched with red bandanas and a black hooded jacket with the words "Fuck You" at the top.

How insufferable was I?

I said to Robert Evans, "I'm not going to roll over and let him fuck me just because he's the director and happens to be married to the head of the studio! You've rolled over so many times that it doesn't even hurt anymore."

How insufferable was I?

When I said that to him, Evans was (and still is) a dear friend of mine.

I was such a big-shot screenwriter that, in San Rafael, California, as I was being wheeled into an ambulance after an artery in my nose burst . . .

I saw a man on the street with his son pointing to me.

"Look," the man said, "there! That's Joe Eszterhas!"

His son said, "Where?"

The man said, "*There! Bleeding.*"

I was such a big-shot screenwriter that I could even keep Mick Jagger waiting.

Mick was calling from Bali, trying to talk me into letting him get an early look at a script I had written about Otis Redding called *Blaze of Glory.*

I told him that I really couldn't do that . . . it wouldn't be fair to the other producers, etc., etc. . . . enjoying every moment of it as Mick started to charm and nearly beg to have a shot to produce it.

Here he was, Jumpin' Jack Flash, the ultimate rock star of my generation, begging just to be able to *read* my words.

So I finally said okay—he was, after all, Mick Jagger, the man every guy of my generation wanted to be. Naomi and I faxed every page of the script over to him in Bali and . . .

He didn't even call me back to tell me he didn't like it.

An assistant called three days later, to say that Mick had passed.

Oh, well, it was worth what had been my opening line to him: "*Please allow me to introduce myself, I'm a man of wealth and taste.*"

A couple years later, Mick Jagger came around again. He was interested this time in acting, not producing . . . playing Alan Smithee, the title character in *An Alan Smithee Film: Burn Hollywood Burn.*

His assistant called the producer of our film.

She said Mick had read the script and wanted to talk about it—not with me . . . but with the director, Arthur Hiller.

The producer, who was a Jagger fan, told the assistant Mick shouldn't meet with Arthur Hiller, who was in his seventies and hardly knew who Mick was.

Mick, the producer said, should meet with Joe Eszterhas, who was a Mick Jagger *freak* and who had all the juice on this movie.

The assistant spoke to Mick and called the producer back. Mick didn't want to meet with Joe Eszterhas, Mick said. Mick didn't have meetings with *screenwriters,* Mick had meetings with *directors.*

Besides, the assistant said, Mick had some script ideas. Maybe Arthur Hiller would hear them and decide to bring in a *new* screenwriter.

The producer told me what Mick Jagger's assistant had said and I asked Arthur Hiller if he wanted to meet with Mick.

"Not especially," Arthur Hiller said and tried to talk me into letting his friend Michael York play the part.

In my insufferable way, I told the producer . . . to tell Mick's assistant . . . to tell Mick, Jumpin' Jack Flash himself . . . to go fuck himself.

I was such a big-shot screenwriter that, in a little Mississippi town near Memphis, I accomplished something Tom Cruise and Danny DeVito couldn't do. I called my boyhood idol Jerry Lee Lewis, introduced myself, told him I was in town, and he said sure, come on over.

I heard later that Cruise and DeVito had made similar calls but Jerry Lee didn't like Cruise's work and he thought DeVito was "a pygmy," so he wouldn't see them.

When I got to his ranch, Jerry Lee came out from behind the steel door of the bedroom he spent most of his time in, wearing a white terry cloth robe and panda slippers. He had an unlighted Dunhill pipe in his mouth.

We looked like two aging geezers who'd seen too many miles of bumpy, potholed road. Two aging geezers who'd used too many unhealthy substances to cushion the bumps.

"*Basic Instinct*—that's one of my favorite movies," Jerry Lee Lewis said.

Then he said, "You know that shot where she sticks her whatchamacallit into the camera? Did they have to shoot that for a long time?"

"How does it feel," an assistant to a director said to me in those post-*Showgirls* days, "to be the most reviled man in America?"

I smiled and said, *insufferably,* "You mean I'm worse even than O.J.?"

She turned archly away and said nothing.

It didn't help that in the week after he was found not guilty and got out of jail, O. J. Simpson went to see two movies: *Showgirls* and *Jade*.

VI

I had very personal reasons for being insufferable.

Screenwriters historically have been treated like discarded hookers in Hollywood: not invited to the premieres of their own movies, cheated out of residual payments, blackballed for their political beliefs.

Many had been treated like hookers because they hooked—working, as the lawyer-turned-successful-screenwriter Ron Bass said, "to serve the director's vision."

I *wasn't* there to "serve the director's vision." As far as I was concerned, the vision was mine and the director was there to serve *it*: to translate *my* vision to the screen.

Film critics and film writers insisted that the director was the auteur of the film, even if the director didn't write the film . . . that a film was "by" Steven Spielberg and Martin Scorsese, not by Melissa Mathison and Paul Schrader. I knew that most film critics and film writers were failed screenwriters who sometimes even forced the screenplays they were clutching on the directors they interviewed . . . so I questioned film critics' motives: here they were, earning their paltry wages, living in their garrets, while screenwriters like me were earning fortunes and living on Maui and in Malibu.

I learned that I shouldn't expect praise from people who either turned green or livid at the mention of my name.

At a graduate school film seminar, Costa-Gavras was asked why one of the characters in *Music Box* behaved a certain way.

"Ask Joe," Costa-Gavras said. "He wrote him that way."

Then another grad student . . . and another . . . and another asked the same question.

"I realized they didn't understand," Costa-Gavras told me. "No matter how many times I said that I shot *your* script and put *your* story and *your* characters on-screen, they had been turned into film school robots who considered *me* the auteur."

I wrote a movie in which two characters were little kids. I named them Steve and Suzi, the names of my first two kids.

Steve and Suzi were happy their names would be on the big screen. We went to the premiere of the movie together and we all sat waiting excitedly for their big moment.

And when it came, "Steve" and "Suzi" weren't in the movie.

"David" and "Jessica" were.

Steve and Suzi were heartbroken and so was I.

In the lobby after the premiere, the director introduced Steve and Suzi to his two beautiful kids . . . David and Jessica.

We all shook hands and the director said we should get Steve and Suzi together with David and Jessica, who were about the same age.

We all said that was a terrific idea!

But somehow or other Steve and Suzi and David and Jessica and the director and I never saw each other again.

Fueled by my anger, I not only pushed my agents into achieving a series of screenwriting breakthroughs, but also made sure the breakthroughs were publicized.

I made record amounts of money on several script sales and kept breaking my own records.

I was the first screenwriter in history to get first dollar gross points (a percentage of every dollar brought in at the box office)—*Tom Cruise points*—from his movie.

My travel budget for each of my scripts included first-class tickets for me, my wife, and my children . . . it also included a limo standing by wherever we traveled . . . two bedroom suites at hotels like the Dorchester in London, the Dolder Grand in Zurich, the King David in Jerusalem, the Ritz in Paris . . . Concorde tickets for all of us to Europe and back.

As opposed to other screenwriters, I held on to the book and theatrical rights to my scripts.

I had to be given the same access to the media as the director and the producer—if they did a publicity junket, I had to be there with them at all the junket's stops.

When I traveled to publicize a movie, my own publicist had to travel with me. All interview requests had to be handled by my own publicity person, not by the studio's.

"*From Joe Eszterhas*" was the bold black line which appeared on the publicity poster (what we call the "one sheet") on my last movie, *An Alan Smithee Film: Burn Hollywood Burn.*

It was the first time in history a screenwriter had been granted this line by the studio.

"*From Joe Eszterhas*" also had to appear boldly on all merchandise connected to the movie: T-shirts, bumper stickers, coasters, matches.

An Alan Smithee Film: Burn Hollywood Burn . . . crashed and burned both critically and commercially.

But I have hundreds of T-shirts . . . thousands of bumper stickers . . . scores of coasters . . . boxes full of matches that say . . . in case I forget . . . "*From Joe Eszterhas*"!

Liz Smith wrote, "*Showgirls* is the reportedly sensational film about strippers that will carry the dreaded NC-17 rating when it is released. Controversy enough? Don't be silly. The *real* hot topic over *Showgirls* has nothing to do with breasts and buttocks. It is the placement of screenwriter Joe Eszterhas's name on-screen that has everybody atingle.

"Eszterhas will see his name appear right *before* that of director Paul Verhoeven. And *after* that of Alan Marshall and Charles Evans—they are the producers of *Showgirls*.

"In the movie industry this is causing a riot. The idea that writers should receive such powerful billing in film credits has producers all over Hollywood acting crazier than ever.

"Writers, on the other hand, are smiling like Cheshire cats that swallowed the whole canary."

Having said all those insufferable things about directors, I have to admit, too, that I am one of the few screenwriters who have worked with the same director twice.

Not only that, but I've worked *twice* with *three different* directors: Costa-Gavras (*Betrayed* and *Music Box*); Paul Verhoeven (*Basic Instinct, Showgirls*); Richard Marquand (*Jagged Edge, Hearts of Fire*).

That means not *all* directors are lying, self-focused, pretentious, homicidal *filmmakers*.

That also means I am not *completely* insufferable.

I was overwhelmed by the money I was making writing screenplays. We were so poor when I was a kid that we mostly ate canned soup for dinner, with occasional fried baloney galas. The clothes my father, my mother, and I wore were from the Salvation Army, the Volunteers of America, or from the St. Vincent DePaul Society.

My shoes were usually so loose that my socks kept slipping down and I had to keep bending down to pull them up. I wore a winter overcoat that was four sizes too big—another kid could have fit under it with me.

In the refugee camps in Austria, we ate pine needle soup for a month and one day my father went through his pockets for crumbs, found some, and gave them to me. I ate them.

VII

Like most Hollywood stars, I even had blond highlights streaked into my hair. My ex-wife took one look at me and said, "Now you look just like Naomi!"

I told her I didn't really think that was fair to Naomi.

Gerri harrumphed.

My first wife, Gerri Javor, and I were married twenty-four years. We had two beautiful children. We grew apart. We divorced.

Gerri and Naomi had a lot in common. They both grew up in small-town Ohio in rusty steel towns: Naomi in Mansfield, Gerri in Lorain. They were both journalism majors at Ohio State University in Columbus. They both worked for the school newspaper, *The Lantern,* and both took photographs of Woody Hayes–coached football teams. They were both Catholics who had gone to Catholic schools. They were both of Central European ethnic origin: Gerri was part Hungarian, part Slovak.

Perhaps most remarkably, twenty years apart, they had both been grabbed at Ohio State by a hooded would-be rapist who knocked them into the snow and then was frightened off by their screams.

After college, they both went on to work for Ohio newspapers: Naomi for the *Columbus Dispatch,* Gerri for the *Cleveland Plain Dealer.*

My father met Gerri Javor before I did. I was still at Ohio University when she was the nationalities editor of the *Cleveland Plain Dealer* and wrote an article about Hungarians' mistreatment of Slovaks after World War I.

My father, a Hungarian writer and nationalist and the president of the Committee for Hungarian Liberation, took great umbrage at Gerri Javor's article and organized a petition drive to get her fired. He asked me to translate the petition from Hungarian to English.

The *Plain Dealer* didn't fire Gerri Javor, but it forced her to have a meeting with my father.

"She's a very attractive young woman," he told me afterward. "You should try to meet her sometime."

I laughed and said, "If *you* like her, Pop, *I* wouldn't."

Two years later, when I met her at the *Plain Dealer,* the first thing Gerri Javor said to me was, "You're that man's son, aren't you?"

I liked her.

My father had lived in Cleveland all these thirty years that I had been in California. He was ninety-two years old and needed around-the-clock nursing. He'd had a heart valve replacement when he was eighty-five and had then suffered a series of strokes.

He couldn't hear very well now and he was on a catheter and most of his teeth were gone . . . but he was happy that he was still in his own house in Cleveland Heights, thanks to my ability to foot all of his bills, and not in an old-age home.

I loved my father but came to the awful, heartbreaking realization in 1990 that I loathed him as much as I loved him, a realization that made our relationship cruelly difficult and painful.

István Eszterhás was a Hungarian novelist and journalist, until 1990 the greatest friend I'd ever had. He was my inspiration and support. He believed in me and cared about me. He loved me.

I knew that without his presence in my life, I would have accomplished very little.

But I tried to stop loving my father in 1990.

I didn't speak to him for a year and a half. I didn't allow him to visit the grandchildren he loved, Steve and Suzi.

All my life my father told me he had a recurring dream.

I was a little boy and we were walking through a labyrinthine train station. He was holding my hand and he somehow let it go and, suddenly . . . he had lost me.

He was sobbing, running up and down, yelling my name, trying to talk to people who didn't speak his language.

No one understood what he was trying to say . . . and I was gone, lost somewhere in this foreign world.

Gerri Javor and I courted while we were both police reporters at the *Plain Dealer*. Part of our courtship was covering stories together.

At a wedding on a Saturday afternoon on the East Side of Cleveland, the former boyfriend of the bride shot the groom and took the bride hostage at an apartment complex only a couple of blocks away from my father's house in Cleveland Heights.

Gerri and I were both covering the story for the *Plain Dealer* as the apartment complex turned into the scene of a media siege. Print and network reporters were there from as far away as Chicago and New York.

As the standoff continued into the next day, I called my city editor from the scene and said, "What if we fly the shooter's mother in here? She lives in a small town in Pennsylvania. We'd interview her, find out everything there is to know about the shooter, and then maybe she could talk her son out of there."

The cops went ballistic. They said if we flew the mother in, we'd be playing

Russian roulette. What if the shooter didn't like his mother? What if her presence triggered more violence?

The *Plain Dealer* decided to fly the mother in anyway on a private plane. Gerri and I met her at the airport. She was a pleasant, white-haired old lady and Gerri immediately made friends with her. We drove her around Cleveland for a couple of hours, interviewing her, getting all the details about her son before we drove her to the scene of the standoff.

The cops tried to tell her to go back home, but she wanted to see her son. I talked her into taking me inside the building with her. The cops seethed.

We went inside the apartment house and up a flight of stairs. Cops with shotguns crouched all over the stairway. The old lady said one word: "*Baby?*"

Her son shot the girl and killed himself.

In the twenty-four years of our marriage, Gerri and I never—not once—talked about what we had accomplished that day at that apartment complex down the street from my father's house . . . while we were courting.

After the shooting . . . at the end of that day . . . I knew that I would ask Gerri to marry me.

Thirty years later, after my divorce from Gerri, I wrote a script about that day for Paramount called *Reliable Sources*.

Paramount paid me $2 million for it.

Were Gerri and I accomplices to the shootings of two people and the shooting death of one of them?

Was I then paid $2 million—thirty years later—for my part in the crime?

Thanks to the details of our divorce settlement, Gerri got some money from the two mil, too.

Gerri's father, George, was an electrical engineer, a graduate of the University of Chicago, who was once arrested for beating his wife in front of Gerri and her sister and her two brothers.

George was an alcoholic who came home from work at four each afternoon and cracked open the bottle of vodka which he finished by eight that night. In the course of those four hours, as he worked on the bottle, George verbally and sometimes physically abused his family. Once he chased Gerri down to the dock on Lake Erie behind her home and threatened to drown her. She ran from the dock and down the street and caught a bus and spent the next week at a friend's apartment in Cleveland.

Gerri's mother, Susan, had an eighth-grade education and didn't much like her husband, let alone love him. Their marriage had been arranged by their old-country Hungarian and Slovak parents.

Gerri's mother was bitter that she, the most beautiful young woman in the town of Castalia, Ohio, had been forced to marry this plain-looking *engineer*.

Gerri and her sister and brothers heard their mother and father arguing all the time . . . because her mother refused to have sex much of the time with her father.

On these occasions, her father would say to her mother: "God bless St. Joseph for what he went through."

And: "The dog will have his day!"

When I was a Hollywood screenwriter and a King Shit agent named Michael Ovitz threatened to destroy my career, that's the last thing I said to him before I left his office:

The dog will have his day!

Ovitz looked at me like I'd lost my marbles and laughed.

Gerri's favorite family member was her maternal grandmother, Sue Balazsik, who lived with her family until her death in her early eighties. The big house on the lake they all lived in was Sue Balazsik's house.

An illiterate Hungarian immigrant, she not only owned and managed Lorain, Ohio's, best Hungarian restaurant, the Cozy Corner (Perry Como came to eat the paprikash every time he appeared in Cleveland), but was also, during Prohibition, Lorain's biggest bootlegger. She made a fortune outwitting the feds, contributed to a lot of local politicians' campaigns, and built the big house on the lake.

When Gerri was a little girl, she and her grandmother watched *The Untouchables* every week. It was the old woman's favorite TV show, the program the former bootlegger called "The Touchables."

And on Lorain Avenue, in Cleveland, twenty-seven miles from Lorain, Ohio, where Gerri and her grandmother were watching *The Untouchables* . . .

My father and I were watching it, too.

It was *our* favorite show, too.

My mother, however, wasn't watching it. She was in the bathroom hiding from the television set, which she believed was filled with rays from outer space poisoning her.

My father and I didn't know as we watched the show—and neither did Gerri and her grandmother—that Eliot Ness became the safety director of the city of Cleveland after he finished with Capone and Nitti and the other little Guinea homeboys in Chicago.

We didn't know that Ness was forced to resign as safety director after, rip-roaring drunk, he was involved in a hit-and-run accident on Cleveland's Shoreway.

We didn't know that Eliot Ness died shortly afterward, drunk and broke.

Many years later, I enlightened a Hollywood studio executive about these things while proposing a movie called *Ness at Twilight.*

The studio executive said, "What are you, *perverse?* Eliot Ness is a greater hero to the American public than George Washington and Abraham Lincoln and Spider-Man combined. And you want to do a movie about him as a drunk driver?"

Not willing to see a several-million-dollar deal go down so fast, I regrouped quickly with that studio executive.

"Listen," I said, "Ness did some truly heroic things in Cleveland, too, when he was the safety director. He fought Fritz Kuhn's American Nazi Bund tooth and nail. Cleveland had a lot of Nazis and Nazi sympathizers among its millions of immigrants and they staged massive parades and protests. Ness stayed on top of them and finally put them out of business. I heard that Costner wants to do something patriotic anyway."

The studio exec thought about it.

"Not bad," he finally said. "But how about we move the story to Chicago? Chicago's about to be taken over by the Nazis and Costner stops them. Cleveland's for losers: Chicago's got Michael Jordan. Kevin would like it in Chicago better than Cleveland, trust me. Maybe we can get Billy Friedkin to do it, he's *from* Chicago and he's old enough to know who the Nazis were."

"That's great." I smiled. "Billy and I did *Jade* together."

"Oh Christ, that's right, I forgot," the studio exec said. "Forget it. Billy won't want to work with you again."

"Billy and I are still . . . friends," I said.

"Well sure you are," the studio exec said with a smile. "So what? But if Billy works with you again, he can't blame your script for bringing *Jade* down. If he works with you again, that means he's publicly saying he thinks you're a good screenwriter. And if he thinks you're a good writer, then it means *he* had something to do with *Jade*'s failure. You think Billy Friedkin is career-suicidal?"

When Gerri's grandmother was in her fifties, her husband left Sue Balazsik and their kids for a younger woman. He married the younger woman and had children with her.

Till the day he died, Gerri's grandmother believed that her ex-husband would come back to her.

He didn't.

As our twenty-four-year marriage was breaking up, Gerri would often say to me: "If you leave me, Joseph, I'm going to be just like my grandmother. I'm going to wait until you come back to me."

Steve and Suzi tell me she's still waiting.

· · ·

The original, rough-draft title of *Basic Instinct* was *Love Hurts*.

VIII

From the refugee camps to the A-list in Hollywood—what a great tag for *Lifestyles of the Rich and Famous,* which used exactly that promo line when I was on the show.

I could even argue that *my* house was in a better Malibu location than Bob Dylan's—mine was right on my own cliff, facing the sea: Bob's was across the road on Birdview Avenue. Bob didn't have his own surfside cliff—but I did!

Plus his house was built from the profits of a *lot* of smash hit records, while I had bought my house from the profits of one *cocktail napkin*—on which I had scribbled the plot of one screenplay—a cocktail napkin (from Le Dome) which I had turned into a four-page outline . . . for which one studio (New Line) had paid *four million dollars!*

And what was the plot outline which had bought my house overlooking the sea? What did the cocktail napkin say?

"Guy meets hooker," it said, "falls in love, leaves wife and kids, discovers she's not a hooker but a wife and mother cheating on her husband."

. . . Success! Redemption! The Streets Are Paved with Gold! Only in America! Hooray for Hollywood!

Lawdy, lawdy, *Premiere* magazine had even picked me as one of the hundred most powerful people in Hollywood, right up there with Eisner and Tom Cruise and Diller and Julia Roberts and Ovitz and Adam Sandler!

A *screenwriter,* a schlub, a leper, a maggot, a nigger—for the first time in history on the Big Shot List! It was something even my own personal hero, Paddy Chayefsky, the only screenwriter in Hollywood who'd ever had any *real* balls, hadn't achieved. (Though, God bless him, he'd slept with Kim Novak, one of the first childhood jackoff loves of my life.)

From the near west side of Cleveland, Lorain Avenue, to the far west side of Los Angeles, Malibu!

Faded stars like Faye Dunaway were calling me at home trying to persuade me to write them *secondary* parts in future scripts. Starlets were leaving their photos (many in thong bikinis) and home phone numbers with the concierge in hotels where I was staying.

I was a Horatio Alger story. I couldn't stand in a ticket line or sit in a restaurant without being asked for an autograph. I was the man who was single-handedly getting even for all the Pat Hobby stories about the million ways screenwriters were abused and humiliated in Hollywood.

I was the schlub, the leper, the maggot, the nigger . . . the screenwriter for Christ's sake as *star!*

I was the rape victim come back as Charles Bronson in *Death Wish*.

Oh how I loved it! I signed every autograph I was ever asked for, even if it meant interrupting my dinner.

According to that *Premiere* magazine list, I was the 78th most powerful person in all of Hollywood.

Less powerful than I were: Denzel Washington (79), producer Arnold Kopelson (80), CAA agent Richard Lovett (81), John Grisham (82), producer Andy Vajna (83), Francis Coppola (84), producer Joel Silver (85), Universal president Casey Silver (86), producer Peter Guber (87), producer Bruce Berman (88), producers Don Simpson and Jerry Bruckheimer (89), Winona Ryder (90), Tom Clancy (91), Savoy chairman Victor Kaufman (92), director Mike Nichols (93), Turner Pictures president Amy Pascal (94), producer/director James L. Brooks (95), agent Nick Stevens (96), Fox 2000 head Laura Ziskin (97), Eddie Murphy (98), producer Wendy Finerman (99), animator Glen Keane (100).

I was a screenwriter who had no interest in doing anything except writing. I didn't have an office or a secretary or a production company. I didn't even own an electric typewriter, let alone a computer. I still used a manual Olivetti.

Yet I was more powerful than Denzel and Eddie and Winona . . . more powerful than *four* studio heads . . . more powerful than film factories Grisham and Clancy . . . more powerful than legendary Hollywood animals like Peter Guber . . . and even my producer friend Don Simpson, who, I was sure, had suffered a near-stroke when he saw me on this list eleven places in front of him.

Oh . . . my . . . God . . . how . . . I . . . fucking . . . loved it!

Bruce Willis was only eleven places in front of me . . . Jack Nicholson only ten . . . and Sharon Stone, my very own Frankenstein monster, three.

GQ magazine wrote: "To his beleaguered confreres, Joe Eszterhas is a superstar, chiefly for having commanded huge fees on his own terms. . . . This ballsy approach, combined with his willingness to wage war with very powerful people when his work was at stake, eventually made Eszterhas something of a Hollywood folk hero—debunking the pathetic, long-held perception of screenwriters as gin-soaked novelties on the career skids, as sweaty and scared East Coast geeks camped out in the bungalows."

Hey, Michael Ovitz:
    The dog had his day!

And when a movie of mine failed or I couldn't sell a script, I had a ready response:

"The hell with it," I said. "It ain't the refugee camps."

IX

When I was in college at Ohio University, it was *From the refugee camps to the White House!*

I was named the outstanding college journalist in America by the William Randolph Hearst Foundation.

I went to the White House, where President Johnson was to award me a gold medal.

But when I got there, President Johnson was busy on his Texas ranch and Vice President Hubert Humphrey gave me the gold medal instead.

I loved that gold medal—heavy, shiny but, alas, brass not gold.

I kept it shined and in plain view on my various coffee tables for almost forty years.

I also got a thousand dollars which I was supposed to spend on my further education.

I still had the White House medal on our coffee table in the living room of the house overlooking the sea in Malibu where Naomi and I lived with our little boys.

It was stolen there by one of the many reporters who came to interview me.

I have no doubt the reporter thought it was gold, not brass.

Going to the White House was my greatest moment at Ohio University. My worst moment came after a night of demonic substance abuse with some friends.

I found myself atop a church next door to a sorority house where I knew a girl who wouldn't sleep with me.

I was hanging on to the cross on the roof of the church, bare-chested, a bottle of Jack Daniel's in one hand, a big cigar in the other.

I was yelling very loudly so the girl I knew in the sorority house could hear me.

I was yelling, "Father, forgive them, for they know not what they do!"

At the time I went to the White House and got a million dollars' worth of publicity for Ohio University, I was on disciplinary probation for:

1. Living in unapproved housing.
2. Living with a girl in unapproved housing.
3. Cutting most of my classes.
4. Bouncing a $10 check at the local A&P grocery store. (The A&P prosecuted.)

Thanks to all the publicity I got at the White House, the university quickly took me off disciplinary probation, but . . .

I never did graduate.

I spent the thousand dollars I was awarded not on my further education but on a used car: a three-year-old blue Ford.

Two years later, in Dayton, Ohio, where I was working as a reporter, I crashed the car into a light post after drinking too many beers. I pretty well demolished my car and broke two fingers on the steering wheel.

I parked it on the street in a no-parking zone and the police towed it the next morning.

I was making so little money as a beginning reporter . . . even one who'd been awarded a brass medal at the White House . . . that I couldn't pay either the towing or the fix-it costs.

I let the Dayton police department keep my blue Ford.

I had no medical insurance and I didn't have enough money to go to a doctor, so I let my two broken fingers heal on their own.

Almost forty years later, they still hurt sometimes.

X

I went to Hollywood for the first time in the early seventies while I was a writer for *Rolling Stone* magazine, then in San Francisco. I was on assignment to meet two priests of a satanic cult called the Process.

I don't know why my devilish priests picked Hollywood as the site of our meeting but they did.

While I was waiting for them, I checked out Grauman's Chinese Theatre and the Hollywood Roosevelt Hotel. I saw a used-car lot with caged reindeer atop its office. I bought an autographed photo of Zsa Zsa Gabor for $3. I stayed in a motel on Hollywood Boulevard and shared some lines of cocaine and his girlfriend with a bass guitarist from Miami who was staying at the same motel.

The devilish priests called me at the motel and switched the meeting site to Palm Springs, so I took a Greyhound over there and waited for them at the old Biltmore, ramshackle and falling apart, but once the meeting place for Hollywood stars sunning in the desert.

I waited three days for Satan's helpers to show but they stood me up. Meanwhile, I read a worn paperback of Mailer's *The Deer Park,* the best book ever written about Hollywood.

I took the Greyhound back to Hollywood, thinking I'd had a total Hollywood experience: Satan, Zsa Zsa, cocaine, a shared bimbo, sun, and Mailer's doomed characters.

. . .

Except for Zsa Zsa Gabor, I was now Hollywood's most famous or infamous living Hungarian.

Through the years, Hollywood had experienced many other famous or infamous Hungarians: Ivan Nagy, Heidi Fleiss's boyfriend; Mickey Hargitay, Jayne Mansfield's muscleman; Adolph Zukor, Jolie Gabor, Thomas Ince, the Korda brothers, Vilma Banky, Ilona Massey, Eva Gabor, George Cukor, Cornel Wilde, S. Z. Sakall, Magda Gabor, Ernie Kovacs, Joe Pasternak, Tony Curtis, Leslie Howard, Bela Lugosi, etc., etc.

There had even been a sign at the cash register of the MGM commissary that said, "It's not enough to be Hungarian, you still have to pay for the chicken soup."

Through the years, people in Hollywood had gotten to know Hungarians and said these things about us:

1. "If a Hungarian is in a revolving door behind you, he will arrive ahead of you."
2. "If you have a Hungarian for a friend, you don't need an enemy."
3. "The difference between a Romanian and a Hungarian is that a Romanian will offer to sell you his sister and the Hungarian will do it."
4. "If you see a Hungarian on the street, go up to him and slap him. He will know why."

Yet even as I was becoming famous or infamous, for many years I kept resisting the town, happy to take Hollywood's money but keeping Hollywood at arm's length, dealing with Hollywood people over the phone or during hurried trips to L.A. but keeping myself aloof from . . .

From what, exactly?

Well, from everything I had heard and read about the place—to put it more exactly: from everything I'd read and heard had happened to writers there.

Writers got fucked there, they got their hearts broken there, they had their balls cut off there, they got screwed, blued, and tattooed.

Look at Fitzgerald, writing his scripts out there, broke, drinking full glasses of gin, taking notes from studio moguls, sleeping with a gossip columnist . . . *dying* there, between her legs, it was said. So tawdry, so *Hollywood*—Fitzgerald *dying* there *between the gossip columnist's legs*—please God! no—think Philip Roth atop Leeza Gibbons or Saul Bellow atop Rona Barrett.

Or look at Faulkner in Hollywood, doing his rewrites at Howard Hawks's beck and call, taking Hawks's notes, slugging bourbon from the silver flask in his tweed coat's pocket, falling down drunk, flat on his face, during a script meeting—William Faulkner sleeping for years with a script girl, a secretary from the studio's pool—but at least he went back to Mississippi after many years of screenwriting, at least he didn't die between the secretary's legs.

What Hemingway said made a lot of sense: a writer, he said, should get as close to Hollywood as the Nevada-California border. He should take Hollywood's money at the border and turn right back around and head east.

And when he left Hollywood and drove back to Mississippi, Bill Faulkner, screenwriter, actually stopped at the California state line and got out of his car.

If it were up to him, he thought, he would erect a sign for travelers going into California: "Abandon hope, all ye who enter here!"

I stayed away from Hollywood for seventeen years while I was working there—*seventeen years* of commuting from Marin County for meetings with studio executives and studio heads, *seventeen years* of dinners at Morton's and stays at the old Beverly Wilshire and the Westwood Marquis.

Even though I always had the feeling deep inside . . . (deep, deep inside, in the refugee camp part of me, in the blackest part of my heart) that I had nothing to fear, that the studios couldn't fuck *me* or break *my* heart. That I'd do the fucking and the nut-cutting, thank you. That I was a hunkie from Cleveland, made not out of Fitzgerald porcelain or Faulkner oyster shell but out of some rusted, red-hot bastard metal—like . . . *Mailer.*

Yes, that was it, Norman *Friggin'* Mailer!

Mailer, who'd gone to Hollywood, had his ass kissed by the whole town, banged Shelley Winters, and left, his only seeming regret that he hadn't been able to nail Marilyn (how it would obsess him that it was that long string of intellectual spaghetti, Miller, who'd done it).

Oh, well, never mind, if not nailing Marilyn was your only regret, that was good enough for me—Mailer, the tough guy from Brooklyn, would be my role model.

I didn't know then that I'd create my own Marilyn and that *I'd* nail *her.* But that nailing her would pale in comparison with the havoc that her presence would wreak with my life.

I'm glad I nailed her, though. Not because I nailed mine (as Paddy Chayefsky had nailed his) and Mailer didn't nail his. Not because nailing her felt all that good (it was okay). But because as a result of Sharon Stone's presence in my life, I met and married Naomi, my one true love.

I didn't attach too much significance to my one-night stand with Sharon.

I had done other one-night stands in Hollywood and so, I knew, had Sharon.

I even knew a producer who said that both he and his son had done one-night stands with Sharon on separate nights, many years apart.

So I didn't think Sharon had attached much significance to our one-night stand, either.

I figured that since I had written the biggest hit of her life for her, she was just saying thank you.

At the end of our night, which was really only just a few hours, I felt *underpaid.*

I knew most screenwriters would have felt *overwhelmed* . . . Paddy Chayefsky never did get over Kim Novak!

And I knew that Sharon thought she was flattering me that night by treating me as if I were a director and not a screenwriter, but still . . . *Basic Instinct* had been the number one box office hit of the year . . . *in the whole world!*

I felt I deserved her.

On the other hand, I thought Sharon's grateful gesture was heartfelt evidence of non-Hollywood values.

Not many actors or actresses would have thanked the screenwriter . . . *at all* . . . *in any way* . . . for boosting their salary so enormously.

Sharon really didn't have to . . .

I concluded that Sharon, like Gerri and Naomi, was a generous, good-natured Midwestern girl after all.

Robert Evans had stirred this unholy brew with Sharon and me by getting me to agree to write the screenplay for Ira Levin's novel *Sliver.*

That's how I met Bill and Naomi Macdonald.

That's how I could introduce my friend Sharon to my friend Bill.

That was the only way, the shrinks would say . . . outside of homicide . . . that I could have Naomi for myself.

Naomi was the real (subconscious) reason I introduced Sharon and Bill.

Such a devilish concatenation of events, no wonder that Evans's favorite movie was *Rosemary's Baby,* a movie about the devil also written by Ira Levin. No wonder that as an actor, Evans had played *The Fiend Who Walked the West.*

The only reason I'd agreed to write *Sliver* was that Evans was broke and down on his luck, curled up in the fetal position much of the time, staring into space, humming.

He had been suspected of murder and had been convicted of possessing cocaine. He adored women but told me he was impotent. He was living off handouts from his brother, Charlie, and Jack Nicholson.

Evans defined Hollywood and the movies to me. His films, either as producer or studio chief, included *The Godfather* and *Love Story* and *Rosemary's Baby* and *Chinatown,* and Ali MacGraw and Phyllis George and Camilla Sparv and hundreds, maybe thousands of gorgeous women were always hanging around his house.

I loved movies and, may God forgive me, I liked Evans a lot, too.

It's only fair, too, that I put my hand on the Bible and state this about Evans: All the lies ever told anywhere about Robert Evans are true.

The script I wrote for *Sliver* was somehow a part of this evil mix.

In my script, Sharon discovered that Billy Baldwin was a murderer and didn't care—because she loved him and was convinced he loved her. She married him. That's how *my* script ended.

And that's what caused that secretary in Evans's office wearing the Blessed Virgin Mary T-shirt to flip out and say I had written a script on the side of evil.

That was the ending which Evans had liked so much that he sent the human telegram wearing only the mink coat over to my hotel.

According to that secretary in the Blessed Virgin Mary T-shirt, then—my script was sympathetic to the devil.

And the fact that it was sympathetic to the devil is, of course, what made Evans, the real devil, like it so much.

When I met him, the devil had just finished making a documentary about Pope John Paul II.

He had done the documentary by court order, part of his sentence for possessing cocaine.

XI

I'd always loved movies. My parents and I arrived in America from the refugee camps in 1950 and went to Cleveland shortly afterward. We lived above the printing shop of the newspaper where my father had just been hired as editor. We lived on Lorain Avenue, a blue-collar "strudel ghetto" made up of the ethnic poor.

I was in love with movies before I ever saw one.

My father went to the Lorain Fulton, the theater down the street from us, once a week and I couldn't wait until he got home. I'd kneel at the window of our apartment overlooking the street, excited to see his roly-poly figure shuffling in the darkness through the snow. He kept a box of popcorn under his coat so it would still be warm and handed it to me as soon as he came through the door.

I ate the popcorn slowly, kernel by kernel, licking my fingers.

. . .

Pretty soon he was taking me with him to see movies like *Open City* and *Paisan* and *Bicycle Thief* and *Bitter Rice*. I was seven years old. My mother was too religious to come with us: she stayed home to say the Rosary, which was broadcast on WERE, in English. She was combining learning this new language with her belief in God.

The Lorain Fulton was playing Italian-made neorealist classic movies because the theater was in an ethnic neighborhood where most people couldn't speak English anyway so they didn't mind the subtitles.

Also, many of the immigrants living on Lorain had picked up bits and pieces of Italian in the refugee camps so they found it easier watching Italian movies than American ones.

Also, these movies were about World War II and most of these immigrants were here on Lorain Avenue *because* of World War II, so it made sense to the theater owner probably that they would feel right at home with the subject matter up there on the big screen.

I felt right at home . . . with that bombed-out building up on-screen—it was just like the one we'd been in that was bombed out in Szombathely: and those soldiers rolling around with that naked girl in the grass on-screen, why that was just like the naked woman I'd seen . . .

I munched my nice hot popcorn. I was watching scenes I'd already experienced. At age seven, I was already educating myself, without even knowing it, without even speaking English—to be an American screenwriter. (A critic who didn't like *Showgirls* would say, years later, "it's obvious English is his second language.")

Sitting in the dark munching hot popcorn, my dad next to me, watching girls rolling around naked in the grass, I liked movies a lot!

The very first movie I saw alone was *High School Confidential!* with Russ Tamblyn.

Yeah, I know, this wasn't Vittorio De Sica or Roberto Rossellini, and the women weren't Anna Magnani or Silvana Mangano, but the real star of the movie for me was Jerry Lee Lewis, who was already one of my true childhood heroes—along with Rocky Colavito of the Cleveland Indians, Shondor Birns, a dapper Hungarian gangster, Lou Teller, a Hungarian bank robber who was from the West Side, too, and Zsa Zsa Gabor, the most famous Hungarian in the world and the reason my *pimpli* (it was what we called it in Hungarian, okay?) was so red raw I could hardly move.

Jerry Lee Lewis, his long blond hair flying, stomping out "Open-up-a-honey-it's-your-lover-boy-me-that's-a-knockin" on top of a piano that he'd already literally set on fire.

Rock and roll! Switchblade knives! Tight angora sweaters with hot milky titties underneath 'em! That's what *High School Confidential!* was about, an obvious precursor to a movie about an ice pick and a tight white dress with milky white stuff underneath it that I'd write many years later.

Russ Tamblyn, too, was close to my heart. Not just because he starred in *High School Confidential!*, the movie that influenced me more than De Sica and Rossellini. But because he also starred in *The Kid from Cleveland,* which featured the entire Cleveland Indians world championship team of 1948!

I met Redford and Hoffman and Cruise and Max Schell and Kevin Bacon and Jeff Bridges and Debra Winger and Glenn Close and blah blah blah over the course of twenty-five years of writing screenplays . . . but I never met Russ Tamblyn.

It is my great Hollywood regret. Mailer never nailed Marilyn and I never met Russ Tamblyn.

My only other Hollywood regret is that I never met Zsa Zsa Gabor, the most famous Hungarian in the world and the dominatrix of my boyhood *pimpli,* either.

When I was already a famous or infamous Hollywood screenwriter, I asked a mutual friend to call and tell Zsa Zsa that I would be calling her soon.

"But no, dahlink, no," Zsa Zsa said to my friend. "I will not speak to such a dangerous man."

I called, left a message, and she never called me back.

I fell in lust for the first time at the Lorain Fulton Theatre, where I'd sneaked in to see a movie the Catholic Church was trying to stop from being shown.

I was an altar boy and this movie was all that the older altar boys were talking about.

And God Created Woman was the title.

Her name was Brigitte Bardot. She was a "sex kitten."

I watched her walk. I watched her eat with her fingers. I watched her pout. I watched parts of her body, which seemed more naked than they actually were.

I heard lines of dialogue like: "She does whatever she wants whenever she wants."

And: "What are you afraid of?" "Myself."

And: "You'd make a good wife." "No, I like to have too much fun."

I sneaked back in to see it two other times and when the *Cleveland Plain Dealer* arrived each morning I attacked it to find anything written about her.

I found that she had held a press conference in New York. Someone had asked her, "What was the best day of your life?" And she said, "It was a night."

Someone asked why she wasn't wearing lipstick. And she said, "I don't like lipstick. It makes trouble. I like to kiss. But if I kiss anyone when I am wearing lipstick, it makes trouble."

I saw a photograph of her in *Life* magazine. She was in a swimming pool wearing a tiny little bathing suit. The pool was filled with milk. According to the story, she had insisted it be "ass's milk."

I marveled at that. I still didn't know the English language very well and the only "ass" I knew about didn't have milk coming out of it.

By then, of course, I was already going crazy.

Hair grew from my palms.

I was going blind.

Even though I loved movies, I never wanted to be a screenwriter. I wanted to write novels.

There was a secondhand paperback bookstore down the street from our apartment on Lorain Avenue which was really a front for a bookie's wire. The bookie let me use the place as a library.

The first book I got from there was William Faulkner's *Sanctuary*. I picked it because of the cover: a young woman who, as the guys on Lorain Avenue said, "was built like a brick shithouse."

I had no idea what being built like a brick shithouse meant.

As a matter of fact, I still don't.

And I had no idea you could do that with a corncob, either.

But I do now, don't I?

I'm a writer whose view of women was permanently affected by Temple Drake on a lurid paperback cover. Just another writer ruined by the influence of the alcoholic, mostly impotent Bill Faulkner, failed screenwriter, who never nailed his Marilyn, who slept with the girl in the secretarial pool.

Heh heh heh.

Come to think of it, I made ice picks as famous as he made corncobs, didn't I?

A casting director at the studio who had read *Sanctuary* told William Faulkner, screenwriter, that she understood that an author always put himself in his books.

"Which character are you in *Sanctuary?*" she asked.

"Madame," Faulkner said, "I am the corncob."

And I am the ice pick.

XII

What, you might well ask, is all this talk about Fitzgerald and Faulkner and Mailer coming from a screenwriter? Why all this high-toned babble about *novelists* in a book about Hollywood? Why not compare myself to other *screenwriters?*

Say what?

Compare myself to other screenwriters? On what basis? Most screenwriters don't even have a body of work that amounts to five let alone fifteen movies. Most screenwriters do adaptations of novels and rewrites of other scripts: they rarely write original screenplays—that is—novels written directly for the screen in screenplay form.

Truth to tell, bottom line, most screenwriters don't want to be screenwriters: they want to be directors so they can tell other screenwriters who want to be directors what to write. For most screenwriters, screenwriting is hopefully nothing more than a temporary stop on the way to the mountaintop, on the way to big bucks, pussy, fame, and auteurhood: *Directing!*

Trouble is, screenwriting, for me, has already led to all those all-American jackpots. I became a famous screenwriter making millions, scoring A-list pussy, picked as one of the hundred most powerful people on Hollywood.

Never mind that most powerful list, but . . .

Godalmighty, a screenwriter scoring A-list pussy?

That drove some people in Hollywood nuts, beginning with writers (usually film reporters and critics) who hadn't sold a screenplay yet and ending with directors—*directors!*—who weren't as famous as I, who were paid less to direct the film than I'd been paid for the script, and who, judging from the trophies on their arms at the wrap parties, weren't scoring the quality pussy that I was, either.

Can you imagine *the hubris of this*?

I was a screenwriter who didn't want to be anything else. I didn't want my own production company. I didn't want my own office at a studio. I didn't want my own parking space on the studio lot. Hell, I didn't even want to go on the damn lot.

I didn't want to be reached. I was busy. *I was writing!* And I didn't want to hear anybody else's ideas while I was writing because I was the writer and they weren't. I didn't want to hear the producer's ideas, the studio exec's ideas, the star's ideas, the director's ideas—especially not the director's ideas because it was usually the director who had the *lamest* ideas.

I understood why. Because the director felt pressured to be creative even when there was nothing for him to do yet—when he wasn't shooting yet. He had to do something and there was nothing to do except make "creative" suggestions to the writer.

I sent a screenplay I'd written to the director Brian DePalma, whose work I sometimes admired.

He called me the next day and said, "You've written a perfect script. I love it. It's ready to go."

I was so happy. "You're going to direct it then?" I said.

He said, "No."

I said, "But why not?"

He said, "It's done. There's nothing for me to do."

I said, "You can cast it, shoot it, direct it, edit it."

He said, "But there's nothing for me to write."

I said, "But you're not a writer."

He said, "I'm the director. It has to be my baby. I have to feel that it's my baby. I have to make it mine. I can't make it mine when it's perfect."

I said, "Maybe I shouldn't have written the perfect script."

He said, "You probably shouldn't have."

I said, "What if you run through it and make it less perfect and then you direct it?"

He said, "I'd always remember how it used to be. It's too late to do that. Its perfection would be in my head."

I said, "Maybe I should have sent it to you in its rough draft."

He said, "Yes, before it was so good."

I said, "Before it was too good for you to direct."

He said, "Yes, next time send me the rough draft."

I didn't even want to go on the *set* of my movies. Most screenwriters begged and pleaded and groveled to be allowed on a set, but I'd never wanted to be there—because I'd learned that if I was there, producers and directors and even the actors—Jesus, even the *grips!*—would approach me with their script ideas—which I absolutely, categorically did not want to hear.

Because of my wild-eyed and frenzied notion that *I* was the writer and that *my* ideas—which were already in the script—were better than *theirs* and that my words on the page should be left the fuck unchanged.

So that when a grip approached me on the *Betrayed* set in Canada (I had to be there because the script I had written was too long and had to be cut), approached me in the lobby of my hotel as I was going up to bed after a long unhappy day eliminating my own words, approached me with "an idea" for the last scene of the script, I did what any screenwriter in that situation *should* do but none ever do.

I picked the pissant up by his shirt and bounced him off the wall and hit him with a beautiful left hook to the liver.

I didn't view the screenplay as a collaborative process. I viewed it as my creation. The rest of the movie was a collaboration between the director and the actors and the editor and some of the technicians.

I viewed myself as the composer. The director was the conductor. The others were part of the orchestra.

It is true that with this attitude I had almost *killed* a couple of directors.

Robert Harmon was the idiot who directed *Nowhere to Run*. He turned my screenplay inside out and I wrote him a long memo explaining his genetic failings to him. He read the memo and suffered a heart attack afterward. Such a young man, too, *tsk-tsk!*

And Arthur Hiller, a very old man, sat next to me in an editing room as I recut the movie he had shot and edited, *An Alan Smithee Film: Burn Hollywood Burn*. He was suffering chest pains as I did my cut and finally got up and drove himself to his cardiologist.

A very tough old man, Hiller took his name off the movie, turning an *Alan Smithee Film* into a real Alan Smithee film, and tsk-tsked jovially when the critics and the public hated my cut.

One director I'd worked with *had died* just before the release of the movie he and I had made. But I hadn't killed him.

I'd urged him to forget the movie we'd just made.

"It's only a movie," I said to him, "it's not worth all this pain."

But Richard Marquand didn't believe me and he had died at forty-eight.

Or maybe I had killed him after all, maybe I had indeed really killed Richard, one of my best friends.

Because the script I had written for him for *Hearts of Fire* was, in my estimation (not in Richard's), awful.

XIII

I realize there is a distinct possibility that the most famous moment from any of my films will be that split-second viewing of Sharon Stone's itty-bitty little hairs in *Basic Instinct*.

More than a quarter century and at least fifteen movies . . . all bubbling down to a few touched-up pubic hairs!

Even more amusing is that that moment—*the most famous moment of any of my films*—wasn't even in the script.

Paul Verhoeven decided that the scene would be more fun if Sharon didn't wear any underwear that day.

In other words, the most famous moment of any of my films . . . was Paul Verhoeven's.

I am a militant . . . and militantly insufferable screenwriter . . . who insists that the screenwriter is as important as the director . . . who insists that the director serves the screenwriter's vision . . . and whose most famous and most memorable screen moment . . . was created by the director, Paul Verhoeven.

That scene in *Basic Instinct* . . . the one I didn't write . . . the one Sharon was now claiming Paul tricked her into, was picked as one of the one hundred greatest moments in the last fifty years of film by *Entertainment Weekly*.

"When Stone's femme fatale uncrossed her legs during an interrogation," the magazine wrote, "she went where few actresses had gone before—straight to Hollywood's A-list."

Other greatest moments: Brando bellowing in *Streetcar;* Kelly dancing in *Singing in the Rain;* Charlton Heston parting the Red Sea in *The Ten Commandments;* the shark attacking victims in *Jaws.*

I loved that: Sharon's itty-bitty little hairs had the same impact upon the world as the parting of.the Red Sea.

I also loved this image: Sharon's itty-bitty little hairs attacking other itty-bitty little hairs.

I have no doubt that writing *Basic Instinct* helped speed up the end of my marriage to Gerri Eszterhas.

Most young women, I found, had seen the movie. Some liked it; others disliked it . . . but almost all of them were fascinated by and on some sexual level *drawn to* the man who wrote it.

If I was a cheating husband before I wrote *Basic,* I became a kind of sexual stuntman after it was released in the theaters.

It all led, finally, to what Evans considered his ultimate compliment: "I saw the movie and thought, 'Damnit, this cocksucker knows more about pussy than I do.' "

(I don't. *No one* will ever know as much as Evans.)

My advice to screenwriters: Be careful what you write. Because what you write . . . can come back and *rewrite you!*

It's possible that in that post-*Basic* period, I was trying to live up to the definition of the Hungarian word *eszterhás:* "a vagabond who sleeps on a different roof each night."

XIV

I couldn't deny that I was a "rogue elephant" of a screenwriter (the *Los Angeles Times*). I not only didn't respect most directors but didn't respect most screenwriters, either.

Which screenwriters were worthy of respect? William Goldman maybe? The Bill Goldman who wrote *Butch and Sundance,* sure, but that was a long time ago and now Bill Goldman was advising young screenwriters to take notes during a meeting with a producer and pretend to like the producer's ideas—even if they were imbecilic—just to get the job. That sounded a whole lot to me like the madam telling the girls how to turn tricks at her bordello, so I told the London *Times* that Bill Goldman was "a hooker from Connecticut." (And Bill, a proud New Yorker, called the *Times* angrily after the piece appeared and said, "Did Joe really say I was from *Connecticut?*")

Or, how about Ron Bass, who rewrote Barry Morrow's *Rain Man* and earned a secondhand ricocheting Oscar? Ron was one of my first attorneys, working for one of the most powerful showbiz law firms in town. (It didn't hurt to still be on the firm's stationery when Ron was seeking screenwriting jobs; studios could curry favor with the law firm hoping to get a break during the next Cruise negotiation by hiring one of its lawyers to write a script.)

Ron was a good lawyer when he had represented me, doing whatever I asked, and he had the same lawyerly attitude working with a director on a script. "My function is to *service* directors," Ron told the press, "to help them realize *their* vision.

"I've got to make the director's vision my own in some way," Ron said. "I've got to find the thing in the director's vision that I'm not just willing to help him with, but that really excites me, so that I can get inspired along his line of thinking. . . . The director was so generous to listen to me. . . . Once I'm commissioned I have a vision that squares with my studio executive's and my director's—whomever I'm working with—and then I'm relaxed. I'm on this job. . . . The director is the author of the film. . . . I wasn't smart enough to get it right away but Steven Spielberg was extremely patient with me. He talked with me until I started to realize this was not only something to get behind but was really a much better way than I'd be doing. . . . These are like the nicest guys, these directors. They're not only great directors, they're also really great people to work with."

As I reread all of Ron's words, I realized that these were really not *lawyerly* terms: "*Servicing . . . the director's vision . . . the director was so generous to listen to me . . . the director is the author of the film . . . Steven Spielberg was extremely patient with me . . . these are like the nicest guys, these directors.*"

No, these were words neither lawyerly nor writerly, these words were the fake and theatrical moans of a hooker performing.

Were screenwriters like Tom Schulman (*Dead Poets Society*) or Michael Blake (*Dances with Wolves*) or Michael Tolkin (*The Player*) worthy of respect? Sure, but they wrote one great script but didn't have lengthy careers.

What about Robert Towne and Alvin Sargent? Were they worthy of respect? Yes, back in the day . . . although Bob, even then, had *talked* his stories to his pals and agents instead of writing them . . . and now he was a "script doctor," a "fixer," a scene assassin hired by the bosses weeks before a film begins shooting to replace the original writer's scenes and ideas with their own. Bob found it relatively easy to do that because, at heart, he wasn't a writer anymore: he was a would-be (and failed) director who had very long ago . . . *way* back in the day . . . written two masterful scripts: *Chinatown* and *Shampoo* (never mind the egomaniacal Warren Beatty's typically actorly assertion that *he* had written that script and had hired Bob to put *his* ideas into the script). And Alvin Sargent?

Way, way, way back in the day, Alvin was something . . . but he wasn't really Alvin Sargent anymore, he was Alvin Sargent Ziskin, the husband of a studio exec and/or producer, the same way that the director of my film *Jade* was Billy Friedkin Lansing. Alvin, like Billy, kept working.

What about Herman Mankiewicz (*Citizen Kane*)? Well, yes sort of . . . Ben Hecht? Yes of course. Ben Hecht wrote over a hundred scripts, but he ground them out one after the other, sometimes working on three or four at a time, sometimes having three meetings a day pitching three different projects—which is something that Ron Bass did, too.

I worked on one script at a time and mostly I wrote spec scripts. That meant I didn't have a deal when I started writing. I finished the script and then sent it to my agent to sell to the studios. It was a *finished* script by the time the studios got it.

I wrote mostly spec scripts for three reasons:

1. I didn't have to play Willy Loman and try to pitch a studio head into giving me a chance to write a script.
2. I avoided the "development" process where all the studio execs had a chance to give me their ideas before I started writing.
3. If the studios bought a "finished" script, it was less likely that they would make changes in it because the script was ready to shoot. Or, at least, they would make fewer changes in it than otherwise.

If a director tried to change my script without my agreement—either by himself or with another screenwriter, I tried to stop him by hook or crook, by baseball bat or heart-attack-inducing memo.

If I couldn't stop a director with a direct assault or by going over his head, I threatened to take my name off the movie.

With *One Night Stand,* I took my name off when the director Mike Figgis made my script unrecognizable to me. Took my name off *after* New Line had paid me $4 million for the script. (I was amazed that New Line allowed Figgis to make so many changes in the script after having paid so much money for it.)

I knew how much I galled some directors and studios. Every other screenwriter could take his name off every other movie in town and nobody cared. But if I did it, it would be on the front page of the trades and jump from there into the dailies and the magazines, which cannibalized the trades for Hollywood news.

And I knew that studio executives believed that bad publicity about a movie—*any* kind of bad publicity—would hurt a movie fatally. Bad publicity gave a movie "the clap."

The studios knew the kind of wildlife they were going into business with whenever they signed a deal with me. It was right there in front of them in black and white—the name of the company I had set up for income tax purposes.

I was *Barbarian, Ltd.*

Naomi and I called our little boys our "barbarians."

The reason New Line allowed Mike Figgis to completely rewrite a script the studio had paid a record amount of money for was explained to me years later, by a New Line executive:

"We loved your script when we got it. People in the office were memorizing lines and saying them to each other. When Figgis first said he was interested, we told him we wanted him to shoot the script. He agreed.

"Then *Leaving Las Vegas,* which Figgis had directed, came out. It was the unexpected smash of the year. Each year there's one unexpected hit that gets a million dollars' worth of publicity. That year it was *Leaving Las Vegas.* Oscars, Second Coming reviews. Figgis was suddenly the hottest director in town.

"Every other studio wanted to sign him up—to shoot the phone book if that's what he wanted to do. And *we* had him with *One Night Stand, your* script. Figgis came to us and said he still wanted to do *One Night Stand,* but he wanted to rewrite it. And we *still* tried to defend your script. 'A little rewrite, okay,' we said to Figgis, 'a polish, but not a major rewrite.' He agreed.

"And then, just then, *your* picture *Showgirls* came out. The critical disaster of the year. You got the Sour Apple Award, you got several Razzies. And here, at this same time, was Figgis rewriting your new script—a script probably raunchier than *Showgirls*—Figgis the artiste of the hour with his Oscar and Golden Globe nominations. Did you see him in his beret at the Golden Globes?

"He turned in his rewrite. It wasn't just not a polish, it wasn't just a major rewrite, it was a tidal wave of a rewrite. *Everything* in your script had been washed away. Many of us hated his rewrite. But Figgis had us. What were we supposed to do? Tell Mike Figgis—think Cimino at the height of his glory, Figgis as the Orson Welles of the month—that we were going to junk his script to find another director to reverentially shoot a script written by the man who'd written *Showgirls?*

"We thought about the publicity *that* would have gotten. We would have looked like idiots. At that particular moment, with the furor of *Showgirls*'s failure, we didn't even like stories which pointed out that we had paid $4 million to the author of *Showgirls.* Many of us felt that was really embarrassing, like—I don't know—did you ever see Steve McQueen in that Ibsen play—*An Enemy of the People*?

"Some of us were actually hoping you'd make a big deal out of being rewritten by Figgis. We knew the kind of publicity together you and Figgis would get and we knew it would only help the movie—especially since the publicity would focus on how the sleaze-meister who wrote *Showgirls* was rewritten by a high-class Oscar nominee.

"It worked, too, for a while. We got exactly that kind of publicity when you announced that you were taking your name off the movie. And for the first couple days, the movie did well. Then, of course, the roof fell in and the movie tanked. Many of us weren't surprised. We knew Figgis's script stunk. Mike is a brilliant and brilliantly atmospheric, stylistic director with an awesome visual sense. But he isn't a writer. He can't write any more than Cimino can or probably Welles could.

"Even you have to admit it would have been impossible to tell Mike that at the height of his days of glory. As I said, every studio in town was offering him everything. He would have taken one of those other offers if we would have said anything to him about not liking his script.

"It helped this company's prestige that he directed a movie for *us* when he could have directed a movie for anybody. In retrospect, from the corporate point of view, it helped us greatly that, at the moment he was the hottest thing in town, he did a movie for us—even if that movie later wound up being a critical and box office failure."

XV

By 1998, when *An Alan Smithee Film: Burn Hollywood Burn* was released, I had become too big for my own britches. Here I was writing a ruthless satire of the industry itself, a savage piece which even used as many real names and situations as legally possible.

I had attracted Sly Stallone and Whoopi Goldberg and Jackie Chan, among others, to my script—but the ads for the movie didn't headline them—they headlined me: "FROM JOE ESZTERHAS" the poster said.

And then, in the making of this movie about power and control in Hollywood, I had persuaded the studio to dump the director's cut and let me *sit in his editing room working with his editor to do the final cut of the movie.*

This wasn't just any director who was getting stabbed in the back either: Arthur Hiller was the former president of the Directors Guild and the present president of the Academy of Motion Picture Arts and Sciences! He was the symbol of the director as titan. He had *led* all directors; he was now *leading* the Academy. And, with the studio as my accomplice, I had stuck a shiv in his back. (At least he hadn't suffered, like Bob Harmon, a real-life heart attack.)

The Directors Guild was so angry at me that they debated changing the name "Alan Smithee" to some other name as their designation for a movie where the director took his name off it. I immediately did a gleeful interview pointing out that a mere screenwriter had stolen "Alan Smithee" from the all-powerful Directors Guild.

Even Paddy Chayefsky—if I was Che, Paddy was Trotsky—hadn't been able to accomplish *that,* although the posters for his movies didn't just have his name on them—they had a *picture* of Paddy in the corner of the poster beating on his typewriter.

I was never able to pull that off, though I did put the actual manual typewriter I used up on the screen in *Jagged Edge*. I don't think any other writer in Hollywood history was ever able to put his typewriter—his actual weapon—up on-screen.

Paddy Chayefsky began working in Hollywood in the fifties, a time when the dean of American screenwriters, Ben Hecht, was quoted as saying: "A screenwriter is a cross between a groundhog and a doormat. . . . All you have to do to make a screenwriter behave is gag him with thousand dollar bills."

Paddy was at dinner once at a studio head's house and he felt the hostess was condescending to him. When he was leaving, she air-kissed him on both cheeks and said good night and thank you.

Paddy air-kissed both of her cheeks and said, "Good night, thank you, and fuck you."

Paddy called NBC critic Gene Shalit a "professional clown."

Paddy insisted that he always be paid at least as much as the director of the movie and was often paid much more.

"The director is an assassin in terms of story," Paddy Chayefsky said. "You have to stand ceaseless guard against the director's ambushes."

He also said:

- "Collaboration in film is fine, as long as it's geared to the realization of the script that I wrote."
- "Becoming a director diminishes a writer—it may give him more power and control, but he loses the writer's perspective."
- "All your life you aim for a time when you're doing what you do for no other reason than that you like it, and I love writing."
- "You spill your guts into a typewriter, which is why you can't stand to see what you write destroyed or degraded into a bunch of claptrap."
- "A writer does not have to compromise his talents in Hollywood. Good films can be made there as well as anywhere else."
- "The worst kind of censorship is the kind that takes place in your own mind before you sit down to a typewriter."
- "Can you believe this? These cruds want rewrites."

Paddy Chayefsky realized every screenwriter's dream—not a word of his script could be changed. It was in his contract.

The studio hired the English director Ken Russell to direct one of Paddy's scripts, *Altered States*. Russell was the classic auteur director.

Russell started changing things in Paddy's script as he shot the movie. Paddy reminded the studio that by contract *nothing* could be changed. The studio reminded Russell.

Russell went berserk. "He started to beat the shit out of the script," the producer of the movie said. "He would make real lousy remarks. Just anything to get Paddy upset. He was really looking to dislodge Paddy from any position of authority, that was obvious. He wanted to debase him."

Ken Russell said to Paddy: "Take your turkey sandwiches and your script and your Sanka and stuff it up your ass and get on the next fucking plane back to New York and let me get on with the fucking film."

Still, no matter how ballistic he was, Ken Russell, the auteur director, couldn't change one word of Paddy's script. Not one word. *By contract.*

And he didn't.

What he did instead was sabotage the film. He had the actors eating when they spoke so no one could understand the words they were garbling. He had them hurry through sentences at machine-gun, nearly stuttering clip. He directed them to get drunk so they would slur Paddy's words.

Paddy went ballistic, too, when he saw what Russell was doing. "You son-ofabitch! You motherfucker!" he screamed at him. But there was nothing he could do. His words were there on-screen, untouched, even if they sounded like gibberish.

The movie was a critical and commercial disaster. Critics blamed not Russell or the actors' delivery but, as one critic said, "the oratorical style" of Paddy's dialogue.

Paddy was heartbroken. He had accomplished what no other screenwriter had ever accomplished. He had protected, by contract, the sanctity of his words—and they had been taken from him and purposely butchered.

"Man, I'm tired of fighting," he wrote a friend. "I truly am."

Within a year, he was dead.

His last words to his wife were "I tried, I really tried."

These words will be on my tombstone: "I tried, I really tried."

Some critic will say: "Even the words on Eszterhas's tombstone aren't original. For most of his career, he lived in penis envy of Paddy Chayefsky (and possibly William Goldman)."

I was discovered as a screenwriter by a studio executive named Marcia Nasatir who'd read a book I'd written and thought I had great potential as a screenwriter.

She was famous in town for writing this memo about a screenplay: "No hope . . . no hero . . . all madness and bullshit philosophy. Script is too wordy. Everything is punched home twice or even thrice."

Marcia was writing about Paddy Chayefsky's script *Network,* for which Paddy later won an Oscar.

I was pleased that she preferred me to my hero, Paddy Chayefsky.

XVI

One of my favorite American novelists never did work in Hollywood, though he wanted to.

"I have listened to writers," Thomas Wolfe said, "who had a book published shudder with horror at the very mention of Hollywood—some of them have even asked me if I would ever listen to an offer from Hollywood—if I could possibly submit my artistic conscience to prostitution by allowing anything I'd write to be made into a motion picture in Hollywood. My answer to this has always been an enthusiastic and fervent yes. If Hollywood wants to prostitute me by buying one of my books for the movies, I am not only willing but eager for the seducers to make their first dastardly proposal. In fact, my position in the matter is very much that of the Belgian virgin the night the Germans took the town: 'When do the atrocities begin?' "

When Thomas Wolfe arrived in Hollywood on a visit, Dorothy Parker threw a party for him where she told a roomful of people that Wolfe "was built on a heroic scale" and that there was no one else "built like him."

Word about his "heroic build" got around quickly all over town and when Wolfe said all he wanted to do was to meet Jean Harlow, Harlow agreed. He met her on the MGM lot and watched her on the set for hours and at the end of the day Harlow, who wore fur-lined tin bras so her nipples wouldn't show through, asked if she could drive the Writer Who Was Built Like No One Else home to his room at the Garden of Allah Hotel.

Everyone on the set noticed the next morning that Jean Harlow and Thomas Wolfe were dressed in the same clothes they had been wearing the night before, but Thomas Wolfe turned down all of MGM's lucrative but dastardly screenwriting proposals and left town the same day.

When William Faulkner, "book-writin' man," first arrived in Hollywood to be a screenwriter, he went to the studio, took a good look around, and fled . . . to Death Valley, where he wandered the desert for a week on a monumental binge.

He went back to the studio, worked in an office for ten hours a day, and stopped by the Hofbrau at night to listen to German music and drink beer. He also played miniature golf and drove down to Santa Monica to watch the surf.

A married man with his wife back home in Mississippi, he went to bed with the secretary at the studio he dictated his scripts to. He wrote poems about her.

He wrote that "her long girl's body was sweet to fuck."

He called her "my heart, my jasmine garden, my April and May cunt, my sweet-assed gal."

Bill Faulkner, screenwriter, brought his wife, Estelle, and their six-year-old little girl to Hollywood. They rented a house in the Palisades. Estelle didn't know that he'd been having an affair with a young secretary for years.

He wanted his secretary to meet Estelle so she could see that Estelle was no threat to his affection for her. The secretary met Estelle at a party and thought her "pale, sad, wasted—not an interesting person."

"Billy," Estelle said to the secretary, "is going to teach me to write." Estelle told her that she was going to become a writer like Zelda Fitzgerald.

At the end of the evening, Estelle said to the secretary, "I hope that you and I will see a lot of each other and become good friends."

From Harlow to Marilyn to Sharon Stone.

A literary tradition for which I did my *bit.* The pen is mightier than the director's sword. It's important to observe that Wolfe and Miller and I . . . what the hell, throw in Paddy and Kim Novak, too, although Novak really doesn't belong in that company . . . it's important to observe that Wolfe and Miller and Paddy and I . . . all used *manual* typewriters.

Screenwriters today don't use manual typewriters anymore, they use laptops which they display to other screenwriters while comparing notes about writer's block at the Rose Café in Venice or at the Farmers Market in L.A.

They don't use *manual* typewriters and they expose their *laptops* to each other—one reason, I think, why this joke is paradigm for today's screenwriters: "Did you hear about the Polish starlet who slept with the screenwriter to get the part?"

A final note about Marilyn which I consider relevant: Cleveland, my home-town, isn't just a place of steel mills and boilermakers. It was home for many years to one of the greatest bar joints in America, the Theatrical Grill, run by a gangster/philosopher named Mushy Wexler.

One night Marilyn Monroe walked in. She was in town on a press tour. She wound up sitting with Mushy, who introduced her to that limp string of spaghetti, sitting by himself in the corner, Arthur Miller, in town for a lecture at the library.

The Theatrical was also loved by Joltin' Joe DiMaggio, who got fantastically drunk there the night the Cleveland Indians stopped his 56-game hitting streak at Municipal Stadium.

The point, obviously, is this: all roads lead not only to Hollywood, not only to sex, but to Cleveland.

Marilyn did *not* leave with Arthur Miller that night at the Theatrical, according to my Hungarian friend Shondor Birns, who was the resident Casanova of the

Theatrical Grill in those days and who was an even bigger poobah racketeer than Mushy Wexler.

Shon was Cleveland's numbers king before the arrival of the King of All Numbers Kings, Don King, who went on to become the infamous boxing manager and promoter. Shon spent a lot of time in jail but whenever he was out, he was back in his green Cadillac, wearing his Italian sharkskin suits, his fedora, and his sunglasses, back hustling the buxom wannabe gun molls at the Theatrical.

According to my friend Shondor Birns, *he* was there the night Marilyn Monroe had drinks with Mushy and another gambler named Fuzzy Lakis when that pointy-headed writer Arthur or Arnold something came over to the table at Mushy's invitation.

But according to Shon, Arthur or Arnold or whatever was introduced and then left and it was *he,* Shon, who took Marilyn Monroe back to her suite at the Hollenden Hotel and spent the night with her.

According to Shon, Marilyn Monroe had skin so pearly white that at a certain moment in the evening he could see all of her veins right through her skin.

Shondor Birns swore to me that all this was true, swore to it till the day he died, his green Cadillac blown to smithereens all over West 25th Street, only a few blocks from where on Lorain Avenue I had grown up.

XVII

Bill Faulkner, screenwriter, woke up one morning at the Knickerbocker Hotel in Hollywood screaming: "Oh, Lordy! Oh, Jesus! They're coming at me! Help me! Don't let them! They're coming at me! No! No!"

He had himself taken to a sanitarium and dried out.

Gérard Brach may be the most famous screenwriter in Europe, author of many of the films Roman Polanski has directed.

One day, while watching CNN in his flat in Paris, something happened to Gérard Brach. He became fixated on the news anchor he was watching.

While the news anchor was unarguably an attractive woman, Gérard Brach had been with many more attractive women. He had even been around Catherine Deneuve, one of the most beautiful women in the world, when she was filming one of his movies.

Gérard Brach watched his news anchor every hour of every day when she was on CNN. Because of the time difference between Paris and Atlanta, sometimes he got up in the middle of the night to watch her.

He stopped going out to make sure he didn't miss her and the doctors told him he had a nervous disorder called agoraphobia—"fear of the marketplace," fear of going out in public.

He wasn't unhappy being home alone all the time. He wasn't home alone. He was at home with his news anchor.

. . .

William Goldman, who got so angry at me after I called him "a hooker from Connecticut" in the London *Times*, has given screenwriters this advice:

- "No matter how much shit you may have heard or read, movies are finally about one thing: THE NEXT JOB."
- "Many, maybe most in the Hollywood community, have a certain contempt for screenwriters. And they're not necessarily wrong."

And this is what Goldman did at a story meeting when he heard an idea from a producer which he knew was absurd: "I wanted to scream so loud: I wanted to choke the asshole—But I was so sweet. I took notes. I grunted and nodded. I smiled when it was conceivably possible."

A couple years after I called him "a hooker from Connecticut," I saw Bill Goldman at Spago. He was with a tableful of Castle Rock executives, obviously pitching something. I was with a gorgeous blonde.

His table was closer to the kitchen. Mine was by the window.

I told my waiter to send him a drink. I watched as the waiter went over. Bill Goldman looked up, glanced at me, shook his head, and looked away from me.

He surprised me. I was sure he'd take the drink.

There are those who claim the reason I've been critical of Bill Goldman for years is that I'm jealous of his Oscars and his critical success.

Oh . . . well . . . *um* . . . I'm not saying it's completely impossible . . . that maybe . . . they're not . . . entirely . . . wrong.

Before I got to Hollywood, when I was a very young newspaperman in Cleveland, I kept hearing from the older reporters about a legendary former reporter who'd wanted to be a Hollywood screenwriter.

He was a legendary drinker and gambler—legendary, too, because he'd been fired from the newspaper for stealing a wristwatch from a jewelry store where he'd gone to cover a holdup.

His name was Ernest Tidyman and when I started writing screenplays in Hollywood, he had just won the Academy Award for writing *The French Connection*.

Overwhelmed with big-money offers to write screenplays, he signed every deal offered him, then hired three young writers to write for him, all of them writing under the name "Ernest Tidyman."

None of the scripts the young men wrote were very good, none of them were made into movies, and suddenly Ernest Tidyman, Oscar winner, wasn't getting any offers anymore.

He died of a heart attack while on a flight to England to meet a director.

I never met him but I spoke after his death to a nephew who told me his uncle had had an extensive collection of watches.

Many years after Ernest Tidyman's death, the director of *The French Connection,* Billy Friedkin, told me that he and Gene Hackman and Roy Scheider had improvised the film and that Ernest Tidyman didn't deserve his Oscar.

But I didn't believe Billy. I figured Billy said that about all the screenwriters who wrote hit movies for him.

Since the movie I wrote for Billy, *Jade,* was a failure, I knew Billy wouldn't say that about me: Billy would say he shot every word of my script.

John Monk Saunders, one of the first screenwriters to win an Academy Award, hanged himself.

XVIII

Are screenwriters ever . . . *triumphant?*

Well, yes, in our evil little ways.

Ben Hecht, the most successful screenwriter in Hollywood history, demanded $5,000 a week from Samuel Goldwyn. This was at a time when houses in Beverly Hills sold for $25,000. He demanded that $2,500 of his weekly payment be made every Monday and the rest every Wednesday.

Goldwyn, one of the most powerful studio bosses in Hollywood, agreed to Hecht's demands.

Then Ben Hecht demanded that if Goldwyn spoke just one word to him the deal would be null and void and Hecht could keep all the money he'd been paid so far. Samuel Goldwyn agreed to that, too.

The weeks went by. Ben Hecht hadn't turned in a page but he'd collected his weekly $5,000. Samuel Goldwyn called him and said, "Ben, this is strictly a social call."

Ben Hecht said, "This cancels the deal," took the $30,000 he'd been paid so far, and was gone.

Charles MacArthur was a celebrated playwright/screenwriter who believed that studio executives were some of the dumbest people he'd ever met and didn't know anything at all about writing. He decided to prove it.

At the gas station one day, he started chatting with the young Englishman who was filling up his tank. The young man lamented that he was only making $40 a week and Charles MacArthur asked him if wanted to make $1,000 a week. The young man said, "Whoever I have to kill, I will happily do it."

Charles MacArthur bought him a new tweed suit and a curved-stem pipe. He took him in to the studio head and introduced him as "Kenneth Woolcott, the well-known English novelist who is against doing any movie writing because he insists there's no room for creative talent in the movies."

The studio boss did everything he could to persuade Kenneth Woolcott, the well-known English novelist, to be a screenwriter at his studio. He finally offered him $1,000 a week. The gas station attendant grudgingly accepted the offer.

The studio was so pleased with Woolcott's work that they kept him under contract at $1,000 a week for a whole year. After which Kenneth Woolcott went back to pumping gas.

We were going to celebrate the fact that Carolco Pictures had bought my script of *Showgirls* and was going to make the movie with Paul Verhoeven directing it.

The producer, Charlie Evans, Bob's brother, was going to throw a lavish party that night at his house in Beverly Hills, complete with mariachi band and Chasen's special chili.

That morning, Paul Verhoeven and I had a script meeting in the dining room of the Four Seasons Hotel. Paul had a suggestion that I rejected. Within minutes our tempers had flared.

"Fuck you!" I said. "I'm not rewriting the script!"

"Then I don't go to party!" Paul yelled in his Dutch but very German-sounding accent.

"Fuck the party, too," I said. "I'm not going to the party, either!"

"Then I get another writer, ja?" Paul yelled.

I got up and stormed back upstairs to my suite.

An hour later, Carolco called my agent to say that, at Paul's direction, they were going to bring in another writer to make changes in my script.

Charlie Evans called my agent nearly in tears. "What's going on?" Charlie said. "What about the party? I can't cancel the mariachi band!"

I called my lawyer, who looked at the Carolco contract and called me back with the news that I hadn't signed it yet. My agent then called Carolco and said *I* owned the script, not them. My agent also said that I wanted another director on the project or I was going to sell my script to another studio.

Charlie Evans called me and said, "What about the party? What am I going to do about the chili?"

During the course of the afternoon, my agent and my lawyer had several volatile conversations with Carolco Pictures. The outcome of these conversations was:

1. I owned the script; Carolco didn't.
2. I had the right to sell it to another studio without Paul Verhoeven's involvement.

3. The party would go on that night anyway because the mariachi band had to be paid and Charlie Evans didn't want all this great Chasen's chili to spoil.

4. No one was under any obligation to go to the party since it was no longer a party that had any connection to *Showgirls* or Carolco Pictures.

By the time Naomi and I got to the party, Paul Verhoeven and his wife, Martine, were already there. The chili was superb. The mariachi band was sensational. The tequila flowed.

Naomi and I were on one side of the room, Paul and Martine on the other.

I was sitting in a thronelike antique chair when Paul came over. He told me he was sorry he'd talked about bringing another writer in to rewrite my script. He said he really wanted to direct the movie. He knelt on the floor in front of my thronelike chair as he said these things. Someone took a picture of the director kneeling in front of the screenwriter.

Paul and I laughed.

He said he'd changed his mind about the suggestion he'd made this morning at the Four Seasons.

Paul and I toasted each other. His wife, a chamber violinist, played some Franz Liszt and dedicated it to me.

I allowed him to direct the movie.

I signed my Carolco contract.

True to his word, Paul made no changes to my script. All the words were mine.

Showgirls made film history.

Right alongside *Ishtar, Waterworld,* and *Heaven's Gate.*

XIX

The worst best-intentioned advice I ever got about screenwriting came from Richard Gilman, the distinguished literary critic, at a party in New York almost thirty years ago.

"Whatever you do," said Dick Gilman to the beginning screenwriter, "don't put your heart into your scripts. You'll get it broken."

For almost thirty years now (and thirty scripts, and fifteen produced movies), I've put my heart into my scripts . . . and my heart is unbroken.

My advice to beginning screenwriters is this:

Put every ounce of heart and soul and guts and passion that you possess into every sentence of every screenplay.

And laugh.

· · ·

She was a fiery, street-smart woman with a nasty temper who'd come to Hollywood out of the world of marketing. She was sexy and no-bullshit with a hank of hair you wanted to press your face into. She had a commercial eye and used it (and her sexiness and toughness) to become first a VP and then head of production. She got a golden parachute, got married, and gave birth to a little girl.

I hadn't seen her for a while and when we had dinner at the Ivy, what struck me was how gloriously happy she was. With her husband, with her little girl. With her life as a wife and a mother. We didn't talk business all night. We talked about our kids.

She wasn't in a hurry anymore. She didn't speak at the rate of a thousand miles an hour. She wasn't looking through me to see who else was in the room. She was almost serene.

I'd always liked her and when I hugged her good night outside the restaurant, I thought—Yes, there *are* happy endings, even real ones, in Hollywood.

A few months later, she was diagnosed with a brain tumor.

And not much later, Dawn Steel died.

My advice to everyone is this:

Put every ounce of heart and soul and guts and passion that you possess into every nanosecond of your life.

And pray!

CHAPTER 2

[Flashback]

Ragamuffin

JONES
What the fuck do you know about what happened half a century
ago in some goddamn part of the world you never even been in?
What the fuck does anybody know about their parents?

Music Box

I was born in Hungary. On the 23rd of November in 1944 in a village near the Austrian border called Csákánydoroszló. American bombs fell. Hungary was a Nazi ally.

The bombs denuded Hungarians, stripping them of their clothes. Women were left wearing nothing but the rubber band inside their panties. They were also left dead, as were many men and children.

My paternal grandfather, Jozsef Kreisz, was a Hungarian teamster. He loved his horses, his beer, his wife, and his three children. He was drafted into the Austro-Hungarian army after the assassination of the Archduke Ferdinand and fought on the Russian front. He fell into a hole, nearly froze, and was captured by the Russians. When he was released, he was half blind. He had aged so much that his wife didn't recognize him.

Hungary had been taken over by a Communist government, run by an angry Hungarian named Béla Kun, whose leather-jacketed, Lenin-capped followers hanged many Hungarians on lampposts. My grandfather took my father, who was a little boy, out into the streets of Budapest and showed him the bodies on the lampposts.

It was my father's earliest memory. He remembered the corpses up there and that they had been hung there by Béla Kun, who was a Communist and a *Zsido* . . . a Jew.

My father grew up in Kispest, a Budapest working-class district, not far from the canning factory where my grandfather now worked, since he was half blind. My grandmother, a devoutly religious Roman Catholic, prayed and raised the three kids, my father and his two older sisters.

They were dirt-poor. When he was a little boy, my father contracted scarlet fever, which infected his hip. Surgery was required. My father had surgery eleven times on his hip without any anesthetic. There was no money for anesthetics, which, after the assassination of the Archduke Ferdinand, were in short supply. The surgeries left him with one leg shorter than the other and a pronounced limp.

He was the baby of the family, doted upon by his mother and two sisters. He stayed in bed and read much of the time. He read *The Count of Monte Cristo, The Three Musketeers,* and his favorite, the German writer Karl May, who wrote of the American West he had never seen (but which my great-grandfather had). My father's favorite Karl May character was the gunslinger called Old Shatterhand.

And there was another little boy living not far away from my father, in Austria, whose favorite writer was Karl May and whose favorite character was Old Shatterhand. This little boy's name was Adolf Hitler.

My father thought, reading so much about Old Shatterhand and the Count of Monte Cristo, that maybe he could write, too. He began writing short stories and sending them to the Budapest newspapers. They were, in the time-honored way, all rejected.

He went to school and excelled, knowing he couldn't support himself with physical labor. He kept writing the stories which kept being rejected. He became a mailman but his hip couldn't take the walking. He got a law degree and was the world's worst lawyer.

Then a story was accepted by one of the Budapest newspapers. And another. And another. A book was published which became commercially successful. And another. And another.

He became an adviser to the Hungarian prime minister. He paid for the eye surgery which restored my grandfather's sight. He was a successful Hungarian writer. A short, balding young man so heavy that a half circle had to be cut out of his desk so he could reach it. He loved Westphalian ham, Csabai kolbász, hard salami, black bread, palacsinta, and dark beer. He still lived with his parents and two sisters, a hardworking responsible young man who only occasionally lapsed.

Like the time he was in a small town on the Hungarian Plains and was arrested for shooting out half the town's traffic lights.

He saw my mother in a Budapest church one day and fell in love. Her name was Mária Biro. She was ten years younger than he, twenty-seven years old, a classic Hungarian beauty: tall, high-cheek-boned, her dark hair highlighted by slanted, deeply brown Eurasian eyes. He inquired about her, discovered that she was a secretary in the Hungarian government's secretarial pool, arranged that she be assigned to his office.

She was the daughter of a tavern-keeper on the grounds of Budapest's largest military academy. Her father was an alcoholic, the size of a swollen buffalo. Her mother, a chain-smoker, had died when she was fifteen. Her father put the extremely shy, fifteen-year-old girl behind the cash register at the tavern—the only woman among the young and sexually aggressive recruits of the military academy.

Six months after her mother's death, her father advertised in the Budapest newspapers for a new wife. He married a prostitute and soon contracted gonorrhea from her. My mother saw her father in the parlor one day: he was trying to clear his penis of pus with a long needle.

She had a nervous breakdown and was sent to live with a Belgian family for a year. When she returned, she moved into a tiny apartment of her own and became a secretary. She was intensely religious. She wore a scapular. She said the Rosary twice a day. She went to Mass every morning.

My parents married in early 1944. She towered over him. He stood on a stack of encyclopedias to match her height. They were startlingly different people. She was inward. He loved the limelight and the applause at the end of a speech. She was deeply private. He was a public figure. She read religious journals. He was literary and political. She was a chain-smoker who liked an occasional sip of brandy. After his arrest for shooting out the streetlights, he was a teetotaler.

I would very much become their son. I was her height and I inherited her cheekbones and her slanted eyes and his jowls and tendency to fat. I was a chain-smoker who liked more than occasional sips of bourbon and beer and wine. I was shy and hid my shyness with a strutting, macho bravado.

I became a public figure whose private life became, on occasion, fodder for tabloids. I felt ambivalent about the limelight, at times reclusive, but at all times enjoying—and then blaming myself for enjoying—the applause at the end of an appearance.

By the summer of 1944, the war was ending. Russian troops were invading Hungary. Hungarians were terrified. The Red Army was on its way. It was the figurative return of the now reviled Béla Kun. The Russians, Hungarians told each other, were barbarians. They were filled with venereal disease. They were raping their way through Hungary. Even old grandmothers weren't safe from the priapic savagery. They were such animals, Hungarians told each other, that they filled their arms with stolen wristwatches—twenty, thirty, on each arm. They drank from the toilets. They urinated in holy water fountains. They ate cats and dogs. They raped anally.

When my mother was five months pregnant with me, my father got her a maid and arranged that they move to a city near the Austrian border, to Szombathely, as far away from the advance of the Red Army as possible. He stayed temporarily in Budapest, in his capacity as an adviser to the prime minister, but would join us when I was born.

He made it through the chaos of the combat lines two weeks after I was born. His father and mother and his two sisters joined us. The Red Army was sweeping through Hungary. American bombs fell hourly from the sky. We all lived in an apartment house in Szombathely. Air raid sirens wailed all the time.

During one bombing, as my mother raced down the stairs with me in her arms, my father next to her, the roof collapsed onto the stairway. I was knocked from her arms as she and my father were propelled down the stairs. When it was over, desperate, they searched for me and couldn't find me. They thought I had been covered by the rubble.

They finally found me. An old woman had picked me up. She had taken her babushka and covered my mouth with it. She had saved my life. The apartment house had taken a direct hit.

My parents lost everything but one suitcase. The suitcase was filled with cartons of cigarettes, not for my mother to smoke, but to be used as currency in this ravaged new world.

We moved to a different apartment house, which took a direct hit the following week. We hid in the basement from the bombs. When we crawled out, my parents heard the screams coming from the basement of the neighboring apartment house, which had caved in and was burning. The people in that basement had sought shelter in a huge furnace. They couldn't get out. No one could get them out. The building atop the furnace burned. The people inside the furnace roasted to death. Slowly.

My father decided after that bombing that we had to leave Hungary, but my grandfather, Jozsef Kreisz, said he wasn't coming. He wasn't afraid of the Russians, my grandfather said, no matter what stories the Hungarians were scaring each other with.

He had met many Russians he had liked in his captivity. He spoke Russian fluently and he knew the Russians couldn't be as bad as the Romanians who had occupied Hungary briefly after his return from captivity. Those bastard Romanians had worn pancake makeup—*pancake makeup on men!*—and say what you want about all the watches the Russians were wearing, they certainly weren't wearing *pancake makeup!*

My father begged him to come with us but Jozsef Kreisz hugged and kissed us, then walked away to the nearest hotel. When the Russians arrived in Szombathely, it was Jozsef Kreisz who, sleepy-eyed and in his shirtsleeves, served as the translator between the Hungarian mayor and the four-star Red Army general.

My father drove us in his small Steir car from Szombathely toward the Austrian border. We were jammed in there—me, my mother, my father, my grandmother, my two aunts, driving through lush green countryside and shadowy black forests. Refugees and retreating Nazis and Hungarian soldiers were everywhere. American fighter pilots buzzed the treetops and machine-gunned the cars (like ours) below. They machine-gunned us, but my father roared the Steir over a ditch and into the trees. We crossed the Austrian border and were incarcerated by the Nazis.

The Nazis took us to a camp called Mauthausen. It was a Zsido extermination camp, filled with Jews from all over Europe. The Nazis put us on the same diet as the Jews: nothing but pine needle soup. A German soldier gave my mother a sliced-in-half gasoline can so she could bathe me. We were at Mauthausen for two months.

One morning the Germans were gone. The war was over. We were free. Some of the Jews went into the countryside and exacted a horrible revenge upon the neighboring Austrian farmers who had abused them as slave laborers.

It was chaos! It was anarchy! It was hell! That's what my father told me and I, of course, believed him.

We don't know the early part. We never know the early part. Our parents tell us and we love them. So we take their word for it.

My father did not tell me that the Hungarians, when the war was clearly over, when they were out of ammunition, marched Hungarian Zsidos to the Danube each day and garroted them with wire or choked them with their bare hands, killing so many that the Blue Danube wasn't blue . . . it was red.

I learned this as an American man, reading history books.

The Nazis were gone and the British and the Americans came. We stayed in one refugee camp for a while and then we moved to another—from Hayd to Kellerberg to Spital, all in Austria.

We lived in barracks, separated from each other by cardboard or hanging blankets. There wasn't any food for months—except polenta, which we called *puliszka.*

One day someone shot a horse and after months without meat, everyone ate it. We got very sick. The smell of shit and vomit was everywhere.

My life was saved by an American soldier who brought me a Hershey bar every day. It was all I had to eat. He had a child my age. He showed us his picture.

I cried all the time. I cried when I had to eat puliszka. And when I saw them shoot the horse. I cried whenever I saw a soldier. Any soldier. Of whatever uniform. I started crying the instant I saw a uniform. I cried whenever I heard a siren, and I heard sirens often in the camps because fires in the barracks were common.

One night the sirens sounded and people were screaming, running out of the barracks. They ran to the outhouse. I ran outside, too, holding on to my mother. They pulled a body out of the outhouse, the body of a little boy. He smelled. He was covered in shit and was dead. He had fallen through the hole into the shit and drowned there.

It is my first memory. I see his body and it smells and my mother is holding me and I'm crying.

I remember my grandmother holding me as she was crying. I wasn't crying, but everybody else was. My grandmother and my aunts were leaving the camp and going back to Hungary. They were rejoining my grandfather. My father was begging them not to go.

I heard the words *Kommunista* and *Komchi* for the first time. My grandmother and my aunts walked away from us and got into the back of a truck. They waved as the truck pulled away until I couldn't see them. My mother picked me up and held me. Her cheeks were wet. My father put his arm around me and held both of us.

I said, "Papa, what are Komchis?"

Komchis are Communists. They were bad guys. They were the worst bad guys. They took kids away from their parents. They killed and executed people. They didn't let people pray. They were the enemy. They were trying to take over the world. They were trying to take good people back to Hungary. Right here in this camp. The Komchis had spies and agents.

I was scared. "Are they worse than the *Krampusz?*" I asked my father.

He said they were.

The Krampusz came to the camp the week before Christmas, dressed as a devil. The Krampusz asked if you'd been a good little boy or girl. He laughed like a witch and howled like a demon.

If you were a good little boy or girl the Krampusz promised St. Nicholas would come for Christmas. But if you were bad, the Krampusz said you'd burn in hell. If you didn't eat your puliszka, if you cried all the time . . .

I was afraid of the Krampusz, the Komchis, the uniforms, the sirens, the outhouse, and of the thing they called TB.

All the children had to line up and stand in front of a machine which would tell you if you had TB. I didn't really know what TB was, but I was afraid of it anyway and I cried. I was already crying when I stepped in front of the machine. But I didn't have TB—I was the only child in the camp who didn't have it.

To try to protect me from getting it, my father took me for long walks every day so we would be away from the camp. We walked the roads outside. There were hills of snow everywhere. It was so cold I felt ice on my eyelids.

My feet froze. We couldn't walk anymore. I couldn't even get my feet off the bed. Now I was crying because my feet hurt.

But I didn't have TB!

Because of the scarlet fever in his hip, my father couldn't do the physical labor most of the men did. He traded some of the cigarette packs we had for a violin, which he had played as a child. He found other violins and other Hungarians who could play them and formed the camp's own Gypsy band. They hired themselves out on weekends to play at nearby Austrian taverns.

My parents were overjoyed. With the few schillings my father made playing the violin, they could buy food in the camp's prospering black market.

Then my father fell on the ice and he broke his wrist. No more Gypsy music. No more violin. No more money.

When we'd had nothing to eat but puliszka for a long time, my father opened the suitcase and brought out a pack of cigarettes to trade for meat. The pack felt light to him. He opened it. It was empty. He opened others. They were empty, too.

My mother had smoked all the cigarettes and had carefully resealed all the packs. My father yelled at my mother, who yelled back at him. I, naturally, started to cry.

Every day from then on, my mother took me for a walk in the countryside. We hunted dry tree leaves together. She rolled the leaves up in a newspaper and sat down on the grass with me and she smoked them. She was happy. Me too.

The Komchis were coming to the camp and my father had to leave. That happened several times. The Komchis had a list with people's names on it and they'd find the people in the camp, drag them to a truck, and take them back to Hungary. My father's name was on the list. So he left.

Somehow he always found out when they were coming. He'd go to one of the other nearby camps and blend in with those refugees until the Komchis were gone from our camp.

Once the Komchis came to our barrack and demanded to see István Eszterhás but my mother said he had left her and she didn't know where he was. The Komchis were very angry and when they got back into their trucks all the Hungarians in the barrack cheered.

Sometimes I heard one of the Hungarians, but never my mother, say "*Büdös Zsidok*" when the Komchis left . . . which means "Stinking Jews."

I asked my father if the Zsidos were bad like the Komchis and the Krampusz. I could tell he didn't like me asking that.

He said, "No, Zsidos are people like other people."

"How do they look?" I asked.

"Like everybody else," he said.

"Are there any here in the camp?" I asked.

"No," he said, "there aren't."

I asked him why not. There were Hungarians, Russians, Poles, Ukrainians, Italians, Lithuanians, Latvians, Estonians, Romanians, and Greeks here. Why no *Zsidos*?

"I don't know," he said.

"Are the *Zsidos* Komchis?" I asked.

"There are some who are and some who aren't," he said. "Just like there are some Hungarians who aren't Komchis and some who are."

"Do they stink?" I asked.

"No," he said, "who told you that?"

I told him some of the Hungarians in the barrack had said it.

"They're crazy," my father said.

"Why do they say they stink?" I asked.

He sighed. "Because they eat a lot of garlic," he said. "It's good for you."

"What's garlic?" I asked.

He laughed and held me in his arms and said, "One day you'll know. One day you'll taste garlic."

As I grew older in the camps, the older Hungarian boys taught me things. Watching a Hungarian woman walk out of a barrack, a small group of us followed her as she walked along a fence and ducked into the back of a garage filled with jeeps. There were American soldiers waiting for her, laughing. There was a mattress on the floor and she got down on it as the soldiers laughed. She took her clothes off. We crept from jeep to jeep, trying to get closer.

After her clothes were off, she twirled around on the mattress, smiling, licking her lips. One after another, the Americans approached her, naked now, their *pimplis* bigger than any I'd ever seen. They moved around individually on top of her.

When each soldier was done, he dropped something on the mattress that one of the older boys said later was a nylon stocking. Then she got dressed quickly and ducked back out. The soldiers laughed some more, got dressed, and left.

A few days later, as we were playing with a soccer ball, the same woman walked by us on the way to the milk line. The older boys started laughing and yelling "*Kurva néni! Kurva néni!*"—"Whore lady, whore lady!"

She put her head down, covered her ears, and ran away.

I asked my mother what a *kurva* was and she slapped me.

I played outside with the other Hungarian kids. I liked the soccer ball that we were always kicking over the barbed wire fence—but the soldiers never minded getting it for us.

One American soldier showed us a strange ball one day we had never seen before. It wasn't round, it was odd-shaped and hard to throw. The soldier kept calling it a football, but we knew it wasn't a football since our soccer ball was the football.

I heard the phrase "*Lofasz A Seggedbe!*" all the time from the Hungarians around me, but never from my father or mother.

It seemed to be the Hungarian way of expressing anger or displeasure or even mild disagreement. It was used casually, almost as casually as "*Hogy Vagy?*"—How are you?—and "*Isten Hozott!*"—God has brought you.

Even though it was used so casually, I was forbidden to say it. I didn't say it, but the older boys said it constantly.

They'd say, "*Lofasz A Seggedbe, Jozsi,* what are you crying about?" Or, if I wanted to play with their ball, they'd say, "*Lofasz A Seggedbe, Jozsi,* go home!"

It means: May a horse's cock enter your behind.

And an English war correspondent covering a Hungarian cavalry charge in World War I wrote: "The Hungarians rode down the hill yelling their ancient tribal battle cry—"Lofasz A Seggedbe!"

This is something else the older boys taught me:

Half a mile from the camp at the edge of the pine forest was a train track. The train came by at dusk each day. There were people, the older boys said, who would wait for the train each day. Then they'd "catch it," the older boys said and laughed. They would lie down in front of the train as it came and let it go over them.

Did I want to see it?

No, I didn't want to see it.

"You're a big baby," they said. "All you can do is cry all the time. All you can do with your *pimpli* is piss with it."

I agreed to go down to the tracks with them. It was winter and there was snow on the ground. Dusk was fast approaching. We waited, hidden behind some trees. We saw no one.

"It doesn't happen every day," one of the older boys said.

"Jozsi is going to shit his pants," another said.

And then we saw her. A very old, birdlike woman, dressed in black. A crow-like apparition against the harsh whiteness of the snow. Her head was down. She wore a black babushka. A rosary was twisting in her hands.

The older boys were excited. My knees felt weak. I felt like I was going to throw up.

"Hold him," one of the older boys said, "don't let him run away."

The old woman went up to the train track and knelt down in the snow, shaking, holding on to her rosary. She was crying. Her lips were moving. It was getting darker. I heard a train whistle.

Some of the older boys hooted. I heard the sound of the train now.

She got up, took a few steps, and fell over into the middle of the track. I could see her body shaking. Her head was down, she was on her knees, crumpled over. A black lump. She faced not the train but the trees where we were hiding.

There was hardly a thud when the train hit her. It sounded more like a squish. Blood sprayed onto the snow.

I smelled vomit. It was mine. I was running, crying. I heard the older boys laughing as they ran after me.

I met my first girlfriend in the camp, the eight-year-old blond Mari Toth, whose father was a Hungarian shoemaker. Her brother, Jozsi, was my first best friend.

We ran from the Krampusz together and played ball together and stood in the milk line together, running home to the barrack with the steaming hot milk which we would share with our parents. I was five and Jozsi was six.

At Christmas, my father made me a toy rifle out of an umbrella and Mari, Jozsi, and I would pretend to go out and hunt Komchis with it. One of the GIs thought we were funny. He'd see us with our umbrella-rifle and grin and shout "Boom! Boom! Boom!" Sometimes he'd even hide from us or sneak up on us and say *"Okay!"*

"Okay" was the first English word I learned. *"Vell"* was the second. Americans used it for everything, but no Hungarian knew exactly what it meant.

Then my father taught me—*"Hallo! Hov arr yu?"* and *"Yez, zir, I lak Amerika very mooch."* I learned to say those things in Spanish, Portuguese, and Italian, because we were trying to emigrate from the camps to those countries, too.

The relief organizations would send their representatives from those countries and my mother, my father, and I would appear before them. I would show off what my father had taught me: *"Okay! Hallo! Hov arr yu? Yez zir!"* Then we would go back to the barrack and hear nothing from them again.

Except once. A relief organizer summoned us to say he had found my father a job as a handyman and janitor in Seattle, Washington. Our sponsor in America would be the judge whom my father would work for. We were overjoyed. We were going to America! The land of the free! Where the streets were paved with gold!

But no. The judge in Seattle changed his mind. He wrote a letter saying he had thought about it and wouldn't feel right about employing a man as a janitor who was . . . a successful novelist, a former lawyer, and who had graduated with honors from the respected Pázmány Péter University in Budapest.

My parents were heartbroken.

I said, "*Vell, okay!*"

And then, in answer to my mother's constant prayers, novenas, Rosaries— appeals to St. Jude, to St. Anthony of Padua, to the Blessed Virgin Mary, Sts. Elizabeth and Margaret of Hungary—a miracle!

We were informed we had another American sponsor. A man who had written that he would personally guarantee our livelihood in America. He was an American citizen but Hungarian-born, a Hungarian actor working in American films, playing mostly American Indians in John Wayne westerns.

His name was Jenö Máté. He lived in New York and Hollywood.

My father didn't know him. He'd never heard of him. He was afraid it was some kind of mistake. Why would a complete stranger guarantee the livelihood of a forty-three-year-old man who couldn't do physical labor? How could he guarantee the livelihood of a Hungarian writer who couldn't speak English?

But there was no mistake. Jenö Máté had written to the authorities specifically about sponsoring István Eszterhás, his wife, and his son.

Plans were made. Dates scheduled. We would be transported by truck from Austria to Bremen, Germany. We would board the American refugee ship, formerly a troop carrier, the SS *Hentselman,* for an eleven-day journey to New York City. There we would be met by a representative of Caritas, a Roman Catholic relief organization. We were even given a five-dollar bill so that we would have some money when we arrived.

All three of us kept looking at and feeling the five-dollar bill. American money. From the land where the streets were paved with gold.

The date arrived. We had our one suitcase with the clothes in it we'd always had. I had my umbrella-rifle in my hands.

It was a rainy summer day. The military truck pulled up in front of the barrack. A GI called our name. We barely recognized it the way he pronounced it. We climbed into the back of the truck.

There were a few Hungarians watching us, my friend Jozsi Toth among them. I threw my umbrella-rifle out of the back of the truck and Jozsi caught it. He was jumping up and down, holding the rifle high.

The truck started to move. We sat down in the back as it rattled and shook our suitcase next to us. I looked out the back. Jozsi was still jumping up and down, his umbrella-rifle raised high.

The camp was smaller . . . and smaller . . . and smaller . . . and then it was gone.

I had never seen a ship before. It was bigger than the steep-cliff mountain I had once seen in Salzburg. My parents taught me another American phrase—"*Zank yu.*"

I spoke English all the time to the soldiers as we stood in the long lines. *Vell, okay, hov arr yu, zank yu.* Some of the soldiers gave me chewing gum and candy. I had never tasted chewing gum before. I didn't know I wasn't supposed to swallow it.

My stomach hurt. I threw up. I cried.

Children my age—I was five and a half in June of 1950—stayed with their mothers on board. The women slept on cots in the biggest room I had ever seen. Thousands of women and their children. The men were sleeping in another endless room.

I slept on a cot next to my mother. When the women went to bed, they took their clothes off. Thousands and thousands of naked women of different shapes and sizes. I studied them.

I was happy studying them. I looked forward each night to my studies.

As a Hungarian boy and then as an American man, I diligently continued the study I began on the ship, a lifelong exploration of the bodies of women.

I dream still about waking early and waiting for the women on the ship to slowly put their clothes on. Sometimes my mother, seeing the intensity of my study, told me to look away.

I looked away, but wherever I looked I saw only more naked women.

During the day, the men and women mingled on deck and the children played. My father was ill. He had the flu and we never saw him.

We visited him in a room where he was lying down. We had to put masks on our faces when we saw him. I didn't know why but I didn't ask any questions.

I thought it was another oddity among people whose streets were paved with gold.

I didn't know what gold was until they showed me it was teeth. An old Hungarian woman in the barrack had heard me ask what it was. So she opened her mouth wide and told me to look deep into it.

In the back, among black teeth, something gleamed. It was the gold. I understood it then.

In America, the streets would be full of these special gleaming teeth.

. . .

A soldier saw my mother on the deck of the ship light up her newspaper filled with tree leaves. He came over and asked to smell what she was smoking. She gave it to him.

He took a drag and started to cough. He threw it over the side, looked at her angrily, and walked away. My mother held on to me. I knew she was frightened.

The soldier came back. He handed her three packs of American cigarettes in a shiny-paper covering. She told him no in Hungarian, but he said *Yez, Yez.*

He opened one of the packs and handed her a cigarette. She put it into her mouth. Her hands were shaking. He lit it for her with a match. She took a deep drag and looked away from him.

I saw she was crying. I looked at him and he was crying, too, but smiling at the same time. Then the American walked away.

A soldier saw me on deck looking at the sea. There were big fish in it, my mother told me, which ate you if you fell into the water. I was trying to see the fish that ate you but I couldn't.

The soldier brought me a rocking horse and a flute. I said, "*Vell, okay, hov arr yu, zank yu.*" He laughed and ruffled my hair.

I loved my rocking horse and my flute. I had the flute in my mouth all day and blew it as hard as I could. My mother said, "Stop. You're all out of breath."

But I blew it and blew it.

It began to rain. The wind howled. The ship pitched forward and back and leaned to the side. We had to stay all day in the room where the women slept. Many of them were throwing up. Needless to say, I was throwing up, too.

But I was happy.

I had my rocking horse and my flute and there were some women who were naked now even during the day.

My mother and father were on deck in the sunshine. I was next to them blowing my flute. Up ahead, we could see the tallest buildings I had ever seen—ten times the size of the sheer-cliff mountain in Salzburg.

They hugged me and said, "Look, Jozsi, look at America!"

I stopped blowing my flute and looked. I said, "They have big barracks here, Papa!"

The soldier who had given me the rocking horse and the flute came and took them back.

I screamed. They were *mine!*

My parents explained that they were for other little boys, too, who'd also come to America on this ship. I didn't care about other little boys. I cared about my rocking horse and my flute.

I screamed at the soldier. I screamed—"*Vell, okay, Hov arr yu, Zank yu!*"—at the top of my lungs. I didn't know any other American words.

He shook his head and walked away with my things. A few minutes later, he came back and said I could keep the flute.

I started screaming at him again, but it didn't work this time. He kept the rocking horse.

We left the ship in a long line. There were relief people on the dock waiting for us refugees, but when we got to the dock, the Caritas official who was supposed to meet us wasn't there.

We were sweating and hungry. A man was selling fruit and my father said he would buy me an apple. I had never tasted an apple. It was big and beautifully red.

My father gave the fruit vendor the five-dollar bill we had been touching and feeling since the refugee camp. The vendor gave me the apple and put the five-dollar bill in his pocket and said, "*Zank yu!*"

Now we had an apple and no money. Then I ate the apple.

Now we had no money and no apple, either.

The Caritas official was finally there and he put us into a car. I had never been in a car before, only jeeps and trucks. It was like a small, beautiful room that moved.

There was so much noise in America that my mother covered her ears with her hands. Cars honked. People yelled. Policemen whistled. The buildings were so big you couldn't see the sky. It was so hot it was hard to breathe. Our refugee camp clothes were covered with splotches of sweat.

My father told the relief official that America must be a very expensive place if an apple cost all the money we had. The Caritas man laughed.

I looked out the car window to see if I could see any gold teeth in the streets. I couldn't.

I asked the Caritas man to show us where the gold teeth were.

He laughed even more, then he took us to a tall tenement apartment building owned by a florid-faced, friendly Hungarian woman, Mrs. Szánto. Her building was filled with other refugee Hungarians.

She gave us a room and she made us food. She spoke Hungarian in a way I'd never heard. The Hungarian words were mixed with vells and okays and also with "*Yu no?*" and "*Alrite, mizter?*"

I stood at the window of our room looking far below at all the cars and blew my flute. There were more sirens in the streets of America then I'd ever heard in the camps.

I cried all night and held my mother.

· · ·

I heard my father tell Mrs. Szánto that he wanted to find our sponsor to America and thank him.

Mrs. Szánto asked him who the sponsor was, and when he said it was Jenö Máté, she started to laugh. She told my father that Jenö Máté sponsored anybody and everybody. That he had sponsored more refugee Hungarians all by himself than entire American organizations. That one day America would put Jenö Máté in jail.

My father was frightened that if America put Jenö Máté in jail, then maybe America would send all the refugees he had sponsored back to the camps. I heard my father say to my mother that he was afraid of the Komchis here, too.

America was in a war with the Komchis at a faraway place called Korea.

What if the Komchis bombed America? What if the Komchis invaded America and started filling their arms with wristwatches again? What if we had come to America for nothing—if the Komchis followed us over here—and the same thing happened here that had happened in Hungary?

My father said maybe we should have gone to Chile or Argentina, countries that weren't at war with the Komchis.

My mother's solution was to pray and sometimes I prayed with her, kneeling down in that airless, overheated little room with sweat dripping off us, the car horns and the sirens echoing from the street.

She continued telling me about Jesus, which she'd begun doing in the camp. I was fascinated by Jesus. More exactly, I was fascinated by his crucifixion. They drove *nails* into his *hands* and *feet* and they put him up on a *cross*.

Why?

Because they hated him, she said.

Who? The Komchis?

No, she said, the Zsidos—the Jews.

The Zsidos killed Jesus?

My father overheard her and was angry. "Stop filling the boy with nonsense," he said.

She got angry, too. "It's true, the Zsidos killed him!"

My father lost his temper. "Jesus *was* a Jew!" he said, and left the room.

"But why did the Zsidos kill Jesus if he was a Zsido?" I asked.

My mother looked away and said I'd understand when I was older.

I was very sick. I was burning up. My throat felt like a wound. It hurt to move.

My father got Mrs. Szánto, who looked at me and used a word I hadn't heard before: *polio*. She knew a Hungarian doctor, Dr. Szo. She would call him. We'd have to meet him at the hospital.

We walked through the garbage-strewn chaotic New York streets to the hospital. My father held me much of the way. My mother had stayed in the apartment. She was afraid of the noise in the street.

At the hospital, Dr. Szo examined me. He spoke fluent Hungarian. He said I was a very sick boy, but I didn't have polio. He prescribed medicines. My father said we didn't have any money. Dr. Szo gave us the medicines.

He hugged me when we left. He shook my father's hand and slipped a twenty-dollar bill into it. My father put his head down and for a moment I thought he was going to cry.

"Go," Dr. Szo said to my father. "Take the boy home. He needs rest." My father carried me much of the way back and told my mother how kind this man had been to us.

"Zsido," my father said to her. She said nothing.

On the way home that day from the hospital, in the withering humidity of the city, my father and I passed a watermelon stand. I had never seen watermelons before. They were the darkest green, lined up next to each other on the sidewalk. My father indicated to the man that he'd like him to cut into one so we could see it.

The man took a big knife, slit the watermelon in half, and the red juice exploded from it . . . and I started to scream.

Maybe it was my fever. Maybe it was something else.

At night in the tenement apartment in New York we heard the shooting begin. Gunshots and mortars and more sirens than I'd ever heard before.

We woke up. We huddled on the floor. War. The Komchis were in the streets. Korea was here.

My mother prayed and sobbed. My father held me. I felt him trembling.

The door burst open. Mrs. Szántó had heard my mother's sobs.

"What's the matter?" Mrs. Szántó cried.

The war, my father said. The gunshots. The mortars. The Komchis. Korea.

No, Mrs. Szántó said. Firecrackers. Cherry bombs. Roman candles.

The Fourth of July.

My father took me with him to visit our sponsor, Jenö Máté.

We walked the streets for hours until we found the address. It was a tenement like ours in a neighborhood like ours. We walked up a long flight of stairs and my father hesitantly knocked on the door. There was no answer. He knocked again. Something roared some muffled words in Hungarian on the other side of the door and we both took a step back and looked at each other.

And then the door was flung open and a giant of a man stood there barechested, wearing only a rumpled pair of pants. His chest was huge and flabby.

His stomach jutted out in front of him. He had a head bigger than any I'd ever seen and his coarse jet-black hair stuck out in every direction. His neck was thick and his eyes were red embers of burning coal. He stood there, glaring, looking like he would erupt. He looked us over like he was sizing us up for lunch.

"*Máté Jenö?*" my father asked timidly in Hungarian.

"Who wants to know?" he bellowed. His Hungarian was perfect and unaccented.

My father told him who we were and began thanking him for making it possible for us to come to America.

"What do you want?" the giant roared.

"Nothing," my father said, "the boy and I came just to thank you."

"Do you want money?"

"No," my father repeated, "I don't want anything."

"I don't have any money," Jenö Máté said. "Don't ask me for money."

"Please," my father said, "I'm not asking you for any—"

"I need money just like you do," Jenö Máté said.

It went on like that for a while and my father asked him why he had sponsored us.

"What's your name again?"

My father told him.

The giant shrugged.

"I've never heard of you," Jenö Máté said.

"But you sponsored us to America."

"Are you sure it was me?"

"Yes," my father said.

"What do you do?" Jenö Máté asked.

My father told him he wrote Hungarian novels.

"I don't know," Jenö Máté said, "maybe I read one of your novels."

"Which one?" my father said.

"Who knows?" Jenö Máté paused a moment and said, "I sponsor everybody. My friends bring me lists. I sign to be the sponsor. It doesn't matter. This is a big country. There's room for everybody. Just don't ask me for money. I don't have any money."

My father thanked him again and shook his hand again. The giant peered strangely from his height at us and we started walking away.

"*Wait!*" he roared. He walked up to us. He handed my father some crumpled money he had pulled from his pocket.

"I can't take this," my father said. "Please. I told you. I don't want your money. I came to thank you." He held the crumpled bill out to him.

"*Take it!*" the giant roared.

"But it's ten dollars!" my father said.

"Buy the boy a hamboorger," the giant said. He turned to me. "Did you eat a hamboorger yet?" I shook my head. "It's the best thing you'll ever eat in America, a hamboorger," he said.

"But this is a lot of money!" my father said.

The giant smiled.

"Buy him two hamboorger!" he said, walked away, and slammed the door in our faces.

In Hollywood as an American screenwriter, I asked about Jenö Máté, who was long dead.

The Hungarians around Fairfax Avenue remembered him. He would sit in the Budapest Restaurant after his day on the movie set, his face still wearing the war paint of an American Indian, a feather tucked into his hair.

He would eat three orders of chicken paprikás, one after the other, drink innumerable bottles of Tokay wine. Then he would sit at the piano and play Gypsy songs over and over again, his war paint mixing with sweat and dripping onto the keys.

Mrs. Szántó found a job for my parents in White Plains, a town not far away. My father would be handyman and my mother a waitress at a place called Margie's Diner. Margie, Mrs. Szántó said, was Hungarian—her mother, now dead, came from Hungary. Margie was born in America, but still spoke Hungarian.

Mrs. Szántó walked us to a bus station. My father carried the suitcase. My mother smoked. I blew my flute.

Margie spoke Hungarian with English like Mrs. Szántó. Her husband was an American named Ed.

My father was "Steve." My mother was "Mary." And I was "Joee." Ed also called me "Heykid!"

When we arrived, Margie showed us where we would sleep—a garage filled with old furniture. My father said there was no room for us. Margie said there would be when he cleaned the furniture out.

I kept blowing on my flute.

Margie said, "Stop that! You're giving me a headache."

We cleared the furniture out. There were no lights, except for a flashlight Margie had given us. We slept in one bed. I was sleeping between my parents.

My mother's scream woke me up. Instantly, my father had the flashlight on. I heard loud chittering noises. And I looked up. The flashlight was illuminating the girders above us.

Rats were watching and talking to us. Laughing. Snarling. Dancing their tails. Flashing their teeth.

. . .

My mother wore an apron and a white uniform. Ed called her "Hanibonch" and "Sveeti." My father was clearing a yard that was overgrown.

I blew into my flute and Margie yelled at me: "Put that thing down!"

My father started to itch. Red spots appeared all over his hands and face. Margie said, "It will go away." But it didn't. He itched more. The spots were all over his body as he cleared the yard day after day.

A Hungarian who ate at Margie's Diner saw him. "He's got poison ivy," the Hungarian said to Margie.

"It'll go away," Margie said.

The Hungarian drove my father to a doctor in town, who gave him something to rub on his itch. Then it went away.

After my father had cleared the yard, Ed said "Heykid!" and took me out there. He had a stick and a ball. He put the stick into my hand and called it a "bat." He threw the ball and I hit it with the stick and Ed ran to catch it.

Sometimes when I'd hit it hard Ed yelled, "*Horun! Horun! Heykid! Horun!*" He laughed when he said that.

I liked doing this very much. I liked this "bazball" very much. My father tried to play with me, too, but he couldn't chase the ball.

I told him to yell "Horun! Horun!" when I hit it. But he didn't.

When I was older, I considered the image of my father, the handyman at Margie's Diner:

A successful novelist. An educated man. A man with intellectual interests. A man unsuited for physical labor, even to exercise. Now clearing yards. Unloading the garage. Sleeping beneath rats. Hearing his wife called "Honeybunch" and "Sweetie." Seeing her in a maid's uniform. In a place where he couldn't even speak the "lingidge."

My flute was gone.

I looked everywhere. My father looked everywhere. My mother looked everywhere. I cried.

Ed saw me in the kitchen, crying. He said, "Heykid!" He said, "Bazball? Come on, horun!" He tried to make me smile.

My flute was gone. I didn't smile.

Margie was there. Ed said something to her in English I didn't understand. She said something to him I didn't understand. He got angry and left.

I sat there, crying. Margie turned to me angrily and told me to go outside and play.

. . .

Ed and Margie took us to the county fair. She gave my father $10 and said, "Spend it on the boy."

I rode in a merry-go-round. I threw a ball at bottles. I ate an apple with candy on top of it. I ate popcorn and a "hoadog."

My father put a dollar on a number on a table and a spinning wheel stopped at that number and we won a big can with ham in it. My father said it was a Polish ham, the best ham in the world. We would eat it the next day.

We were very happy.

But when Margie and Ed drove us back, she asked my father for the ham. He was holding the big can in both hands. He told Margie that he'd won it. Margie said that he'd won it with money she'd given him. My father said this wasn't fair. Margie asked him if he wanted to lose his job. He gave her the ham and mumbled something under his breath.

She turned angrily and said, "What did you say?"

My mother whispered, "*Jaj, Jézus Mária.*"

"Nothing," my father said to Margie.

But I'd heard what he said: "*Kurva.*"

I was drinking milk in the kitchen of Margie's Diner. Margie and my mother and father were there. My mother was making "sanviches" for the diners from the big Polish ham my father had won.

I said, "This milk doesn't taste good."

Margie tasted it. "It's fine," she said.

I drank some more. "It's spoiled," I insisted.

My father tasted it. "The milk isn't good," he told Margie.

"It's good enough for *your* son," Margie said.

My father took the milk and threw it into her face. She started screaming at him. He started screaming at her. He called her a "*diszno*"—a pig—and a "*kurva.*"

She screamed, "You dirty Nazi! You're lucky I hired you!"

He screamed, "*I am not a Nazi!*"

She screamed, "You're all Nazis, all you dirty DPs!"

DPs were "displaced persons." Everyone, even Mrs. Szántó, called us that.

My mother, whose hands were shaking now as she made the sandwiches, ran outside. Ed ran in.

Margie and my father were still screaming at each other—then Ed and Margie were screaming at each other. Ed slapped Margie and she ran outside.

Ed looked at my father and shook his head. Then, quietly, he said, "Get out, Steve! Go!" He jerked his thumb at us.

We stood at the side of the road near Margie's Diner, the suitcase between us. My father had his thumb out.

Okay. Hov arr yu! Zank yu! Heykid! Kurva! Jaj Jezus Mária! Horun! Horun!

We weren't there long. Only two or three cars passed. Then a big black car stopped. Two men got out. They were Hungarian.

They introduced themselves—the Reverend Benedek Biro and the Reverend Ipoly Dési. They were Franciscan priests. They had come to Margie's Diner to look for István Eszterhás, the Hungarian novelist. They had read and admired some of his novels. They owned a Hungarian language newspaper called the *Catholic Hungarians' Sunday.* They were hoping he'd be interested in being its editor. They took our suitcase and put it into the trunk. They helped us inside their big black car. They drove us away.

As a successful American screenwriter, I told that story to my friend Alan Pakula, the director, and he laughed until he had tears in his eyes.

"At the side of the road!" Alan said. "Hitchhiking. And God comes along! It's unbelievable! *Louis B. Mayer wouldn't have believed it! Of course I believe it. It's life."*

And many years after that conversation, Alan was driving along the Long Island Expressway in New York when a pipe fell out of the truck in front of him and went through his windshield and killed him instantly.

Just casually driving along. And God came along. It was unbelievable! *Louis B. Mayer wouldn't have believed it!*

Of course I believed it. It was life.

The priests took us to a house in Fairfield, Connecticut, where they lived next to their church. We went to church every day. The house was big and magnificent and we had our own big and magnificent room.

I had never seen a room like this. It was snow-white, filled with fresh air. There were no rats, no sirens outside. There were yards all around the house, perfect to play bazball, although the priests told me they didn't play it.

I took walks with my mother in the woods nearby. We saw birds with many colors. We fed ducks and squirrels. My father talked with the priests. There would be a delay until they could get rid of the old editor of their newspaper. They would find my father a job for six months and then we would go to a place called *Klevland* where my father would edit the paper.

The priests said, "The boy is too skinny. He must eat."

An old Hungarian woman who was their cook made us heaping dishes of sausage and mashed potatoes and paprikaed beef and pork chops and spare ribs. I ate everything but never put any weight on.

The priests bought us new clothes—all we had were the clothes from the camps. They bought me pants and sweaters and a jacket with a fur lining. They bought me gloves and rubber boots.

And one day Father Benedek, an old man who had difficulty breathing, bought me a flute.

I took the flute into the backyard and blew it. Sometimes Father Benedek sat on a porch swing watching me and saying, "Good, Jozsi, blow it! Louder! Louder!'

I blew my new flute until I was as out of breath as he.

I heard my father talking to the priests about the Komchis as we had dinner in their house. I heard about Komchis named Stalin and Malenkov and Molotov and Beria. I heard about a Hungarian Komchi named Mátyás Rákosi, just as bad as Stalin.

"Zsido," one of the priests said.

My father glanced at me and nodded. My mother said nothing during these discussions about the Komchis except once, when they were talking about a man named Hitler, who was a Nazi, not a Komchi.

"*Bolond*," my father said—crazy.

My mother said, "Maybe."

My father said, "Absolutely. A madman."

When my father and I were walking in the woods in Fairfield, I asked him, "Papa, who were the Nazis?"

"They were bad people," he said.

"Worse than the Komchis?"

"They hated the Komchis, but they were just as bad," he said.

"Why were they bad if they hated the Komchis?"

"They killed Zsidos," my father said.

"Why did they kill Zsidos?"

"Because they were crazy," he said.

"Did they kill the Zsidos because they didn't like the smell of garlic?"

"Yes," he said, "something like that."

I said, "I like the smell of garlic. I smell it on you sometimes. I don't mind."

"Good." He smiled.

I said, "Why don't the Zsidos stop eating garlic if people want to kill them for eating it?"

My father said, "Nobody has the right to make anybody eat or not eat something."

I said, "You made me eat puliszka in the camps!"

"I was afraid you were going to die," he said. "You had to eat something."

"It would have been better with garlic," I said.

"Yes," he said, smiling, "for certain."

When I walked in the woods with my father, we never watched the birds or looked at the leaves or fed the squirrels and the ducks. We marched along briskly together, holding hands. He didn't say much, unless I asked him something, but then he answered me at length.

I never walked in the woods with both my mother and father. It was always one or the other. The two of them never walked in the woods, alone, without me.

Father Benedek got my father a job in Washington, D.C., with a friend of his, Joseph Tischler. We lived in the Tischlers' house outside the city, in Takoma Park. The Tischlers were a kindly couple who treated us like we were part of their family. Mrs. Tischler found my mother a job in the kitchen of a restaurant in the city. And I was enrolled in the first grade of an American school.

My father took me to my first day of school. I had my flute. I walked into the school and the teachers led me from one place to another. The other children smiled and I smiled back. But I couldn't understand what anybody was saying. I said, "*Hov arr yu? Okay! Zank yu! Heykid!* And *Horun!*" I blew my flute and a teacher took it away. But I didn't cry. I said, "Okay." I knew I was making too much noise.

At the end of the day, when my father came to pick me up, the teacher gave the flute back to me.

It was like that every day. Everybody smiled. Everybody called me Joee. Everybody said okay when I said okay.

As an American man, I considered the image of my father in Takoma Park. He left with Joseph Tischler every morning and he came home with Joseph Tischler every night.

He had spent the whole day looking at documentary film footage recovered from the Nazis in Hungary.

He who had survived the bombings was spending his days in America examining film of it, identifying for Tischler the bombed-out Hungarian cities. He even saw film one day, he said, which he was certain was the apartment house in Szombathely where we'd been bombed.

Some nights when he came home he looked dead tired, but he had reason to be, didn't he?

The teachers in school asked to see my parents. The Tischlers came along to translate. I was there, too. I had my flute but I didn't blow it.

The teachers said I did nothing in school. I didn't do the numbers. I didn't look into the books. I didn't play with the other kids.

The teachers also said I was friendly and smiled a lot. I was smiling right then, too, as they were saying it, holding my flute. They were smiling at me right then, too, along with my parents.

My parents and the teachers asked me why I was behaving that way. I said it was because I didn't understand what they were saying. Then I said, "Okay?"

They laughed and I laughed and the next day in school I didn't do the numbers, didn't look into the books, and didn't play with the other kids.

But I smiled.

One night the Tischlers took my father and me to the restaurant where my mother was working in the kitchen. My mother seemed very happy we were there and introduced me to her restaurant friends.

They were people I'd never spoken to before, but had seen among the GIs in the camps and on the streets in New York. They were Americans with black faces.

Her black-faced friends gave me candy and Coca-Cola and some of them picked me up and held me. A big black-faced man said something my father and I didn't understand. The Tischlers translated it: I looked just like a famous American named Havdi Doodi.

I said "Horun! Horun!" and the big black-faced man said "Havdi Doodi! Havdi Doodi!"

And I told that story when I was an American man to some people.

To Delia, a young American black woman I was in love with. "Howdy Doody?" Delia said. "Alfred E. Neuman would be more like it."

To Carl Stokes, a friend and the first black mayor of a major American city. "Washington, D.C.," Carl said, "in the fifties? That was deep backwater cracker country."

To Ahmed Evans, a month or two before he and his black nationalist followers killed seven policemen in Cleveland. Ahmed said, "Ain't no more black men workin' in no more fuckin' kitchens kissin' the white boy's ass!"

To the Reverend Martin Luther King, Jr., whom I was interviewing. Reverend King stopped the interview and asked me for ten minutes about what the refugee camps had been like.

To Jimi Hendrix, sitting in a little Hungarian restaurant, surrounded by older Hungarians looking at Jimi as though he were a purple-haired and beringed Martian. Jimi Hendrix said, "My dad worked in a kitchen like that much of his life."

To Otis Redding, the day before he got on an airplane that killed him. Otis told me a story in return. "I worked in a kitchen in a hospital once," he said, "and I was in an elevator singing a song that I was working on. And this white doctor said, 'Shut up, nigger!' and I slammed him so hard against that elevator wall that he went down. And, man, I walked out of that elevator singing that song real loud!"

And I wanted to tell that story to O. J. Simpson, who was at the pool of the Ritz-Carlton with his wife, Nicole, and my wife, Naomi. But I never got a chance to tell it because Nicole was angry at O.J. about something and because O.J. kept telling me how much he'd loved a mystery I'd written about a famous man who kills his wife and gets away with it.

While we were living with the Tischlers, we went to visit a friend my father had known in Hungary, Paja Balázs, and his wife and daughter in a town in Maryland. They lived next to a slaughterhouse where Paja, also a Hungarian writer, was employed. My father and mother were happy to see Paja and his wife and I was happy to see Erzsi, who was twelve years old and whom I'd never met.

At night the adults went out to see a movie and Erzsi stayed home with me. Erzsi asked me how old I was. I told her I was six. She wanted to see my *pimpli*. I showed it to her and she showed me her little breasts. Then she took me into a bedroom and we lay down on the bed and she showed me her behind and what was between her legs. She licked my *pimpli* and asked me to lick between her legs.

I was happy that she licked me and happy to lick her. She told me what we had done was a secret and I shouldn't tell anyone. I didn't.

Paja Balázs had seen me hysterical as a police car went by outside with its siren wailing.

"The boy has to be toughened up," I heard him say to my father.

He and my father took me down the next day to the slaughterhouse where Paja worked. Paja changed into rubber clothes and grabbed the longest knife I had ever seen.

He went up to a pig and slit its throat. The pig shuddered and gushed blood. Then he went from one pig to another and did the same thing. There were five or six pigs shuddering and spraying blood. A sticky sweet smell filled the air.

My father held my hand but didn't look at me. I watched the pigs bleed and shudder, but I didn't cry.

Paja came over with his bloody rubber suit and said, "Huh, boy? Tomorrow we make sausage!"

The Tischlers gave me a black "kovboy" suit for Christmas. Leather pants. A black kovboy hat. A leather vest. A leather belt. A leather holster on each side. Two guns with rolls of red paper that made sparks.

I was no longer Havdi Doodi. I was Hopalon Kesedi.

After I got my guns, I forgot about my flute. I slept with my guns the way I'd slept with my flute.

From the time I was a young American man, I've always kept a gun near me when I sleep—on a nightstand, on top of a dresser, under the mattress.

I've never fired any of these real guns, but I've always been aware that they were there, ready to be fired.

. . .

The Tischlers hugged me and cried when we got on the train to Klevland. I looked at them with a mean face and fired both guns they had given me. They laughed and hugged me again.

I was wearing my kovboy clothes and my black hat.

On the way to Klevland, I looked out the train window looking for the Komchi Indians Joseph Tischler had told me about. I had my guns drawn but my father told me I couldn't shoot them. As I held my guns, my mother clutched her rosary, praying that this place called Klevland would be kind to us. My father slept.

I saw no Komchi Indians, but when I saw a rat on a train platform when we were stopped, I fired at it. My father woke up and took my guns away.

CHAPTER 3

I Kill Rocky Balboa

COLT
You stir up the shit, you get down to the sludge.

Hearts of Fire

Hollywood beckoned in 1974.

I was a writer at *Rolling Stone* who, after growing up in the gray and rusted Midwest, had fallen in love with California. But Jann Wenner, the publisher of *Rolling Stone,* was moving the magazine to New York from San Francisco and I desperately didn't want to go. I wanted to stay in the sun.

I had serious responsibilities. Gerri and I had two babies and sometimes things were so tough that we'd go through clothes in the closet looking for change. Unless a miracle happened, it was clear that I was going to New York with Jann.

And then the miracle happened. Out of the blue, I got a phone call from an executive name Marcia Nasatir at United Artists. She had read my book, *Charlie Simpson's Apocalypse,* which was a National Book Award nominee. She thought the book was cinematic and asked if I had any interest in doing screenplays.

Screenplays!

I had loved movies all of my life, had even taken some film courses in college, but the plot I'd always had in mind was to do some journalism, learn about life, and then write novels.

Never mind what I had in mind . . . the gun was at my head . . . the wolf was at the door . . . there were babies in the house crying for their Similac . . . Jann was going to New York . . . and I didn't want to leave Marin County.

I flew down to L.A. to see Marcia Nasatir. She was an intelligent, caring woman who was looking for new screenwriting talent.

"Why don't you go back home," she said, "and think of some screenplay ideas and send them down to me."

I went back home and did that. It wasn't easy. The house we were renting was so small and Steve and Suzi were so loud that I had to put an earplug into each ear to try to think. After about a week of doing that, both ears got infected and now I had doctors' bills on top of all the other bills.

I finally got a note together to Marcia with some ideas. One of them, in very brief outline form, was about a screenplay to be called *F.I.S.T.,* about a truckers' union.

Marcia liked the concept and asked me to come down to L.A. again to talk about it. She asked what I had in mind. I explained that from my reading and the stories I'd heard from old union people on the West Side of Cleveland, where I grew up, I understood that the early years were a war, that people had died in the struggle, that the reason some unions became intertwined with the mob was that union members were immigrants fighting a brutal WASP power structure and were forced to turn to other immigrants for help just to stay alive.

What I had in mind was a big, sweeping historical piece that would necessitate a lot of research and would explain the intertwining of labor and the mob on a human level.

Marcia said, "Fine."

I said, "I beg your pardon?"

She said, "Let's do it."

"Just like that?"

She laughed. "Just like that."

I laughed. "Well, what do we do?"

"Do you have an agent?"

"I have a book agent."

"Fine," she said, "we'll work it out with your book agent."

The deal they made with me was what they called "a step deal." I would do the research, then write what they called a "treatment," then write a screenplay, and then make revisions on the screenplay—and if the movie was made, I would earn a total of $80,000. I was told that at any time along the line they could decide to end the process and end my payments.

It was, I knew, a risky proposition. I didn't know anything about writing a screenplay. What if they just took my research and said "Thank you very much"? What if the research took me longer than I thought it would—what would my family live on?

But it offered the possibility of freedom if it worked out. I wouldn't have to go to New York with Jann, I wouldn't have to go through closets for change, I wouldn't have to leave the sun. And it sounded like fun when it didn't sound scary. I'd always enjoyed doing historical research and that's how this would begin.

Before everything was finalized, Marcia asked that I meet with Mike Medavoy, the head of the studio. He was pleasant and friendly. His back wall was filled with photographs of himself with actors, politicians, and public figures.

"It sounds fine to me," Mike said. "But how do I know you can write a screenplay?"

"His book is really cinematic," Marcia said to him. "You'd see this is no problem if you read it."

"Yeah, but it's a book," Mike said. "I'm talking about a screenplay. How do I know he can write a screenplay?"

I said nothing. My Adam's apple was probably bobbing, butterflies were making their way through my esophagus toward my open mouth.

"Mike, I'm telling you," Marcia said.

"We're not making a book deal with him, we're making a deal for a screen-play."

"Oh," I suddenly blurted. "That's no problem. I took a couple of film courses in college. *I wrote a couple scripts.*"

He looked at me a long moment, a twinkle in his eye. "Fine," he finally said, "no problem then. Let's do it."

Twenty years later, Mike Medavoy said to me. "I knew it was bullshit, but that wasn't the question I was really asking you. The question I was asking you was if you really wanted to do this and the lie told me that you did."

The research took longer than I expected. I drove across the country to places like Ypsilanti, Michigan; Sandusky, Ohio; Johnstown, Pennsylvania; Passaic, New Jersey; talking to veterans of the labor movement—to people who'd been gassed and beaten because they stood up for their rights as working men and women against a cruel conglomerate made up of bankers and company heads with goon squads and National Guardsmen at their beck and call.

I knew I could put my heart into this piece. I had been called a "greenhorn" and a "hunkie" and "trash" as I grew up on the streets of Cleveland. They were the same epithets hurled at those in the labor movement.

It was time to write a treatment and send it to Marcia. I had no idea what a treatment was. I knew what an outline was, but a treatment was evidently not that, nor was it a screenplay.

I wrote an eighty-page exegesis which bore the results of my research and also included some rudimentary notes in search of a story and characters.

To my utter amazement, Marcia called to tell me she liked the alleged treatment very much and also to say that the studio already had a director interested in making the movie.

"But there's no script," I said.

"It doesn't matter," she said, "he likes the idea."

"There not much of an idea there, either," I said.

"Don't worry. There's enough there to interest him. You'll work out the rest of it together."

"Together?" I said. "He's not writing it, *I'm* writing it. He's *directing* it."

She laughed at me. "It's part of directing," she said.

"What—writing?"

"Yes."

"But has he written anything before?"

"No," she said, "he's not a writer, he's a director, why would he have written anything before?"

Bob Rafelson was the director. I knew his work and had greatly admired one of his movies: *Five Easy Pieces*. I also knew that he was a very in-demand director, a star director, and I was flattered that he was interested in directing my script even though it wasn't a script.

"There's a great movie in here somewhere," Bob said when we met in L.A., "all we have to do is find it."

"How do we do that?" I asked.

"You'll find it, all I'm going to do is give you directions."

What we had to do, Bob said, was talk. We had an awful lot of talking to do, he said, and somewhere in all that talk we would find the words that would go into the script.

"Fine," I said, "but I'll write the script, right?"

"Of course you'll write the script," he said, "I don't know anything about writing."

We made plans to do our talking in Aspen, where Bob had a home.

"You better plan to stay awhile," he said. "A couple weeks."

"A couple *weeks?*"

"Well, we've got a lot of talking to do."

The morning of the day before I was to leave for Aspen Bob called, got my flight information, and said he'd meet me at the Aspen Airport.

That afternoon, Marcia Nasatir called me and told me I wasn't going to Aspen.

I said, "Yes I am, Bob's going to pick me up."

"No he isn't," she said.

"Yes he is, I just spoke to him."

"He's off the project," she said.

"No he's not, he's really into it, he's got all kinds of ideas."

"We *took* him off the project," she said.

"You said he'd be perfect for this."

"We saw the rough cut of *Stay Hungry*." It was Bob's new movie.

"Yeah?"

"It's awful."

"You said he was one of the most talented directors in the business."

"He is," she said, "but the movie's awful."

"How can the movie be so awful if he's so talented?"

"I don't know. That's why we're taking him off *F.I.S.T.*"

She said the studio would start looking for a new director. Meanwhile, she advised me, I should "sit tight."

The next afternoon, my phone rang.

"Where the hell are you?" Bob Rafelson said.

I said, "I'm sorry?"

"I'm at the Aspen Airport and you're not. Your plane just got in and you aren't on it. What the hell's going on?"

I didn't know what to say. For a long moment, I said nothing.

Bob kept saying: "Hello? Hello?"

I said, "They told me not to go."

He said, "Who told you not to go?"

"UA."

"UA?"

"Yes."

"But—why?"

I said nothing again. Bob said, "Hello? Are you there? Is something wrong with this connection?"

"They took you off the project."

"UA took me off the project?"

"Yup. That's what Marcia told me."

"But why did UA take me off the project?" I could almost hear a snicker of disbelief in his voice.

"Because of *Stay Hungry*."

"*Stay Hungry?* What does *Stay Hungry* have to do with this?"

"They said it was awful."

"*They did?*"

Bob Rafelson hung up shortly afterward and moments later Marcia Nasatir called, very angry.

"What did you tell Bob Rafelson?" she asked.

"I told him I wasn't going. Why didn't *you* tell him I wasn't going?"

"It was an oversight. Did you tell him I said *Stay Hungry* was awful?"

"Yeah."

"Why in the world would you tell him that?"

"Because you told me it was awful."

"But I didn't tell you to tell him that."

"He was at the airport. He wanted to know why I wasn't there. What was I going to tell him?"

"I don't know," she said, "anything else. Tell him anything else, but don't tell him I said his movie was awful."

The phone didn't ring for weeks after that. I didn't know what was going on.

When the phone finally did ring, Marcia sounded very happy. She kept calling me "honey" and "darling" and it sounded like I'd been forgiven for my Rafelson indiscretion. She was calling, she said, with great news. We had a director who was "just perfect."

Karel Reisz was a very wired, chain-smoking man who seemed like he wasn't even sure that he liked my "treatment." He didn't call it a treatment. He called it a "*document.*"

"I think it's a very interesting document," he said, "with a great many interesting things in it."

We talked a lot about the labor movement during our meeting in L.A. and I recounted some of the more powerful anecdotes I'd picked up in the research.

"It could be a tough, hard-hitting movie," Karel said.

"Not *Zhivago.*"

"*Zhivago?*" he said. "My God no. I don't see this as a love story, do you?"

"God no," I said. It was a great relief to me that at least we agreed about that.

Karel was going home to England and we made plans for me to join him there so we could continue to talk about the movie that was possibly there in the "document."

The week before I was to leave, Marcia Nasatir called and told me that Karel Reisz was off the project. The UA executives had seen *The Gambler* and agreed that it was nearly "unwatchable."

"Will you tell him he's off of *F.I.S.T.?*" I said to Marcia.

She laughed. "I'll tell him."

"Will you tell him today?"

"I'll tell him today."

"Do you promise, Marcia?"

"I promise."

Three days later Karel Reisz called from London saying he was looking forward to my arrival and asking about my hotel reservations.

"Have you talked to UA?" I asked.

"Not since I left," he said. "Why?"

"I'm not coming," I said.

"You're not coming?"

"No."

"Why not?"

"Because you're off the project, Karel," I said.

"Why am I off the project?" he asked.

I'd learned my lesson. I wasn't about to tell him that the UA executives felt *The Gambler* was "unwatchable."

I said, "I don't know, Karel. You'll have to ask them."

Fourteen years later, on a set in Lethbridge, Canada, I met Karel Reisz's wife of many years, Betsy Blair, a distinguished and gutsy woman who defied the blacklist. I asked about Karel's health and mentioned how much I'd liked him during our *F.I.S.T.* discussions.

"You know," Betsy Blair said to me, "I remember you were supposed to come to London and then you didn't. Karel still doesn't know what happened to him on that project."

By then I had learned the truth about why Karel Reisz was suddenly gone from *F.I.S.T.* It had nothing to do with *The Gambler* being unwatchable. It had everything to do with a man named Norman Jewison and his former agent, the head of production at United Artists, Mike Medavoy.

At the time I met him, Norman Jewison was forty-eight years old and one of the superstar directors in town. He'd had big-hit movies—*The Cincinnati Kid, The Russians Are Coming, In the Heat of the Night, The Thomas Crown Affair, Fiddler on the Roof*—and he'd directed them without condescending to his audiences. A Jewison movie was accessible, it was *about* something, and was never pretentious.

Medavoy had been his agent years ago and had somehow managed to get my "treatment" to him. When Norman finally read it and liked it, Mike Medavoy dumped Karel Reisz, and poor Karel's new movie became "unwatchable."

The first thing Norman Jewison said to me, holding my seventy-some-page exegesis of *F.I.S.T.*, was, "I don't know what the fuck this is. It isn't a treatment, it isn't an outline, it sure as hell isn't a screenplay. It's neither fiction nor nonfiction. It's some sort of bastard mutation."

I liked him personally immediately. There was an orneriness about him, a feistiness. He viewed himself as a combatant against the studios, but his combat was not only confrontational, more often it was charming. He mainly lived in Toronto, had another place on a lake in Ontario, but he also often stayed at his house in Malibu next to Blake Edwards and Julie Andrews on the beach.

One early morning he was staring at the surf and when I came up behind him he fixed me with those elflike eyes and said, "Do you know why I live out here at the beach?" He turned back toward town and the eyes suddenly narrowed. "So I don't have to look at those fuckers over there."

By "fuckers" he meant the world of the studios, the world he'd succeeded in but tried to keep at arm's length, the world that he was convinced was a creative enemy but could occasionally be either beaten or cajoled into being a temporary ally.

"I'll tell you what they're good for, kid," he'd say. "They put up the money."

I *was* a kid. I'd come off *Rolling Stone,* watching Hunter shoot ether into his navel or hearing about Hunter spraying fire retardant on Jann, into this world that I didn't understand and that I often found intimidating. As it turned out, Norman Jewison would become my mentor and, through the years, my internal guide. I often found myself thinking: Well, what would Norman think about this? How would Norman play this? Would Norman tell 'em to fuck off or would he put his killer grin on and take them out to lunch?

I didn't know that then, though. All I knew was that I liked the man, I liked his movies, and while there was a whole worldful of stuff I didn't know about, I took pride in being a writer and intended to be one on this screenplay. A writer who would write a script out of his own heart and gut the way he wanted to write it. Norman, a shrewd judge of people, knew what he was dealing with quickly, of course.

A kid with a chip on his shoulder looking at Hollywood warily while at the same time ready to be seduced by it.

The first step was to take my bastard mutation exegesis of a treatment and talk it to death, which is what we proceeded to do.

I marvel at Norman's patience now. This was *my* script and no one was going to push me around, including Norman big cheese Jewison, so I said a lot of things about making a movie that didn't *sell out,* that wasn't *Hollywood,* that had true *street smarts*—using words that I hoped would push buttons on a man who was a big "commercial" director.

We started talking about the story that would wrap itself around all of my research. The discussions would begin early in the morning and go all day. Norman had been asked to direct *Ragtime,* E. L. Doctorow's best-seller, and he often took calls during the day about that project.

"I thought you were doing *F.I.S.T.,*" I said to him.

"I don't have a script of *F.I.S.T.,*" he said. "I don't have a script of *Ragtime,* either. I'll do whichever script I like."

"You want me to compete with *Ragtime*? It's an international best-seller," I said, "written by one of the great writers of our time."

"What are you," Norman asked, "chopped liver?"

"I don't *think* so."

He grinned. "I don't think so, either, but we'll see."

What fascinated him at the core of my bastard mutant exegesis of a treatment was the shadow of Jimmy Hoffa, who, as far as I was concerned, wasn't even in the damn bastard mutant exegesis of a treatment.

"This guy Kovak, your hero," he said, "he's Hoffa."

"He's not—I took him as far away from Hoffa as I could, considering that he heads a truckers' union."

"That's one of the things that's wrong with it—get Kovak closer to Hoffa."

"I'm not writing a roman à clef."

He held the treatment up. "So far I haven't seen you writing anything except this mutation."

When we were finished with our discussions, he said—"Remember this, kid. We've talked about a lot of things. You're a writer, I'm not. Use what you think will help you and discard the rest. Write it with your heart, put yourself into it. I can't ask you to do more."

Then he said, "Call me when you're done."

A week later he called me.

"They're really pushing me on *Ragtime*," he said. "I've got a first draft that's pretty good. Send me the pages you've got."

"That wasn't our deal," I said. "I said I'd send you *the script* when it was done. I'm not going to send you pages and then listen to your suggestions on the pages as I'm writing. *I'm* writing this—*you're* not."

"Well, okay," he said, "but they're really pushing me to do *Ragtime*."

I said, "Fine. Do *Ragtime*."

He laughed. "I'll make a deal with you. This script is going to be in two parts [we envisioned an intermission in the middle of the movie], send me the first part when you're done."

"What if you don't like it?"

"Then I'll do *Ragtime*."

"What if I don't send it to you?"

He laughed again.

"I'll still do *Ragtime*."

About a month and a half later, I sent him the first half of the script. I was petrified. I felt like I didn't know what I was doing. This wasn't journalism, which I'd done all my life. This was making things up out of the air.

"Well, I read it," he said when he called me.

"And?"

"And keep writing."

"Did you hate it?"

"No."

"Did you like it?"

"No."

"Are you doing *Ragtime*?"

"No."

"What are you doing?"

"I'm waiting for the second half of it," Norman said.

A month and a half later I sent him the rest of the script. The two halves of the first draft came to 387 pages. A page of script, I'd learned, equaled one minute of screen time. Three hundred eighty-seven minutes: a six-hour-and-some-minute movie.

Pat Palmer asked me to come down to L.A. and see Norman three days later. When I walked into his office, Norman was grinning like a loon. "Three hundred eighty-seven minutes," he said. *"Three hundred eighty-seven minutes!"* He ruffled through the script. "A monologue that goes on for eight minutes." He started to laugh, holding the script up—"It weighs like *War and Peace*, kid," he said, "but it doesn't read like it."

I said, "What's wrong with an eight-minute monologue?"

He said, "They'll throw tomatoes at the screen, that's what's wrong."

"Not if the words are good."

Norman and Pat Palmer thought that was hilarious.

We started to go through the script page by page, scene by scene, over and over again—at his house in Malibu, at his house by the lake near Toronto. We argued incessantly. I was green at this and I knew it, but I wanted to save the script from the kind of slick theatricality that I hated in Hollywood movies.

As Norman and I continued working on the script, we continued arguing. He could have said thank you very much and moved on to another project. He could have replaced me with other writers and kept working on *F.I.S.T.* I really have no explanation for why he didn't do those things except for the patience and generosity of spirit that epitomizes the man to me now.

We just kept going over the script, cutting, rewriting, restructuring. When I look back on it now I realize that what I was getting was a graduate seminar in film from a man who had more than proven his ability to make commercially successful and award-winning movies.

Oh, he did now and again give me some not so subtle hints to be less intractable. After a particularly difficult day of back and forth, exasperated with me, he took me out sailing on the lake in Ontario. I'd never been sailing before.

A wind kicked up and a storm came in. The damn boat was flopping around in the water—this *thing* kept swinging by my head on the boat, barely missing me. I was dry-mouthed, scared shitless.

Jewison looked at me with his killer grin: "A little dry-mouthed, are we?" he said. "This will teach you not to fuck with me."

In Malibu once, in the middle of our Sturm und Drang, I found an envelope on the table in my guest bedroom. It was addressed to Norman Jewison from an accounting firm. It said "Personal and Confidential." The thing was just lying there on the table. It hadn't been there before. It wasn't sealed. I stared at it for a while, then turned away. All I could hear was the lapping of the sea but this envelope was screaming at me. I finally gave up and opened it. It was a statement from Norman's accountant of his net worth.

Norman Jewison was a very, very rich man.

The next morning, on his deck, we resumed the battle over the script. After I'd said something particularly obnoxious and probably insulting, he got up and stretched. He looked at the crashing surf for a while.

Without looking at me, he said, "Did you open it?"

I said, "What?"

"You know what."

"I don't know what you're talking about."

"Yes you do," he said, "and if you'd just listen to me sometimes and stop being so goddamn pigheaded, it's just possible that you'll be worth that kind of money someday."

I said nothing and, as we both looked at the crashing sea, we both started to laugh.

We finally finished the script—it had taken us almost six months working together. I liked it. I knew it was as much his as it was mine, but I liked it.

"It's a good script, kid," he said. "I'm proud of you. You did good."

I said, "Thank you. Does this mean you're going to direct it?"

"Maybe." He smiled.

"If," Pat Palmer said, "we get the right budget and good casting."

"What if you don't?" I said to Norman.

"Well," he said, not cracking a smile, "we had a lot of fun, didn't we?"

I felt nauseated when he said that, but as I got older and wiser I understood that we'd had more fun than movie people usually do.

Norman sent the script to Robert De Niro. We waited. Weeks went by . . . a month went by . . . another month went by. De Niro didn't say yes and he didn't say no. His agent said he hadn't yet had a chance to read it.

At the same time, we ran into budget problems with United Artists. Norman needed $14 million to make it the way we wanted to make it: a big, epic, three-hour-long movie with an intermission in the middle. UA would only go as high as $11 million. Norman asked to have the project in turnaround, making it possible for him to take it to any other financier. UA agreed.

Norman took it to every financier in town. Everybody passed (a classic Hollywood word: projects pass the way kidney stones and people do).

He wouldn't take no for an answer. He went back to United Artists and begged and pleaded. He got nowhere. He got on a plane and flew to New York to meet with Arthur Krim, the corporate head of United Artists, a nearly mythical elderly man known for his taste and liberal political beliefs. And he talked Arthur Krim into making the movie . . . but only for the $11 million they had earlier agreed to.

It meant we had to cut the script. It meant that our three-hour movie would be down to two hours and some minutes. It meant that the intermission was gone. It was a very painful process.

"Is it worth truncating this script?" I asked him.

"We're not truncating it," he said, "we're cutting it."

"Is it worth cutting it radically just to get it made?"

"Would you rather it sit around in a drawer?" he asked. "That's our only alternative. You've spent years on it. I've spent more than a year on it. But if you tell me that it's better it sit in a drawer, we'll stop right here."

"No," I said, after a moment's thought, "I'm not telling you that."

"I didn't think you were." He smiled.

Then he said, "I think you'll have a long career in this town."

. . .

We cut forty pages out of the script and then, suddenly, Norman cast it. His agent was Stan Kamen at William Morris. Stan was also representing the hottest actor in Hollywood, an actor whose face was on the covers of *Time* and *Newsweek*, whose last movie, *Rocky*, had become an American icon: Sylvester Stallone. Through Stan, Norman persuaded Sylvester Stallone to star in *F.I.S.T.*

The day after Norman and Stan and Stallone met and agreed, Robert De Niro's agent called to say that De Niro wanted to do the movie. It was too late. There was a verbal agreement with Stallone.

The day after De Niro's agent called, Norman, Pat, and I were sitting at Norman's patio in Malibu. All three of us were muted. Robert De Niro was the best actor in the world. Nobody really knew whether Stallone could act. We had the most publicized young star in the world and none of us were happy.

I went back home to Marin County and Norman started pre-production on *F.I.S.T.* Thanks to Stallone's involvement, it was suddenly the most publicized movie being made in town. The whole world had wondered what he'd do to follow up *Rocky*.

I suddenly was being hustled by agents and producers who, in most cases, hadn't even read my script, but were aware of the fact that I'd written a film starring Sylvester Stallone.

Army Archerd in *Daily Variety* devoted most of his column to the fact that Stallone was going to star in *F.I.S.T.* He talked a lot about Jewison, too, and even mentioned me.

He said that I "would stop playing for the Rolling Stones" and would now be doing screenplays full-time. That, of course, was news to me, but then so was the fact that I'd stopped singing with Mick and Keith.

What came leaping out at me was this line: "Stallone plans to immediately begin working on his rewrite of *F.I.S.T.* with director Jewison."

What? WHAT?

I called Norman in a near lunatic state. He sounded busy, distracted, but blasé.

"Oh, that," he said, "don't worry about it."

"But—but—is it true?"

"No, not really."

"Not—*really*?"

"Stallone considers himself a writer, not just a star. He wrote *Rocky*. He's got his ego in writing, too. He's going to be on the cover of *Writer's Digest*. It's a part of his deal."

"What—deal?"

"His acting deal. I had to agree to let him do a polish to get him to star in the picture. I'll let him do a polish, so what—it's not going to make any difference to the script."

"But it's *my* script." I said. "*I* wrote it. I spent nearly three years on it, now he's saying—"

"It doesn't matter what he's saying. Everybody in town knows it's your script. It's just star ego. Everybody in town knows what that's about."

I didn't say anything and Norman knew I was seething.

"Aw, come on," he said. "You'll take it to the Writers Guild. You'll get sole screenwriting credit, I promise you."

I tried to settle down, but just when I thought I was handling it, I read an interview with Stallone in the *Pacific Sun*. The *Pacific Sun* was my hometown Marin County paper. And in the *Pacific Sun*, Stallone was quoted as saying: "*I've written a new script called* F.I.S.T."

"Is it a sequel to *Rocky*?" the interviewer asked him.

"No, I know it sounds like a boxing movie," Stallone told the *Pacific Sun,* "but it's about labor unions."

I had a routine doctor's appointment and my doctor said, "Why did you tell me you'd written that movie—*F.I.S.T.*"

"What are you talking about?" I said. "I did write it."

"I know who wrote it," he said. "I read it in the paper."

On the way out of his office, I was afraid he'd ask me to pay him in cash.

I seethed and seethed and just at my boiling point, I got a call from a writer named Saul Pett who wrote features for the Associated Press. Pett was interested in writing a nice cuddly human interest story about how it must feel for a novice screenwriter writing his first script to attract the hottest star in the world.

I said: "Sylvester Stallone is a thief."

I said: "He is trying to steal my screenplay."

I said: "He's Apollo Creed. I'm Rocky Balboa here—I'm the refugee kid who was born in Csákánydoroszló, Hungary."

I said: "I'll fight him anyplace, anytime."

I said: "Besides, I've been in more barroom brawls than he has. He fights like a sissy."

Saul Pett wrote it all down and the story appeared on the front page of more than two hundred newspapers that Sunday.

My father read it in Cleveland and called me. "It's okay if you threaten to fight him," he said, "but I saw *Rocky,* too. *Threaten* to fight him, but don't fight him."

Norman called, laughing. He said "Sly"—as he was calling him now—was ballistic.

"You've really done it now, kid," he said.

Norman said he was sorry, but for the sake of the production, he couldn't allow me on the set of the movie.

"I can't believe you're doing this, Norman," I said.

"I'm not doing this," he said, "*you* did."

On the set that I wasn't allowed to visit, in Dubuque, Iowa, Norman Jewison was having his own problems with Sylvester Stallone.

The first problem was that some of the town fathers were getting very upset about the number of young high school cheerleaders who were seen entering and leaving the star's hotel suite. The second was more serious. In the script that he signed on to, the character that Stallone plays, Johnny Kovak, dies. He is shot to death by the forces who were once his allies. He is forced to go to the mob for help against the bankers and the companies . . . but the mob, twenty years later, feels forced to kill him.

It was Greek tragedy, the logical ending to a tragic story. Except . . .

Sylvester Stallone did not want to die.

He argued it with Norman over and over again: "The public will not accept me dying," he said. "I'm Rocky. I'm a hero. It's going to hurt the movie commercially and it's going to hurt *me*. It turns the movie into a *downer*."

Norman dug his heels in. "You have to die," he told Sly. "We're not making *Rocky* here, we're making a tragedy about the labor movement. Without your death, there is no ending to the movie. It won't hurt your career, it'll help it, it'll show your range."

"I'm a star," Stallone said.

"You're an actor," Norman said.

Stallone went to his agent and then he went to the studio. They told him he had read the script which he had agreed to do. He had signed a contract.

"I'm not doing it," Stallone told Norman.

The day they were supposed to shoot the scene where Johnny Kovak is shot-gunned to death and falls down the stairs, Sylvester Stallone said he couldn't work. He had hurt his neck, he said.

Lawyers got into it now. Stallone threatened to walk off the movie. He threatened not to do any publicity for the movie. The studio threatened to sue. Norman threatened to sue. Two orthopedic specialists were flown from Beverly Hills to Dubuque to examine Sylvester Stallone's neck. One was chosen by the studio, the other by Stallone. The studio's specialist said there was nothing wrong with Stallone's neck. Stallone's specialist said he had sprained his neck muscles and couldn't work.

Filming stopped for a day until Norman and Stallone and the agents and the studio people and the specialists and the insurance company and the completion bond people worked out a compromise.

Stallone would do the death scene once.

Just once—that was it.

If Norman somehow blew the scene, that would be it. We'd have to redo the ending of the movie.

So Norman shot the scene just once.

He shot it perfectly.

And Sylvester Stallone died the way he was supposed to.

Norman showed me the rough cut. I liked what I saw for the most part. Yes, I missed the forty pages we had cut out at the end and I kept wondering what De Niro would have been like in the part, but I liked the movie. I even liked Stallone in it most of the time.

The big change that Sly had made to the script involved the killing of his best friend and near-brother. In my script, Johnny Kovak ordered that his life-long brother be killed. In the movie, the mob did the killing *without his knowledge.*

"There is no way I could get him to play it that way," Norman said. "He didn't want to even die, let alone look like he was orchestrating his best friend's death. It's a star thing."

As far as my credit was concerned, Norman, Patrick, and Marcia all believed that I would be awarded sole credit by the Writers Guild on the screenplay.

Norman had kept his word: except for the "star thing" change prettying his character, Stallone hadn't been allowed to, as Norman put it, "put his fingerprints on the script."

Since Stallone indicated through his attorneys that he wanted screen credit, I made plans to submit the issue to the Writers Guild.

Meanwhile, my book agent in New York, Lynn Nesbit, astounded the world by selling the novelization of the screenplay for a record $400,000. Part of the high price, I understood, was because publishers liked the script and thought it would make a good paperback novel. Part of it was they thought I could write it: *Charlie Simpson* had been a National Book Award nominee. And part of it, no doubt, was because Sylvester Stallone was an overnight, huge star and his picture on the cover of the book would really sell it.

That overwhelmingly good news was tempered by the fact that I had signed a first-time screenwriter's contract with the studio which gave them 90 percent of any novelization money. No one, of course, at the time that contract was signed could imagine that Lynn Nesbit could transform a novelization into this kind of money.

I called my lawyer in Los Angeles, Barry Hirsch, one of the industry's most respected attorneys, and explained the situation to him. I had worked for nearly three years on this script for $80,000. I used up a good part of that money just for the research.

Was there anything we could do, I asked, to get around the 90-10 contract with UA?

He asked me for time to think about it and then asked me to come down and see him at his office.

Barry Hirsch is a low-key man with his own gestalt psychology practice on the side. Outside his office door is a framed pair of blue jeans. His usual dress is jeans, a checked shirt, and tennis shoes. When I saw him at his office in L.A., the first thing he said was "I checked the contract, there's nothing we can do."

"Jesus, Barry," I said, "you asked me to come down to L.A. to tell me this? Couldn't you have done it over the phone?"

"Unless—" Barry Hirsch smiled. His blue eyes were ice.

"Unless what?"

"Unless they think you're so crazy and out of control that you'll do something rash."

"Like what?"

"Like telling them that you'll call Jimmy Hoffa's son to tell him that this script became more and more about Jimmy Hoffa as it went along."

"You mean blackmail them?" I said.

"I wouldn't use that word," Barry said and smiled.

"How do I convince them that I'm out of control?"

"You call them up and yell and scream."

"Who would I call?"

"UA. Marcia's your closest person there. I'd say you should call Marcia."

"You mean," I said, "I call the person who got me into movies, whom I'm very fond of, and call her a bunch of names—"

"She won't take it personally anyway. She'll figure out this is business."

"—and threaten to blackmail her company by getting Jimmy Hoffa's family involved in this?"

"It's up to you," Barry said, "you want the money or don't you?"

"Are you sure she won't take it personally?"

"She's been around," Barry said. "This kind of thing happens all the time in this town. She'll forgive you. It's in her interest to forgive you. She wants to work with you again."

"But I will have hurt her," I said.

Barry smiled.

Barry said, "She won't allow herself to feel any pain."

I made the call from Barry's office with Barry sitting next to me, although I didn't tell Marcia that. I called her a bunch of terrible names, used a lot of obscenities, and pretended to have Jimmy Hoffa's son's phone number in my hand and then hung up before she could say too much.

"That was great." Barry smiled. "I've never seen anybody make that kind of phone call better."

"Now what?" I said.

"Now." He smiled again. "We wait for the phone to ring."

It rang no more than ten minutes later, Marcia Nasatir for Barry Hirsch. I sat there as Barry took the call.

I heard Barry say that yes, I was obviously a man out of control—he was doing his best, but . . . Then I heard Barry not saying anything for a while and he finally said, "Seventy percent—his way."

Barry listened for a long time again, I could hear Marcia's voice loud and upset, and then Barry said, "Sixty would be fine."

They hung up shortly after that and Barry turned to me and said: "Sixty percent of $400,000 is $240,000, that's what you're getting for the novelization."

We laughed a bit and celebrated and Barry said, "Call her tomorrow and apologize."

"Won't she find that a little suspicious? That I'm under control so fast?"

"She knows what it's about," Barry said. "She *likes* you. She'll appreciate the call."

I called Marcia the next day and apologized. She accepted my apology graciously, called me "honey," and said she was pleased we were "one big happy family again."

That left the matter of screen credit to deal with—or so I thought.

Lynn Nesbit informed me that Dell, publishing the novelization, intended to use a picture of Sylvester Stallone on the jacket cover.

I said, "So?"

Lynn said, "So we have a big problem. Stallone has to approve the cover art. If he doesn't approve the cover art, Dell isn't publishing the book."

I called Barry Hirsch and told him. He said he'd call Jake Bloom, Stallone's lawyer.

Barry called me back the next day. Jake had spoken to Sly and Sly said he'd be happy to approve the cover art.

I said: "That is fantastic!"

"If," Barry Hirsch said, "you don't take the credit issue to the Writers Guild and agree to give Stallone co-screenplay credit."

"Let me get this straight," I said to Barry. "We manage to get $240,000 by blackmailing UA and now if I don't agree to Stallone's blackmail, I don't get any of the money."

"I wouldn't use that word," Barry Hirsch said. "We made an arrangement with UA. We'll just make another arrangement with Sly."

We did: I got the $240,000, from which I was able to buy my family our first house. Sylvester Stallone was very cooperative with Dell Books and approved the cover art.

The credit of *F.I.S.T.* reads—Story by Joe Eszterhas, Screenplay by Joe Eszterhas and Sylvester Stallone.

The check for $240,000 from Dell Books arrived via Special Delivery mail at the house we were renting in Mill Valley. I kept staring at it. It was more money than my father had made in the twenty-five years he'd been in the United States. I lit up a joint and kept staring at the check. The zeroes seemed to be dancing around the living room.

The next morning Gerri and I drove into San Francisco for a meeting with a team of accountants that Barry Hirsch had recommended. It was an entire roomful of suits and I still felt a little stoned.

This money, I soon learned, was a big problem. We had IRS payments to consider, California tax payments, insurance policies, trust funds for the kids, stocks and bonds, real estate maybe. I kept saying all I wanted to do was buy us a house.

One of the suits said, "It might be smarter to put it into windmills. They're a better investment now."

"I don't want a windmill," I said, "I want a house that's ours for the kids."

"A house may not be the best investment you can make," another suit said.

"I don't care about it being a good investment," I said, "I just want to live in it. I want to eat and sleep in it. I want to go to the bathroom in it."

"We can get you a great deal on a limited partnership for some windmills outside Palm Springs," one of them said.

The meeting went on interminably. We had all kinds of forms to sign. We were setting up checking accounts, savings accounts, we were setting up a company.

"A what?" I said.

"A company. We can get you a real tax break by setting up a company and having you paid not to you but to the company."

"But this check here"—I kept looking at the zeroes—"This isn't made out to a company, it's made out to my name."

"We'll send the check back," one of them said.

"Dell would be happy to make it out to a company once we set one up," another one said.

"Of course we'll have to redraw the contracts," said a third.

"No," I said. "*No!* I am not sending this check back! Do we all understand that? We are not sending this check back! We are *cashing* it!"

"*Cashing* it?" one of them laughed. "You can't just *cash* a check like that— you have to put it into an account of some kind."

"Fine," I said, "we're putting it into an account, but we ARE NOT SEND-ING IT BACK!"

I was exhausted when we got home. The check was no longer in my hands, the bastards had put it away into some kind of an account. I couldn't see the dancing zeroes on the ceiling when I lit up that night's joint.

I slept restlessly, my head full of windmills and tax payments and redrawn contracts. When I woke up in the morning, I felt like my heart was going to blow out of my chest. My breathing was funny.

We called the paramedics—by now I thought I felt my left arm starting to hurt. They put me into an ambulance and headed for Marin General Hospital.

On the way there, a construction crew held up traffic. I jumped out of the ambulance with the paramedics running after me and started screaming at the head of the construction crew. He wore a hardhat with the name "Brinkerhoff" stenciled on it.

"I'm having a heart attack, goddamnit," I yelled at Brinkerhoff, "you've got to let us through."

He took one look at me and started shepherding his guys off the road.

At Marin General, they told me that I was not having a heart attack.

My doctor came over and said I'd had an anxiety attack. He told me to stop drinking coffee and to stop smoking dope.

"Have you been under any stress lately?" he asked.

"Well, no," I said, "everything's cool. As a matter of fact, I've just gotten a lot of money."

"Well, shit," he said, "that'll do it every time. I've seen quite a few cases of guys having anxiety attacks after they made a lot of money."

I thanked him and he offered to drive me home.

"By the way," he said, "what did you make the money on?"

"On *F.I.S.T.,*" I said.

"Oh, that's the thing Stallone wrote, isn't it?" he said.

Meanwhile, I was still throwing up every morning. It had begun when I had actually begun writing the screenplay and it was still with me now. I was beginning to think that this was just part of being a screenwriter.

I woke up, thought about the writing I had to do that day, and then I threw up, I had some orange juice and an English muffin, and then I sat down at my typewriter and worked on my script. Part of it, I knew, was that I was afraid I didn't know what I was doing and, with the babies in the house, there was a lot of pressure.

Gerri was concerned about my health and I went to see doctors and specialists. Invasive and humiliating tests were performed on various private parts. The doctors said I was in perfect health.

"Is it perfectly healthy to be throwing up every morning?" I asked my doctor. It was the same doctor who'd told me he'd seen many cases of sudden money leading to anxiety attacks.

"Did this ever happen to you when you were poor?"

"No. I was hungry when I was poor but I was never nauseous."

"There you go," he said. "It's part and parcel of the same big-gift package."

Approaching release, *F.I.S.T.*, Norman told me, had "a terrific buzz."

"What's a buzz?" I asked him.

"An advance word of mouth."

"That's great," I said.

"It doesn't mean anything."

"It doesn't? Why not?"

"Because very few people have seen it."

"How can there be a buzz if few people have seen it?"

"It beats me," Norman Jewison said, "but it happens in Hollywood all the time."

"Well," I said, "it still sounds good. Maybe we'll have a hit movie."

"Don't buy the mink coat on it yet." Norman laughed.

Stallone, meanwhile, Norman told me, had set up a punching bag and written the name "Eszterhas" on it. He'd had himself photographed while punching it.

Jewison thought that was funny. "It's getting a lot of press," he said. "It's like the Hatfields and the McCoys now. The whole town thinks it's a great publicity stunt."

"It's not a publicity stunt," I said, "the goddamn guy—"

"Yeah, I know." Norman was laughing. "Save it for the reporters."

I was invited to the movie's premiere. It would be a big Hollywood gala, the opening of Los Angeles's Filmex film festival. There would be red carpets and photographers and television coverage. Stallone would be there.

My father, at the age of seventy-one, was flying out from Cleveland. My wife was shopping for an evening gown. I had to rent a tux. We were on our way to our first Hollywood premiere—and the studio was picking up all the costs.

There was a suite waiting for us at the Beverly Wilshire. A limousine would meet us at the airport and would stay with us until we flew back. None of us had ever been in a suite or a limousine before.

We got into the limo at LAX and there was a chilled bottle of Dom Pérignon in the back seat, courtesy of United Artists. I popped the champagne open and sprayed it all over myself.

When we checked into the Wilshire, an attractive assistant manager led us up to our suite.

"Why is she coming with us?" my father whispered to me in Hungarian.

"She's taking us to the room."

"Does she want money?"

"I don't know."

"She must want money, that's why she's coming."

"I'll give her some money."

"Why should you give her money? We didn't ask her to come."

"It's okay, Pop."

"Will the studio give it back to you?"

"I don't know, Pop."

"Can you call them to find out?"

The suite had two bedrooms and was magnificent. There were vases of flowers everywhere.

I thanked the assistant manager and offered her a $5 tip. She smiled and took it and left.

"How much did you give her?" my father asked me in Hungarian.

I told him.

"*Five dollars?* You gave her *five dollars*? All she did was open the door."

My wife was checking out the flowers: cards were attached from Norman and Marcia.

I wanted this to be a Hollywood day for us. We trooped back into the limo and went to Scandia for lunch. United Artists had made the reservation for us. Scandia was the best seafood place in town. A bottle of Dom Pérignon was waiting for us when the maître d' led us to our table, courtesy of United Artists.

We looked at our menus and ordered.

My father said to the waiter, "Corn beef sandwich." He spoke with a thick accent.

The waiter said: "Excuse me?"

"Corn beef," my father said, louder now.

The waiter looked at me. "I'm sorry," he said, "I'm having difficulty understanding—"

"My father would like a corned beef sandwich," I said.

"We don't serve corned beef sandwiches, sir," the waiter said to me a little haughtily.

I told my father in Hungarian that they didn't have corned beef.

"*No corn beef?*" my father said, acting as though he'd been insulted.

"What kind of place did you bring me to?" he said. "This is the biggest place in Hollywood and they don't have a corn beef sandwich?"

When we got back to the hotel, my father decided to take a nap before the night's festivities. Gerri was getting her hair done and I had an interview in the hotel bar with another reporter who wanted to do a story about my feud with Sylvester Stallone.

While I was passing through the lobby on the way to the bar, a receptionist suddenly stopped me. "Mr. Eszterhas," she said, "I have a phone call for you."

I stepped to the phone and heard my father on the other end.

"Get up here!" he said in Hungarian. He sounded very upset.

"Where are you?"

"Where do you think I am? I'm upstairs!"

I hurried up. I couldn't imagine what was wrong. I'd left him seconds earlier and he was fine, still grumbling about having to eat herring and sour cream instead of a corned beef sandwich.

When I got off the elevator at the seventh floor, I saw him. He was at the end of the hall with his back to me. He was crouched over the hall phone. He was wearing only his boxer undershorts. I hurried to him.

"What are you doing out here in the hallway in your *gotchis,* Pop?" I asked him.

"I locked myself out."

"How did you lock yourself out?"

"There are too many rooms in there," he said. "I was going from the bedroom to the living room and I found myself out here."

That night, when the limo pulled up to the theater—there were spotlights in the sky, flashbulbs going off, policemen everywhere—I thought we all looked good. My father and I had our rented tuxes on. Gerri was wearing her new evening gown and new shoes.

We got out of the limo and started walking down the red carpet as photographers were snapping and flashing away. Gerri was in the middle, her arms crooked into my father's and mine.

"Who the hell is that?" one of the photographers yelled.

"The screenwriter," another photographer said.

"You're kidding me," the photographer said, and stopped wasting his film.

Halfway down the red carpet, Gerri suddenly stopped.

"Oh my God," she said.

"What's the matter?"

"I lost my shoe."

I glanced back. I saw her shoe about five feet behind us on the red carpet. The three of us turned, arm in arm, and she very gracefully stepped into her shoe.

There were *F.I.S.T.* belt buckles and yellow *F.I.S.T.* trucks on the tables at the ABC Entertainment Complex's largest banquet hall. I noticed that we were seated very far away from the main tables, far in the back. As a matter of fact, I didn't even know some of the others at our table.

Norman walked the half mile from his table to ours and asked if I wanted to come over and meet Sly. The twinkle in Norman's eye was pulsing.

"Aw come on," I said.

But Gerri and I followed Norman across the vast hall and we finally got to Stallone's table, which was surrounded by bodyguards. The bodyguards turned and stared at me as I approached.

Stallone got up with a big grin and stuck his hand out. I'd never met him, of course, and what struck me was that he was short standing next to me.

"Hey," he said. He drew the word out.

"How ya doin'," I asked.

I introduced Gerri. Stallone put his hand out to shake hers.

And Gerri hit him. Playfully, sort of, but hard enough. With her fist. Right in the gut. Stallone wasn't expecting the sucker punch. He groaned a little, then turned it into a laugh.

"She hit you!" Jewison yelled. "*She hit you!*"

Everybody laughed and we went back to our table, where someone had stolen our yellow *F.I.S.T.* truck. (We wanted it for the kids.)

There was another premiere we were invited to days later—this one in Dubuque, Iowa, where the movie was filmed. Stallone was not attending this one. Studio rumors said that the father of one of those high school cheerleaders was very mad at him.

Our flight connected through Chicago and at the Chicago airport, I found the new issues of *Time* and *Newsweek,* which had reached the stands an hour earlier.

Time's review said "J.U.N.K." and *Newsweek*'s said "Sylvester Hoffa." The reviews were scathing.

"We're dead meat, kid," Norman said when I saw him in Dubuque.

I couldn't believe what he was saying to me so casually: three years of work . . . "great buzz" . . . a red-carpet L.A. premiere . . . the hottest star in the business . . . and we were *dead meat*?

"Are you sure?" I said.

"I'm sure."

"Now what do we do?"

He laughed. "We smile till our faces are sore."

The studio sent me out on a publicity tour during the movie's opening week. Marcia told me it was the first time they'd ever sent a *screenwriter* out on tour, but my Hatfields and McCoys act with Stallone had attracted so much attention from the press—*Esquire* had even done a long feature on it—that they thought it'd be worthwhile.

It wasn't. Nobody in any of those cities—Cincinnati, St. Louis, Pittsburgh—knew what to do with me. *A screenwriter for Christ's sake?* Most of the people interviewing me had never even *met* a screenwriter before.

I was a relief to the young PR woman who had been assigned to squire me around. Her previous tour had been with James Caan. James Caan, she said, did most of his interviews in his hotel suite with a towel wrapped around him. And if the interviewer was young . . . and female . . . he would find a moment during the interview to sort of move the towel around in a way so that she would . . .

In Pittsburgh I met a salt-of-the-earth white-haired old exhibitor who insisted on showing me the real Pittsburgh. He took me to every good kielbasa place in town and drove me to the airport when I left.

"You're a good kid," he said, as I got out of the car, "but that goddamn piece of shit movie you wrote—I had eight people in my two theaters last night!"

In St. Louis, the last stop of the publicity tour, I met a young married woman who was at the Park Chase Hotel attending an emergency room nurses convention. She told me she had seen my movie *F.I.S.T.* a few days earlier and hated it but allowed me to escort her up to my suite anyway.

She called her husband from my suite while, naked, she knelt on the floor in front of me.

She told him how much she missed him and loved him and then she hung up and got busy with me.

When she was finished with me, she told me in great detail how the screenplay of *F.I.S.T.* should have been changed to make it a better movie.

Many years later, I put that hotel room scene at the Park Chase Hotel in St. Louis into my screenplay for One Night Stand.

I've often wondered if that no-longer-young woman saw the movie and recognized herself kneeling on the floor naked and telling her husband how much she loved him.

F.I.S.T. was a complete critical and commercial stiff and when that was clear, Sylvester Stallone apologized to me. He did it publicly, in *Us* magazine.

"I feel like a man who's been burgling Joe Eszterhas's house for the past year and a half," he told *Us* and went on to say that he'd done no real work on the script: it was *all mine.*

I called Norman and said, "Well, what do you know? He's a stand-up guy.

He admits that he lost his bearings with all those magazine covers. How many times have you seen a big star actually do a public apology?"

"You schmuck," Norman said. "Don't you get it? The movie failed. All he's doing is washing his hands: he's saying *your* script is to blame. Not his—*yours.* He didn't apologize when the movie had great buzz, did he?"

The day after *Us* magazine appeared on the stands, Sly's manager, Herb Nanas, called and said Sly wanted to get together for lunch "so bygones can be bygones."

We had lunch at the Universal commissary. Sly was working on *Paradise Alley,* a movie which he'd really written, and was in the middle of a blazing affair with his co-star, Joyce Ingalls.

A gigantic blowup of Joyce Ingalls and other Universal stars faced us as we ate. He wore a black T-shirt and black jeans and looked very *cut.* He was having vitamins and sprouts for lunch and I was eating a cheeseburger and French fries. He'd sneak his hand over every couple of minutes and steal some of my French fries.

"That woman is hot," he said, staring at Joyce Ingalls's blowup. "She's driving me crazy. Certifiable, you know what I mean? Not as bad as Melinda Dillon on the movie, though. One night she just took off and started driving. She was in about the next state when they finally caught up with her."

We talked about our feud.

"Did you really say I fight like a sissy?" he said.

"Yup. I sure did. Maybe I was stretching things a little, though."

He looked at me and smiled.

He said, "Uh-huh."

"Well, listen," Sly said, "I'm sorry I said that stuff. My life has been so insane. This stuff just—like happened overnight to me. It doesn't matter, though. Everybody in town knows it's your script."

"Yeah," I said, "but the movie failed."

"That fucking Jewison," he said. "I told him. He wouldn't listen to me. The public doesn't want to see me die. I'm Rocky Balboa. You kill Rocky Balboa and there's gonna be a price to pay."

"You were supposed to be Johnny Kovak," I said.

"Johnny Kovak is nothing compared to Rocky Balboa. He's just a character you made up."

"But isn't Rocky Balboa," I said, "just a character *you* made up?"

"Not anymore," Sly said. "Rocky Balboa is an American myth now. He's Superman with heart and vulnerability."

He ate some more sprouts and he said, "Yo, Adrian," and started to laugh.

"You know what I told Jewison? I said—Break this thing into two movies and release them a month apart in the theaters. *F.I.S.T. I* and *F.I.S.T. II*. The first one ends on a high—Kovak wins against the bad guys. Rocky Balboa triumphant. The audience would have eaten it up. Then, a month later, you put the other one out and get into *The Godfather* stuff.

"It would have worked," Sly said. "I'm telling you it would have worked. But no—Jewison won't listen to me. Directors, God help us. I'm gonna direct all my stuff from now on."

A group of Universal executives sat down in the roped-off area near us and all nodded or waved to Sly, who grinned and waved back.

He ate some more of my French fries and shot them a glance.

"Those smiling motherfuckers," he said. "They'll spit me out like bad meat if I ever stop being hot. They think I don't know it."

He took me upstairs after our lunch and showed me his offices, furnished with expensive antiques, and took me over to the Moviola to show me some footage from *Paradise Alley*, which he had also directed.

He was watching himself on film and smiling and when Joyce Ingalls came onto the film his smile turned to a leer.

"Look at her," he said, "just look at her."

"You think she's going to be a big star?" I asked.

"I don't know," he said. "Who knows? Who the hell knows anything in this town? Probably not, but she is sweet. She . . . is . . . sweet!"

These were his final words: "You tell Jewison we could've had a hit movie! Two parts would have done it! We could've had *two* hit movies!"

When I saw Marcia Nasatir that same afternoon, she told me that my novelization of *F.I.S.T.* had also badly failed. (The editor who had agreed to pay the record $400,000 price was in danger of losing his job.)

Marcia and I went for a walk around the studio backlot, our conversation echoing around blocks of false facades.

"Jesus, Marcia," I asked her, "what's going to happen now? Is my screenwriting career over?"

"Not a chance, honey," Marcia told me with a smile. "You wrote a brilliant script—everybody in town read it. Sly Stallone is going to be a very big star. Norman Jewison will go on to direct many other movies."

"You mean," I said after a while, "there is no responsibility?"

We stopped and were staring at one of the false fronts—a huge brick wall with nothing but air behind it.

"When you called me on the phone and called me all those names . . ."

She let the sentence dangle and wasn't looking at me. Our eyes were on the false facades.

I said—"Yes?"

"Did I make you take responsibility for saying those horrible things to me, calling me those vile names?"

I said—"No."

We looked at each other then and she slowly smiled.

"It's just Hollywood, honey," Marcia said.

The Pool Man

Henry took care of our swimming pool at the Malibu Colony. He was sixty-nine years old and lived in the Valley:

I knew all the big stars when I was about seventeen, eighteen. Cary Grant came into the house once and the first thing he said was, "It's very nice to see you, Henry." He was really looking at me. I was a good-looking kid.

They'd all come to the house to see my dad. He was at Paramount then. He'd been at RKO before then and later on went to Columbia.

I went to Beverly Hills High School where I was a really shitty student. I spent all my time in the pool at home and we also had a place out in Malibu so whenever I wasn't in the pool I was out at the beach, riding the waves and getting a tan.

Man, I had a great tan but that wasn't what I really cared about. That just happened by itself because of all of the time I happened to be out in the sun but what I cared about was being in the water.

All this time later I could still take you out to the best beaches out there. There's a place off of Dume just south of Zuma that very few people would go to. You'd swim out fifty feet and you were in so deep you could bump into whales out there, I'm not kidding.

Well, okay, maybe a couple hundred feet, but then you'd run into schools of dolphin romping around just like I was. I had my arms around a dolphin's neck once, I really did. I know what it sounds like, but I really did. I had that sucker around the neck, hanging on to him as he was joyriding around.

It has something to do with how deep how quickly the water is out there. The currents attract the whales and the dolphins. They're the same currents that used to wreck a lot of ships.

I was around the Colony in Malibu a lot, too. My dad's place wasn't far from it although the Colony then wasn't like the Colony now. It was just a bunch of fancy beach shacks and the person living there then that everybody was talking about was this nutty guy in a big straw hat and a beer gut and a walrus mustache. A writer. Saroyan.

I saw him once out there. He was collecting stones off the beach. I asked him what he was doing and he looked at me like I was screwy and said he was collecting stones off the beach. Oh-kay. Whatever. I asked my dad about him and he said—Well, I don't think he'll ever be a screenwriter. Later on I read something by him but it didn't do anything for me. It was about a guy who was a writer who collected stones off the beach.

Being out there at the beach all the time and having the pool at home in Beverly Hills was about the worst thing for me. That's all I cared about, you see. The water. The damn water. I fell in love with the water. Can you believe that? My dad would say to me—I can fix you up with any job you want on any lot—and I didn't want any of it. I just wanted to be around the water. If it wasn't the pool, it was the beach.

It's not just that I wasn't studying anything . . . I wasn't even around a lot of kids my age; not even around a lot of girls. Girls weren't like the water. Girls were complicated and sometimes they'd downright bite you in the ass for something you said or did. With a girl, I'd get hung up. With the water, I'd glide.

It completely messed my life up, really. My parents got divorced. My dad couldn't get any other studio jobs and went to New York to run a clothing company. My mom moved to Paris. We had to sell the house in Beverly Hills first, then the one in Malibu.

I stayed in L.A. I didn't go to college, I just hung around the beach. It was all I had left. I didn't have a pool anymore. I got a job at a hamburger stand on the beach in Santa Monica.

A guy I worked with at the hamburger stand quit and went to work for a pool company. He was cleaning and servicing pools all over Bel Air and Beverly Hills. They had another opening and he asked me about it and I said fine.

I've been working on pools for almost forty years now. It keeps me around water. I'm around water six days a week, ten hours a day. I've got my own company. I hate the maintenance part of it, the motors and heaters and wiring problems. But I like the water. I like putting the chlorine in it, I like putting my hands in it. If there's a problem with the light-

ing, I'll wade in and fix it. I've got a place in Tarzana. I've made enough money so that I've got my own pool at home.

On the weekends, I go down to the beach.

I think about my dad sometimes. He was smarter than I was. He was always with his big stars or on the phone to their agents. I never saw him in the pool, he was hardly ever out at the beach. I don't think he even knew how to swim.

CHAPTER 4

Michael Ovitz
Fondles My Knife

DAVID

You're in charge here.

CLIFFORD

You know, when I met you I didn't know what a pain in the ass
you'd be.

Jade

United Artists, feeling, I think, that I'd worked nearly three years on a
screenplay for not very much money, threw me a bone. It was an adaptation of Brian Moore's novel *The Doctor's Wife.*

I loved Brian Moore's novels and my idea of an adaptation was to stick as
close to the book as I could, using as much of the novel's dialogue as possible.
That was not, however, the producer's idea.

His name was Frank Rosenberg. He was in his early seventies and he had
begun working as legendary studio boss Harry Cohn's publicity man in New
York in the thirties. Harry Cohn was legendary not just because he'd run
Columbia for many years but because he had a thick white shag rug in his office
and an elevated desk.

Frank Rosenberg wore a very ill-fitting toupee and arrived at his office
each morning with a fresh bag of Winchell's donuts which he offered no
one else. I asked him the first time we met about Robert Mitchum pissing
on Harry Cohn's rug but for some reason Frank took offense at the question
and launched into a diatribe about the changes we'd have to make on Brian
Moore's novel.

I disagreed with everything he said. Then he launched into a harangue about the manner in which we'd work.

"You'll sit here," Frank Rosenberg said, pointing to a small desk in his office, "and I'll sit here," pointing to his desk, "and when you finish a page you'll hand it to me."

"You mean I'll work in your office and hand you the pages as I write them?"

"You got it," he said, munching a chocolate donut.

I went to see Marcia Nasatir.

"This guy is some kind of moron," I said. "I can't do this."

Marcia did two things: 1. She called Frank Rosenberg and told him that it was "unreasonable" that I be asked to work that way. 2. She brought in a director to put some distance between Rosenberg and me.

The director was Karel Reisz. Even though UA had thought his last movie was so "unwatchable" they wouldn't let him direct *F.I.S.T.*, it was evidently not so "unwatchable" that they wouldn't bring him in to direct *The Doctor's Wife*.

Karel and I met, scrupulously avoiding any mention of *F.I.S.T.*, and we agreed to take a crack at Moore's novel. Then Karel met Frank Rosenberg, listened to his ideas, observed his style, and went to Marcia and said: "This man and I are not in accord in any way. I can't do this."

Marcia convinced him that my presence put some distance between them, so the three of us, Karel, Frank, and I, sat down to discuss the adaptation.

The book was set mostly in Belfast and in Villefranche, in the South of France. I had never been in those places and a few hours into our discussion, it became obvious that I didn't know what I was talking about.

"How could they give me a screenwriter who's never even been in the South of France?" Frank asked.

He called Marcia and asked for a new screenwriter and, instead of bringing one in, Marcia had a better idea. I would go to Belfast and I would go to Villefranche before we resumed our discussions.

And so I did. I had to do, not factual research, but as Marcia called it, "emotional research." I had to get a "feel" for those places.

I went to Belfast and did a lot of walking about, stayed at a great hotel, and ate at the best places. Belfast was a singularly barren and threatening place and after about three days, I felt I had "the feel" down just right.

Then I went to Villefranche, a luxurious resort location not far from Nice. I walked about, stayed at a great hotel overlooking the marina, and ate at the best places. There were a great many "best" places here, though, and the sun was out—and while I had gotten "the feel" in Belfast after three days . . . it took me nearly three weeks to get "the feel" in Villefranche.

I came back to L.A. tanned and refreshed and Karel, Frank, and I resumed our discussions. Karel and I quickly allied forces and all we did was argue with Frank.

Finally, Karel, as the director, spoke up and said: "Perhaps we should just let Joe go back to Marin County and write his script."

"I'm not gonna like what he writes," Frank said.

"Oh, you never know." Karel chuckled. "He might surprise us."

"I know he's not going to surprise me," Frank said.

But Marcia supported Karel's suggestion and I was quickly back in Marin, still throwing up every morning, adapting Brian Moore's novel.

I hated doing it. I had a reverence for the novelist's words, didn't want to change any of them, and felt like I was doing nothing but a translation of form—putting Brian Moore's words into a scripted format.

When I turned the script in, Frank Rosenberg hated it and wanted me to start from scratch.

I wasn't about to start from scratch and wasn't about to napalm Brian Moore's novel and so I quit.

When Karel Reisz heard that I'd quit, he quit, too.

When UA heard that Karel Reisz quit, UA quit.

Frank Rosenberg had a problem: he had no screenwriter, no director, and no studio. He was out in the cold, starting all over again with a project that only a few months ago had looked like a movie.

Marcia was right. Never mind *F.I.S.T.*'s abject critical and commercial failure, Sly was already booked two movies ahead and Norman was mounting his next movie. And I was the newest "hot" screenwriter in town.

I got two offers that were particularly intriguing:

1. David Obst and Peter Guber were setting up a new publishing company and wanted to sign me up to write a novel. David was the founder of the Dispatch News Service, which had broken the Seymour Hersh stories of the My Lai massacre, and Peter, already the former head of Columbia Pictures, now the head of Casablanca Film Works, was an industry wunderkind.

2. The director Alan Pakula (*The Sterile Cuckoo, The Parallax View*), respected by both the critics and the industry, wanted me to write a script about the Alaska pipeline.

I met with Obst and Guber and decided to do the novel.

They put an ad in *Daily Variety*, full-page, that I framed: "David Obst and Peter Guber take pride in announcing the signing of Joe Eszterhas for his new novel."

I called Pakula and told him that I hoped he understood, I'd always wanted to write novels, this was a particularly good offer, blah blah blah.

"What do you mean you expect me to understand?" Pakula said. "Understand? I thought we had an understanding that you'd do this script."

"I hadn't agreed to do it," I said, "we don't have anything in writing."

"*Writing?*" Pakula said. "How dare you talk to me about what's in writing?"

My agent called me that night and summoned me to a hasty meeting in L.A. "Pakula called me," he said.

"I told him we didn't have anything in writing."

"Nobody has anything in writing," he said. "Most directors don't even sign their contracts until they finish shooting the movie."

"I didn't know that," I said. "I thought having something in writing means something."

"Not in this town, not unless it's a shooting script that's been green-lighted and cast."

"What did he say to you?"

"He said," my agent told me, "that *you'll never work in this town again* if you don't do this script for him."

"*Alan Pakula said that to you?* He's got a reputation for being a sensitive, caring guy."

"He *is* a sensitive, caring guy," my agent said. "He is sensitive about you not doing his script and cares about it maybe being his next movie."

"Can he sue me?" I asked.

"How could he sue you? There's nothing in writing."

"Well," I said, "does he really have the power to stop me doing screenplays if I want to do one again?"

My agent shrugged. "He's a very respected part of this community. This is the smallest town in the world, you know."

"Well *what the hell are we gonna do?*" I said. "Obst and Guber have already run their ad in *Variety.*"

"A lot of people run ads in *Variety* announcing new projects," my agent said, "half of them never happen. Everyone who reads *Variety* knows that."

"You mean they ran an ad and nobody paid attention to it anyway?"

My agent shrugged again.

"Did you sign your contract with Obst and Guber?" he asked.

"No."

"Well," my agent said, smiling, "then *they* can't sue you."

I didn't know what to do. I went back to the Beverly Wilshire where I was staying, compliments of Obst and Guber, of course, and sat down at the bar and asked for a double Jack Daniel's on the rocks.

A woman was sitting down the bar from me. She was in her fifties, coiffed, manicured, and wearing tasteful gold jewelry with a mink coat. She kept staring at me.

I was aware of her presence but I wasn't interested. I looked into the bottom of my Jack Daniel's and thought about Todd's painting in Nathanael West's *Day of the Locust: The Burning of Los Angeles.*

"Excuse me, do you mind if I speak to you?" she asked.

I said, "Sort of."

She laughed and came over to sit next to me. She spoke with what sounded like a British accent. Her perfume was subtle and meadowy.

"I have to tell you this," she said. "I read auras. You have an amazing aura."

She went into it: She was from South Africa. She was a diamond merchant with offices in Johannesburg and Tokyo. But what she really did was auras. She could also "read" people.

"Would you like me to tell you about yourself?"

I thought: *This screwy town. It really is lalaland.*

Within thirty seconds, she told me these things: I was a writer. I had recently made a lot of money. She told me the exact figure—$240,000. I would be rich and world-famous. The key was to continue doing what I was doing *now*. I should not be tempted by doing anything else. She gave me her card, listing her offices in Johannesburg and Tokyo, wished me luck, and left.

I thought about it that night as I fell asleep. She was clearly a complete wacko. I came from good hunkie peasant stock, my feet on the ground, far from auras.

But she did tell me the *exact amount of money* I had recently made. She did tell me I was a writer—most people thought I was a Hells Angel.

She told me I would be world-famous—but screenwriters not only weren't world-famous, most people didn't know what it was they did. And she said I had to continue doing what I was doing right *now*.

But what was I doing right now? Yes, I'd written two screenplays, but on the other hand I had agreed to do a novel.

Was I screenwriting right now or planning the novel right now?

The next morning I called my agent and told him I was doing the script for Alan Pakula.

"I think you made a really good decision," he said.

"You won't believe how I made it."

"Try me."

"Well, I was sitting at the bar at the Wilshire—"

"Right."

"And this woman was sitting near me—"

"Right."

"And she was a diamond merchant—"

"Got it. And you figured it'd be easier buying diamonds with screenplays than novels. See ya later."

He hung up on me.

· · ·

Alan Pakula certainly seemed like a sensitive and caring man, not the kind of street punk who'd tell you you'd never work again. He was literate and literary, charming and friendly. His reputation was that he was always involved in many projects and had some difficulty deciding to commit himself to actually directing one of them.

His offices were in New York, high up in the Gulf + Western Building, and his offices swayed while we spoke—there was a gusty wind that day. He didn't deny that he often worked on a project that wound up in his drawer.

"There's always the fear that one day my phone will stop ringing," he said. "And that day I'll know that I have some good scripts in my drawer ready to go. I've got a Pat Resnick script in there and an Alvin Sargent script and maybe there'll be a Joe Eszterhas script in there, too. But that's not so bad, is it? You'd be in good company."

His idea was to do a story about the heroic construction of the Alaska pipeline. He wanted me to research it extensively and then capture a kind of old-timey frontier spirit within a modern-day context.

"That's it?" I asked.

"That's it," he said, "go do it."

Alan's nephew by marriage, a young man named Jon Boorstin, was to be the co-producer of the project. He would travel with me. Jon was the son of Daniel J. Boorstin, the historian. He was very intellectual and prone to abstractions and by the time we got to our first stop on the research trip—Tulsa, Oklahoma— I knew we were not ideal traveling companions.

But the pipeliners were wild, larger-than-life characters. They'd worked on pipe all over the world. A union in Tulsa had a lock on the welders—so if pipe was being laid anywhere in the world by any American company, these guys from Tulsa had to be the ones doing the work. They'd been everywhere—Abu Dhabi and Singapore and Kuwait—sported gold, diamond-encrusted Rolexes and thick gold chains, and were never without a beer can nearby.

They were a raw-meat, no-bullshit, fuck-'em-if-they-can't-take-a-joke group very much like a lot of the guys I'd grown up with on Lorain Avenue in Cleveland.

We found an entire colony of them in a place called Grand Isle, Louisiana, down on the bayou two hours out of New Orleans at the tip of the Gulf of Mexico, deep in Cajun country where the stop signs looked like swiss cheese from all the target practice everybody took as soon as the sun went down.

There was one motel in town and one bar where all the pipeliners hung out—it was a vast U-shaped bar decorated with hardhats. There was one bartender and she was the only beautiful woman in town.

Jon Boorstin and I went in there and Jon started telling the bartender that we were from Hollywood and were doing a movie that he was going to produce.

She liked that. "Oh yeah? You gonna put me in it? I can be sexy." She laughed, swayed her hips, and licked her lips with her tongue.

There were fifty of the roughest-looking guys I'd ever seen listening to all of this and they sure didn't look like happy campers. The only relatively beautiful woman in town was acting like she was ready for the casting couch with these two Hollywood assholes who had no business down here on the bayou.

I tried to tell Jon to cool it but Jon was into it, he was having fun and, from what I could tell, so was she.

It went on for a while—she was full of all kinds of questions about Hollywood, not questions really but periodic quasi-observations like: "That Robert Redford, he must be really somethin' huh" or "Burt Reynolds, now he can park his boots under my bed anytime!" and as she and Jon kept talking I noticed two Cajuns glaring at us.

They were rip-roaring sky-high drunk, the empty Pearls a fort around them, and after a while they got into an argument with each other which, the best that I could make out, had to do with their scars.

They took their shirts off and one of them said—"Lookit this here, now this a .38 Magnum went clear on through." The other said, "This one here, it's that Bowie knife Willie Joe got for Christmas year fore last."

They kept giving us glances as the enumeration of wounds went on.

Then they suddenly started yelling at each other about something and it ended with one of them saying to the other, "Fuck you, motherfuckin' sonofabitch fuck! I'm gonna kill you!"

The one using the words jumped up and tore ass out of the bar.

I grabbed Jon by the lapels of his sport coat, said, "Okay, we're out of here," and dragged him outside and down the stairs while he all the while kept saying, "Are you completely nuts? What's wrong with you? Have you lost your mind?"

We had turned the corner and were heading into our motel court—the ground was littered with seashells—when we heard the gunshots. The Cajun had meant it. He'd gone to his car and gotten his gun and gone back into the bar, where he shot his friend and two others.

Had we still been in there, I'm convinced, the two Hollywood assholes would have been the first two dead men.

I went back home, happy to be alive, and wrote the script based on my interviews and research, still dealing with my now familiar morning ritual: first you throw up and then you write the screenplay.

I went to New York to discuss it with Alan Pakula. He hated the script and gave me the best writing advice I ever got from anyone.

"Forget the research," he said. "Go back home and use your imagination, make it up. Don't lean it on great lines and great characters you've heard and seen, just, *make the whole thing up.*"

I went back home and did exactly that. It was the most fun I'd had writing anything. It was the first fun I'd ever had writing a screenplay, the greatest natural high I'd ever felt. Out on a high wire every morning, way out on an edge, playing God, just . . . *making . . . it . . . all . . . up.*

And, after nearly three years of my morning ritual, I stopped throwing up.

I sent the new script to Alan and he loved it. He had the script budgeted and started sending it out to cast it. He was thinking about Burt Reynolds and Jane Fonda. The budget came to $40 million.

Forty million dollars?

Forget about it, the studio said. *Heaven's Gate* had just put United Artists out of business. *Forty million dollars?*

We had to cut the script—but we couldn't cut the script, Alan pointed out. Most of the money was in rebuilding and re-creating pipeline conditions in Alaska, with the inherent dangers of blizzards and windstorms delaying shooting.

In the middle of the budget hassle with the studio, both Burt Reynolds and Jane Fonda passed. "If you want a star to do a movie," Barry Hirsch, my lawyer, said, "don't set it in a blizzard in Alaska for God's sake."

When Burt and Jane passed, Alan Pakula called to tell me that my script, entitled *Rowdy,* was going into the drawer with Pat Resnick and Alvin Sargent.

"Well," I said, "will you let me find another director for it?"

"Absolutely not," Alan said. "It's a great script and if my phone stops ringing one day, who knows . . ."

"Yeah, I know, I know," I said, but I almost didn't care.

First he'd threatened to put me out of business if I didn't write his script. Now that I'd written the script and written it well, he wasn't allowing anyone else to put it up on-screen; he was hiding it in his drawer.

The damn script had almost literally left me a dead man in Bayou Country, but he had given me the best writing advice I've ever had and I will be forever grateful to him.

Alan Pakula also told me one of the truest stories I've ever heard about film journalists:

"When *Sophie's Choice* was coming out, one of the news magazines sent a writer to do a major feature on me. He came to my office to do the interview and, during it, he told me about a script he had written. He just happened to have it with him and he gave it to me.

"Three days later, he called me and asked if I'd had a chance to read his script yet. He told me that he was in the middle of writing his profile about me.

I knew what he was doing: he was shaking me down. While he was in the middle of writing a profile of me which would be read by millions of people, he was asking me what I thought of his script.

"I told him that I'd been very busy, but hoped to read his script that weekend—which I knew was past his deadline for submitting my profile.

" 'Oh,' he said, sounding disappointed, 'I was hoping you'd have it read before then.'

"I thought about it. A favorable profile in a magazine with that kind of mega-circulation would certainly help the movie. I was worried about *Sophie*'s box office anyway. The subject matter itself would scare some people off.

"I called him back and told him that I'd finished reading his script and loved it. I told him that I wanted to produce it—not direct it, but produce it like I had produced other movies earlier in my career.

" 'Oh,' he said, sounding disappointed, 'I was hoping you'd direct it.'

"I called him back the next morning and told him I'd thought about it more. I told him I liked his script so much that I wanted to *direct* it. As my next movie.

"There was a pause and he said, 'I hear you're an honorable man. Do I have your word on that?'

" 'Absolutely,' " I said to him. 'I give you my word. You've written a brilliant script.'

" 'Thank you,' he said, 'this is probably the greatest moment of my life. By the way, I think you're going to like the profile I'm writing.'

"We made plans to get together in a week—way past his deadline—to celebrate.

"When the profile came out, it was long, glowing, and flattering and I'm sure it helped the movie's success.

"He called me after the article came out and he kept calling for days, but I wouldn't take his calls.

"He sent me an anonymous note in the mail, but I have no doubt it came from him.

"All it said was: 'You fucked me masterfully. I applaud you. I deserved it.' "

My agent, Bob Bookman, was leaving the agency to be head of production at ABC Films, an attempt by the network to go into film production. I liked "Bookie," as everyone in Hollywood called him. He was one of the few people in Hollywood I'd met who actually loved to read. A fanatical Francophile, he was the kind of guy who'd carry a wine tip sheet listing undiscovered new brands and vintage years into a restaurant.

I asked Bookie to recommend another agent. He said he'd have to think about it.

The man he finally recommended was Guy McElwaine.

Guy McElwaine, then in his forties, was the premier actor's agent in town and one of the heads of the agency. He had represented everyone from Peter Sellers to Yul Brynner to Burt Reynolds.

"What writers does he represent?" I asked Bookie.

"He doesn't represent any writers."

"What writers has he represented?"

"He's never represented any writers."

"You think I should be represented by an agent who's never represented a writer?"

"Yeah, I think you'll like each other," Bookie said.

He spoke to McElwaine and I made an appointment to see him. I did some research on him. He was an ex-jock, known as "The Golden Beef" in the days when he outpitched Don Drysdale in high school. He began as a publicist for Frank Sinatra and then Judy Garland. He was famous for the large number of gold chains he had once worn around his neck. He was now on his sixth marriage.

I was nervous the afternoon I was supposed to meet him. This person sounded like a real Hollywood animal to me.

Had I hurt Bookie's feelings somehow? Was McElwaine some kind of twisted Francophile revenge? I knew, after all, how much Bookie loved Proust.

Our appointment was at 2:30. I was in Guy McElwaine's outer office at 2:15. The outer office had a framed photograph of John F. Kennedy with the words: "To Guy, All My Best, Jack" written on it. JFK's pal wasn't there at 2:30. He wasn't there at three o'clock. He wasn't there at 3:15.

"I had an appointment at 2:30," I said to his assistant, "it's now 3:15, I know I'm only a writer, but—"

She was sweet. "I'm sorry, I'm so sorry, I'm really very sorry," she said, "he got delayed, he's on the way."

At 3:30, Hunter Thompson arrived.

Hunter Thompson? Here?

In Guy McElwaine's outer office? Wearing his Hawaiian shirt and shorts and safari hat and carrying his doctor's bag? Was I *hallucinating?* I hadn't seen him since I left *Rolling Stone.*

"What the fuck are you doing here?" I said.

"In the building," he mumbled, "heard you here. Wanna beer?"

He took out a cold Heineken from his bag and handed it to me.

"Fuck motherfuckers," he said. "Don't take any shit, vultures, jackal screenwriters, Sunset Marquis, call me," and Hunter was gone.

At five minutes to four, as I was finishing Hunter's Heineken, Guy McElwaine floated in.

I mean, he *floated.*

He was dressed immaculately in a beautifully tailored suit and he was inside a cloud of fumes that smelled like Jack Daniel's fine sipping whiskey to me.

With him was Peter Falk, wearing his Columbo raincoat.

First Hunter Thompson and now *Peter Falk in his Columbo raincoat*?

Maybe I was having some sort of bizarre acid flashback that had kicked in after all these years.

"Come on in, come on in," Guy waved. "Peter left his keys."

No apology for being late, no hello, just a wave to the butler to follow him into the house.

Peter Falk couldn't find his keys. He started doing his Columbo number.

"Jesus, I'm really sorry here," he said, looking around couches and on the floor, "I know I held you up here, kid, it's all my fault, Jesus where could I have put 'em, I thought I left 'em right here, you don't see any keys around anywhere, do you, kid?"

I shook my head no. As Columbo stumbled around, McElwaine poured himself a drink at his own private bar. He didn't offer me one.

I saw what he was pouring for himself: it *was* Jack Daniel's!

"Here they are!" Falk suddenly said. "Well what do you know? I must've dropped 'em. How about that? I thought I looked there—my eyes must be gettin' worse—Jesus, maybe I should see my eye guy. See you, Guy. Great lunch, huh?"

"Always a pleasure," Guy McElwaine said.

"Good luck, kid." Peter Falk winked at me and stumbled, Columbo-like, out of the office.

Guy McElwaine and I looked at each other. I felt my ears burning. My blood pressure must have been through the roof. McElwaine looked cool, professionally unperturbed. He looked at his gold watch and sat down at a couch across from me, his Jack Daniel's in hand.

"So, tell me," he said, sipping his drink, "what ambitions do you have in this business?"

He glanced at his watch again. I think it was that second glance that did it.

"You've got a lot of balls," I said. "You come in here an hour and a half late—you don't even apologize—you sit down like King Shit condescending to some servant! I don't care who you are! Or who you represent! I don't care if I'm just a writer and not one of your big stars! But you don't have a right to treat another human being this way!"

He stared at me, his eyes cold, his face expressionless, and took another sip of his drink as I was carrying on.

I ended my tirade eloquently.

"Go fuck yourself," I said, got up, and headed for the door. I was almost there when I heard him.

"Come back here and sit down."

I turned but I wasn't going back.

"I'm sorry. I apologize. It'll never happen again."

"You're goddamn right it won't," I said, and turned back to the door.

"For Christ's sake!" he said, his voice low but hard. "Come back here and sit down and have a drink with me!"

I looked at him. He was shaking his head and grinning. I went back and sat down on the couch across from him.

"What can I get you to drink?" he said.

"Jack Daniel's sounds great."

"I think I'm gonna like you," Guy McElwaine said.

Sometime during that first meeting, Guy McElwaine, grinning, drink in hand, said to me: "Remember this. There is no heart as black as the black heart of an agent."

I grinned back, drink in hand, and promised to remember it.

I went into what everybody in town called Development Hell, writing scripts that I enjoyed writing but that weren't made. My price per script jumped each time—I sometimes suspected that studio executives were simply not prepared to be dealing with Guy McElwaine, superstar agent, wheeling and dealing on behalf of a freshman writer.

I had countless meetings with countless executives over countless projects, getting to know people. I was also getting to know Guy, who sort of adopted me, taking me to places like La Scala, Le Dome, Ma Maison, and the Bistro and introducing me around.

What a piece of work this Golden Beef was!

We were on our way to La Scala for lunch one day—Guy was a permanent resident there with his own banquette.

The sun was in our eyes and an attractive woman, walking toward us, stopped us.

"Guy, how are you?" she gushed.

"I'm just fine, thank you," he said.

He was peering at her, his Gucci shades on. I could tell he didn't know who she was.

"Well you look really great," she told him with a smile.

"Thank you." He smiled back. "So do you."

"Guy, don't you recognize me?" She laughed.

"Well sure, of course I do," he said but she and I both knew he had no idea who she was.

"But Guy," she said, "I was your first wife."

Another time we were having dinner and there was a stunning woman in her forties sitting near us with a white-haired man in his seventies. When the man went to the restroom, she turned to us and said, "Guy, you never call me anymore."

He oozed charm and said he was very sorry but that he certainly would.

"It's been such a long time," she said, "I miss you."

"I miss you too, darlin'," Guy said, smiling.

When her friend came back from the restroom they left.

"Who was she?" I asked him.

"I don't know," he said.

"You don't know?" I laughed.

"Well, I remember her. I don't think I ever knew her name, but twenty years ago she used to give the best head in this town."

Another night at La Scala with Guy, I also met a young agent who had just started his own agency. Michael Ovitz was with Sally Struthers and they stopped at our table on their way out.

At the moment they stopped, I was holding a hunting knife that I'd bought on Wilshire Boulevard at Abercrombie & Fitch that afternoon.

I was showing it to Guy and the six-inch blade was open when Ovitz and Struthers stopped.

Guy introduced me to them and after a few moments of agent banter, Ovitz suddenly turned to me, glancing at the knife, and said: "Do you eat dinner with that thing?"

"No," I said, "but I carry it into all of my meetings."

"You'll probably go a long way in this town." Ovitz laughed.

Sally Struthers asked to see the knife, so I handed it over, its blade open.

"This thing is really lethal," she said.

She handed it to Ovitz, who checked it for heft, rubbed it admiringly, and made some stabbing motions with it.

"Maybe I'll borrow it sometime," he said with a smile.

"Not while I'm around," Guy said.

We all laughed.

"Anytime," I said to Michael Ovitz and he smiled and handed the knife back to me.

One of the more memorable meetings in Guy's office was with Jann Wenner, my old boss at *Rolling Stone,* whom I'd always called Napoleon, partly because of his size and partly because of his accomplishments.

Jann had just gotten a three-picture producing deal at Paramount through his friendship with studio head Barry Diller and we were now talking about my writing a script for him.

The irony didn't escape me. I'd written magazine articles for him all those years and now here he was, back as my potential "producer."

The only problem with the meeting was that Jann was zonked out of his mind—not on grass or coke or some of the other more arcane highs that we'd shared (*ibogaine? belladonna?*) . . . but on vodka.

Even Guy, who must've been a part owner of Jack Daniel's, was sort of taken aback. I was amused: when I was at *Rolling Stone,* Jann knew so little about alcohol that when Yevgeny Yevtushenko (a world-renowned drinker) came to visit us, I had to draw up a liquor list for his arrival.

Now, in Guy's office, Jann was lurching around and fixated on the boots I was wearing.

"*Those are Beatle boots!*" he said.

"No they're not."

"Yes they are. They're Beatle boots. I can't believe you're wearing Beatle boots."

"I am *not* wearing Beatle boots."

"Cleveland, you're from *Cleveland.* It makes sense. No wonder you're wearing Beatle boots. Guy, don't those look like Beatle boots?"

"Well, a little, I guess," Guy said. "Maybe."

"Beatle boots!" Jann crowed. "*Fucking Beatle boots!*"

I also met Don Simpson during that period of time. He was the head of production at Paramount, working with and under a stellar cast of people that included Craig Baumgarten, Jeff Katzenberg, Michael Eisner, and Barry Diller.

I was in Don's office to discuss adapting one of my books, *Nark,* to the screen, and in the room were Craig Baumgarten and a producer Barry Hirsch had recommended to me. I knew that Simpson had come out of the music business and I was immediately drawn to his let's-kick-some-ass, passionate, rock and roll style. He was firing ideas off in machine-gun bursts and at one point in the meeting he got so excited about what he was saying that he got up from behind his desk and started hurling himself around the office.

I knew that the producer Peter Guber was known in town as "The Electric Jew" but Simpson truly was some kind of dervish-like force.

As Simpson hurled himself about the office, waving his arms, nearly boogalooing, I got up from the chair I was sitting in and wandered behind his desk, sat down in it, and put my feet up on it.

Simpson gaped at me. He looked frozen.

"What are you doing with your feet up on my desk?" he whispered.

"I'm stretching my legs," I said.

He stood there, riveted to the spot, and smiled, then he started to giggle. Then we all started to giggle.

"Make the fucking deal with him," Simpson said to Craig. "Now I know what I'm dealing with."

And then, turning to me, he screamed—"GET THE FUCK AWAY FROM MY DESK!"

I did.

It seemed sometimes that the Beverly Wilshire Hotel was becoming my temporary home.

The suite I favored looked across Wilshire Boulevard down Rodeo Drive.

I sat on my patio one night watching an army of policemen and SWAT team members as they cordoned Rodeo off. Helicopters buzzed the night sky. Spotlights turned night into day. Police sirens wailed.

I wondered what movie they were shooting and was looking for the sound trucks when a bulletin on my TV set announced that a robbery had gone wrong at Van Cleef & Arpels Jewelers on Rodeo. Hostages had been taken. Police were on the scene.

Maybe it wasn't a movie being filmed, but what difference did *that* make?

I had a great front-row seat!

Steven Spielberg was an old friend of Guy's. When Steven was starting out in the business, Guy would let him drive his car and offered him a spot at his Thanksgiving table each year. Now Steven was thinking about doing a remake of *A Guy Named Joe* and Guy wanted to bring the two of us together.

I went to Steven's house in the Palisades. It was filled with toys and miniatures of sets from his movies.

Steven told me he was going through a tough time: he was breaking up with Amy Irving and he wanted to get into another project as soon as possible— meaning *now*.

We watched the movie together at his house and when it was over he told me he had read a couple of my scripts and wanted me to do it. Was I interested?

Yes I was, I told him, but I couldn't get to it for at least another six months because I had agreed to write an idea from my old agent, Bob Bookman, for ABC Films, about migrant wheat farmers in the Midwest.

"Did you sign a contract?" Steven asked.

"No, but I agreed to do it," I said. "Besides that, I hear nobody in town signs a contract."

"But you didn't sign one, right?" he said.

"No."

"I'll talk to Guy," Steven Spielberg said.

Guy spoke to me the next day.

"It's no problem," he said, "I can get us out of the ABC thing. We didn't sign anything."

"But I gave my word to Bookie that I'd do it."

"This is Steven Spielberg we're talking about here," Guy said.

"I'll do it in six months," I said.

"He can't wait," Guy said, "he's going through this breakup with Amy Irving. He wants to work on this *right now.* You're probably going to have to go to London for a couple months to baby-sit him through it."

"I'm not a baby-sitter, I'm a writer."

"Well, you know what I mean," Guy said. "Think about it."

I did and called him back.

"I don't feel comfortable with this," I said. "I've given my word to Bookie and I've never been good at baby-sitting anybody—"

"Forget the baby-sitting part. I just meant spending time together, hanging out. Steven needs a friend right now."

"I don't even know the man. I met him once and liked him but—"

"Do you really want me to tell Steven Spielberg that you won't work with him because of some dipshit ABC project about farmers?"

I said: "Yes."

He called me back and said he had spoken to Steven.

"What did he say?"

"He's pissed off at you."

"How can he be pissed off at me? What if I'd made an agreement with him and then did something else?"

"Nobody does that to Steven Spielberg."

"Does what?"

"Turn him down."

"What did he actually say to you?"

"He said—'I can't believe Joe's turning down a chance to work with Steven Spielberg.' "

I went off to Nebraska and Iowa and hung out with the migrant farmers instead of Steven and sent ABC an outline.

"This is a great outline," Bookie said in his new corporate digs, "but we want you to do something else."

"Something *else?*"

"I'll tell you the truth," he said. "We market-researched this idea. Market research says a movie about migrant wheat farmers won't be a hit movie."

"Why didn't you market-research it before we made an agreement that I'd write it?"

"We probably should have, but we didn't. Jeff was right." Jeff Katzenberg, at Paramount, had issued a recent edict that movies with "dust" weren't to be made because they were a box office turnoff. Wheat farmers meant *a lot of dust.*

"Don't worry about it," Bookie said, "we'll find something else for you to do."

"But I've already done the research and I've spent a lot of time figuring out a story."

"What can I say?" Bookie said. "I'm sorry."

Guy wasn't sorry when he heard what had happened, he was apoplectic. As I sat in his office, he called Bookie.

"You're *sorry?*" he said. "You made a deal with him to write this script on this subject. He began to perform. Now you don't want him to perform because of market research? Well fuck market research! You pay him out completely and have the check on my desk in an hour! If you want to make another deal with him to write something else, we'll consider it! If the check isn't here within the hour, this agency will cease doing any business with ABC Films!"

He slammed the phone down and made himself a drink.

"I always did like Bookie." He smiled.

Then he turned to me and said: "The moral of the story is don't ever turn down Steven Spielberg."

My kids were growing and I was starting to make a lot of money, but it was screwy. No movie had been made from any of my scripts since *F.I.S.T.,* but my price was escalating and I was more and more in demand.

I was commuting to Los Angeles more often, still living in Marin County, being the dad, cooking hamburgers for the nursery and grade schools, getting involved in Little League, but my day-to-day life was as much about Hollywood as it was about Marin County.

Gerri felt estranged from the world that I was spending increasingly more time in.

One night at dinner in San Francisco with Paramount vice president Craig Baumgarten and his then-wife, the actress Vicki Frederick, Gerri suffered an allergic attack that I thought was more about Hollywood than about the pine nuts she had accidentally eaten.

Vicki, starlet-slick and cat-eyed, kept tossing her hair back theatrically and vetting the other diners and Gerri's face started to swell. Her eyes became webbed and finally her breathing became choked and I wound up rushing her to Marin General Hospital.

She knew what had happened, too, I think, because she said, "I never want to eat dinner with people like that again," when she recovered.

We were living in bucolic Marin County because we felt it was a peaceful place to raise our kids.

At three o'clock in the morning on a rainy winter night—when Suzi was four and Steve five—there was a banging at our front door in quiet San Rafael.

I looked through the glass and saw a figure in a camouflage outfit, his face blackened, carrying an M-16.

I almost shot him on sight with the .22 Beretta I had in the pocket of my robe. He must've seen my hand move in my pocket because he yelled: "No! Don't! *Don't!* My name is Officer Guerra of the San Rafael Police Department. Call this number right now!"

He gave me his office's number and they told me that he was a member of the SWAT team. They also told me that in the house right next to ours, a teenage boy had taken his parents hostage.

I let Officer Guerra in and he told Gerri and me that since our house was in the teenager's gunsight, we'd have to wake Steve and Suzi and evacuate our house.

Gerri and I, terrified, woke the kids, but before we could leave our house there were gunshots next door and newly arrived policemen told me we couldn't leave our house now . . . we had to get down on the floor in a room of the house that was away from the line of fire.

Steve and Suzi screamed and were so terrified we could hear their teeth chattering as we lay down on the floor of a spare bedroom.

Our house became a command post for the SWAT team. Men with blackened faces and M-16s and semiautomatic weapons kept opening the door to the room where we were lying on the floor.

As Gerri and Steve and Suzi lay on the floor, I crouched at the window to see what I could see.

I saw men with weapons crouching by all the bushes.

And I saw our kitty-cat go promenading up the middle of the street in the glare of the police lights.

At noon the next day the teenager gave himself up and we were allowed to get off the floor of our spare bedroom.

Steve and Suzi went back to bed and slept for twenty hours.

I drank a half bottle of Tanqueray gin and Gerri and I talked about how awful it was that our children could be so horribly traumatized in such a peaceful place.

The teenager went to a psychiatric facility for a month, came home, and blew his brains out.

His older brother, we discovered, had killed himself a decade earlier by jumping off the Golden Gate Bridge.

Some months later, the teenager's parents made a complaint to the Humane Society that one of our dogs was keeping them awake at night barking.

I responded that the dog had been traumatized by all the shooting which their dead son had done.

The Humane Society ruled that their complaints about our dog were without merit.

There had been strains in our marriage before and Hollywood did nothing to ease them. Gerri never wanted to come to L.A. on my commutes, sensing that the world there was a very different place from Marin, then noted for its rustic and harmonious vibes.

Hollywood in the seventies was movie excess—coke on silver platters at all the parties, "chicks" ready and willing to do anything and everything to somehow get involved in the business. I'll never forget a famous director at a party one night, on his hands and knees on a thick white shag rug. He was trying to snort up the coke he had dropped, a very difficult business with a white shag rug.

When my son Steve was six years old, he fell in love with *Jaws*. He watched it over and over again. Then he watched the sequels over and over again. He learned all the dialogue in *all* of them.

He walked around the house wearing a shark tooth all the time. Then he started collecting shark teeth and shark jaws.

Steven Spielberg called one day and Steve picked the phone up and introduced himself to Steven as the little boy in *Jaws* who died.

I met a young woman who was an assistant to one of the more powerful producers in town. He was wooing me to do a script for him so it seemed I spoke to her incessantly: the guy would call all the time and insisted that we meet whenever I was in L.A.

I liked her. She was from a small town in Texas and had a raunchy and lively sense of humor. She liked to drink and had a seemingly inexhaustible stash of coke. She also had a cynical wisdom about the business and had a Dallas Cowboys cheerleader body and face. It began with drinks and then a dinner and before I knew it we were having an affair.

I realized I was compartmentalizing my life—there was Hollywood and then there was Marin County, schools, and pediatricians—but it was difficult to compartmentalize this affair simply because she'd call three times a day, placing the calls for her boss but managing to have very personal, sometimes intimate conversations with me before she put her boss on. After a while I realized she was getting too involved and decided to end it.

I saw her for dinner in L.A. and tried to tell her it was over but we had both had too much to drink and wound up back at my hotel. We got into the coke then and I wound up breaking the news to her at four o'clock in the morning.

She flipped out and called me a bunch of names. I agreed that they were all accurate. She went home to her apartment in Westwood.

She called me about an hour later and said, "I can still smell you."

I said, "Take a shower."

She hung up and called me back in ten minutes and said: "If you don't let me come back there right now I'm calling your wife to tell her what's been going on."

I knew she had my home number and I knew from the sound of her voice that she meant it.

"Come on over," I said.

She came back and after a while I managed to calm her and she fell asleep. I went into the living room of the suite and called her boss. It was five o'clock in the morning.

He kept saying, "Oh my God, Oh my God," and asked if he could come over and talk to her.

He arrived forty-five minutes later, went into the bedroom, and they left together.

She called me later that day and apologized. Her producer boss called shortly after that.

"Did she call you to apologize?" he asked. I said that she had and thanked him for cooling her out.

"I didn't cool her out," he said. "I told her she'd *never work in this town again* unless she left right now and called to apologize to you.

"Hey," he said, "you owe me one. You gonna do that script for me now?"

I did not write the script for him but she called me about a year later and asked me to recommend her for a job she was applying for at a studio. I recommended her and she got the job.

I had known Jim Morgan since we were both reporters at the police beat in Cleveland. I worked for the *Plain Dealer* and he worked for the *Cleveland Press*.

He left the *Press* and went to Germany to edit an army publication, the *Overseas Weekly*. He came back with his wife, Karen, a high school sweetheart, edited the *Overseas Weekly* in California for a while, and then started to free-lance. He was having a tough time making a living; Karen, an executive secretary in the corporate world, essentially supported him.

We became the best of friends. We had writing and backgammon in common, as well as Cleveland. When I started writing screenplays, Jim got interested, too, and I started telling him my Hollywood adventures.

He came to me one day with an idea for a screenplay that he thought we should write together. It was about a blue-collar guy who worked in the service department of a car dealership, an ordinary sort of all-American husband and father who winds up getting into politics because the streetlight in front of his house goes out and nobody wants to fix it.

I thought it sounded like a fun idea and we started working on it without telling anyone. Jim did a draft and then I did one and then he did one and after about three months we had a screenplay: *City Hall,* by Joe Eszterhas and Jim Morgan.

. . .

I called Guy McElwaine and told him I had written a new screenplay with my friend and Guy was not happy.

"You don't write scripts for nothing," he said.

"It's not for nothing, I'm hoping you can sell it."

"But when you wrote it, you weren't being paid to write it, were you?"

"No. But I will be if you sell it."

"That's not the point," Guy said. "The point is that only amateurs write for nothing in this town. By the time real screenwriters sit down at the typewriter, they have money in hand."

I tried to tell him that I had fun writing this with Jim. I didn't have to have any inane discussions with studio executives about it, I didn't have to listen to their innocuous ideas. As a matter of fact, it was the most fun I'd ever had writing a script.

"Only unknown writers write spec scripts," Guy said. "They do it as a writing sample so they can get hired on real jobs."

But he agreed to read it. We sent it down to him and he said, "Okay, I can sell it but don't ever surprise me like this again."

What Guy planned to do was to send it out to several financiers and try to get them to bid against each other. He singled out Warner Brothers, Universal, Paramount, and MGM.

The day of the auction was the final game of the World Series between the Kansas City Royals and the Philadelphia Phillies. Jim and I were at my house. He was so nervous he kept walking around my dining room in crazed dizzying circles. He kept pouring himself shots of vodka.

At two o'clock in the afternoon, Guy called and said Warner Brothers was offering $200,000. Jim literally started jumping up and down.

I said to Guy, "What do you think?"

He said: "I think there's more."

"Have we heard from any of the others?"

"Universal and MGM passed."

At 2:30 Guy called to say that Paramount had also passed.

"What do you think?" I said.

"I still think there's more, from Warner's," Guy said.

"They're bidding against themselves."

"Yeah," Guy said, "but they don't know that."

At three o'clock Guy called to say that Warner Brothers had upped their bid to $300,000 with this codicil: we had to accept it by the seventh inning of the World Series game or they would withdraw their offer. The game was now in the third inning.

Jim kept pouring the vodka as he listened to my side of the conversation.

"What do you think?" I said to Guy.

He laughed this time. "I think there's more."

He called them when the game got into the seventh inning and rejected the offer.

"What did they say?" I asked him.

"They said fine, they were out," Guy said.

It hung there between us.

"*They're out,*" I said.

Jim hung his head between his hands, slumped on the dining room table.

"That's what they said," Guy said.

Jim and I sat down in my living room and watched the conclusion of the game—without saying much to each other, both of us slugging the vodka now.

I was walking Jim to my front door when the phone rang.

"I just got home," Guy said. "Frank Wells [one of Warner Brothers' top executives] was waiting for me in my driveway. I'm sitting with Frank in my living room now. Warner Brothers will pay you and Jim $500,000 for the script."

I raised five fingers up to Jim and he started pounding his chest like he was having a heart attack.

"What do you think?" I said to Guy.

"No, no, no, no, no," Jim started telling me in the background, "don't ask him that! *Take the deal!*"

Guy heard Jim in the background and said, "I think we should take the deal."

It was the highest amount of money ever paid for a spec script in Hollywood. We had the check three days later—before, of course, any contracts had been signed.

I stood with Jim at a bank in Marin County as he deposited his half into a checking account that had $89.22 in it. When we left, he started war-whooping up and down the streets of San Rafael.

Two weeks later, Frank Wells and John Calley, who had bought the script for Warner Brothers, left the company. The new head of production was an ex-agent named Robert Shapiro who had had nothing to do with the purchase and who'd read it only the morning of the day Jim and I met with him.

"Well, what are we going to do with this piece of shit?" Robert Shapiro said as we shook hands.

Jim and I glanced at each other. We had sold a script for the most money ever paid in Hollywood and the new studio head was calling it a piece of shit.

He had some ideas what to do with it, though.

"I think it would be perfect for Dolly Parton," Robert Shapiro said.

"You mean for the hero's wife," I said. "Isn't she too big a name? It's not that big a part."

"Not for the wife," Shapiro said, "for the hero."

"The hero's a guy who works in the service department and is married," I said.

Jim said not a word—it was his first Hollywood meeting and he was taking it all in.

"Change him. Change him to Dolly Parton."

Jim started to laugh.

Robert Shapiro looked sharply at him and said, "Did I say something funny?"

"You sure did," Jim said.

We tried to change Shapiro's mind but he was adamant—*City Hall* would become a Dolly Parton movie.

As we were leaving, I opened the wrong door: it was Shapiro's bathroom door instead of his front door.

"That's the john." Shapiro laughed. "But you can use it if you want."

"Considering your taste," I said, "it must be a mistake you make all the time."

Neither Jim nor I was interested in turning our script into a Dolly Parton vehicle, so Shapiro was bringing other writers in. But the script had circulated around town and was getting rave reviews. I told Jim that he could get other screenwriting jobs off of it and Guy agreed to help him.

We went down to L.A. together a couple months later on the morning shuttle. Jim was knocking the vodka and orange juice back on the flight. He had meetings scheduled with two producers and I had a meeting with Richard Gere.

Jim Wiatt at Guy's agency, ICM, was going out to lunch with Jim. Wiatt was an up-and-coming young agent who had worked for Senator John Tunney.

When I came back from my meeting with Richard Gere, Guy told me what had happened. Jim and Jim Wiatt had gone to lunch. Jim had had so much to drink that he couldn't make his meetings and was now sleeping it off in the ICM conference room.

Jim and I took the same flight back to San Francisco and he could hardly talk. He apologized the next day but said he didn't think he'd want to have any more meetings with "those assholes down there."

Every time I saw him after that, he was drunk. His wife was desperate. He was spending the money indiscriminately. A Porsche for himself and a matching Porsche for Karen. Drinks for the house when he'd walk into a bar. He decided on a whim to fly to Tokyo for a weekend with Karen and spent most of the time in his hotel room drinking.

"Did you have anything from the minibar, sir?" they asked him when he checked out.

"Everything," Jim said. He wasn't kidding.

I found the name of a good detox place in Napa and went to see him. I said I'd made the reservations and was paying for everything. All he had to do was get in the car with me.

"There's nothing wrong with me," he said, "I'm fine."

He was knocking down a quart of vodka a day, Karen told me. He had had two incidents of esophageal hemorrhage and had been ambulanced to the emergency room.

"Jim," I begged him, "you're going to die."

"I lost my porn collection," he said.

I asked him what the hell he was talking about.

"I had a great porn collection I started collecting when I was in Vietnam, all kinds of Asian stuff. When I had my hemorrhage, I thought I was going to die and didn't want Karen to find it. So I put it in the garbage before the ambulance came. When I got back from the hospital, the garbagemen had taken it away."

A few months later, Karen came home from work and found his body on the living room floor. An autopsy revealed that he died of cardiac arrest. Karen said he had finally decided to stop drinking. He went from a quart of vodka a day to nothing. Cold turkey. It killed him. He was forty years old.

I was the living embodiment of the Peter Principle.

None of my scripts were being made . . . the only one of my scripts which had been made was a critical and commercial disaster . . . yet my price was escalating and more and more people wanted to work with me.

Richard Roth was one of the hottest producers in town. He was independently wealthy; he came from oil money. His brother, Steve, was a successful agent at CAA. Richard had produced the critically praised and commercially successful Jane Fonda–Vanessa Redgrave movie *Julia*.

He had just bought Lucian Truscott IV's best-seller, *Dress Gray*, which Herb Ross had agreed to direct for Paramount. I knew Lucian and liked him and his work. He and I had spent an insane week together covering Evel Knievel's Snake River Canyon Jump—he for the *Village Voice* and me for *Rolling Stone*. Richard Roth wanted me to adapt Lucian's novel for the screen.

"I've done one adaptation," I told Richard. "It was a terrible experience. I don't want to do another one."

Richard begged me to at least take a meeting with Herb Ross and Jeff Katzenberg at Paramount. To convince me, he flew up to San Francisco and staged an ornate private-dining-room dinner at Chez Panisse in Berkeley, then beginning to be recognized as the tabernacle of fine dining in California. After about the seventh course and the third bottle of the finest California red, I agreed to take the meeting.

I had never met Jeff, known even then as one of the hardest-working executives in town, and only knew Herb Ross by reputation. A former choreographer, he had directed *The Owl and the Pussycat* and *The Sunshine Boys* and was known as a studio favorite.

Jeff talked about what a commercially viable project he thought this was and Herb, who had read my unproduced scripts, talked about how perfect he thought I was for this material. I hadn't said a word and finally Jeff looked at me and said, "What do you think?"

I said, "Listen, guys, I appreciate this, I really do, but the only experience I've had with an adaptation was a nightmare and there's no way I'm going to do this, thank you very much."

They looked at each other and then looked at me again—this time with a certain blankness of expression.

"Thank you," I said, and got up.

"Wait a minute," Jeffrey said, "if you had no intention of doing this, why did you take the meeting?"

"Because Richard asked me to," I said, "even though he knew how I felt."

"That's true," Richard said. "I thought we'd talk him into it."

I started shaking hands on my way to the door and Jeffrey said: "This is it? The meeting's over?"

"It is," I said.

Herb Ross laughed. "Well," he said, "I've never seen a writer end a meeting before."

A couple of months later, the road led back to Jeffrey when Michael Cimino was suddenly interested in directing my script *Nark,* which was under Jeffrey's aegis at Paramount. The script had been on Paramount's shelf. Although everyone there professed to like it, no one had made any moves to start getting it made.

Cimino had gotten the script somehow and called me. He said he knew Paramount was not interested in making it, but he liked it and wanted to do it at another studio. I asked if he wanted to sit down and talk about the script and he said he didn't want to do that unless Paramount gave it back to me first . . . for him to take elsewhere. Then, once I had it back from Paramount in turnaround, we'd sit down and talk.

I had mixed feelings about Michael Cimino. I thought *The Deer Hunter* was a brilliant movie that captured a kind of ethnic feel on-screen better than any movie I'd ever seen. And I thought *Heaven's Gate* was an abomination, as awful as *The Deer Hunter* was dazzling. I suspected that part of the problem with *Heaven's Gate* was that Cimino himself had written it.

I had been witness to one of the sorriest moments in film, a New York press and VIP screening of *Heaven's Gate,* attended by Jeff Bridges and Kris Kristofferson and Cimino and many of Cimino's friends. Michael was pacing around the lobby before it began looking like he hadn't slept in weeks; the word was that he had been editing the movie only an hour ago. Twenty minutes into the showing, the audience began to catcall and hiss—this was a *press and VIP* screening, for God's sake!

When it was over, I saw Kris Kristofferson nearly hurl himself into a limo.

The next morning, in the *New York Times,* Vincent Canby called it "the greatest disaster in the history of American film."

So I called Jeffrey Katzenberg after hearing from Cimino and asked to have *Nark* back in turnaround and he said, "Absolutely not."

"Jeffrey," I said, "please. The script is on your shelf. You're not making it, give me a chance to get it made somewhere else. You know you'll get the script price back with interest. What can you lose?"

"It's our policy not to give anything back in turnaround," Jeffrey said. "It's company policy. That's it. I'd like to help you, Joe, but I can't."

I pleaded with him and in the course of the pleading blurted out the phrase "personal favor."

"A *personal favor?*" Jeffrey stopped me. "Between you and me?"

"Yes."

"Well why didn't you say so," he said. "Of course I'll give it to you as a personal favor."

"You will?" I couldn't believe my good fortune.

"Of course I will," he said, "but you will owe *me* a personal favor. Will you promise that you'll remember that?"

"I will," I said, and I had *Nark* back, free to set it up anywhere else with Cimino.

Michael was ready to discuss the script now and we set a time at Shipp's Coffee Shop on Wilshire Boulevard. When I walked in, he was there already, wearing sunglasses and making himself his personal toast on the toaster at the table.

He made me a couple of pieces of toast, too, and then he said, "Let's do the bottom line first. This is how it's going to work. You give the script to me—I own it—I take it wherever I want, I do whatever I want to it and then I shoot it and you come to see it when it's locked."

The toast I was chewing definitely needed more jelly.

"You mean you just *take it,*" I said.

"That's right," Michael Cimino said, "that's the way I work."

"Tell me why I should do that," I said. "I've got a script that I wrote that I like. Maybe it'll get made someday and maybe it won't. But it will be *my* script and the story *I* want to tell. So why should I just give it to you and forget about it?"

"Is your script being made?" he asked.

"No."

"I can get it made. That's why you should do it."

"What if I'd rather it remain unmade unless it's made the way I wrote it and want it made."

"Then I'm not the man to make it," he said.

We had a two-ton chunk of ice now between us and ten minutes later, I was out of there as Cimino sat waiting for his huevos rancheros.

I called Jeffrey and said, "I don't want *Nark* back anymore. You hold on to it. I changed my mind."

"You can't change your mind," he said, "you've got it for twelve months. And you owe me a personal favor."

Now *Nark* was up on my own shelf instead of Paramount's, but at least Michael Cimino wasn't making it—and, the way I figured it, that was a big plus.

Guy McElwaine, meanwhile, was leaving the agency business. He was going to head a studio, Rastar, the producer Ray Stark's production company, which, considering Stark's power in town, was like a mini-studio itself. It was not the first time Guy had headed a studio. Sometime in the early seventies, before I met him, he was the head of Warner Brothers.

"Well that's just great," I said. "Now I don't even have *you* anymore."

"You'll always have me," Guy said. "Just because I'm heading a studio doesn't mean I can't look over your deals."

At Rastar, the first thing he did was make a deal with me.

It was to do a five-day polish on a script called *Blue Thunder* that John Badham was about to shoot with Roy Scheider, also one of Guy's clients. Badham had directed *Saturday Night Fever* and every studio in town wanted to work with him. What the movie needed was an ending. In five days, I came up with one.

Guy wanted to buy me a new Jaguar for my five days' work, which, considering my contribution, was eminently fair.

My new agent, Guy's protégé Jim Wiatt, didn't.

"What's our commission?" Jim Wiatt said, "a wheel?"

Jane Fonda wanted to do a project that I loved about a young woman named Karen Silkwood who gave her life in a battle with a corporate behemoth more interested in profit than in the common good.

I had known Jane since I was a young reporter in Cleveland and she was busted as she flew from Canada to Cleveland for carrying a joint. I had interviewed her in jail and covered the legal proceedings. I admired Jane's politics and her balls-out approach.

When she learned, shortly after that, that I had written a book about Kent State, she read the book and took it around with her, holding it up, on just about every talk show that she did.

She asked me to fly down to L.A. to see her and, together, we went to see the studio people at MGM, where her production company was housed, to talk about Silkwood.

We were both impassioned about the Silkwood story. We both felt there was a profoundly disturbing movie there that said volumes about corporate greed and insensitivity.

The executive we spoke to said, "This is politics, isn't it?"

We both said no—it was a stirring human story about a courageous young woman who would not be intimidated.

"It's a lefty thing, though, isn't it?" the executive said.

"It's not a lefty thing, it's a human thing," I said.

"But it's sort of like propaganda."

"No," Jane said, "it's not. We will dwell on the human aspects of it."

"I guarantee you there will be no preaching in this movie," I said. "Whatever message there is will come out of the facts."

"Facts are rarely black and white, though," the executive said.

"They're pretty black and white in this case," I explained.

"There's no proof, though, right? Nobody went to jail or anything."

Jane said, "Why don't you let the lawyers worry about the legal stuff instead of worrying about it now?"

"I'm not worrying," the executive said. "I'm just offering guidelines." The executive laughed. "We're just spitballing here, aren't we?"

We agreed that yes, indeed, that's all we were doing here, spitballing.

"I like it," the executive said. "I'm not sure how commercial it is. It *is* sort of a downer. She dies at the end, but *I* like it. I'll pass it on upstairs."

We thanked the executive and left. We knew we didn't have a prayer.

Jane Fonda said, "There are so many idiots in this town. I don't know how I do it."

Silkwood was made years later from a brilliant script by Nora Ephron and Alice Arlen.

While Guy was gone on his studio adventures, I bounced back and forth between agencies like a berserk shuttlecock. Even when I was with an agent, I was allowing myself to be wooed by others.

I had a breakfast scheduled with an agent once, got back to the hotel at five in the morning, realized I'd never make the breakfast, and called him—at five in the morning to break our eight o'clock date.

"I've never had anyone call me at five in the morning to cancel before," he said.

I said, "I didn't want to be rude," hung up, and laughed.

First I was with Jim Wiatt at ICM, a smart, down-to-earth man who liked to drive out to the desert in his Porsche occasionally, park it at Joshua Tree, and live among the cacti for a few days "to keep it all together." Then I switched to Michael Ovitz's rising CAA, where I was represented by Steve Roth, Richard Roth's brother. Steve was a free spirit much drawn to long getaway weekends with people like Debra Winger. Then, when Steve left the agency business, I switched back to Jim Wiatt at ICM, drawing, for the first time, the ire of Michael Ovitz. He called the producer Don Simpson, with whom I was working at the time, and said, "Who is this fucking bum to do this to me?"

Ovitz didn't care at all about me personally at the time, he just didn't want it to appear that Roth's departure (Roth was one of the original CAA founders) would cause any of his clients to leave CAA.

Then, after being with Wiatt again for a while, I switched back to Ovitz's CAA to be represented by Rosalie Swedlin, a young, bright "literary" agent who had spent time in London and spoke with an English accent.

The accent drove me nuts after a while . . . she hadn't spent *that* much time in London . . . but what bothered me more was that she was a "literary" agent. I didn't know what a "literary" agent was doing in Hollywood, but she did. She felt the main part of her job was to give me advice about the scripts I had written.

"The third act needs cutting," she'd say to me and I finally asked her if she had ever written anything in her life.

She took umbrage at that.

"Is that meant to be an insulting question?" she asked.

I met a bunch of other agents from other agencies and was unimpressed by all of them, even though all of them said the same flattering smarmy things and were more than willing to fly up to San Francisco at the drop of a dime.

I finally wrote Rosalie, whom I personally liked very much, a note explaining our dramaturgical incompatibility and the note brought Michael Ovitz directly into my life for the first time. He was rapidly becoming one of the most powerful people in town and CAA was beginning to be viewed as the New York Yankees of tinseltown.

Michael had a new plan in mind. He would represent me himself, along with another CAA agent, Rand Holston. I knew that when he said he would represent me himself it meant that he would send me presents for Christmas and that Rand Holston would do the actual work.

It was, I had been told, a common CAA ploy.

Holston came up to Marin County and arranged a lunch in a fancy place. He was in his early thirties, an earnest robotic yuppie. Well, I thought, I'm not marrying the guy and maybe Guy McElwaine would become an agent again one of these days.

· · ·

During the same period, I wrote three screenplays without a contract. I'd loved the freedom of *City Hall*—no discussions, no meetings, no advice from anyone, just the pure bald pleasure of writing a story I believed in.

The first was called *Platinum.* It was about a rock and roll singer who is thought to have died. His brother, a Cleveland cop, thinks his death is suspicious and winds up very much out of his element tracking his brother's glitzy and highly connected friends. My agent sent the script out to over a hundred financing entities in town. Every one of them passed. The script, the universal opinion held, was "too dark."

The second was called *Magic Man.* It was a poignant, nostalgic piece about the relationship between a rock disc jockey in the early sixties and a sixteen-year-old refugee Hungarian kid very much patterned after me. It involved payola and was about loyalty and values. My agent sent the script out to the same financing entities who had passed on *Platinum.* They all passed again.

The third script was called *Checking Out* and was about a man in his thirties who suddenly realizes that he is going to die. He becomes obsessed with death and the obsession changes everything in his life. It was a dark comedy.

My agent sent the script out to the same financing entities who had passed on *Platinum* and *Magic Man.* They all passed once again—except for the producer Ned Tanen, the former head of Universal, now an independent producer, who had been ill, found the script very funny, and wanted to think about it.

He thought about it and then he passed.

"They all thought it was too dark," my agent said.

"It's a dark comedy," I said.

"They thought it was too dark for a dark comedy."

"Well, I can't lighten it any," I said, "it's about dying."

"Tough subject," he said, "I get it."

The good news: my price was higher than ever before, I was making more money than ever before, agents and producers and studio heads were now wooing me more than ever before.

The bad news: the only movie I'd had made had flopped. None of the scripts I'd written on contract had been made or looked like they'd ever be made. Three spec scripts I'd written hadn't sold. The only spec script I'd sold, *City Hall,* was now being turned into a Goldie Hawn vehicle by other writers. (Dolly Parton had passed.)

I got a call from a young guy in Marin County. He was working behind the counter at the Book Depot in the middle of town, serving coffee and selling books. His name was Ben Myron. He had formerly painted addresses on curbs without the homeowners' permission and had then presented them with a bill for his "services." Now he wanted to be a producer.

Ben Myron asked if I had anything "in the drawer" that he could try to sell in Hollywood.

"Do you know anything about Hollywood?" I asked him.

"I grew up in L.A."

"Do you know anything about the movie business?"

"Truthfully," he said, "no."

I let him have *Checking Out*. It was the one I liked the most.

"What are you going to do with it?" I asked.

"I don't know," he said, "but I'll figure it out. Should I pay you any money for the option?"

"Do you have any money?" I asked.

"I don't, but my girlfriend has some," he said.

"Forget about it," I said. "Call me when you sell it."

Guy called to see how I was doing. He always said, "What trouble are you getting into?"

I told him that the new producer of *Checking Out* was working behind the counter at the Book Depot in Mill Valley and had once painted addresses on curbs.

"Perfect," he said, "just perfect. Do you know what you're doing? You're establishing a real reputation for writing scripts that no one wants."

He went on and on. The spec scripts, he said, were going to destroy whatever career I had.

"I love writing them," I said, "I don't have to hustle anybody, I don't have to be nice to people I can't stand—"

"From what I hear you're not nice to people you can't stand anyway," he said.

"It's more honest for the studios, too, isn't it?" I asked. "They don't have to take a chance on the fact that maybe I'll write a good script. They can read the finished script—take it or leave it. It ain't a pig in a poke."

"You're too ornery for your own good," Guy said. "You oughta be out making nice instead of carrying knives around with you. That's what screenwriters do."

The two houses were close together, and she was my father's neighbor, divorced, raising her two little boys.

I had met her once on a previous visit to my father as she stood in her front yard, pruning her roses.

On this visit I ran into her at a friendly bar called Nighttown not far from my father's house. It was humid and sticky outside and we had a couple of cold beers together, then started chasing them with shots of tequila.

She asked me about Hollywood and I could tell she read the tabloids: What was Sylvester Stallone *really* like? Did everybody in Hollywood *really* do drugs? Was it true that so-and-so was gay? Was it true that I had made *millions* writing screenplays?

When Nighttown closed she asked me if I wanted to have "one for the road" at her house—a very short road because I was sleeping at my father's house that night.

We had another and another in her dark living room, then went back to the cold beer because her house wasn't air-conditioned. Her little boys were asleep.

After a while we went up to her bedroom and couldn't wait to get our clothes off because we were so sweaty.

A light went on in my father's house and as I made love to her I looked out the window and saw my father sitting there in the blistering heat of his own bedroom—bare-chested and sweating and staring off at nothing.

Afterward she told me that she saw my father sitting there and staring all the time.

We slept for a couple of hours and one of her little boys woke up and she told me I had to go. I kissed her goodbye, got dressed, went downstairs quietly, and used my key to open the door to my father's house.

I went upstairs and he was still sitting in the chair, slumped back. He was asleep. I kissed him on the top of his head and glanced out the window and saw her.

She had her little boy in her arms. She was rocking him back and forth. She saw me looking at her and turned her light off.

CHAPTER 5

[Flashback]

Commies in Klevland

KARCHY

Hey, Pop, how come you still call yourself *Dr.* Jonas?

KARCHY'S FATHER

I still doctor.

KARCHY

No you're not. That's old-country stuff. You don't work in a
hospital or anything.

KARCHY'S FATHER

I doctor law, got Ph.D. degree in Hungary. I *doctor.*

KARCHY

It doesn't mean anything over here. Nobody cares.

KARCHY'S FATHER

I care. It mean something . . . to me.

Telling Lies in America

Priests met us at the railroad station in Klevland and drove us through the
dark streets. It was late at night in the winter. Mounds of snow covered
the ground.

They stopped at a building next to a building with a large neon sign and led
us up a long stairway into an apartment with no furniture. Bare lightbulbs hung
from the ceiling. There was no heat.

We lay down on the floor in our coats. There was no food. My mother cried
and smoked a cigarette.

I clutched my cowboy guns.

The apartment was small. One bedroom, a living room, a kitchen, and a tiny office for my father.

The priests, who were Franciscans like Father Benedek and Father Ipoly but younger, brought us some furniture. I slept on a couch in the living room. There was a small concrete yard in the back between our apartment and the printing shop where the newspaper was set into type and printed. I played there and in a private alleyway that ran on the side of our apartment. Beneath us was the newspaper's circulation office, where more priests sat.

I ran around the concrete yard and the alley firing my guns at the priests.

Our address was 4160 Lorain Avenue, which was also the address of the newspaper my father was going to edit, the *Catholic Hungarians' Sunday.*

Since the paper's printing shop was behind our apartment, the smell of burning lead was pervasive. Also filling the air was the smell of burning potatoes: the Num Num Potato Chip factory, a tall red-brick building, was on the other side of our apartment.

We were at the epicenter of Cleveland's West Side Hungarian neighborhood. Right out our living room window to the left was Papp's Bar . . . across the street was the Korona Kavehaz, also known as the Crown Café . . . down the street were the Debrecen Restaurant, Sarosi Dry Cleaners, Gerzeny Movers, Sam Finesilver's Hardware Store, and the Louis A. Bodnar Funeral Home.

Lorain Avenue was a main artery furnishing Hungarian goods to people who worked at Republic or U.S. Steel and stayed close to other Hungarians in what they called their "strudel ghetto." There were 150,000 Hungarians in Cleveland living mostly in blue-collar neighborhoods whose boundaries were populated by Puerto Ricans, Appalachians, Irish, German, and black residents. To either side of Lorain Avenue were old streets with little houses intersected by an intricate, mazelike network of dark and garbage-strewn back alleys.

The focal point of the West Side Hungarian community was the church, St. Emeric's, behind the block-long West Side Market on West 25th Street, sixteen blocks from our new home.

I was enrolled at St. Emeric's, the Hungarian-American grade school. The teachers were Hungarian nuns in black clothes, the Daughters of the Divine Redeemer. The school was attached to the parish, whose pastor was Father John Mundweil. A gruff man in his forties, he scowled a lot. Even the sisters were afraid of him.

The school grounds were at the edge of a bluff overlooking the city's flats. From the field at the edge of the bluff, you could see a river—the Cuyahoga—flowing between the factories. The river smelled of sulfur and chemicals. The closer you got to it, the more it stung your eyes.

The river made me cry.

. . .

My mother walked me to school on my first day. I wore my cowboy outfit.

It was the last time I wore it. One of the other kids knocked my hat off at recess and stomped on it and when my mother arrived to walk me back from school, my fancy vest and pants were covered with mud.

Because the nuns and most of the kids in school . . . kids named Csaba and Tibor and Geza and Gyuszi and Arpi . . . were Hungarian, I couldn't get away with not saying or doing anything like I had in Washington.

I hated school.

The Daughters of the Divine Redeemer, who taught mostly in Hungarian, were scary. If you didn't know an answer . . . if you misbehaved . . . they slapped you . . . pulled your hair . . . hit your hands with a ruler . . . pulled your pants down and hit you with a paddle . . . said you were going to burn forever in hell . . . said they'd call the police to take you to jail . . . said they'd tell Immigration to take you back to the old country.

Sister Rose told us that America, like our school, was named after St. Emeric, Hungary's heroic Prince Emeric, St. Stephen's son. The Italian mapmaker Amerigo Vespucci was baptized after Hungary's St. Emeric. Not only did it mean that America was named after a Hungarian, it meant that had St. Emeric not lived, there would not be a place called America.

Only thanks to Hungary was there an America!

Shortly after we arrived, the circulation office of the newspaper downstairs was burgled.

All that was taken, I heard my father tell my mother, were files the Franciscans had kept about the things my father had achieved in Hungary.

My father said it was the Komchis . . . coming after him.

They were afraid of the Komchis in another way, too. They mentioned the names of Hungarian men . . . who'd been sent back to the Komchis . . . back to Hungary . . . by America.

I asked why America would send Hungarians back to the Komchis and was told that there were Komchis everywhere, even in America.

I was frightened, too. I was afraid that one morning I'd wake up to find that the Komchis had taken my father away. I stood at the living room window which faced our street—Lorain Avenue—with my cowboy guns in hand, looking for Komchis.

I didn't see any but one day I saw two Hungarians yelling at each other outside Papp's Bar, talking of course about the horse's cock that would enter their behinds. Then I saw one of the men take a knife out of his coat and push it into the other's stomach.

The man fell and blood gushed out of him the way it had gushed out of the pigs at the slaughterhouse. I stared until I heard the siren that was getting closer and closer.

When it got very close, I ran into the bathroom and covered my ears.

Rats were in the alley and the concrete yard but, probably because the Franciscans placed traps in the stairs, there were no rats in our apartment.

But the building next door to ours was the Num Num Potato Chip factory and the rats had overrun it. We could see the rats scurrying on the ledges leading to the factory windows.

An old Franciscan named Father Ákos collected the trapped rats in the yard and in the alley every morning. He took them to a shed behind the printing shop where he grilled and smoked them.

My father said Father Ákos came from a part of Hungary called Transylvania. And that this was a custom there.

My father had what he called a green card. It was very important, I heard, because if you didn't have one you couldn't be in America.

My mother took my father's pants to Sarosi Dry Cleaners across the street and left his wallet in the pants. The green card was inside the wallet. First my mother and then my father went to Sarosi, but Sarosi said there was no wallet in the pants.

My parents were desperate. I heard my father say that he was afraid to go back to the Immigration and tell them he'd lost his green card. My mother prayed to St. Anthony of Padua, the patron saint of lost objects.

A week later the mailman brought my father's wallet with the green card in it. Someone had taken the few dollars inside and put the wallet in a mailbox.

The Franciscans paid my father $100 a month plus the apartment. I didn't know how very little this was but I knew it was little because I heard my mother saying, "How will we be able to buy food and clothes for the boy?"

I went with my mother as she shopped. Two-day-old bread at Timar's Bakery, fruit and vegetables hardly spoiled at the West Side Market. We ate soup often and eggs, Spam, hot dogs, cans of sardines, and rice with hot milk and raisins.

We had an icebox that we couldn't keep in the kitchen because the kitchen was too small. So we kept it at the top of the stairway leading to the apartment. It was mostly empty.

Every day, as my mother walked me to school through the outdoor stands of the West Side Market, an Italian fruit vendor threw me a shiny red apple and said, "Heer ya go, Joee!"

On days when the West Side Market wasn't open, the outdoor stand area—which my mother and I had to walk through to get to St. Emeric's—was overtaken by bums. As my mother was walking me to school, we saw a bum by a dumpster, looking at us and laughing. His pants were open. He had his *pimpli* in his hand and was pulling it.

When my mother saw what he was doing, she picked me up and we ran away.

I woke up on my living room couch and heard my parents moving around quickly in the darkness. I grabbed my cowboy guns. My mother shushed me.

Someone was at the top of the stairway by the icebox. My father was standing by the door. We heard whispering voices out there. We heard the icebox door open and close. Then we heard footsteps going down the stairs and footsteps again at the private alley at the side of our apartment. We ran to the living room window and watched them as they came out of the alley.

A man and a woman, nicely dressed, carrying a brown bag. They walked to a car and drove away. The next morning we discovered that they had taken a package of hot dogs from the icebox.

"The Komchis," my father said.

"But why?" my mother asked.

"To let me know they're watching me."

My mother said, "Maybe it was just two people from the bar who were drunk and hungry."

My father said, "Mária, you saw them. They weren't drunk. They were nicely dressed. They had a car. Why would they take our *frankfurters*?"

The Komchis stole everything in Hungary, my mother said. They broke into the poorest and the richest homes. They stole anything and everything.

They told men to take their pants off but let them keep the jackets they didn't want. Or they took the jackets and let them keep the pants they didn't want. Or in some cases, they took both the jacket *and* the pants and even underwear or even socks or eyeglasses.

They had machines which beeped when they found gold or silver. They opened people's mouths, and if they had gold teeth, they pulled them out with pliers.

I was happy *I* didn't have any gold teeth!

Rákosi was one of the most evil Komchis, my mother told me. He had worked for Béla Kun, the Komchi who had hung people on the lampposts when my father was a boy.

I saw pictures of him. He was a big, fat, bald man. My father said he had been in a Hungarian prison for years, but had then been released and exchanged for some flags the Russkis had stolen from Hungary many years before.

This, my father said, had been a very big mistake. Now Hungary had a Communist flag.

Rakosi, my mother said, had a gang of evil men who helped him hang people, put them in jail, and torture them with rubber hoses, pliers, and burning cigarettes applied to their eyelids and armpits.

Their names were Ernö Gerö and Jozsef Révai and Zoltán Vas and Mihály Farkas. All of them, my mother said, were Zsidos.

My father told me when we were alone that this Mihály Farkas began his days by peeing into the mouths of prisoners.

I told my father that my mother said that the gang were all Zsidos like Rákosi and Béla Kun.

My father said, "Your mother is right. But the fact that they are Zsidos doesn't matter."

The rapes were the worst, my father said. Many of the Russki Komchis were sick in their *pimplis*. Their *pimplis* had big boils and were full of pus.

When they stuck it into the women, the boils and pus grew inside them. The women sometimes killed themselves so they wouldn't feel the boils and the pus in there.

Bishop Vilmos Apor was a great Hungarian hero. He hid women in the church cellar so they wouldn't get the boils and the pus. When the Komchis came to the church, Bishop Apor stood in front of the cellar door. The Komchis shot him. Then they opened the cellar door, opened their pants, and did their boiling and pusing.

I was happy *my pimpli* didn't have boils or pus.

The man I kept hearing about—from my parents, the Franciscans, my father's friends—was Cardinal Mindszenty, the Hungarian saint.

He was in a Komchi prison in Hungary now, being tortured. He had already been beaten with a rubber hammer between his legs and on the soles of his feet, kept awake for months, and forced to wear a clown costume every day.

I asked if his fingernails had been torn out with pliers and if Mihály Farkas had pee-peed into his mouth.

I asked if the Komchi women had forced him to put his *pimpli* into the boils and pus inside them.

My mother got angry at me and told me to stop asking such stupid questions.

I didn't think they were stupid.

· · ·

I was sick in bed a lot with endless tonsillitis and fevers and nosebleeds—the result, the Hungarian doctors said, of vitamin deficiencies and the rickets I'd had in the camps.

I was thin as a toothpick, freckled everywhere, with overgrown fly-away ears. My carrot-colored crew cut was especially bizarre. Our Slovak barber, for some reason, had shaved the widow's peak atop my forehead.

Bristly little wartlike hairs grew there!

I was learning English at St. Emeric's quickly. When I first played kovboys and Indians with my classmates at recess, I spoke mostly Hungarian, then after a while, smattering the Hungarian with English words.

When we spoke English—Steve Wegling and Paulie Szabo and David Markovics and Willi Krassoi and I—we spoke with Hungarian accents. When we played bazball and Yook-Yook, a game where we tried to hit each other with a rubber ball, we'd call each other's names in Hungarian, then switch to English.

Jozsi, gotcha!

My father asked me to accompany him sometimes on an errand. I knew hardly any English; I was picking some up.

We went inside a furniture store where he had seen a desk in the window.

The man inside said, "Thirty dollars."

My father said, "Five dollar!"

The man started yelling, "Fok you!" He called us bums and DPs and green-horns.

My father said, "Ten dollar!"

The man yelled, "Get the *fok* out of here!"

We left.

It was the first time I'd heard that word. I didn't know what it meant. When we were out on the street, I saw the tears welling in my father's eyes. I understood his humiliation.

I've been wanting to say this to that man at the Polster Furniture store on Lorain Avenue for fifty years. I know what it means now.

No, fok you! Fok you!

I saw an old Gypsy violinist who played next door at Papp's Bar on weekends walking slowly down the street, inspecting the gutter. He was drunk.

"*Sanyi Bácsi*," I said to him, "what are you doing?"

"What do you think I'm doing, boy? I'm looking for the gold."

"What gold?" I said.

"You must be a very dumb boy," he said. "Don't you know that in America the streets are paved with gold?"

He cackled and slapped me on the shoulder.

Then he picked a cigarette butt up from the gutter and lit it. He took a satisfying drag and smiled.

"You see, boy?" he said, laughing. "It's true. I have found the gold."

At the same time I was learning to read English at St. Emeric's my mother taught me to read Hungarian at home. We sat at the kitchen table and read about King Mátyás and St. Stephen's Holy Crown and St. Stephen's Preserved and Uncorrupted Holy Right Hand. Every time I made a mistake, my mother slapped me. They were casually administered and hard slaps that hurt. Sometimes during the course of a lesson, she'd hit me ten times.

I learned to read perfectly in Hungarian very quickly.

But for the rest of my life, as perfectly as I could read Hungarian, I didn't read it. I would read books in English about Hungary and Hungarians, but I would never read my . . . mother *tongue.*

St. Stephen, my mother taught me, was the founding father of Hungary. He united all the Hungarian tribes and taught his people to pray to God. That's why his right hand was still alive today, thousands of years after his death, paraded through the streets of Hungary before the Communists took it over.

St. Stephen was no one to trifle with. He cut an enemy's head off and then chopped his body up into little pieces and let the wind blow it away. St. Stephen's son was St. Emeric, who didn't become king because he was gored to death by a wild boar as big as a horse.

King Kálmán, my mother taught me, was the greatest Hungarian king after St. Stephen. He was known as Kálmán the Bookworm because he loved to read and encouraged all Hungarians to read.

When he was dying, King Kálmán the Bookworm was afraid that his brother, Álmos, would try to be king instead of King Kálmán's son, István. So King Kálmán the Bookworm summoned Álmos and Álmos's son, Béla, to his deathbed.

And King Kálmán the Bookworm had his soldiers stick fiery-red swords into their eyes. King Kálmán died peacefully, knowing his son would be king.

The Tartars, my mother taught me, invaded Hungary from Russia before there were Komchis in Russia.

They burned all the houses down, raped all the women, and cut all the men's heads off. Tartar children used Hungarian children as human targets when they wanted to practice with their bows and arrows.

The year before they invaded, Hungarians knew there would be bad news. Wolf packs came down from the mountains. The sun disappeared from the sky at noon. And on a summer night, a blazing star with a long tail crossed the sky.

Then came the Tartars.

· · ·

The Turks invaded Hungary, my mother taught me, and cut Hungarian heads off with curved swords. They took women and children to Turkey, where they sold them in the slave markets. Beautiful Hungarian girls could be bought for a pair of boots.

The Turks were helped by a Romanian named Vlad Drakul, who, my mother said, was the greatest monster in the history of the world. She didn't tell me why, but my father did.

Vlad Drakul made men sit on spikes that went through them. He boiled people alive and decorated his castle with their severed heads. He cut women's breasts off and hung them on his walls.

The Hapsburgs, my mother taught me, spoke German, invaded Hungary, and made it into the new country of Austria-Hungary. They didn't burn or rape or cut heads off, but they treated Hungarians like slaves and forced them to speak German. Until Lajos Kossuth, the Hero of Freedom, the Torch of Liberty, the Greatest Hungarian, organized a revolution against them.

Kossuth, my mother told me, was like my father. A writer. An editor. And when Kossuth lost his revolution, he had to leave Hungary. But he continued writing. He worked for Hungary's freedom in America. Like my father.

Kossuth's dream was freedom for Hungary. Like my father's dream.

But it didn't happen. Kossuth died in Italy. Old, half blind, and poor.

My mother worked in the printing shop at a linotype machine with the Franciscans and other Hungarian men and women. I watched her sometimes as she typed, her eyes squinted, the cigarette ever present in her mouth, while a few inches from her face a red-hot bar of lead melted into the machine.

She came back from the printing shop once crying. She closed the door to my father's office but I could hear her through a crack near the linoleum floor.

She was alone, she said, and she was locking up, and she heard a noise in the back. She went to see what it was and she saw one of the priests, Father Peter . . . naked, on top of one of the other women who worked there.

"What kind of priests are these?" my mother cried.

We shopped for our clothing at the Salvation Army on Bridge Avenue near West 25th Street. All three of us would go.

My father bought suits for a dollar. My mother was very excited to find a black velvet dress with a matching black hat. They bought me a winter overcoat, but it was so big I could have fit in it twice.

After I wore the coat a few times my mother said to my father, "What kind of man are you? How can you stand to watch your son wearing something like that?"

They started to argue.

I kept saying, "It's fine, Mama. It's a nice coat."

And when I was a rich American man, I found myself obsessively buying winter jackets and overcoats of the finest quality, Polo and Sulka and Giorgio Armani. In California, where it was never cold, where I couldn't even wear them.

At noon every Monday, the city had a civil defense air raid drill. America was in a cold war with the Communists. Atomic and hydrogen bombs could turn all of us into watermelon juice.

At noon every Monday, thousands of sirens all around the city began to wail. More sirens than I'd ever heard. I started to wail, too. I shook so badly I couldn't get into the closet to which I was assigned to hide from the atomic bombs. I screamed and shook until the sirens stopped.

The nuns at St. Emeric's tried to calm me, but couldn't. My father told me to stop acting like a hysterical girl.

My mother started coming to my school five minutes before noon every Monday. She held me as I screamed, and when the sirens stopped, she left.

There was a famous American man, my father excitedly told my mother and me, who understood about the Komchis.

He was a *zenator*. And a Catholic like us. Mekarti. Zenator Jozsef Mekarti from a place called Viskonzin. Mekarti was a hero. Not afraid to speak out. Not afraid of the Komchis. He knew there were Komchi spies everywhere.

My father wrote about Mekarti in his newspaper. All his friends talked about him too.

Mekarti! Mekarti! Mekarti!

As a young American man, I learned about Senator Joe McCarthy. The hero. Tail gunner Joe. The opportunist. The liar. Who had varying lists of innocent men he slandered as Communists. Who had no decency. Who was condemned by the Senate. Who died a drunk and a broken, humiliated man. Joe McCarthy, my father's hero.

My day began at 5:30, when I dressed quickly and walked the block to Timar's Bakery to pick up a fresh loaf of rye bread with caraway seeds.

Mrs. Timar, a second-generation Hungarian, had an agreement with the Hungarians in the neighborhood. If we bought the bread before six in the morning, we could have it for half price.

I raced home with the hot bread and my mother made the two of us strong black coffee. My father drank tea. She put a load of sugar into the cups and we dunked the bread into the sugary coffee.

I heard the word *Nyilas* often as my father spoke to his friends.

What is a *Nyilas*? I asked him.

They were Hungarian Nazis, he said, the Arrow Cross. Their symbol was an arrow and a cross. They were crazy like Hitler. They wanted to kill the Zsidos.

There were many of them in Hungary, he said, and many of them had come to America. He didn't like the Nyilas, my father said, and they didn't like him either. He said he was proud that when millions in Hungary were joining the Arrow Cross Party, he had never joined.

"Tell me about Hitler," I said to my father.

My father told me this: Hitler ate chocolate bars for breakfast and vegetables the rest of the day. Hitler hated cigarettes and loved his dog, who was named Blondie. Hitler farted so much that they had to open all of the windows after he had a long meeting. His *pimpli* was so small, it barely stuck out between his legs.

Hitler vacationed all the time when he was a boy at Spital, the location of our last refugee camp. When we were walking around outside the camp avoiding TB, we were probably walking in Hitler's footsteps!

There was a Hungarian printer and linotype operator named Oszkár Moldován, younger than the priests in the printing shop.

He always had a radio on near his machine with the sound of a man talking and sometimes yelling in English. The word that I heard yelled from his radio, as I ran about the print shop in my kovboy hat and with my guns was, "*Horun! Horun!*"

"Bazball?" I asked Oszkár in Hungarian. "Do you like bazball?"

Oszkár smiled. "Do you, Jozsi?"

I told him yes, I loved bazball.

He asked me if I liked the Indians.

"No," I said. "I am a kovboy—I shoot Indians."

"The Klevland Indians." Oszkár smiled.

"There are Indians in Klevland?" I asked.

"Al Rosen," he said. "Bobby Avila. Bob Feller. Larry Doby. Dale Mitchell. Don Mossi."

I saw Father John Mundweil on the way to school. He was with the bums in the alley by the market. He was wearing a white T-shirt over a pair of black pants. He was yelling at the bums.

"You leave these kids alone!" he yelled. He had a slight Hungarian accent. "If you bother these kids, I'm going to come back here with the police! You hear me?" His face was red. The bums nodded and mumbled.

"Get out of here!" Father John yelled. "Now! Get the hell out!" The bums started walking away from the market.

Father John stood there, and then he lit up a cigarette. He saw me watching him.

"Do you want to be late for school?" he growled in Hungarian.

"No, Father."

"Then go!" he said.

I ran.

"Who knows who invented the telephone?" Sister Rose asked.

"Tivadar Puskás," I said.

Everyone in class laughed.

"Thomas Edison," Carol Ann Hill said.

"Alexander Graham Bell," Joey Kish said.

"No," I insisted. "Tivadar Puskás! My father told me."

Everyone in class laughed again.

When I got home, I told my father what had happened.

"You are right," he said. "Tivadar Puskás invented the telephone. We will prove it."

We went down to the Carnegie West Library at Lorain Avenue and Fulton Road. The book said Tivadar Puskás had been Thomas Edison's assistant.

"But it doesn't say he invented the telephone," I said.

"If he was his assistant," my father said, "they worked on it together. If they worked on it together, he invented it, too."

He looked at the book again.

"Puskás," he read, "also invented the *telefon hirmondo*," the speaking newspaper—which sent news to subscribers.

"You see?" my father said. "The telephone—that is nothing. Tivadar Puskás also invented the speaking newspaper. *That* is something!"

Edward Teller, a Hungarian, my father said, had invented both the atomic and the hydrogen bombs. All Hungarians, he said, were proud of Edward Teller.

Before I told anyone in class, I went down to the library and read about Edward Teller in an American book. It said Edward Teller had worked with a man named Einstein and had persuaded Einstein to make the atomic bomb.

But then it said Edward Teller *was* "the father of the hydrogen bomb" which could kill "ten million people with one flash."

I wasn't sure whether I was proud of Edward Teller or not. Ten million people!

One flash!

I learned about Klevland in school. It was founded by a man named Moses Cleaveland, an investor in the Connecticut Land Company. The company had bought the area called the Western Reserve west of Pennsylvania. Moses led an expedition to survey the land. The principal settlement, it had already been determined, would be where a big lake (Erie) met a little river (the Cuyahoga).

Moses arrived at the site and found an old and crooked river, its banks marshy and boggy. Silt stuffed its mouth. Sandbars made passage nearly impossible. The flatland around the river was nightmarish. Side pools smelled like rotten eggs. Foot-long snakes slithered on the shore. Clouds of ravenous mosquitoes obscured the sun.

Moses Cleaveland finished his survey in one day, named the place after himself, and went back to Connecticut. He never returned.

George Washington, Sister Margaret told us, was not only the father of America, but he was also the man who looked at a map and told Moses Cleaveland to build a city there.

So George Washington was not only the father of America, but the father of Klevland, too.

My father gave me a lesson about America.

"Everybody says '*Hov arr yu?*' " he said. "But they don't mean it. If you tell them how you are, if you say—'So-so, I have a headache, I think I'm getting a cold, I'm worried about money, my wife and I had an argument,' they look at you like you're crazy.

"What they want to hear is *fein. Hov arr yu? Fein.*

"If you are dying, if you have nothing to eat, if your best friend has betrayed you, if you are about to kill yourself, and if they say *Hov arr yu? Fein fein fein.*"

On those summer nights when the windows were open and the drunks left Papp's Bar, I received Hungarian lessons, enriching my vocabulary with words my parents never used:

AZ ANYÁD PICSÁJÁT—Your mother's pussy!
LE VAGY SZARVA—You are shit upon!
SZARHÁZI KURVA—You're a whore from a house of shit!
SZAROK RÁD—I shit on you!
BASZD MEG—Fuck you!
BASZD MEG AZ ANYÁD PICSÁJÁT—Motherfucker!

One of the men who came to my father's office was Dénes Kacso, a Hungarian poet. He was a short, overweight, but fierce-looking man with blazing black eyes. He cleaned toilets at an old-age home.

"I clean *their* shit," he said, "and I write *my* shit."

He lived in a shack on a little street not far from us. The shack had no electricity or heating. Dénes filled the shack's fireplace with limbs he sawed off the trees on neighborhood streets. He had bought a saw at the Sam Finesilver hardware store and he lurked around in the predawn dark collecting his firewood.

He ate mostly dog food. He came to my father's office with his pockets full of different cans and explained that America was such a rich land that even dogs ate the finest meals.

I was on the linoleum floor in the kitchen, watching the ants, and I listened to my father yelling at two of the Franciscans. He was yelling about a priest named Father Galambos, who wrote a column for the newspaper. My father was saying he was the editor and he wouldn't run a column this priest had written because it was "*Zsido ellenes*"—against the Jews.

"Stop it! Stop this madness!" my father yelled at the priests. "You can't say these things here! Didn't you learn any lesson?"

When the Franciscans left, he turned to me and said, "Remember this, Jozsi. Jews are people like any other people, some good, some not so good. Just like Hungarians. Some good, some not so good. Never judge a man by his nationality or his color or his religion. Judge him by his character. Whether he is a good man or a not so good man."

My mother said, "Politics. Always politics. Always yesterday."

"No!" my father said angrily. "Not yesterday! Today! This is about America." He pointed to me. "This is about his life. This is about him!"

And as an American man studying the Holocaust, I discovered that many of the Nazi butchers who got away—Mengele, Eichmann, Bormann—got away thanks to an underground which shuttled them from one monastery to another and then smuggled them onto boats which took them to South America.

It was an underground operated by Franciscan priests and monks.

I overheard my mother reading to my father from a book containing the now-being-tortured Cardinal Mindszenty's words:

"Dearly beloved faithful, my brethren. We Hungarians are frequently reminded of the sins of the past. Sometimes it seemed that other peoples considered us Hungarians the dregs of European society, the scum of the earth, and a cursed race living among a choir of angels. Other nations have openly reviled us. In fact, there is no end to the sins others lay at our door. The whole world has acquired a distorted view of Hungary's role in the war. My conscience will not allow me to believe that Hungary is truly responsible for all the crimes she is accused of."

I got up off the linoleum floor and walked into my father's office and asked, "What are we accused of? What's a 'crime'?"

"Nothing," my mother said. She seemed angry that I had overheard them.

"You are too young, Jozsi," my father said. "When you are old enough, I will tell you."

"Is it true?" I asked.

"Is what true?" my mother said.

"What we are accused of."

"No, Jozsi," my father said. "Go play. It is not true."

Oszkár Moldován took me out into the alley behind the printing shop and handed me a stick he had found on the floor. He threw me a red rubber ball.

And when I hit the red rubber ball over the cyclone fence of the Num Num Potato Chip factory, the American drivers standing around their trucks threw it back and cheered.

One of them yelled, "Attaboy, kid! Horun! Horun!"

Dénes Kacso, the Hungarian poet, smelled of wine every time he came to my father's office. Every time he came, he brought my mother and me a piece of strudel from Timar's Bakery.

As I was playing ball by myself in the concrete yard, I heard shouts from the circulation office. Then the door from the office burst open and one priest after another ran out and fled into the printing shop. Father Gottfried was last and behind him, screaming and swearing, was Dénes Kacso, who had a pocketknife held high in his hand.

Father Gottfried got away—Dénes said he had insulted one of his poems.

Sometimes I went out into the alley alone when Oszkár was working or when he had his days off. And I hit the red ball against the brick wall of the Pep Up soda bottling company, which faced the cyclone fence of the Num Num Potato Chip factory.

And sometimes one of the drivers from Num Num or one of the American men working at Pep Up would come into the alley and throw me the red ball so the others could yell "Horun! Horun!" and "Attaboy, Joee!"

We got the *Plain Dealer,* the morning newspaper, early each morning and I read it after my father was finished with it. I used the Hungarian-English dictionary to translate it for myself.

I read about the Cleveland Indians and the player named Al Rosen. I read about a man named Lou Teller, who was of Hungarian descent and robbed banks with his girlfriend, Tina Mae Ritenour, who had big breasts. I read about a man named Papa Joe Cremati who ran what I translated in the dictionary as *kurva* houses.

I was very excited about all these things and hoped Lou Teller would rob the Cleveland Trust Bank two blocks down at the corner of Lorain and Fulton.

I kept an eye on passing cars in case Al Rosen drove by.

I wondered if Papa Joe Cremati knew the *kurvas* at Papp's Bar.

. . .

When we got our report cards, Father John handed them out to us in class. He looked at each card carefully and made comments in front of the rest of the class. When he looked at my report card he said, "Do you want to be a dummy?"

I said, "No, Father."

"Are you stupid?"

I said, "No, Father."

"Then why does this report card say you're stupid?"

"I don't know, Father."

"Is this report card lying to me?"

"No, Father."

"Then you *are* stupid."

"No, Father."

"We'll see."

He almost threw it at me.

The radio said a tornado was coming. My parents didn't know what a tornado was. There were no tornadoes in Hungary or the camps.

The sky blackened. Hail the size of golf balls fell. We heard the sound of a roaring locomotive, although there were no train tracks near us. The apartment started to shake. A window in my father's office exploded.

We ran to the living room and held each other. The electricity was gone. Police and ambulance sirens sounded all night. My mother held on to me as I shook and cried.

The next morning, my mother walked me to school and my father came with us. As we walked down Bridge Avenue, we saw houses collapsed and trees down everywhere. My father stopped and looked at the devastation.

"It's nothing compared to a bombing," he said.

Dénes Kacso told me about witches while he was whittling a piece of wood with his pocketknife in the concrete yard.

Witches, he said, were beautiful women who hovered in the air from midnight to dawn singing beautiful songs. Witches could saddle young men and ride them like airplanes. No grass ever grew where witches met. A circle of mushrooms grew to show where they had been. Witches drank from the hoofs of horses and oxen and feasted on human flesh. The surest way to keep them away from you was to keep a horse's skull nearby.

"Where can I see some witches?" I asked Dénes Kacso.

"You will see them when you're older," he said. "Every man sees his share. Before he dies."

. . .

Father Gottfried went out of his way to be mean to me when he saw me in the concrete yard playing ball. He would roughly push me, once even knocking me down. At another time, he picked the ball up as it bounced from the wall and threw it on the roof. I told my father and he told me to stay out of the priest's way. But I had a better idea.

I stood on the iron grille patio above the concrete yard and waited for Father Gottfried to come from the circulation office toward the printing shop. I had pieces of lead I had picked up near the linotype machines in my hand.

When I saw him, I fired. I hit him in the side of the head. He was bleeding and screaming.

He came running up the stairs and charged through our door. He and my father yelled at each other. Then my father yelled at me. Then my mother slapped me. But Father Gottfried never bothered me again.

My father insisted that my mother and I go to his speeches, which were three hours long. He spoke with broad gestures, his face red, his voice falling and rising dramatically.

He spoke over and over again about the danger to the world posed by Communism. He referred always to Stalin and Lenin and Marx and to Mátyás Rákosi in Hungary. And he spoke of the Treaty of Trianon and how it had unfairly taken Hungarians away from Hungary.

At the end of the speech, he was drenched in sweat.

The hundreds of Hungarians who were there applauded him loudly. That's when I usually woke up, asleep in my mother's arms.

When I was a grown American man and considering the image of my father speaking to one of his many audiences, I thought his oratorical style similar to: Fidel Castro, Everett Dirksen, John L. Lewis, George Wallace, Jimmy Swaggart, the Reverend Ike, and . . . Adolf Hitler.

The other speaker at many of these events was a Franciscan named Father Dobay. He was a fat and effeminate man who sometimes wore rouge. He had a haircut unlike any I had seen—combed straight down his forehead almost to his eyebrows. He was extremely shy and nervous.

So that when he spoke at these Hungarian events, he spoke this way: He read his speech into a tape recorder in the basement of our apartment house. Then the tape recorder was driven to the place of the gathering. It was placed center stage. The spools started spinning and we heard Father Dobay's voice coming from the tape recorder. Sometimes we stared at the tape recorder on the stage for two hours, listening.

Father Dobay stood backstage, listening, too.

. . .

I became an altar boy. My mother was very proud of me. All of us altar boys were petrified of Father John.

He caught Steve Wegling and me tasting the wine in the sacristy before Mass. He slapped us so hard our faces burned for hours.

At the altar early one morning, as I was pouring the water and wine over his hands at the offertory, I spilled the wine all over him. Father John looked at himself, looked at me, slapped me . . . right there at the altar in front of the congregation . . . and continued saying the Mass.

Besides witches, Dénes Kacso, who sat in the courtyard whittling with his pocketknife, told me stories of princes and horses, of trees that reached up to the sky, of magic ships and frogs with diamonds in their eyes.

He also told me how God created women. God took a rib out of Adam but a dog came along and grabbed the bone out of his hands. God chased the dog and grabbed the dog's tail. The tail stuck in God's hand but the dog got away with the rib.

Tired from the chase, God just turned the dog's tail into Eve. That explained, Dénes Kacso said, why women acted the way they did.

On my eighth birthday, my father announced that he was taking my mother and me for a special dinner at Nick's Diner, just down the street from us on the corner of Lorain Avenue and 41st Street. It was the first time I'd ever been in a restaurant. I'd passed Nick's each day on the way to school with my mother. I'd stared at the big steamed window with the grilling hot dogs behind it.

My father wore his Salvation Army trench coat and beret. My mother wore her black Salvation Army velvet dress. We sat in a booth and everyone stared. Everyone else was wearing rolled-up T-shirts, tight black pants, and ducktail haircuts.

A waitress came over, smiling, and asked what we wanted. In his broken English, my father said "Tree franfoorter." But it sounded like "Ree Foorter."

The waitress said, "What was that, hon?"

He repeated it, louder this time, but she stood there smiling blankly. He repeated it again, still louder, his face red, but she still didn't get it. The place was pindrop silent, all eyes on us.

Finally, in a near roar, he said, "Hoat dog! Hoat dog!"

And the waitress smiled brightly and said, "Okay."

My days ended sitting on the living room couch waiting for my father's friends to leave so I could go to sleep there.

His friends were people like Gyula Kovács, a former Hungarian army general who worked on a factory assembly line . . . Jenö Szebedinszky, a Hungarian journalist who came to visit him from Pittsburgh . . . Lászlo Ágh, a quiet, good-looking man, the president of the MHBK, the Hungarian Soldiers Friendship Association . . . Imre Ács, a poet who went up and down Lorain Avenue reciting his verses in a loud, staccato tone accompanied by arm movements suited to a symphony conductor.

My favorite among his friends was the pipe-smoking Gyula Bedy, a novelist, short story writer, and poet, the only one ever to say: "Let's get out of here so this boy can sleep."

When I was eight years old, I was allowed to walk to school and back by myself. I took a different way home one day and saw a group of American kids playing bazball. I watched for hours, studying the way the game was played.

At home, I started listening to Jimmy Dudley describing the Cleveland Indians games on the radio. Jimmy Dudley said, "And that ball is going, going, and gone for a home run!"

When Oszkár Moldován or the American men at Num Num or Pep Up couldn't play with me, I practiced bazball in the concrete yard behind our apartment.

I stood facing the towering furnace wall of the potato chip factory. I threw the red rubber ball with my right hand. It bounced back at me off the wall and I swung at it with my stick left-handed. I dropped the stick and chased the ball as it came off the wall again.

And all the time, quietly, I'd narrate the play just like Jimmy Dudley narrated it on the radio: "The pitch from Vitey Ford! Rosen svings! A hi fly ball to zenter! Mantle go back! He gots!"

I learned new English words each day, sometimes even on my way to school.

Older boys as old as eighteen hung around Nick's Diner. They wore black leather jackets and smoked cigarettes. Some of them owned old cars whose motors were loud and sounded like something was broken inside them.

As I tried to walk by them, sometimes they would grab me and push me from one of them to the other. As they did, they taught me new English words.

"Come here, you wimpy little fuck!"

"Hey, fuck you, asshole, speak English!"

"What did you say, motherfucker?"

"Come on, pussy! Hit me, hit me!"

"Well son of a fucking bitch!"

"Shit, look at that! The little pussy's crying!"

On Friday nights, when my father was away making a speech, my mother and I would stay awake past midnight. We had so much fun.

We couldn't eat meat on Friday, the Catholic Church said, so my mother and I waited until midnight and she sliced the Hungarian bacon she'd gotten that day at the West Side Market. She made tiny strips she called soldiers and put them on bread.

She talked to me about her mother and how much she'd loved her and about Hungary and how beautiful it was. Sometimes, when we were finished with our soldiers, she cried.

But even when I saw her crying, I was happy.

I heard my father tell his friends once that he was trying to obtain copies of all the books he had published in Hungary.

"Just so I can convince myself," he said with a smile, "that I really did write them, that they still exist, that the war didn't blow them away."

He said he'd written some letters to American libraries and that the one book he thought he'd have trouble finding was *Nemzet Politika*—National Policy—that he'd written when he was twenty-seven years old.

My father bought a broken violin at the Salvation Army for $3. He glued it back together.

He played it often, standing in his office, looking out the window, playing mournful Hungarian folk tunes and bright upbeat *csárdáses*, his expression the same while playing both: his eyes lost somewhere out the window, staring at the sky.

I listened to the sound of his violin sometimes as I played bazball with myself against the Num Num Potato Chip factory wall.

At noon on Good Friday, my mother knelt on the kitchen floor with two other Hungarian ladies, saying the Rosary.

A Trappist monk had predicted that the world would end this Good Friday at three o'clock in the afternoon and my mother and her friends were preparing themselves.

My mother urged me to kneel down and pray but, instead, I went into my father's office. He was beating away at his typewriter.

"Papa," I said, "they say the world will end."

"Maybe it will," he said.

I said, "Really?"

"Sure," he said, "sometime."

"But not today?"

"No," he said, "not today."

At 2:30 in the afternoon the sky turned black, chunks of ice fell from the heavens, and zigzag lightning flashed through the air.

My mother and her lady friends were working themselves into a frenzy on the kitchen floor.

I could still hear my father's typewriter beating away.

I went back to his office to see him.

"Are you sure?" I said.

"About what?"

"Are you sure it's not going to end?"

"What?"

"The world."

"I'm pretty sure"—he smiled—"but I could be wrong. I've certainly been wrong in my life before. Many times, actually, to tell you the truth."

"Should I pray?" I asked.

"Prayer never hurts," he said.

I knelt down with my mother and her friends and prayed while he kept beating away at his typewriter.

At ten minutes after three, the sky cleared and my mother said to me, "God has answered our prayers once again!" She was very happy.

I was, too.

My father came into the living room and saw us hugging each other joyously.

"Still here, eh?" He smiled.

My father was trying to learn English by reading American novels. They were paperbacks with brightly colored paintings of half-naked women on them.

His favorite American writer was Mickey Spillane. My father said Mickey Spillane was so wealthy from his writing that he had a typewriter that was solid gold.

When he saw me take a great interest in the covers of Mickey Spillane's books, he started tearing the covers off and ripping them into little pieces. My mother caught me trying to reassemble a Mickey Spillane cover on the living room floor.

"What are you doing?" she asked.

"I'm trying to learn English like Papa," I said.

She took the ripped-up pieces of paper away from me.

"I see," she said.

Josef Stalin was dead. The radio said he had killed twenty million people and put another twelve million in prison.

My father knew he was dead last night, before the radio told us. He knew because on our shortwave, Moscow radio was playing music all the time and not saying anything. The Russians do that when a leader dies, my father said, they stop talking and play music.

I heard new Russian names on the radio now: Malenkov, Bulganin, Mikoyan, Molotov, Khrushchev.

My father said, "This is the happiest day of my life!" But he didn't look happy.

My father took me to the soccer games on Sunday, across town on the East Side at Latin Field. We rooted for the Hungarian team, the St. Stephen's Dramatic Club team.

The championship showdown was between the Hungarians and a German team.

The referee, a small pudgy bald man named Lieberman, called a foul on the Hungarian team in the final moments with the score tied. The Germans got a free kick and won the game.

The Hungarians chased Lieberman down the field into his car. They were screaming things at him. One of the things I heard them—but not my father—yell was "*Büdos Zsido!*"—Stinking Jew!

I scrounged garbage cans, fields, and back alleys collecting pop and beer bottles to return to grocery stores for the pennies with which I bought bazball cards.

I collected the Indians—Al Rosen especially. I had six Al Rosens, but I also had six of Hank Sauer of the Cubs and Elmer Valo of the Philadelphia Athletics—because Sauer was Hungarian and Valo was Slovak.

I was laying my cards out in the concrete yard when Father Peter picked one of them up.

"Rosen," Father Peter said, "*ez Zsido.*"

On a weekend night when my father was gone making a speech and my mother and I were alone, two Hungarian drunks from Papp's Bar came up the stairway and beat on our door.

They said, "Open the door, pretty Mari, we know you're alone."

They said, "We'll make you feel good, pretty Mari, the boy can watch."

They said, "Don't you want to teach your boy?"

They said, "Our horse's cock will enter your behind."

They said, "Open the door, pretty Mari, you know how much you want to!"

They said, "Open wide! Open wide!"

Then they laughed and left.

My mother had said not a word, holding me tight to her, her arm around me, a rosary in her other hand.

Somebody passed me a note in class.

It said, "Why can Jesus walk on water?"

On the other side, it said: "Shit floats."

Sister Rose saw me laughing and came over to my desk. She put her hand out for the note. I thought about eating it. But I gave it to her. She hit me so hard I almost fell out of my chair.

She called Father John and showed him the note. He slapped me so hard my mouth bled.

Father John called my parents down to school. He showed them the note. My mother slapped me so hard my face swelled up.

"It's a very old and bad joke," my father told me that night. "I heard it when I was a boy."

"Did you laugh?"

"Of course I laughed." He smiled. "I was young and stupid like you."

My father told me a story to inspire me:

"When I was eighteen, I was picked as one of ten Hungarian students to be a guest of Lord Razmeer in London. Lord Razmeer owned the *London Daily Mail*, one of the greatest newspapers in the world. I met the lord and Ward Price, the editor of the paper. At the end of our visit, they gave us all gold watches."

"What happened to the gold watch?" I asked. "Do we have it? Can I see it?"

"We traded it in the camp for a Polish ham," my father said.

I hated Christmas each year. My parents told me there was no Mikulás or Kis Jézus—Santa Claus or Baby Jesus—that the gifts came from the money we didn't have.

On Christmas Eve, the three of us took the bus to the May Company near the Terminal Tower in downtown Cleveland. We went to the bargain basement, where, after two in the afternoon, prices were the lowest of the year. We picked out one piece of clothing as our Christmas present for each of us.

We hurried to get the bus back to Lorain Avenue so we could stop at Gerzeny Brothers Movers before six o'clock. That's where we bought our Christmas tree and they closed at six sharp. Between five and six on Christmas Eve we could buy a tree for one dollar.

We carried the tree the two blocks home and decorated it with strips of paper my mother had scissored from the *Cleveland Plain Dealer*.

When I was a young American man and a reporter for the Cleveland Plain Dealer, *I wondered if anyone else on the staff had ever decorated their Christmas tree with the newspaper they now worked for.*

CHAPTER 6

Michael Eisner Pimps the Teamsters

> TONY
> Come on, give me a break here, willya? Even a prick deserves a
> break sometime, am I right?
>
> DAWN
> Never.
>
> *Showgirls*

In 1981, Don Simpson, the head of production at Paramount, had a script called *Flashdance* written by a former journalist named Tom Hedley. Simpson thought the script needed a rewrite and sent it to me.

I'd been screenwriting for six years now, though I'd still only had one movie made. But I'd been in innumerable meetings and shucks and shine-ons . . . and I'd heard and told too many worn-out lies to and from too many producers, directors, and studio heads. By no means a Hollywood animal, I was no longer the fresh-from-the-underground, *Rolling Stoned* Hollywood naïf, either. Head honchos like Simpson didn't scare me anymore.

I read the script and thought it needed not a rewrite, but a total re-creation from page one. It was about a group of kids at the Fashion Institute of Technology who band together against a Hells Angels–type cycle gang which is threatening their neighborhood. At the center of the piece was a young woman designer who falls in love with a married man in his sixties. What I liked about the piece, I told Simpson, was the title and the kind of arty fashion-oriented stripping that some of the girls did on the side.

"What would you do for the story if you redid it?" Simpson asked.

"I didn't say I was interested in redoing it," I said.

"I know that," Simpson growled, "but what would you do?"

"If you make me an offer I can't refuse, then I'll tell you."

"Fuck you," Simpson said, "you want me to make a deal with you to rewrite it before I know what you want to do?"

"I don't want to do anything until you make me an offer I can't refuse."

He hung up amidst a torrent of obscenities and called my agent. He wanted to pay me $125,000 for a rewrite and my agent told him he'd have to pay me my full fee for an original screenplay ($275,000 at the time), considering the work I'd want to do.

"You tell your client," Simpson said, "that he is a greedy pig! I will *never— never—never* pay that kind of money for a rewrite."

Simpson and I had a special bond between us. I enjoyed teasing him. He still talked about the time I sat down in his chair and put my feet up on his desk. And then, too, there was a more recent and painful (to Simpson) incident which took place at the bar of the Sherry-Netherland Hotel in New York.

Simpson and I were knocking down Tanqueray shooters late one afternoon when we were joined by Hillary, a beautiful young woman who was an editor at the *Village Voice*. Simpson prided himself on being a stud—"I know more about pussy than anybody in Hollywood with the possible exception of Robert Evans"—but two hours later she left with me, not with Don.

He had called me the next morning, sputtering.

"You motherfucker!" he ranted. "I don't get it. I'm the head of a studio, you're just a writer. No, you're a *screenwriter!* You're *nothing!* and she leaves with you? The bitch! The fucking bitch!"

Three weeks after he told my agent I was a greedy pig, he called him back and made the deal with me. "Tell that pig I want him down here!" Simpson said.

He told me about the background of the piece and introduced me to the others involved. Peter Guber and Jon Peters had originally been involved; Lynda Obst had developed the screenplay with Hedley. Hedley had based the script on a particular kind of stripping/dancing that was being done in some of the clubs in Toronto.

They were all gone from the project now. Adrian Lyne, a hip Englishman who had directed a beautiful little movie called *Foxes,* was now involved to direct. Dawn Steel, a vice president of production at Paramount, was the executive in charge of the project. He filled me in on Dawn. She had begun her career as an assistant to Bob Guccione at *Penthouse.* She had then, on her own, started manufacturing Gucci toilet paper and made a lot of money until Gucci stopped her.

Now that we had a deal, Simpson said, now that he had made me an offer I couldn't refuse, maybe I'd condescend to tell him what I had in mind for the story.

Not yet, I said.

"Excu-u-u-u-use me?" Simpson said in a voice I was sure you could hear over the lot.

Well, I said, if Hedley based his script on something that was actually being done in Toronto—then why didn't we begin by going up to Toronto and speaking to some of the young women who were "flashdancing."

"Jesus, *Toronto?*" Don said. "You want to go to Toronto? We're not talking about Miami Beach here or Vegas. Toronto is the boonies."

I didn't just want to go to Toronto, I explained. I wanted him to come with me, along with Adrian Lyne . . . and Dawn if she wanted to come.

"I am not going to *Toronto!*" Simpson said.

But a week later we were there—Don and I and Adrian and a young producer who would also be involved in the project, Jerry Bruckheimer, lean and sharp-eyed, who had produced a funny movie called *Young Doctors in Love.*

Toronto, we discovered, was sex-crazed. Not only were there dozens of clubs where "exotic dances" and "exotic acts" were performed, but the weekends were sexual extravaganzas.

A promoter would rent out a hall—I mean a hall with seating for ten thousand or so people, a hall where rock acts would usually perform, and into that hall the promoter would book a Penthouse Pet or a Playboy Centerfold. The Pets and Centerfolds would take most of their clothes off in front of this hooting, foaming-at-the-mouth, slobbering mob and receive $50,000 for the weekend. Sometimes there would be three of these arena-strips going at the same time and the papers would have ads for "The Battle of the Busts."

We focused on the more intimate clubs where "flashdancing" was being performed. We discovered that several of these young women began wanting to be classical dancers. Some had even had formal training. Most regretted that they hadn't followed that path for one reason or another—usually having to do with boyfriends and unexpected children and putting food on the table. One young woman cried as she spoke softly about not "following her dream." Another told me of her very talented younger sister who could have been an Olympic skater had she only pursued it. What was her sister doing now? I asked. She was stripping, too, I was told, in a very grungy after-hours club where "she took it all off."

After one of the flashdancers got off the stage, I ran my hands through her hair, sopping with sweat, and an aura of perspiration exploded into the bright lights and Adrian said, "I have to get that effect on-screen."

On the way back to L.A., Don and I talked about it. What if our lead, I suggested to him, was a girl who had a dream to be a dancer? What if she was uneducated, blue-collar, and got sidetracked into stripping just to survive? What if the piece really was about "following your dream"?

What if we put the entire piece within a blue-collar context—if her love interest was also a blue-collar guy, who finally had to understand that it was more important for her to follow her dream than to marry him?

What if he loved her so deeply that he was willing, finally, not only to accept that most painful of all acceptances, but to help her realize the dream?

Simpson thought it was a good beginning but wondered what it was she actually did—blue-collar sounded intriguing, but what did she do?

"She welds," I blurted, "she's a welder." All the research I had done with welders on *Rowdy*, the Alaska pipeline piece, suddenly came back to me.

Adrian, a visual wizard, loved it instantly.

"She has a torch in her hand," he said, "she has a mask. The torch flares. She flips her mask up."

I started working on the script and was summoned to L.A. days later. There was an . . . unexpected . . . problem. Don was out as head of production at Paramount. The project, I was told, was "up in the air." He was now negotiating an independent production deal with the studio. If the deal worked out, he and his friend Jerry Bruckheimer would produce *Flashdance*. If the deal didn't work out . . . nobody knew what was going to happen to the project.

Adrian, Jerry, and I talked about the script for a couple days with Simpson absenting himself from the meetings . . . sort of. He would occasionally chime in on the speakerphone from home, but he was wired and edgy.

The negotiations, I was led to believe, were not going well. Don said that Michael Eisner, in charge of the studio, was "a motherfucker." Jeff Katzenberg, who had replaced him, was "a little bitch."

Don sounded like he was out of control and I knew that the "sinus infection" that was turning his voice very nasal had more to do with soothing his very obvious anxieties than it did with bacteria.

I went home to Marin County to continue working on the script and Don concluded an independent production deal with the studio. I thought he'd settle down then but he seemed to be more cranked up than ever before.

He'd call me at midnight or two o'clock in the morning with script ideas. He was full of words like "catharsis" and "epiphany" and "second act overdrive" and "redemptive arc."

He sounded like he had been to some literary critic's rummage sale.

"For Christ's sake," I finally said to him one night. "It's four o'clock in the morning. Put the goddamn powder away and stop bothering me. I've got a script to write."

I could *hear* him snorting another line over the phone.

"This is important," he yelled into the phone. "I've got everything riding on this. This is the only movie I've got now! I don't have a slate of them anymore. I've got this one. *I've got you!* I have to have a hit movie!"

· · ·

The day after I sent him the finished script, he sounded ecstatic.

"It's sensational!" he said. "It's just what I wanted. We're going to have a big hit movie! Thank you! *Thank you!*"

He sent me a case of Dom Pérignon.

The day after I got the champagne, he sent me a forty-three-page single-spaced memo. The memo literally took the script that he had thought "sensational" apart.

I felt like beating him to death with a bottle of Dom Pérignon.

What particularly galled me was the tone of the memo. It was supercilious and patronizing and command-like. "*We*" feel this and "*we*" think this should be changed.

I wrote him a twenty-four-page memo back that took apart his forty-three-page memo. I began by asking who the "*we*" was.

"You may not have noticed it," I wrote, jabbing him about the fact that he no longer spoke for the studio, "but the emperor has new clothes."

I also demanded a face-to-face meeting with him and Dawn and Adrian and Jerry Bruckheimer.

When we met in Dawn's office, I immediately demanded a stenographer.

Simpson couldn't believe it! "You want a *what?*" Simpson said.

"I want a stenographer. Call for one. You can get one from the studio pool."

"What the fuck do you want a stenographer for?" he asked.

"I want every word to be on the record. I want posterity to know what asshole, stupid, benighted, moronic suggestions you're making."

It looked like smoke was coming out of his ears.

"Call a fucking stenographer," he growled at Dawn.

We sat there in that room—Dawn and Jerry and Adrian and I—waiting for a stenographer, not looking at each other. Don went back and forth to the bathroom; each time he came back, his sinus condition was worse.

Fifteen minutes later, the stenographer arrived. The stenographer was a transvestite.

Don stared in dazed and blinking disbelief. I started to go through my rebuttal to his memo. The stenographer was writing everything down.

Don interrupted me. "Can I speak to you for a moment outside?"

We went outside the building. He looked like he was going to have a stroke. "We gotta do this with this fucking freak in there?" he said.

"I don't have any problem with her."

"Him! *Him!* Did you see the hair on *his* arms?"

"You want to call for another stenographer, it's okay with me."

"I don't want to call another stenographer! I don't want any stenographer in there! I wanna do it with just you!"

"You and me—nobody else, is that the deal?" I said.

"No—Jerry, Adrian, Dawn—"

"All they're gonna do is agree with you. You're stacking the deck. At least having a record will prove what an idiot you're being."

"I could fire you! I could fire you and not pay you out!"

I hadn't yet been paid my full fee.

"I'd sue you!" I said.

"Fucking sue me!"

"Okay, I'll fucking sue you!"

We went at each other like that and he finally agreed to it.

He and I, alone, would have discussions. When we were done talking about the script, we'd ask Dawn and Jerry and Adrian to join us.

We went at each other for days then—back and forth, arguing, cajoling, swearing, screaming. At one particularly difficult moment, we even walked into Michael Eisner's office to see what he thought.

Michael seemed amused. We were like two kids taking it to daddy. He wouldn't take a position agreeing with either one of us. He started talking about O. Henry and how much he admired him. I admired O. Henry, too, but I wasn't sure how relevant he was to a discussion about the dreams of a flashdancer.

At the end of those days, Don and I were still somehow friends. My script was still intact, but I had agreed to make some changes that I liked.

"You're a prick!" Simpson said as I left. "You're a no-good fucking Hungarian prick," and then he mock-punched me goodbye.

The project went on a very fast production track and two weeks before the start of photography, Simpson scheduled a final script meeting. It would be at Caesars Palace in Las Vegas, I was told.

"Why are we having a *script* meeting at Caesars Palace?" I asked him.

"Because we're going to be *auditioning* at the same time we're having the script meeting."

"Auditioning whom?"

"Dancers for the movie," he said.

My suite at Caesars was glaring red. Red walls, red ceiling, a red shag rug—and, outside my window, a red neon sign. Simpson's suite, the size of a house, had a Jacuzzi in the middle of the living room.

That's how I first saw him in Vegas. He was sitting in the Jacuzzi with Adrian and Jerry on chairs nearby. He had a bottle of Tanqueray on the edge of the Jacuzzi, a gram of coke on the rug behind him, and a cigar in his mouth.

Over the next few days, we would discuss the script and interrupt our discussion to meet some nineteen-year-old nubile young woman who wanted to dance in the movie. Adrian held a full audition one afternoon where a hundred young women in bikinis and leotards bumped and grinded as the Stones's "Start Me Up" exploded in a Caesars Palace conference hall.

One night Don held a party in his suite. It was Don, Jerry, Adrian, and I, and fifty of the most beautiful young women in Vegas, all desperate to be in the movie.

I saw him early in the evening sitting next to a voluptuous young woman in a see-through dress. He was earnest and shy speaking to her. She was so airheaded and stoned I'm not sure she was picking up a word of it; she had her hand on his thigh.

Around three in the morning, when I was leaving, I wanted to say good night to him.

"He's in there," Jerry said, pointing to a door. I opened the door and saw him. He was naked and had a naked young woman up against the wall with her back to him.

I said, "Good night, Don."

He looked back and grinned but didn't stop what he was doing.

We started at noon the next day, none of us too fresh. It was at this moment that Adrian launched his big creative idea. Until now, he had pretty much kept his suggestions to visual ones, but now he had a whopper.

Adrian very strongly felt that our lead character, the young woman welder who wanted to be a dancer, was raped by her father when she was eight years old.

I was trying to shake the cobwebs out of my head. I realized that we were at Caesars Palace and realized that we'd had a bacchanalian evening and that we were in a room that had a Jacuzzi in the middle of the floor, but I couldn't have heard Adrian right, I just couldn't have.

But Adrian repeated it. He felt she needed "motivation." He felt the script needed "an additional layer."

"You don't mean just telling the actress that," Simpson said, "you mean actually putting it into the piece—that her father raped her when she was eight years old."

"Yes," Adrian said.

He went on to talk about *Last Tango in Paris*, which was his favorite movie of all time. *Last Tango* had those kinds of "layers" he said.

"Adrian, this isn't *Last Tango*," I said. "We're not going to have a butter scene in this one. This is a little fairy tale of a movie. It's innocent, it's romantic—the fact that it retains that innocence and romance in a seedy world is what makes it different."

Don leaned back in the Jacuzzi, poured himself some Tanqueray on ice, and lighted a cigar. Jerry, as is his wont, didn't say much.

Adrian and I went at it. "You're destroying this movie," I said.

"I'm giving it some solidity."

"It's a fairy tale! You don't have a butter scene in a fairy tale!"

"I didn't say anything about a butter scene!"

We went on and on until suddenly it was too much for me. I turned from them, went out the door, went up to my red suite, packed my suitcase, checked out, and went home.

Adrian, Simpson told me later, came up after me five minutes later and found that I was gone.

"He's checked out!" Adrian said to Simpson, still in his Jacuzzi. "He's bloody left the hotel."

"When the gorilla shits in your face," Simpson said to Adrian, "get out of the way."

My sudden departure from Vegas had its desired effect.

Don was able to convince Adrian that a rape at age eight did not belong in this movie.

Auditions were also held on the Paramount lot.

A two-hour wait to get into the room . . . a sweltering day on the lot . . . a musical . . . a dance picture . . . an audition for *Flashdance* . . . a movie about following your dream.

She's a dancer or so she says . . . auditioning for stardom . . . for survival . . . following her dream.

She's pretty . . . but not all that special . . . skinny but still fuckable . . . edgy but still vulnerable . . . but . . . but . . . oh, Lord . . . she can dance.

You did great, you really did . . . We've got your phone number right here . . . We'll call you . . . Don't call us . . . *Ha ha.*

Two hours later . . . the audition long over . . . she's back suddenly . . . "You won't believe this." She smiles . . . We don't believe it . . . But we pretend to.

She was supposed to get a ride . . . her girlfriend's clunker broke down . . . she wonders if any of us . . . are headed toward Westwood?

Yes . . . miraculously . . . one of us is.

Yes . . . one of us will give her a ride.

And then we'll tell her that . . . she's good . . . don't . . . give up . . . ever . . . give up . . . follow . . . your dream.

Casting Alex, our lead character, came down to three finalists. Demi Moore, a young actress who'd been in *Young Doctors in Love;* Leslie Wing, a New York model; and Jennifer Beals, a young model from Chicago.

The studio couldn't decide whom to cast.

Michael Eisner finally directed that each young woman do an audition reel in full costume with Adrian directing them under "shoot" conditions—the use of a professional cinematographer and lighting man.

When the reels were done, Michael Eisner, who in his heart of hearts is a Mike Todd–like showman, organized one of the most unusual test screenings in the history of Paramount Pictures. He gathered together two hundred of the most macho men on the lot, Teamsters and gaffers and grips, and sat them down in a screening room.

He got up onstage to tell them what was about to happen. That they would see a reel from three young actresses auditioning for the lead in the movie called *Flashdance*.

"I want to know one thing from you guys after you've seen it," he said. "I want to know which of these three young women you'd most want to fuck."

The men cheered and threw fists into the air and after they saw the reels they voted overwhelmingly for Jennifer Beals. She was cast in the part.

The shoot was uneventful—Pittsburgh looked glorious on-screen (I wanted to set it in Pittsburgh; when I was living in Cleveland, Pittsburgh was where we escaped to on weekends), and at the end we felt we'd have a visually startling and romantic movie.

Simpson started to work on the music. He was a genius with film music. He had an instinctive rock and roll feel and he came up with a brilliant idea. He gave the script or showed the rough cut to musicians he liked—people like Irene Cara and Michael Sembello and Kim Carnes—and asked them to write songs that might work in this movie.

Adrian, meanwhile, worked on the cut. His director's cut was two hours and twenty minutes long. It was, I thought, beautifully done—the characters were fleshed out—it wasn't just the story of a welder who wanted to be a dancer; it was also the story of a young comedian who fails and gives up, of an ice skater who compromises her talent, of a young man . . . (played by Michael Nouri after Mickey Rourke turned the part down, feeling, at the time, pre–*Wild Orchid*, that he couldn't do love scenes) . . . who comes to realize what loving someone really means.

But the studio—Michael Eisner, Jeffrey Katzenberg—hated the cut and insisted that Adrian make deletions. Every time Adrian made a cut, they insisted on more, until all that was left, finally, was dancing, a very bare story line, and music.

Adrian felt his movie had been raped at the age of eight.

I felt like the writing was gone from the piece. Simpson was having a nervous breakdown, especially after he discovered that Paramount had so little faith in *Flashdance* that the studio sold off 30 percent of its own potential profit to a private investors group. We all knew, of course, that studios only did that with movies that they were absolutely certain would stiff.

The weekend we opened, we stiffed. The reviews were vicious—most reviewers dismissed the movie as "soft porn." The opening weekend's grosses were a blip on the screen—$3.8 million—in Hollywood terms, "zilch."

The Thursday after we opened, Simpson called me. "I don't know what's going on," he said, "but something's going on."

Theater owners were reporting that they were getting repeat business— especially among young women. People were leaving the theaters in tears, humming the music. The owners also had to order triple the amount of popcorn they usually ordered.

"This could be a popcorn movie," Simpson said.

"What's that?"

"An audience picture. The audience comes, has fun, tells their friends. The movie becomes critic-proof."

The following weekend, we did $4.3 million—it was still a very small number, but the fact that we'd gone up instead of suffering the usual second-weekend drop meant that we were getting great word of mouth.

And from then on, the movie just kept getting bigger box office each weekend.

Irene Cara's "Flashdance" and then Michael Sembello's "Maniac" went to number one on the *Billboard* chart. Within a month, we knew we had a phenomenon. It played in the theaters for eight months and made more than $400 million worldwide.

Everyone took credit for it, a sure sign of a huge hit. Peter Guber and Jon Peters bragged about producing it, although I had never even met them in the course of the production.

Lynda Obst bragged about developing it, although the script she worked on with Tom Hedley was junked. Tom Hedley said that he wrote it, although all that was left of his script was the title and the dance style (enough, though, in my mind: without his original creativity, there would have been no movie).

The truth is that it was really one person's movie. It was Simpson's baby from beginning to end and it made a lot of us involved a lot of money.

I had a very few net profit points in residual earnings, what Eddie Murphy referred to later as "monkey points"—meaning that they never paid off, that the studio accounting system was always able to deny net point participants money because no movie ever made *so much* money that they had to pay monkey points off.

My monkey points on *Flashdance* amounted to over $2 million.

When Art Buchwald sued Paramount years later, Paramount asked me to testify on its behalf. The studio needed an example to show that net points sometimes meant real dollars.

I turned the request down.

I didn't want to be known as the one writer in Hollywood the studios wouldn't cheat.

You're never hotter in Hollywood than when you have a raging hit movie out in the world and *Flashdance* was so hot around the world that Europeans had a new craze: trading cards consisting of five hundred shots from the movie.

I wondered how some United Artists executives were feeling: at a time when "the buzz" on *F.I.S.T.* was good, they had authorized the manufacture of thousands of brass *F.I.S.T.* belt knuckles, which were now, no doubt, filling up a warehouse somewhere.

When it was clear that *Flashdance* was a gold mine, Guy McElwaine called me to advise: "You are going to get avalanched with offers. Do none of them. Wait. Take all the meetings, but accept nothing till they offer you what you should have."

I was making $275,000 per script.

"What should I have?" I asked Guy.

"Six hundred thousand a script," he said.

So that's what I did. I met with everyone and turned everything down. I wanted to sit down and write a new spec script on my own but I was so busy that I didn't have the time.

It was a swirl of meetings, lunches, and dinners in both L.A. and San Francisco. Congratulatory cases of champagne and breathtaking bouquets of flowers were arriving from producers and studio heads I'd barely shaken hands with.

I was busy in Marin with my other life.

My son Steve was first in soccer and then in Little League. I went to every game. I won an award as the only parent who attended all seventeen Little League games.

Sometimes, I thought, dealing with Little League was as difficult as Hollywood. I was almost escorted off the field at a Little League game for berating a teenage umpire who, I felt, didn't know what constituted a balk.

My daughter, Suzi, had decided she was going to be the next Dian Fossey. She was eight years old.

Gerri and I took her to every zoo and animal preserve in the area.

My father, approaching eighty, enjoyed accompanying me to L.A. He still lived in Cleveland but he was flying out a lot to Marin, and often, when I had a meeting, he'd come with me. He had friends in L.A. While I was having meetings in L.A., he was visiting his friends there. When I was free, my father and I would trip around the town together.

We made an odd couple, but we had fun: a shuffling old man in his black suit, carrying a cane, his arm held by a younger man with hair over his shoulders, a mountain man beard, and wearing tattered jeans.

We were a long way from the Lorain Fulton Theatre now, as we visited Grauman's Chinese or walked the Hollywood Walk of Fame, but we still enjoyed ducking into a matinee before my meeting with David Begelman, the head of MGM.

We liked meeting at midnight, after I'd had a dinner at Morton's with yet another producer who wanted to be allied with one of the hottest screenwriters in town.

My father and I would sit in the El Padrino Room at the Beverly Wilshire sharing a Caesar salad and talking about the old times on Lorain Avenue.

He had remarried, unhappily, after my mother died, and we talked about my mother a lot. Thanks to the movies, I was able to support him. He had been fired without warning when he was seventy-three by the Franciscan monks who owned the *Catholic Hungarians' Sunday*. I started making money at about the time he got fired and the money allowed him to publish new Hungarian novels that he wrote—and whose publication costs I covered. It gave him a sense of worth and, more than that, it gave him something to do. Without the money Hollywood was paying me, my dad, I knew, would quickly have become a candidate for an old-age home.

Instead, I was able to show my father the better restaurants and walked around the Warner Brothers lot with him and I even got a map of the stars' homes one afternoon and we drove around Bel Air and Beverly Hills.

"I wouldn't know how to do this," my father said to me one day as we were walking down Rodeo Drive, arm in arm.

"What, Pop?"

"This Hollywood business," he said in Hungarian.

I asked him what he meant.

"Sometimes I see you at night when you come back," he said, "and you have had meetings and lunches all day and meetings again and I see you very tired."

"Everybody gets tired," I said.

"Yes, but you look *very* tired. And I know in my life sometimes I have gotten very tired, but I have gotten tired from the writing and not the meetings."

"Well, tired is tired, isn't it?" I said.

"No," he said, "there are very different ways of being tired."

I thought about it for a while and then I took my father into Café Rodeo. He ordered a corned beef sandwich—they had it, thank God.

He and I laughed over something from my childhood . . . I felt the setting sun on my face, and I didn't feel so tired anymore.

The Smart Girl

A plain woman in a town filled with beautiful ones, she began as a studio reader, assigned screenplays which the studio execs, all men, were too busy to read because they were too occupied with beautiful women.

She worked fourteen, sometimes even sixteen hours a day, reading diligently and carefully, not just critiquing scripts like the other readers but offering suggestions about how to make them better.

One of the execs took credit for her suggestions and, thanks to her, developed two hit movies.

He offered her a job as his special "creative assistant."

She participated in meetings with screenwriters now but never said anything, putting all of her thoughts into memos for her boss, who, thanks to her memos, was rewarded for a series of hits by being named the head of production.

Word had leaked out about her memos and box office instincts and when she was offered a VP job at another studio, she took it, knowing she had to get away from the boss who would always take credit for her ideas.

Her new studio job was ideal for her. The studio chief, one of the town's great lovers, was also known to be remarkably dumb. There was no possibility he would get any credit for her work. Even better, he didn't try to hog the credit. He knew no one would believe him and he was also way too busy trying to bed various models who wanted to be actresses.

When he was finally fired—the men in New York had tired of his personal excesses—she was the logical choice to replace him. The East Coasters liked her work ethic and were amazed to find someone smart in Hollywood. She was appointed head of production on her twenty-eighth birthday.

She had never had much of a personal life but it really hadn't ever mattered to her. It still didn't. Men bored her and beautiful women intimidated her and she loved nothing more than her work. It was enough. She was happy.

CHAPTER 7

Blood and Hair on the Walls

BILLY

The night is young.
The tide is red.
There are pigs in the sea.

Foreplay, unproduced

Richard Marquand, an English director who had directed *Eye of the Needle,* one of my favorite thrillers, was in Marin shooting George Lucas's *Return of the Jedi.* A wry, down-to-earth Welshman in his early forties, Richard and I were introduced by a mutual friend and were instant mates.

He and his wife, Carol, a smart, cigar-smoking woman, were renting a house in Tiburon. George Lucas was driving him nuts—"he just bloody stands there, right behind me, watching"—and Richard and I enjoyed sharing moments at local pubs dwelling on the glories of Guinness stout.

Jedi was a big-budget, high-profile production, and Richard, who had spent many years scuffling in L.A. trying to get a directing job, was near the top of the heap. He remembered those years in L.A. all too well, though, hanging out at Barney's Beanery—"I lived on that damn chili"—and living in a succession of ratty Hollywood Hills apartments.

"You're only as good as your last picture if you're a director," he said to me. "It's different if you're a writer. Your profile is lower, you can get away with much more. But I can't. And I know I can't."

In the course of spending time together, we talked often about our kids. We were both devoted fathers and we both felt that the children in our lives had opened inner doors which we had mostly kept shut. Our children were humanizing, softening, sensitizing influences which we both greatly welcomed and treasured in our lives.

Richard remembered a moment when he was watching Sam, his three-year-old, as Sam watched a butterfly alight on a windowsill. Sam made a movement to touch the butterfly and then held back, his hand still up in the air. As the butterfly flew away, Sam started to laugh in delight . . . and Richard, watching him, started to cry.

I started talking about writing a script which would be about an inheld man, a man who had walled his heart off from most people . . . a man who, thanks to children that he loves, finds himself reborn.

"I'll direct that movie, Squire," Richard said.

"You will?"

"I give you my word," Richard said, and we shook hands.

I sat down and wrote the script and called it *Pals*, the name with which both Richard and I often addressed our kids. It was about a convict named Sam Bragg (named, of course, after Sam Marquand) who escapes and holes up in woods neighboring a farm.

The farm is run by a widow with two little kids and the story focused on the convict being brought back to inner life by the love he felt for the children.

Richard cried when he read it, formally committed to do it as his next movie, and the script was quickly sold to Paramount for $400,000.

"You're crazy," Guy told me when he heard about the sale. "You should have held out for $600,000."

"It's a labor of love," I told him, and told him about the butterfly on the windowsill that Sam Marquand had watched.

A month after I sold the script, with Richard in post-production now on *Jedi*, he and I went to have a production meeting with Paramount about *Pals*. Richard wanted to go into pre-production right away.

"We don't want to move quite that fast," Jeff Katzenberg, Paramount's head of production, said.

"Oh?" Richard said. A month earlier they had bought the script *very fast*, literally *overnight* after receiving it.

"Why not?" I asked.

"It's a brilliant script," Jeffrey said, "it's moving, it's poignant, it makes you cry."

"Yes?" Richard said.

"And you are a terrific talent," he said to Richard. "The word of mouth on *Jedi* is fantastic. It's got a great buzz."

Oh, oh, I thought. There's that "buzz" word again. *F.I.S.T.* had had great "buzz," too.

"Yes?" Richard said.

Jeffrey looked down at his desk for a moment, and Richard and I glanced at each other.

"I'll tell you the truth," Jeffrey said. "It's essentially a character piece set on a farm, a relationship piece on a farm."

"That's what it was when you bought it," I said.

"Well, we're just not certain that farm movies are working right now."

"Dust," I suddenly said.

Jeffrey nodded.

"What did you say, Squire?" Richard said.

"Dust," I said, "there's lots of dust on a farm. No dust."

"No *dust?*" Richard said. He looked like a man trapped in a straitjacket now.

"No."

The damn dust, it had me again. First at ABC Films and now here.

Our butterfly wasn't going to flutter.

Guy McElwaine was now the number two man at Columbia Pictures under Frank Price, known as the Sphinx, a studio head made famous for passing on the opportunity to make *E.T.*

"Do you know who Marty Ransohoff is?" Guy asked me one day.

"He's the wild boar of the business, from what I hear."

"You'll like him. He's got a great idea, come on down and meet him."

Marty Ransohoff, I knew, was one of the all-time, all-star producers in Hollywood. The producer of *The Beverly Hillbillies* and *Mr. Ed* on television, he had then produced *The Americanization of Emily, The Cincinnati Kid, The Sandpipers, Catch-22, The White Dawn,* and *Silver Streak.*

He was obviously larger than life; mythical stories attached themselves to him.

He had had a blazing affair with Kim Novak . . . he owned much of the Big Sur coastline . . . he was close to the top business honchos at Columbia, especially to Herb Allen, and had been integral in the studio's ouster of former studio chief David Begelman, caught forging a check . . . during the making of *The Americanization of Emily,* he had chosen to stay loyal to Paddy Chayefsky and had fired the director William Wyler . . . Budd Schulberg, the writer, had called Marty "The messiah of the New Hollywood" . . . Joyce Haber, the columnist, had called him "L. B. Mayer without the overhead" . . .

Knowing all of that, I still wasn't prepared for our meeting. He was loud. He spoke in four-letter words. He had a Buddha-like gut. He wore a wrinkled Banlon top with wrinkled pants. He had a few wisps of white hair that were artistically placed across a mammoth bald skull.

"Blood and hair on the walls, that's what I want," he growled. "You got that? It ain't gonna work without blood and hair on the walls."

What he had in mind, specifically, was a courtroom drama involving a shocking, bloody crime. There hadn't been a courtroom drama made in years. One of Marty's favorite movies was *Anatomy of a Murder.*

"If you make it a woman lawyer," Guy said, "I think I can get Jane Fonda into it."

"She's a pain in the ass," Marty said. "What do we want to get her into it for?"

"She's a big star," Guy said.

"You just want to boost your boyfriend's deal," Marty said, nodding at me.

"I don't know what you're talking about." Guy smiled.

"I'll tell you what I'm talking about," Marty growled. "Fonda gets attached and your boyfriend will get more money for writing the script than he's ever gotten before."

"You know what your problem is?" Guy said. "You've been in this town too long."

He laughed; so did I.

"Fuck both of you," Marty said.

The next day Guy, Marty, and I met with Frank Price, the studio head, and two young creative assistants.

I understood quickly why they called Frank Price the Sphinx. He listened to what we had in mind with an utterly stone-faced blank expression. He lit up a cigarette and looked blank. He lit another and looked blanker. He lit another and . . .

"It's gonna have blood and hair on the walls," Marty said. Frank looked blank, the creative assistants nodded.

"It's gonna have a fuck-'em-if-they-can't-take-a-joke ending," Marty said. Frank looked blank, the creative assistants nodded.

"It's gonna have great word of mouth on it," Marty said. "Fuck the critics, it'll be an audience picture."

More blankness, more nods.

Marty's litany went on: Nastier than *In Cold Blood,* lots of sex, scare-'em-pissless moments, forget *Witness for the Prosecution,* forget *Anatomy of a Murder,* forget that bullshit Perry Mason confess-at-the-end bullshit. We were gonna scare the living shit out of all those assholes out there.

"What assholes?" I said.

"The audience," Marty said.

"I think I can get Jane Fonda," Guy said.

The Sphinx finally spoke. *Mirabile dictu!*

"*You can?*" Frank Price said.

"I think so," Guy said.

"That'd be great," Frank Price said.

"That'd be great," a creative assistant said.

"That'd be great," another creative assistant said.

Frank Price lit up another cigarette and looked blank.

The meeting was over.

I looked at the assistants and said, "Do you guys ever do anything but nod?" The assistants laughed nervously.

Frank Price looked at me, his expression blank.

That night Guy and Marty and I met with Jane Fonda at a Japanese sushi place in Century City. We had to take our shoes off.

"I'm not taking my shoes off," Marty said.

"For Christ's sake," Guy said, "it's a sushi place. She picked it. You gotta take 'em off or you can't come in."

"I hate these places where you gotta take your shoes off," Marty said. "What the fuck kind of place is it where you gotta take your shoes off?"

"It's a sushi place," Guy explained.

"I hate fucking sushi," Marty said.

"You should eat more of it." Guy smiled, glancing at Marty's very swollen belly.

"Don't tell me what the fuck to eat, okay?" Marty said.

"I'm looking out for your health, that's all," Guy said.

"Don't, okay?" Marty said. "Look out for your own fucking health, not mine."

Marty finally got his shoes off—it wasn't easy; he looked like he'd burst when he bent over—and Jane joined us ten minutes later, looking radiant. She had just come from taping an exercise video.

She and I talked for a while about Kent State and the Silkwood project we'd tried to put together and then Guy started telling her about what we had in mind.

"It'll be a big classy piece, like *Witness for the Prosecution*," he said. "You'd play an attorney fighting a seemingly impossible case—"

"It'll have blood and hair on the walls," Marty said.

Jane lowered her sunglasses and stared at him.

"What?" she said.

Guy cut Marty off.

"The crime itself will be shockingly violent, but not the movie," Guy said. "We probably won't even show the killings."

"Are you out of your mind?" Marty said. "We gotta show the killings."

"Well, not necessarily," Guy said, "there are ways of doing it without—"

"It's nuts," Marty said, "you gotta show it."

"It's up to Joe," Guy said. "He'll decide whether we show it or not."

"He'll show it," Marty said. "Did you see *Flashdance?*"

"I liked *Flashdance*," Jane said.

"I don't know whether I'll show the crime or not," I said. "It depends on the material."

"We're not making a fucking art movie here," Marty said.

"You don't have to make an art movie to make a classy one," I said.

"You're damn right," Guy said. "I suggest we let Joe write the script he wants to write."

Jane looked at me and smiled.

"Do you want to write it?" she asked.

"Yeah," I said, smiling at her, "I think it'll be fun."

She held my smile a moment and said, "Okay, I'm in."

"That's great." Guy smiled.

"I still think we gotta show it," Marty said.

We all laughed.

Marty pushed his sushi away. He hadn't touched it.

The next day Guy went to Frank Price, told him Jane Fonda had become "attached" to the project, and suggested that Columbia pay me $600,000 for the script.

Frank thought the number too high and said he'd make the deal for $500,000. Guy suggested that at that rate the studio would be wise to make a three-picture deal with me. Frank agreed to the three scripts at $500,000 apiece and Guy informed Marty.

"It's bananas," Marty said, "it's fuckin' bananas. The guy's had two pictures made and on both of them he got a shared screenplay credit. He's never written a movie that he had sole credit on. And you're paying him $500,000 for *three* of 'em? *Bananas!*"

From then on, that's always what Marty called me: Joe Bananas.

Marty and I took off for Chicago and New York in an effort, as Marty said, to make the script "authentic." I tried to tell him that I had covered trials as a reporter, had even been hauled in front of a grand jury once in a prosecutor's attempt to force me to divulge my sources, but Marty said this would give the script "the seal of approval."

In Chicago we had an appointment to see a woman criminal attorney who had won all forty-three of her felony cases. It was sweltering when we got to her office and Marty's gargantuan head was soaked in sweat.

The attorney told us that she felt she had won most of her cases in jury selection.

"If you get the wrong jury," she said, "no matter what you do, no matter how good a case you present, no matter how articulately, passionately you present it, you're going to lose."

"That won't work," Marty said.

"On the contrary," she said with a smile, "with the right jury, it's worked for me all the time."

"Not in the movie it won't," Marty said. "We're putting blood and hair on the walls, we're not doing a movie about jury selection."

"Well," she said. That's all she said.

I asked her if she had ever represented a client she knew in her heart was guilty.

"I've never known any of my clients to be guilty," she said.

"Do you ever ask them if they did it?"

"It's the one question I never ask."

"Is it important for you, as a human being, to know if you are possibly freeing someone who committed a crime?"

"It's more important for me to know that I am doing the best job I can, as a professional, in behalf of my client."

"Do you ever feel badly about maybe turning a guilty person free?"

She looked at me.

"Whoa, whoa there, Bananas," Marty said, "she's not on trial here. She's helping us."

"Jesue Christ, Bananas," Marty said in the street outside, "what the fuck were you doing in there?"

He seemed to be gasping for breath in the dank, humid air.

"I was just asking some questions that I thought might be relevant in the script."

"Don't go off track here," he said. "I don't want this to be a Jane Fonda movie."

"It *is* a Jane Fonda movie," I said.

"It doesn't have to be a Jane Fonda movie just because she's in it," Marty said.

We went to New York to interview Judge Burton Roberts, a Runyonesque New York character, an old friend of Marty's, and later a model for one of the characters in Tom Wolfe's *Bonfire of the Vanities*.

"I don't understand what we're talking to this guy for," I said to Marty. I explained to him that I knew all about the court system. I had even spent an enjoyable afternoon with F. Lee Bailey once during the second Shepard trial in Cleveland.

"He's very well liked, very well known, and very respected," Marty said of Judge Burton Roberts.

"That may very well be true. But I still don't understand why we need to interview him."

"He's going to be our legal adviser on the movie," Marty said.

"Great," I said, "but what will we interview him about?"

"We'll take him out to lunch and chat," Marty said, "and that will be the interview. We'll pay him some money for him to be our legal adviser and then, when those fuckheads at the studio put their fuck-you shoes on and try to find some legal flaw in the script, Burt's going to tell them they're full of shit and they'll throw their shoes back in the closet."

"Got it," I said.

"You got a lot of learning to do, Bananas," Marty said.

We had a very pleasant lunch with Judge Burton Roberts at an Italian restaurant near the courthouse. Judge Roberts told some timeworn brightly polished anecdotes, signed on as our legal adviser, and thanked us for the lunch.

"We flew all the way to New York for this?" I asked Marty afterward. "Couldn't we have made the deal with him over the phone?"

"You still don't get it," he said. "We've got a personal connection now. *You've* got a personal connection now. He liked you. You may not have any sole credits, Bananas, but occasionally you're likable. So when we need him to write a letter defending *your* script on a legal basis to the studio, he'll write a good letter. He'll *care.*"

"Wouldn't he do the same thing if we just had a deal with him?"

"This isn't about the money," Marty Ransohoff said. "That's one of the things you still haven't learned. This business isn't always about the money."

I was ready now, thanks to all of this stimulating, extensive, and in-depth research, to write the script, but Guy stopped me.

"Frank wants an outline," he said.

"I don't do outlines. My deal doesn't call for an outline."

"I know that," he said, "I made your deal."

"So what are you asking me for an outline for?"

"I'm not asking you, Frank Price is."

"Tell him it's not in my deal."

"He knows it's not in your deal," Guy said. "He's asking you as a favor."

"I don't owe him any favors."

"You owe me some," Guy said.

"I know I do," I said.

"So I'm asking you."

"You said Frank was asking me."

"That was before. Now *I'm* asking you."

Frank Price, he explained, had started as a writer. He had written a great many television dramas and had then gone on to be a TV executive and then a movie executive.

"That's why he's so good at what he does," Guy said. "He's a writer. Don't you have any respect for your fellow writers?"

"For my fellow *screenwriters*?" I asked. "You know the answer to that. He isn't even a screenwriter. He's a TV writer."

. . .

I wrote the outline, finally, as a favor to my new friend, the Sphinx. Guy "loved" it. Marty said, "It'll work."

It was the story of a newspaper publisher in San Francisco, Jack Forrester, who is arrested for killing his wife and her maid in a brutal "blood and hair on the walls" way. He is defended by a woman named Teddy Barnes who believes in his innocence and then begins to think that he is guilty. To my amazement, Frank Price spoke as soon as we began the meeting about my outline. He was still smoking, his expression was still blank, but he was speaking.

"Your ending won't work," is what he said.

In my ending, Jack Forrester is guilty of the killings and Teddy Barnes shoots him to death. She shoots him after they have had an affair during the trial.

"We have to have an upbeat ending that audiences will love," Frank Price said. "You can't break their hearts and then have them walk out of the theater."

"Why not?" I asked.

"Because they'll hate the movie, tell their friends they hate the movie, and nobody will come to see it."

"This is a mystery," I said. "If you fake them out of their seats, if you shock them at the end, won't they walk out having gotten their money's worth?"

"They don't like to be faked out at the end of a mystery," Frank Price said. "They don't like to feel stupid. If you make them feel stupid, they'll hate the movie."

The two creative assistants nodded with such gravity that I was afraid their heads would hit the table. Guy and Marty said nothing, looking as blank now as Frank.

"You mean you give them a predictable ending and they'll be pleased? If they figure it out before they see it, then they'll like it?"

"Exactly," Frank Price said.

"Exactly," the creative assistants echoed.

"Bullshit," I said.

Guy cleared his throat. Marty kept touching the few strands of hair across his head, atop which was a halo of sweat.

"Is that the kind of mystery you like?" I asked Frank Price. "Where you can figure out what happens before it happens?"

"No," he said, "it's not."

"There you go," I said.

"But I am not your audience. I am more intelligent than your audience."

"You're more intelligent than the audience and your intelligence tells you that they're dumb."

I phrased it as a statement. I wanted the Sphinx to give me a flat "yes" to that.

He didn't, though. He gave me a look that said: Are you getting cute with me here?

Then he said, "You cannot use this ending."

Then he said, "This is the ending I want you to use."

He detailed it for me. The movie had to end with Jack Forrester and Teddy Barnes holding each other. He was innocent. She had mistakenly thought for a moment that he was guilty, but he was innocent.

"You mean she's dumb, too," I said.

The Sphinx was glaring at me now. I was using this word "dumb" too many times in one meeting.

"Why 'dumb'?" he asked. It was like he didn't even want to say the word.

"Because she mistakenly thinks for a moment that he did the killings."

"That doesn't make her dumb," Frank Price said.

"What does it make her?"

"A woman who fell in love and lost her head," Frank Price said.

He laid it down again. This was the ending I had to use. This was the movie the studio would make. If I insisted on *my* ending, the studio wouldn't make it and would bring in some obedient writer who'd change it.

There was a chill in the air now and, in an effort to warm it a little, the Sphinx suddenly became avuncular. "I know what I'm talking about, Joe," he said, "believe me." He told me of all the TV things he'd written and supervised.

"I know you've done all those TV things, Frank," I finally said. "I understand what you've done. That's exactly the problem, all the crap you've done."

When Marty and I went back to Guy's office, Guy said, "Well, you just have to burn *all* of your bridges, don't you?"

I was a little dazed, I think, because I asked the same question that I had never gotten an answer to in the previous meeting.

"Do those assistants ever do anything but nod?"

Guy didn't think that was funny, possibly still sniffing the ash from those burning bridges, but Marty laughed.

"They're hall mice," he said.

"What are hall mice?"

"They scurry up and down the halls every day picking up little pieces of cheese—information—and run the cheese back to Frank. Hall mice nod. Everybody knows that, Bananas."

"What do we do now?" I asked.

Guy just shrugged. Marty asked me to walk back with him to his office.

"You can't use his ending," Marty said.

"I don't intend to," I said.

"Good. A writer who actually believes in what he writes. I can't believe I'm seeing it, but good."

"He'll just bring somebody else in to rewrite me," I said.

"Not if he doesn't have the script," Marty said.

"What do I do—not write it?"

"You write it but you don't turn it in. You say you're still working on it. You say you're a perfectionist and want to get it right. You say you've got writer's block."

"How long do I keep saying that?"

Marty Ransohoff smiled a beatific smile and said, "Until he gets fired."

"Frank Price is getting fired?"

The smile positively glowed now.

"They all get fired sooner or later, Bananas."

"Will this be sooner or later?"

He chuckled now. "Sooner rather than later."

"Did Herb Allen or one of the corporate guys tell you that?"

"Bananas! *Bananas!*" Marty Ransohoff said. "You always ask so many *fucking* questions!"

I went back to Marin and finished the script in eight weeks.

Two weeks later, Columbia called my agent and formally asked when I would deliver the script.

Two weeks later they called again.

Two weeks later, they were threatening to sue me.

My agent said I was a perfectionist. And that I was suffering from writer's block.

"I don't know how long I can keep dodging," I said to Marty. "Their lawyers are into it now."

"It's your call, Bananas," Marty said. "View this as a test of conscience. Are you a writer or are you a two-dollar whoor?"

Frank Price was fired a week later. The man who replaced him—the new president and CEO of Columbia Pictures!—was the Golden Beef himself, Guy McElwaine.

His first phone call as the top man was to me.

"You've got your ending," he said. "Write it the way you want to write it."

"You'll have it in three days," I said.

"You sonofabitch." He laughed.

The men Guy appointed as his top vice presidents at Columbia were Craig Baumgarten, with whom I'd worked at Paramount; my old agent, Bob Bookman; and one of the nodders at the meeting with the Sphinx, Robert Lawrence, now suddenly known as the Hall Mouse Who Went to Heaven.

Craig Baumgarten was assigned as the executive in charge of my script, which was to become the film entitled *Jagged Edge*. The appointment from Guy was Craig's biggest break in the business. He had begun in a way that he now tried to keep hush-hush. He had not only produced a porn movie called *Some-*

time Sweet Susan but had also starred in it. He had moved from porn into independent production, then on to Paramount, then to another independent production company, and now here he was at Columbia.

Originally from Chicago, from an upper-middle-class background, he was opinionated, temperamental, sometimes abrasive, and smart. He spoke with a sense of passion about the projects he was involved in, a rarity for a studio executive.

Marty Ransohoff knew, of course, that Craig and I had been friendly in the past—"You've sure got a lot of boyfriends, Bananas"—and seemed threatened by it.

"You've got one loyalty here, Bananas," he said, "and it's to me. Forget McElwaine, forget Baumgarten. I'm the one who okayed you for this. I'm the one getting this piece of shit script of yours made."

"I've got one loyalty here, Marty," I said, "and it's to my script."

"You're a typical fucking egotistic sleazy dime-a-dozen screenwriter," he said. "Chayefsky was the worst."

I knew he didn't mean that; I knew that he was actually paying me a great compliment in his gruff, wild-boar way. He had gone to the wall for Paddy the way few producers ever go to the wall for a writer, when he fired the director who'd wanted to change Paddy's script.

When Guy got the script of *Jagged Edge,* he read it immediately and called to tell me he loved it. He gave it to Craig and Craig felt the same way. The studio formally sent the script to Jane Fonda.

My attorney, Barry Hirsch, who was also Jane's attorney, called me on a Sunday night to tell me that Jane didn't like the script. He also told me that the Columbia executive who gave her the script told her that Columbia didn't like the script either and that other writers would have to be brought in before it would be a movie.

According to my attorney, what this executive said to Jane tainted her reading. She was reading something that, she thought, the studio *disliked.*

I called Marty, who became apoplectic. He knew that both McElwaine and Baumgarten loved the piece and he now knew that someone had sandbagged us with Jane Fonda. He discovered the villain the next day.

It was Robert Lawrence, Frank Price's nodder, the Hall Mouse Who Went to Heaven.

Lawrence denied everything, but we knew from Hirsch, Jane's attorney, exactly what he had said. Guy threatened to fire him and I called him from Marin and threatened to break his knees the next day at ten o'clock in his office.

When I got to his office the next day, I discovered that the Hall Mouse had called in sick.

We had a serious problem now, though. Jane Fonda didn't like the script and she was putting together a memo asking for specific changes. When I got her memo, a week later, I realized that if we were to take her suggestions, it would mean a complete, page-one overhaul of the material. What she had in mind was a different movie.

I read Ransohoff, who had been out of town, part of her memo when he called me from Los Angeles Airport. I could hear a lot of people around Marty, who was in a phone booth. He suddenly started to bellow: "The stupid fucking sleazy cunt! What does she know? Jane Fonda went down on the Vietcong!"

The studio now had a decision to make. Guy McElwaine could either fire me and bring other writers in to do a rewrite at Jane's behest . . . or he could remove Jane from the project and look for other actresses.

My attorney and Jane's, Barry Hirsch, tried to mediate.

"You and Jane have been friends for a long time," Barry said. "It's silly to end a friendship over a script."

"What do you suggest I do, Barry?"

"Rewrite it. She'll do the movie if you rewrite it."

"She wants a totally different movie."

"But she'll do it," Barry said.

"I can't do that, Barry."

"Joe, it's only a script," said Barry, the gestalt psychologist, "we're talking about a relationship here."

Marty Ransohoff, God bless him, told Guy that if I was taken off the project, he would remove himself, too. He eloquently defended the script in a lengthy memo and said Jane "doesn't know what she's talking about."

I called Barry Hirsch back and said, "Talk to Jane for me, Columbia's going to take her off the project. I think she'd be great in it. She's making a creative mistake."

Barry scoffed at me. "Never," he said. "Jane Fonda is a very big star. I know you and McElwaine are close, but no studio head is going to begin his run by firing one of the biggest stars in the world . . . because of a *screenplay*," Barry said.

But that's exactly what Guy did. To the amazement of Hollywood's trade press, Jane Fonda was off a movie because of a "creative difference" with a screenwriter.

"This is better than William Wyler and Paddy," I said to Marty Ransohoff. "This is a movie star getting canned."

And Marty shot back: "Don't you dare bring Paddy up in this context."

"All I know," Guy said, as he was fielding phone calls from Liz Smith and Army Archerd, "is that this movie better work or I'm going to look like the biggest asshole in the universe."

. . .

We decided to look for a director before a star.

Craig Baumgarten, Marty Ransohoff, and I went over a list of six directors. At the bottom of that list was my friend Richard Marquand, finished with *Jedi* now and available. He was at the bottom of the list and not the top because Marty said he didn't like his work.

The real reason, I realized, was that Marty knew Richard and I were friends, knew as well that Craig and Richard were friends, and didn't want to be surrounded by people in the making of a movie who had close personal relationships.

"Everyplace I look, Bananas," Marty said, "I see one of your *fucking* boyfriends."

The arrangement we made with Marty was that if the other five passed . . . then . . . *and only then* . . . would we go to Marquand.

Craig and I both badly wanted Richard to direct it. We knew he could do a mystery thriller well. And the three of us liked each other. This could actually be one movie where we could have fun.

Each week Craig called Marty to tell him that one of the five directors at the top of our list had passed. After five weeks and five passes, per our arrangement, we sent the script to Richard with Marty's blessing and Richard agreed to do the movie.

At our first dinner with Richard, Marty casually asked him when he had read the script and Richard said, "Oh, about six weeks ago."

I saw Marty's Adam's apple bob. He looked at me for a moment, knives in his eyes. The next day he called the directors who'd been the top five and learned they had not even been submitted *Jagged Edge*.

It was too late for him to do anything about Richard—Columbia had formally made an agreement with his agent to direct *Jagged Edge*.

"You and your boyfriends," he raged to me, "you sold me out! You fucked me behind my back!"

"I didn't know anything about it," I said. "Craig sent those scripts out—I didn't."

"He *didn't* fucking send them out!" Marty screamed.

"Well, then *Craig* didn't send them out," I said.

He called Craig and screamed at him, too, and Craig, armed with his own volatile temper, screamed back.

"You don't run this studio!" Craig said to Marty Ransohoff. "We do!"

"You better find a new boyfriend," Marty told me one night, strangely whispering over the phone, "your old boyfriend is a dead cocksucker, Bananas."

.   .   .

As we began casting, Marty called Craig's office to inform him that he was going to New York that weekend to look at off-Broadway actresses for one of the smaller parts.

It was a routine notification. While a producer had to inform the studio that he was making such a trip (the studio was funding it) the notification was pro forma. With a producer as powerful and as successful as Marty, this kind of call was always a notification and never a request.

Craig's secretary called Marty back an hour later to notify him that Columbia was not approving the trip.

Marty could go to New York, but only at his own expense.

Marty went berserk. He launched into a tirade with me over "my boyfriend" that exceeded all the others and ended this way: "You tell that sleazy cocksucker boyfriend of yours that I've got his porno tape! I've seen his fat white ass pumping away up on the big screen! The tape is in my possession! I can send it to whomever I want! *Do you understand me, Bananas?*"

"Have you gone nuts?" I asked Craig. "What does a three-day tab in New York matter? Columbia's got the money."

He repeated the same words to me that he had said to Marty. "He doesn't run this studio, we do."

"He's got your tape," I said.

"What tape?"

"The porn tape."

There was a slight pause on the phone and Craig said, "So what."

So . . . *a lot* . . . I explained to him. Columbia was owned by the Coca-Cola Company. The Coca-Cola people were very conservative, rah-rah red-white-and-blue, old-values types. Marty's closest connection to corporate Columbia was the powerful New York investment banker Herbert Allen, also known as a very conservative straight arrow.

"Does Coca-Cola know about your porn tape?" I asked Craig. "Does Herbert Allen?"

There was a longer pause on his end of the line. "Are you kidding?" he finally said. "They never would have hired me. Guy knows about it."

"Is Guy going to cop to the fact that he knows about it—that he hired you knowing about it—if the shit comes down on him from the Coca-Cola people?"

Craig said nothing.

"What if Guy feels his own job is going to be endangered by the fact that he hired you knowing about the porn tape? What do you think Guy's going to do?"

"He'll take care of me," Craig said, "he needs me here. We're so close, I even pick him up every morning and drive him in to the office."

I tried to tell Craig that he was being stupid, that he was playing Russian roulette with Marty—not a healthy thing to do.

"What do you think I should do?" Craig said.

"Have your secretary call him back and let him go scout in New York anytime he wants."

He said nothing.

"Come on, Craig," I said, "if it were any other producer, you'd approve the trip."

"I'll think about it," he said.

I called Marty back and told him I had spoken to my boyfriend and that I expected Craig's secretary to call him and authorize his trip to New York.

"That's all I want, Bananas," he said. "I don't even want an apology and I deserve an apology."

Three days later, Marty called me and said, "Your boyfriend's secretary never called me. I'm sorry, Bananas."

Craig Baumgarten was relieved of his duties at Columbia Pictures a week later. He sobbed on the phone when he told me.

The Coca-Cola Company had found out about his porn tape. They'd come down on Guy for hiring someone with this background. Guy told them he had no idea Craig had ever been involved in a porn film. Craig said Guy cried when he told him he couldn't stand up for him—his own job was on the line.

"I see in the papers you've lost a boyfriend," Marty Ransohoff said to me. "Don't worry about it, Bananas. You make friends easy. You'll find lots of others."

The Wild Boar chuckled softly as he hung up.

Richard Marquand and I went to London to talk about the final shooting script. Bob Bookman, my old agent, became the executive in charge of the project.

Our trip to London was partly a getaway. Richard and I liked being around each other. He showed me his world as I had shown him my Marin County world. We went for long lunches to his club (the White Elephant), spent time at his Kensington flat, and drove out into the countryside to stay at his seventeenth-century estate, complete with pond, in Kent. The script was nearly ready: Richard made one insightful suggestion that had a great beneficial impact upon the script. Sam Ransom, the private eye, Teddy Barnes's partner, Richard thought, should be more of a comedic character, an aging private eye with a burned-out sardonic wit.

Richard had a single concern about the shoot. He was afraid of Marty Ransohoff.

Marty, we had discovered, was really a frustrated director. When a director let him know that he didn't really need any help directing, thank you very much,

Marty would try to fire him. It had happened with Sam Peckinpah and with Lewis John Carlino—both of them gutted and discarded by the Wild Boar two weeks into the shoot.

Then, too, there was the pregnant postcard Marty had sent me in London with the simple scrawled words: "Old age and treachery will always defeat youth and Bananas."

When we got back to L.A., we began casting in earnest. Richard met with Kathleen Turner and said that their meeting was a "chemical mismatch." He met with Michael Douglas, an old friend of his, but Michael wasn't interested in doing a mystery-thriller.

We made a formal offer to Glenn Close, who wasn't a star, who'd never had a box office hit, but who, we both felt, was a brilliant actress. She accepted it but wanted to have a "discussion" with me.

We met in L.A. She was wearing a baseball jacket from *The Natural.*

"The only thing that bothers me," she said, "is that this is a revenge piece."

"What do you mean?"

"Well, she kills him at the end. It's almost like a vigilante thing, a right-wing thing."

It was the first time in my life I had ever been accused of writing a "right-wing thing" . . . I had been involved in the civil rights movement, the antiwar movement, and I tried to explain to her that it was a "self-defense thing." Jack Forrester tries to kill her at the end of the movie and she kills him in self-defense.

"But she knows he's coming to the house and takes a gun up there to wait for him."

"She doesn't use the gun until he comes at her to kill her."

"But do you think people are going to focus on this as a vigilante movie?"

"It's a mystery-thriller," I said. "I don't think they'll focus on it politically. It's a genre piece."

"Well, I know some of my friends in New York will."

"I can't help what your friends in New York will do," I said. "We're not making *The Song of Bernadette* here."

"No," she said with a half smile, "we're not."

Richard and I were both great admirers of Jeff Bridges's work and pushed Guy to make him an offer to play Jack Forrester.

"He's a great actor," Guy said. "There's no actor I admire more. I personally love to see his movies. But he's death at the box office. Anything he's in, it bombs."

We thought Jeff would be ideal casting. He could play Jack Forrester with boyish charm, innocence, and warmth. The more he played him that way, the more startling our ending would be.

"What the hell," Guy said after a while, "Glenn Close isn't a star, that's for sure. We might as well make it an all-nonstar team."

Marty Ransohoff adamantly opposed casting both Glenn and Jeff.

"Have you ever seen her sexy?" he kept saying about Glenn. "She's a matron in training. There's a love scene in this movie. Would you want to fuck her? I wouldn't want to fuck her!"

And about Jeff: "Sure, put him in a cowboy movie. Put him in a farm movie. But he's supposed to be the editor of the San Francisco newspaper! He can play a T-shirt. But he can't play a suit!"

Partly to assuage Marty, we agreed to his choice to play Sam Ransom, Teddy's private eye sidekick. Marty was an old friend of Robert Loggia, an actor known more for playing the Beverly Hills dinner circuit than for playing great parts. We felt Loggia was shopworn, "a TV face," as Richard said, but Marty wanted him, and the Craig Baumgarten Moral of the Story was that it wasn't a bad idea to try to keep Marty at bay.

"Thank God I've never done any porn films," Richard said.

For a small but significant part—a woman who had had an affair with Jack Forrester and was now testifying against him—we chose Leigh Taylor-Young, who just happened to be Guy McElwaine's most recent wife . . . the seventh or eighth, no one seemed to know for sure.

Richard and I knew there were already strains in their marriage. We were both present one night at Guy's house, sipping Jack Daniel's and talking about casting, when Leigh came in and asked Guy to sign a check.

Guy looked at the check and the bill and said, "Jesus Christ! You spent *ten thousand dollars* at Fred's?"

Richard and I sat there in pained discomfort as they went back and forth about the bill until Guy said, "Goddamn it! I can't believe this!" and signed it.

A few days before the shoot was to begin, Jeff arrived looking trimmed down and lean. He had put himself on a regimen of diuretics and vegetables and had lost twenty pounds in three weeks. And he looked just sensational, never mind Marty, in his Armani suits!

He was having trouble figuring out the part, though. As Richard and I listened to him, we realized that he was over-intellectualizing it. He was reading Scott Peck about the nature of evil.

"Just play it like you didn't do it," Richard told him. "Play it like you're innocent."

"You mean I shouldn't try to get into the psychology of it?" Jeff said.

"You're not evil," Richard said. "You're Jeff Bridges. You're a sweet man. Play it like that."

"Don't act?" Jeff smiled.

"Don't overact." Richard smiled back.

One of the early scenes shot was the lovemaking sequence between Glenn and Jeff. "She's nervous about it," Richard told me. "She's not comfortable with the nudity."

I said, "She knows there won't be any real nudity up on-screen."

Richard and I had agreed that the scene wouldn't be explicit—that less was more. Their lovemaking would be shadowed by lighting and camera angles.

"She's not comfortable with being nude just for the shoot."

"I don't blame her," I said. "I wouldn't be comfortable naked in front of a bunch of strangers and bright lights, either."

Richard closed the set and limited the number of people in the room to the essential camera and lighting people.

Marty wanted to be in there.

Glenn Close said absolutely not.

"I'm the producer of the movie," Marty said. "Nobody can tell me I can't be there during a shoot."

"She's not comfortable with you . . ." Richard began.

"I don't want to fuck her for Christ's sake," Marty raved. "She's got a fat ass. Who'd want to fuck her? I'm not gonna get any jollies looking at her fat ass. I want to make sure there's heat in the scene."

"That's *my* job," Richard said.

"You need all the help you can get," Marty said.

The issue went all the way to the top: to Guy.

Guy denied Marty's demand.

From that moment on, the Wild Boar started telling everyone at Columbia that Glenn Close looked awful and the movie was going to be a disaster. He openly criticized the dailies. He called Richard a "traffic cop." And he kept talking about Glenn Close's "Fat Ass."

Word of what Marty was saying got back to Glenn, of course, and now she began being critical of the dailies—more specifically, of how she looked . . . most specifically, about how her . . . *ass* . . . looked.

It became the Great Ass Controversy of *Jagged Edge*. Marty was urging Guy to fire Richard. Glenn was urging Guy to fire the cinematographer. Richard was being critical of Glenn's costume designer, Ann Roth, who was there because Glenn had chosen her.

And it was all because of how everyone perceived . . . Glenn's ass.

"I'm not firing anybody," Guy said. "I think her ass looks fine. I do think she could be put into some suits that don't deliberately emphasize that part of her anatomy."

It is not an exaggeration to say that everybody was at everybody's throat. Marty was angry at Richard and Glenn and Guy.

Glenn was angry at Marty and the cinematographer and at Richard—for not firing the cinematographer.

Guy and Richard were angry at the costume designer.

And Marty and Glenn were very angry at me because all I was doing was backing Richard up.

"You're destroying your own movie, Bananas," Marty railed. "All because you're so in love with your boyfriend. You're blind. Your boyfriend is destroying what you've written."

On a more sinister note, he said: "I thought maybe you'd learned your lesson with your first boyfriend [Craig Baumgarten]. Now you're just as much in love with your second one. Didn't you get the postcard I sent you in London?"

In a courtroom scene one day, I saw Glenn Close get even with Marty Ransohoff. He had brought his daughter—a gawky young woman who looked somewhat like her father—to the set. Marty was excited about having her there. He was in an unusually jovial mood and, the proud dad, introduced her to everyone.

Glenn was doing a scene in which she paces across the courtroom, making a speech to the jury. Marty and his daughter were out of camera range, watching Glenn. Marty had his arm around his daughter.

As Glenn paced across the room, she stopped dead suddenly and, on this packed set, pointed at Marty and his daughter. "I can't do this with them in here!" She was spitting her words. "They are in my line of vision! *Get them out of here!*"

Marty looked mortified. His daughter was frozen. He put his arm around her and, with their heads down as everyone stared, they left the set.

Glenn watched them leave and turned to Richard with a satisfied smile. "Are we ready now?" she said.

"The cunt!" Marty raged. "The fucking slimy cunt! She does that to me with my daughter there! She's gonna regret what she did till the day she dies!"

He knew what he wanted to do in revenge. The love scene, he told me, was terrible. It would have to be reshot.

"I'm gonna make that cunt go in there and take her clothes off," Marty Ransohoff said, "and I'm gonna be standing there watching her fat white ass and I'm gonna be fucking it with my eyes. She's gonna know it, too. She's gonna know I'm standing there, fucking her with my eyes!"

He launched a campaign. He showed everyone at Columbia the love scene. He made sure that as many people as possible at Columbia saw Glenn Close naked. He tried to convince everyone that the scene lacked "heat" and had to be reshot.

Richard and I knew what he was doing and went to Guy.

"Forget it," Guy told Marty, "the scene will not be reshot."

When the shoot ended, Richard and I felt we had a good movie. Guy was just happy that the shoot was over.

The Wild Boar said, "This was all your fault, Bananas. You and your three boyfriends, you put me into a gang bang."

Every movie mystery needs a McGuffin, a smoking gun, a clue that ties the killer inextricably to the crime.

In *Jagged Edge* it was the old typewriter that Glenn Close finds in Jeff Bridges's closet, an antique machine which as she types the phrase "he is innocent" inverts the letter T and that matches the notes the killer had sent earlier.

The idea came from my own work process. I have always used a manual typewriter. I learned to type when I was twelve on one of my father's discarded machines, using two fingers—the middle fingers of my right and left hands.

"If Marty's got fuck-you shoes," Richard Marquand once said, "then Joe's got fuck-you fingers."

But since I learned to type that way, I've been unable to use either electric typewriters or computers. I hit the keys so hard with the two fingers that I would destroy an electric typewriter or a computer in a week—besides bringing five other keys down for every one I intended to hit. Even the old manual machines I use are worn out at least once a year.

Through the years, when manual typewriters became scarce, I collected old ones at flea markets and office sales. Almost every machine I used had some sort of imbalance with the letters—either an up or a down. The old Royal I used to write my script of *Jagged Edge* had just such a natural inversion and as I typed my script, I came up with the McGuffin.

The McGuffin would be . . . *the typewriter itself.*

Not only the typewriter itself, but *the very same typewriter—the old Royal—I was using to write the script.*

I showed the old Royal to Richard at my home in Marin and he liked the look of it so much that when it came time to shoot the discovery of the McGuffin, he asked if they could use my machine itself for the scene.

I loved the poetry of it: here was an old machine that beat out a story about an old machine that leads to a killer . . . and now this old machine itself would be up on-screen.

"Please," I said to Richard, "take care of this. I've written a lot of things on it and I'm very attached to it. It's okay if it becomes a movie star, but I want it back to write other scripts with."

"What do you want it back for?" Guy said. "Reading a script on it is like spending a weekend with the Vietcong."

Richard understood the value and meaning of it. He assigned someone on the set to keep an eye on it at all times and when they finished the scene, he assigned someone to pack it carefully, swaddled in Styrofoam.

He didn't trust regular mail or Federal Express, so he sent my old Royal back by private express. A messenger took it to the airport in L.A. and a messenger waited for it in San Francisco.

But the messenger in San Francisco was told it wasn't on the plane, even though it had been put on the plane in L.A. At the last minute, he was told, it must have been rerouted somewhere.

A search was conducted.

"Nada," as Robert Loggia said in *Jagged Edge*. "Zilch. Nothing."

Instigated by Columbia Pictures, an investigation was begun by United Airlines.

Nada. Zilch. Nothing.

My old Royal was gone. The typewriter which, as far as I was concerned, was a star in the movie, had been stolen.

McElwaine, pondering his weekends with the Vietcong, said it was a benevolent act of God.

Marty said, "It wasn't a very good typewriter, and it wasn't a very good McGuffin, either. Who the fuck cares?"

As Richard and I watched the rough assembly, we felt the performances were superb. Glenn had just the right amount of vulnerability combined with strength, Jeff's boyish charm made the ending impossible to predict, and Robert Loggia was a diamond in the rough: Marty's call was right; Loggia almost stole the movie.

Marty had distanced himself from the movie, even though Richard had agreed to hire one of his sons as part of the editing team.

"It's your movie, you and your boyfriends," Marty said to me. "I never did like a ménage."

We realized the movie would be controversial when, at an early screening, during the first scene, a woman got up in the dark and started to scream.

"I'm not going to watch this exploitative piece of shit!" she yelled. "Let me out of here."

I followed her out to the lobby with Guy and some of the other Columbia executives. She was continuing her tirade.

"Who's the drunken sailor who wrote this piece of shit?"

Guy thought that was funny and pointed to me.

"He's right there," he said.

The woman started coming for me and I ducked back into the darkened theater.

. . .

We premiered the movie at the Toronto Film Festival. The two-thousand-seat theater sold out. Richard and I sat high up on the top step of the balcony and, at a certain moment near the climax, when a window unexpectedly shatters on-screen, we saw the audience practically levitate.

At that moment Richard turned to me and said, "We've got a hit movie."

The next day festival goers picked *Jagged Edge* as the festival's "audience favorite."

Our next stop was at the Mill Valley Film Festival on my home turf, in Marin County. Glenn had agreed to fly in—she had not yet seen the picture.

I also flew my father in from Cleveland. I warned him before the screening: Glenn, we were hearing, was still very nervous about the picture's ending. She was, she was telling Columbia, unsure about doing any publicity for it. She had a movie called *Maxie* scheduled to come out two weeks before *Jagged Edge* and, from what we were hearing, she was putting all of her efforts behind *Maxie*.

"So," I said to my father, "whatever you do, don't say anything to her about 'revenge' or 'vigilantes.' "

Glenn sat next to me at the theater in Mill Valley. Sitting near her was Craig Baumgarten, whom Richard and I had invited to the festival. Still unable to find a job, Craig had been our ally from the beginning and we wanted him here now at the end.

Richard and I said a few words to the audience, introduced Glenn and Craig, and then sat down to watch it with them. The response was identical to the one in Toronto. They literally jumped out of their seats, stayed through the final credits, and applauded for a full minute.

When the applause ended, I turned to Glenn and asked, "What did you think?" Richard, a few seats away, was intensely watching our conversation.

"I thought my ass was too big," Glenn said.

I felt more than I saw Richard put his head in his hands and start to giggle.

That's all Glenn said. Period. Not a word about her performance, the others' performances, or the movie itself. I suddenly realized she had her head up her ass.

At dinner afterward, I introduced her to my father, who went through the elaborate Hungarian hand-kissing routine I had seen him perform too many times through the years.

But Glenn was charmed. I heard the two of them talk about the years I spent in the refugee camps and then I heard my father, at his most charming, say: "You were wonderful. You were unbelievable. With your hair—your hair wet and then the gun . . ."

I was agape at what I was hearing my father saying and I turned to him as he finished the thought: "*You were an avenging angel!*"

"A what?" Glenn said. Her smile was frozen and her mouth was open.

"*Avenging angel!*" my father repeated, very loudly this time so others could hear it.

"Did you think so?" Glenn said, her smile gone.

"Absolutely," my father said.

"Avenging angel," Richard repeated, a smile on his face, "well I guess that pretty well says it, doesn't it?"

He started to laugh and reached for his glass of champagne.

It was no surprise to us then that Glenn informed Columbia that due to her other movie, *Maxie,* she would do little publicity for *Jagged Edge.*

We watched her do every big and piddling TV show as *Maxie* came out and had mixed feelings when it died a mean box office death its first weekend.

We were concerned about what effect the death of one Glenn Close movie would have on another one opening right behind it.

Marty's opinion was not a surprise.

"She sucks, that's what it says. The public doesn't want to see her. We'll die the way *Maxie* died."

"A lot of people saw her on a lot of those shows," Guy said. "Maybe they like her but didn't like *Maxie.*"

"If they like her they would have gone to see *Maxie,*" Marty replied.

The weekend *Jagged Edge* opened, the numbers were flat—a little better than *Maxie,* but not much. The reviews, for the most part, were dismissive and negative. The *New York Times* took care of us in about seven paragraphs.

And then, suddenly, it was like *Flashdance* all over again—the second weekend, the numbers jumped up, miraculously up—and *Jagged Edge* was the number one movie in America.

The third weekend the numbers were up again. We stayed number one for four weeks and played for six months.

Once again, I had an "audience movie," a movie that defied the critics and spread solely on word of mouth. And it was the ending that Frank Price wanted to change so ferociously that seemed to startle people the most.

Siskel and Ebert, reviewing the movie late, spun off an entirely different phenomenon. Once the ski mask came off the killer at the end, they said, it wasn't clear to them who the killer really was—was it Jeff? Or was it actor Marshall Colt, who played the part of the red-herring tennis pro, Bobby Slade.

The exhibitors began reporting that people were going back to see it a second or third time just to be sure that it was Jeff when the mask came off.

Various lawyers' groups began attacking the movie for "inaccuracy," claiming that lawyers never had affairs with clients—a charge the public found absurd.

Robert Loggia, meanwhile, on his way to an Oscar nomination, was claiming that he had improvised all of his funny lines, hoping that if producers didn't want to hire him for his face, maybe they'd hire him for his wit. (If any did, they must have been disappointed.)

And a knife shop in Saginaw, Michigan, sued us, claiming that we'd gotten the title of the movie from the name of their shop: the Jagged Edge.

A very nervous Columbia lawyer asked me, "Have you ever been in Saginaw, Michigan?"

I told him that, thankfully, I had not.

"Did you ever buy a knife from a store called the Jagged Edge and use either a credit card or a check?"

I told him that, thankfully, I had never bought anything from any shop in Saginaw, Michigan.

While Richard and I reveled in the fact that we had a hit movie, Marty Ransohoff and Frank Price were unyielding.

"We got lucky," Marty was telling people, "the script overcame the acting and the direction."

And Frank was saying, "If they would have used my ending, they would have done thirty million dollars more. Their ending cost them thirty million dollars."

"*You're a screenwriter,*" my lawyer, Barry Hirsch, said to me, "but you're a star."

I had had two big hit movies, now.

"I'm a screenwriter," I said, "*screenwriters aren't stars.*"

"You are," he said. "You need a PR person."

"What for?"

"To deal with the interviews you're doing."

"I'm doing them," I said, "what more is there to it?"

"Plenty," he said.

He took me to lunch with Pat Kingsley, the most successful PR woman in town. She represented a lot of stars, including Jessica Lange and Julia Roberts, but she'd never represented any screenwriters.

"What can you do for me that I'm not doing for myself?" I asked.

"I can get you profiles in the *New York Times* and in the big magazines," she said.

"I'm doing those already."

"I can pick the writers," she said.

"*You can pick the writers?*"

I was astounded. I was under the impression that editors picked writers to do stories. "How can you do that?"

"I can pick a writer that I know will be friendly to you."

"How?"

"They all want interviews with my *other* star clients. I can tell them they can get someone like Jessica or Julia *if* they interview you. They know that if they write a negative profile of you, they'll never get Jessica or Julia."

"The magazines let you do that? Pick the writer?"

"Sure. They want Julia or Jessica on their covers. Julia and Jessica sell magazines. The magazine editors want to be very nice to me."

"What if a writer lies to you and stabs me in the back?"

"Impossible. He'll never get interviews with any of my other clients. He won't be able to make a living."

"I guess that's why I see so many star profile puff pieces," I said.

She laughed and said, "I can do something else for you, too. In some cases I can get you the story before it gets to the editors. If you don't like something in it, we can change it or take it out."

"You mean I can edit the guy's story?"

"Yes," she said. "Officially he can say he sent it to me and I sent it to you just to make sure your quotes are accurate. It's all done in the interest of journalistic accuracy."

"Don't the writers care about the fact that they are being censored by the people they're writing about?"

I was curious. I was a former journalist who had fought an editor sometimes if he wanted to change *punctuation marks* in my story.

"No," she said, "they care about getting access to big stars. The better access they have to big stars, the more money they'll make."

"I guess they don't have a real strong sense of artistic integrity," I said, laughing.

Pat Kingsley laughed with me. "Not yet," she said. "They all want to be screenwriters. They have scripts they leave with my clients during interviews. What they really want to do is direct. Then they'll develop some artistic integrity."

I was going to sign up with her but not long after our lunch I had an ugly public disagreement with Michael Ovitz, the most powerful agent in town, whose agency, CAA, represented most of Pat Kingsley's clients.

I ran into Sean Connery at the Warner Brothers commissary. A studio executive introduced us. He was wearing a safari jacket, jeans, and sandals. We shook hands.

He looked me up and down. I was wearing a red Cleveland Indians T-shirt, jeans, and mud-splattered tennis shoes.

"Do you act?" he asked.

"I write," I said.

"You should act," he said, smiled, and walked away.

I worried that maybe he'd read one of my scripts.

. . .

There is no better feeling than sharing a hit movie with a director who is your friend (and no worse feeling than sharing a disaster with a director who is your friend: Norman Jewison and I had never even had one phone conversation since *F.I.S.T.*).

But Richard and I raged on together as our movie raged on week after week at the box office. We took innumerable meetings as a team.

"I'm only directing it if Joe's writing it," he told studio heads.

"I'm only writing it if Richard's directing it," I told producers.

One memorable evening at Morton's, in the company of three studio executives trying to involve us in a project, we drank six bottles of Cristal champagne . . . then moved to the El Padrino Room of the Beverly Wilshire, where I was staying, and started on the cognac.

John Madden and Howard Cosell, the TV football announcers, were at a nearby table and for a while we carried on with them—they had both seen *Jagged Edge* and were full of questions.

"Jeez, Glenn Close was great," Madden said.

"You didn't think her bum was too big?" Richard asked, his eyes merry.

"Her what?" Madden asked.

"Her ass," Cosell translated.

"Christ no," Madden said, "I thought she was great."

And then, after they left, we were joined by two young women who had been sitting at the bar and had overheard some of the conversation. They were, naturally, would-be actress-models and they had, naturally, loved all of my movies and Richard's.

Richard left with one of them for more drinks in his suite at the Westwood Marquis and I took the other one upstairs for drinks in my suite. The suites, naturally, were compliments of Columbia Pictures.

At seven o'clock the next morning, Richard called me.

"Can you get up here right away?" he said. "I need help."

I raced over to his hotel and banged on his door, unprepared for what I saw when he opened it. He was stark naked. His hands were handcuffed behind his back. He had an erection.

I started to laugh.

"This isn't funny," he said.

I said, "*Oh yes it is!*"

"I fell asleep," he said. "When I woke up, she was gone. It took me a half hour to figure out how to call you. Have you ever tried making a phone call with your hands handcuffed behind you?"

"You dumb fuck," I said, "you didn't know her well enough to let her handcuff you."

"Please don't be judgmental," Richard said.

"Where's the key?" I said.

"I'm afraid I don't know," Richard said. "I don't see it anywhere. I think she took it. I think she took my wallet and my watch, too."

"How come you've got a hard-on?" I said. "Does this situation turn you on?"

"I *always* have a hard-on when I wake up," Richard said. "*Always.*"

"It must come with being a director," I said.

"Will you just shut the fuck up and help me look for the damn key?" Richard said.

We looked everywhere. The key was gone.

"What do we do now?" Richard said, pacing around the suite stark naked, his hands handcuffed behind him, his penis still standing at attention.

I said, "I'm stumped."

He said, "You're the damn screenwriter. Figure something out!"

I put his pants on for him, then his shoes and socks. I called hotel security and said we needed help.

Two security guys came up and I told them who we were and what we did for a living and said we'd been trying to act out a scene in my script where a man has to free himself of handcuffs.

The damn prop department, I said, had given us real handcuffs accidentally and of course we didn't have a key.

The security guys stared at us, glanced at each other, and one of them said, "*Oh—kay.*"

They first tried to pick the lock on the cuffs with a toothpick and then with the innards of a ballpoint pen. Then they called hotel engineering.

"Handcuffs," I heard one of the security guys tell hotel engineering. "That's what I said. *Handcuffs.*"

Two men from engineering came up. I saw them try to hide their smiles.

I didn't even want to think about what they were thinking.

They tried to pick the lock on the handcuffs with various pliers. No luck.

"These are real high-quality cuffs," one of the engineering guys said admiringly.

"Can't you call your prop department at the studio?" one of the security guys said. "Maybe they've got the key for it."

"It's Saturday," I said quickly, "the prop people are closed Saturday."

Richard said, "Christ, can't you just saw the bloody things off?"

"No, sir," one of the engineers said. "Like I said—these are real high-quality cuffs you got here."

"*Fuck me!*" Richard said.

"Excuse me?" one of the engineers said.

"It's a Brit expression," I said.

"Oh," the engineer said, eyeing me oddly.

"What do we do?" I asked.

"We'll have to call a locksmith," one of the security guys said.

"It's Saturday, it's early," the other security guy said.

"*Fuck me again!*" Richard said.

Three hours later, a locksmith took Richard's cuffs off.

The minute they were off, Richard was in excruciating pain. With the locksmith, the engineers, and the hotel security guys standing there, I called the hotel doctor. He said that Richard had strained his back muscles by being handcuffed for so long.

He was flying back to England and I offered to drop him at the airport. He thanked me and asked that we stop on Sunset Boulevard for a moment first.

"Why?" I said.

"You'll see."

"Does it have anything to do with the handcuffs?"

"You truly are a writer," Richard said. "No director should ever have a writer for a friend."

I was driving down Sunset when he suddenly told me to stop.

Across from us was a gigantic billboard of *Jagged Edge*. We looked at it.

Richard said, "I just wanted to see it again."

Six months later, the movie was still playing in New York, and one night Richard and I, there for different reasons, had dinner and a couple of drinks and as we were walking down Madison Avenue, we saw the big lighted-up marquee for *Jagged Edge* and said, what the hell, let's go see it.

They were sold out. We told the ticket taker who we were and she didn't believe us.

We asked her to summon the manager. We pointed to our names on the poster and the manager asked to see our IDs.

We showed them to him and he stared at us and said, "I don't believe you guys, okay? If you don't get the hell outta here, I'm gonna call the cops."

Richard and I stumbled down Madison Avenue, arm in arm, howling at the moon.

Many years later, when there was a hip-hop group called Jagged Edge making hit records, my son Steve told me how much he admired my title.

"There are a lot of titles for movies that you forget, Pops," Steve said. "But you remember *Jagged Edge*. How did you come up with it?"

My policy with my kids is to never lie to them. Steve's question was a test of my policy.

"Well," I finally said, "I *didn't* come up with it."

He said, "What?"

"My title, if you can believe it, was—*Hearts of Fire*. The studio hated it and decided to change it."

"But then who came up with *Jagged Edge*?" Steve asked.

"They assigned some secretary at the studio to go through my script letter by letter, word by word in the effort to come up with another title. The secretary found 'jagged edge' in my description of the murder weapon: 'a knife with a jagged edge.' "

Steve smiled. "It's *your* title then," he said, "it was in *your* script. You just didn't know you had it."

My children love me.

Even though Richard Marquand and I both hated *Hearts of Fire* as the title of *Jagged Edge*, we still liked the sound of it.

We changed the title of the next movie we did together—*American Rocker*—to *Hearts of Fire*.

CHAPTER 8

It's Only a Movie

CARL

I had me eight ice-cold Budweiser beers. I'm probably still drunk.
But you know what? Everything else is so damn cockeyed . . . to
hold on to your balance, I figure you gotta get just as cockeyed.

Foreplay, unproduced

Ben Myron, my wannabe producer friend from the Book Depot in Mill Valley, had been knocking on every door in Hollywood with my unsold spec script *Checking Out* in hand for two years.

All the doors shut in his face, and then one of them was suddenly open a crack.

George Harrison, the Beatle, owned a small film company called Handmade. George liked *Checking Out* and said he had a director in mind who was the "flavor of the month."

David Leland was the flavor of the month. He had just written and directed a movie which whiz-banged the film festivals: *Wish You Were Here,* starring a bright English actress named Emily Lloyd. David, who had worked up through English television, was suddenly being offered everything in town.

I was more than pleased, then, when he read *Checking Out,* the story of a suburban husband and father who becomes obsessed with the notion that he is dying.

It was a dark comedy, which came from that very personal moment in my life when, at the age of thirty-three, after a lifetime of good health, I woke up one morning thinking that my heart was about to blow out of my chest like the *Alien,* called the paramedics, was ambulanced to a hospital, and told that my heart was fine, but that I had to stop smoking and drinking black coffee.

I sat down with David Leland in a suite at the Beverly Hilton with a pool table and a living room Jacuzzi compliments of Handmade and I said, "David, I own this script. It's very personal for me. I want to know one thing. Please tell me the truth. You're a writer-director. Are you going to change this script?"

David Leland, a pleasant, clear-eyed young Brit, looked me right in the eye and said, "Not one word."

We shook hands. I agreed to sell the script to Handmade, with David directing it and Ben Myron producing; and talked Jeff Daniels into starring in it.

David started shooting. He called a couple of times a week to tell me everything was playing wonderfully. He came up on a weekend and amazed Steve and Suzi. David was double-jointed. He made magic tricks with his fingers.

He called and asked me to come down to see a rough assembly.

I stared, my jaw slack. *Not one word would he change, he had said. Everything was playing wonderfully, he had said.*

He'd lied. He'd looked me right in the eye and lied . . . because there were new subplots I was seeing on-screen and new characters who weren't in my script.

Worse, much worse, tragically worse: the new characters he had created were buffoon-like and had clichéd stereotypical Jewish names. David Leland had managed to create a movie which in my opinion was anti-Semitic.

I was in utter and absolute disbelief. *My name* was going to go on an anti-Semitic movie?

I wrote Warner Brothers, the distributor, a letter demanding that my name be taken off and demanding that the anti-Semitism be cut out of the movie. I carboned my agents, my lawyers, Handmade, George Harrison—anyone I knew who was involved in the production.

David Leland took most of what I was objecting to out and I put my name back on.

The movie was minimally distributed and bombed. The night it opened in San Francisco, there were eight people in the theater.

David Leland, double-jointed flavor of the month, went back to England.

Sylvester Stallone called to tell me how much he had liked *Jagged Edge.* He also said he wanted to do me a favor.

"I owe you one," he said.

Well, I thought, at least he doesn't have short-term memory loss.

He was directing a movie called *Staying Alive,* he explained, with John Travolta. It was the sequel to *Saturday Night Fever.* They were halfway through the shoot and he and John were having differences over the script. He needed, he said, a fast rewrite. A two-week rewrite and "I can get you $500,000."

"I owe you one," he said again.

I told him that I had no interest in doing a rewrite, and was thinking about what my next original screenplay would be.

"Come on down," he said, "we'll talk on the set. We'll have dinner. We'll put you up in the Presidential Suite of the Wilshire, how's that? We're friends. Friends help each other."

Well, okay, I thought, so now we were *friends.*

I had called him a thief and he had said he'd been burgling my house and he'd had a picture taken of himself hitting a punching bag with my name on it . . . but now we were *friends.*

I flew down the next day to speak to him.

We met in Sly's trailer. We gave each other hugs. He badmouthed Norman Jewison, and John Travolta walked into the trailer. He was wearing a black motorcycle jacket and had the emaciated look that stars often do during shooting. He struck me as a very earnest and nice . . . boy. Say whatever you want about Sly Stallone, he was no boy.

He and John started talking about the script. Sly wanted to do one thing with the script and John wanted to do another. Sly kept talking about emphasizing Tony Manero's "cool" and John kept talking about his "vulnerability." They were on different planets and were interested in writing different scripts.

"What do you think?" Sly asked me.

"I think you guys have a real problem here," I said, "and you've gotta work it out."

"You'll help us work it out," Sly said.

"Not me, guys," I said to them.

"Come on," Sly said, "you can do this."

"No, I can't," I said.

For the first time I saw Travolta smile.

"Sure you can," Sly said, "we'll talk it through today, we'll have dinner tonight, I got you the Presidential Suite at the Wilshire, we'll finish up tomorrow."

I started to laugh. Both of them watched me. John kept smiling; Sly looked puzzled.

"Sly," I said, "you fucked me once on *F.I.S.T.* What do you want to fuck me again for now that we're friends?"

Then John started to laugh, too, and after a moment so did Sly.

"Maybe you're right," Sly said. I was out of there.

I used cabs in L.A. whenever I commuted from Marin for meetings. The cabbies asked me what I did for a living and I told them the truth: I was a screenwriter.

And I discovered that most of the cabbies in L.A., including the Russians, were either writing a screenplay or had written one which they wanted me to read, co-write, or at least sell for them.

Scripts were dropped off with the concierge of my hotel. Cabbies prowled the lobby waiting for me as I got off the elevator. A Russian cabbie showed up in the bar of the hotel where he'd dropped me off—showed up with his wife, his infant daughter, his mother-in-law, and his script, written in a language which I discovered to be neither Russian nor English.

After a while, whenever a cabbie in L.A. asked me what I did, I said, "*This, that, or the other, you know.*" And one cabbie smiled and said, "What does that mean—criminal activity?"

But I still had a problem with those cabbies who either dropped me off or picked me up at studios, so I started using limousines on my trips—the cost didn't matter, the studio was picking it up anyway.

My son Steve was eleven years old. We did everything together—played catch together, swam together, collected baseball cards together, and watched batting practice at the Oakland Coliseum in the bleachers together. We even caught foul balls at the ballpark together.

I started thinking about the special closeness there is between fathers and sons at this age in a boy's life and it led me to write a script about a little boy whose dad dies unexpectedly and he suddenly has to cope with the world alone.

I sent the little boy whose dad dies, Obie, off on an adventure with a little black kid whom he meets, Scam. The script, I knew, was really a very personal gift to Steve. Obie was Steve—in appearance, shyness, and style, right down to the vernacular that skateboarding kids of his age used, words like "Sau-sage!" when they got excited about something.

I sent the script down to my agent and we decided to send it out to auction. Our expectations weren't high. This was a little arty piece about two little kids becoming friends and discovering the world. As my agent pointed out, "There aren't even any women in it."

To our surprise, *Big Shots* captured the interest of both Twentieth Century Fox, headed by Barry Diller and the producer Larry Gordon, and Lorimar, headed by Merv Adelson and Lee Rich. My old ally Craig Baumgarten had found a job there as head of production.

Fox and Lorimar bid against each other for the script and, at the end of the day, Lorimar bought it for $1.25 million. It was a new record high for a spec script in Hollywood. (Jim Morgan and I had set the previous high six years ago when *City Hall* sold for $500,000.)

I was amazed. The script had been a labor of love with seemingly noncommercial qualities and now a studio had paid a fortune for it.

Lorimar needed "product" and Craig was anxious to show his new bosses that he could put a movie together, so *Big Shots* suddenly became Lorimar's top priority. He made it his twenty-four-hour obsession to find an A-list director—someone whose attachment to the project would send a message to the town that Lorimar, with Craig Baumgarten as the head of production, was a "player."

It was as important for Craig to find a top director as it was for Lorimar. He had had some difficulty finding a job after his porn film ouster from Columbia. After his firing hit the papers, everyone in town had quickly rented a tape.

Ivan Reitman was the A-list director he found. He was about as A-list as you could get—the director of *Ghostbusters*, of *Meatballs* and *Stripes* and *Legal Eagles*, although no one liked to talk about *Legal Eagles*. The movie, with Redford and Debra Winger, had been such a disaster that Winger had threatened to leave CAA, claiming that she'd been snookered into taking the part because the agency was more interested in putting together a "package" than considering her best interest.

With great press fanfare, Lorimar announced that Ivan Reitman would direct *Big Shots*.

Alas, an hour after meeting him, I knew that wasn't true. His "attachment" was for Lorimar's press release, but not for my screenplay.

Yes, there was a chance that he'd direct it, Reitman allowed, but he would probably produce it. He had a production company that he was intent on making an entity of its own, producing not just movies that he directed.

I found Ivan Reitman, the directing king of big-budget Hollywood comedies, to be one of the most humorless men I'd ever met. Getting a laugh out of him was like getting a reaction out of Frank Price. The man was downright dour—in his dress (all black), in his style (nervous, angst-ridden), in his attitude (he seemed to *drag* himself around).

He would read a scene in the script and say "That's funny" deadpan, straight-faced, as though he were saying "I'm dying."

"Why does the kid say 'sausage' all the time?" Ivan asked me. He seemed morose, depressed, almost prosecutorial as he asked the question.

"I don't know. My boy says it all the time and his friends say it all the time. It's just a kid thing, I think."

"But why '*sausage*'? People don't eat much sausage anymore."

"They don't?"

"It's not healthy for you," Ivan Reitman said gravely. He paused a moment and looked out his window. "Maybe it has some significance," he said.

"*Sausage?*"

"Yes."

"Like what?"

"I don't know," Ivan Reitman said, carefully choosing his words, looking ponderous and suspicious. "But it must have significance."

"I'll ask my boy," I said.

The next time we met, he brought it up right away.

"Did you ask your boy about 'sausage'?"

It was like he was trying to unearth the identity of Deep Throat.

"I did."

"And?"

"He said it was just a word that all his friends use."

He nodded.

I knew the explanation wasn't good enough for him. I almost felt like he was waiting for me to *confess* something.

I tried to make him understand it—judging from the seriousness of his expression, the stakes were awfully high here.

"It's a kid thing, you know? Like when we were kids, we'd use certain words and phrases all the time because they were cool."

"Like what?" Ivan Reitman grilled.

"I don't know." I laughed.

I stopped laughing. *He* wasn't laughing. And he didn't seem to like the fact that *I* was laughing.

"Like—'It's no big thing.' "

"It's no big thing?" He seemed to be dissecting the words.

"Yeah."

"It's no big thing?"

He didn't like what he was dissecting.

"I've never used that phrase," he said.

"Well, I did, all the time."

"You did?"

"Yeah."

Ivan Reitman looked at me for five seconds, his face stony, and shook his head.

" 'Sausage,' " he said. " 'Sausage.' I don't think that's cool."

"The *kids* think it's cool."

He stared at me for another ten seconds and said nothing.

When I saw Craig I said, "This guy is *weird*. He's got some thing with 'sausage.' "

"He eats a lot of sushi," Craig said.

"No," I said, "with the word. With the word '*sausage*.' In the script. He keeps asking me about it."

"Change it," Craig said. "Use 'sushi' instead. He'll like that."

"I can't do that," I said. "The kids don't say 'sushi,' they say 'sausage.' "

"I'll bet the kids in Beverly Hills say 'sushi.' "

"We're not making this movie for the kids in Beverly Hills."

"Well, we're not excluding kids in Beverly Hills, are we?"

"Don't you think that kids in Cleveland, for example, will relate to 'sausage' better than 'sushi'?"

"I don't know," Craig said, "that's a market research question."

The director that Craig and Ivan agreed on was Bob Mandel. In his thirties, thin, Mandel was as grave as Ivan but his super-seriousness was offset by a jittery, nervous twitchiness.

If Reitman's expression read "We're all dying," then Bob Mandel could have been an underpaid professional mourner. Mandel, a child prodigy with the violin, had directed a hit movie, *F/X*—a movie, I noted, with no kids in it.

I looked at his other movies and realized that no movie that he had ever directed had kids as stars in it. It also became quickly apparent to me that while Bob Mandel was always nervous, being around Ivan Reitman made him *very* nervous. Maybe it was the fact that Mandel would be working for another director, maybe it was Ivan's leaden prosecutorial style, but when Bob was around Ivan, he didn't just twitch . . . he nearly *twittered* twitching.

At our final script meeting, Ivan said, "I've given this a lot of thought." He stopped and gave whatever it was he had given a lot of thought to . . . even more thought. "Take the 'sausages' out."

"What do you suggest I replace the sausages with?"

"Nothing." Ivan Reitman said, "Just take them out. Nobody will get it."

"I think it's funny," Bob Mandel said.

Ivan glared at him. "I don't."

"Fine," Bob Mandel said, looking away, his hands skittery on the table, his crossed legs tap-tapping the air.

"Maybe Craig should market-research it," I said.

Ivan thought about that. He even closed his eyes a few seconds to think about it.

"No," he said.

Lorimar launched a nationwide hunt for kids to play Obie and Scam. As the search went on, Gerri came by Ivan's office one day with Steve and Suzi to pick me up.

Ivan kept staring at Steve, and before we left, asked to speak to me alone a moment.

"He'd be perfect as Obie," Ivan said.

"Steve *is* Obie," I said. "Every nuance of Obie is Steve."

"Let's cast him," Ivan said.

"No way."

"He'd be great in it."

"He's a kid. He's a normal, well-adjusted, happy kid who lives in Marin County, rides his skateboard, and collects baseball cards. I'm not going to mess his life up by putting him into a movie."

"We'd have tutors on the set," Ivan said.

"Give me a break," I said.

"You're really that against it?"

"Duh!" I said.

"What?"

" 'Duh!' It's what kids in Marin say when they want to say 'No shit.' "

"*Duh!*" Ivan Reitman said. "*Duh!* I like that. *Duh!* Put it in the script."

On our way out, he said to Steve: "Why do you say 'sausage'?"

Steve looked at me.

I nodded and then he looked at Ivan.

"I don't know," Steve said.

"But you say it?"

Steve nodded.

"Say it for me."

Steve's look to me said: Dad, who is this crazy guy and why do I have to be talking to him?

Steve said, "*Saw-sage!*"

Ivan stood there a moment, never cracked a smile, and said, "I still don't get it."

Lorimar found two very talented child actors to play Obie and Scam and I went down to the set with Gerri and Steve and Suzi on the last day of the shoot. We took some pictures with our kids and the two actors and as the pictures were being taken, the kid who played Scam said to me—"Man, this is the most fun I've had all the way through the shoot."

I thought to myself: If *this* is the most fun you've had, we're all in trouble here.

When I saw the rough cut, I knew we were in big trouble. There was no zip between the kids. In a movie that was about the relationship, the kids were flat and seemed to be going through the motions.

The movie came out and failed miserably. I saw it on the Friday night it opened, with Gerri and Steve and Suzi at the Montecito Theatre in San Rafael. In a theater that held four hundred people, there were twelve people there—including the four of us. Of the other eight, four walked out during the movie.

Afterward, in the parking lot, trying to soothe our depression, I said, "Well, the hell with it, let's go get a pizza."

Steve turned to me with a big smile, his braces gleaming, and said: "*Saw-sage!*"

. . .

Thanks to Ivan Reitman, Dustin Hoffman and I were having a story meeting at a table on the terrace by the pool of the Westwood Marquis Hotel.

Ivan was there with us telling us his idea of a hit movie: Rip Van Winkle as a Vietnam vet, set free thirty years after the war.

Three attractive young women came to the patio and sat at the table next to ours. They recognized Dusty and started whispering excitedly to each other.

Dusty saw them recognize him, turned halfway their way, unbuttoned the top three buttons of his shirt, and lounged back on the chair sexily.

I turned halfway to them, too, unbuttoned the top three buttons of *my* shirt, lounged back on the chair sexily, and smiled into Dusty's eyes.

After our meeting, Dusty told Ivan he had another writer in mind to write the Rip Van Winkle story.

I had an idea for a new script and I called Guy to tell him about it. He told me his days at Columbia were numbered. Of some fifteen movies that he had put into production, only one—*Jagged Edge*—turned out to be a hit.

That was somehow emblematic, considering our friendship, but it wasn't good enough as far as his production record was concerned.

I asked him what he was going to do and he said he thought he was going to go into business with Jerry Weintraub, whose *Karate Kid* movies had made him one of the most successful producers in Hollywood. He suggested I take my idea to Jerry, who had just been made the new head of United Artists.

My idea came from walking around Marin County's playgrounds with Steve. I kept seeing racial epithets like "*Kikes!*" and "*Fuck the Niggers!*" and "*Die Nigger Die!*" scrawled into benches and graffitied onto playground walls.

And Marin County was one of the liberal bastions of California, a place where liberal left-leaning candidates usually got 70 to 80 percent of the vote. I wondered what was going on in the rest of the country.

I had been involved in the civil rights movement as a journalist. I had even found myself one sunny day in Philadelphia, Mississippi, with a shotgun pressed against my stomach. It was held by a deputy sheriff named Cecil Price who had been indicted for the killings of the civil rights workers Goodman, Chaney, and Schwerner. I was there to try to interview Deputy Price about the charges and his response was to stick the shotgun into my belly across an office counter and tell me to "get your ass out of Neshoba County."

Two sheriff's cars had followed me to the county line.

Now, many years later, I thought we had put that kind of ugliness behind us. But the newspapers were saying that groups of neo-Nazis, styling themselves as American patriots, were robbing armored cars and killing people in a guerrilla terrorist movement aimed, ultimately, at toppling the American government. They had even murdered a liberal talk show host in Denver.

My idea was to write a script which would show us the insides of this move-ment. I hoped that by putting it up on-screen, I would draw attention to the dangers it posed and that the attention would force a crackdown by the govern-ment and the populace.

I loved America, felt a chill go down my back when returning from abroad or hearing the national anthem, and felt that my involvement in the antiwar and civil rights movements had helped make the country I loved a better place.

I called Jerry Weintraub, whom I'd briefly met, and told him that I wanted to talk to him about what I thought would be an important script. He sent his driver to pick me up and thirty seconds after I told him what I had in mind, he said, "Let's do it. It's a great movie."

I asked him who the executive at UA would be in charge of the project and he told me it would be Robert Lawrence, newly hired at UA, the Hall Mouse Who Went to Heaven, the executive who queered *Jagged Edge* with Fonda, the executive whose knees I'd threatened to break.

I told Jerry that Robert Lawrence would be unacceptable to me and told him why.

He picked the phone up, said, "Get in here right away," and within moments a very pale Robert Lawrence was standing there as Jerry said to him, "I'm making a deal with Joe. If you fuck with Joe . . . if you get in Joe's way in any way, if you get near this project in any way, I'm gonna throw you out this fucking window."

He then dismissed Lawrence (whose knees, I thought, seemed to be shak-ing), walked me to the elevator, and his chauffeur drove me back to my hotel.

My phone rang immediately when I got back to the room.

"I want to get you together with a producer, he just called me with the same idea. Do you know Irwin Winkler?" Jerry Weintraub said.

I didn't know him, but I would have to have been deaf, dumb, and blind not to know about him. He was one of the most successful producers in Hollywood. He had produced the *Rocky* movies and had even won an Academy Award for Best Picture. He had produced *Raging Bull; New York, New York;* and *'Round Midnight*. His reputation was that he was smart, shrewd, and had great taste.

Irwin and I clicked instantly. There was a special communication between us. As I began to talk about what I had in mind with the script, he was almost finishing my sentences for me.

A poor kid, he had worked his way up. He had begun as a hired "laugher" for live TV shows and had then become an agent, representing Jackie Mason in days when he and his wife were so poor that Irwin had to take his agent's cut at the door so they'd have something to eat. He had been married to the same woman for thirty years and they had three grown sons.

He had made so much money with the *Rocky* movies that he didn't need to do anything anymore. He was probably the most selective producer in town. He had very close relationships with people like Martin Scorsese and

Robert De Niro and CAA agent Ron Meyer, the number two man to Michael Ovitz, whose agency was now representing me. Irwin was close to Ovitz as well—two of his sons had served internships at CAA.

We found that we agreed on most things. We both were voracious readers and we both liked sports. We had a great many things in common— backgrounds, kids, liberal political beliefs. I liked his style, his sense of humor, and his sensitivity. There was a shrewdness and a toughness to him, sure, but there was great gentleness as well. He spent much of his time in Paris with Margo, his wife. He wanted to keep his horizons broad and stayed mostly away from the Hollywood party circuit.

We started to talk about a director who'd be good for this project and I mentioned my good friend Richard Marquand. Irwin had liked *Jagged Edge* and suggested we meet with him. I told Richard about the project and he jumped at it.

But when I told him about Irwin Winkler producing it, he jumped back. "He's a very powerful producer, Squire," Richard said.

I agreed that he was, but told Richard my impression of Irwin.

"He sounds wonderful," Richard said, "but I have no intention of working with him."

I didn't understand what he was saying.

"One Marty Ransohoff is enough for a lifetime," Richard said.

"Irwin's no Ransohoff."

"No, he's worse," Richard said, "he's more powerful than Marty is."

I told Irwin what Richard had said and Irwin smiled.

"Well," he said, "I like working with strong people. If I intimidate him before we've even met, he's probably not the right person for me to work with."

When Richard heard who was going to direct the movie instead of him, even he was impressed.

So was I.

Costa-Gavras, Konstantinos Gavras, at the age of fifty-three, was one of the world's most respected directors. Born in Greece, he went to Paris when he was eighteen, graduating three years later from the Sorbonne with a degree in literature. He then studied filmmaking in Paris and after apprenticing to René Clair and Jacques Demy, he debuted with a classic suspense-thriller, *The Sleeping Car Murders.*

He followed it up with one of the most revered films in history, *Z,* a blistering, dazzling indictment of the Greek junta. He followed *Z* with two other hardhitting political thrillers—*The Confession* and *State of Siege.*

His most recent film was the CIA exposé *Missing,* which had garnered a flock of Oscar nominations.

Costa, I found, as we began to talk about the script I had in mind, was a lowkey, down-to-earth, gentle man with a passion for exposing political excess. He knew in his heart, probably from personal experience as a boy in Greece, that power corrupts and that absolute power corrupts absolutely.

He was a left-leaning liberal but most important he was a great and practicing humanist . . . unafraid, for example, of going after the left in a movie like *The Confession*. He also fervently believed that you could do a movie about a political subject that at the same time could be entertaining.

That's how he felt about the movie we would ultimately call *Betrayed*—its social impact, he felt, could be enormous: by calling attention to this new, burgeoning neo-Nazism in the American West, we would be doing something socially constructive.

At the same time, he felt that the piece's underlying themes—rugged individualism and the American cowboy myth perverted into poisonous racism and anti-Semitism—would make for exciting drama.

The creative mix among the three of us was superb. Our discussions were egoless and stimulating. References were more literary than filmic. The sessions were fun. We laughed a lot and told a lot of stories.

"I am not a writer," Costa said. "I am a director. I will not tell you what to write. I will try to direct as best as possible what it is that you have written."

"I'm not a director." Irwin smiled at Costa. "I won't tell you how to direct. I'll try to make your job as easy as possible."

I almost felt off-balance with this good-natured camaraderie.

Was it possible that this was how movies could be made? Without Wild Boarishness? Without somebody twitching all over the place? Without backstabbing and ego?

"Go write your script," Irwin said.

"Write it with passion," Costa said.

On the way out, Costa asked me if I remembered the time he had called me nearly ten years ago.

I remembered very well. It was in the months after I had finished *F.I.S.T.* A man who spoke with a very thick accent whose name I had difficulty understanding said that he had read my script and loved it. He said he couldn't speak English, but was taking Berlitz courses and would call me back when he had completed them.

"I finish all the courses now," Costa-Gavras said with a smile. "Now we will do our movie."

I traveled to Idaho and Montana and Wyoming, attending jamborees organized by the Aryan Nations Brotherhood in their effort to recruit new members. I posed as Joe Ezdras, a bartender from San Francisco who was looking for some answers.

Most of the people I met were not secretive about their beliefs. They were mostly blue-collar people, mostly rural, who felt that the government had become a cancerous behemoth invading their privacy and stripping them of their civil rights. They talked of destructive taxes and repossessed farms, of affirmative action denying their sons and daughters a chance, of a world where smoking had become a worse offense than drugs.

Their grievances led them to two villains: blacks and Jews. The government, they said, was a Zionist Occupation Government, ZOG, and the only way anything would change, they said, was if ZOG was brought down. Their obsession with blacks and Jews put them into a surreal and dark netherworld that encompassed and perhaps put into action the demented fantasies found in a novel called *The Turner Diaries*, in which black people were hunted down like animals and murdered.

I heard some dark and drunken ramblings about various "mud hunts" that had allegedly taken place in Idaho and Wyoming—but I was never sure whether the alleged participants were recounting reality or fantasizing.

What I found most bizarre and sometimes poignant was that most of these people discussing these ugly, heinous things led exemplary, all-American lives devoted to family and church.

Back in the Bay Area, I found a person who had once been part of a neo-Nazi group called the Order and, on the basis of my research at the jamborees and my interviews with the defector, I wrote the script.

I tried to be as realistic as possible. What I found most frightening and what I thought posed the greatest danger to society was the lethal and mind-boggling paradox: they loved their kids, they prayed every day, they had served (sometimes heroically) in the armed services, and they were capable of injuring and killing people just because they were black or Jewish.

When Costa-Gavras read the script, he said it was the best script he'd ever read. I was flattered and thrilled and when Irwin read it and said he felt the same way . . . we were ready to cast and shoot . . . I thought it was the greatest compliment ever paid to my screenwriting.

Costa had never been in the American Midwest, the farm country where the piece was set, and I agreed to accompany him and show him around. We went to Scottsbluff, Nebraska, where Tom Berenger, who had been quickly cast as the neo-Nazi Gary Simmons, joined us.

Tom, who was originally from Chicago, knew and got along easily with Midwesterners, and he and I introduced Costa to hog farmers and iced tea lunches and hamburgers grilled in the backyard, drenched with ketchup.

We also introduced him to the drink known in Nebraska as "The Colorado Motherfucker," but after the introduction, and half a tall glass of it, Costa went back to the Ramada Inn and left us alone to do further research for the evening.

There wasn't a whole lot of other research to do at night. Tom and I drank oceans of beer and I'd find him in the pool each morning doing a hundred laps, trying to get rid of the aftereffects of the night before.

We were so desperate to find a really good meal that one night we crashed the local country club in our jeans and long hair, announced who we were to those in charge, and ate a great steak.

Costa, the sophisticated Parisian, seemed bemused the night we took him to the biggest local attraction. There was Costa-Gavras atop a Conestoga wagon! As it made its way back and forth across a dirt field in emulation of the Pioneers!

Tom Berenger, whose movie *Platoon* was still in the theaters, was the biggest star to hit the town of Scottsbluff, Nebraska. He looked the part, too. He was tan, slim, his outfit consisting day to day of a pair of worn jeans, a T-shirt, and a baseball cap.

Word spread very quickly that Tom Berenger was in town and spending lots of nighttime at the bars. A lot of the cowgirls in their rhinestones would come by and ask us about Hollywood.

One day we had lunch at a hog farmer's house. He had three daughters in their late teens and early twenties. They couldn't keep their eyes off Tom. They rushed to bring him his hamburger, kept asking if he wanted more potato chips, and finally asked if they could take a picture with him. Tom looked embarrassed by the whole thing—Costa and I kept laughing at him—but graciously allowed it.

One of them went up to him and whispered something into his ear and I saw Tom blush, then laugh.

"Where?" he said, and she motioned toward the back of the house. The other two sisters were standing nearby, giggling.

"I'll think about it," Tom said.

"Don't do it," I said when she moved away. "This is farm country, man. They'll bushwhack you. They'll put you in jail. You'll have to marry her."

"All she wants is an autograph," he said.

"What? In the back room."

"For her and her sisters."

"All three of you in the back room?"

"Well, she wants me to autograph their panties."

He wandered into the back room after a while and Costa and I and her parents sipped some more iced tea and heard a lot of giggling back there and when Tom emerged, only a couple minutes later, the sisters were all blushing and hugging each other.

"How was the autograph party?" I asked him later.

"Wet surface," he deadpanned. "Tough to write."

· · ·

Back in Hollywood, meanwhile, Irwin Winkler relayed disturbing news. Jerry Weintraub, the studio head who'd contracted this project, was out.

Costa and I were worried. Usually in Hollywood, when the studio head who'd contracted to do a project was fired, it meant that the project died with him.

"Don't worry about it," Irwin told us.

The new heads of the studio were Lee Rich, the former head of Lorimar, and Tony Thomopoulos, the former head of ABC Entertainment.

"Tony's close to Mike Ovitz," Irwin said. "So am I. Mike will work this out."

When we got back to L.A., Lee Rich and Tony Thomopoulos told us that they were as committed to this project as Jerry Weintraub had been.

"I have only one suggestion," Tony said.

Costa and I waited breathlessly. Tony was a TV guy, a nice guy, but a TV guy. We had no inkling what the suggestion would be. It could be *anything*.

"A tattoo," Tony said. "I think the guy—the neo-Nazi, Berenger, should have a tattoo. Then when our girl, the FBI agent, is in bed with him, she discovers the tattoo and it is in that intimate moment that she knows that the man she's falling in love with, the man she's just had sex with, is the enemy."

"Hmm," Costa said.

"I don't know," Irwin said, "it's pretty old. I've seen it before."

"I think we can come up with something better," I said.

"Well, it was just a suggestion," Tony said.

We all smiled and thanked him.

"By the way," Tony said, "I have some notes."

"Notes?" I said. "What notes?"

"Script notes." He handed Irwin a document that looked like it weighed a pound.

"I didn't know you had any script notes," I said. I kept eyeing the pages in Irwin's hands.

"*We* do," Tony said.

"It's okay," Irwin said. He quickly got up to say goodbye.

"Should we discuss them?" I asked Tony.

"*We'll* discuss them first," Irwin said. He looked like he wanted to race out the door.

"I don't mind discussing them now," I said.

"That's okay," Irwin said, "we'll discuss them later."

"Whatever you want to do," Tony said.

Irwin led us out. When we got to the parking lot, I said, "They've got all those notes? Let me see 'em."

"Are they formidable?" Costa asked Irwin. He pronounced it the French way—*for-mi-da-ble.*

"I don't know," Irwin said. "It doesn't matter."

"It doesn't matter?" I said. "They're the studio's notes. This is how movies get screwed up."

"Will you settle down?" Irwin said.

He took the notes and started tearing the pages into pieces.

When he was done tearing up all the pages, he smiled and said, "Good meeting, see ya later," got into one of his antique Ferraris, and drove off.

Costa and I stood in the lot a moment and laughed.

"He is a very good producer," Costa very formally added.

Our major piece of casting was still undone. Katie, the FBI agent sent undercover among the neo-Nazis, was the star of the movie.

We heard that Debra Winger—my attorney, Barry Hirsch, her attorney as well, had gotten her the script—was interested. Costa, Irwin, and I drove to Winger's house in Point Dume one day and after a thirty-minute discussion, she agreed to do the movie.

Winger had a fearsome reputation and, while happy that she was in (we admired her work), we feared that we'd all get gray hairs in the course of the shoot.

"Well, so far so good," Irwin said in his understated way.

"So far too good." Costa laughed.

"Well, this is as far as I go," I said.

I was finished with the script; Costa's task was just beginning.

"The easiest movie to cast and get made," Guy McElwaine told me, "is a sexual thriller set at a resort location in the tropics. Every movie star wants a paid vacation, tropical sunshine, swimming in the moonlight. Every movie star wants to have real sex on the beach with his co-star."

I wrote a sexual thriller called *The Bouncer* set at a resort location on Maui. It was a story of seamy seduction with lots of hanky-panky on the beach and in the moonlight.

No star was interested. No studio was interested. I couldn't sell it. It's still in my drawer.

While Costa planned the *Betrayed* shoot, Richard Marquand flew up to Marin to tell me that he'd found the next film he wanted to make. It was a script called *American Rocker* by a songwriter named Scott Richardson.

"I want you to rewrite it," Richard said.

I read it and told him I thought it was awful. And I didn't understand why he wanted to do it.

"You've just had a big hit movie," I said, "you can do anything you want to do. And you want to do *this*?"

He told me how much he had always loved rock and roll—one of his early directing efforts was a brilliant little film about the Beatles for the BBC which I had admired. This script was about a young woman who wanted to be a rock star.

"There's never been a really good rock and roll piece," Richard said. "I like *The Rose* very much, but even that didn't quite completely work."

He told me that Craig Baumgarten and Lorimar wanted to make a big deal with him to put the movie on a fast schedule for distribution.

"We're not going to have much time," Richard said, "they want to put it into the pipeline quickly. They need product."

I was against it.

"I don't think there's a movie here, Richard," I said.

"I can do it if you help me," he said. "Besides, it'll give us a chance to be together. I miss you. I know you're gallivanting about with these world-renowned directors, but I miss you."

I missed him, too, and besides, I found it almost impossible to purposely disappoint him. We had shared too many laughs and good times together.

"Aw, fuck it," I finally said. "Okay, I'll do it, what the hell."

He laughed.

"You're the only man I've ever met who can accept an absolute fortune so ungracefully."

We sat in the rain in Palm Springs for a week going over the Scott Richardson script, which, I thought, was basically an excuse for Richardson to put some of his songs—which were quite good—into a movie.

During our discussions, we evolved a romantic triangle featuring a young rock singer who wants to be a star caught between an English pop idol and a washed-up and retired American rocker.

In my more frustrated moments, I kept muttering, "This is a mistake, Richard."

And Richard smiled and said, "We'll work it out."

I had to have the rewrite done within two weeks. I met the deadline, but hated what I'd written. Richard liked it, Lorimar liked it, and we went right into casting.

For the part of the young woman, we cast Fiona, a New York club singer who the record companies were convinced would be a big star. I looked at her screen test and said she couldn't act. Richard and Craig felt she was fine.

For the part of the English rocker, we cast Rupert Everett. I couldn't argue with that; I thought him to be a marvelously gifted actor. And for the part of the washed-up American rocker, we cast . . . ta-dum! *Bob Dylan*.

"Can Dylan act?" I asked Richard.

"No, certainly not."

"But we're casting him."

"We are. All he has to do is to be himself."

I repeated my mantra.

"We're making a big mistake here, Richard."

"Do you like Bob Dylan?" he asked.

"I revere Bob Dylan," I said. "I have every single one of his albums. I have every single one of his bootleg albums. I will travel a thousand miles to see him in concert. But I don't think we should cast him in this movie. I don't think we should do this movie. I think we should give them their money back and pull out of this movie."

"You wrote a brilliant script." He smiled.

"Aw, fuck you," I said.

He knew damn well how I felt about my script. I kept trying to rewrite the damn thing behind Richard's back even though it had been cast and budgeted.

We met Dylan at a sushi place in Malibu to discuss the script. He was wired and uptight—he wore black leather and motorcycle boots—and hardly said a word. His leg kept jiggling. He hardly ate and then he left.

We met him again in Denver, where he was appearing in concert at Red Rock with Tom Petty and the Heartbreakers. He was friendly and seemed pleased that we had flown in to talk to him.

"What's your favorite Bob Dylan song?" he asked me almost shyly, phrasing it exactly that way and I told him it was "Mr. Tambourine Man." To my delight, he played it at the concert that night, introducing it only with the words "Hey, Joe, this one's for you."

We congratulated him after the show and agreed to meet at the bar of his hotel that night to talk about the script. But when we met at the bar, Bob Dylan said, "Can you fly to Portland? We're in Portland next."

Richard and I both knew a thing or two about game playing, so Richard said, "Bob, we have flown *here*. To Denver. We will not fly to Portland. We have flown to Denver. We are *here*."

When Richard said it, he sounded like Richard Burton, which made sense, because for a time in his career he had served as Burton's professional voice, filling in for him at looping and radio interviews that Burton didn't want to do.

Bob Dylan grinned when Richard said that and said, "Yeah, you're *here* in Denver, that's *true*," and we agreed to meet him in his hotel suite at eight o'clock the next morning.

When Richard and I walked into the suite the next morning, greeted by a roadie, we were told to sit on the couch, Bob would be right out. There was a quart bottle of Jim Beam on the table, about a quarter gone. We waited for about ten minutes. Three stunning black women, his backup singers, came out of the bedroom, smiling demurely at us and telling us that Bob would be right out.

When Bob did come out, he was bare-chested and barefoot, wearing only a pair of jeans. He said "Hey" quite affably, reached for the Jim Beam, took a huge slug, and sat down facing us.

Richard did the talking. He said that it was very important within the dynamic of the script for him to meet Fiona as soon as possible, since his love story with Fiona was at the heart of the piece.

"I don't know about that, man," Dylan said. "I can't kiss her. I don't believe in that stuff."

"You don't believe in kissing?" I asked.

Dylan thought that was hilarious and started to laugh. "Not kissing her, no," he said. "Not up on-screen. I don't do that."

Richard kept going on and Dylan kept laughing and slugging on the Jim Beam and then he said he was sorry, he had to get ready, "The bus is heading to Portland."

Richard told him that we really did need more time to talk to him and Dylan said, "You want to fly into Portland? I can see you in Portland. I know you're *here* and I'm *here*, but I'm going to *Portland*."

When we left, Richard said, "Don't worry, it'll work out."

"How?"

"I'll talk to him on the set."

"What if you don't convince him on the set?"

"I will."

"You know, this is *Bob Dylan* here," I said to Richard. "It may not be that easy to convince him."

"Trust me," Richard said.

He went to England to shoot the movie and every time he called me he told me how wonderfully it was all working out. Fiona and Dylan and Rupert Everett, he said, were great friends.

"Dylan and Rupert are friends?" I asked.

"Great friends."

"They're not supposed to be," I said. "They're supposed to hate each other."

"Well, they do, sort of, in the script."

"*Sort of?* This is a romantic triangle. Where's the drama going to come from if they don't hate each other?"

"Don't worry," Richard said, "trust me."

He brought the rough assembly to L.A. with his editor and showed it to me along with three or four Lorimar executives. He and his editor kept laughing at moments that weren't funny.

Bob Dylan did not kiss Fiona on-screen. He and Rupert Everett did not hate each other. The romantic triangle was gone. The movie had no humor, no energy, and no dramatic tension.

The Lorimar executives, including Craig, made their usual disingenuous disclaimers—*It's great, but it needs some work*—and quickly left the room.

I didn't say a word until Richard and I wandered outside and were alone.

"It's awful, isn't it?" he said.

"It is," I said. "I'm sorry, but it is."

He had tears in his eyes.

"I blame myself first," I said. "I never gave you a script that was any good. Fiona can't act. Dylan can't act and it's not Rupert's movie. I'm sorry, Richard."

"Is there anything we can do to fix it?" he asked.

"I don't know."

We tried everything—recutting, tightening, expanding. I wrote some new scenes, but we couldn't persuade Lorimar to do any reshooting—no good money after bad money, the rule in Hollywood says.

Richard took the negative back to England with him and would work on it until dawn, exhausting himself, trying everything he could think of.

He called me near dawn one day and he was crying. "Nothing works," he said. "It's just a bloody bad movie."

"It's only a movie, Richard," I said. "Remember that. Please. We'll have some hits, we'll have some misses, but it's only a movie."

He called me about a week later to say he had thought about what I'd said to him and was going off to Greece with Carol to sit in the sun for a week, swim, and walk in the sand. He sounded good for the first time in a long time.

"Think about what we should do next, Squire," he said. "I've got some thoughts myself."

I said I would and said that I was happy he was taking the time off. He had a wonderful wife, beautiful children, he was one of the most successful directors in the world and this was—

"Only a movie," he said at the same time that I did.

He called from London two weeks later to tell me that he and Carol had had a delightful time in Greece.

"I feel like I'm twenty years old again," he said with a laugh.

Carol called me the next day to tell me that he had sat down to dinner after my conversation with him and during dinner he had stood up suddenly and then collapsed.

He had suffered a massive stroke. A few days later, my great friend Richard Marquand was *dead*. He was forty-eight years old.

· · ·

I couldn't believe it. I was in shock. I lost myself in a whiskey fog for days. I cried and grieved for the man I had loved.

I understood the full horror of the lesson here: If you allowed Hollywood to infect your soul . . . not your brain, not even your heart, but your *soul* . . . you became vulnerable to the *shiv* with which Hollywood could kill you.

Hollywood had handed my friend Richard Marquand that platinum and diamond shiv and he had taken it and plunged it into himself. He hadn't died of a stroke after all. He'd been killed by a very bad movie called *Hearts of Fire*.

Lethbridge, Canada, where Costa was shooting *Betrayed,* is farm country two hours south of Calgary in the Canadian West, where the jukeboxes blared Anne Murray and Lynyrd Skynyrd, and where the big deal on a weekend night was to get rip-roaring "toasted" on tequila shooters.

The driver who picked me up at the Calgary airport was a longtime Lethbridge resident who gave his twisted version of a Junior Chamber of Commerce speech.

"We've got a real nice town," he said, "this part of Canada has the lowest AIDS rate in all of North America. We've never had a movie filmed here, most of our residents don't do a lot of traveling, and we have some damn pretty women. You feel free to enjoy yourself."

As he drove me to the Lethbridge Inn, where I was to meet Irwin Winkler, I saw that the town was decked out and ready for the film crew. The liquor store had big signs that said: "French *champane*." The restaurants had signs that said: "Caesar salad now being served."

Irwin had called and asked me to come. "Something's up," he had said in his laconic way. He was already in the dining room of the inn, waiting, when I got there. He looked strangely pensive. Irwin Winkler's usual style is cool, inheld, and controlled.

We had a problem, Irwin explained. Costa was about halfway through the shoot and he and Irwin suddenly realized that the script was too long. If Costa shot the rest of it as it was written, the movie would be two hours and forty-two minutes long.

"Didn't anyone time the script before he started shooting?"

Irwin shrugged.

"Evidently not. Or if someone timed it, they timed it wrong."

"What can we do?" I asked.

"We have to cut from the scenes that have not yet been shot," Irwin said.

"That's nuts. It's bad enough to have to cut so much out, but to have to cut from only what hasn't been shot—it can throw the whole balance of it off." Shaking my head, I said, "Is there any good news?"

"Plenty." Irwin smiled. "The dailies are terrific and Debra's a dream."

Winger, he said, was the ultimate pro. All that talk about how difficult she could be was just talk. She was going through a tough time, too. She had recently given birth, put herself on a crash diet to be ready for the movie.

When the shoot began, Irwin said, Tom Berenger was obviously intimidated by her. Debra noticed it and started going out of her way to put him at ease. She'd make coffee for him and kid with him. The crew, Irwin said, was terrified of her. Winger started playing poker with them—on the night when they got paid. Now the crew was in love with her. They had discovered that Debra Winger was an ace poker player. They didn't even seem to mind losing most of their money to her.

I saw how much Winger was the heart and soul of the set the next day, when I arrived on location. It was 12:30 in the afternoon when I finally got there and Debra was in the middle of a scene.

She stopped cold when she saw me and very loudly said, "Well, look who's arrived. At 12:30 in the afternoon. *The writer* has graced us with his presence. Will somebody *please* get him a cup of coffee?"

I started trying to cut the script from what had not yet been shot. It was a terrible, frustrating process that kept me at it in a small office behind a loading dock until well past midnight every day.

As I worked, I saw what made Irwin Winkler such an exceptional producer. He was on the set every day, from seven in the morning till seven at night. It was 100 degrees outside and under lights inside a barn it was much hotter than that, but Irwin was there for every moment. One day he was so exhausted and dehydrated that he got very dizzy.

"Irwin," I said to him, "it's only a movie." It was painful for me to even say the words I had so recently said to Richard.

He nodded.

"I know it," he said, "but all directors are a little nuts. The best directors are more than a little nuts. I want to be there to make sure we don't experience any unexpected improvisations."

When I finally was finished, Costa said he wanted to sit down with me and Irwin because he had had "a formidable inspiration."

He explained his inspiration formidably indeed, with his customary passion. The script as written ended with Winger coming back to see Berenger's children, some time after she had killed him. What if, when she came back to see the children, Costa asked, she was pregnant with Berenger's child. "It will accentuate the tragedy," Costa said.

I didn't think that Debra's pregnancy (from Berenger) would "accentuate the tragedy." I thought it would move the piece closer to . . . *Peyton Place.* Irwin adamantly agreed with me and after nearly a day of discussions, Costa termed his suggestion "not so formidable maybe" and forgot about it.

· · ·

There is nothing quite like a location shoot for Hollywood romance. You're in a strange town with strange restaurants and bars. You're in a completely isolated land whose Constitution is the shooting schedule and whose president is the director.

And since you're in a strange town and a tough world where deadlines have to be met and there isn't a lot of time to sleep, you get lonely.

There are no class distinctions on a location shoot, either, as opposed to a shoot on a studio soundstage, which means that the star can relieve her loneliness with the stuntman or the makeup person.

Egalitarianism is in the air: that cute little extra, the daughter of the town's mayor, can be admitted into this insular world, too, albeit temporarily (the length of the shoot), if she so desires and if she is willing to ease the loneliness of one of these deadline-pressured out-of-town celebrities.

Also very much in favor of romance is the understanding that whatever relationship began on location will . . . *and has to* . . . end at the wrap party, where the romancers will appear with their mates and air-kiss those who willingly and knowingly swallowed their well-meant lies about love.

When the shoot ended, Costa took the negative back to Paris and began editing it there. A week into the edit, he called and asked me to fly over to Paris to help him. I worked with him for three weeks.

I loved what I was seeing. He had somehow—beautifully, almost lyrically—captured the visual nuances of the American Midwest. A director who had never been in the Midwest before I took him there, he had made perhaps one of the most authentic films ever made about the heartland.

Lee Rich and Tony Thomopoulos flew over to join us and after they saw the rough cut, they called my agent and wanted to turn our one-picture deal into a three-picture deal at $750,000 per script.

When Costa finished the final cut, Irwin and I and the studio felt that it was a movie we would always be proud of—daring, visually stunning, finely crafted with superb performances. We felt we had pulled it off and, startlingly, had remained as allied at the end as we were at the beginning.

When the movie opened its first weekend, we had reason to rejoice. It did more than $6 million. There were block-long lines in L.A. and New York. Some exhibitors were reporting that some audiences found the movie so disturbing that people started yelling in the theaters.

The next weekend the movie died. It fell from $6 million to $3 million. The same word of mouth that had turned *Flashdance* and *Jagged Edge* into box office juggernauts had killed *Betrayed*.

People wanted to see it the first weekend very much. They had high expectations of it. They saw it, they disliked it, they told their friends they disliked it, and, in less than a month, *Betrayed* was gone.

We knew we had also been hurt by the critics, who damned it universally. They felt we had created an "unrealistic . . . apocalyptic vision."

People like these heartland neo-Nazis didn't exist, the critics said—or, if they did, they were part of bizarre microscopic cults which posed no danger to America.

One columnist disliked the movie so much that he attacked Costa and me as "foreigners trashing America." The columnist was Patrick Buchanan, future presidential candidate of the Republican right wing.

I wonder what those critics were thinking eight years after *Betrayed*'s release when Timothy McVeigh, the reification of the Tom Berenger character, blew up the Federal Building in Oklahoma City.

CHAPTER 9

[Flashback]

Sins and Zip Guns

KARCHY

Maybe I'll join the priesthood. You don't have to work, you live in
a nice house, you don't go hungry.

FATHER NORTON

Is that what you think the priesthood is about, Mr. Jonas?

KARCHY

Well, you don't get laid, but I'm not getting laid anyway, Father, so
what's the difference?

Telling Lies in America

My mother was having severe stomach pains but she wouldn't see a doctor. She went a couple of blocks down Lorain Avenue and saw the Hungarian pharmacist, Alex Sajo, instead. Alex Sajo gave her a tin can filled with medicine.

I watched her eat her medicine at dinner. She opened the can and put six round pieces of charcoal on her plate. She ate one piece after the other. Her mouth and her lips were black.

"I didn't know you could eat charcoal," I said.

"Oh yes," my father said. "It is an old Hungarian cure."

"Do you want to try a piece?" my mother asked me.

"No thanks."

"I'll take one," my father said, and popped it into his mouth like a peanut.

. . .

Every year I went with my classmates at St. Emeric's to the Kraus Costume Company in downtown Cleveland and rented a Hungarian Hussar's outfit. High black boots. A cockade cap. Red peasant vest. Billowing white shirt. Tight black pants.

All decked out, we stood on the back of a flatbed truck in a parade down Lorain Avenue as Hungarian csárdás music blared from a loudspeaker. My father and mother were very proud of me. One of my father's friends took lots of pictures. I hated it. I felt like a geek.

Howdy Doody as a Hussar!

I was looking at the girls' bodies in school. Their breasts and their behinds and the way they crossed their legs. I felt my *pimpli* grow and become rigid sometimes when I looked at them.

When I was in the apartment alone once, I touched my rigid *pimpli* and pulled it and the most amazing thing happened. White juice came out of it and I felt an overwhelming warmth spreading through my body.

I discovered that if I focused my imagination on girls' bodies, on the women I'd seen on the ship, on the things I'd seen on Erzsi, my *pimpli* would grow rigid and I could make myself feel this miraculous warmth by pulling on it.

I did it to myself over and over again in the dank darkness of the apartment basement. In the bathroom. On the couch at night when my parents were asleep.

Sometimes there was so much juice my stomach was wet and I had to use a towel.

My mother was sick, she had a high temperature and was throwing up. Her stomach hurt and her skin was yellowish. A Hungarian doctor named Bognar came to the apartment and said she needed to have her gallbladder removed.

My father had an old Hungarian friend now living in Canada, Dr. Laszlo Szöllösy, who was a surgeon. My father didn't trust the American surgeons in Cleveland. Neither did my mother.

They took the train to Canada. By the time they arrived in Hamilton, eight hours away, she was in a near coma.

They left me alone in the apartment. My mother's friend, Dora Szakács, would bring me food every day and check on me.

I started throwing up about an hour after they left for the train. I felt like I was burning up. I lay down in my parents' bed and felt so weak I couldn't get up. I had to go to the bathroom but I couldn't get up, so I went in the bed. It smelled and it was all over me and the bed but I couldn't get up. I was very thirsty but I couldn't even get up for a glass of water. Everything was spinning around very fast.

Dora Szakács forgot to come.

She came the next day, when the bed was dripping to the floor with everything that was coming out of me. She called a doctor. I had a 105 degree temperature.

Dora Szakács took me to her home and I stayed with the Szakácses until my parents got back. Her husband, Zoltán, a kindly man, bought me marbles to make me feel better.

In school the nuns said that playing with ourselves was a mortal sin. We would burn in hell forever. Hair would grow on our palms and we would go blind. We would go mad and have to be taken to asylums where jackets would be put around us so we couldn't touch ourselves.

As Sister Rose was saying these things, I was watching Karen Buganski's breasts. Karen was eleven and had breasts you could see clearly, dark, flashing big eyes and long brown hair. I felt my *pimpli* grow rigid as Sister Rose talked. I said I had to go to the bathroom.

I went to the bathroom and, thanks to Karen Buganski's breasts, made myself feel wonderful.

My father read the *Plain Dealer* in the morning, his English-Hungarian dictionary at his side, desperate for news about Josef Stalin's successors.

And I read the *Plain Dealer* when he was done, his English-Hungarian dictionary at my side, desperate for news about the Hungarian bank robber Lou Teller and his big-breasted girlfriend, Tina Mae Ritenour.

I was scissoring the photographs of American women whom I liked from the *Plain Dealer*.

Zsa Zsa Gabor, Mamie Van Doren, Betty Grable, Esther Williams, Jane Russell, Marilyn Monroe, Lana Turner, Joanne Dru, Debra Paget, Dana Wynter . . . and Tina Mae Ritenour.

Tits!

It was a new American word I had learned!

My father was gone a lot now. He was traveling on the Greyhound and making speeches to Hungarians in Youngstown, Ohio, and Detroit, Michigan, and Windber, Pennsylvania.

He was also forming friendships with American women who came to his office that he introduced me to. Huldah Kramer, an American magazine writer, and Katherine Webster, the librarian at the Carnegie West branch at Fulton and Lorain.

While I was walking with him at night to the library he told me a story about a man named Casanova who was the greatest lover of women in history. He said that when he was a young man in Hungary, he had been Casanova.

"Don't tell your mother about this," he said. "I'm talking to you as a man now."

I was a ten-year-old man.

In the fall of 1954, I ran after school each day to the corner of West 25th and Bridge. On this corner, behind the store windows of a furniture store, stood six Zenith television sets.

On each of these sets, the Cleveland Indians were playing the New York Giants in the World Series. I watched Willie Mays catch a ball impossible to catch off the bat of the Indians' Vic Wertz. I watched Al Rosen and Larry Doby and Wally Westlake strike out again and again.

I watched a lumbering man named Dusty Rhodes, a pinch-hitter for the Giants, hit so many home runs that I hated him as much as the Komchis and the Krampusz combined. The Indians lost four games in a row. I cried.

To make me feel better, Oszkár Moldován bought me a Cleveland Indians American League Champions pennant. It was my prized possession: glaring red and yellow, featuring a grinning Chief Wahoo, the Indians' mascot. It had the name of every player on it.

I climbed to the roof of the printing shop and waved it at the truck drivers in the Num Num Potato Chip factory lot. They cheered.

My mother's teeth had always hurt. Now, within two weeks, she had all of them pulled.

When she got her false teeth, she stopped working in the printing shop behind the linotype machine and got a job as a bookkeeper at the Central National Bank on West 25th Street. She spoke little English but she was a whiz with numbers and many of the other bookkeepers were also Hungarian women.

She worked from nine to six, but even when she was home there were long silences between my parents I hadn't noticed before.

She complained of severe headaches and my father urged her to smoke less. She switched brands instead, from unfiltered Philip Morrises to filtered Herbert Tareytons. But then she cut the filters off the Tareytons with a razor blade and smoked them that way.

She said they tasted better.

Huldah Kramer drove my father and me on a rainy Sunday to a small town nearby, Mansfield, Ohio. My father asked my mother to come but she said she had a headache.

"You go with Huldah," my mother said.

"And the boy," my father said.

"Yes, of course, the boy," my mother said.

We were going to see the farm of the famous millionaire American writer Louis Bromfield.

Huldah drove her beautiful new car and my father sat in the front with her. I sat in the back. She was teaching my father words in English but they also spoke in German. Huldah spoke German fluently, and my father spoke a little. Classical music was playing on the car radio.

I hated Huldah. I didn't know why.

We got letters from Hungary sometimes, from my grandfather Jozsef Kreisz and my grandmother and aunts. They said they were happy and well. They said they were praying for us.

My father got angry whenever we got a letter. He said the letters were lies. He said the Komchis had forced them to write these things. He said no one was happy and well under Communism. He said they were being forced to write these things because the Komchis were trying to lure him back to Hungary.

"What would happen if you went back to Hungary, Papa?" I asked him.

"The Komchis would hang me."

"Why?"

"Because I have spent my whole life fighting them."

"I want to help you fight them," I said. "Please, Papa?"

He smiled and patted my head.

"When you are older, we will fight them together—good, Jozsi?"

I envisioned us together—our silver guns blazing, wearing our black cowboy hats, getting the Komchis!

All three of us went to see the movies *Quo Vadis?* and *The Robe*. They were about Jesus.

My mother loved them. She said they were like watching a prayer. I loved them, too. The women in the movies hardly wore anything. My father said he was bored.

Sometimes when I told my parents I'd have to go to the public library after school, I walked over the bridge to the stadium when the Indians were playing. After the fifth inning, they let kids in for free.

When the game ended, I hung around outside hoping to get autographs. I saw Mickey Mantle come out. I ran up to him. I asked him for an autograph in my thick accent. He grinned at me and kept walking.

Suddenly I saw Billy Martin was there. I asked him, too. He grinned and kept walking, too.

"Hey," I heard someone say. "What's wrong with you guys? Sign the kid's book."

I looked. I saw a squat and homely man: Yogi Berra. Whitey Ford was with him.

"Get over here, Mick," Whitey Ford said, as he was signing my book. Mantle and Martin came back sheepishly and signed my book.

"You happy now, asshole?" Mantle grinned at Yogi and walked away.

"Yeah, you're damn right I'm happy," Yogi Berra said.

The others got into the car and Yogi Berra turned to me.

"You German or somethin', son?" Yogi Berra said.

I told him I was Hungarian.

"I'm Italian." Yogi Berra smiled, winked, and walked over to the car.

I stood there, staring as the car drove away. Yogi Berra turned back, grinned, and waved.

Thanks to his friend Katherine Webster, the librarian, my father was occasionally getting copies of the books he had written in Hungary. Every time he brought one home from the library, he was overjoyed. He immediately sat down and read it.

"Why do you read it if you wrote it?" I asked him.

"To make sure I wrote it well," he said.

"Did you write it well?" my mother asked him as he was reading one of his books.

"So far so good." He smiled.

The Hungarian bank robber Lou Teller and his gun moll, Tina Mae Ritenour, were captured by the police in an apartment in Detroit, where the Detroit Tigers played.

There were pictures of them in the *Plain Dealer* trying to hide their faces from the camera. They had been captured without firing a shot.

I was disappointed in Lou Teller. How could he let them take the beautiful Tina Mae Ritenour from him without firing a shot?

And as a young American newspaperman, I tried to arrange interviews with Lou Teller and Tina Mae Ritenour, now out of jail, no longer together, and trying to lead ordinary lives.

They both turned me down, but I spoke to Tina Mae Ritenour over the phone.

"Why do you want to do a story about something that no one cares about anymore?" she asked.

I had my reasons.

Heh. Heh. Heh.

. . .

On the 23rd of October, 1956, when I was twelve years old, Radio Free Europe told us that a revolution had broken out in Hungary.

We hardly turned the radio off. We hardly slept. All we did was listen to Radio Free Europe. Oszkár Moldován had gotten me a Davy Crockett raccoon hat.

All the time we listened to the radio I wore it.

October 23 Tens of thousands of Hungarians pour into Budapest City Park, where stands a twenty-four-foot-high statue of Josef Stalin with the inscription "To the great Stalin, from the grateful Hungarian people." They yell, "Mindszenty! Mindszenty! Mindszenty!" They wind cables and ropes around the statue's neck to pull it down. They can't do it.

Acetylene torches appear. They try to melt Stalin's knees. Stalin finally topples. They yell: "*Russki haza!*"—Russians go home! The crowd breaks the statue into little pieces with iron pipes and hammers.

Stalin's two bronze feet, each six feet tall, are left intact on the pedestal.

October 24 Russian tanks are in the streets of Budapest, firing on the crowds. Boys and girls flush the pavements with soapy water. The tanks swerve and spin into each other. Boys and girls approach the tanks with bottles of gasoline, a lighted rag sticking out of them, and hurl them at the tanks.

October 25 At Parliament Square in Budapest, secret police and Russian tanks fire on the demonstrators. Five hundred demonstrators are killed.

Students, union members, teenage boys and girls, bandoliers over their shoulders, hand grenades in their belts and tommy guns in their hands, hurl themselves at the troops and the tanks. They call their tommy guns "guitars."

October 28 Radio Free Europe tells us that the Red Army is withdrawing its troops from Hungary.

The freedom fighters have won!

The Komchis are fleeing!

My parents stand in front of the shortwave radio hugging me and crying.

"Hungary is free!" my father says.

"We can go back home!" my mother says.

I think: *Home? This is home. The Num Num Potato Chip factory is home. Pep Up is home. Bazball is home. Al Rosen is home. Jerry Lee Lewis is home. Tina Mae Ritenour is home. Davy Crockett is home.*

. . .

November 3 Cardinal Mindszenty has been freed from prison by Hungarian freedom fighters and is on the radio. The world's press is reporting a massive Russian troop buildup on the Hungarian border.

Cardinal Mindszenty says, "The great powers of the world quail before the Soviet army while schoolchildren fight on the streets of Budapest and in the mutilated torso of Hungary. The West is blind as well as impotent."

"What is impotent?" I ask my father.

"A man whose *pimpli* doesn't stand up."

Well . . . I certainly didn't have to worry about that!

November 4 Sixteen Russian armored divisions equipped with two thousand tanks launch an attack on Budapest. The scale of the attack is as large as Hitler's attack in World War II.

Most of the troops are from Manchuria and Mongolia. They don't even know they are in Hungary. They think they are at the Suez Canal. They ask Hungarians to show them the canal.

They begin collecting watches and lining them on their arms. They rape women aged seventy and girls aged six.

November 6 My mother is keening. Her head is lowered, she moves it from side to side, and moans. My father is rigid and pale.

Radio Free Europe rebroadcasts a message from a radio station in Budapest: "The last flames begin to go out. The Soviet army is trying to crush our troubled hearts. Their tanks and guns are roaring over Hungarian soil. Save us! SOS! SOS! Our ship is sinking. The light vanishes. The shadows grow darker from hour to hour. Listen to our cry!"

As my parents cry, I try to hide my happiness.

It means we won't leave America . . . *my home.*

November 11 It's all over.

Twenty-five thousand Hungarians—as many as five thousand children— are dead. Another thirty thousand Hungarians are wounded. Another twenty thousand will be deported to Siberia. Twelve thousand are imprisoned and one thousand will be executed.

Cardinal Mindszenty has been granted political asylum at the American embassy in Budapest. He will live in the building, saying daily Mass for embassy staffers, for fifteen years.

West Side Hungarians formed a caravan of cars to a rally in Public Square in honor of the freedom fighters who had lost their lives to Red Army tanks.

Everyone wore a black armband. It was a cold winter day. My father was the main speaker. He said America had let Hungary down. He said President Eisenhower wasn't a true anti-Communist. He said the blood of thousands of Hungarians was on President Eisenhower's hands.

"Why do you attack America?" my mother asked my father afterward.

"What I said was true," he said.

"They will send us back if you attack them," she said.

"I have to tell the truth."

"You!" she said. "You have to hear applause!"

My mother's father, Antal Biro, who had married the *kurva,* was dead. My mother got her stepmother's letter. Inside were black and white photos of the dead Antal Biro in his casket.

They were close-ups. A very swollen, fat face, his eyes closed, rouge on his face, his mouth slightly open showing bad teeth.

"What kind of human being sends photographs like this?" my father said, throwing them to the kitchen table.

My mother was crying and staring at her dead father's face.

Very quietly she said, "*Jaj, Papa . . . Jaj, Papa . . .*"

Dénes Kacso, my poet friend who taught me about witches and how God created women, who hated Father Gottfried as much as I did, was dead, too. Drunk, he had passed out and fallen into his blazing fireplace.

He burned to death.

My mother's weight was fluctuating wildly. She put thirty pounds on, took forty off, put fifty on.

She was suffering such severe headaches that she was forced to quit her bookkeeping job at Central National Bank.

She sat at the kitchen table for hours, razor-blading her Herbert Tareyton cigarettes, an iced towel wrapped around her head to ease her pain.

Father Benedek Biro, who had picked us up on the road outside Margie's Diner, who had told me to blow my flute louder and louder, was dead, too.

He was one of the greatest émigré Hungarians, my father told me, respected by Americans as well, a personal friend of a man in New York named Dewey who had almost become America's president.

Father Biro, my father said, wasn't like the Franciscans in Cleveland, who would now become the newspaper's publishers and my father's bosses. These Franciscans here were "stupid" and my father worried that they would try to force him to print "ugly" articles in the paper.

"What kind of articles?" I asked.

"About the Zsidos," my father said.

After school or on weekends, I was out on the playgrounds playing bazball. We played with balls held together with masking tape. Few of us had gloves. Many of the bats we used were cracked.

I was a solid line drive hitter and a good fielder. I chased a ball down in the outfield and made a catch that was better than Willie Mays's catch off Vic Wertz of the Indians in the World Series. I lunged after the ball, my back to the batter, my hands outstretched, running as hard as I could. I caught the ball, lost my balance, did a perfect somersault, and came up with the ball in hand.

Then I yelled "Fuck you!" at the kid who'd hit it.

My teammates rolled around on the ground in laughter. The kid who'd hit the ball was so angry he chased me for two blocks, the bat in his hand.

I felt increasingly at home on the playgrounds and in the alleys with new friends who weren't Hungarian . . . José, who was Puerto Rican and had biceps the size of my thighs . . . Chuckie Chuckles, a bantam-rooster hillbilly kid with more freckles than I had.

We pitched baseball cards against the curbs and that led to pitching pennies. (We dug through the maggots in the garbage cans looking for more bottles to return.) José and Chuckie had pairs of dice in their pockets and soon I had my pair, too. We rolled the dice for anything—pennies, baseball cards, sometimes even to tell the future.

Okay, let's see whose mom is gonna live the longest, yours or mine?

There were always older kids around who tolerated us condescendingly—kids with lipsticked and mascaraed girlfriends, kids who had brown paper bags with bottles of Thunderbird or muscatel inside which they shared, kids with smokes who'd let us take big drags.

I loved the very first drag of a cigarette I tasted on a playground. I was twelve years old.

From then on, I started stealing some of my mother's or borrowing them from José, who'd started smoking when he was eight.

Going to school one morning, I saw Father John Mundweil up ahead at the West Side Market and quickly shoved the lighted cigarette into my pocket. When my mother washed and ironed the pants, she found the pocket burned inside.

"Don't do this," she said, "please. I've suffered more from this my whole life than anything else."

"Will you tell Papa?" I asked.

She looked at me and shook her head and said, "May God forgive me."

. . .

Time magazine picked "The Hungarian Freedom Fighter" as its Man of the Year.

My father was very happy. *Time* magazine, he said, was run by a good man named Henry Luce, who had been a friend of Father Benedek Biro's in Connecticut.

"Luce is as good an anti-Communist as Zenator Mekarti," my father said.

We stole cars and took them for joyrides.

We went out on the Shoreway sometimes and stomped the gas pedal and got the speedometer up to a hundred miles an hour.

It was scary, exciting, exhilarating, criminal, and a helluva lot of fun.

My favorite joyride was to take our newly acquired car to the drive-in theater in a suburb called Parma.

That's where I saw Elvis in *Jailhouse Rock* . . . at a drive-in . . . sipping beer . . . in a stolen car.

Chuckie had a transistor radio that changed my life. There was music coming out of it that made me feel like I was exploding somewhere deep inside. Jerry Lee Lewis. Elvis. Chuck Berry. Little Richard. Fats Domino. Jackie Wilson. Sam Cooke. The Platters. Buddy Holly. The Everly Brothers.

At home in the apartment, when my parents were asleep, I'd sneak from the living room couch back to my father's office and put the big Philips shortwave on. I found the AM band, turning the knob back and forth, its green cat's eye flickering on a station, trying to listen through the static to WLS in Chicago and CKLW in Windsor besides WERE and KYW and WHK in Cleveland.

My father watched me listening when he wasn't working in his office.

"Jungle music," he said in Hungarian. "What's next?"

Every morning my mother made me a sandwich to take to school—salami and baloney and kolbász and szalona. And every morning, on my way out, I'd dump the sandwich into a small supply closet at the bottom of the stairway leading to the street.

I didn't want these Hungarian foods. I wanted hot dogs and hamburgers. The Franciscans found a prospering colony of rats in the supply closet one day and when I got home from school, my father, who rarely struck me, slapped me hard across the face.

"You will never amount to anything!" he raged. "You do nothing with yourself! You stare out the stupid window! You play the stupid bazball! You throw away good food when we starved for all those years in the camps! Why? Why do you act this way? Why did I come to this country? Why did your mother and I sacrifice *everything for you*?" His arm hurt so bad after he hit me that he had to go to a doctor. The doctor put his arm in a sling. My father had dislocated his shoulder.

Walking back home through the alley from Greenwood Pool, I cut through the Alex J. Kozmon Funeral Home parking lot and saw Father John Mundweil in his black Ford coupé kissing the funeral director's blond wife.

Father John saw me, too, watching him.

The next day in school, he asked me if I wanted to be the altar boy at funerals and weddings, where I'd get nice tips. I thanked him.

Funerals, I discovered, paid off better than weddings if you played it right. A few sympathetic tears in the altar boy's eyes and the bereaved relatives always took good care of him, appreciating this goodhearted boy's great sensitivity.

Walking home from a playground at dusk, I saw a group of older boys in an alcove on the ground floor of William Dean Howells Junior High.

They were hovered around a naked girl I'd seen with other older boys in the alleys. One of them was covering her mouth with his hands, the others were holding her legs apart.

I stopped and stared.

"Hey, Joey, you want some?" one of them yelled.

"Come on, Goofy," another said, "you're old enough."

I started to run.

I heard them laughing behind me.

Sister Rose, furious that I hadn't cleaned my desk the way I was told, grabbed me by the hair and dragged me to an empty classroom.

She knelt me down in front of her and screamed, "You don't listen! You never listen! Listen to me!"

She picked up an empty Coca-Cola bottle near her and raised it above my head.

Before I knew what had happened, I had knocked the old nun against a wall and onto the floor. The Coca-Cola bottle was in my hand and I smashed it to the floor next to her.

When my father heard what had happened, he raged: "You hit a sister? You knocked a sister down? Do you want them to throw you out of school? Do you want to go to jail?"

My father wanted me to take violin lessons. I didn't want to take them. I wanted to take saxophone lessons.

He arranged for my violin lessons to be given to me by a man named Wenger, who lived in a part of Cleveland far from us.

My father gave me the money to pay Mr. Wenger and then I took the bus to go to his house for my lessons . . . but I didn't make it there.

I got off downtown and went to see the Cleveland Indians lose to the Boston Red Sox again.

"How was the violin lesson?" my father asked me.

I said, "Fine."

He said, "Fine?"

I said, "Fine."

Wasn't that the advice he had given me? If they ask you anything in America, say "Fein."

"Pig," he said and started to slap me. But he winced as he raised his arm and then held it, grimacing in pain.

Mr. Wenger had called.

On a muggy, sticky night in the summer, my father took me for a long walk. We went halfway over the Lorain-Carnegie Bridge, which connected the west side of the city to the east, arching over the industrial flats.

My father stopped on the bridge and looked at the flame-topped towers of the steel mills and the iron ore hills on the Cuyahoga's banks. The smell from the mills on this night was gagging.

"This is where you will work if you don't make something of yourself," my father said. "You will live your life in this stink and hell among oil monkeys who have to be drunk to forget the misery of their everyday life, their bodies covered in oil and filth no soap can take off. Smell it. Breathe it in. Get your first taste of the rest of your life."

When Chuckie and José and I were in an alley at night in the stifling heat, slumped against a wall, smoking Lucky Strikes, it was Justine Corelli on *American Bandstand* we talked about. She was the most beautiful girl I'd ever seen.

"Jeez, those fuckin' tits," Chuckie said.

"That blond hair?" José said. "I want to shove it in that fuckin' hair."

"I wanna fuck that sweet ass," Chuckie said.

"You can't fuckin' do that," I said, "that's not what it's fuckin' for."

"What the fuck you fuckin' talkin' about?" Chuckie said.

"It wouldn't fuckin' fit in there," I said, "it's not what it's fuckin' for."

They all laughed at me.

"Man, it makes fuckin' room!" José said.

"Fuckin' Goofy don't even fuckin' know you can fuck an ass," Chuckie said. "Fuckin' Goof's fuckin' goofy."

I heard my mother and father arguing about me.

"We are Hungarian," she said. "He is more American every day."

"He is Hungarian," my father said. "He knows his heritage. He is proud of it. We have taught him."

"He should be in the Hungarian Boy Scouts."

"He doesn't want to be in the Boy Scouts."

"He should be in the Hungarian choir."

"He doesn't want to be in the choir."

"Do you want him to grow up to be an American and not a Hungarian?" she asked him.

"He lives in America," my father said. "I don't want him to be a foreigner—like us. Why should he have a life like ours? He is a boy. He can learn everything."

"He is learning bad things," my mother said.

"Mária, please," he said. "All boys learn bad things. Then they forget those things and become good men. He would have learned these bad things in Hungary, too."

"Did *you* forget the bad things that you learned in Hungary?" my mother asked my father.

"What exactly are we talking about, Mária?" my father said.

"I would have liked him to learn bad Hungarian things," my mother said, "instead of bad American things."

"Boys learn bad things in a universal language," my father said. I could hear the smile in his voice.

"I'm not just talking about that," my mother said.

"Then I don't know what you're talking about."

My mother said, "Yes you do."

"*Read!*" my father said to me. "What are you doing with your life? *Read!* It's the key to knowledge, the key to success. Always this bazball! You will grow up to be one of the stinking-feet people." That's what he called athletes: *stinking-feet people.*

"*Sitzfleisch!*" he said, using a German word for the ability to sit on your own posterior. "*Sitzfleisch!*"

I begged him to take me to an Indians game or to give me the money to go to one. He said I was too young. I kept asking him. Finally he said, "If you get all As on your next report card, I will take you to see the stinking feet." I was getting Cs and Ds.

On the day I brought him the report card with all As, he let me pick the day we would go to the stadium. I picked a Saturday afternoon. The Indians against the Yankees.

My father wore his beret and his trench coat. It was summer. He watched the game for a while. I tried to explain it to him.

"This is stupid," he said. "Nothing happens. They stand around and wait. Where is the action?"

He took a Hungarian-language book out of his trench coat pocket and for the rest of the game he read. Dostoyevsky. *Crime and Punishment.*

And when I was a successful American screenwriter and kids asked me how they could learn to write, I said, "Read! Read! It's the key to knowledge, the key to success!"

I even said to them "Sitzfleisch! Sitzfleisch!"

But then I added this sentence: "There aren't many German words I like, but . . ."

At that baseball game, my father saw people around us eating frankfoorters and gave me a dollar to buy some. When I got to the hot dog stand, they had just run out.

There was a pizza stand next to it and I bought two pieces with slices of kolbász stacked on top. I had never tasted this wondrous-smelling thing before.

I took the slices to my father and he said, "What's this?"

I told him it was an American food called pizza, that they were out of frankfoorters.

He looked at it suspiciously, tasted it, and said, "This is *magnificent!*"

I tasted it and agreed.

He told me to go back and buy two more slices and then he sent me back again to buy two more for my mother.

"How was the bazball?" my mother asked when we got home.

My father said, "Mária, they serve the most magnificent food at these American games!"

He handed her the slices we had bought for her.

"This is *wonderful!*" my mother said. "What's it called?"

"Pizza," I said.

"It sounds Italian," she said.

"American!" my father said. "It's American food!"

My father gave me advice about America. "Didn't I tell you Americans are crazy? They are producing an electric can opener. I read it in the *Plain Dealer.* Who needs an *electric* can opener? Is it too much work to open a can with a regular opener? Don't they know that no one will ever use something so stupid?"

I was lying to my parents all the time about what I was doing after school.

I told them I had to go to the public library downtown to study a special project.

I went instead to Jean's Fun House and the Roxy Burlesque on East Ninth Street and watched a stripper take her clothes off.

One Sunday I told my parents I had to play in a special baseball game and went with José instead—Chuckie was sick—to the Cleveland Arena where we watched Jerry Lee Lewis play the piano and howl like the devil. He didn't just play his piano, he put it on fire with matches and lighter fluid.

José and I went out on Euclid Avenue afterward and broke some store windows with other kids, then ate a cheeseburger at a Royal Castle and listened to the jukebox play "*Come along-a-baby, whole lotta shakin goin on!*" about ten times.

José paid for the whole thing. He'd stolen an old lady's purse as she was coming out of the seven o'clock Mass at St. Patrick's.

When I was an American journalist, I told Tempest Storm how I would sneak down to the Roxy and watch the strippers when I was a boy.

We were in Tempest Storm's dressing room in Dayton, Ohio, and Tempest appreciated my story so much that she took her sweaty G-string off and put a fresh one on while I was doing the interview.

Tempest said she had played the Roxy but I was sure the show I got in her dressing room was better than anyone ever saw at the Roxy!

I got a zip gun like Chuckie's and José's. We didn't really know what to do with these homemade, sling-shot-style guns, so we shot rats in the alleys with them.

We were walking down an alley at night when a drunk came staggering toward us. José went up to the drunk and smashed him in the face with the zip gun. The drunk's nose broke and he fell to his knees and wailed like an old woman. Chuckie kicked him in the Adam's apple and he started to gag on his own blood. I kicked him in the nose and blood burst from his ear. José took his wallet out of his pants and we ran.

Seven bullshit dollars but we got away clean.

I have never told anyone about that helpless, pathetic man and the blood that burst from his ear. I probably shouldn't have told you.

One night we hit the jackpot.

We didn't plan it . . . it was a stultifyingly hot day . . . We'd been down at Greenwood Pool and we'd prowled around the alleys . . . and we saw the old lady who owned the little grocery store on Bridge Avenue lock up her shop and get into her shiny new Buick and drive away. Word was that she lived in Rocky River, where the rich Irish lived.

We messed around for another couple hours . . . trying to get into the pool hall, drinking coffee and listening to the jukebox at Nick's . . . until it got darker . . . and then we went back to the store and got in through the back where the window looked out onto the alley.

As soon as we touched the window, the burglar alarm went off, but that didn't stop us.

José went right to the cash register—he knew what he was doing—and opened it. Chuckie and I went to the front window, waiting for the cops. We both had our zip guns.

Chuckie suddenly started to laugh nervously and took his dick out and started to piss all over the floor and the window.

José said, "What the fuck is wrong with you, man?" But he was laughing, too. He was still going through the register, trying to get some drawer in there open.

We heard a siren approaching from far away.

Chuckie yelled, "Let's go, let's go, let's go!" and was zipping up his pants.

José yelled "Wait!" then whooped and hollered and held up a white envelope.

We ran toward the back and Chuckie, for no reason, took his zip gun out and blasted the cash register a couple of times.

We dove out through the window and ran down the alley as we heard the siren much louder now, coming closer on Bridge Avenue.

The white envelope had $800 in ten-dollar bills. We divided the money up.

I was afraid to keep that kind of money on me or hidden in our apartment.

In the Num Num Potato Chip factory parking lot, I found a loose red brick in the wall.

It became my first bank.

I was rich now. I sat for long hours at the Royal Castle on Lorain near Fulton, eating cheeseburgers, sipping black coffee, smoking Lucky Strikes, my T-shirt rolled up, my hair in a greasy ducktail, a silver comb in my back pocket, a zip gun in my jacket pocket, listening to the jukebox, my face full of angry red-pus-dripping zits that I clawed and scratched at.

I was a cool . . . rock and roll . . . DP . . . *geek*.

I didn't have a room of my own in our apartment, no place where I could read or study or listen to the radio or jack off or smoke in peace.

At night I slept on that couch in the living room that folded open.

I had a Cleveland Indians pennant and a Rocky Colavito photo I wanted to put on a wall.

"The boy needs a room of his own," I heard my father tell my mother.

"Why?" my mother said. "What's he going to do in there?"

He started building my room the next day. We had a small extra bathroom in the apartment with a toilet and a washbasin.

He screwed a wooden board into the wall above the washbasin and got a small chair that fit in front of it at the Salvation Army.

Now I had my own table.

He built a wooden box that fit over the toilet.

Now I had my own cabinet.

I read and studied there and listened to my portable radio. I put my Indians pennant and my Rocky Colavito photos up on the wall.

Now I had my own room!

There was a penny arcade on West 25th Street run by a white-haired American named Timmy. In the back room he sold dirty pictures. I bought one for ten cents and put it in my wallet. It showed a naked woman kneeling.

My father said one afternoon that he wanted me to come to the public library on Bridge Avenue at Fulton Road with him. He sat down on a bench in front of the library. He reached into his pocket, pulled out my wallet, and opened it to the picture of the naked woman.

"Well?" he said.

I said nothing.

"Your mother found it," he said. "She's very upset."

"I'm sorry," I said. My face was burning. It was all I could say.

"I know you're masturbating," he said.

I felt myself flush even more. He was looking right at me. I looked away from him. I felt tears welling in my eyes. He looked away and sighed and contemplated the library's lawn.

"I'm sorry," I stammered. "I know it's a sin."

He didn't look at me for a long time, then nodded and looked at me with a sudden smile.

"Who said it's a sin?" he said.

"Sister Rose."

"*Ha!*" my father said. Just that one word. "*Ha!*"

"Isn't it a sin?" I said. "She says I'll go blind."

"Are you having any difficulty with your vision?" he asked, still smiling.

"No."

"You won't go blind," he said. "Nothing will happen to you. Everybody does it. It's normal."

I was astounded. "You too?" I said.

"At your age," he said, shrugging.

"Sister Rose? The other sisters?"

"For certain," he said, grinning widely now. "Especially the sisters. Much of the time."

"*Much of the time?*"

I was laughing. So was my father.

"I have one question I want to ask you," my father said. "Why did you pick a woman with such a big *fenék*?" (It meant posterior in Hungarian.) "Some men like big *fenéks* and some men like little *fenéks*, but the *fenék* on this woman is *really* a big one."

And with that, my father handed me my wallet. "You don't have to throw the picture away," he said, "but hide it someplace where your mother can't find it."

I said, "Yes, Papa."

"And do a better job of hiding it than you did with your mother's sandwiches."

"Yes, Papa."

He looked at me a moment. He seemed to be studying me. I saw tears welling in his eyes suddenly.

And in English—it was the first time he had ever spoken to me in English—he said, "You American now—yes, *Joe?*"

I felt tears in my eyes and in Hungarian I said, "*Nem, Papa.*"

And in English he said, "*Ohhhhkay,* Joe," and walked away.

[*Freeze Frame*]

The Phone Man

*I*met the wealthiest telephone repairman in Los Angeles. He's got a house with a pool in Calabasas, a Ferrari and a Porsche, and hot bimbette girlfriends all over town.

It started accidentally. He was up on a pole, repairing a circuit, and he heard a voice in his ear he recognized immediately. Jack Nicholson. He couldn't stop listening—Jack was talking to a girlfriend—and after an hour he knew a lot, a whole lot, about Jack's intimate life.

He called the National Enquirer and they sent a reporter out and he sold everything he had learned about Jack Nicholson for $10,000.

He went back up on his pole and traced Jack calling all of his friends—Marlon Brando and Warren Beatty and Bob Evans and Lara Flynn Boyle. Then he went up on poles near all of their houses and listened to all of them and learned all about their intimate lives and made another $30,000.

Then he traced all of the numbers they called and climbed up on other poles and pretty soon he felt like he had the whole movie industry wired.

He was dating a famous television starlet now. She'd showed up on one of his traces and he learned everything about her as he listened to her talking to her mother and her boyfriend and especially her girlfriends. Then he just happened to be at the Viper Room when she was there with her sister and he just happened to start a conversation with her about Costa Rica, which was her favorite place in the world. And then he just happened to be at the same hotel at the same time she was in Costa Rica without her boyfriend.

His income from what he heard up on the pole was endless. He was thinking about becoming a producer.

CHAPTER 10

I Coldcock Ovitz

DAVID
You're such a cynical sonofabitch.

MATT
That's why we're friends.

Jade

I was being represented in the summer of 1989 by CAA, Creative Artists Agency, the most powerful agency in Hollywood. My career was skyrocketing . . . it was after *Flashdance* and *Jagged Edge,* after the *Big Shots* auction, after a six-picture deal at $750,000 a script with United Artists.

Most of those "scores," as CAA agents liked to say, had been orchestrated by my two agents . . . the young, preppie-like Rand Holston . . . and the Kingfish Himself, the Thousand-Pound Gorilla—*Michael! Ovitz!*

I didn't know Ovitz very well, but I liked what I saw of him. I thought he was probably the most intelligent and dynamic agent I'd met. On a personal level, Michael had once offered to fly his acupuncturist to Marin when I badly injured a disc while vacationing in Santa Fe.

I was in Longboat Key, Florida, surfing warm Gulf waters with Gerri, Steve, and Suzi, when I got a call from Guy McElwaine. After an eight-year absence from the agency business, running various studios, Guy told me he was going back to ICM, Creative Artists' biggest competitor, and becoming an agent again.

Before Guy could say anything else, I said, "You've got your first client, pal."

My instant decision had nothing to do with CAA or with Michael Ovitz.

Yes, CAA had done a superb job representing me.

Yes, Michael had stayed personally involved in my deals.

But I *loved* Guy . . . it was as simple as that . . . he had helped me from the day we'd first met. And now, for the first time in my life, as my career was sky-rocketing, I could help *him*.

I would become his first "star" moneymaking client at a time when he had none.

Guy thanked me, his voice a little hoarse, and said it meant a lot to him. "It's not going to be as easy as you think," he said. "Ovitz isn't going to like this."

"Come on," I said, laughing. "He knows our history. He knows you created the monster."

"That I did," Guy laughed. "Call Barry Hirsch, see what he thinks."

Barry had been my attorney for more than a decade now. At fifty, he was powerful, low-key, and engaging, still doing his gestalt practice on the side. He had given himself a little red Porsche for his fiftieth birthday.

I called Barry from Longboat Key and told him casually that I was leaving CAA and Rand Holston and Michael Ovitz and going over to ICM and Guy McElwaine.

"You can't do that," he snapped at me. "They've done a great job for you." He said I was making a "silly and sentimental decision that will hurt your career.

"Guy doesn't know anything about being an agent in this town anymore," Barry went on. "He's too old to be an agent. It's a young man's game. The only reason he's an agent again is because he busted out of Rastar and Columbia and Weintraub and he needs to make a living."

"I don't care," I told Barry. "I owe him. And I like him. And it's going to mean a lot to him right now to be representing me."

"You're not in the charity business," Barry said. "You've got your wife and kids to consider. You've got your career to consider."

"I feel a loyalty to Guy," I said. "He's always been loyal to me."

"What about your loyalty to Michael? To CAA? Haven't they done right by you?"

"It's not the same thing," I said.

"It *is* the way I see it. Michael likes you. He's going to be hurt personally. You don't want to make an enemy of him."

"An *enemy?* What do you mean an enemy?"

"An enemy. You know what it means."

"Just because I'm going to go back to a person who *made* my career—because for the first time in my life I can help *him*—that's going to make Michael Ovitz my *enemy?*"

"Bet on it," Barry Hirsch said, "and put it in the bank."

I told Barry my mind was made up and asked him to notify CAA that I was leaving.

"Not me," Barry said. "I don't want to have anything to do with this. If you're really going to do this, then *you* tell Michael personally. You owe him that much."

"You're right," I agreed.

"Joe," Barry said, his voice softening. "I mean, really think about this. I don't think I've ever given you bad advice, have I? Don't make an emotional decision here. You do not want Michael Ovitz to be your enemy."

I called Guy back from Longboat Key and told him what Barry Hirsch had said.

He laughed and said, "I *told* you it wouldn't be easy."

Gerri and the kids and I stayed on the Florida beaches for another month, doing our annual beach/wildlife/sun crawl, moving from Key West to Captiva to Longboat to Disney World to Boca and Palm Beach, and I kept thinking about the decision I had made, as Barry had suggested. The more I thought about it, the more I was convinced I'd made the right decision. It was a personal choice and had nothing to do with business. It was a payback for Guy's many years of caring.

Maybe Barry was right. Maybe Guy *had* busted out of the studios. Maybe it *was* impossible to be an agent when you were pushing sixty in a town dedicated to eternal youth and new meat. I didn't care about any of that. All I cared about was that now, finally, after all these years, I could help Guy.

We got home to Marin from our Gypsy-like beach bum binge and I called Barry to tell him I was setting up an appointment with Ovitz. I told him that my decision to leave CAA and Michael Ovitz was final.

Barry said, "You're making the biggest mistake of your life."

I called Ovitz's secretary to set up the appointment and flew down to L.A. Rested from the long Florida trip, I was tan. I wore a beach shirt and shorts and grungy sneakers. My producer friend Ben Myron, whom I'd met in Marin, picked me up at the airport and drove me to the meeting.

I told Ben I knew this wasn't going to be pleasant, but I thought it'd work out okay. Ovitz, I said, *had* to be enough of a human being to understand my motivation. He had to understand that my decision had nothing to do with his agency's performance.

I'd never been inside the new CAA building before. I'd never seen the new Lichtenstein painting on the wall in the lobby. I was impressed—it was the classiest-looking agency headquarters in town.

I announced myself and an assistant came down to the lobby and led me up to Ovitz's office. Michael was sitting behind his desk, waiting for me. He was smiling.

I was struck by how small the office was compared with Guy's old barn-sized lounge-bar.

We shook hands warmly and he asked me to sit down facing him. He stayed behind his desk.

He was buttoned-down, impeccably dressed in corporate Armani wear—I was a bizarre counterpoint, I realized, in my beach clothes and grungy sneakers. I hoped the sneakers didn't smell. I hadn't had time after the trip to buy new ones.

He asked me about Gerri and the kids and our vacation. I noticed his eyes fix on, then flit away from my sneakers.

I cleared my throat.

"Well, I guess you know why I'm here," I said.

He looked at me a moment and said, "Barry told me."

I explained to him about Guy and went on at length about the great loyalty I felt to him, about how, even during his corporate years, Guy had kept looking out for me.

Michael listened impassively, nodding. Then he said, "What about your loyalty to me?"

He had a thin and strained smile on his face.

I tried to tell him that I *did* feel a great loyalty to him and to CAA. That, indeed, there was no other possible *reason*, no other possible *person*, that would cause me to leave.

"You mean all the deals we made for you don't count?" he said. "The three-picture deal, then the six-picture deal, the *Big Shots* sale, all the casting we've done for your movies."

He mentioned Debra Winger and Tom Berenger in *Betrayed* and Jessica Lange in *Music Box*, all CAA clients.

"We've made you the highest-paid screenwriter in the world. That doesn't count?"

"Of course it counts," I said.

"But not enough." We were looking right at each other, that thin strained smile still on his face.

"No," I said.

For a moment his smile disappeared as we looked at each other evenly. Then his face broke into a broad grin. He leaned forward over the desk, leaning closer to me.

"You know what, Joe?" he said quietly. "You're not going anywhere. You're not leaving this agency. If you do, my foot soldiers who go up and down Wilshire Boulevard each day will blow your brains out."

I wasn't sure I'd heard him right. What did he say? *Foot soldiers? Blow my brains out?* His grin was frozen now, his eyes right on mine, his voice soft, friendly, avuncular. I could hear my own heart beating like an echo chamber in my ears. He went on in a calm monologue. It almost sounded rehearsed to me. I glanced at his desk to make sure he didn't have notes in front of him.

He said that he was going to sue me.

"I don't care if I win or lose," he said, "but I'm going to tie you up with depositions and court dates so that you won't be able to spend any time at your typewriter. If you make me eat shit, I'm going to make you eat shit."

When I said I had no interest in being involved in a public spectacle, he said, "I don't care if everybody in town knows. I *want* them to know. I'm not worried about the press. All those guys want to write screenplays for Robert Redford."

I knew that he (and Barry Hirsch) represented Redford.

He said, "If somebody came into the building and took my Lichtenstein off the wall, I'd go after them. I'm going to go after you the same way. You're one of this agency's biggest assets."

He said, "This town is like a chess game. ICM [Guy's agency] isn't going after a pawn or a knight, they're going after a king. If the king goes, the knights and pawns will follow."

He facetiously suggested that maybe he'd make a trade with ICM. He'd keep me and give ICM four or five clients.

Almost as an aside, he said that if I left, he'd damage my relationships with Irwin Winkler, who'd become a close friend, and with Barry Hirsch, whom I also viewed as a good and trusted ally.

"Those guys are friends of mine," he said. "Do you think they'll still be good friends of yours if you do this?

"I like you," Michael Ovitz said. "I like your closeness to your family. I like how hard you work. I like your positive attitude. I like the fact that you have no directing or producing ambitions. You write original screenplays with star parts—your ideas are great and so are your scripts.

"I like everything about you," Michael Ovitz said, smiling good-naturedly, "except your shirt." He looked at my shirt, the floral Hawaiian knockoff I'd picked up at a roadside T-shirt shop facing the beach in St. Pete.

"You know what you're like?" Michael Ovitz smiled. "You're like one of my kids. He builds these blocks up real high and then he knocks them all down. I'm not going to let you do that to yourself."

I couldn't believe what he had said. I felt like leaning over his desk and hitting him.

Who in the fuck did this smug, self-absorbed asshole think he was?

But I realized another part of me was scared.

He was the most powerful man in Hollywood—that's who this asshole was.

He was telling me he'd put me out of business and, knowing from many years of experience what a chickenshit town Hollywood was, why did I think that he couldn't do that?

That he *wouldn't* do that?

. . .

"You're not leaving, Joe," he said, "that's all there is to it." His smile broke into a sneering little laugh. Here he was—Michael Ovitz, the Thousand-Pound Gorilla—laughing right in my face after telling me his "foot soldiers . . . would blow [my] brains out."

I stared at him and didn't say a word. I felt frozen.

I felt like I'd been witness to some obscenity that would come back in flashes till the day I died.

He was watching me assessingly, his smile gone, like a referee watching a guy on the apron of the ring, eyeing him for signs of life.

"Think about it," he said, his words quiet as a whisper.

He put his hand out to shake hands. I hesitated a second in shocked disbelief and then, may God forgive me, I shook his hand.

He gave me a big grin and said, "I'll walk you out." He opened his door for me and we walked down some stairs and through the full lobby. People stared.

Michael Ovitz, I suspected, didn't walk clients to the front door himself very often. When we got to the front door, he cut the black doorman off and opened that door for me, too.

"You're not going anywhere, Joe," he said again. "Call me."

He slapped me on the back as I stepped out the front door, his grin so toothy now I could almost see his molars.

My friend Ben Myron, who had been waiting for me in the lobby, stepped quickly around the black doorman . . . *what was CAA, the model of liberal political correctness, doing with a black doorman in 1989?* . . . took one look at me and said, "Are you okay? You're white as a sheet."

"No," I told Ben, "I'm not. I've just been fucked by a thousand-pound gorilla."

When we got to Ben's car—a long, antique white Cadillac with fire-red interior—we sat there for ten minutes as I told him what had happened. It was now Ben's turn to pale.

"*Foot soldiers?*" Ben said. "*Blow your brains out?* Is he nuts? He sounds like Captain Queeg. Did you see any brass balls?"

"He might have 'em in his pocket," I said, "but he wasn't playing with 'em."

Ben said, "What are you going to do?"

I had no idea what I was going to do, I was still reeling, but I knew I had to tell Guy what had happened as quickly as possible.

Ben drove me over to Guy's house high in Beverly Hills, just down the street from Mary Pickford and Douglas Fairbank's legendary Pickfair estate. Guy was watching a football game with a bunch of the Monday Night Regulars—Alan Ladd, the producer, was there . . . and Jim Aubrey, the famed "Cobra," former television mogul, and a cherubic man named Mr. Katz, Bookie to the Stars.

They were all in Guy's den, where the cocktail table was littered with hundred-dollar bills (these guys bet handoff-or-pass) and where the walls were lined with framed photos of Guy with Peter Sellers and Yul Brynner, Burt Reynolds, and Sinatra, Sinatra, Sinatra.

I drew Guy away from the others and told him what Ovitz had said. He was stunned. He kept shaking his head.

"I can't believe this fucking guy," he said. He noticed the expression on my face and added, "You need a drink." I glugged half a glass of straight gin and Guy said, "Lew Wasserman would pull some hard-assed shit in the old days, but nothing like this."

He called Jeff Berg, the head of International Creative Management, gave him a summary, and handed me the phone.

Jeff, known to friend and foe as "the Iceberg," asked me to give him a detailed rundown and I did. Jeff wasn't surprised.

"It's their old game," he said. "Ovitz sits a guy down who wants to leave and threatens him. They run it all the time. I think they hold on to half their clients this way. Most people soil their drawers and stay. I'll tell you this, Joe. If you leave there and they try to hurt you, this agency as an agency will do everything it can to protect you. And we can do a lot."

I thanked Jeff, hung up, and told Guy I was seeing Rand Holston that night for dinner. I'd scheduled it earlier to tell him in person that I was leaving.

"He'll play good cop," Guy said. "They've got it down to a cabaret act. Ovitz beats the shit out of you. Holston's going to tell you how much he loves you . . . all Hungarians, your kids, your pets, whatever."

Guy understood how shaken I was. "I want you to do whatever you want to do," he said. "If you're not comfortable leaving there after what he told you, then don't do it. It's not worth it to me to see you this upset. Just do what feels good to you. But remember this—if you write a good script that people in this town think they can make money off of, Michael Ovitz and all his yuppie wimps won't matter. *This town runs on greed.* If people think they can make money with a script, they'll go with Eszterhas over Ovitz—no matter how many stars Ovitz or CAA represents."

That made me feel a little better.

"Are you sure about that?" I smiled.

"Well." Guy grinned. "It'd better be a *real* goddamn *commercial* script."

I went to meet Rand Holston at Jimmy's, CAA's quasi-official clubhouse. Holston, whose usual style was humorless and robotic, was waiting for me in the bar when I got there, looking grim. It didn't look to me like Guy's good cop/bad cop prognostication was going to happen.

Holston said that after his meeting with me "the veins were bulging out" of Ovitz's neck. He added that Ovitz was the best friend anyone could have and the worst enemy.

If I left, Rand said, "Mike's going to put you into the fucking ground."

He listed the particulars. If I left CAA, no CAA star would appear in any of my scripts. "You write star vehicles," he said, "not ensemble pieces. This would be particularly damaging to you." In addition, no CAA director would direct any of my scripts. Ovitz would go out of his way with studio executives and company executives "like Martin Davis"—Paramount—to speak about me unfavorably. He would tell them that while I was a "pretty good writer," I was difficult and hard to work with. He would say that I wrote too many scripts and cared about none of them.

"There's no telling what Mike will say when he's angry," Holston said. Ovitz would make sure, Holston said, that studio people knew that I was "on his shit list."

Since most studio executives desperately wanted to use CAA's stars in their pictures, Holston said, executives would "avoid me like the plague" to curry favor with Ovitz and his CAA stars, who were the biggest names in town: Redford, Streisand, Stallone, De Niro, Cruise, Hoffman, Scorsese, Sally Field, Kim Basinger, Bill Murray, Barry Levinson, Sydney Pollack.

Holston added that since I was late turning in my latest script to United Artists, I was technically in breach of contract on my overall six-picture deal.

He said that if I left CAA, United Artists would sue me.

Rand and I never got to the dining area at Jimmy's. I lost my appetite. I had another double Tanqueray and went back to my suite at the Westwood Marquis, paid for by United Artists.

Three messages from Barry Hirsch—all marked urgent—were waiting for me. I put a "Do Not Disturb" on my phone, plunked a Willie Nelson cassette into the player, and stretched out on the living room rug.

I had a headache.

I had a very bad headache.

It was particularly exacerbated by the fact that Gerri and I had just bought, but hadn't yet moved into, a big new house in San Rafael—a house that would steeply raise our mortgage payments each month.

And now Michael Ovitz, the Thousand-Pound Gorilla, was threatening to blow my brains out and put me into the ground?

How could I leave CAA, I thought as I fell asleep on the rug, and live in our expensive new house after what Ovitz and Holston had said they were going to do to me? But . . . damn it . . . I'd already bought the house . . . Gerri and the kids were overjoyed. We were so badly cramped in our old one that two of the bathrooms were unusable because they had become storage areas.

If I left Ovitz after what he'd said, I'd have to get rid of the new house, hope for not too much of a loss on it, and break my kids' hearts. If I stayed with Ovitz, I'd have none of these problems.

But what about Guy? Could I look him in the eye?

And what about me? Could I look myself in the eye?

I woke up on the floor shortly before dawn, sat at a little secretarial desk for the next two hours in the living room of the suite, and wrote detailed notes of everything that Ovitz and Holston had said. I wasn't sure why I was doing this but an inner voice told me it was important to note all the details while they were still fresh.

Then I went down to the pool area of the hotel and watched the sun cut through the L.A. smog. When I got back to the suite there were two more messages waiting from Barry Hirsch.

"We've got to talk," Barry said when I finally called him. "Michael's going crazy."

I met Barry in his office that morning. Michael had called him several times since our meeting.

"He was screaming into the phone," Barry said, "I've never heard him like this."

When I related the specifics of what Holston had said, Barry said, "I guarantee if he puts the word out it'll have the same effect on producers. No producer will want to hire you if—right off the top—it means he has no chance for Cruise or Redford or the others."

I sat there, still somewhat in shock.

"You can't do this," Barry said. "You just can't. I can't let you do this, Joe."

Now even more disturbed, I went over to Guy's house. He got dressed and, as he nearly sputtered with anger, we went back over to Barry Hirsch's office.

On the way over, Guy said, "This doesn't have to do with me. Don't think about me in this, think about you. But this is wrong. What they're doing to you is wrong. I know this is Hollywood and I know this is a mean town, but this isn't a fucking Mafia town."

By the time we got to Barry's office, Guy was red-faced mad. Barry sat there cool as a cucumber, inheld, almost remote.

"Let me understand something, Barry," Guy said. "You're Joe's attorney. You're an official of the court. Your client's getting the shit beat out of him, he's being blackmailed, and you're advising him to give in to the blackmail. You're not saying you'll go to the D.A.'s office. You're advising Joe to give in to all of it, is that right?"

Barry said, "I'm acting in my client's best interest."

"Who's your client," Guy said, "Ovitz?"

Barry kept his fabled, gestalt-trained cool.

"Joe's my client, as you know," he said icily to Guy. "My client of more than ten years. And my friend of more than ten years. It's true that I have a lot of clients represented by CAA. It's true that this firm does a lot of business with CAA. That's no secret."

"You're damn right it's not," Guy said.

Barry also pushed the dangers of the prospective United Artists suit against me with Guy.

"It's a bluff," Guy said. "It's bullshit and you know it. No studio is going to sue anyone just to make Mike Ovitz happy."

Barry smiled. "How much do you want to bet on that?"

"Anything you want," Guy said.

"Do you want to bet his career?"

Guy's face darkened even deeper. He got up and walked to the window in Barry's office. He stared out, his back to us. His shoulders looked slumped.

Under his breath, I heard him say, "You son of a bitch."

Barry pretended that he hadn't heard it.

"Are you going to give me a piece of paper?" Barry said to Guy, "from ICM that says ICM will cover all of Joe's legal costs if United Artists sues him? Will you give me a piece of paper that says if Joe has to return any of the moneys UA has advanced him—that ICM will pay those moneys for Joe?"

Guy turned from the window and said, "You know I can't do that. ICM as a corporate entity will never do that."

"My case is closed," Barry said.

"But they'll never sue Joe!" Guy said.

"If they'll never sue, then it should mean nothing for ICM to give me a piece of paper. According to you, ICM has no risk."

Guy never even said goodbye. He went straight to the door and walked out.

I caught up with him at the building's front door. When I grabbed him by the shoulder he turned, tears in his eyes.

"I'm sorry," I said. I couldn't look him in the eye. "I can't leave Ovitz."

"Yeah," he said, "I know."

Guy forced a tight smile. "I told you I didn't want you to do anything that made you uncomfortable."

I called Barry from the lobby and told him I was staying with CAA. I could easily have walked back upstairs but I didn't want to see him.

"I don't think you've got any choice," Barry said. "But it's a good decision. I think you should tell Michael."

I said, "*You* tell Michael."

"Fine," he said.

I heard the smile in his voice.

. . .

I went back to the Westwood Marquis, sat down at the bar, and had a couple of beers. I felt like dog shit. I'd betrayed my friend and I felt like I'd betrayed myself.

The bartender tried to cheer me with stories about the times Dustin Hoffman would come into the bar barefoot and play the piano. I wasn't listening. All I thought about was that Dustin Hoffman was a CAA client.

And then suddenly, surreally, Rand Holston was there, bubbling over. Barry had let them know and Rand had raced down here to tell me how happy he was and what a good decision I'd made.

He put an arm around me and actually kissed me on the cheek as the bartender stared.

I ran upstairs, dumped all my beach gear into a suitcase, and raced out to LAX to get the hell away from this lethal place.

The next morning Ovitz called me in San Rafael. He sounded bright and upbeat.

"How's the Thousand-Pound Gorilla this morning?" I said.

"Hanging from the rafters," Ovitz said. "He's been fed some bananas." Then he said, "You made the right decision. I *knew* you would."

That hurt.

I said, "You did, huh?"

He said, "Yeah, I think I know you pretty well. If you need anything, just call."

He laughed. "Business as usual," he said.

Rand Holston called every day talking about new deals and new projects. I was waiting for Guy to call . . . but he didn't.

Gerri and the kids and I were spending a lot of time at the new house we'd bought in the Dominican section of San Rafael, talking about knocking walls out and the decor . . . but my heart wasn't in it.

"Are you okay, Dad?" Steve asked me.

Suzi said, "Don't you like this house, Dad?"

I felt awful being there. I felt like I'd violated something deep within myself. I'd allowed someone to beat me up, to treat me like dirt.

I kept stewing about these things, feeling a leaden depression as, a week later, I went back to L.A. with Gerri and the kids for a research screening of *Music Box,* my new film. I hated these demographically fine-tuned research screenings but had been through my share of them. They always ended with a focus group, a collection of dunces who, with varying degrees of pomposity, played Siskel and Ebert for an evening, knowing that every little thing they said would make a big difference to the studio people observing.

Sure enough, at the end of this focus group, some fool got up and vehemently suggested a new ending for the movie . . . finding Jessica Lange's war criminal father innocent, thereby, in my mind, turning the movie into a tool for those right-wingers who wanted war criminal prosecutions ended.

As I was walking out of the theater, smiling to myself about what the amateur moron/critic was suggesting, I felt an arm go around my back. I looked and it was Rand Holston, saying, in his most unctuous tone: "Joe, don't listen to him. You wrote a brilliant movie. I'm proud of you and CAA's proud of you."

And I knew at that moment that it was over . . . that Ovitz and Holston were out of my life . . . that I just couldn't do this . . . that I was leaving Ovitz and Holston and CAA and going back to Guy. It was like I'd gone into anaphylactic shock at Holston's touch and the greasy taste of his words.

I looked at him and laughed suddenly. He looked at me bewildered.

Gerri and the kids and I went back to the Westwood Marquis, to the same suite where I'd fallen asleep on the floor the night Ovitz had muscled me.

I laid it out for them. I couldn't stay with CAA after what Ovitz had done to me. I couldn't betray Guy. I couldn't betray myself.

I didn't know, I explained to Gerri and Steve and Suzi, what the consequences would be . . . but I was *afraid.*

It might mean that my career in Hollywood would end. It might mean that we'd have much less money.

And then I came to the most painful part.

It meant, I explained, that we couldn't live in the big house we'd just bought. I couldn't risk a mortgage payment like this with Ovitz's threats hanging over my head. We were going to have to sell the new house, I said, and live in the old one.

They were kids—Steve was fifteen, Suzi almost thirteen—they were deeply disappointed, but they understood. Gerri, who'd been married to me for twenty-one years, was, as usual, unconditionally supportive although I knew how much she loved the house. I was moved and thanked her.

Over the next two days in Marin, I thought about what I was going to do. Okay, Ovitz swore by his teeny little volume of *The Art of War* (he'd even sent me a copy years ago) . . . but I grew up in the back alleys of Cleveland's West Side.

I was going to write him a letter.

I would recount all the ugly things he and Holston had said to me. And at the end of the letter I would tell him to go fuck himself. I would cc this letter to Holston, Barry Hirsch, Guy, and Irwin Winkler. And I would make sure that this letter leaked all over town and into the papers.

It was, as I saw it, a preemptive strike. It would be more difficult for him to "put me into the fucking ground" and "blow my brains out" if the whole world was watching him and his *Art of War*–trained foot soldiers.

It would be more difficult for him to persuade United Artists to sue me if United Artists knew that *the world would know* that Michael Ovitz had put them up to it.

It would be more difficult for him to destroy my relationships with Barry Hirsch and Irwin Winkler if they knew *the world would know* they were so afraid of Michael Ovitz that they blew me off.

And it would be more difficult for studio heads to do no business with me if the world would consider them Ovitz's pawns.

The publicity . . . the fallout . . . would, I thought, be my best armor to keep my career from being put into the ground. I told no one what my plan was, not even Gerri and my kids. I wanted to be able to credibly deny leaking this letter when it hit the fan.

And I knew just how it would leak. My friend Costa-Gavras was back in Paris. I didn't have his Paris address, so I was going to send a Xerox of my letter to Ovitz to Costa . . . through his agent at William Morris, John Ptak.

But I wasn't going to *seal the envelope* to Costa. I was betting that Hollywood being Hollywood, Ptak wouldn't be able to resist taking a peek at what was inside the envelope addressed to Costa.

I was further betting that if Ptak read it, he'd show it to William Morris super-agent Sue Mengers, the biggest Ovitz-hater in town. I was sure that if Mengers got her hands on it, she'd get it all over town.

Three days after Rand Holston put his arms around me, I sat down at my manual typewriter, the notes I had taken at the Westwood Marquis nearby, and wrote my letter to Michael Ovitz. It came out of me in a blind-hot fury. I wrote it in forty minutes and then retyped it in another hour.

With notes in hand, I recounted the things Ovitz and Holston had said to me . . . and then I concluded this way:

> To say that I was in shock after my meeting with you and Rand would be putting it mildly. What you were threatening me with was a twisted new version of the old-fashioned blacklist. I felt like the character in Irwin's new script whose career was destroyed because he refused to inform on his friends. You were threatening to destroy my career because I was refusing to turn my back on a friend.
>
> I live in Marin County; I spend my time with my family and with my work; I've avoided industry power entanglements for thirteen years. Now I felt, as I told my wife when I came home to think all this over, like an infant who wakes up in his crib with a thousand-pound gorilla screeching in his face. In the two weeks that have gone by, I have thought about little else than the things you and Rand said to me. Plain and simple, cutting out all the smiles and friendliness, it's blackmail. It's extortion, the street-

hood protection racket we've seen too many times in bad gangster movies. If you don't pay us the money, we'll burn your store down. Never mind that in this case it wasn't even about money—not for a while, anyway: I told you that ICM didn't even want to split the commissions with you on any of my existing deals—"Fuck the commissions," you said, "I don't care about the commissions."

Even the dialogue, I reflected, was out of those bad gangster movies: "blow your brains out" and "put you into the fucking ground" and "If you make me eat shit, I'm going to make you eat shit."

As I thought about what happened, I continued, increasingly, to be horrified by it. You are agents. Your role is to help and encourage my career and my creativity. Your role is not to place me in personal emotional turmoil. Your role is not to threaten to destroy my family's livelihood if I don't do your bidding. I am not an asset; I am a human being. I am not a painting hung on a wall; I am not a part of a chess set. I am not a piece of meat to be "traded" for other pieces of meat. I am not a child playing with blocks. This isn't a game. It's my life.

What I have decided, simply, after this period of time, is that I cannot live with myself and continue to be represented by you. I find the threats you and Rand made to be morally repugnant. I simply can't function on a day-to-day business basis with you and Rand without feeling myself dirtied.

Maybe you can beat the hell out of some people and they will smile at you afterward and make nice, but I can't do that. I have always believed, both personally and in my scripts, in the triumph of the human spirit. I have abhorred bullying of all kinds—by government, by police, by political extremism of the Left and the Right, by the rich—maybe it's because I came to this country as a child and was the victim of a lot of bullying when I was an adolescent.

But I always fought back; I was bloodied a lot, but I fought back. I know the risks I am taking: I am not doing this blithely. Yes, you might very well be able to hurt me with your stars, your directors, and your friends on the executive level. Yes, Irwin and Barry are friends of yours and maybe you will be able to damage my relationships with them—but as much as I treasure those relationships with them, if my decision to leave CAA affects them, then they're not worth it anyway. Yes, you might sue me and convince UA and God knows who else to sue me. And yes, I know that you can play dirty—the things you said about Guy in your meeting with me are nothing less than character assassination.

But I will risk all that. Rich or poor, successful or not, I have always been able to look myself in the mirror. I am not saying that I don't take

*your threats seriously; I take your threats very seriously indeed. But I have
discussed all of this with my wife, with my fifteen-year-old boy and my
thirteen-year-old girl, and they support my decision.*

*After three years of searching, we bought a bigger and much more
expensive house recently. We have decided, because of your threats and the
uncertainty they cast on my future, to put the new house up for sale and
stay in our old one. You told me of your feeling for your own family; do
you have any idea how much pain and turmoil you've caused mine?*

*I think the biggest reason I can't stay with you has to do with my
children. I have taught them to fight for what's right. What you did is
wrong. I can't teach my children one thing and then, on the most elemental level, do another. I am not that kind of man.*

*So do whatever you want to do, Mike, and fuck you. I have my family
and I have my old manual imperfect typewriter and they have always
been the things I've treasured the most. Barry Hirsch will officially notify
you that I have left CAA and from this date on Guy McElwaine will
represent me.*

I went down to the stationery store in San Rafael, made six Xerox copies,
drove home, addressed the envelopes, and took them to Federal Express in
Larkspur Landing. I drove back to San Rafael, bought two hot dogs on the
street, took them into the Positively Fourth Street saloon, and ate them with two
cold Beck's beers. Hendrix was on the jukebox. I felt high. *I felt like I could kiss
the sky.*

I called Guy that night and said, "I want to read you a letter I sent Michael Ovitz
today."

I read him the letter and Guy started to cry. He didn't say anything, he just
cried.

"I'll call you back," he said.

When he did, in fifteen minutes, he was still choked. "It's the proudest
moment of my life," he said.

The first call came shortly after ten o'clock the next morning. It was Michael
Ovitz. Gerri took the call. "Joseph's not in," she told his secretary.

Ovitz got on the line with Gerri. I was listening in on another phone.

"Gerri, please," Ovitz said. "I've got to talk to him." His voice was high. I'd
never heard him sound like this. "It's very important. I've got to talk to him."

I gave her a hand signal and she hung up on him. I loved the moment.

The Thousand-Pound Gorilla was *scrambled.*

The dog was having his day!

· · ·

The phone rang again immediately. This time Michael had dialed himself.

"Gerri, listen," he said. "Please don't hang up. I'll take a plane up there. I'll be there in an hour. I've got to talk to him."

The Thousand-Pound Gorilla was *begging*.

I thought: *You punk. You bully.*

You tell someone you're going to put him into the ground, you tell him your goons are going to blow his brains out, you tell him he's a fancy painting on your architecturally splendid wall . . .

I thought: *Beg!*

I gave Gerri the hand signal and she hung up on him again.

He called again mid-afternoon. This time the Thousand-Pound Gorilla sounded very tired.

"Gerri," he said, "I know you're going to hang up on me. Please don't. Tell Joe I'm sorry. I'm very sorry. I just want to come up and talk to him for fifteen minutes." His voice was plaintive and defeated this time.

Gerri hung up on him again.

I got calls from other agents at ICM throughout the day so I knew news of the letter was already making its way around the agency, but the call I was waiting for came the next day.

It was John Ptak, Costa-Gavras's agent from William Morris.

"I opened your note to Costa," Ptak said. "I hope you don't mind, but the envelope wasn't sealed."

He expressed his outrage over what Michael and Rand had said and praised me for not giving in to their threats.

And then he said, "Would you mind if I share this with my colleague Sue Mengers?"

"No," I said, very casually, "that's okay."

The next morning, by Federal Express, I received a letter from Michael. It said:

> When I received your letter this morning I was totally shocked since my recollection of our conversation bore no relationship to your recollection. Truly this appears to be one of those Rashomon situations, and your letter simply makes little or no sense to me.
>
> As I explained to you when we were together, you are an important client of this company and all that I was trying to do was to keep you as a client. There was no other agenda. If you have to leave, you have to leave and so be it. I have talked to Guy and told him that whatever we can do to be helpful in this transition we will do. Of course, as you assured me, I am expecting that you will pay us whatever you owe us.
>
> I am particularly sensitive when people bring families and children

into business discussions. If someone said to me what you think I said to you, I would feel the same way as you expressed in your letter. I think your letter was unfair and unfounded, but it does not change my respect for your talent. I only hope that in time you will reflect on the true spirit of what I was trying to communicate to you.

I want to make it eminently clear that in no way will I, Rand, or anyone else in this agency, stand in the way of your pursuing your career. So please, erase from your mind any of your erroneous anxieties or thoughts you may have to the contrary. Best wishes and continued success.

Never mind how plaintive and defeated he'd sounded over the phone, now I was enraged all over again.

Rashomon? Erroneous anxieties? Unfair and unfounded? The true spirit of what he was trying to communicate to me?

I found one sentence especially slick. In no way, he wrote, would he or Rand stand in the way of my "pursuing" my career. He couldn't stand in the way of my "*pursuit*" of it. What he'd threatened to do was to put the career itself "into the fucking ground."

I wrote him another letter in response to his!

> *A brief response to your letter dated October 3, 1989.*
>
> 1. *You can quote* Rashomon *as much as you like, but words like "my foot soldiers . . . will blow your brains out" and "he'll put you into the fucking ground" leave little room for ambiguity.*
>
> 2. *I am particularly sensitive when people bring their families and children into business discussions too—and I hope that in the future you will reflect that keeping important clients isn't worth haunting families and children the way you haunt mine.*
>
> 3. *I understand very well "the true spirit" of what you were trying to communicate to me in the meeting and will live my life accordingly.*
>
> 4. *My "erroneous anxieties" notwithstanding, we are selling our new house anyway.*
>
> 5. *Please understand that after the things you and Rand said to me, I can hardly take your "best wishes" for my "continued success" seriously.*

By noon of the day after John Ptak called me, Guy called to tell me that people all over town were faxing around my original letter to Michael.

People were Xeroxing faxes and then sending them on again.

Debra Winger, who'd had her own problems with CAA, was in the Middle East desert filming *Sheltering Sky* when her fax machine kicked out my letter to Ovitz.

Marvin Josephson, the corporate head of ICM, was in the South of France. His wife read it to him in the back of a limousine and he started clapping his hands.

Producer Ray Stark, whom I'd barely met, got his fax and sent Guy a $2 million check made out to me—"no strings"—so I could buy our new house. (I called Ray and thanked him but said no thanks to "the most generous thing that's ever happened to me." "You're an idiot, take the money," Ray said.)

Producer and old friend Don Simpson sent me a note that said, "Read your Ovitz letter. My pulse is at 200 beats a minute. You are a *bad* motherfucker!"

Shortly thereafter, the *Los Angeles Times* led its Calendar section with an account of my letter. The wire services picked it up and I was suddenly besieged by *Stern* and the *Times* of London and *Paris Match*, who all wanted to run it. (The next issue of *Harper's Magazine* would run it in full.) It was turning into a media circus.

Liz Smith quoted the letter and talked about Ovitz's "gangster tactics." The *Los Angeles Herald Examiner*, trying to find follow-ups to the story, found a young screenwriter who'd been threatened by CAA the same way and had audiotapes to prove it.

Ovitz denied to the press that he had ever said those things to me . . . no foot soldiers . . . no threats . . . I'd made it all up.

He had friends like Michael Eisner and Sydney Pollack quoted about the "theatricality" of my letter's account of what had "allegedly" happened. Interestingly, I noted, Rand Holston issued no denials and sent me no letter denying my allegations.

Meanwhile, I started getting phone calls and letters from others who'd been similarly threatened. The producer Bernie Brillstein even remembered the same words being used to him—"My foot soldiers will put you into the ground."

The producer Edward Feldman, who produced *Wired*, the John Belushi movie taken from Bob Woodward's book which Ovitz was desperate to stop, remembered the same threats.

The actor Mark Harmon wrote me a chilling letter detailing the things CAA agents had done to damage his career after he left the agency.

Late one night as the story was raging in the press, I got a call from a friend of Ovitz's. He was whispering.

"Joe," he said, "this call never happened, okay? Michael is crazy with this stuff. Watch your driving, check the brakes of your car, see if you're being followed."

I felt my blood run cold. *Were we really talking now about literally putting me into the ground? About blowing my brains out? Were we talking real flesh and blood now and not career?*

"What are you telling me?" I said to Ovitz's friend.

"Be careful, that's what I'm telling you. Be careful."

I felt my knees a little weak. I had two beautiful children I adored. I had a wife who'd been good to me for very many years.

Is this where all this was going? To some insane netherworld where I had to check my brakes and my rearview mirror?

"Do you think maybe we should just leave the country for a while and disappear?" I said to him.

"I think that's a great idea," he said.

I hung up and I sat in my tiny office/den, shaken.

I told Gerri what the friend had said and she started to cry.

We made a list of places where we could go and settled on Zurich and the Dolder Grand Hotel, which Steve and Suzi had loved.

I started thinking about it. We'd have to take the kids out of school when they were just getting adjusted to the new year. And what would it look like if I suddenly disappeared? The media was all over this. Even *60 Minutes* was trying to get me to talk about it.

It would look, I thought, in the face of Michael's heated denials, like I had something to hide.

I called my friend Irwin Winkler in Paris. I knew how well he knew Ovitz and I knew how close he was to Michael, Ron Meyer—Ovitz's number-two man at CAA—and CAA. But I trusted Irwin.

I woke him up. I didn't tell him what Ovitz's friend had said to me, all I said was that I was sorry I'd woken him but that I had to ask him the most important question I'd ever ask him.

"Is Michael crazy?" I asked. "Should I be afraid for my life and Gerri's and the kids' lives?"

"He's crazy like a fox," Irwin said flatly. "There's no reason you should be afraid for your life or your family's."

I thanked Irwin and decided we weren't going anywhere.

We got the first phoned death threat the next day.

"Joe Eszterhas?" a male voice said, "you're a dead man."

We got another call the next day, same voice, same message.

A couple days later our housekeeper went out into the driveway to get the morning *Chronicle* and she found a black skull-and-bones bandanna wrapped around the paper.

I hired a Marin County private investigator to tap our phones and trace the calls. He notified someone at the San Rafael police department and they put our house on a special watch.

. . .

Don Simpson called me and asked me to come down to see him. He said it was important and he didn't want to discuss it over the phone. We met at his house.

"I want to tell you something," he said. "Watch your ass when you're down here. No bimbos, no parties. Don't drive anywhere. Use a limo. Watch what you drink. Beer or wine, have them open it at your table. Stay in different hotels. Don't register under your own name."

"What's going on?" I said.

"I like you."

"What else is going on?"

Don smiled. "Life in the fast lane."

I saw Craig Baumgarten, who said Ovitz had showed up at his house in a sweat suit on a Sunday morning. They weren't close. Ovitz had never been to his house before.

"He asked me about you and other women," Craig said. "I told him you were married. I said I didn't know anything about you and other women. He said, '*Come on, I know there are other women.*' I told him he knew more than I did."

I had dinner with Irwin Winkler, now back in L.A. He picked the place and the one he picked was odd.

Irwin liked places like Spago and Morton's and Le Dome, places where, I always felt, we were showing each other off. This time he picked an obscure little neighborhood Italian place on Pico.

He wasn't happy. And he was frank about being in a difficult position. He told me how close Ron Meyer had gotten to him and his family, how often Ron stayed with them as a house guest. Irwin disagreed with what I had done, with both my decision to go back to Guy and with my letter.

"He's wounded," Irwin said about Michael. "He's not a guy you wound. He's very upset. Judy [Ovitz's wife] is very upset. He's worked hard on his image. He wants to be known as a good guy, a philanthropist. He gives a lot of money. He wants to be a captain of industry. He might even want to be president someday. You ruined his image. It'll never be the same for him."

Irwin said the smartest thing I could do would be to get out of the business for a couple years.

"Go to Europe and write a novel," he said.

Giving me even more pause on this particularly Kafkaesque L.A. trip was the meeting I had with one of Barry Hirsch's law partners. He called me at my hotel and asked to meet in my suite. We'd known each other a long time. He was a former rock and roller who'd played in a hit band a long time ago.

"I'm risking my career telling you this," he said. "You need a new lawyer. Our firm handles too many of CAA's clients. We work hand in hand with CAA. If they get a new client, they send him to us. If we get a new client, we try to steer him to CAA."

His words were like kicks to my ribs that made me feel breathless. *What? I needed a new lawyer? Now? When I was in the biggest fight of my life?*

My imagination went into overdrive and I felt the Jell-O-like, showbiz ground shift seismically beneath me. I felt like I was adapting a le Carré novel, but I was not only its screenwriter . . . I was also its angst-to-the-max central character, my inner bearings lost and manipulated by powerful and sinister forces.

What was this lawyer telling me? Was it possible that I was a pawn in a deceitful and amoral Hollywood game? Was it possible that Barry Hirsch, who had been a guru and ring doctor in my life, had too many strings binding him to Ovitz, who had overnight become Darth Vader in my life?

I found myself suddenly in a maelstrom of my own fears and *melo-dramaturges,* face-to-face, nose-to-nose, eyeball-to-eyeball with Darth Vader. I had the heebie-jeebie willies. I imagined myself to be both Joseph K and John Galt, trusting no guru or ring doctor, no matter how many faithful years he'd loyally spent in my corner, patching up my cuts.

I decided to end my relationship with Barry and his law firm, thereby ful-filling Darth Vader's dark and sad prophecy.

I went back to Marin and thought about it. We had gotten another death threat while I was gone—the call, of course, too brief to be traced. I could simply fire Barry Hirsch or . . . I could use him.

I called Barry at his office and told his secretary it was an emergency. He called me back from a pay phone.

I told him *60 Minutes* was trying to talk to me about Michael. I said that if I got any more threats or found any more skull-and-bones scarves on my drive-way, I'd agree to speak to them.

Barry was silent for a long moment and then he said, "You don't want to go on *60 Minutes.*"

I said, "No I don't."

From that day on, I got no more death threats, no more black scarves.

No star clients, meanwhile, were deserting CAA.

Robert Redford, so it was said, was upset by my letter and flew into town to meet with Michael. Michael convinced him that his *Rashomon* account was the truthful one.

I knew from several sources how enraged Michael was as he was forced to keep making his denials. Judy Ovitz, at lunch one day, went across the room to a table with Tom Cruise and screenwriter Robert Towne and, with no preliminaries, said, "Can you believe the lies this horrible man is telling about Michael?"

A CAA agent had told me that Michael had bought a new sculpture of a Cadillac wrapped around a telephone pole.

"You see that?" Michael said to friends. "That's Joe Eszterhas's career."

I wrote Barry Hirsch a brief note telling him I was firing him but stating no reason. He never wrote or called in response.

Now, *right* now, under these circumstances, I *really* needed a lawyer and I needed a powerful one, somebody who had the will and the strength, if needed, to stand up to CAA.

I asked Guy which powerful entertainment lawyer disliked Ovitz.

"You mean which one will *admit* to disliking him," he said with a laugh.

I spoke to Skip Brittenham, a fiercely independent man and the head of one of the most powerful firms, and while Skip didn't admit to disliking Ovitz, he did say that what Ovitz had done to me was wrong and he had no doubts that Ovitz had said what I was alleging he'd said.

"If I represent you," Skip said in his mild-mannered way, "it's going to cause me business problems, but I'm going to do it."

We shook hands on our agreement and when word got out the following week that Skip was representing me, Bill Haber, one of CAA's top agents closest to Michael, called Skip and said, "If you represent Eszterhas, you are never getting any business from this agency."

And Skip, in his mild-mannered way, said, "Oh, fuck you."

Haber meant it. Skip's firm got no CAA referrals for years.

About a month after my letter became public, *Music Box* had its Hollywood premiere at the Academy Theatre on Wilshire. I was curious how I would be treated at this gala industry event and I got my answer as soon as Gerri and I walked in with Steve and Suzi. *People fled from us.*

Studio executives I'd known for a decade looked right through me. Even Jessica Lange, a tough cookie, looked nervous around me, and I suspected it was because of the hovering presence of Pat Kingsley, Jessie's PR person (also CAA's favorite), who was casting daggers at me.

Dawn Steel, my old friend from *Flashdance,* a woman I greatly admired, was the only person there who didn't seem frightened or embarrassed by my presence. She nearly ran across the lobby, hugged me, and then hugged Gerri and Steve and Suzi, whom she had never met.

But something strange happened inside the darkness of the theater. As the credits rolled and my name came up, the applause was explosive . . . more applause even than for Jessie or Costa, an unheard of position for any screen-writer to be in.

It told me there were a lot of people here who admired what I'd done—that was the *good* news.

The *bad* news was that, considering the way they'd treated me in the lobby, there were a lot of very frightened people here, too.

Afterward, at a Wolfgang Puck–catered reception at Irwin Winkler's house, I saw how nervous Irwin was, too. He seated us at the far end of the tent, about as far away from the main table as he could. And he hardly spoke to us all night. I was hurt but tried to understand it: I counted at least six CAA agents, including Ron Meyer, inside Wolfgang's elaborate tent.

Stephen Farber, the writer and critic, told me this story: "I was teaching an adult education film course at UCLA. When your letter to Ovitz surfaced in the media, I did a lecture in class about Hollywood agents and how much I admired your letter. I got a phone call from Mike Ovitz a few days later. I couldn't believe it. I'd never met Mike Ovitz. I didn't even know anybody who knew Michael Ovitz. He asked me to have lunch with him at his office. *Wow!* I was stunned. *Lunch with Michael Ovitz at his fancy CAA office? Who? Me?*

"The lunch was catered. Very elaborate. Ovitz was charming and very curious about me. He even asked me if I had any scripts in the drawer I wanted to sell. Then he got to what he wanted. He wondered if I could do another lecture about your letter and Hollywood agents. A lecture that wouldn't be quite as one-sided in your favor as the one I'd done.

"Why? Why was it so important what *I* said in a classroom about him and you? Because his father was in my adult education class. His father's feelings had been hurt by the things I'd said.

"I found that quite touching. Mike Ovitz may have been the tough guy super-agent, but he really loved his father."

I stayed as far away as possible from Hollywood for the next few months, working on scripts to fulfill my United Artists contract. Three months after I sent Ovitz my letter, I saw a headline in the *Los Angeles Times* that got my attention.

A front-page story announced that a screenwriter had set a new record price for a screenplay in Hollywood. His name was Shane Black. The title of the script was *The Last Boy Scout.* He had received $1.75 million for it.

The story didn't make me happy. I had held the record for a screenplay price in Hollywood since 1980, when I had sold *City Hall* for $500,000. I had stretched that record in 1986 to $1.25 million for *Big Shots.*

I had no problem with any other writer making lots and lots of money. I wanted *all* writers to make lots and lots of money and rooted for them to do so. But I was competitive. *Very* competitive.

. . .

I was thinking about film noir. I'd never written film noir but I loved the genre and thought writers like Jim Thompson and Cornell Woolrich and David Goodis were twisted, possessed geniuses.

In an effort not to be pigeonholed in Hollywood . . . and to keep challenging myself . . . I'd cut across a lot of genres. *Flashdance* was a musical, *Big Shots* was a kid's movie, *Checking Out* was a dark comedy, *F.I.S.T.* was a historical drama, *Jagged Edge* was an old-fashioned mystery, *Music Box* was a political thriller.

So I started thinking about a noir piece with a strong sexual content. I had also written three movies where men manipulated the women who loved them—*Jagged Edge, Betrayed,* and *Music Box*.

I thought it would be fun to flip the dynamic: to do a movie about a man being manipulated by a woman who is brilliant, omnisexual, and evil. I wanted to touch on thrill killing and homicidal impulse, concepts I found especially frightening.

The piece wrote itself. I improvised all the way through. I made no notes for myself, no outline. I simply put the things down which the characters said to me.

I immersed myself in the Rolling Stones. For some reason I didn't really understand, their music was at the core of the piece.

Three weeks from the time I started thinking about it, I finished the piece. I called the script *Love Hurts*.

The morning that I sent it to Guy, I changed the title to *Basic Instinct*.

Both Guy and Jeff Berg were knocked out.

"Now *this* is what I mean by commercial," Guy said, harking back to the advice he'd given me when I was thinking about leaving Ovitz . . . that the best way to overcome Ovitz was to write a script that everyone felt would make money.

I sent the script to Irwin Winkler, vacationing at the Hôtel du Cap in Antibes, and asked him to produce it. "It's not the kind of thing I usually produce," he said, "but it's a helluva script. Sure, I'll produce it."

What Guy and Jeff had in mind was to do a "full, broad-based auction" . . . to send it to every production entity in town with any kind of money and to try to get them to bid against each other.

My first question to Guy and to Jeff when they told me their plan was, "What about Ovitz?"

"Fuck Ovitz," Guy said. "Remember what I told you? *This town runs on greed.* This is a $200 million hit movie."

"Ovitz can't hurt us on this one," Berg said. "He won't dare to try to stop this. If he does, the media will be all over him in a nanosecond thanks to your letter. A year from now, when we go out with another script, *that's* when we have to watch him."

"You know what?" Guy said. "In a funny way, Ovitz just might work *for* us. A lot of people don't like him or resent CAA's power. Maybe they'll want to send him a message by bidding on this."

The bidding began at ten o'clock in the morning.

By noon, we had offers up to $2 million.

"The whole town's playing," Jeff Berg told me. He was excited.

"Joe," he said, "this is where I live and breathe.

"I'll tell you where I think this is going," Jeff said. "I think I can get you four million dollars for this, without Winkler, or I can get *you* three with a mil as Winkler's producing fee. If you want my advice, we don't need Winkler. Take the four million and whoever buys it will put on a producer."

I told Jeff I didn't want to do that. I'd asked Irwin to produce it. He was, in my mind, the best producer in town. And he'd stayed my friend, albeit a little shakily, through the Ovitz mess.

"You're handing the guy a million dollars on a silver platter," Jeff said. "He didn't have anything to do with developing this. His name isn't helping us sell this. The studios don't care who's going to produce this. Many of them would prefer to use their own producers. I'm not going to say to you that Irwin Winkler is ever exactly a liability, but he doesn't bring anything to the party here."

I told Jeff I was sticking with Irwin and at three o'clock that afternoon, the auction ended. Mario Kassar, the head of Carolco, bought *Basic Instinct* for $3 million (and another $1 million for Irwin to produce). More significantly maybe in the context of Michael Ovitz's threats, every studio entity in town with the exception of Fox had bid for it.

You talk about kissing the sky? Six months after foot soldiers were going to put me into the ground, I had set a staggering new writer's record. It was more money than most directors and some stars were getting.

Guy was right: The town ran on greed.

Daily Variety put a big bold headline across the top of the front page that said, "A NEW ERA DAWNS IN HOLLYWOOD." The story said, "In what must have felt like vindication for Eszterhas in his battle with Michael Ovitz . . ."

It was big news everywhere, even on the wire services and in the daily papers. CBS even put an interview with me on its *Nightly News*. Most stories mentioned my letter to Ovitz in their second paragraph.

The day after the sale, I took Steve to a baseball card show in San Jose and bought him six Rickey Henderson rookie cards.

The best news to me was that we could buy our big house now. I'd made so much money on *Basic* that whatever Michael Ovitz did or tried to do, Gerri and I and Steve and Suzi would be okay.

· · ·

Gerri and I hadn't made love for years . . . until now, down here in Captiva, Florida, on this balmy summer afternoon. We were sky-high, celebrating the $3 million I'd gotten for writing *Basic Instinct.*

Steve and Suzi were outside playing on the beach. The day was sun-kissed. There was a tropical breeze.

We spoke afterward about the money—how it would free us, how we could now buy a house big enough for the kids to have their own bedrooms, how all the years of struggle and battle had been worth it.

We didn't realize until years later that even though we could buy our big house now . . . *we weren't free* . . . that, on that afternoon in Captiva, we should have been talking not about money . . . but about why we hadn't made love in years.

I was driving by the CAA building one day and, without giving it a thought, I stuck my hand out the window and gave the building my middle finger.

It was a kind of reflex action.

It felt so good that I did it every time that I passed the building from then on.

It felt so good that I was still doing it ten years later, when Michael Ovitz was long gone from CAA.

I even did it on film for ABC's *20/20*. They didn't get the shot right so we kept driving around the building over and over again as I pumped my middle finger into the air.

A reporter asked me after my letter became public if I was afraid of Michael Ovitz.

I listed the reasons why I wasn't afraid of him:

1. He didn't grow up in refugee camps.
2. He didn't grow up on the West Side of Cleveland.
3. He never carried a knife strapped to his wrist.
4. He never owned a zip gun.
5. He was the president of his college fraternity.
6. He went to college at UCLA.
7. He was short.
8. He was nearly bald.
9. He grew up middle-class in the Valley.
10. He took karate lessons from Steven Seagal.

[Quick Cut]

"You Know I Love You"

Hollywood Lies:

You look terrific!
My answering service keeps screwing my messages up.
We've got half the financing.
I was working on the script with Kubrick when he died.
Did you lose weight?
He's a writer's director.
We're messengering the check to your accountants.
I never read the trades.
I never read my reviews.
I didn't see the movie.
I'll read your script tonight.
I'd love to be there but we're in Aspen this weekend.
I really respect his artistic integrity.
It's not about the money.
I'll read your script tomorrow.
Tom and Penélope are coming.
Steven almost committed to it.
I'll read your script this weekend.
I couldn't get it past business affairs.
I wrote that movie but the Writers Guild screwed me out of the credit.
I'm only halfway through your script but I love it.
This is just a suggestion.
Don't make any changes in your script you don't want to make.
I love this ending but market research doesn't.
I believe in redemption.
I love ambiguity.
I want it to be like Network.

Think Oscars, not grosses.
It did great foreign.
The studio took it away from me and recut it.
All your script needs is a little touch-up.
This isn't about ego, it's about getting it right.
I don't believe in control.
We're friends, aren't we?
Harvey's interested.
We had creative differences.
You know I love you.

CHAPTER 11

[Flashback]

Attempted Murders

OBIE

Lots of things aren't fair, are they, Mom?

OBIE'S MOM

How do you mean?

OBIE

In life.

OBIE'S MOM

No. But we live with them.

OBIE

I know. But they hurt.

Big Shots

I'd been begging my parents for a pet and my mother brought home a kitten she'd found huddling in a gutter. We named her Caesar, kept her in a box with a clock, and fed her with a baby bottle.

As the kitten got older, she went pee-pee in only one spot: on my father's newly typed manuscripts. My mother thought that was funny.

My father said Oszkár Moldován and the other linotype operators were laughing at him because his writing always smelled like cat piss. My mother thought that was funny, too.

When I got home from school one day, Caesar was gone. I looked every-where in the apartment, in the circulation office downstairs, in the printing shop, in the concrete yard, in the alley. I even looked in the Num Num Potato Chip factory truck lot. I was frantic.

"Stop looking for the cat," my mother said without warning at dinner. "Your father killed it."

My father said, "*What did you say?*"

"You killed it," my mother said, looking him right in the eye.

"How can you say such a horrible thing?" my father said. His voice was high. He looked like he was in shock.

"You and your precious writing," she spat at him. "Caesar knew its worth!"

"What's wrong with you, Mária?" he said. "Why are you angry with me? What have I done to you?" He looked like he was going to cry.

She said nothing and literally ran out of the room.

Radio Free Europe said the Communists had launched a Sputnik with a dog named Laika in it.

I found my mother sitting at the kitchen table one day, the ice bag on her head, pressing on her temples as hard as she could.

"Are you all right, Mama?" I asked.

My mother said, "It is up there."

"What?"

"The Sputnik. It is up there going around and around shooting out its rays. Around and around, it never stops."

On another day when I asked her how she was feeling, she said, "I couldn't sleep all night. I kept hearing that poor dog howl."

I said, "What dog?"

"That Laika," she said, "up there howling, going around and around. Didn't you hear her?"

I said, "No, mama."

She said, "Honestly, I really don't understand how you and your father can sleep through that poor dog's misery."

"*Ex Libris*" is what it said on the bottom of the pieces of paper which my father was sticking into his books.

It said "Dr. István Eszterhás" on the top next to a design which he had drawn: a globe with the holy crown of St. Stephen on top of it.

My mother was holding one of these pretty pieces of paper.

"How much did these cost?" my mother said.

"Not much," my father said, "hardly anything." He said one of the Franciscans had printed it for him downstairs in the printing shop.

"But still *something*," my mother said. "There must be the cost for the paper it's printed on."

My father shrugged. "Almost nothing," he said.

"We live like paupers," my mother said. "There are lice in the clothes that we buy. We eat fruit that is almost spoiled with worms inside sometimes. The boy's shoes fall off his feet. And you buy fancy decorations for the books that your *kurva* gives you—"

"*Stop it!*" my father cried.

"—Your *kurva* gives you at the library."

"*Stop it now!*" he cried, slamming a book to the table. "*Enough!* I have nothing! *Nothing!* I can at least have this in my books like I had in my books in Hungary! *At least this!* Do you understand me, you crazy woman? *At least this!*" He was trembling. His face was purple.

"Ex Libris!" She laughed in a high, tinny voice. "Ex Libris!" I saw she was shaking, too.

I came home from school one day and she was at the kitchen table cooking something. I kissed her on the cheek as was my usual custom when I got home from school. She wouldn't even look at me.

I started talking to her but she didn't respond. She kept her eyes on the stove. I asked her what was wrong but she didn't say anything. I was sure that my parents had discovered something awful that I had done.

"Did I do something wrong?" I asked my mother.

She didn't answer me. She wouldn't look at me.

I found my father in the printing shop wearing his dark green visor and looking at the page proofs of that week's newspaper.

"What's wrong with Nana?" I asked.

"I don't know," he said. He didn't look up from the proofs.

"Did I do something, Papa?"

I saw him smile slightly. "Probably," he said, "but if you did I don't know about it yet."

"She won't talk to me," I said.

"She won't talk to me, either."

"Did something happen?" I asked. "Did you have an argument?"

"No," he said. "She woke up this morning and never said good morning and hasn't said anything all day."

"Is she okay?"

"Her head hurts," he said. "I saw her put the ice bag on it."

That night at dinner she was mute. There was a faraway look in her eyes. She served the soup, ate little, and smoked her cigarettes.

My father and I tried to talk to her.

"Did I hurt you somehow, Mária?" my father said. "If I did I'm sorry."

And: "Please tell us what the matter is, Mária. Please. Whatever it is it will be all right, Mária."

And: "Don't do this, Mária, please. Don't do this to the boy."

I was sitting at the table, crying.

"Nana," I said, "what's wrong? Tell me what's wrong. I'm sorry, Nana. If I did something, I'm sorry. Please, Nana."

She was stone-faced, unblinking, her jaw set. She didn't say a word. I fell asleep on my living room couch. For the first time in my life, she didn't kiss me good night.

I couldn't focus on anything in school the next day and ran the sixteen blocks home from school.

She was in the kitchen again, a cigarette in her mouth, her face stone, her jaw set.

As I moved to kiss her, she moved away from me. I started to cry and ran for my father in the printing shop. He hugged me.

"She must be sick," he said. "We'll try to talk to her tonight."

"What's wrong with her?"

"I don't know," my father said.

That night at dinner she sat there unblinking, mute, eyes distant again. My father tried again.

" Mária, are you sick? I'll call the doctor. What's wrong, Mária? Please, we love you. I love you. The boy loves you."

He was choking up and started to cry.

"We only have each other, Mária," he said. "Just the three of us. We have nothing else. Just us."

And then she suddenly started to laugh. It was a high-pitched and hyena-like sound that I'd never heard before from a human being. It put chills down my back.

My father's face flushed deep red. He got up and held on to the kitchen table— he had high blood pressure and suffered dizzy spells—and he started to yell at her. "Stop this! This isn't funny! You think this is funny? Look what you're doing to the boy!"

I was shaking. I felt tears running down my cheeks.

My mother got up from the table and, her eyes wild, started to scream words at my father. She screamed that he was in love with the woman at the library . . . that he and the priests were teaching me to be a "pervert" like them . . . that I was spilling my filthy and smelly seed into the living room couch at night and she had to scrub it away with Ajax every morning . . . that I had perverted sick pictures in my wallet and . . . she suddenly threw something she had in her apron pocket onto the kitchen table.

I stared at it, horrified. It was a prophylactic that I had no use for but that I had recently hidden in the fold of my wallet.

My father was yelling back at her. "What is wrong with you? Are you crazy? Have you lost your mind, Mária? How can you say such filth?"

And always the words: "Look at the boy, Mária! *My God, look what you're doing to the boy!*"

I was shaking so hard that I startled myself with my own movements.

Everything in the room was somehow blurry to me.

And then my father collapsed suddenly. He fell onto the linoleum floor, reaching for the table as he fell, then rolled over onto his face.

I was screaming now, screaming for him not to die, atop his body on the floor, trying to roll him over so he could breathe better. His face was ashen, thick sticky drool came out of the side of his mouth. He was taking big gulps of air as I screamed and then the color came back into his face and he was struggling to get up, leaning on me.

My mother stood there watching us, laughing again in that spine-chilling way, a cigarette in her hand, taking fast little puffs on it. I helped my father into the bedroom to lie down and she followed us in.

"*Drama!*" she cackled at him in a screeching-high voice. "Drama for the boy! Anything for sympathy! *Liar! Liar!* I believe not a word anymore! *I have heard all the lies! I have seen through all the lies! I know!* I know what you are! Devil! *Devil!*"

She was screeching that word in Hungarian: "*Ördög! Ördög!*"

I looked at her and caught her eye for a moment and she looked right at me and screamed "*Ördögök*"—*Devils!* looking for a long moment at the two of us.

She went back to the kitchen and sat at the table, staring hollow-eyed at nothing, chain-smoking her cigarettes.

My father said he was better and needed to rest. I stayed with him until he fell asleep and went to my couch in the living room and tried to sleep. I could hear her out in the kitchen striking matches for her cigarettes.

The next morning my father woke me when it was still dark and told me my mother wanted to go to Mass. We went with her to the seven o'clock Mass at St. Emeric's.

She said not a word as we walked the sixteen blocks, her jaw set, but my father whispered that she would like it if I could serve the Mass. So when we got to church I asked Father John if I could serve because my parents were there. He looked at me a little strangely but said yes.

I was the only altar boy and I saw my parents were in the front row. I kept craning my neck around all through the Mass to see them—I was afraid my father was going to collapse again and die. I was afraid my mother would start to scream or laugh that terrible laugh.

Father John noticed me craning around and hissed, "What is wrong with you?"

. . .

My father met me in the sacristy afterward and told me not to worry. He felt fine now, he said, he had just gotten dizzy last night. Everything would be "okay." He would call a doctor when they got home.

I asked where my mother was and my father said she was still sitting in church. I saw the bags under his eyes and his pallor as he stood in his old trench coat, his beret in his hands. I hugged him close to me.

I felt the tears on his face and he looked at me through his thick, horn-rimmed glasses and with the twinge of a smile said, "It okay, Joe" in English.

I glanced into the dark church from the sacristy and saw my mother sitting in her pew, staring blankly ahead. She was smoking a cigarette. In church. Very calmly. Taking long deep puffs.

When I got home from school, the doctor was there. His name was Michael Varga-Sinka and he had been with us in the refugee camps. He was a friendly man and he was smiling now, talking calmly with my mother, who was screaming at him.

"Why are you with *them?*" my mother screamed.

"Whom, Mária?"

"With *them!*" She pointed to my father and me. "Why are you trying to hurt me?" I saw she was wearing her rosary around her neck.

"I'm trying to help you, Mária," Dr. Varga-Sinka said. "They're trying to help you. You're tired. You need some rest."

"No!" she said. "You're trying to put me to sleep so I won't see their filth. I have to scrub that couch every morning! He puts his seed into it. My own boy! He *sins!*"

She went on that way. All the while Varga-Sinka kept talking to her calmly, cajolingly, telling her she needed to rest, trying to persuade her to allow him to give her a shot.

"Please, Nana," I said. "Let him give it to you. It's good for you."

"Why did you join them?" she said to me. *"I loved you, Jozsi."*

She started to cry and so did I and she suddenly put her arm around me and kissed me.

"All right, Jozsi," she said, "all right." She held her arm out to the doctor and Varga-Sinka, seizing the moment, plunged the needle in. She fell into a deep sleep within minutes.

"She'll sleep for a long time," Varga-Sinka said at our kitchen table. "I think she's having a mental breakdown." My father told him about the breakdown she had suffered as a girl in Hungary when her father had advertised in the newspapers for a new wife.

"What can we do?" my father asked.

"I don't know," the doctor said, "let's see how she is in the coming days. This is not uncommon. I have had other Hungarian patients, other women who came through the camps and the war that this has happened to. Maybe it's everything together that causes it—coming to a new country, their fears, abuse, poverty. You two have to stay strong to help her."

She was still asleep the next morning when I left for school but when I came home that afternoon I could hear her screaming from half a block away.

When I burst through the door, I saw that Dr. Varga-Sinka was there again.

"Take him away, Jozsi," my mother begged me when she saw me. "Don't let him poison me. Please. *Don't let them poison your own mother.*"

She was wearing her rosary around her neck again. She didn't have her false teeth in and the words and kisses she was suddenly showering me with were filled with spittle.

"Don't be with them, Jozsi," she said, and her voice suddenly grew harsh. "*Do you want to go to hell? Is that what you want, Jozsi?*" She was yelling at me now. "To burn in hell? *You're going to burn in hell, you filth!*" and she started to laugh her hyena laugh.

My father moved me quickly out the door and down the stairs while Dr. Varga-Sinka stayed with her.

She had been sleeping peacefully, my father told me downstairs, when he went to the printing shop in the morning. Two hours later, when he went back upstairs to check on her, she was sitting calmly at the kitchen table reading her prayer book.

She had put glue into all of the electrical outlets. She had cut the cords of the radio and the lamps. She had unscrewed all of the lightbulbs and smeared bacon fat into their housings. She had glued all the windows shut with rubber cement. She had broken her false teeth into little bits with a hammer. She had stripped the cover off the couch where I slept and jammed as much of it as she could into the toilet.

We went back upstairs and Varga-Sinka was still trying to calm her. She was ranting about rays coming out of the electrical outlets, poisoning her, torturing her. *They* were trying to kill her, to poison her, to drive her crazy. *They* were putting thoughts into her head. *They* were watching her—when she went to the bathroom even, when she wiped herself, *they* were laughing because she smelled so bad.

We were back at the kitchen table with Dr. Varga-Sinka, who had given my mother another shot.

"She's very ill," he said, "she's ill not in her body but in her mind. I'm not a psychiatrist. She needs a psychiatrist. This is paranoia, this business with the rays, the watching. She's always been such a shy woman."

"Who can we go to?" my father said.

Varga-Sinka said there were no Hungarian psychiatrists in Cleveland; he would find the name of an American one.

"An American?" my father said. "She can hardly speak any English. How can she be helped by someone who doesn't understand her?"

"I don't know, Steve," Dr. Varga-Sinka said. "But we have to try." He left some pills for her to take and when my mother woke up the next day the first thing she did was flush them down the toilet.

She wasn't going to see any other doctors, she said. She wasn't going to tell anyone else that she smelled bad when she wiped herself. Besides, all the doctors were in cahoots with my father and me.

For about a month or so she became mute again. She continued cooking our meals but wouldn't speak or respond to us.

I kept repeating to myself what my father kept repeating to me: that I mustn't take her actions personally, that my mother loved me and was sick.

But it was hard to believe it. She was *so* cold, *so* distant.

I stopped trying to kiss her when I came back from school.

One morning I woke up and she was staring at me, the ice-towel around her head. The crucifix which my parents kept on their bedroom wall was in her hand and she was pointing it at me.

I looked up at her and smiled tentatively and said, "Hi, Nana."

She hissed, "Clean yourself! *Clean yourself of your filth!*" and backed away from the couch, still pointing the crucifix at me.

Then she did it again: rubber-cemented the windows, cut the cords to the electric outlets, bacon-fatted the lightbulb housings. This time she even took our old Philips shortwave and hammered it into bits.

She refused to have new false teeth made because she said the teeth were "receptors for the transmitting rays."

And then, suddenly, unbelievably, miraculously, she was her old self. Affectionate, loving, warm.

Yes, she said, she had been sick but now she was fine and she loved me so much, she said, and I was growing up to be such a big boy . . . and the next day she was mute again . . . and the following week she was cutting the cords again . . . and the week after that she was her old self again.

In the beginning I prayed to God at night to make her well, because I missed my mother so awfully much, but after a while I just prayed for day-to-day improvement. *Please, God, don't let her be silent today, please, God, don't let her cut the cords tomorrow.*

I started doing screwy things, knowing they were screwy even as I did them: I waited for Tuesdays because St. Anthony of Padua was her favorite saint and she had dedicated Tuesdays to St. Anthony and the chart I kept of her behavior showed me that she had never cut cords on a Tuesday.

And I rolled my dice at night sometimes to tell me how she'd be the next day: doubles meant she'd be better the next day; snake eyes meant we'd have to call the doctor again.

I tried to stay off the playgrounds and the alleys and tried not to touch myself at night. I feared that she was listening to every rustle of my couch and I felt guilty about touching myself. In some part of me there was a nagging and paralyzing fear that I had *caused* my mother's illness, that my nighttime seed spillings had somehow *driven* her into this madness.

So I cut a deal with God: If you make her better, I won't touch myself.

My father bought a blue 1950 Nash at Dunajszky Brothers' secondhand cars on Lorain Avenue and West 65th Street.

I washed it and polished it and Simonized it every week.

The back seat of the car folded down into a bed and my father planned a vacation to Pennsylvania. We were going to fold the seat down and sleep in the car at night on the way there.

We pulled the car over to the side of a rural road on the first night of our vacation and my mother, my father, and I changed into pajamas and tried to sleep.

It was a steaming hot summer night and the mosquitoes were eating us alive.

Just as we were falling asleep, the police arrived. They told us it was illegal to sleep at the side of the road.

"I will never understand America," my father said. "Why do they sell cars where the seats fold into beds—if it's illegal to sleep at the side of the road?"

We were driving along on a highway. My father was afraid of highways; the Hungarian roads he had driven weren't jammed with big tractor-trailers. My father drove with his beret pulled low and both hands gripping the wheel.

A highway patrolman pulled us over. He asked my father for his driver's license.

"You're driving too slow, Steve," the highway patrolman said. "Minimum's forty."

"I am no Steve," my father said, "I am Dr. Stephen Eszterhás." He pronounced it "Steffan Eszterhosh."

My father had a law degree from a Hungarian university; anyone who had a law degree in Hungary referred to himself as "Dr."

"Sorry." The highway patrolman smiled. "Didn't know you were a doctor."

"No doctor," my father said. "Lav-yer."

The highway patrolman said, "What?"

I said, "Lawyer. My father was a lawyer in Hungary."

The highway patrolman looked at me and then at my father. "Gotcha," he said. "But tell him he's going too slow. Minimum's forty, he was going thirty."

Before I had a chance to translate it, my father said, "Free country."

The highway patrolman stared at him and said nothing.

"Translate it," my father said to me in Hungarian.

I said, "He says it's a free country," to the highway patrolman.

My father said, "*America free country.*"

The highway patrolman was still staring at him. He said, "Yes sir?

"What's he mean by that?" the highway patrolman said to me.

I said, "I think he means America's a free country."

My father said, "Eef vant, drey-ve shlow. America free country—no?"

The highway patrolman said, "Yeah. For sure. But there's still a minimum," he said. "Listen, I don't wanna have to give you a ticket, okay?"

My father said, "No tick-et—America free country—no?"

The highway patrolman said, "Yes sir, but—"

My father said, "Zank you ver-ry mooch. Goo-bye," and drove away.

I looked back and saw the highway patrolman standing at the side of the road, staring after us.

Every time we bought gas for the car on that vacation, my father tipped the attendant.

One attendant looked at the coin my father was pressing into his hand and said, "What's this?"

"Five cent," my father said.

"What the hell for?"

"Teep," my father said.

The attendant smiled at him and said, "Big spender, huh?"

"What did he mean by that?" my father asked as we drove away from the gas station.

I said, "I think he meant that you didn't have to give him any tip."

"You know what I think, Jozsi?" my father said. "I think these Americans find it hard to say thank you."

My mother was mute for a couple days after we got to Scotty's Cabins in Cook Forest, Pennsylvania, and then she was suddenly affectionate and then one day shortly before dinner she started again: We were devils and we were poisoning her with our rays and our filth and we were watching her in the bathroom as she wiped herself.

She was screeching at us and shrieking that awful, bloodcurdling laugh.

My father got out his violin, turned his back to her, and played a *csárdás*.

I bolted out the door of the cabin and started to run . . . wildly . . . blindly . . . desperately. I could hear the shrieks and the violin blending into each other and fading slowly.

I ran down a lane and up a hill and jumped a fence and ran across a farm field and then another and now there were cows around me and I kept running, barely able to breathe now, until I fell.

I was gasping for air. My nose was bleeding. Every part of me was shaking. I heard myself sobbing, my moans echoing across these lovely green hills.

I started to throw up . . . and I passed out.

When I woke up it was pitch-black and for a moment I didn't know where I was. Then it all came back—the shrieking, that awful laughter, the violin.

I got up and started to walk back to the cabin. Something, I knew, was different now. A part of me had either died or a part of me had been born. I felt that my mother could never hurt me again. *I felt that nothing or no one could ever hurt me like that again.*

When I was married in California to Gerri, I had an affair with a woman in Cleveland and drove her one weekend to Cook Forest.

We took a cabin for the weekend at Scotty's Cabins and we walked the hillside where I had run and fallen down.

We did nothing but drink Jack Daniel's and red wine and make love . . . and one night I heard a violin solo on a static-filled radio station that sounded like it was very far away.

A few years later, I took Gerri to Scotty's Cabins for a month in the winter and I finished my first book there . . . this time in the very same cabin where I had been with my mother and father.

Gerri and I had fun in that little cabin. We kept the fire in the fireplace going for a full month . . . and I tried to find the same faraway radio station on which I'd heard that violin solo, but I couldn't.

Gerri and I were at Scotty's during Valentine's Day and one night as the snow fell we came out of our cabin to take a walk. We passed Scotty's restaurant's front window.

It was late and the place was empty and closed but completely lighted up inside. The hardwood floor had just been washed and was gleaming; a wall-sized stone fireplace was blazing; above the fireplace, spotlighted, was a huge woodcut of a bright red Valentine's heart.

Gerri and I stared at that scene openmouthed and held each other, sure that we'd live together happily ever after.

I was back in the alleys and on the playgrounds. I didn't want to be home and around my mother, and my father understood and didn't try to stop me. Whenever she started to rant and rave, he took out his violin and turned his back to her and played. Sometimes the violin seemed to settle her down.

At other times she screeched as he played, almost as though they were performing a duet.

I never knew what I was going to find when I got home. Sometimes she was okay and sometimes she was ranting or laughing and sometimes she stared vacantly and mutely at the wall.

My father and I were almost afraid to talk to her, certainly afraid to initiate any conversation. We never knew what would set her off.

Dinner was especially difficult. My father read at dinner now and she'd usually smoke and stare and I'd scarf the food and listen to the radio. My father had bought a small, battery-powered Arvin radio so she couldn't cut the cord.

One afternoon I stopped at a playground on Franklin Avenue and there was a pickup ball game in progress. I knew some of the kids. Most of them were a few years older. One of them was an Irish kid named Jimmy Murphy.

He was a big, good-looking, "cool" kid, his hair ducktailed like Conway Twitty and Fabian, cigarettes rolled up in his T-shirt. He was a kind of neighborhood playground hero, a home run hitter on the field (I had trouble hitting line drives, never mind homers) who always had pretty girls around him.

He'd always disliked me. He imitated my accent. He called me "DP" and "greenhorn" and "asshole" and "creep" and the one that hurt the most, the title of a hit song, "Jo Jo, the Dog-Faced Boy." I tried to fight him twice and got beaten up twice.

After my last beating, he called me "numbnuts."

On this day he didn't say anything to me at all. He saw me, grinned a supercilious grin, and stepped up to the plate. I was just lolling around the batting cage, feeling one of the bats there, watching Jimmy Murphy, and I calmly sauntered up behind him, bat in hand, and swung as hard as I could at the back of his head.

He went straight down on his face, blood gushing from his head, his nose, his ears, his arms and legs jerking. I heard screams and yells and one of his friends hit me in the mouth with his fist, but I hardly felt the punch.

I wasn't crying. I wasn't shaking. I wasn't upset. I was calm. Police and an ambulance were there within minutes. Jimmy Murphy's friends screamed at me and kept trying to hit me. The cops put me into the backseat of their car. Kids spat at the backseat window.

"Did you hit him with the bat?" a cop asked.

I nodded.

"What'd you hit him for?"

I shrugged.

"I asked you a question!" the cop said, hard.

"I don't know," I answered.

"Jesus," the other cop said quietly, "you better hope he doesn't die."

They took Jimmy Murphy to Lutheran Hospital, not far away, and the cops took me there, too, and put me in a little room that they locked from the outside.

When they came back they told me that Jimmy Murphy had a cerebral hemorrhage and was going into surgery and asked me where my parents lived. I told them.

A little while later a police car brought my father, wild-eyed, his face very red. He was wearing a white undershirt and pants, an unusual sight. My father never went out on the street in anything but one of his Salvation Army or Volunteers of America suits.

He sat down in the little room next to me with the policeman there—there were more policemen there now in suits—and he said to me in Hungarian, "Did you hit this boy?"

I said yes.

He said, "Why?"

I said, "I don't know, Papa."

"Did he hit you?"

"No."

"*Te Jó Isten*," my father said—My good God—"What have you done?"

I looked at him. He was covering his face with his hands. I felt numb. Suddenly I felt exhausted, like I'd run for miles, like the day in Cook Forest when I'd run and fallen down.

I reached into my pocket and pulled out a cigarette. One of the policemen gave me a look and I said, "Can I smoke?"

"How old are you?"

"Thirteen."

He looked at another policeman, shook his head, and shrugged.

I lit up. My father stared at me.

Father John Mundweil arrived. My father had called him when the police came to the printing shop to bring him to the hospital. Father John was in all black, wearing his priestly collar, and he spoke to the police in fluent but Hungarian-accented English and then he spoke to us.

"I'm calling a lawyer who will meet us at the juvenile," Father John said.

"Will he go to jail?" my father asked. His voice was hoarse.

"If this boy dies," Father John said, "he will go to jail."

My father put his head between his hands and started soundlessly to cry.

"Why did you hit him?" Father John asked me in Hungarian.

"I don't know," I said. "I wanted to."

"Did you know what you were doing?"

"Yes," I said. "I wanted to hurt him."

Father John's eyes narrowed at me a moment and he said, "Don't tell that to the police."

The policemen drove us downtown to juvenile hall, where a Hungarian lawyer, John J. Vasko, tall and very in charge, was waiting for us.

They took my fingerprints and papers were filled out and Father John signed a paper which said he'd be responsible for making sure I would go to court when I had to. The attorney drove us home and on the way he dropped Father John off at the hospital.

My mother was on her knees in the kitchen, praying, the rosary around her neck. She never looked at me. The telephone rang. Father John was calling from the hospital to say that Jimmy Murphy was out of surgery and the next two or three days would determine if he'd live.

When my mother heard my father tell me that, she stopped praying and began a long, wailing cry.

"Do you want something to eat?" my father asked.

I shook my head.

He looked like he wanted to say something to me but turned away.

"Go to sleep," he said, "you're tired."

I lay down on my couch in the living room and stared at Papp's Bar's blinking neon sign. The apartment was dark. I could hear my father snoring in their bed and I could hear my mother, still on her knees praying in the dark kitchen.

I thought about what I had done. *Had I killed a human being?* Is that what it felt like to kill a human being? Was it possible not even to feel very much after killing a human being? How could I have done that? Why did I do this to this particular kid? Other kids had called me names, other kids had hit me. What was going to happen to me? Was I going to live in a jail?

I thought about trying another deal with God. *Please, God, let Jimmy Murphy live. Please, God, don't let me go to jail.* If you do that, God, I won't do any of the bad things I've done anymore.

But I couldn't bring myself to make a deal with God. I'd tried a deal with God about my mother and what had happened? My mother was gone. There was a scary stranger on the kitchen floor in her place, gibbering away with her toothless mouth, dodging rays coming out of the electrical outlets.

So much for deals with God.

So much for God.

. . .

The next morning two men in suits from the Juvenile Bureau came and so did John J. Vasko and asked me endless questions about what had happened.

I told them the truth. I didn't know why what happened had happened. I told them about the fights Jimmy Murphy and I had had and the names he had called me. But I told them I'd had fights with lots of other kids who had called me names.

That afternoon Father John called to tell us that Jimmy Murphy was better and the doctors thought he would live. My mother stayed on the floor praying for most of the day. Soon afterward we heard that Jimmy Murphy would fully recover with no brain damage.

John J. Vasko said he had worked out an arrangement with Jimmy Murphy's parents. If we paid the family $5,000, they would urge the juvenile authorities to file no charges against me. Vasko said he had a friend, a Hungarian judge, who could persuade the juvenile authorities to file no charges—but only if Jimmy Murphy's family urged them first.

"*Five thousand dollars?*" my father said in shocked disbelief. His salary at the newspaper was $100 a month.

"I'm sorry," John J. Vasko said, "it's the only way. You somehow have to get the money."

My father asked the Franciscans for the money—the newspaper's circulation was booming, thanks to his efforts, many of the Franciscan priests were driving shiny new cars—but the Franciscans turned him down.

He went to see Father John and asked to borrow the money but Father John said he wouldn't lend it to him.

Father John said that he might, however, lend it to me.

"*Me?*" I said.

I went down to the rectory. It was the first time I'd been inside Father John's house. He was wearing a battered pair of black pants and a white T-shirt. Classical music was booming. A half bottle of Tokay wine was on the cocktail table in the living room. He was a barrel-chested, muscular man in his forties with thick silver-black hair. He spoke to me in Hungarian.

"Let's go for a walk, young man," he said.

He came out that way, in his T-shirt and sandals, and we headed toward the West Side Market, which was closed on this day. He lit up a cigarette as we started to walk. When I lit up one of mine, he reached over nonchalantly and backhanded the cigarette out of my mouth.

"You haven't been to confession in a long time, have you?" Father John said as we walked.

"No, I guess not."

He grinned. "Do you think your sins are too great to be forgiven?"

I said, "I don't know."

"I do. We all sin, Jozsi. We're all human. We're all weak." He looked at me. "Me too," he said. "You *know* that."

I knew he was talking about the night I'd seen him kissing the funeral director's wife.

"Are you stealing?" he asked.

"No, Father."

"Don't lie to me, Jozsi," he said. "I don't lend five thousand dollars to liars. Are you stealing?"

"Yes, Father."

"And you are doing other things that you shouldn't be doing and you *know* you shouldn't be doing, aren't you?"

"Yes, Father."

We stopped and sat down on a wooden stall at the market. There was no one else around.

"Do you know what I do on my weekends, Jozsi?"

"No, Father."

"I go down to the jail looking for Hungarians. There are always Hungarians in jails on the weekends. Sometimes I talk to them. Sometimes I pray with them. Sometimes I pay a few dollars and bail them out so they can go home. I would be particularly sad, Jozsi, if I found you in one of those jails when I went visiting. Do you know why?"

"No, Father."

"Because you don't belong there," he said. "*Because you don't belong there!* But unless you do something with your life, you will go there. You're too smart to go there. You have too much potential to go there. Do you understand me?"

"Yes, Father."

"*No you don't!*" he said, louder now. "You have no idea what I'm saying to you! Do you listen to your parents? Do you listen to your father? What does he say to you?"

"He tells me to make something of myself. He tells me to read."

"And do you?"

"No."

"Why not?"

"I don't know. It's boring."

"Because *he* reads! Because you see *him* reading and you think he's nothing but a stupid hunkie. He doesn't know anything. He doesn't know anything about America, all he knows is *hunkie business*—is that what you think?"

"I don't know, Father."

"Oh, stop all this goddamned foolishness," John Mundweil said to me. "Yes, Father, no, Father, I don't know, Father. We're not in the confessional now. I'm talking to you like a man. I'm not talking to you like a boy in a class. *Talk to me!*"

"I don't know," I said. "Maybe that *is* what I think. I think that sometimes, but then. . . ." I felt myself choking up.

"What?"

"I look at my father working, or with the damn Franciscans, or on the street, and I feel . . . I feel . . ."

"What?"

"I feel so sorry for him, for *both* of them."

He looked at me a long moment, nodded, and looked away.

Finally, very quietly, he said, "So you run from them—from both of them—so you don't have to feel sorry for them, so they don't cause you pain. You run—on the street, in the alley, running, stealing, hitting people with baseball bats—that's how you run. Yes?"

"I don't know, Father," I said. "Maybe. She's . . . my mother is . . . she's . . . sick."

"Yes," he said, "I know."

"You do?"

"I hear your mother's confession. And I hear your father's confession. A priest always knows too much. A priest always knows things he doesn't want to know."

He grinned suddenly and I smiled a little bit. He lit up another cigarette. I badly wanted one but there was no way I was going to reach for one.

"Your father and your mother are the best thing you have in your life," Father John said. "Don't reject them. Embrace them. Listen to them."

I started to cry. I didn't say anything for what seemed a long while and John Mundweil put his arm around me.

"I can't," I said. "I don't know her. She's somebody else."

"Try," he said. "You must. I know it's not easy. I know more than you know about your parents. They are good people. Human. Like you. Like me. But *good* people. Both of them."

I nodded and didn't say anything.

"That's the promise I want from you," John Mundweil said. "Try. If you promise to *try*, to listen to your parents, to do something with your life I will give you the five thousand dollars."

I said, "How can I ever pay it back, Father?"

"I said '*give*' not 'lend,' " John Mundweil said.

I looked at him.

"If you promise to try," he said.

I nodded slowly. "I promise to try."

"Then you will make something of your life," he said. He was smiling at me.

"We will go back to the church," he said. "I will hear your confession and then I will give you the money. Good?"

I nodded.

We went into the dark church and he got into the confessional in his T-shirt and sandals and I confessed my sins.

I told Father John about all of it . . . the drunks that we had kicked and rolled in the alleys, the break-in at the grocery store, the stolen cars, the circle jerks, the whore whose wig fell off, the zip guns, the knives, all of it.

I never choked up. I just told it and he never interrupted me. I felt I wasn't confessing all this to God. I felt I was confessing these things to a friend who cared about me. At the end he said, "Say ten Our Fathers and ten Hail Marys and I'll meet you back in the rectory."

I said the prayers but my mind wasn't on the words. *I wasn't going to jail.*

Father John was at the screen door of the rectory when I got there. He handed me the check, pointed his finger in my face, and gruffly said, "You made me a promise, young man!"

I said, "Yes, Father."

He said, "And stay away from Puerto Rican whores. They're all sick and your *fasz* will rot off."

I said, "Yes, Father," and he slammed the door.

He had used the word *fasz* and not *pimpli. Pimpli* was a boy's penis; *fasz* was a man's.

CHAPTER 12

Your Basic Shit Storm

CATHERINE
I'm a writer. I use people for what I write. You write what you
know. Let the world beware.

Basic Instinct

W hile we were in Florida celebrating the *Basic Instinct* sale, Irwin Winkler stayed behind to mount the movie with Mario Kassar at Carolco. Irwin called me after his first couple of meetings. He wasn't happy.

"They're not interested in what I think about casting or a director," Irwin said. "They're treating me like some rookie producer."

Without even consulting Irwin, Carolco had signed Michael Douglas to play the lead—Nick Curran, the burned-out homicide cop. It was, Irwin and I agreed, perfect casting, but the fact that it was done without even consulting Irwin, my producer, gave us pause.

I was happy about Michael's commitment to the movie for another reason: Michael Douglas was one of CAA's premier clients.

"Does this mean an easing of tensions with CAA?" I asked Guy.

"Forget it," he said. "Carolco's trying to hush it up but they're paying Michael *fifteen million dollars* to do it. For that kind of money, Ovitz himself would've signed to do one of your scripts."

It was the most an actor had ever been paid in Hollywood history.

I was amused by the irony: a screenwriter finally bursts into the stratosphere with his price . . . and is almost immediately *dwarfed* by the actor's price.

Irwin and I decided to move quickly on our own to find a director who was in sync with our vision of the movie.

I viewed my script as a psychosexual thriller with erotic content but I didn't want it to turn into porn. All the scenes in the script with any nudity had a descriptive tag line: "*It is dark. We can't see clearly.*" Irwin and I wanted those scenes to be about shadows and arty camera angles, not about skin, and certainly not about full-frontal nudity.

Our choice was Milos Forman, whose work we both admired, who had directed *One Flew Over the Cuckoo's Nest* and *Amadeus*.

Irwin reached Milos's agent, who said Milos was on a bicycling tour in the South of France. We somehow finally got him the script and his agent said he liked it very much and wanted to talk. Irwin and I were happy.

With Milos directing it, *Basic* would be the kind of classy daring movie we wanted it to be.

It was then that Carolco announced that, without even consulting us (once again), they had made a deal with a director: Paul Verhoeven.

He had recently directed *Total Recall* (which I'd hated) and *RoboCop* (which I'd loved). Before that, he had made a series of daring and sexually explicit films in his native Holland. In one of them, a penis was severed . . . and then levitated . . . over opening credits.

Milos Forman he wasn't.

When I got back from Florida, I flew down to L.A. for a "creative meeting" with Michael and Paul at Irwin's house. I knew Michael slightly but had never met Verhoeven.

Within minutes, it became obvious to Irwin and me that we were involved in a fiasco. Because neither Michael nor Verhoeven *liked my script*—for which Carolco had paid this record amount of money.

"But what is this script about? What is it about?" Verhoeven kept yelling in a thick Dutch, Germanic-sounding accent. When I told him it was about evil and psychological and sexual manipulation and homicidal impulse, Verhoeven looked at me blankly.

Michael kept talking about redemption.

"Where is the redemption here?" he asked. "You can't do a picture where evil triumphs at the end. Is that the message we want to send? That evil triumphs?"

Michael's actor's ego was also involved.

"I'm the star of the movie and she one-ups me at every turn," he said.

I thought: how absurd. I'd written a script that everyone in town wanted to buy. I'd sold it for a headline-making fortune. And now, after paying me that fortune, the buyer wanted me to turn my creation inside-out.

Verhoeven was listing the many changes he wanted. I argued each one and said I wasn't going to do it.

His answer was the same each time. "I am the director, *ja?*" he said, "and you are the writer, *ja?* You will do what I say, *ja?*"

I said no—*no jah, no jah!* I wasn't going to do that.

I told him he was right. He was the director—not the writer. He didn't know anything about writing, so he should do what he was supposed to do, shoot the damn script, *ja?*

Verhoeven, really yelling now, said, "*I am the director and you are the writer, ja?*"

And this time I yelled back into his face: "If you say that to me one more time, I'm going to come across this table at you!"

Michael jumped up and said, "Gentlemen, gentlemen!"

Irwin tried to make the arguments in defense of my script, but I saw that these guys weren't having any of it. They wanted their changes. Verhoeven also made it clear he wanted the film to be sexually explicit with full-frontal nudity.

The meeting ended so acrimoniously that as Michael and Verhoeven stormed out, Irwin yelled "Fucking Nazi!" at Paul.

This, I knew, was going to be a disaster. I wasn't going to make these changes. Period. I wasn't going to mutilate my own child. It was what screenwriters in Hollywood had always done and were always doing to their creations . . . making changes they despised just to get the money and the screen credit.

It wasn't ego that was keeping me from doing that to my script; it was self-defense. I didn't see how I could have any respect for myself as a writer if I did that. And if I didn't have any respect for myself as a writer, then how could I ever write anything I believed in? How could I sit down and write anything again?

I had only two choices: either make the changes or withdraw from the project. I knew how I'd look to much of Hollywood if I withdrew.

Like an ego-mad ingrate.

I could hear the dialogue at Morton's: "Can you believe the guy? They pay him $3 million and then he's got the balls to piss on the movie because they want him to make some changes? He's a screenwriter—that's why you need 'em—to make changes!"

I also knew there was no way to withdraw quietly after the banner headlines about the sale of the script.

And, too, there was the never-ending presence of Michael Ovitz. I could just hear what he'd have to say to the studio heads about the kind of team player I was.

But I had never made a change on a script that I didn't agree with. I wasn't about to start now.

"What can we do?" I said to Irwin, who was shocked by what had happened.

"I don't know," he said. "I haven't had a meeting like that in all these years of producing. Let's think about it."

I went to Guy's office, told him what had happened, and told him I wanted to withdraw from the project.

"Christ," Guy said, "you don't want to do that. A lot of people in this town will never understand that. For three million dollars, they'd kill their mothers, and their kids, never mind some words in a script. You're going to look like the ultimate prima donna. You've got enough people who are just jealous about a *writer* getting three mil. There must be hundreds of screenwriters who want to kill you on sight. I'm not even going to mention what Ovitz is going to be saying."

"Thanks," I said, "please don't."

"Can't you just make the changes?" Guy said.

"I can't," I said. "They're wrong. Verhoeven's wrong. Michael isn't thinking about the movie, he's thinking about his star image. The changes would destroy the movie."

Guy said, "Let me talk to them and see what their take on the meeting is."

I went back to Irwin's house and told him my mind was made up.

"Yeah, I agree with you," he said, "but you're going to take some flak."

I shrugged. He smiled.

"I'll withdraw with you," he said.

I knew that if Irwin withdrew, he wouldn't be paid because the movie wasn't yet in production. I *would* be paid because my payment was for having already written the script. I told him he didn't have to do that.

"The only reason I'm involved in this is because of you," Irwin said. "I don't want to work with Verhoeven. God knows what this movie is going to look like when he is done. If I withdraw *with* you, you're not going to look as bad. No one's ever accused *me* of being hard to work with. If I pull out, too, it'll signal that you're right to a lot of people."

I knew he was withdrawing to help me. I thanked him and called Guy to tell him Irwin was withdrawing as well.

Guy said, "What if I can convince Carolco to take their three mil back and give us the project back?"

"Are you kidding me?" I said. "That'd be great!"

"Hold on," Guy said. "Understand that if we get the script back, and try to sell it again, we might not get as much as the first time. It'll look to some people like something's wrong, like it's got the clap."

"Do it," I said.

But Carolco refused to give the project back to me and the next morning's *Variety* had another banner headline: "ESZTERHAS, WINKLER WITHDRAW FROM *BASIC*."

I issued a statement:

Due to philosophical and personal differences with the director Paul
Verhoeven, I have decided to withdraw from *Basic Instinct*.

At a meeting with Verhoeven and Michael Douglas on August 8, it
became clear to me that Verhoeven's intention is to make *Basic* as a
sexually explicit thriller.

In a current issue of *Premiere* magazine, he discusses his willingness
to show an erect penis on-screen.

My intention when I wrote the script was that it be a psychological
mystery with the love scenes done subtly. Every love scene in my script
begins with the words: "*It is dark; we can't see clearly.*" On a personal
level, I discovered Verhoeven's attitude toward the collaborative
process was, as he very loudly explained it to me, "*I am the director, ja?
I am right and you are wrong, ja?*"

The wires picked it up because of the record script sale and the story blasted
its way into the daily papers.

Guy told me Mario Kassar was so angry he was threatening to sue me for
"publicly injuring" the project he'd paid $3 million for.

I went back to Marin and heard that Paul was working with Gary Goldman,
a screenwriter friend of his, on the rewrite.

Meanwhile, Carolco was trying to cast the part of Catherine Tramell and was
having problems. Lena Olin called Mario Kassar after a meeting with Verhoeven
and said she liked the script but couldn't work with Paul, whom she described as
"an animal." Most actresses, afraid of the nudity and Paul's decision to make the
movie sexually explicit, were turning it down. Kelly McGillis and Mariel Hemingway wanted to do it but had done screen tests that weren't very good.

And then there was Sharon Stone. She was a B movie starlet who had
worked with Paul on *Total Recall*. A former model, she'd scratched and clawed
for more than a decade trying to get star parts in movies. None of it had worked.
Her own agency (CAA), even her own accountants, had fired her.

Her agents described her this way: "If she can get into the room, she'll close
the deal." A producer told me, "She knocked on my door at midnight at the
Deauville Film Festival. I wouldn't let her in."

Sharon Stone was in love with the script, in love with the part, and cam-
paigning to get it. She did a screen test that Verhoeven and everyone at Carolco
loved. But they were reluctant to cast her.

"Sharon Stone?" Guy said. "Sure. With Long John Holmes. But with
Michael Douglas?"

A few months after Irwin and I pulled out of *Basic,* Andy Vajna, the head of the
production company Cinergi, called to tell me of a lunch he'd had with Ver-

hoeven. Paul told him he wanted to send me the final *Basic Instinct* shooting script.

"What does he want me to do?" I asked Andy. "Have a stroke while reading it?"

"He says he didn't change your script," Andy said.

I said, "I bet he says that to all the girls."

I got the final shooting script from Verhoeven and as I was reading it, I thought Verhoeven had mistakenly sent me the wrong draft. But there it was—on the front page, "Final Shooting Script."

Because *not a word* had been changed.

It was *my* first draft, *word for word, scene for scene*, even with the exact ending that Michael Douglas had so disliked.

I called Verhoeven and asked, "Is this some kind of joke you sent me?"

He very affably said that it was no joke—it really was the final shooting script. He said that he and Gary Goldman had done two or three drafts that hadn't worked and at the end of that process, he'd realized that my original script was "genius."

Paul said he had then convinced Michael Douglas and now even Michael "loved" the script.

I was so bewildered I didn't know what to say.

"How do you feel about coming back in?" Paul asked.

Well, I said, still dazed, I guessed I felt fine about that.

I asked about bringing Irwin back in as well and Paul said that it was unfortunately too late for that, he had brought in his own producer, Alan Marshall, a line producer with a take-no-nonsense reputation.

I went down to L.A. a few days later and Paul, Guy, Michael Douglas, and I had a very public prime-table dinner at Morton's.

Paul said how pleased he was that Carolco had finally decided to cast Sharon Stone as Catherine Tramell.

"She *is* Catherine Tramell," Paul said.

Since Catherine Tramell was an ice-pick-wielding, manipulative, omnisexual, sociopathic killer, I asked Paul what exactly he meant by that.

"Sharon is evil," he said.

"You mean as Catherine Tramell."

"No, as Sharon." Paul laughed. "She is perfect."

The next day Paul and I met with *Daily Variety* and Paul publicly welcomed me back to the project. He said he had made a "mistake." He hadn't understood "the basement, the foundation" of my script. I was impressed. The same man who had yelled "*I am the director, ja?*" at me was now publicly saying he'd made a mistake. I didn't know of many directors who'd make such an admission privately, let alone publicly.

This was some kind of screenwriter's dream I was living here: first $3 million for a script, then a public admission from the director that *he* had screwed up.

Sure enough, there it was on the front page of *Daily Variety* the next day: "VERHOEVEN ADMITS TO MAKING 'BASIC' MISTAKE."

A few days before the shoot began in San Francisco, I went to an actors' read-through at a Fisherman's Wharf hotel.

Michael was there, looking trim and tan after a few weeks in the sun in Mexico . . . "I'm gonna go down to Mexico and get beautiful," he had told me at Morton's . . . George Dzundza . . . I'd seen Willie Nelson in the Dzundza part when I wrote it . . . the willowy and dark Jeanne Tripplehorn . . . was it possible there were *already* sparks between Michael and Tripplehorn?

And Sharon Stone.

She was wearing a sweat suit and didn't strike me as being a sex goddess. She had a cuddly, little-girlish quality about her and an open freshness.

"Who am I?" she asked me, wearing Catherine Tramell's shoes.

"You're charming and warm," I said. "And you've got a great smile. And you're manipulative and cold and enjoy hurting and killing people. *You are evil.*"

She held my eyes and she said, "*Yes!*" and we laughed. I liked her.

She flashed me that wonderful smile and she said, "You're *so sly.*"

"Why?"

"Catherine's last name. *Tramell.* I researched it. I know what it means."

I smiled at how proud she seemed of herself.

"What does it mean?"

"You *know* what it means," she said.

We were smiling at each other.

"Will somebody end the suspense, please?" Michael Douglas said.

"A *tramell* is a funeral shroud in Scottish mythology," Sharon said. "Isn't that brilliant?"

"That's very good," Paul said to me.

Michael said, "I'm impressed."

"Actually," I said to Sharon, "I didn't know that. I like to name my characters after baseball players. Alan Trammell of the Tigers is one of my favorites."

"*Oh don't you try pulling that stuff with me!*" Sharon said, suddenly an irate little girl, and we all laughed.

. . .

As the shoot approached, there were stories in the papers that San Francisco's large and politically powerful gay community was going to mount a major protest against the movie. The trouble had begun with a Liz Smith column that described the script as being about "ice-pick-wielding lesbians."

Though I'd lived in the Bay Area for nearly twenty years and though I'd made many gay friends, I wasn't concerned about the protests.

To begin with, I didn't consider Catherine Tramell to be a lesbian. She was clearly *bi*sexual in the script, which to me meant that she was both heterosexual *and* homosexual. To say that this was an ugly negative portrayal of a *homosexual* was, I felt, silly.

The real point to me, as I saw her character, was that she was psychotically *omnisexual*. She used her sex and her brains for manipulation.

It was the manipulation and the seduction that she really enjoyed, not the sex.

A group of prominent gay community leaders approached Paul and asked him to have a meeting with them to discuss the script. Paul turned them down.

Angry at being flatly rebuffed, they called me. I knew some of them . . . I particularly admired one of them, San Francisco supervisor Harry Britt . . . and said I had no problem sitting down with them.

I called Paul at his hotel on the wharf and told him I thought we should sit down for a meeting with the gay leaders.

"I am not sitting down with anybody!" he said. "This is censorship. I will not allow a political action committee to stop my creative expression!"

I said, "You don't have to agree with them. What's wrong with an exchange of ideas?"

"They are blackmailing me to attend this meeting by threatening their protests. I will not be blackmailed and I will not attend!"

He sounded like he was back in his "*I am the director, ja?*" mode.

"Well fine," I said. "If you don't want to sit down with them, then I will."

"You are a *traitor!*" he yelled. "You are betraying me!"

Mario Kassar called Guy moments later, screaming, threatening to sue me again.

"Well, I'm sitting in the bunker again," Guy said to me. "I'm thinking about taking the next plane to Paraguay."

The San Francisco papers carried the story prominently. There would be a meeting with gay protesters. The screenwriter would be there, but the director wouldn't.

Paul called me screaming. "What are you doing to me? Now I *have* to go!"

I was getting tired of it.

"You don't have to go," I said. "You do what you have to do. I'm *going*."

"I will look like an asshole if I don't go," Paul said. "You are *making* me look like an asshole, *ja?*"

I said, "You *are* an asshole if you don't go."

"What?" Paul Verhoeven sputtered. "*What?* I am not an asshole!"

"Fine," I said, "then I'll see you there."

I got to the meeting, held in a conference room at a San Francisco hotel, a couple minutes late.

Paul and his producer, Alan Marshall, a big, bearded New Zealander, were sitting at one end of a very long table with an oily Carolco PR man and two local PR guys, both gay, both clearly here to mollify the gay community.

Sitting very far away, at the other end of the table, were about a dozen people . . . Harry Britt among them . . . men and women, mostly very young, a couple of them wearing cool Queer Nation T-shirts.

I introduced myself and picked an empty chair among the protesters, sitting *with* them . . . facing Paul.

The Carolco PR man began to spiel about making a corporate contribution to a local AIDS fund and I laughed to myself. It was a simple-minded, insulting gesture, a bribe offer, really, and Harry Britt nicely backhanded it by saying he wasn't there to discuss AIDS, he was there to discuss *Basic Instinct*.

"There is nothing to talk about except this," Paul said. "I am not a racist! I am not a homophobe! I will make the movie I want to make! You will not tell me what to make! I will not accept censorship!"

It was the worst way to begin, exacerbated, I saw, by his style and his accent. The style was blazing hot and the accent awfully Germanic.

I knew Paul Verhoeven hated the Nazis, I knew he had even been the victim of Nazi bombings as a child, but he acted and sounded like the stereotypical screen Nazi.

"Paul," I said, "I don't think anybody here wants to censor you. I don't think anybody in this room believes in censorship, but I, at least, as the screenwriter, want to hear how people here feel about the script. There can be no harm in listening."

Alan Marshall was glaring at me.

Paul, I could tell, didn't even want to look at me.

The people in the room had gotten the script somehow and started to talk about it. They viewed Catherine Tramell as a lesbian and felt her depiction to be negative.

Since she was, the script implied, having sex with a woman friend (Roxy) who was a convicted murderer, they saw *two* lesbian killers in my script.

They thought the reference to Catherine and Roxy by the George Dzundza character as "dykes" was offensive.

They believed Michael's sexual scene with Tripplehorn to be "date rape" and felt that showing date rape on-screen would lead to real-life imitation of it.

I argued that neither Catherine nor Roxy were lesbians but *bi*sexuals—*part* straight and *part* gay—so it wasn't fair to view them simplistically as gay.

But as far as the group in the room was concerned, bisexual *was* gay.

"I don't get it," I said. "If someone is bisexual, he or she is not just homosexual—he or she is also heterosexual."

"If they're bisexual, they're gay," someone said.

"By whose definition?" I asked.

"By ours."

"I don't agree with the definition," I said.

"It doesn't matter," someone said. "If you were gay, you'd know what you were talking about."

"What does that mean?" I said. "Does that mean only gay writers can write about gay characters?"

"Yes," someone said.

I said, "Aw, come on. That means Tennessee Williams and Edward Albee can't write about *heterosexual* characters. That means they shouldn't have written their plays."

No one said anything to that.

Paul said to the group, "Do you mean that gay people on the screen can't be *bad* people? Gay people on the screen have to be *saints?* Are there no bad people in real life who are *gay?*"

"Why do they *always* have to be bad people on-screen?" Harry Britt said. "Why haven't there been *any* movies where the good guy just *happens to be gay?* Why haven't we seen any action heroes *ever*—who just happen to be gay?"

Harry went into a very moving description of his childhood in Port Arthur, Texas. "The only gay role model I had growing up," he said, "was Liberace. Why aren't there ever any gay role models in the movies?"

"You've got two lesbians in this movie," somebody said to me, "they're both killers."

"Even if you view Catherine and Roxy as both lesbians," I said, "and I disagree with you . . . that's not true. By your definition, you have the police psychiatrist, the Tripplehorn character—by your definition, she's lesbian, too, and she's a victim, not a killer."

Somebody said, "If we're not killers in movies, then we're victims. Why does it have to be that way?"

Somebody else said, "What do you mean the Tripplehorn character isn't a killer? She's revealed as the killer at the end of the movie!"

I said, "No, she's not, Catherine's the killer," and I suddenly realized that *Basic* was such a *tangled* mystery that some people here didn't know who the real killer was.

As I watched the young people in this group, I was moved by their passion and their conviction. I had always identified with blacks and Jews and gay people . . . the words "nigger" and "kike" and "faggot" weren't far from the "greenhorn" and "hunkie" and "queer" that I'd heard as a child and as an adolescent.

"Why do we have to have these 'dyke' references in the dialogue?" somebody asked me.

I explained that the words came out of the mouth of a veteran, hard-boiled old-school cop and that, realistically, George Dzundza's character would use that word.

"But why do we have to hear it on a screen?" someone else said. "We hear it so often in real life."

I thought about those words that had hurt me so much as a kid and I suddenly said, "Maybe you're right."

Paul said to me, "What do mean she's right? It's part of *your character's* language. *You* just said so."

"He doesn't absolutely have to use the word 'dyke' for us to understand his character," I said.

There was silence in the room.

Paul and I were looking at each other.

His look said: Traitor, how can you be doing this to me?

Harry Britt looked at me and said, simply, "Thank you."

"Let me look through the script," I said. "Maybe I can find some changes that don't affect the plot or the characterization."

"No," Paul said, his voice rising. "We will make no changes! I am the director! I am shooting the movie I want to shoot and I want no changes!"

"This isn't your baby," I said to him. "It's mine. If I want to make changes to *my* script, I can."

"You can make all the changes you want," Paul said, "but I am not putting them into the movie."

Then he turned to the group and he said, "I will not make a movie you will find offensive. I will not make a movie the public finds offensive to you. Your date-rape scene, for example—it will be obvious to everyone that scene will be consensual sex, not date rape."

"How do we know that?" someone asked.

"Because I tell you," Paul said.

"How do we know that's true?"

"Trust me," Paul said.

Harry Britt said, "That's just not good enough."

It was all over the television news in San Francisco that night—Eszterhas was willing to make changes, but Verhoeven wasn't.

I saw myself interviewed, saying, "They made some points I agreed with."

The next day the papers played Paul as the bad guy and said I'd become a hero to the gay community.

Mario Kassar called Guy and said, "That's it! I'm suing him!"

"If you sue him," Guy said, "you're going to have every gay militant between California and Paris on the set of your movie."

"*Fuck him!*" Mario Kassar screamed. "I'm going to put a contract out on him!"

"*What did you say?*" Guy McElwaine screamed so loudly that the secretaries down the hall heard him.

"Oh for God's sake, Guy," Mario said. "You know I'm not going to do anything like that. *But why is he doing this to me?* I paid him three million dollars to do *this* to me?"

The *New York Times* did a story about the San Francisco protests of *Basic Instinct* which pointed out that this was probably the first time a screenwriter was battling to change his own words . . . against a director who wanted to use the screenwriter's words unchanged. The *New York Times* also pointed out that this was the *same* screenwriter who'd walked off the project because this *same* director wanted to *change* his words.

I sent Paul a series of changes which, I felt, violated neither the story nor the characters.

Paul once again said publicly that he would make no changes.

A columnist who applauded Paul's position said this was the first known case of a director maintaining the integrity of a script against the efforts of a screenwriter who wanted to destroy what he'd written.

The protests began as the movie started shooting. The protesters carried signs and yelled loudly and blew whistles but were, I thought, harmless. Alan Marshall didn't think so, however, and started making "citizen's arrests" of kids in Queer Nation T-shirts and carrying them to nearby police vans.

I couldn't believe that the producer of a Hollywood movie was actually carrying out "citizen's arrests" on the streets of San Francisco and attacked Alan for using "Nazi tactics." I referred publicly to a book in which Bill Cosby, who'd worked with Marshall, called him a "racist."

My criticism of Alan Marshall caused a trash fest in the press. Michael Douglas, an icon of liberal politics who had become the main target of the protesters, called me a bunch of names in a national magazine, the nicest of which was "opportunist."

Paul was quoted as saying that since I lived in the Bay Area, I was physically afraid of the wrath of the gay community. (When *Basic Instinct* was released, Paul sandbagged parts of his Pacific Palisades home, afraid of being physically harmed by Queer Nation kamikaze squads.)

Paul kept filming. He suffered a nosebleed one day which required hospitalization and my spies said Michael Douglas had punched him, although Paul denied it. (Not that unusual in Hollywood: Sly Stallone broke several of director Ted Kotcheff's ribs on *First Blood*.)

Stone and Michael were at each other's throats.

I remembered Michael's complaint that "she one-ups me every time" . . . when I heard that, in a scene near the end of the movie, he refused to move toward Sharon, but insisted Stone move toward him. Stone refused to do it and Paul was forced to shoot it both ways.

At the end of the shoot, still trying to mend fences, Michael attended a gala San Francisco AIDS benefit, sat on the dais, and announced a big-buck donation.

I was invited to no screenings and was left off the invitation list for the premiere. Gay groups announced massive protests in San Francisco, New York, and Los Angeles for opening night. T-shirts were made that said "Catherine Did It" and kids with Queer Nation T-shirts and loudspeakers walked up and down San Francisco streets saying "Don't See It—Catherine Did It!" hoping to ruin the mystery and the box office.

I saw the movie on opening night in my local Marin County theater with Gerri and Steve and Suzi. I stood in line, paid money to see my own movie, bought everybody popcorn, and sat down. A bank of TV lights waited outside for my reaction.

When it was over, I walked outside and stepped to the cameras and said, "I loved it. Paul Verhoeven has directed a brilliant movie. My hat's off to him. He was right when he said there wouldn't be anything injurious in this movie to gay people."

The public agreed with me. The movie opened huge—$15 million in 1992—against sometimes fulminating reviews. The protests ended after two days.

While protesters were right about harmful Hollywood depictions of gay people, many of them soon realized they'd picked the wrong movie as their target. They should have gone after *Bird on a Wire* with Mel Gibson instead of *Basic Instinct.*

I did notice, though, as I watched the movie, that Paul had removed all the references to "dykes" in the dialogue just as I'd suggested.

As we walked out of that Corte Madera Theatre, Steve, my fifteen-year-old son, seemed orgasmic.

"Dad! Dad!" Steve said. "How did you come up with that scene where she crosses her legs?"

It was the scene which my friend Robert Evans would refer to as "the hundred-million-dollar pussy-hair shot."

I realized I was at a cathartic moment with my son. *Why oh why had I told my kids I'd never lie to them?*

"I didn't," I said.

He said, "*What?*"

I said, "It wasn't in the script. It was Paul's idea. In the previous scene in the script, as Sharon was getting dressed, Michael saw that she wasn't wearing underwear. But to have that flash of hair in the interrogation scene, that was Paul's idea."

Steve seemed shocked.

The most controversial, most talked about scene in the movie, wasn't even his father's idea.

I sent Paul Verhoeven a case of champagne congratulating him and told the *L.A. Times* that "Paul was right and I was wrong" about the points the protesters had argued. *Basic Instinct,* I said, was in no way a homophobic movie.

Now some of the leaders of the gay community were calling me a "traitor" and accusing me of "using and betraying" them.

I noticed that in the interviews that he did, Michael Douglas seemed somehow befuddled about the movie's success. He kept talking about "redemption" and how this movie had no "redemptive value."

I noticed, too, that a lot of people who had seen the movie were coming to me and asking whodunit? They'd enjoyed the movie but weren't sure who the killer was.

It reminded me of *Jagged Edge,* where Siskel and Ebert had set off a national guessing game by saying they weren't sure that it was Jeff Bridges who was wearing the ski mask in the final scene of the movie.

. . .

A woman in Toledo, Ohio, who saw *Basic* killed her husband by sticking an ice pick into his heart.

She had seen the movie.

The media was all over me.

I told them he probably died a faster and less painful death than if she had used a butcher knife or a gun.

Basic Instinct, the script I'd written in three weeks, went on to gross more than $400 million around the world. It was the number one box office hit of the year in both the United States and around the world. A French news magazine picked it as the event of the year. Not the *movie* event of the year. The *news* event of the year. The magazine said that a hundred years from now, 1992 would be remembered as the year *Basic Instinct* was released.

Ah, the French! In France, Mickey Rourke is a superstar.

Thanks to *Basic Instinct,* Gerri, Steve and Suzi, and I were undergoing a very personal crisis in Tiburon.

Gerri's brother, Bob, developed schizophrenia in his early twenties. "Voices" took over his life. "God" began speaking to him, telling him, among other things, to build a cuckoo clock with the figures of the apostles.

Among the "other things" was the notion that I was "killing God and America" with the movies I was writing and that I was "fornicating with harlots."

When I wrote *Big Shots,* a movie about a white and a black kid learning to be friends, "God" whispered to my brother-in-law that I was Satan and that Steve and Suzi were "Satan's spawn." This was because "God" told Bob that "the color black represented evil."

His condition worsened and Bob entered a psychiatric hospital in Ohio.

Just before *Basic Instinct*'s release, I got a phone call from the doctors at the psychiatric hospital. They told me to flee my house in Tiburon with my wife and kids. My brother-in-law had broken out of the hospital, stolen his mother's car, grabbed two rifles from the attic, and was headed west to kill me.

He had seen some television ads for *Basic.* "God" told Bob he didn't like the ads for *Basic.* "God" talked to Bob about "harlots and Satan."

It wasn't easy to flee my house. My eighty-two-year-old father was in an upstairs room with round-the-clock nursing recuperating from a heart valve replacement. My kids were in high school. I had other scripts to write.

Instead of fleeing, I hired an army of private detectives and security agents. Armed guards stood in front of our house. Camouflaged agents with high-scope rifles prowled the fields in back. They started wearing bulletproof vests after the private eyes discovered that my brother-in-law had won an expert marksman award while at a private military school in his teens.

There were guns and shotguns hidden in different parts of our house in Tiburon—under pillows and couches, atop cupboards.

We waited and cowered. Nothing happened. There was no trace of my brother-in-law, although police agencies had been notified across the country.

Suzi, I saw, was petrified and I realized I couldn't do this to my kids any longer. We decided to flee to a hotel in Hawaii, leaving the security army behind to guard my father, the nurses, and the house. The high school my kids attended distributed mug shots of my brother-in-law to all the teachers.

Three weeks later, while we were in Hawaii, my brother-in-law called a relative in Ohio. He was in Mexico City. He was broke. He needed money.

I sent two of the security agents—off-duty federal marshals—to Mexico City. They found my brother-in-law at his fleabag hotel and "observed" him. He spent much of his time in the hotel lobby, ranting and raving about God and Satan and *Big Shots* and *Basic Instinct* and me.

My security agents had a legal problem. They couldn't just kidnap him and take Bob back to his Ohio psychiatrists. They had to get my brother-in-law across the border legally somehow.

I called Robert Evans. I knew that Evans had ties to the Bush White House, especially to press secretary Marlin Fitzwater. I told him about my brother-in-law problem. He went to Fitzwater, who got the ambassador to Mexico involved. FBI agents and Mexican federales hooked up with my security agents in Mexico City.

My brother-in-law was arrested for vagrancy and taken to jail. He was left there for three days. After three days, my security agents went to see him. They gave him a choice. He could either rot in that Mexican jail or he could accompany them back to his psychiatric hospital in Ohio. Bob didn't much like that Mexican jail. He agreed to accompany my security agents.

The security agents handcuffed him and sat on the plane with him to Ohio. The plane stopped in Houston, although, thanks to Fitzwater, they didn't even have to get off and go through Customs.

As the others were getting off the plane in Houston, Bob started raving at the black people passing him, black people who were "the color of evil." He ranted and raved about *Basic Instinct*. He asked the other passengers if they'd seen *Basic*. He told them they'd go to hell if they did.

When the plane landed in Cleveland, my security agents whisked my brother-in-law to a limo I'd hired standing by the plane. The limo drove him to his psychiatric hospital. When they got there, my brother-in-law, still hand-cuffed, head-butted one of the security guards and made a run for it. When they dragged him inside, he was yelling, "Joe is Satan. Joe Eszterhas is Satan."

My private detectives found his car abandoned at the side of the road in Connecticut. They found the two rifles, recently oiled and loaded, in a locker at the Greyhound station in Houston, where Bob had left them on the way into Mexico.

Seven months after I sold *Basic*, I wrote another spec script—this one called *Original Sin*, a thriller about lovers who'd met in a past life.

I sent the script to Guy and Jeff Berg, who said they were going to stage another auction.

My first question to them was: "What about Ovitz?"

Jeff said, "We'll watch him."

Guy said, "We surely will."

I had once again asked Irwin Winkler to produce it and he had once again agreed.

"Does Irwin have the script?" Berg asked.

"Of course he does," I said. "How could he read it otherwise?"

"That means Ron Meyer's got it, which means Ovitz has it."

I said, "Irwin wouldn't do that to me."

Berg said, "Okay," and hung up.

Two days before the scheduled auction date, Andrea King of the *Hollywood Reporter* wrote a front-page story about *Original Sin* being auctioned. The story lavishly praised the script and said it was so commercial that it would go for an even higher price than *Basic Instinct*.

It was obvious from her story that Andrea King had a copy of the script.

Berg was thermonuclear.

"You know what this story does?" he yelled. "It scares everybody away. It says they don't have a chance to get this because the price is going to be so high. *That* means we won't be able to bid people against each other to get the price up. She sandbagged us. She purposely wrote this and praised it to the heavens to kill the sale. How did she get the script? Tell me that."

"I don't know," I said, "you've got the only copy."

"Our copy's in the safe, we haven't even Xeroxed it yet."

"I don't know how she got it."

"I do," Berg said. "Winkler."

He pointed out that Andrea King covered CAA for the *Reporter*.

I called Irwin and asked him if he'd shown the script to anyone. "Are you kidding me?" he said. "Absolutely not."

The day we went out to auction with *Original Sin*, Jeff's fears were proven right. The studios claimed to like the script but said they were afraid to bid on it considering what they'd read it was going to sell for in the *Reporter*.

We discovered they were hesitant for another reason, too: the Thousand-Pound Gorilla was working the phones. Himself.

"Ovitz is calling everybody," Jeff said. "He's not talking about you. He never mentions you. He's putting it in terms of the industry. He's talking about the escalating price spiral, especially for screenwriters. He's saying that for the health of the industry, screenwriters' prices have to be kept down. He's saying it would be a bad precedent if we sold this for even more money than we got for *Basic.*"

Jeff laughed. "He's got nothing personally against you. He just wants to be the studios' pal and give them good advice."

I said, "What can we do?"

Jeff said, "We can sell this sonofabitch script."

ICM went to war with CAA over *Original Sin.* ("Jeff and I must have made eight hundred calls," Guy told me later.) For two weeks . . . as the battle went on . . . the script stayed unsold.

During that time, a young assistant at ICM told her boss that she had seen a Xerox copy of *Original Sin* at her boyfriend's house five days before we took it to auction.

In other words, while the script I'd sent to ICM was still in their safe.

I called her from Marin and asked who her boyfriend was. He was, she said, one of Ron Meyer's assistants at CAA. I asked if she could possibly retrieve her boyfriend's copy.

I think one of the saddest moments of my life was when I opened the brown envelope she sent me. It was a Xerox copy of my *typescript* of the script done on my manual typewriter . . . the typescript copy of *Original Sin* I'd sent only to Irwin Winkler . . . the script I'd sent to ICM had already been typed on a computer by my typist.

What froze me to my bones at that moment was that I knew that at least one thing Michael Ovitz threatened had come true: *my relationships with Barry Hirsch . . . and now my dear friend Irwin Winkler . . . were over.*

I called Irwin, shattered and angry, and said, "How could you have done this to me?"

"What?" he said. "What's wrong?"

"You gave the script to Ronnie Meyer."

"I didn't," he said. "I told you. I didn't give it to anybody."

"You're lying to me, Irwin," I said. "I trusted you."

"We're friends," he said. "I wouldn't lie to you."

A part of me believed Irwin even as I knew I would end my relationship with him. I knew it was possible that one of Irwin's secretaries or one of his assistants had gotten my script to CAA without Irwin's knowledge.

I didn't feel I had the freedom, though, to dwell on that possibility. I was caught up in . . . *overwhelmed by* . . . my war with Ovitz and his asshole foot soldiers. I was made uncomfortable by the very fact of Irwin's undeniable closeness to Ovitz, Meyer, and CAA.

It's possible that I ended my relationship with Irwin for that reason alone . . . that my bloodlust for the battle made the breakup a self-fulfilled prophecy.

At the end of the two weeks, we sold *Original Sin* to Andy Vajna and Cinergi for $1.25 million. ICM had won its war with CAA.

Vajna, my fellow Hungarian, facing intense pressure from Ovitz not to buy the script, agreed to buy it only after ICM promised to help him with casting on other projects.

"Ovitz never mentioned you," Vajna told me later, "he was arguing for the future financial health of the industry."

About a year later, over dinner in Hawaii, Wolfgang Puck, a very decent man and an immigrant, like me, from Europe, turned to me and said, "Michael never forgets, Joe. Remember that. I know him. I've done business with him. Watch your back."

I watched my back for many years as Michael Ovitz kept denying over and over again the things I alleged he had said to me at our meeting in the fall of 1989.

Then, in an authorized biography published in 1997 called *Ovitz,* written by Robert Slater, I was astounded to read the following paragraphs:

> The question that was on the minds of everyone connected to the Eszterhas Affair, and that certainly was uppermost in the author's mind as he talked with Ovitz, was this: Had he or had he not made the notorious threat to march his foot soldiers down Wilshire Boulevard and blow the screenwriter's brains out?
>
> The question was posed: What in fact had he said to Eszterhas in that regard?
>
> Then came Ovitz's startling response:
>
> "Eszterhas and I were joking with each other when I said: 'You don't want our foot soldiers going up the street gunning for you, do you?' "
>
> Until that moment, Ovitz had denied ever making any foot soldiers' remarks of any kind. Was this the first time he had admitted to making the infamous remark?
>
> "Yes," said Ovitz, "it was."

We had been joking!
That was funny!

· · ·

Two years after I sold *Original Sin,* I got a script from Andy Vajna, the head of Cinergi, with a note that said, "Read immediately!"

I started reading it and recognized it as *Original Sin* with a different title and by a writer I'd never heard of.

Someone had Xeroxed my script and put a new cover and title on it.

I called Vajna and he told me the story:

The script in front of me had been sold to Hearst Television the previous week for $250,000.

Cinergi's lawyers had discovered that the "author" worked in Chicago as a mailman and lived with his aged mother. He had taken a screenwriting course at a local community college where *Original Sin* had been part of the course and where copies of my script had been distributed to the class.

The mailman Xeroxed my script, changed the title, put his name on it, and sent it to a Chicago agent who sent it to a Hollywood agent who sold it to Hearst Television.

Cinergi's lawyers were now threatening the mailman with the tortures of hell.

You couldn't expect to sell *every* script you didn't write, of course. Cinergi's lawyers determined that the mailman had tried to sell another of my scripts, too—*Sacred Cows*—but this time had failed in his efforts.

The Dentist

He had very bad teeth and the reason he went to Dr. Abramson in the first place is that he was ashamed of his teeth and didn't want them to become part of industry gossip.

Abramson wasn't a dentist to the stars; he had a small office in a dingy part of mid-Wilshire.

Abramson took one look at his teeth and said, simply, "Ah, we have some work to do." He didn't give him a sermon, he didn't tell him that he had ruined his teeth by rarely brushing and never flossing them.

Abramson asked him what he did and he told him he was a producer. Abramson revealed that he saw at least six movies each week. They spent the long painful hours in the chair discussing their favorite movies. After a while he began telling Abramson the plots of scripts submitted to him and Abramson started giving him advice on which ones to make.

He scoffed mostly at the dentist's advice but he took it once and the movie turned out to be a hit. He took his advice again and had another hit. As a result, he was made the head of the studio.

He made a quiet deal with Abramson then. He paid him a significant amount of money to read every script he was considering green-lighting. He had one hit after another.

When Abramson, a fat man badly out of shape, had a heart attack and died, the studio head almost had a heart attack himself.

He tried to find other Abramsons—a parking lot attendant, a waitress, a high school classmate, but none of them had the dentist's encyclopedic knowledge of hit movies.

He green-lighted one stinker after another and was fired at the studio. He didn't fare any better as a producer.

Industry gossip said he was spending much of his time in dentist's offices. He had developed gum disease from neglecting his teeth. He was, it was said, in great and ceaseless pain.

CHAPTER 13

[Flashback]

Me and Anastas Mikoyan

KARCHY
I can't say "the." My tongue. I can't get it right.

MAGIC
Put a rubber band on it.

KARCHY
I never thought of that.

Telling Lies in America

The first book I read was Jules Verne's *Michael Strogoff*, set in the world of czarist Cossack horsemen. It had been a Christmas gift from my father's friend, the novelist and poet Gyula Bedy, and had been on a shelf unopened for two years. Suddenly I found myself out in the Russian steppes, far from back alleys, juvenile caseworkers, and my mother's loony laughter. I moved on to *The Three Musketeers, The Man in the Iron Mask,* and *The Count of Monte Cristo,* books my father had read when he was a boy.

I read either on my living room couch, if my mother was okay, or, if she wasn't, in my nonbathroom sitting on my non–toilet seat with wadded-up Kleenex in my ears.

Sometimes I told my father I was going down to the public library after school . . . and this time I really did, sitting in the Reading Room with the bums who came there to either warm up or cool off.

I started to haunt a used paperback store on West 30th and Lorain, a front, I discovered, for a horse racing wire. They sold paperbacks here with many of their covers torn off for either two cents or five and I moved on to Faulkner and

Fitzgerald and Hemingway and Steinbeck and Salinger and C. S. Forester and A. J. Cronin and Mickey Spillane and Eric Ambler and Mary Roberts Rinehart.

The horse bettors, moving through to the back room of the store with big cigars in their hands, would sometimes give me literary advice.

"Hey, kid, didja read Henry Miller yet?"

"No."

"Read him. He'll make your dick grow."

"I can't sell him Henry Miller," the owner said, "he's a minor. They'll put me in jail."

But I begged the man and he sold me *Tropic of Cancer* and *Tropic of Capricorn* for ten cents. So I read Henry Miller and he didn't make my dick grow but I widened my eyes sometimes when I read his descriptions. And I read Wolfe and Tennessee Williams.

I was a catholic (small c), ecumenical, and promiscuous reader. I read anything and everything that appealed to me. I hung around so much the owner asked if I wanted to help him in the back with the wire for $5 a day. I was tempted—$5 was a lot of money—but I remembered my promise to Father John and turned him down.

I told him I had made a promise to a priest to make something of my life. Touched somehow by that, he let me have the paperbacks for nothing as long as I brought them back when I'd read them.

I felt myself *transported* when I read a book. Nothing else existed when I was reading. *I* didn't exist, either. *I* was Michael Strogoff and Tom Joad and Gatsby and Nick Adams and Mike Hammer. Their problems were my problems; their loves were my loves. *I* was in love with Daisy Buchanan because I *was* Gatsby.

My father gave me one of his beaten-to-death Hungarian-language typewriters—he typed with two fingers and smashed the keys—and I started making lists for myself of the books I had read.

Each listing had the author's name, the major characters' names, and a summary of the plot.

I also made lists of words that I hadn't understood, their definitions in English, and their Hungarian translations.

I read only in English, to my father's consternation. I refused, even, to read his own novels, copies of which were slowly gathering from subscribers who'd seen his ad asking for copies of his books.

"Why won't you read Hungarian?" he asked. "You know how. Your mother taught you."

"It's easier for me to read in English," I said.

"Are you ashamed of being Hungarian?"

"No."

"Then what?"

"You told me to read," I said to him. "I'm reading. You didn't tell me to read in Hungarian."

"Yes." My father smiled. "Unfortunately that is absolutely true."

Besides getting copies of his books from Katherine Webster or subscribers to his newspaper, my father would also steal them. Well, he wouldn't really steal them because he'd pay for them—but he'd take them from the public library, and then say that he'd lost them.

I was with him one day when he told a librarian that he had lost four books and wanted to pay for them. The librarian wrote down the book's titles and she wrote down the author and my father paid her $20 and she wrote my father a receipt.

When she wrote the receipt she stopped suddenly and said, "But this name—your name—is the same as the author's!"

"This name," my father said, deadpan, "Eszterhás—this name is as common in Hungarian as Smith or Jones."

"Really," the librarian said.

My father said, "True!"

"Well, you learn something every day," the librarian said.

We were laughing as we left the library that day . . . Eszterhás was most definitely not a common Hungarian name. It was such a rare Hungarian name that we knew of no other Eszterháses in the whole world.

"Did you get a copy of *Nemzet Politika* yet?" I asked my father.

"Why do you ask me about *Nemzet Politika*?" My father smiled. "You don't read my books anyway."

"You said it will be the most difficult to find."

"No, I don't have a copy yet," my father said.

"When I grow up," I said, "I will find it for you."

"Thank you." He smiled. "Will you read it, too?"

"All right," I said, "I promise you that if I find *Nemzet Politika* I will read it."

"Thank you," he said, his arm around me. "That means very much to me. I will hold you to your promise."

Glancing through the *National Catholic Register* one day, I saw an announcement for a contest. If I answered 250 questions relating to American history, art, literature, and religion correctly, I'd win $1,000.

I told my father I was going to go down to the library after school every day and dig into all the books there and win $1,000.

"What will you do with the money?" he asked.

"I'll buy a record player and I will buy every Jerry Lee Lewis, Elvis Presley, Chuck Berry, and Little Richard record ever made."

He shook his head and said *Ohkay!* And *Fein!* And when I got back from the library the next night I found a stack of musty and rain-damaged *World Book Encyclopedia*s on the kitchen table.

"For *Elvész*" (the word means "lost" in Hungarian), my father said. "*Elvész Prezli*" (the lost pretzel).

I worked for a month answering the 250 questions and when I was finished my father drove me in our blue Nash to the downtown post office and we mailed my thick envelope Special Delivery to the *National Catholic Register* offices in Denver.

A week later I got a postcard back informing me that I'd lost but that I could subscribe to the *Register* at a special rate.

My father saw how disappointed I was and tousled my hair.

"There is an old Hungarian saying," he said.

"I know all the old Hungarian sayings," I said. "I don't want to hear another one now."

"You don't know this one," he said. "*Nem minden papsajt, van papszar is.*"

It really made me laugh. "Not everything is priest's cheese; there is priest's shit, too."

I even thought I detected, shockingly, a glimmer of a smile on my mother's set and stern face.

"You worked very hard," my father said. "You lost. But you learned many things. Correct?"

I shrugged. All I knew was that I'd lost.

"So," he said, "as far as I'm concerned, you won and to reward you for winning, I will give you two dollars every week from now on."

I laughed and hugged him and I saw that my mother was smiling, too, and in my joy I moved to hug her, too. She backed away from me and left the room.

I stood there. My father was looking at me evenly.

"She doesn't mean it," he said.

I won my spelling bee at St. Emeric's School and my father and I studied the dictionary together for the West Side finals.

I was eliminated in the first round of the finals for misspelling a word.

I ran home and my father and I looked it up in the dictionary and there it was: I had spelled it correctly.

Dictionary in hand, he came back to the school with me to confront the teacher with the evidence.

The teacher looked at the dictionary, then at the flyleaf, shook his head, and said, "This is an English dictionary you have here, published in Great Britain. They spell it differently over there."

My father said, "It correct. Boy study in dic-cherry."

"Sorry," the teacher said, "wrong dictionary. Where did you get it?"

"Voloontair America," my father said.

The teacher smirked.

On the way home, my father said to me in Hungarian, "I read an article in the *Plain Dealer* about a famous American writer, he knows all the big words, but he can't spell them. So he pays someone to spell all the big words for him—a lawyer, I think. When you are a famous American writer, you will pay a lawyer to spell words, too."

I passed the playgrounds slowly sometimes but kept walking. The alleys and streets were not the lure they had once been. The rawness and edge of the alleys didn't amount to much compared with the worlds I lived in in Tennessee Williams and Faulkner and Mickey Spillane.

I ran into Chuckie Chuckles on the way home from school. He had a brown paper bag of Manischewitz and offered it to me but I shook my head.

His family was heading back to Kentucky, he said, and José's older brother had been killed while holding up a grocery store on Clark Avenue.

"Dumb shit," Chuckie said. "He goes in with a zip gun and the guy behind the counter has a real Luger he brought home from the war."

My father made me a soccer game with his own hands. It was a piece of wood painted green with wire mesh nets at each end and metal rims around the sides.

The game was played with buttons. Larger coat buttons were the players and a little white shirt button was the ball. We took turns flicking "the ball" with the larger coat buttons toward the net.

The coat button "players" soon had distinctive "personalities" and my father and I rummaged through the button jars at the Salvation Army and the Volunteers scouting new player buttons. It was the first time that going to the Salvation Army or the Volunteers was ever fun.

I played the game so much either with my father or by myself that my thumb got badly blistered.

For Christmas he bought me a toy printing set with rubber letters and its own ink supply. I decided to publish my own newspaper, the *St. Emeric Herald,* which I left on the desks at school early one morning.

It was filled with local news—"Frances Madar Seen Necking with Robert Zak in Cafeteria" was one headline.

I wrote an editorial that said, "Masturbation is not a sin. It will not make you blind. Everybody does it, even Father John, Sister Rose, and the other sisters, especially the sisters."

Sister Rose immediately summoned Father John, who, I thought, was going to kill me. All copies of the *St. Emeric's Herald* were collected by Sister Rose and burned in the alley.

"Are you forgetting the promise you made to me?" Father John scolded.

"No, Father," I said. "Look. I wrote a whole newspaper. All by myself. It was hard work."

"I don't know what will become of you," he said, "I just don't," but he was smiling . . . sort of . . . just a little.

My father bought me a BB pistol that I had been eyeing in the front window of Sam Finesilver's hardware store. It was for the two of us, he said, to be used only for target practice.

We drove out to Metropolitan Park in our old Nash, put bull's-eye paper targets on the trees, and fired away. We were laughing and having fun together.

I loved that BB pistol and just couldn't leave it up there on top of the bookshelf until the next trip to Metropolitan Park.

When my mother was in the kitchen or my father in the printing shop, I snuck to the living room window with the pistol and waited for targets to come along.

My favorite target was a fat Hungarian prostitute with a huge derriere. Each time she passed beneath our window I'd shoot her in the butt. All she did was smack herself back there as though she'd been stung by a mosquito.

Then I started on the big blazing Papp's Bar neon sign right next to our window. First I shot out all the green lights, then all the red lights, then all the yellow lights . . . until the big neon sign was dark.

When the policemen came, I couldn't even deny it . . . they'd picked all the BBs out of the gutter right underneath our window.

When the policemen left—after my father had agreed to pay old man Papp for the damage—my mother went completely berserk, screaming that my father was teaching me to shoot people.

I said, "All she did was scratch her behind, it didn't even hurt the fat *kurva*."

My father turned calmly away and started to play his violin.

My mother screamed at him. "A murderer," she said. "*Your* son. *Your* son. A murderer. Like you!"

I said, "Nana, really, she didn't even feel it."

She kept screaming about murder. My father kept playing the violin.

I went into my nonbathroom, stuck the Kleenex in my ears, and read *War and Peace*.

I read:

> *Kon-Tiki* by Thor Heyerdahl and wondered if it was possible to take a
>   raft across Lake Erie.
> *The Little World of Don Camillo* by Giovanni Guareschi and wondered

if, like Father John, Father Camillo had a funeral director's wife in
his life.

The Catcher in the Rye by J. D. Salinger and wrote the words "*Colder
than a witch's tit*" into a notebook.

East of Eden by John Steinbeck and hoped I'd meet a "monster" like
Catherine when I grew up.

The Blackboard Jungle by Evan Hunter and thought high school was
going to be a lot of fun.

Andersonville by MacKinlay Kantor and was very happy I wouldn't
have to go to jail.

Mandingo by Kyle Onstott and imagined Tina Mae Ritenour, Brigitte
Bardot, Justine Corelli, Mamie Van Doren, and Zsa Zsa Gabor as
my slaves.

And I read *The Rains Came* by Louis Bromfield, whose farm and
mansion I had visited with my father and Huldah Kramer. I
hated it.

My father was at home more, making fewer speeches and rarely out of town.
Huldah Kramer didn't come to see him in his office anymore and I heard nothing about his librarian friend, Katherine Webster.

I hardly ever saw him reading a Hungarian book or a classic. He was only
reading his American paperbacks now—not just Spillane but writers named
Macdonald and Hammett and Chandler and Woolrich.

During one of my mother's better periods, my father said we would go on a
vacation. I would be the navigator, he said. I could pick out where we would
go—as long as it was in Michigan or Pennsylvania, not too far away.

I went down to the library and to the automobile club on Euclid Avenue
and studied vacation spots. I announced my choice—a place in Michigan called
Houghton Lake. I gathered the maps and we set off. My father drove—my
mother sat between us. It took us about eight hours to get there.

For the first seven hours of the trip she was fine—smiling, friendly. Then
she turned on us.

"You are not Mindszenty," she said to my father. "*Torturer!* You are Mindszenty's torturer!"

"*Diszno!*" she said to him—"Pig! I know what filth you do to the boy!"

She made the Sign of the Cross.

I started to shake. I braced my arms against the dash and watched my arms
as they shook like feathers.

My mother looked at me and smiled.

"Stop acting," she said sweetly to me. "You and your father are such actors!"

. . .

We found a cabin at a place called Chet's Resort, which was right on the lake. We were there for a week.

The first day, we went into the water. It was filled with little fish that nibbled at us. When the first fish nibbled at my mother, she ran screaming from the water and never came back in again.

"That's why you picked this place!" she said angrily to me. "You knew that the fish would torture me!"

My mother said, "*Torturer!* Just like your father."

Staying in the cabin next to us was a family from Detroit, the Jacksons. Mr. and Mrs. Jackson and their sixteen-year-old daughter, Karen. I thought she was prettier even than Justine Corelli.

We swam together and rode a boat together. We talked about *American Bandstand* and Elvis and I told her about the windows José and I had broken after seeing Jerry Lee Lewis.

"How old are you?" she asked.

I lied and told her I was sixteen, not fourteen.

There was an old unused trailer behind the cabins and we went in there and smoked a cigarette.

It was *colder than a witch's tit in there.* She let me kiss her and touch her breasts. The day after I touched her breasts, she and her parents left, their vacation over.

My father bought me a portable transistor radio. I kept it near me twenty-four hours a day—at night it was next to my pillow.

"Don't let your mother get her hands on it," he said. "God knows what she'd do to it. Boil it maybe, ha?" He smiled.

It was the most beautiful radio I'd ever seen. It even picked up a station from Memphis, Tennessee, where *Elvész* and Jerry Lee Lewis lived, a station the Philips shortwave had never picked up. It picked up baseball games played by the Brooklyn Dodgers and the Chicago Cubs and White Sox.

I listened to it nonstop, hearing masterpieces like "Get a Job" by the Silhouettes, and "At the Hop" by Danny and the Juniors.

My father heard me listening to it and he even sat and listened to "Great Balls of Fire" by Jerry Lee Lewis, who was more famous, I told him, than Franz Liszt.

"Please," my father said, "if you tell me that again I'll *give* your radio to your mother to boil."

But he even found a song he liked, forced to overhear the jungle music he didn't like on the radio he had given me.

He looked up every time he heard it. I even heard him humming it. The first American song he had ever liked. Doris Day sang it.

Que sera, sera, whatever will be, will be, the future's not ours to see, que sera, sera, what will be, will be.

The Cleveland Indians had a player I liked a lot. He was young—a hard-line-drive hitter who always hustled. He was exciting to watch, particularly good in the clutch when the game was tied. He looked like he could be an All-Star some-day. The Indians traded him.

His name was Roger Maris. He would soon break Babe Ruth's home run record.

He wanted to write a book, my father said, in English, not in Hungarian. He couldn't speak English, but I could. Maybe I was a little young, at fourteen, to be a translator, he said, but he didn't know any other translators.

If I translated his book, he would get the Franciscans to print it and send it to American newspapers through the mail. The American newspapers would write about it and then Americans would buy it.

And if enough Americans bought it, we could buy a mansion and a farm like the one owned by Louis Bromfield. We could also buy a car beneath whose rusted-out floor we couldn't see the street.

We could go to vacations not to Cook Forest or Houghton Lake but to Viareggio in Italy, where my father said he had vacationed as a young man and had eaten fresh oysters from the sea. We could eat Westphalian ham and Hertz salami not just at Christmas but every day. We could wear clothes not from the Salvation Army but handmade by Italian tailors, who had made the silk suits he wore as a young man.

It was, my father said, up to *me*. If I agreed to translate his book, all those things could . . . no, no, probably *would* happen.

And just to be fair—because this was going to be a lot of work—he would pay me *before* I did the work.

He would buy me a television set.

We carried the set home together from the furniture store. When we got it through the door, my mother started yelling.

"No!" she said. "Enough rays! You won't bring any more rays into this house and torture me with them!"

"Do you want the boy back out on the streets?" my father yelled at her.

She was so upset she was dancing around us, stomping her feet.

He laid down rules. I could watch the set for two hours on weekdays and four on weekends.

I watched *American Bandstand* every afternoon and I watched the Cleveland Indians and *Naked City* and *Peter Gunn* and *M Squad* and *The Lineup*.

Sometimes my father watched with me but my mother never did. She stayed as far away from the rays as possible, in the kitchen.

My father's favorite program, which he never missed, was *I Led Three Lives* starring Richard Carlson. It was about the underground FBI agent Herbert Philbrick who was spying on Communist spies. Each week Philbrick uncovered more spies and each week when the show ended my father said "*Jó volt*"—"That was a good one."

He tried to persuade my mother to watch the capture of the Communist spies but my mother said the Komchis were just trying to get her closer to their rays by putting on a program about Communist spies.

We worked on his book after school and on the weekends. He read it to me sentence by sentence and I wrote it down in English in longhand after consulting the three Hungarian-English dictionaries on the kitchen table.

Then he took my longhand English sentences and typed them up. We did that sentence by sentence, paragraph by paragraph, page by page, day by day, week by week, month by month. I understood very little of what I was translating. The book was about political science and filled with words like "autonomy" and "interdependence" and "hegemony."

He knew I wasn't having any fun and one day, after we'd worked for seven hours, he took a package out of the refrigerator and opened it on the table.

It was a few slices of Westphalian ham.

"A preview," my father said, "of all the Westphalian ham we will eat after Americans buy this book."

My mother risked the rays inside the television set for one hour every week. She sat down next to my father and took little sips of her cognac. I joined them sometimes as they watched Lawrence Welk.

It wasn't my kind of music, but it was the one hour each week when we were really all together, when we were having fun. My father talked about how wonderful the champagne lady, Alice Lon, was. My mother talked about how wonderful the accordionist was. I imagined how wonderful the youngest Lennon sister, Kathy, the one with the hair and the freckles, would be.

Life was just a-wonderful, a-wonderful!

The Franciscans printed the book, now entitled *Social Proportion*, and my father went down to the public library and made a list of a thousand of America's newspapers.

He wrote a cover letter which I translated giving his address and telephone number and saying that he would happily make himself available for interviews. He and I put the books into brown envelopes, went to the post office downtown, and mailed them.

"I couldn't have done this without you, Jozsi," he said. "Thank you."

We waited for the American newspapers to write or call. *Viareggio vacations! Oysters! Italian clothes! Westphalian ham every day!*

We waited.

And waited.

Nobody wrote.

Nobody called.

After three months without a response from the American newspapers' book editors, my mother made a detailed list of how much *Social Proportion* had cost.

We owed the Franciscans $500 which they would deduct from my father's salary, plus the money for the envelopes, plus the money for the stationery for the cover letters, plus the money for the stamps.

My mother handed him the list and said, "This is what you have wasted."

He turned red and I thought he was going to yell at her, but he didn't. Instead he said, "Oh, Mária, what have I done to make you hate me so?"

In 2002, after I did a Hardball with Chris Matthews *show in Cleveland, an old man stopped me with a book in his hands.*

It was Social Proportion.

He asked me to autograph it and as I did, I noticed my father had already signed it . . . in 1958.

"Where did you get this book?" I asked him.

"I was at the Volunteers of America down by the West Side Market," the old man said, "and I saw it on a shelf. I thought it was one of your books."

I told the old man how I had translated this book when I was a kid and the old man said, "Both of you signing it—this is gonna be worth a lot on that eBay, don't you think?"

The Volunteers of America near the West Side Market . . .

My father's book had wound up on the shelf at the Volunteers . . . the same store where he and I had shopped for our clothes, the same store where we'd found buttons for the soccer game we played.

The butcher of Budapest, Anastas Mikoyan, the Soviet foreign minister, was coming to Cleveland to visit his friend Cyrus Eaton, the international tycoon and multibillionaire, Cleveland's wealthiest resident, once John D. Rockefeller's personal assistant.

Mikoyan was the Soviet leader, the press informed us, who had secretly flown into Hungary to plan the Red Army's deadly attack against the freedom fighters.

Hungarians in Cleveland hated Cyrus Eaton because he was Nikita Khrushchev's friend—Khrushchev had given him a Russian troika—and because, after a trip to Hungary after the revolution, Eaton had said America was "more of a police state than Hungary."

My father, as the newly elected president of the Committee for Hungarian Liberation, organized a demonstration at the downtown Hotel Cleveland for Mikoyan's arrival.

My father and I and hundreds of Hungarians filled our pockets with rotten eggs. When Mikoyan got out of his limousine in front of the hotel, protected by a police cordon, we screamed "*Russki go home!*" at the top of our lungs and fired our eggs.

And the egg that I threw . . . with the arm strengthened by all those games of baseball, the American pastime . . . hit Anastas Mikoyan on the side of his butchering dirty Commie-rat face.

I was a hero among the Hungarians on the West Side.

My father said, "I have never been prouder of you than I am today."

"It is because of all the bazball I've played," I told him.

My father said, "Don't say that!"

Many years later, when I was a reporter for the Cleveland Plain Dealer, *I got a note from Cyrus Eaton telling me how much he liked a story I had written and asking me to visit him at his office.*

He was a friendly, courtly, and grand old man in his eighties and we talked about our mutual loathing of the war in Vietnam.

"Do you remember that day Mikoyan visited you and there was a demonstration against him at the hotel?" I asked.

"Yes, of course I do," Cyrus Eaton said.

"Do you remember that egg that hit Mikoyan in the face?"

"I'll never forget it." Cyrus Eaton smiled. "He was mad as a hornet. I thought for a moment that silly egg was going to affect the course of Soviet-American relations. He's Armenian, you know. He has quite a temper."

"I threw it," I said.

"You did what?" Cyrus Eaton said, thinking he'd misunderstood me.

"I threw the egg that hit Mikoyan," I said.

"Why, you scamp!" Cyrus Eaton said, and laughed so hard he had to ask for a glass of water.

CHAPTER 14

I Climb the Hill
of Broken Glass

TONY

You got something wrong with your nipples?

NOMI

No.

TONY

They're not stickin' up. Stick 'em up.

NOMI

What?

TONY

Play with 'em a little bit.

Showgirls

When *Basic Instinct* turned into a worldwide event, Guy said, "Boy did we dodge a big one. Imagine a three-million-dollar screenplay, imagine all the publicity over the record sale, and then imagine it going into the toilet. We would've been in deep shit."

Mario Kassar at Carolco called me to say, "*Joey,* that three million dollars for your script was the best investment I ever made. I paid you peanuts for a money tree."

I knew how much Mario was enjoying the fruits from his money tree. He had been soundly trashed by a lot of people in Hollywood for paying a writer, any writer, $3 million.

It was payback time for Mario now.

He'd paid $3 million to make $450 million.

. . .

A few months after the release of *Basic,* my Marin County producer friend Ben Myron, who'd just produced the powerful independently made *One False Move* directed by Carl Franklin, came up with a movie idea.

"A dark musical," Ben said, "like *Flashdance* but much darker, about Vegas. The underside of Vegas. The real Vegas, the one the casino PR people try to hide." I told Ben I thought it was a great idea. A dark musical seemed like a fresh and original concept to me in 1992.

Then Ben said, "Verhoeven!"

I laughed. "He'll kill *me,* I'll kill *him,* life is too short."

"He's never done anything like this," Ben insisted. "He's got a jazzy style. He'd be perfect for it."

"Call him," I told Ben. "See if he wants to have lunch with us. He might just say he never wants to see me as long as he lives."

"Let's bet," Ben said. "You gave him the biggest hit he's ever had. He'll be there."

We met at the Ivy on Robertson. I hadn't seen Paul since our session with the protesters in San Francisco. He was friendly, but wary, with an edge.

Ben pitched his idea and Paul loved it.

"We do it honest, *ja?*" he said. "We go there, we research."

"You mean you're committing to do it?" I asked.

"Of course not. I commit when I see a brilliant script."

"Why don't you commit to develop it with a studio?"

"Oh no," Paul said. "So you can get three million dollars because the studio thinks I'll direct it? I'm not going to do that for you."

"I got three million dollars without you being anywhere near the project on *Basic,*" I said.

"True. But you also had a finished script. You do what you did with *Basic, ja?* Then I see if I will direct."

"This is different, Paul. I wrote it, then we sent it out to the studios. You came into it after Carolco bought it. If I do this as a spec, and the town knows I did it with you or with you in mind—and you pass—I'll never sell it."

"That's the risk you run to get me," Paul said.

Ben said, "What if we don't talk about making a deal now? What if we go to Vegas, the three of us, and see what we find there. We'll do the research, we'll interview people. Then we'll decide if we want to do it."

"Who pays for Vegas?" Verhoeven asked.

I laughed. I knew that while I had made $3 million on *Basic,* Paul had been paid $7 million to direct it.

"I'll pay for it," Ben said.

"You are not rich." Paul smiled. "You are a struggling producer. Joe is very rich. He should pay for all of our expenses."

"Fine." I laughed. "I'll pay for all our expenses."

"The beginning of some justice, *ja?*" Paul said.

Ben hired a researcher to lead us around and we flew into Vegas. What we found was a hidden sexual carnival. There were no hookers walking the streets anymore thanks to the town's new corporate-run squeaky-clean image. But the Yellow Pages listed hundreds of escort services.

You could order a woman the way you'd order a pizza . . . short, blond, tall, brunette, anchovies, etc. And she'd be at your hotel room door in an hour, dressed to look like somebody's date or wife so no questions would be asked by hotel security.

On the fringes of the downtown area, lap dance clubs, many still run by the mob, welcomed tour groups of men bused there by the hotels. The lap dancers were, for the most part, stunning, statuesque Playmate-types who picked up as much as $1,000 in tips each night.

A lap dancer took you into a dark back room, took all her clothes off, and danced on your lap stark naked, often bringing you to climax.

She was allowed to touch you but if you touched her—and didn't tip her—security would bounce you out. If you touched her and tipped her *enough*, everybody looked the other way.

The showgirls, meanwhile, who'd often been used as hotel-comp hookers in the past, didn't do that (or as much of that) as before. Their world was a catty and competitive place where women worried about their understudies, and put ice on their nipples and coke in their noses before they went onstage.

As we did the interviews, I resolved to make this script as real as possible, even though much of it was grim, especially the part that had to do with sexual violence.

Over and over again, we heard stories of rape. A young dancer brutally raped by a high roller who then bought her a $10,000 diamond ring to shut her up . . . a lap dancer gang-raped by a group of male Chippendale dancers in Hawaii . . . a showgirl on vacation with her boyfriend in Mexico raped by police responding to her calls that the boyfriend was having a heart attack. (The boyfriend died and, after the rape, police forced her to drive his body back across the border.)

Back in L.A., Paul said he agreed there was a powerful, original, but very dark story here.

"Are you going to commit to direct it?" I wanted to know.

"Not until I read your script."

It was the same ring-around-the-rosie as before.

"I'm not going to write it for free and take the chance of not selling it if you decide not to direct it."

"Then," Paul announced, "I say to you goodbye."

We were stuck. He wouldn't commit to direct it and I wouldn't write it for free with him already involved. When Robert Evans heard about the stalemate, he howled.

"Eszterhas and Verhoeven together again after *Basic Instinct*? Lap dancers, music, tits and ass and pussy? You tell me who's not going to want to see that movie!"

Evans told his independently wealthy brother, Charles, about it and Charlie, in his late sixties, asked me how much it would take for me to write the script. I told him to call my lawyers.

My lawyers set the terms. Charlie would have to give me a $2 million advance. After I wrote it, if we sold the project to a studio, Charlie would get his $2 million back—and a $1 million profit. He would also be a producer of the movie.

If I wrote the script and couldn't sell it, Charlie would be out the $2 million. Charlie knew that if Paul committed to direct it, we could sell it anywhere. He asked to meet with Paul.

"Tell me the truth," Charlie said to Verhoeven. "What are the chances you're going to direct this?"

"I don't know, *ja?*" Paul smiled. "It depends on the script. If it's brilliant, yes. If it's shit, no."

"I'd like to have a better idea of what you're going to do before I lay out two million dollars."

"Very understandable," Paul said.

"So how about it?" Charlie said.

"Oh, I can't tell you that until I know if it's shit."

"But Joe won't write the script until he gets paid," Charlie said.

"That's right." I smiled.

"But is that fair?" Charlie said to Paul. "That I just write him a check for two million dollars under these conditions?"

"Certainly not," Paul said. "If I were you, I wouldn't do it."

Charlie sighed.

"Also," Paul said, "you have to understand, you can be a producer but you won't be a producer."

"What do you mean?"

"You can't *do* anything. You will have your name on the movie but that is all. I have my own producer, Alan Marshall, and Ben Myron will be a producer."

"But I don't want to do anything," Charlie said.

"Then why do you want to be a producer?"

"I want my own trailer on the set," Charlie said.

"A trailer, fine. You can have a trailer."

"I want to meet the girls in the movie."

"That's okay, too," Paul said.

After the meeting, Charlie drew me aside and asked me what my hunch was. Would Verhoeven direct the script if Charlie paid me $2 million to write it?

"Yeah," I said, "I think he's into this. I think he will if the script's good."

"You think the script will be good?"

"Well, *Basic Instinct* was pretty good, wasn't it?"

"This is a musical not a mystery," Charlie said.

"That's true. But *Flashdance* was pretty good, wasn't it?"

"You rewrote that. That wasn't your original," Charlie said. "I did my homework on you."

"That's true, too, Charlie."

"I wish I could be sure you'll write a good script. I wish I could be sure he'll commit to direct it."

"That'd make it easier for you, Charlie, wouldn't it?"

Charlie said, "Yes it would."

He decided to take the chance.

The morning after he wired my lawyers the money—$2 million up front—Charlie Evans woke up and had himself taken to the hospital.

He was having heart palpitations.

Verhoeven just laughed.

"Who wins?" he said. "Joe wins."

I had a $2 million advance to write the script called *Showgirls,* but it would have to wait. There was something else I had to write first . . .

A few months after *Basic*'s release, I was at dinner in Robert Evans's fabled house around the corner from the Beverly Hills Hotel. The dinner was our first in-depth discussion of the script I would write, *Sliver,* and Bob, now in his mid-sixties, his skin sun-tooled to nearly black leather, had asked two bimbos to join us, a fortyish mother and her young daughter.

Halfway through the dinner I said, "This is the way it's going to work, Bob. I write the script the way I want to write it. You have no input. You give me no ideas. When I'm done, I give you the script and you get it made."

When the dinner ended, he drew me aside and asked, "You want mom or the kid?"

I wanted neither.

I didn't want to be compromised by Evans, as so many in Hollywood had been through the years. He had a shoeboxful of Polaroids he had shown me . . . explicit, *Hustler*-like shots of women who were now married to famous and powerful men.

"Pussy hair, my boy," Evans said to me, "is stronger than universal cable."

He was famous for greeting new screenwriters with a special present. There would be a knock at the screenwriter's hotel door and the screenwriter would open it to find one of Bob's stunning bimbos standing there.

One poor schmuck with an Underwood (Jack Warner's phrase) even fell in love with one of these young women, a romance that ended when he discovered that part of his new love's job was to report the details of his sexual performance to Evans. That kind of personal knowledge, to Bob, meant power and deals and movies made, and . . . *input* into a screenplay.

I was doing *Sliver,* an adaptation of Ira Levin's novel, as a favor to Guy, who was urging me to do it as a favor to Evans. Bob's career, which had reached the pinnacle of Hollywood success during his years as the head of Paramount and his fabled marriage to Ali MacGraw, was pretty much over.

He and his brother, Charlie, had been busted for cocaine; Bob had even been implicated but ultimately cleared on a murder charge. He had spent, by his own admission, "years in the fetal position," unable to get up in the morning. His office was filled with framed, yellowing headlines and photographs which his staff called "The Hall of Shame."

But there was a disarming candor about Evans. In a town of pretentious phonies, Evans almost bragged about how broke he was. And he was a flatterer.

"The only reason *Sliver* is going to get made," he said, "is because of you."

It was only partially true.

Yes, I was the hottest screenwriter in Hollywood and my presence meant a lot to the project and to Bob, but studios didn't green-light movies because of the screenwriter's name.

Evans had been desperate to get me to do this project.

"This movie," Evans said of *Sliver,* "is all about pussy."

I didn't think Ira Levin's well-crafted novel was about *that* . . . but what Evans said didn't surprise me. Evans thought everything was about *that.* And from his point of view, from inside this grand house full of mirrors and candles and vivacious, uninhibited young women frolicking in the pool and the guest-house and Bob's mink-rugged bedroom . . . maybe it was all about *that* . . . although Bob claimed, "I haven't been able to get it up since 1978."

The house, I thought, smelled of scented candles, mildew, and come (one reason maybe for all the scented candles).

Evans's charm kept me interested. The day we had our first meeting with the studio, Bob insisted we have lunch at his house first. It was a feast of freshly flown-in caviar and lobster and bottles of Dom Pérignon, with the butler and the maid in hovering attendance, and I thought there was something deeply touching about this man, broke and supported by his brother, making such a grand *event* out of a meeting with a studio.

Evans was *so happy* to be back in business! *So happy* to be having a meeting with the studio about a film that looked like it might actually be made!

A block-long limo took us to the meeting. Evans was dressed in his mono-grammed slipper shoes and as he went through the doors of the administration building at Paramount . . . I stopped him and wiped some white powder off his black cardigan sweater.

"Jesus, Bob," I said.

After *Basic Instinct* was released, I started spending time with the biggest star in the world.

Sharon Stone was funny and bright and I thought I saw occasional flashes of Catherine Tramell: a world-weary cynicism sometimes clouded her eyes.

"She *is* Catherine Tramell," I remembered Verhoeven saying, "*she is evil,*" but I didn't believe him.

His observation, I thought, was probably the result of Sharon refusing to sleep with him unless Paul left his wife.

Sharon and I had fun together; we made each other laugh.

"You created me," Sharon teased me and sent me notes signed "Catherine."

I bought her two hundred roses when she was nominated for a Golden Globe and a gold wildlife bracelet made in Hawaii.

One memorable night I picked her up at her tiny house off Mulholland over-looking the Valley. Sharon brought out a bottle of frosty Cristal, we put James Brown on, and then she brought out some grass that she said was Thai. We shared a joint and it blew the tops of our heads off.

We were crawling around her living room rug, around the dollhouse she loved so much, slugging from another bottle of Cristal. We were ripped out of our skulls but we thought we should have something to eat and somehow made it down to Citrus, the industry's flavor of the month, after what seemed the longest ride.

"Holy Christ," I kept saying.

"I know, I know," Sharon giggled, almost trilling the words.

Citrus was jammed full of the usual industry faces and we must have been an odd sight sitting in our booth, our eyes rolling around in our heads.

Sharon blinked at the other diners and said, "Who are these fucking people?"

I looked around and identified certain producers and agents, all trying not to stare at the spectacle we were creating. Sharon smiled at them and good-naturedly said, "Fuck 'em." She had some white sauce running down her chin and I wiped it off with my napkin.

"That felt nice," she said and smiled.

Another bottle of Cristal later we were ready to leave and I asked the maître d' to ask our driver to pull the limo as close to the door as he could so we could fall into the car and not have to walk. The maître d' gave us a signal a couple minutes later and we wobbled and lurched across the restaurant as the other diners, frozen, stared.

We fell into the car and Sharon, somewhat revitalized, said we had to hear some more James Brown. Now. Right now.

The driver took us to Virgin Records on Sunset, pulled up as close to the door as he could, and we wobbled and lurched inside. James Brown CDs were upstairs.

I wasn't sure I could navigate the steps but Sharon went zigzagging up. A few minutes later, she reappeared on the top step, holding a stack of CDs. She threw her arms wide and yelled, "I'm coming down!"

I heard laughter from some of the people in the store and then some of them started to applaud. Sharon came zigzagging back down the stairs, her arms wide, and threw herself three steps up into my arms. Now I heard more applause.

We somehow paid for the CDs and were trying to leave the store when the security guards came over. We were trying to leave, they explained, through the front store window. They graciously led us to the door, where our driver was waiting for us and helped us into the car.

In the limo, we put James Brown on, Sharon pulled out another joint, and the rest of the night turned into a blur. There was a moment when I put my hand on her thigh—she was wearing chocolate-brown suede pants—and she said, "I knew you'd put your hand there, that's why I wore these."

We had a brief and insane argument.

"My ass hangs halfway to my knees," she said.

"You've got a beautiful ass," I told her.

She said, "I'm pushing forty. This should have happened to me twenty years ago. Why didn't you write this script twenty years ago? *Why?*"

She got suddenly, briefly depressed and said, "I crawled the hill of broken glass and I sucked and I sucked until I sucked all the air out of my life."

We had another bottle of Cristal back in her house and crawled around the doll-house some more. I discovered that her body was doughy, too much peanut butter and Wonder Bread maybe. And then I went back to my hotel. The phone rang as I was walking in the door to my suite.

It was Sharon. She sounded hysterical. "My burglar alarm went off," she said. "I woke up in the living room. I grabbed a butcher knife from the kitchen. I started to look around, then I got scared and ran down the street and the security people picked me up."

I could visualize the scene: Sharon Stone, the biggest star in the world, the ice pick queen, running down her little suburban street with a butcher knife in hand.

"Where are you?" I asked.

"They brought me back home. The burglar alarm was off. The security people said it had never gone off."

"Do you want me to go over there? I'll be right there."

"No," she said. "I'm okay now. I think I'm okay now."

I said, "You just freaked on the dope."

"This happened to me on Ecstasy once," Sharon said. "I had to go to the hospital. I thought I was having a heart attack."

"Are you sure you don't want me to go over there?"

"No," she said. "It's okay." She paused and in a little girl's voice she said, "We had fun, didn't we?"

"Yeah." I laughed. "We sure did."

At my recommendation, she hired Guy McElwaine as her agent and, thanks in no small part to Guy, she agreed to do *Sliver*.

She had reservations about doing another movie with erotic content, but she thought I was her good luck charm.

I had, after all, as she kept saying, "created" her. And we had fun spending time together.

Guy told me he was devastated. His marriage had broken up. It was his eighth or ninth marriage. I'm not sure. He was married at least twice to the same woman.

Guy is the world's last romantic. Each time he marries, he is in love. He thinks it'll last forever each time.

When he told me that this marriage had broken up, I told him that I was sending him to Hawaii for two weeks—all expenses paid—at the Mauna Kea Beach Hotel resort on the Big Island.

An hour after I told him, his secretary called me to ask if my offer was for Guy alone or for Guy and "a friend."

"Don't tell me Guy and his wife are getting back together again," I said. "That's terrific."

His secretary said, sadly, that they weren't . . . but that Guy had a friend—formerly married to an actor and a rock star—and if it was okay with me, he wanted to take her to the Mauna Kea "to cheer him up."

I said that was fine with me: let the cheering up begin!

· · ·

When Robert Evans heard that Sharon was doing *Sliver,* he was overjoyed. He was suddenly a big shot again, producing a movie starring the world's newest screen sensation. But when Evans found out the condition with which Sharon was doing the movie, I thought he was going to go into cardiac arrest.

Sharon's condition was simple, flat, and nonnegotiable: Evans could not go to the set of his own movie when Sharon Stone was filming.

She did not want to be around Robert Evans. Sharon did not want to *cast her eyes* on Robert Evans. And, since the biggest stars in the world always get what they want, Paramount had happily agreed to Sharon's condition.

The problem was a girl in a dog collar. According to Sharon, a friend of hers from her modeling days wound up as one of Bob's house bimbos. According to Sharon, Bob supposedly kept the young woman naked and in a dog collar for weeks at a time. Sharon said that her friend needed psychiatric care for months after leaving the Evans house.

According to Evans, Sharon's story was whole-cloth fiction. He was enraged. "You talk to any girl who's ever been in this house," Bob said. "There are no dog collars here. This isn't that kind of a house."

I felt he had a point. The girls that I had met in Bob's house all seemed very fond of him, treating him like a classic Hollywood "daddy."

"She can't kick me off my own set!" Evans raged. "Who the fuck does she think she is? A dog collar? The name is Evans! Robert Evans! Not the Marquis de Sade!"

Sharon, however, was adamant and unyielding and, as the shoot began, Evans was not allowed to go within one hundred yards of his own set.

Our director was Phillip Noyce, a big, shambling Aussie whose first big hit was *Dead Calm* and who had directed the recent hit *Patriot Games.*

Sharon, perhaps sensing that she intimidated the physically gawky Noyce on a sexual level . . . Phillip seemed to *gaze* at Sharon a lot . . . didn't like him. She called him "the Creep" and "the Bozo."

Evans, who had always had ego problems with directors—"The best time to hire a director is right after they've had a great failure," he'd said—didn't like Phillip either. He called him "that lummox."

I was almost feeling sorry for Evans, banned from his own set, desperate to contribute, frantic to be the creative hero of yore. Evans was now down to meetings with the music supervisor and the costume designer.

I knew his musical tastes . . . Nat King Cole was his favorite; he knew nothing about Enigma or UB-40, the groups we were talking about using.

He told the costume designer he thought Billy Baldwin should be wearing the clothes he wore—not the *kind* of clothes Evans wore—but the *clothes themselves.* So he had a grip from the set bring his clothes from his house to his office:

white shoes and white belts and lavender slacks and monogrammed slippers were everywhere.

Evans was also conducting a guerrilla campaign against his own movie. He said he hated the dailies.

"That lummox can't direct," he said about Noyce. "That scene where they're supposed to be making love. They don't make love, they don't even fuck. They *rut*. They're wild hogs. Horses. We've got a script about pussy by a writer who knows pussy with a producer who knows pussy and it's being directed by a lummox who thinks his dick is something to pee with."

He loathed Sharon for banning him from his set and took it out on her dailies. "You can't even shoot her ass anymore. It's too spongy. Her tits hang down. She's over already. She's too old. Who'd want to fuck her anymore? Who's gonna buy their popcorn and *come* watching her?"

He didn't like Billy Baldwin much, either.

"All those big *schwantz* brothers in that family and we had to pick this goony *putz*."

I don't know how many times my son Steve saw *Basic Instinct,* but I know the videotape I had of the uncut European version was worn out pretty fast.

I got Sharon to sign a sultry bathing suit picture which Steve put up on his wall. It said, "To Steve—All My Love, Sharon."

Sometimes when Sharon and I were hanging out together, enjoying each other's company, I wondered what was going on in Steve's head. I was certain they were the same kinds of goings-on that had gone on, when I was Steve's age, between me and Mamie Van Doren, me and Zsa Zsa Gabor, me and Brigitte Bardot.

In a very complex and intimate way, I knew, I had introduced Sharon to Steve.

I was at a party at a producer's house in the flats of Beverly Hills and I had to pee.

The line to the bathroom was long, though, and everyone standing there seemed to have the sniffles, so I thought it would be some time before I could get in there.

I left, jumped into my rent-a-car, and thought I could wait till I got back to the hotel.

A few blocks away, though, still in Beverly Hills, I realized I couldn't wait anymore. Not one minute longer. Not even thirty seconds.

I jumped out of the car on a dark side street and spotted a high wall surrounding an estate and peed against the wall.

I was still in midstream when bright lights from all directions illuminated me and a loud alarm went off.

I was still zipping myself up when two Beverly Hills police department cruisers pulled up, sirens wailing, cherries whirling.

The cops put me against the wall and frisked me and told me what I'd done was a crime and they were going to arrest me for it.

I told them that I had just come from the producer's party and that Don Simpson, the producer who'd made *Beverly Hills Cop,* was a good friend of mine.

I recited my credits for them.

One of the cops said, "Did she know her pussy was getting shot for that scene?"

I said she did indeed, and the Beverly Hills cops sent me on my way.

Besides Sharon, I had also become good friends with Bill Macdonald, the head of Evans's production company. Bill was in his late thirties and liked to have a drink and a good time.

Bill was a man of many *implications.* He *implied* that he had an offshore fortune and he *implied* that he had a Texas ranch and he *implied,* oh so delicately, that he'd been involved with the CIA in certain vague and unmentionable Far East exploits.

Pinned down, Bill blithely admitted that his father was a San Francisco surgeon famous for the pub crawls that even Herb Caen wrote about . . . but he *implied* that his mother was General Douglas MacArthur's illegitimate daughter.

I thought Bill's *implications* were a hoot and had fun matching yarns and tequila shooters with him.

I liked Bill's girlfriend just as much as Bill. They had been together ten years and were about to be married soon. She was thirty-two years old and drop-dead gorgeous. She had a razor-sharp wit . . . and she was from Ohio.

Her name was Naomi Baka.

From the time she was a little girl, Naomi wanted to leave Mansfield and Ohio.

She dreamed of a place with broader horizons—it was something most of her family—her father, her older brothers, her sister—didn't understand. They loved Mansfield—it was a great, crime-free place to raise kids.

Only her mother and her younger brother, Jeremy, got it. Her mother, who grew up in a small mining town in Illinois, always encouraged her to broaden her horizons, to *live,* to "color every page."

Naomi did. She read. She took photographs. She saw lots of movies. She drew. She was Richland County Fire Queen. She went to Ohio State and became the first person in her family to graduate from college. She worked in factories to pay her tuition; she was a busgirl at the local Ramada Inn. After college, she worked as a stringer for a newspaper in Columbus and then as a public relations rep at the phone company in Mansfield.

She wanted to get out of Mansfield, but she was still in a relationship with her high school boyfriend. Her boyfriend worked in Mansfield, too, and talked about moving to Kansas City.

Naomi didn't want to live in Kansas City. She wanted to live in New York, the city she'd dreamed about since she was a little girl. Her mother kept urging her to go; her father kept telling her she was crazy.

She rented a U-Haul, put a few pieces of furniture into it, and said she was going to New York. She had $800 in her pocket. Her father didn't even kiss her goodbye when she left. He shook her hand and said, "You'll be back. With your tail between your legs."

She went to New York and with the little money she had, she became the roommate of a woman subletting one room of her apartment. She went to all the big firms with her résumé and got lucky with Warner Communications. They hired her as a secretary and moved her quickly to public relations. She was making enough money now to have a small apartment of her own.

She gloried in New York—a dazzlingly beautiful young woman from Ohio, of all places, sweet and seemingly naive. Men found her "charming" and "different." She went to places like "21" and the Oak Room bar and Trader Vic's. She loved the mad swirl of Manhattan streets and the food in the neighborhoods—Chinese and Brazilian and Caribbean—exotic and exciting foods they'd never even heard of in Mansfield.

But they didn't understand, back there in Mansfield, what she was so excited about. She persuaded her sister to visit her in New York but her sister thought the city was dirty and dangerous and hurried home.

She got an even better job in public relations at American Express, flying to corporate retreats in Arizona and Vermont and Florida. She was even flown to a conference in Rome, where she met the pope. No one took her for a naive farm girl from Ohio anymore. She persuaded her little brother, Jeremy, to go to New York and he got a job in public relations there, too.

She met a young man named Bill Macdonald, who said he was in the import-export business. She settled into a relationship with him. They went to parties with the Kennedys; they crashed the Petrushka Ball; they spent holidays with the Armours of Texas and visited the Biddles of Philadelphia.

When Bill Macdonald decided to move to L.A. to get into the movie business, she followed him to California and got another, higher-paying job in public relations. She and Bill lived in Venice Beach and then in Marina Del Rey. She drove a little Mercedes 280 SL. She started drawing portraits of James Dean and Elvis and Brando and displaying them in galleries. She persuaded Jeremy to follow her to California and get another PR job.

· · ·

Shortly after I met Naomi, I was watching her at dinner with a group of people. She was elegantly dressed and was talking about working on Wall Street with her WASPy friends.

Her hands were moving in the air and her eyes were flashing and she suddenly reminded me of a girl I'd known once in Italy.

I interrupted what Naomi was saying and said, "You're a Guinea, that's what you are, a little Guinea."

She stared at me curiously for just a moment and then she said, "Yes, that's what I am," holding my eye.

She told me that her Polish father had always called her Italian mother "the Little Dago."

Bill Macdonald became my wingman on my prowls through San Francisco's and L.A.'s clubs, though I noted he wasn't interested in picking up any women— all he was interested in was his tequila.

On one of those prowls, I wound up in a tiny house in Larkspur, California, making love on the living room floor with a waitress I had picked up . . . while Bill lay on a couch inches from us, feigning sleep.

I didn't know that Bill was relating every detail of these club prowls to his girlfriend, Naomi, telling her even about the moans that he had heard and the sights he had seen on that living room floor in Larkspur, California.

I didn't know that "little devil" Naomi was keeping a journal.

CHAPTER 15

[Naomi's Journal]

Robert Evans
Kneels in Prayer

NOMI
What are you doing here?

CRISTAL
What am I doing here? I'm doing the finest cocaine in the world,
darlin'. You want some?

Showgirls

April 8, 1989

Someone is stealing Evans's shoes. Bill's not even that
upset about it, since the shoes Bob owns are those sort of
half boots that zip up the sides that they wore in the seventies (that's how long he's had them). Bill has been trying
to encourage Bob to get a more "modern" look.

But Bob is perplexed and devastated. The suspects are a
man-and-wife team that works there. God knows what they want
with Bob's shoes.

Now all he has left are the shoes he got from the movie
The Two Jakes. I've seen them. Sort of brown and white saddle shoes out of the forties. He loves them. From the seventies to the forties . . . but they actually look pretty good
with his bolo ties . . .

May 4, 1989

Over the weekend we went up to Bob's. I haven't been there for a while. There's a new girl at the house named Bridget. She is beautiful but looks about fifteen years old.

When we arrived, she answered the door sweetly. She was wearing a tiny black maid's outfit with a little ruffled white slip and white panties peeking out from underneath. It had a tiny white apron and she wore a little cap.

I said, "Oh, you should wear that at Halloween."

She looked at me sort of blankly.

As we headed to the screening room Bill whispered to me "She wears that every day—Bob likes her in it!"

June 8, 1989

Bill is an exhausted nervous wreck ever since he drove Bob to Scripps for his stint in rehab. When he arrived at Bob's house, he found Evans nearly incoherent, stuffing hundreds of photos of nude women he has known (most of them now other men's wives) into a briefcase. Bill had to practically drag him into the car.

Then on the way down Bob kept desperately trying to get Bill to turn around. At the "intervention" with his friends and family it had all seemed like a good idea, but in the reality of day he was having a nervous breakdown.

They passed some sort of resort hotel and Evans shrieked "Turn in here! Turn in here!" but Bill kept going.

Then Bob pulls an absolutely *huge* dildo out of his briefcase and tries to shove it out the car window.

"What is that!?" Bill says to him.

"Bridget gave it to me—I have to get rid of it!" Evans says as he struggles to force it out the window.

"For God's sake Bob! We're going to get pulled over! Have you lost your mind?!" Bill is yelling at him.

They finally get to Scripps and Bill leaves him there.

The next day Evans calls and I answer. He's frantic. "I've got to get out of here. I can't sit here in a room full of women with blue hair . . . I'm going to lose my mind . . ."

I just said, "Bob, you need help. You promised everyone you love you would get it. You have to stay there . . ."

The very next day he checked himself out, called a limo

which came and picked him up, and went home. Thus ends
Evans's rehab.

July 14, 1989

Bill and I had dinner with Bob, his son Josh, and Ali
MacGraw last night. It was the most fun I've ever had with
Bob. He was in his element and I found him hysterical—
telling old Hollywood stories as only he can.

There was one really interesting part of the evening.
Every time I see Ali she rushes over to me and says, "You
look *gorgeous!* You look absolutely incredible! What are you
doing with yourself?"

The first time it happened (I ran into her at Tribeca) I
was flattered. It was so spontaneous and I just glowed with
the compliment.

But then the next time I saw her she said "You look
absolutely beautiful tonight!" and I thought "Well, maybe
she just thinks I'm pretty."

But last night was very revealing. Josh was imitating
Bob—his baritone voice, his mannerisms. We were howling.

Then he said, "Yeah, I can do my mom, too . . ." and he
said, "You look *fantastic!* You look absolutely *gorgeous*
tonight! My God, you look incredible."

I felt my ears get hot and I knew my face turned red, but
I don't think anyone noticed.

They were all laughing at Josh (including Ali). All
I could think of was, "You idiot, you actually
believed her . . ."

April 4, 1990

It seems Lotto has reached somewhere near $70 million.
Evans, who is desperate for cash, has decided Lotto
might save him. He bought hundreds of tickets hoping that
some miracle would bail him out of the debt that keeps
growing.

When we entered the screening room last night, there
on the large round table were hundreds and hundreds of
Lotto tickets. Daphne and several other visiting bimbos
were gathered around the table reading off the numbers.
(Daphne is Evans's latest fixture at the house. She told me
they met in St. Tropez on the beach when he admired her

tattoo.) Even Darryl the tennis pro, dressed in his whites with his racket leaning against his chair, had come in off the court to lend a hand. It sounded like one of those telemarketing calls with the hum of voices droning in the room.

"Can you fucking believe this?!" Evans was shouting and pacing around the screening room. "Not one fucking winning number in the bunch! I'm the unluckiest Jew that ever lived!" He was nearly spitting, waving his glasses around and screaming at the bimbos not to mix up the ones that had been rechecked with the ones that had been re-rechecked.

We decided not to stick around. He was in no mood to discuss setting up a monthly budget, which was the purpose of Bill's visit. Besides, we would have ended up sitting at the table checking Lotto tickets.

July 8, 1991

Bill came home last night with stars in his eyes. The Evans overall deal with Paramount was signed. Bill said Bob cried. They've decided to move into Evans's old offices on the lot. Bill said to Bob, "Let's take the Robert Evans Company sign off the garage door, shine it up, and put it back on the Paramount lot."

July 11, 1991

Bill and Evans spent last night writing the press announcement for the Paramount deal. Just the two of them— Bill seated at the computer and Bob spouting grandiose plans.

July 17, 1991

Bill and Evans rode in their new company car (a white Jag) to the studio today to look at temporary offices.

Evans is flipping out. This is all happening so fast.

I think that in June of 1988, when Bill met him, Evans had one foot in the grave (at least psychologically and emotionally).

The day he met Bill, Evans said, "I need you more than you need me, you just don't know it yet."

July 31, 1991

Bill came home excitedly bearing his Paramount parking access card and paycheck.

Finally he's in an office.

August 20, 1991

Evans took *The Saint* bolo tie he always wears and put it over Paramount executive John Goldwyn's head and dragged him down the hall by the bolo and the neck to David |Kirkpatrick's office. David is the head of production.

Evans was screaming at Goldwyn "to have some balls and make *The Phantom*. Your grandfather would have made it! This place needs to make movies, not memos."

September 19, 1991

Bill spent the afternoon on Friday with Joe Eszterhas, whom he has decided he likes very much. They have a lot in common. Joe's favorite vacation spot is near Reggiomaggiore in Italy (which is one of Bill's favorite spots in the world).

Joe lives in Marin County near San Francisco and is a real family man. He and Bill will get along fine.

September 28, 1991

Bill and Evans went to a screening of a movie with Michelle Pfeiffer. He and Bob were given the red-carpet treatment.

Bob was sitting next to the director of the film, and Bob fell asleep and started to snore. A woman sitting near them said to Bill, "Is Bob commenting on the film or is he snoring?"

Bill said, "He's snoring."

The woman said "Oh my God" in this wonderfully clipped English accent.

September 30, 1991

I talked to Evans for over an hour on the phone. Bill wasn't home when he called. Evans read me the preface to his upcoming autobiography and a letter he wrote about Alzheimer's disease.

We chatted awhile and Evans convinced me to look up a
new word every day in the dictionary, write it down five
times, use it in a sentence five times, and then do a quiz at
the end of two weeks.

The first word I've chosen is *contumelious:* "insulting."

October 1, 1991

Bill was up at Bob's house and found a goodly amount of
the forbidden fruit—cocaine—in one of his couches. He
brought it home and is going to confront Bob.

October 5, 1991

Poor Bob. Evidently his new nickname at the office is "El
Cid." This refers to the old story of the great Spanish
warrior who crusaded against the Moors. In the final scene of
the movie (with Charlton Heston I think), El Cid is dead and
they strap him to a warhorse and send him into battle. Seems
no one knows he's actually dead.

Bill and Gabrielle Kelly, the Evans Company's head of
creative affairs, say it's like they've got this dead leader
and they're fooling everyone into thinking he's still alive.
Poor Bob. Poor El Cid.

Christmas Day, 1991

On Friday, the 13th of December, a fire caught behind the
kitchen refrigerator while I was out Christmas shopping. Our
house burned down and we lost our beloved golden retriever,
Jake.

I'm hurt beyond repair.

Robert Evans offered us no support, not even words of
consolation.

January 19, 1992

All of Evans's bank accounts were frozen this week by
the state of California due to the $33,000 he owes in state
taxes. He spent the week running around planning his son
Josh's twenty-first birthday party, paying no heed to either
his financial or business issues.

January 27, 1992

Evans is busy moving pieces of furniture from his home,
just in case the IRS shows up.

February 1, 1992

Evans broke out in hives in the office today and felt
very dizzy. Bill thought Bob was having a heart attack, but
he wasn't.

February 18, 1992

I heard today that Arthur, Bob's Polish butler, is writing screenplays and trying to sell them to Paramount.

February 19, 1992

Evans got Stanley Jaffe, the Paramount head honcho, to
agree to use Billy Friedkin to direct *The Saint.*

Everyone's furious because: *A.* Billy Friedkin hasn't had
a hit in years; *B.* They won't be able to attract any big
name actors if Friedkin directs.

Goldwyn went into Evans's office literally screaming.
Evans hemmed and hawed and didn't have much to say in his
defense.

Joe Eszterhas has been working on another script, *Nowhere
to Run,* while he's under contract to Paramount to do
Sliver. Instead of handling it diplomatically, Evans
called Eszterhas half stoned at 9:30 A.M. Evans provoked
Joe to such a degree, Joe hung up on him and called
Bill to say: "I'm sending back the half-million-dollar
Sliver advance and burning what I've written so far!"
Bill somehow calmed him down and Joe has agreed to stay
on the project.

February 20, 1992

Joe Eszterhas called Bill, laughing about a letter of
apology he got from Evans. Evans sent him some thirty scented
candles with a letter that said something like "to light up
your abode with prayer . . . to conquer the surrounding darkness." And ending with "I'm sending prayers to whoever's up
there."

The IRS wants $250,000 from Evans in three days. So what
does Evans do? He gets on a plane for Mexico. He says he's
going to work on his autobiography.

February 24, 1992

Evans was screaming at everyone in the office on Friday because he was trying to dictate a congratulatory letter to Jack Nicholson, who recently had another child. The letter made reference to the penis size of the baby.

A sheriff's deputy was at Bob's house inquiring about an unpaid florist bill. Bob thinks it was really the IRS taking a peek around at the furniture.

February 25, 1992

Every few months at Evans's house there appears a new "honeybee," a term I use to describe a very young, pretty girl flitting around. Evans will soon start to talk about how "important" she is to him and how he couldn't have imagined life before she came along, and she then becomes the "Queen Bee." Sometimes Helmut Newton even takes nude pictures of her.

She then is the "lady of the house" and attends all functions with Bob, helps with dinner parties, decorates the tree (depending on the time of year) and becomes a permanent fixture. Before long, a new honeybee appears.

The Queen Bee accepts cohabitation with this new beauty, a little wary but still thinking her position is sound.

Suddenly the Queen Bee is gone, the new honeybee assumes her role, and the cycle starts again. It never fails. Anytime I go up I can usually spot the new one.

One time Margaux Hemingway became the Queen Bee (she never entered as a honeybee, she just swooped in as Queen). Bob even redecorated the guest bedroom for her. But then, alas, a honeybee buzzed in one day (I think her name was Brandy).

Bob was frantic. He said to Bill "I just don't know how to get rid of Margaux . . ." Then he had a brainstorm. He sent her to New York to have all her teeth done. He was very pleased with this bit of ingenuity.

She left for New York happy and starry-eyed, her cozy guest room awaiting her return. I never saw Margaux again.

February 28, 1992

Evans spent the day yesterday writing a letter to the archbishop of New Orleans which was completely unintelligible.

It seems that Bob has done such a superb job promoting and hyping his cocaine-conviction court-ordered documentary about Pope John Paul II that the Catholic Church now wants a piece of the action. (Because the Church believes, erroneously, that money was made.)

March 2, 1992

Our weekend with the Eszterhases in Marin was fabulous. Joe Eszterhas and his wife, Gerri, are great people. Both are from Ohio, she from a small steel town. While "the men" talked business, the "wives" went to Stinson Beach to view the latest Eszterhas purchase—a splendid old Victorian near the beach. Bill was his wonderful usual self and I think both Joe and Gerri liked me, too.

March 4, 1992

Ever since Bill asked Gabrielle Kelly to read the letter Bob had written to the archbishop of New Orleans out loud (Gabrielle has a lilting Irish brogue), Bob has been cornering her to read everything aloud to him. This galls Gabrielle horribly.

Yesterday Evans had an author in his office and Bob's brother, Charles, was there. Of course Bob had never read the visiting author's book but called Gabrielle in to read a passage out loud which referred to him.

As Gabrielle began to read, she became more and more appalled at the way the author (who was in the room!) described both Bob and Charles. Gabrielle refused to go on.

Bob and Charles were both so out of it they didn't even comprehend how bad the descriptions were.

March 8, 1992

Evans looked at his desk and said, "What I don't understand is what *everybody is doing?* Look at my desk! There's nothing on it but some pictures of some women, a letter to the archbishop, and Tootsie Rolls. I don't understand it! I should have some important books and papers on this desk!"

March 12, 1992

Evans showed up at work Monday wearing worn flannel pants, his shoes from the movie he never played in, *The Two Jakes,* and a soiled white shirt with brown stains all over the front of it.

He had his hair slicked back and he was wearing his *Saint* bolo tie. The staff now calls him "the Lizard King."

He is meeting every day with Charles Michener, the ghost-writer of his autobiography. Michener is a Princeton grad and a historian and Bob hadn't read a word he'd written before he hired him. He hired him because he was told that Michener was "a hot ghostwriter."

When Bob read what Michener had written, he called Bill in and said, "What is it with this guy? He writes like some stuffy Harvard graduate."

Bill said, "Princeton, Bob."

Bob said, "Well, I told him that when I was sixteen, I used to hang out in bars in Harlem because the waitresses there could pick tips off the table with their cunts. He changed it! He uses the word 'vagina' all the time. I've never used that word in my life. Now I've got to go back and change all of Michener's *vaginas* to my *cunts.*"

March 18, 1992

Evans is now calling Sigourney Weaver to try to get her into some old script Charles, his brother, had commissioned ten years ago.

Charles recently bid against *himself* on a home he wants to buy. He forgot that he'd made a bid, then he heard about another bid, forgot that that was his bid, and topped it with another bid.

April 27, 1992

Bill met for three hours with Joe Eszterhas in San Francisco—they discussed Bill's next career stops. Joe says that Bill must establish relationships at other studios and set up projects there. He said that within the Industry a lot of people think he is a former CIA guy or a drug dealer.

Why else would a bright, educated guy be this diligent
in his efforts for Evans, a known drug addict? Bill's
import-export background reinforces these rumors. Joe said
that if Evans is busted for drugs or drops dead, Bill should
be prepared with other projects or he risks going down with
Bob.

May 1, 1992

A smoky haze fills the air this morning. Four thousand
National Guardsmen have been deployed in the city.

Bill met with Brad Pitt, a potential candidate to play
The Saint.

On the way home, Bill was terrified as he drove through
smoky streets, rioters, and screaming sirens.

When someone was shot three blocks from the Paramount
lot, all employees were ordered to go home.

Evans insisted that his staff stay to write a memo to
John Goldwyn.

May 14, 1992

Yesterday Evans was making a point by waving his hand
around and in his hand he was unconsciously holding a vial
of coke. In the office!

He was dictating a letter to his secretary and he said,
"Now let's get this straight. I'm crossing my fingers and
toes and balls for good luck."

Then he dictated a memo to the director Larry Kasdan and
he said, "I'd give up a blow job to direct this picture
myself."

May 18, 1992

Evans has a new girlfriend named April. She came into
the office in her underwear.

Larry Kasdan was so offended by Evans's memo that his agent
called Bill to tell him Kasdan will never work with Evans.
Evans's response: "Kasdan's a whore! Anybody can be bought!"

May 22, 1992

When Bill got to work on Friday morning, everyone was in
a frenzy. Rumors were floating about that Eszterhas was not

going to deliver the *Sliver* script that day as planned—that
he was going to miss the deadline. Bill told everyone to
calm down and he called Joe. As it turned out, the script
was being typed and did arrive as scheduled.

June 6, 1992

When Bill arrived in the morning to pick him up for
work, Bob was meeting some "potential investors." Appar-
ently they are also very religious.

They suggested that perhaps it would be good to pray for
guidance. So there is Evans (in his slippers) kneeling with
his head bowed in the living room with these holy rollers.

As they pray, two bimbos come out of Bob's bedroom and
go tiptoeing past behind them. One is wearing only a pajama
top, the other only the bottoms.

They hold their fingers to their lips and stifle giggles
as they pass by Bill. They get a glass of juice from the
kitchen and go tiptoeing back, as God is invoked by the
investors.

June 11, 1992

Evans called one of Sharon Stone's agents and offered
her the lead part in *Sliver*. The agent called Bill back
and said, "Sharon says—'I'll never work for that slime
Evans and I'm not showing my pussy for Joe Eszterhas
anymore.' "

July 8, 1992

At his first meeting with a writer yesterday, Evans
fell asleep and proceeded to snore. Bill, Gabrielle Kelly,
Bobby Jaffe (Stanley's son), and John Goldwyn were all
there.

Bill kept coughing and dropping things to try to wake
Evans up. Gabrielle nervously tapped her pencil to try to
rouse him—to no avail.

The entire scene climaxed when the writer, courteously
trying to ignore the snoring Evans, said, "Well, as Bob said
earlier . . ."

And all heads turned to look at Bob, who sat slumped and
snoring in his chair.

At the end of the meeting, John Goldwyn said, "If someone will please wake Mr. Evans, we will adjourn."

August 4, 1992

The word around Paramount about why Sharon Stone agreed
to star in *Sliver* is that Eszterhas "convinced" her. I hear
they're "close" but I don't know what that means.

[Dissolve]

The Souvenir

She was twenty-three years old and had just broken up with her boyfriend and, on the spur of the moment, she walked into the office of a travel agent and told him she had to get away from Harrisburg.

She found herself days later in the Austrian Tyrol at a place called Igls in a hotel called the Sport sipping hot schnapps on the heated patio.

She saw him there. He was the most famous movie star in the world and she was a gorgeous young woman from Harrisburg, Pennsylvania, with a broken heart.

He came over and offered to buy her a schnapps and she saw what a perfectly beautiful man he was. He was here, he told her, about to film a skiing movie. He asked her to dinner and she thought about it and refused, knowing she wasn't ready for any new adventures of the heart. She knew, too, that he was very publicly married.

He knocked on her door at midnight as she knew he would. He had a chilled bottle of Dom Pérignon in his hand and flashed the most famous smile in the world at her. She was wearing nothing but one of her ex-boyfriend's blue Gant button-down shirts. She let him in.

They made love three times, drank the Dom Pérignon, and hardly spoke. She drifted off to sleep and when she awoke, he was gone. The next day, she flew back to Harrisburg.

She's happily married now to the man who was temporarily her ex-boyfriend. She is the somewhat matronly mother of three grown children. She's never told anyone about that night in Igls. She still sees him on the big screen sometimes.

She kept that bottle of Dom Pérignon for a long time but it's gone now. She doesn't even know what happened to it. Tossed out or down in the basement in some box maybe.

CHAPTER 16

My Hollywood Mistress

DR. PALME
He likes games and danger, courts it. He's sociopathic, a great
danger to women. His defense system is extraordinarily developed, an acute schizophrenia, nonparanoid, classic Jekyll and
Hyde syndrome.

Sliver

Cleveland was back in the news again. Even the *Wall Street Journal* was doing stories about "the Cleveland Resurgence."

It was all thanks to a Republican mayor named George Voinovich, who, among other things, had lighted up the Terminal Tower, Cleveland's vest-pocket version of the Empire State Building.

I read one day that George Voinovich's little girl had run out into the street in front of her house and been dragged to her death by a passing car. The first on the scene was her older teenage sister, Betsy.

I was at home in Tiburon in Marin County when an old friend called to say he was coming to town and would like to visit . . . with him would be a young woman who wanted to meet me and wanted to be a screenwriter, the governor of Ohio's daughter, Betsy Voinovich.

She was twenty-six now, a coltish blonde who had studied writing under John Barth and Joyce Carol Oates, wrote startling short stories set in the world of grunge rock, and was the world's biggest John Lennon fan. She'd played in her older brother's band around the Cleveland area and had barnstormed for her father, whom she adored, around the state of Ohio.

She had dinner with my friend and me and Gerri and Steve and Suzi in Tiburon and the next day I took her, along with my friend, down to Stinson

Beach, where the three of us checked out my old Victorian and walked on the beach.

I told her I was scheduled to do a writing seminar at Ohio University in a couple of months and she suggested I visit her father at the Governor's Mansion in Columbus on my way back to California.

"Will you be there?" I asked her.

"No," she said, "I'll be moving into my apartment in L.A."

"Why should I visit your father then?"

"Because he's an interesting man," she said, "and so are you."

I looked at her; I was forty-seven years old, old enough to be her father.

"Is your father a more interesting man than I am?" I smiled.

"No," she said, "you're a much more interesting man than he is. But you'll like him, I think, and he'll like you and then you can call me in L.A. and tell me how much you liked him. Or you can come down and tell me in person and we can listen to my John Lennon collection."

Gerri saw me air-kiss her goodbye, but Gerri didn't see the look in my eye as I did it.

Betsy met my eye, smiled, and said, "See you in L.A."

At dinner in the Governor's Mansion in Columbus, I liked George Voinovich immediately.

I thought him a sensitive and caring man who viewed his stewardship of the state in the manner of a secular priest. He and his wife lived monastically at the mansion, using only a tiny apartment upstairs. We talked a lot about his Croatian background and my Hungarian one and I noticed a jangled, skittish quality about Betsy's mother. It made me wonder whether anyone ever got over the loss of a child.

They were both afraid for Betsy, away from home, out there in L.A., and afraid that her dreams of becoming a screenwriter would come to naught.

"Maybe you can keep an eye on her out there for me," George Voinovich said, looking me in the eye. "I would consider it a personal favor."

"I'll do that," I said.

"I'll be in your debt," he responded.

A lone butler served a simple pasta and vegetable dish and the portion was so small that on the way back to the hotel I stopped at McDonald's and ate a quarter-pounder.

I went from Columbus to Cleveland to see my father and ran into a barmaid at the Ritz-Carlton who recognized me and told me how much she'd loathed *Basic Instinct*. She said it was sexist and homophobic and she hadn't seen a movie she'd disliked so much in years. She also showed me her nipple ring.

She came up to my room when she got off work and we killed a bottle of Dom Pérignon and continued our discussion of *Basic* and fell happily into bed.

When she left in the morning, I called Betsy and told her how much I'd liked her dad.

"He asked me to keep an eye on you," I said.

"What did you say?"

"I told him I would."

"So when are you coming to L.A. so you can start doing that?"

"Soon," I said.

I hung up and walked into the bathroom to shower.

Lipsticked words had been scrawled on the mirror. They said, "Welcome to the wonderful world of AIDS."

I wasn't worried. The same message had been left for me by another young woman on another mirror in Vegas recently.

It was the new practical joke going around.

I saw Betsy in L.A. for the first time on my forty-eighth birthday. I had lunch with her at the Café Rodeo and told her the scripts she'd left behind for me to read were awful.

I meant it: Her short stories were wonderful. Her scripts sucked.

"I can get better." She smiled. "I'm glad you told me the truth. Most people don't."

She asked me what I was doing that night for my birthday and I told her Guy McElwaine was throwing a birthday party for me at Dominic's.

"Can I go?" she asked.

"Sure."

"Can I go with you?"

I laughed and said, "I like you—you're very appealing and attractive, but I'm married. I have two children, I—"

"I've met them," she said with a smile. "They're very nice. I *like* them. But I'm a big girl."

"Okay," I said.

"I'm a big girl," she repeated, laughing at me.

I took her to the party that night and watched her. Sharon Stone was there ... Tom Berenger, wearing a Confederate hat and drunk out of his mind ... Phillip Noyce ... Bill Macdonald. Betsy held her own with all of them. She seemed to put Sharon off somehow; I thought it was Betsy's youth.

We all drank too much and wound up at Guy's house. Guy found an ancient mud-colored joint he'd hidden in a jewelry box in 1976 and he put Frank Sinatra on.

Betsy and I drifted away from the others and found ourselves in a child's room filled with mobiles and stuffed animals. I kept a close eye on her . . . as I had promised her father, the governor of Ohio . . . all night.

I saw Betsy steadily after that whenever I went to L.A. She said she was falling in love with me. I knew I liked her very much. I knew this was a relationship, but I didn't think it was love.

"I'm going to wind up hurting you and I don't want to do that," I said.

"You can't hurt me," she said, "you're a big old softie."

It made me laugh.

"I think you should leave your wife and kids and run away with me and live happily ever after," Betsy said.

I said, "I can't do that."

"Sure you can. What's the best place we can run away to? I'll bet you've seen some places."

"Useppa," I told her.

"What's that?" she said.

"A tiny island in Florida. It's hidden away. The CIA used it to train the guys who were slaughtered at the Bay of Pigs."

"Perfect," Betsy said. "Poetic. Tragic. Idyllic for us."

We were in a suite at the Four Seasons in Beverly Hills.

"I'm going to dream about being on Useppa with you," Betsy said, turned over, and went to sleep.

But she didn't dream about Useppa. I woke up at dawn to her choked sobs. She was dreaming, as she often did, about the little sister she'd found broken to pieces in the street just down from her house.

"I want you to leave Gerri and your kids and come to Useppa with me," Betsy said.

"I can't," I said. "I just can't. Sometimes I think I wish I could but I just can't."

"You really don't love me, do you?" Betsy said.

"I really don't know. There are moments I think I do."

"When? When we're making love?"

"Please stop this," I said, "I haven't lied to you."

"Fuck you," she said, "asshole."

She went for a long walk with her father and told him she was in love with me.

"He reminded me," Betsy said, "that you were married and had kids and that we were good Catholics and that this was wrong. Then he said that he liked you and that you'd looked lonely to him. Finally he said that he loved me very much and would be there to support me whatever happened between you and me."

"What a great dad," I said.

"*Asshole*," Betsy said to me, "don't you realize how much fun you'd have in our family?"

I had to be in Cleveland to make a speech. Betsy wanted to come back with me but couldn't—she didn't have the money.

I flew there and late at night my phone rang. It was Betsy. She was two hours from the city on the turnpike—she had driven all the way from L.A. just to be with me.

I was happy Betsy called.

I got the barmaid with the nipple ring who didn't like *Basic Instinct* out of my suite quickly.

Betsy said she was running out of money. I believed her. I had seen George Voinovich's home in Cleveland and was convinced that if there was one honest politician left in America, he was it.

Betsy couldn't afford her apartment anymore; the new one she'd picked out was in a high-crime gang area in Venice.

"You can't live there," I said. "You'll get raped or killed or both."

"I want to stay in L.A. for two years to see if I can make it writing scripts," she said.

"What would it take for you to live on for two years?"

"Fifty thousand dollars."

"I'll lend you the money," I said.

"Now I'm a kept woman." She smiled. "A Hollywood mistress."

"You have to promise to pay me back," I told her.

"I'll pay you back," she promised.

I gave a close producer friend a $50,000 loan and he gave Betsy a check for $50,000. That way Gerri Eszterhas wouldn't suspect anything.

Sometimes Betsy and Bill Macdonald and I would go out to a club and drink and listen to live rock and roll. Bill and Betsy and I liked each other and the three of us almost always had fun together.

Bill told me he had told Naomi about my relationship with Betsy and said that Naomi was very curious about her.

"What did you tell Naomi?" I asked Bill.

"I told her Gerri is your anchor in life and you'll never leave her," Bill said.

I was supposed to fly to Paris to shoot a Chanel commercial I'd written that Roman Polanski would direct. Bill Macdonald asked if he could come with me. We'd hang out in Paris for a week while Naomi went up to Marin to hang out with Gerri. I was taking the Concorde from New York. Bill was taking a charter flight from Washington. We'd meet in Paris. That was the plan.

When I got to New York to catch the Concorde, I got a message that my father had suffered a stroke in Cleveland. I turned around and headed back to Cleveland. It was too late to inform Bill, who was already on his way.

I reached him in Paris. He turned right around and flew to Cleveland to be with me at a difficult time.

When he got to the hospital in Cleveland I thanked him and he said, "Hey, I love ya, man."

And I said, "I love you, too, Billy."

Betsy was with me, too. She came to be by my side.

The night I took Sharon Stone out to dinner . . . the night I wound up on the floor crawling around her dollhouse . . . the night Sharon went down her street wearing bra and panties and carrying a butcher knife . . . Betsy was in my suite at the Four Seasons waiting for me when I got back.

I told Betsy some of what had happened and Betsy kidded, "Damn. We could've had *some* threesome!"

"Go back to Cleveland," I said. "You've been out here too long."

"Three months."

"That's what I mean."

Betsy thought that was funny.

Sometimes, when Betsy and I were in Cleveland together, I did feel there was a possibility I was falling in love with her.

She came alive in Cleveland, she *radiated*. Her eyes sparkled and she walked down the street with a strut, letting her boot heels clomp the concrete. She sipped white wine in L.A. but she gulped tequila shooters as we watched hard-rock blues bands in the Flats in Cleveland in bars decorated with old, battle-scarred Cleveland Browns helmets.

She was, of course, the governor's daughter, the former mayor's daughter, recognized by passersby who always greeted her with a smile.

At times, with her Slavic cheekbones and blue-collar style, she reminded me of young women I'd known on Lorain Avenue as a kid. She was as ethnic as I was, enjoying tripe with eggs at a factory café and stuffed cabbage at the Slovenian Home. We both had more fun in those places than at Spago or at the Ivy in L.A.

I was going out to dinner in L.A. with Betsy, but I'd never visited Bill and Naomi at their apartment in Marina Del Rey, so I stopped by on my way to dinner. Their place overlooked the beach and they had a fireplace going when I got there. Naomi had bought two bottles of Cristal and smoked salmon and Hungarian salami, all my favorites.

I couldn't take my eyes off Naomi. She wore tight jeans and cowboy boots and a Western shirt and as she walked across the room to bring some more smoked salmon, I couldn't stop myself from saying, "Hey, look at *you!*"

She turned and gave me a special smile and I knew that she knew that I had been looking at her body.

Bill seemed oblivious to all of it, maybe because, he confessed, he'd had four or five screwdrivers.

We drank the Cristal and I told them I had to go. I said I had to have dinner with Stanley Jaffe and Sherry Lansing of Paramount, but I could tell from her expression that Naomi knew that was a lie—she knew I was going to see Betsy.

"You just got here," she said.

"I'm sorry," I said, "but I've gotta go."

I gave Bill a hug and then Naomi and headed out the door. Naomi stopped me and handed me something in an envelope—two perfectly rolled joints.

"Two for the road," Naomi said.

I knew how very carefully she had picked her words. She knew that *Two for the Road* was my wife's favorite movie of all time. She knew that the movie was about the relationship between a philandering husband and his wife. And I knew that she knew that Gerri's husband was going off into the night to do some philandering.

I broke up with Betsy the next time I was in L.A. I wasn't going to leave Gerri and Steve and Suzi for her. I wasn't going to offer her any kind of future. I'd wind up hurting her even more than I was going to hurt her now.

She was in love with me but it wasn't reciprocal. She was too moody for me, too prone to black-dog depressions, too scarred maybe by the broken body of the little sister she had found in the street.

I'd continue to use her body, I knew, unless I ended the relationship . . . like I'd used the bodies of too many others and I didn't want to do that to her. I liked her too much. She was an intelligent and attractive young woman who deserved a real future and a man who'd love her.

I told her that I was breaking it off because I was married and had kids and didn't want *us* to hurt my family.

"You're nuts," she said. "You're one of the loneliest people I've ever met. You stopped loving your wife a long time ago. Your kids are grown—they're hardly home and off with their own friends. You've spent most of your life taking care of others and have neglected only you. You've got a great heart that's sort of atrophied and unless you give yourself the freedom to really love another woman, you're going to engage in the same kind of self-destructive behavior you've engaged in for much of your marriage. If you keep doing that, your atrophied heart is going to die."

I thought about what she said for a couple moments and then I reached over and took her hand and brought it to my lips and kissed it.

"You're right about everything you said—except one thing. You're the wrong 'another' woman. I don't love *you*."

Betsy looked at me, her eyes wet, shook her head slightly, said, "Oh, man," and walked out of the room.

She sent me a forty-four-page letter after I broke up with her. It was more a long short story than a letter and my feeling was that she should try to get it published somewhere.

George Voinovich was elected to the United States Senate.

Betsy went back to Cleveland. She met a guy she loves . . . and who loves *her* . . . and had a baby they named after John Lennon.

[Dissolve]

The Lovers

T hey met at a store on Melrose, where they were both clerks, helping out Leo or Cruise or Brad when they came in to check out the new Lori Rodkins or Chrome Hearts or the freaky Gothic stuff Peter, the owner, brought back from Morocco or Mexico or Bali.

They liked the gig and they liked each other. Lisa was nineteen and wanted to be a model. Sarah was twenty-two and wanted to design clothes.

They started hanging out after work at the Viper Room or the Sky Bar and when Lisa got a tat of a snake on the small of her back, Sarah got one, too. They moved in together in a little place two blocks up from the Strip. They were both vegans and sometimes, even though they ate little, they both came home from a night out and forced their fingers into their throats and rid themselves of the poisons and slept much better.

It was Lisa who came up with the idea, having heard about it from a girlfriend of her brother's, who was a junkie and an ex-con and had actually hung out with Robert Downey when they were both in the joint.

They went down to one of the antique stores on Montana in Santa Monica and found the perfect blade but the weight of the old-time razor frightened them and they put it away in a drawer. A week or so later they snorted a little smack and Lisa got the straight razor out of the drawer.

They examined the gleaming blade and Sarah handed it to Lisa and Lisa started but couldn't do it herself.

She handed the razor to Sarah and begged her, showed her the spot on her arm where she wanted it and Sarah took the razor and slashed a perfect cross into her forearm.

They watched the blood trickle and drip to the floor, snorting a little more smack, and Sarah handed Lisa the blade and then it was her turn to slash a cross into Sarah's arm.

They became lovers that night, licking and kissing each other's slashes, and the next day they showed everybody at the store and everybody thought it was so really cool.

They talked about doing it to each other's beautiful faces but they weren't stupid. This was still a new relationship and they weren't sure if they were ready for that kind of commitment.

Peter checked out their slashes and went to Mexico in search of straight razors, coming back with ivory and ebony and crucifix-bedecked razors which quickly became the hottest thing in town.

CHAPTER 17

[Flashback]

Howdy Doody
with a Ducktail

RAY

Hey—winning isn't everything.

JOEY

That's what you said, Dad.

RAY

There are more important things.

JOEY

Like what?

RAY

Happiness. Health. Enjoying each and every moment. What do
you think, Joey?

JOEY

Bullshit, Dad.

Checking Out

Two Catholic high schools were supposed to be the best in the city—St.
Ignatius was a Jesuit school only six blocks from where we lived. The
other was Cathedral Latin, across town on the East Side, an hour and a
half by bus from us.

I wanted to go to neither school. Both were all-boys schools. I wanted to go
to West Tech, ten minutes away from us by bus, where there were girls.

But my parents insisted that I go to a Catholic school. I wasn't admitted to St. Ignatius but Cathedral Latin accepted me.

My mother knelt down and thanked God.

On my first day at Cathedral Latin, I felt disoriented. The other boys had names like DeSapri and DeGrandis and Boravec and Bolan and Ondercin and Cudnik. There were Italians and Irish and Slovaks and Slavs, but there were no Hungarians.

Many of them, East Siders, had known each other in grade school and in Catholic CYOs and banded together here quickly. Relative to where I came from, they were rich kids. They wore colorful sweaters of fine weave and light, tan-colored pants, blue button-down shirts and shiny, pointy-toed black shoes. I wore the gray flannel pants we had bought at the Salvation Army. And a white shirt my father no longer wore which was baggy and bunched out of my pants. And the shoes which were too big. And I had my Hungarian accent.

Many of these kids had their own cars, most of them shiny and new.

I still looked like Howdy Doody, but Howdy Doody with a ducktail haircut.

I heard the word "asshole" directed at me soon and, more commonly, the word "greenhorn." My ears stuck out and the kids sitting behind me flicked them with their fingers.

When I turned around to hit back, the teachers said, "What are you doing, Mr. Esterhose?" and the kids laughed.

It became my Cathedral Latin name: Joe Esterhose.

The teachers were Marianist priests and brothers, most of them young men in their twenties and thirties. None of them seemed able to pronounce my name. It came out "Esterhash" and "Esterhanz" and "Esterhaze" and "Esterass" and "Esterhose."

I sat alone at lunch. I hated the three hours each day that I spent going back and forth on the buses and the rapids to Cathedral Latin.

I wore the same clothes almost every day—I had two pairs of pants my father had bought and two of his shirts.

One day, when I switched to my other pair of pants, a brother said to the class, "Well, Mr. Esterhose has a new pair of pants today." The kids laughed.

"How was school?" my father asked me each day.

And I said, "Fine."

I couldn't tell him that I was miserable, that I hated every moment of it, that the kids and the brothers made fun of my name, my clothes, my ears, and my accent. My father had enough problems.

"*Fein*," he said. "Always *fein* like all the other Americans. You, too, Jozsi, a liar like the other Americans."

"I'm not lying, Papa," I said. "I'm fine. Everything's fine."

"I am glad to hear it, Jozsi." My father smiled. "Me too. I am *fein*, too. Everything is *fein* with me, too."

The Indians had a player I liked as much as the now departed Roger Maris. His name was Rocky Colavito. He was a home run hitter. He was exciting to watch. He'd put the bat over his shoulders, stretch his muscles, point his cap, step up to bat, and a lot of times hit a home run. The whole city was excited about him.

The Indians traded him.

Jerry Lee Lewis wasn't on TV or on the radio anymore. His songs were out of the jukebox at the Royal Castle. The *Plain Dealer* said preachers were putting his records into stacks and burning them. All because he had married his thirteen-year-old cousin.

Even Elvész Prezli was gone, off the radio and the TV and out of the jukeboxes. In Germany, in the army, his ducktail gone, too, wearing a crew cut, signing autographs on the breasts of Nazis now probably.

My portable radio broke. A kid at Cathedral Latin named Jack Harrison knocked it out of my hand as I was putting it into my locker.

I hit him in the mouth. A brother started screaming at me and took me to the principal's office.

The principal took a file out of a drawer, studied it, and looked at me.

"Mr. Eszterhas," he said, pronouncing it right, "if you're ever brought into this office again for something like this, I will expel you from Cathedral Latin."

"He started it," I said.

"I don't care who started it," the priest said. "I won't care who started it. Do you understand me?"

I said, "Yes, Father."

I took the radio home and was trying to tape it together.

"What happened to it?" my father asked.

"I dropped it," I said.

"How?"

"It just fell out of my hands."

"Clumsy of you," my father said.

I looked at him. He was looking into my eyes.

"Yes," I said.

"Maybe I can help you fix it," he said.

Even my mother helped. That shocked me because she had to touch the tubes which she believed emitted the rays that tortured her. We taped it together with black electrical tape, all three of us, and it worked.

"You see," my father said, "I am a genius!"

"You did nothing," my mother said, "I fixed it."

"We did it together." My father smiled.

After I broke Jack Harrison's teeth, none of the other kids at Cathedral Latin shoved me or flicked my ears or knocked things from my hands.

They just pretended I wasn't there.

The brothers ignored me, too, and hardly called on me in class.

One of them, though, said to the class, "Look, gentlemen, Mr. Esterhose has a new haircut today. Doesn't he look handsome?"

I didn't much look forward to Christmas.

"You're older now," my father said. "You know that everything costs money. You know that we don't have much money. So from now on I will ask you what you want for Christmas each year and then we will discuss it. We will find out how much it costs and if it's too expensive, I will ask you to pick something else. That way you'll be helping us with the money.

"So," my father said, "what do you want for Christmas this year?"

I said, "Nothing."

I got nothing and they got nothing for each other, either.

I was seeing my father less.

We weren't playing much of our button soccer game. He was going out at night often again. He was taking a political science night course at Case Western Reserve University and a drawing course at an art school.

"I have to try to make more money," he said to me. "Maybe I can teach political science somewhere. Maybe I can draw things and sell them to the magazines."

He kept his drawings in a big case that was always tied together. Alone in the apartment one day, I opened it. All I saw were drawings of naked women.

When my mother was in the printing shop downstairs, I asked my father why he only drew naked women.

"How do you know I draw only naked women?" he asked.

I shrugged and he glanced at his case and knew.

"The course I am taking at the art school is called figure sketching," he said. "There is a model sitting there naked and the students draw her."

"She is naked *sitting right there?*" I asked.

"Yes," he said, "that's what models do."

"Can I learn figure sketching, too?" I asked.

He laughed. "Whatever you do, don't tell your mother," he said. "She doesn't know what I'm drawing."

I didn't tell her and he hid his case filled with his drawings in the same tiny alcove where I had hidden my discarded sandwiches.

My mother found them.

My father stopped going to art school.

I discovered Joseph Conrad and Turgenev and Hawthorne and I kept reading Steinbeck. I realized that there were people in America who were even poorer than we were. And I realized from reading Steinbeck that there were Komchis, Reds, who spent their lives trying to help these poor people. I didn't say anything to my father, though, about the good Komchis I was reading about.

Conrad particularly interested me. He was Polish, an immigrant who'd lived in England. Polish was his mother tongue. He couldn't even speak English until he was in his forties. For the rest of his life, he spoke it with a pronounced accent. And yet he had learned to write in English so well that he was a world-famous, immortal writer.

I discovered a whole new world on television: boxing. My new heroes were Archie Moore, the Old Mongoose, who ate steaks by spitting them out and swallowing only the juice . . . Floyd Patterson, who played peekaboo with his gloves as he fought . . . Carmen Basilio, whose face looked like raw meat at the end of a fight . . . Joey Giardello, a brawler who sometimes hit below the belt.

When Ingemar Johannson and his right hand of "Toonder" knocked Floyd Patterson out, I felt like crying.

My father watched me listen to the fight on the radio and said, "Why do you like people hurting each other?"

I couldn't answer him.

One of the radio stations, WJW, began a program which I never missed with an announcer named Tom Carson. Tom Carson drove at night in a car with the radio station's letters on its side and went to the scene of crimes.

He reported from there, live, describing holdups and shootings and bar fights. I listened to Tom Carson prowling the streets of Cleveland every night.

Once he said, "The shooting is at the corner of Fulton and Lorain. I'm at 65th and Lorain now, I should be there in three minutes."

I ran to the living room window and waited and here he came, right by our window, Tom Carson with the car that said WJW on its side!

As a newspaper reporter in Dayton, Ohio, and in Cleveland, I drove cars with "Journal Herald" and "Plain Dealer" painted on their sides.

When I cracked my own car up in Dayton, I "borrowed" the Journal Herald *car and drove it to Cleveland on weekends.*

The Plain Dealer *car even had a telephone in it and, sometimes, driving through the city, I'd hold the phone to my ear to look important.*

Even when there was no one on the line.

The only part of Cathedral Latin I liked was the pep rallies. I had never seen anything like it. All nine hundred of us packed into the gym. All boys. All boy cheerleaders screaming their lungs out: "Beat Ignatius! Beat Ignatius! Beat Ignatius!" Or "Beat Holy Name! Beat Holy Name! Beat Holy Name!" Or "Let's Win One for the Purple and Gold!"

It went on until we were red-faced and out of breath, hoarse-voiced, and foaming at the mouth. Even the brothers were foaming at the mouth, waving their fists and screaming.

I took the bus alone to our game against Holy Name High School. I sat alone in the stands rooting . . . for Holy Name High School.

I heard the best cheer I've ever heard anywhere. I heard it from the father of a Holy Name player.

The dad yelled, "Fuck 'em in the belly, Jimmy!"

The most revered people at Cathedral Latin were the jocks, the stars of the pep rallies.

They proudly wore their letter sweaters and made speeches: "What did I say? *Beat Ignatius!* Who we gonna beat? *Ignatius!* What are we gonna do? *Beat Ignatius!*"

The letter sweaters were a snowy white with the letters C and L in purple and gold sewn on them along with your first name. You were awarded the letter sweater by the priests and brothers for achievement.

I resolved that I, Howdy Doody, the Greenhorn, the Asshole, the Creep, would somehow achieve such a Cathedral Latin letter sweater!

I joined the Cathedral Latin Speech and Debate team. My debate partner was a midget. He wasn't even four feet tall.

We must've been a sight—Howdy Doody with a ducktail and his midget sidekick, pontificating about whether or not America should withdraw from the United Nations. One debate we were for it and the next debate we were against it. We never knew which side we would represent until the judge told us.

We couldn't *believe* in either position but we had to be persuasive in advocating either position. The midget and I traveled to different high schools, debating the differing sides between ourselves.

Sometimes by the time we got there we were so confused my partner and I argued different positions while debating the other team. But the other team was confused, too, and the same thing happened to them sometimes.

"What kind of foolishness is this?" my father said. "How can you put your soul into both sides of an argument?"

"This is how they do it in America," I told him.

"They are teaching you," my father said, "to believe in nothing. They are teaching you to lie expertly. They are teaching you to be American politicians."

I failed algebra. The brother who failed me was the same one who had said, "Look, Mr. Esterhose is wearing a new pair of pants today." But he wasn't wrong to fail me. I was as bad with numbers as my mother was good.

I told this brother I hated numbers.

He said, "Unfortunately, Mr. Esterhose, you need to know about numbers in life. How are you going to keep track of your money in life if you can't count? How will you be able to pay your taxes?"

I said, "I will be very rich and will pay others to keep track of my money and my taxes."

"How will you become very rich?" he asked, trying not very successfully to hide a sneer.

"Like Shondor Birns," I said.

He said, "Who is this?"

I said, "Shondor Birns is a pimp, a gambler, a numbers king, a gangster. A great Hungarian."

He looked for a moment like he couldn't believe what I'd said.

Then he smiled and said, "Of course."

"How could you fail algebra?" my father said. "Now I will have to pay to send you to summer school."

"Do you know algebra?" I asked him.

"Somewhat."

"What use has algebra ever been to you in life?"

"That's not the point," my father said.

"Was there any moment of your life—ever—when you thought, 'Oh, I am so happy I know algebra!'?"

My mother spoke up unexpectedly.

"I have worked with numbers," she said. "I have even worked as a book-keeper. I don't know algebra. I never studied algebra."

"You see?" I said to my father.

"Why are you saying these things to him?" my father said to my mother.

She said to him, "You aren't right about everything. Sometimes *I'm* right, too.

"You're wrong a lot," my mother said to him. "You've *been* wrong a lot. But no, we never talk about that! Oh, no! You are the great leader! *Everybody applauds!*"

She stopped as suddenly as she had begun and turned back to her stove.

"Look what you started by failing algebra!" my father said to me.

I went to West Tech for summer school—the place were I'd wanted to go to high school—and I saw most of the kids I'd met in the playgrounds and the alleys near Lorain Avenue.

They were kids like me, dressed like me. No one called me names. The teachers pronounced my name as best they could but mostly called me "Joe." We ate lunch together out on the grass behind the school from brown paper bags. We shared our smokes and an older kid even shared a can of beer with me sometimes. No one flicked my ears; no one knocked things out of my hands.

And when we took the final test, a girl named Marcy Jacobs secretly shared her answers with me, which was the only possible way I could pass algebra.

There was a new kid at Cathedral Latin. His name was R. J. Wilkinson. He wore a Nazi uniform—the black uniform of an SS officer complete with gleaming silver skullheads. He had a black Nazi cap and a flashing cape with swastikas on it.

He was a freak. His face was pale, his skin saggy. He wore thick glasses. He spoke with a lisp and stuttered. He stuttered about Hitler and Jews. He walked into a classroom, looked at the teacher, threw his right arm into the air, and yelled "*Sieg Heil!*"

I avoided R. J. Wilkinson, but watching him at a pep rally, screaming "Beat Ignatius! Beat Ignatius!" in his Nazi uniform, his face red and his fist in the air, he looked like he was in his element.

He wasn't at Cathedral Latin long. Word was that a teacher had ordered him to stop wearing his uniform and Wilkinson had refused.

I told my father there was a kid at Cathedral Latin who came to school each day in a Nazi uniform and he stared at me.

"I told you," he said, "Americans are crazy."

Whenever I saw that Bob Hope was going to be on TV, I always watched. He was Cleveland's most famous native son, besides John D. Rockefeller, of course.

He was in town often—to throw out the first pitch at an Indians opener or to cut the opening day ribbon at the National Air Races. He was sometimes seen at the Theatrical Grill on Short Vincent in the company of Shondor Birns.

Bob Hope on TV always made me laugh, almost as much as Larry of the Three Stooges or Spanky on the Little Rascals. I loved his nose—probably because, from what I could tell, it was even longer than mine.

I wondered if, when he was growing up, the other kids had called him "Schnozz."

And when I was a famous American screenwriter, I asked Bob Hope that.

"My friends all called me Schnozz," Bob Hope said.

We were at a party in Beverly Hills thrown by Guy McElwaine, who was also Bob Hope's agent. I saw that his nose was actually longer than mine and when Guy told him that I, too, was from Cleveland, Bob Hope was so happy that he sat down in a corner with me.

We had a lot of things in common, besides our noses. Schnozz was an immigrant, like me. He came to America from England when he was five. He grew up just down the street from Cathedral Latin—on East 102nd and Euclid. He hung out on the corner of East 105th and Euclid, where I caught the bus to go back home after school each day. He was part of a gang of Irish kids and got into some juvenile trouble. He went to East High School, which was part of the same conference as Cathedral Latin.

He told me that he sold the Cleveland Plain Dealer *on the corner of 105th and Euclid and each day John D. Rockefeller stopped in a limousine and bought a copy. One day John D. Rockefeller gave him some advice: "If you want to be a success in business, trust nobody. Never give credit and always keep change on hand."*

I asked Bob Hope how well he knew Shondor Birns and Schnozz laughed and said, "Shondor Birns! Did I know Shondor Birns? Oh boy did I!"

I told him the story Shondor Birns had told me about the night he made love to Marilyn Monroe.

"Shondor Birns said he made love to every famous woman who came through Cleveland," Bob Hope told me with a laugh.

"Now if you want to know about Marilyn"—he winked—"I can really tell you about Marilyn."

We both laughed and Bob Hope said, "You know, she had the most amazing translucent skin. You could just about see the veins under her skin.

"At certain moments, that is." And Schnozz winked again.

Our old blue Nash was dead, its transmission left in the street on 28th Street near Bridge Avenue.

My father and I went down to Dunajszky Motors on Lorain Avenue, where all the West Side Hungarians shopped for their used cars. We picked out a light green 1952 Ford, only seven years old, with only fourteen thousand miles showing on the odometer. Old man Dunajszky said it had been owned by a widow lady who hardly ever drove it.

I was fifteen years old, a year away from being able to get a temporary driver's license, and my father said that he would teach me to drive.

We began slowly, moving back and forth in the parking lot of Fisher Foods when there was no one there. Then he let me take the wheel on small streets like Whitman Avenue. When it was time to use the brake, he yelled "Brake! *Brake!*" and stomped the floor with his foot, as though he were braking.

He wanted me to use my horn all the time—as I turned, at stop signs, at green lights. "The most important weapon in America with all these crazy Americans is your car horn," he said. "They *know* they are crazy, that's why *they* use *their* horns so much. If they are close to you, shout at them with your horn before they shout at you."

I drove up and down the West Side tooting my horn. My father and I were our own parade. The American drivers looked at us. Sometimes they tooted back at us. Often they waved in the American way—with their middle finger.

My father didn't know about this American wave with the middle finger. I explained it to him.

"*Baszd meg,*" I said, "that's what it means."

"The pigs!" He laughed. "They wave all the time."

"Only when *we* are driving," I said.

He gave me a look. "How do you say '*Baszd meg*' in English?"

"Fuck you," I said.

He practiced it quietly a couple times but it came out "Fucky you."

The next time I honked and an American waved at us with his middle finger, my father yelled, "Fucky you!"

The American looked at my father, his middle finger held high above the beret on his head . . . the American stomped on the gas . . . and got *the hell* away from us.

The Hungarian old-age home in Chagrin Falls, a rustic Cleveland suburb, held an annual St. Stephen's Day celebration. My father was the featured speaker.

I still didn't have my temporary license, but my father allowed me to drive. My mother sat between us in her velvet dress. She looked terrified.

My father stomped his foot each time I braked. I hit the horn every ten seconds. Somebody gave me the finger—my father waved his middle finger back at him and cried, "Fucky you!"

"What did you say?" my mother asked him.

"Move over," my father said, "that's what I told him."

"Why did you point to him with your finger?"

"It is an American custom," my father said. "Jozsi taught it to me. I am teaching Jozsi to drive and he is teaching me how to behave with Americans."

When we got to the old-age home, I drifted away from them as my father made his way with her to the stage. I went back to the car and when he started to orate, I started the Ford up and took it out on the road. I knew from bad experience how long my father's speeches were. I figured I had plenty of time.

I took the car out on the two-lane rural roads and stomped on the gas, getting it up to eighty and ninety. I turned the radio up as high as it would go. The sun was shining. The smell of burning leaves was in the air.

I was in bliss.

I don't know what happened. Maybe I lost myself somehow in the speed, the music, the sun. But when I got back to the old-age home, most of the cars were gone. Standing there in the parking lot, waiting for me, were my mother and father. His face was purple. Hers was snow-white. I could tell she'd been crying. I pulled the car right up to them and got out.

My father shook his head and looked like he wanted to say something, but didn't. My mother looked away. We got into the car, my father behind the wheel, my mother between us. We drove in utter, absolute silence.

My father honked and honked and at an intersection an American driver gave him the finger. My father stared grimly ahead, but my mother smiled suddenly and waved at the American with her middle finger.

I started to laugh. I couldn't help it. She kept waving happily with her middle finger. My father, without looking at me, started to laugh, too. I laughed harder and so did he as my mother kept waving her finger.

Offended, my mother said, "What's so funny? I can be American, too."

I read about the movie *Psycho* in the *Plain Dealer*. It was an American sensation. There were long lines for the movie in every city. I asked my father to take me to see it. He agreed, and my mother said she wanted to come, too.

"It is very violent, Mária," he said. "You wouldn't like it."

But she kept insisting and he finally agreed.

It was the most exciting movie I had ever seen. Not just because of Janet Leigh in the shower but because of how frightening so many scenes were. At each frightening scene, my father laughed, I stared, and my mother softly said, "*Jaj*."

When we walked out, she said, "I am never going to a movie again."

"I told you it wasn't for you," my father said.

"Then why did you bring me?" she said.

"Because you insisted, Mária."

"No," she said. "You brought me because you knew it would upset me. I am upset. Are you satisfied now?"

"I thought it was really good," I said.

"You have corrupted the boy," my mother told my father.

A famous Hungarian actress named Zita Hamori was appearing at a Hungarian theater on the East Side. I saw her picture in the Hungarian daily, the *Szabadsag*.

She was an attractive blonde. All the Hungarians who came to my father's office were talking about her.

My father said he had known her in Hungary and she was asking him now to introduce her at the start of her program.

"I'm not going," my mother said.

He pleaded with my mother, but she refused to go.

"She wants to see *you*," my mother said to my father, "not me. She's *your* friend, not mine."

"For God's sake, Mária," he said, "we were friends, that's all."

I wanted to see Zita Hamori, too, but the day of the event, he said, "I don't like leaving your mother here alone. Maybe it would be better if you stayed home with her."

When he got back from the East Side that night, it was very late. I was asleep. My mother's screams woke me.

She was screaming at him. She was calling Zita Hamori a painted *kurva* and she was calling him a pig.

"We were friends, that's all," he yelled at her. "We're friends, *friends*."

She came out of the bedroom, slammed its door so hard it shook the floor, and went on into the kitchen. I heard her crying.

"Go to sleep, Jozsi," my father said from behind the closed bedroom door. "Everything is fine."

He said the word in English: *fein*.

Tom Cruise
Is a Mousy Little Guy

*P*amela Anderson Lee's (and Naomi's) manicurist seemed to know everything about Hollywood and, after a while, we started writing her revelations down:

Debbie Reynolds called Zsa Zsa Gabor a "cop socker."
Palm Springs is death's waiting room.
Jennifer Grey's career was ruined by her nose job.
Charlie Sheen has EMA tattooed on his shoulder. EMA stands for "Eat my ass."
Errol Flynn and Howard Hughes had sex together.
Howard Hughes offered Hedy Lamarr $10,000 to pose for a rubber dummy he wanted to have sex with.
Jack Nicholson never wears condoms.
George C. Scott beat his wives.
Woody Allen likes to chew gum that's already been chewed by a midget.
Steve McQueen was into orgies.
Mel Gibson in the eighties was arrested for drunken driving in Canada.
John Wayne drank a quart of whiskey a day for three decades.
If Mama Cass had given Karen Carpenter her sandwich, they'd both be alive.
Jayne Mansfield never turned anything down except the bedcovers.
Nancy Reagan's godmother was Alla Nazimova, the silent film star.
Clint Eastwood always asked Sondra Locke if she had flossed before they had sex.
Truman Capote wanted Marilyn Monroe to be in Breakfast at Tiffany's.

Robert Mitchum was Elvis's favorite actor.

Shirley MacLaine is Warren Beatty's older brother.

Quentin Tarantino sucked Cameron Diaz's feet.

Loretta Young worked with a full-length mirror next to the camera.

Richard Gere takes his shirt off in almost every movie he makes.

Yul Brynner loved black or white leather suits.

Tom Cruise is a mousy little guy.

Tony Curtis called Jill St. John "a sack of shit."

Burt Reynolds beat his wife.

Bob Hope used wars to publicize himself.

Sarah Miles wore her beloved terrier as boots after he died.

Raquel Welch's father was a plastic surgeon.

Jan-Michael Vincent stomped his ex-wife's kitten to death.

Tommy Noonan acted in films with Marilyn, Jayne Mansfield, and . . . Mamie Van Doren!

Mamie Van Doren said Burt Reynolds was "amusing but small."

CHAPTER 18

[Naomi's Journal]

In the Fetal Position

SLADE

You think you're really something, don't you? You twist everything
around, don't you? You don't care who you hurt.

Jagged Edge

August 28, 1992

Bill and I sit waiting to take off for San Francisco for
a visit with Joe Eszterhas. He's offered to let us stay in
his new Stinson Beach house. Joe came into town this week
and met with Evans and said it is grossly unfair that the
studio is attempting to cut Bill out of a credit on *Sliver*,
especially since Bill was responsible for Joe's prompt
delivery of the script.

Thank God Joe is on Bill's side.

August 31, 1992

Joe and Gerri were wonderful and generous as usual. I
confided to them about how vicious the movie business has
been for Bill and they offered sage advice. Watch your back
and don't take any of it too seriously. Joe showed us the
letter he is sending to John Goldwyn to make sure Bill will
get a credit on *Sliver*. We are most grateful for his friendship and support.

September 1, 1992

Bill came home at 1:30 this morning, exhausted after a grueling day. Sharon Stone walked off *Sliver*, but she's back on. It promises to be a stormy few months.

September 28, 1992

Joni, Bob's secretary, has lost her mind. She came into the office on Monday and announced that she had made an earthshaking discovery. She had spent the weekend reading and rereading the *Sliver* script and had discovered that—

1. It is a satanic message from the devil.
2. Joe Eszterhas is Satan himself and she had a vision of him with his long hair levitating from a dark pond.
3. Phillip Noyce, whose address is "666" something, is in cahoots with the devil.

Even Evans, insane as he is, turned to Bill and said, "She's lost her mind, hasn't she?"

Others at Paramount claim they have seen an actual ghost roaming the halls in one of the old buildings on the lot.

This has resulted in a group of Jerry Falwell's fanatics meeting in Evans's office when he wasn't there. Bill walked in to take a meeting and discovered there were religious fanatics there whispering in hushed tones to the professed "ghost sighters."

Bill discovered that Joni had conducted a séance in Bob's office last Friday night to try to communicate with the restless ghost.

Joe gave Bill his copy of his original *Sliver* script and signed at the bottom of the first page—"To Bill Macdonald, without whose friendship and support this script would never have been written."

Bill had tears in his eyes when he showed it to me. We're going to have it framed.

Bob is now desperate for cash because the latest bank loan failed because he failed his physical. They found cocaine in his blood.

October 27, 1992

Bob shrieked at Bill today, "Can't someone find me some money?"

October 29, 1992

Bill had a screen test for a part in *Sliver.* The casting agents thought he'd be perfect for the part of Sharon Stone's boss, who, much to Bill's dismay, is described as "40ish, balding, and tweedy."

Joe Eszterhas told the casting agents that if they use Bill they could cast every movie he makes in the future. Guess he loves Bill.

November 4, 1992

Bill and Joe were chatting with Sharon Stone on the lot yesterday. Of course she took an immediate liking to Bill. As they chatted and laughed, Bill discovered she is very well read and very bright. Joe says that he has never seen her open up as quickly to anyone as she did to Bill.

She finally said to Bill, "What do you do?" completely unaware that Bill is actually a co-producer of *Sliver.*

Bill, in his typical way, answered, "Well, I'm in the import-export business."

She said, "What do you import and export?"

And he said, "Everything but drugs and arms."

Stanley Jaffe walked by. Bill said he was thrilled that Stanley saw him standing there with Sharon and Joe.

November 6, 1992

At around 4:00 P.M. yesterday, Bill said he went in to watch *Sliver* dailies. He was alone. Then Stanley Jaffe himself walked in. Bill said he then spent the next forty-five minutes with Stanley Jaffe, talking about *Sliver* and *Jade,* the next Eszterhas script for which Bill just finalized the deal.

Stanley said, "What do you think of Sharon in the dailies?"

And Bill said, "Well, for one thing, I think she's wearing too much makeup."

Stanley Jaffe wholeheartedly agreed, Bill said.

November 11, 1992

Bill went onto the *Sliver* set yesterday and Sharon Stone
was calling him "buddy."

Evans has entered into a deep depression and has not
returned anyone's phone calls. He is doing massive amounts
of cocaine and takes Nembutal suppositories at night to
bring himself down. He told Bill he is "in the fetal position."

Joe Eszterhas wants to really stick it to Paramount and Bob
for what he considers horribly unjust treatment of Bill.
Joe's idea is to let everyone, including Sherry Lansing and
Stanley Jaffe, call him and beg him to do *The Saint* rewrite.
He will say no.

Then Bill will talk to him and he'll agree to do it. Only
Joe could come up with such a plan—or should I say only
Bill and Joe, since those two devious minds seem to flourish
together.

November 16, 1992

Bill and Joe have been on the phone constantly, plotting
a joint production company tentatively called "Renegade."

Joe said, "It sounds like you should get up here and we
should talk."

Evans is still "in the fetal position," still not
returning phone calls.

November 23, 1992

Bill arrived at Joe's only to find that two cameramen who
were shooting locations for *Sliver* in Hawaii were trapped
near a volcano. Another disaster.

Sharon Stone is apoplectic because she says she's being
forced to direct herself since Noyce is so weak. And Evans
is in Acapulco in the fetal position.

November 24, 1992

Bill came home from Joe Eszterhas's birthday bash—at a
small place on Sunset—at 3:30 in the morning. Sharon Stone
was at the party.

She told Bill that he looked "world-weary" and that she bet he was thirty years old when he was ten. He filled her in a bit on his background (God only knows how much, he was staggering drunk when he got home).

She said she wants to tell Bill something the next time she sees him. She wants to "formulate it" in her mind first.

I comfort myself with the knowledge that *at least* she's my age.

November 27, 1992

Bill and Joe keep talking about Renegade, the production company they're thinking about setting up. The company logo on their films will show a skull and crossbones and say "Renegade Presents."

Then the screen will go black and silent, only to be shattered by the sound of a gun firing, leaving a bullet hole in the black screen. It's too perfect for Bill.

December 2, 1992

The studio, which Evans always calls "The Mountain," has decided they very much want Joe Eszterhas to rewrite *The Saint*, so Bill is meeting this morning with Evans, Goldwyn, and Sherry Lansing.

Sliver is $700,000 over budget and still shooting. The studio wants to cut three days' shooting from the script.

They approached Joe and he said, "No way. I'm not cutting any pages. It's a thirty-million-dollar movie, what's another seven hundred thousand? If you cut any pages, you'll really screw the movie up and it's already pretty screwed-up." The studio backed off.

December 4, 1992

Evans wrote a letter to Sherry Lansing that says he can get Joe to rewrite *The Saint*, which we all know is hogwash.

December 5, 1992

Joe heard about Evans's letter and said, "Fuck him."

December 6, 1992

Bill told "The Mountain" he was meeting with Roger Moore to appease him and quell his apprehensions about the lack of direction for *The Saint*. Bobby Jaffe, who'd never read *The Saint* contract and didn't know that Roger is contractually bound to be in the movie, said, "Why do you keep bothering with Roger Moore?"

Bill almost shrieked, "Read the fucking contract!"

Bobby looked stunned and said, "Oh, I thought it was just some goodwill thing that he be in the script."

December 8, 1992

Yesterday Bill went on the *Sliver* set and Sharon said, "Oh, not you again!"

But I know she was clearly glad to see him. I don't care what Bill thinks, *I* think she likes him. She always compliments his clothes and managed to use his office while Bill was in San Francisco.

I'm *glad* she likes him. It can only be good for his career. Also, he has never given me any reason not to trust him.

I hope I get to meet her.

December 15, 1992

Joe came to L.A., to work out the deal to do *The Saint* rewrite. Several problems developed.

1. His attorneys got involved in the negotiations. It got complicated, as things do when lawyers get involved; 2. Joe asked for a deal so rich that Bill and Evans couldn't even consider taking it to Paramount.

This after Evans wrote Sherry Lansing that Joe would do it for free!

Evans was livid. He couldn't believe that after his brother, Charles, gave Joe $2 million to write *Showgirls*, Joe's "sticking it into me."

"That sonofabitch Eszterhas humiliated me," Evans said to me, referring to his letter to Sherry Lansing. "I feel used! I feel like a woman who opened her legs for a guy on Friday, opened them for another guy on Saturday, and another guy on Sunday, and on Monday, not one of them called her. I detest him."

December 26, 1992

Christmas Day at Joe's house was fun. I spent the day in the kitchen with Gerri preparing a turkey feast, which was delicious. I like Joe's kids very much.

December 27, 1992

We're on Maui. Gerri, Suzi, Joe's daughter, and I went on a hike to see one of the sights of Maui. I originally planned not to go but Joe said he wanted to talk to Bill some more about Renegade.

December 29, 1992

There's a tension to Joe here, a kind of moodiness, that I haven't felt with him before. Sometimes he doesn't look me in the eye. If I move toward him, he moves away. He never speaks directly to me.

Combine this with the fact that I'm walking around in a bikini all day, and you may get an idea of how uncomfortable I feel.

At lunch today Joe said, "You know, when he drinks, Bill has a point of near insanity that he reaches sometimes. You can see it coming."

I said, "That's true. You know him very well. The only difference is that while I try to keep him from getting to that point, you act as a catalyst to get him there quickly."

He looked at me (for the first time in days) and smiled. "That's right," he said, "I knew you and I were destined to be enemies."

December 30, 1992

The tension with Joe was so thick you could cut it with a knife. Maybe I'm flattering myself, but there was also, it seemed to me, sexual tension. Every time I was near him I felt naked.

January 1, 1993

There were a whole bunch of people in Joe and Gerri's suite when I got there last night. They were all Industry people also on vacation here. Bill was already there when I came in.

It looked like a subdued group and when I commented on it, Joe said, "We were just waiting for you to get here."

So I said, "Well I'm here. Let the games begin."

When we all went out to get in the cars, there were two limos and a van awaiting us. Gerri got into a limo with Suzi . . . with one of Joe's lawyers and his wife . . . and others quickly jumped in. Bill and I got into the van. At the last second, so did Joe and Steve.

After dinner the plan was to go to a New Year's Eve party at the home of Shep Gordon, a music producer who used to own a record company.

It was raining but the party was a blast. Steve and Suzi got really drunk, as did Bill. Then, at midnight, we lit sparklers and blew noisemakers. The kids were smoking cigarettes (unbeknownst to Joe or Gerri).

Woody Harrelson and his wife were there and he and Joe did some kind of elaborate high-five I've never seen.

The ride home was one of the best adventures of my life. The kids, Joe, Bill, and I poured ourselves into the van. Bill and the kids all fell asleep. Gerri stayed with the lawyer and his wife in the limo.

Joe and I talked. The tension I felt earlier was gone. It was like we were alone in the van. We were both a little high, not from booze but from the joint that we'd smoked at the party.

I don't remember everything we talked about, but I remember we talked a lot about Ohio, about growing up. His shoulder was touching mine and I remember being very conscious of his shoulder. The Pretenders were blasting.

When we got back to Joe and Gerri's suite, the kids promptly passed out on their beds. It was then that Joe suggested Gerri and Bill and I play the "question game." Each person asks another person a question and that person has to answer truthfully.

Joe said, "I'll go first." He said, "My question is for Naomi. What happened when Bill first tried to make love to you?"

With that, Bill exploded from his drunken stupor and said, "Good Lord! You can't be serious! She has to answer that?!"

I answered, "*Nothing* happened the first time Bill tried to make love to me." We all roared.

Then I asked—"What is your greatest strength? What is your greatest weakness?" of everyone.

Gerri: "My greatest strength is loyalty. My greatest weakness is lack of self-discipline."

Joe: "My greatest strength is my instinct. My greatest weakness is self-destructiveness."

Bill: "My greatest strength is that I like everyone I meet. That, however, is also my greatest weakness."

The game went on till six in the morning.

Joe asked, "When did you have your first orgasm?"

Gerri said, "On my honeymoon."

Kidding, I said, "On my honeymoon. Three months ago. After *ten long fucking years!*"

The room exploded as Bill said, "That's it. I'm leaving," once again erupting from his almost comatose state.

Joe asked: "What is your greatest fear?"

Bill: "I'm afraid that it's all not worth it. That you strive to get there and find that in the end, it's just not worth it."

Gerri: "That my family will die."

Joe: "My own insanity."

Me: "I'm afraid to love someone too much. I'm afraid to care too much. Because it would be my own self-destruction if it were taken away."

January 5, 1993

When Joe saw me writing in my journal on the plane back to California, he asked if he could make a guest entry.

TO NAOMI, WISE AND BEAUTIFUL WOMAN, PARTY GIRL, BILL'S BETTER HALF—

WHO MADE OUR TRIP TWICE AS FUN—

I LOVE YOU.

Joe

January 20, 1993

Joe's wife, Gerri, has asked me to visit for the weekend. Joe is out of town somewhere. She sounded lonely. I can't refuse. I like her a lot.

January 23, 1993

My trip to San Francisco to visit Gerri was wonderful.
We shopped, had lunch, cooked, watched videos, and generally
enjoyed our time together. Gerri wants to do a TV project
with me. It would require lots of research but it could
potentially work.

January 27, 1993

Sunday night Joe arrived and we proceeded to uncork a
bottle of Cristal. Bill and Joe are both excited about the
prospect of this coming week. They're strategizing about
announcing Renegade.

Joe liked our condo and the new Jake, who instantly recognized a dog lover and cozied up to him for constant attention. Joe was quizzing me on what I did to Gerri during my
visit to San Francisco.

It seems that Gerri has a renewed sense of herself.
She's even exercising each day. I think Joe is pleased about
my friendship with Gerri.

February 10, 1993

Bill had lunch with Joe, Sharon Stone, her manager,
Chuck Binder, and some Italian guy from the *Sliver* set.

Bill, who had been speaking Italian to the guy from the
set, mentioned that he had lived in Europe for a while.

Binder said, "What were you doing in Europe?"

Bill said, "I was in the import-export business."

Joe said, "Why don't you tell the story about the condoms?"

And Bill said, "Well, the only reason Joe likes the
story is that it reaffirms his conviction that Japanese technology is overrated."

So Bill proceeded to tell the story of how, when he was
in Asia, he was making a deal to manufacture condoms in the
U.S. and ship them to Asia. The only problem, they discovered, is that all of the machinery was too big . . . i.e.
condoms designed for Americans were way too big for Asians.

Then Sharon, following Joe's lead at giving Bill a hard
time, said, "How did you discover this?"

Bill said, "You mean, did we market-research?" Joe and

Sharon were laughing as Bill mumbled something about what an asshole Joe could be.

February 11, 1993

Yesterday Joe went to Maxfield's to buy a Valentine's Day present for Sharon—a silver Chrome Hearts hash pipe!

While they were there, Bill saw an antique Rolex inside a silver case. It was priced at $7,000. He said to Joe, "Look at that, isn't it gorgeous?" Bill told me he thought to himself—Maybe one day I'll be able to come in here and buy something like that.

Later in the limo, Joe leaned over and put a box from Maxfield's into Bill's pocket and said, "Hey, Happy Valentine's Day." Bill immediately knew what Joe had done and said, "I absolutely cannot accept this."

Joe said, "Please, don't spoil it for me."

They argued about it, but when Bill came home in the wee hours of the morning, he said, "Turn on the light. You've got to see this."

It is so perfect for Bill and he is so moved by the gesture.

February 12, 1993

Bill had a meeting yesterday with a woman who owns the rights to Ayn Rand's *Atlas Shrugged*. The woman said, "I've never had a meeting with anyone in Hollywood who understands the book like you do."

An hour after the meeting, there was a loud rap on Bill's office window. It was Sharon Stone.

Bill raised the window and said, "Hey, did you ever hear of *Atlas Shrugged*?"

She said, "Yeah, it's been done. Patricia Neal."

Bill said, "That's *The Fountainhead*. I'll get you the book."

She said, "I've got it at home. I'll read it."

And Bill said to her, "Joe will write it, I'll produce it, and you'll win the Academy Award."

February 13, 1993

Joe and Bill went up to Guy McElwaine's house and Sharon dropped by to visit. It was her sister's birthday and she

couldn't stay, but she did stay long enough to hear Bill
say, "The day you win your first Academy Award, I'll give you
$10,000 if it *isn't* a movie that Joe and I produced." She
laughed.

Bill talked to her about *Atlas Shrugged* and she's primed
to do it.

February 14, 1993

I knew that later that evening was the wrap party for
Sliver and though I would have loved to go, Bill hadn't
asked me yet.

Finally I said, "Are you going to the wrap party
tonight?" And he said yes.

And I said, "But I'm not."

And he said, "Well, it's just that Joe's going to have
Betsy, his girlfriend, there and it might compromise every-
one if we all go together"—since I am a friend of Gerri's,
Joe's wife, is what Bill meant.

I said "Oh" and he said, "You're disappointed."

It really hurt my feelings. I felt that people would
think that Bill didn't want to bring me. So Bill started
insisting I should go but it seemed like I had pressured him
and it just didn't feel right.

Finally I agreed to go and look the other way if Joe and
Betsy were overly affectionate.

I got all dressed up and drove to the Four Seasons
Hotel, where I was to meet Bill and Joe and we'd all ride to
the party in a limo.

When I arrived, Bill was standing out front.

He said, "You're not going to believe this, but we're
having a crisis. MGM-UA has heard we're doing Renegade—in
fact, it's all over town. The problem is, Joe owes MGM three
scripts and now they're threatening to sue and destroy Renegade before it's even off the ground. Joe's on the phone now
with Guy, who's at his golf course. We're not going to the
party, we're having an emergency meeting at Guy's house
instead.

"So," Bill said, "you can go to the party, but I don't
know when or if I'll even get there and I don't know if you
want to go alone to an L.A. nightclub."

So I said—"Maybe I should just go back home."

I felt *so* bad. First I had to ask if I could go and then I got all dressed up and drove to Beverly Hills for nothing.

He took a box from Maxfield's out of his pocket and said, "Here. I got you this for Valentine's Day."

It was a Kieselstein-Cord keychain. It had a little leather strap and on its end was a silver object. I looked at it closely in the darkness.

It was a broken heart.

Every Breath You Take

The newest royal Young-and-Hip movie star couple, they were in L-U-V, hanging out together in their tank tops and razor-sliced jeans and incognito goofy shades on Venice Beach . . . Riding their refurbished antique Indian bikes in the Malibu Hills . . . Getting some sun, stripped down to the bone at Joshua Tree.

They hit the Viper Room together wearing matching silver-studded Chrome Hearts leather jackets. They tattooed each other's names into the small of their backs. They fed each other strips of albacore and eel at a patio table at Zuma Sushi.

Wearing trucker hats and big kahuna Maui Jim shades, they held each other and watched the little kids play in the sand pit at Cross Creek, where they had come in his Lamborghini after listening to the violinist play Edith Piaf torch songs at Granita, just across the PCH.

But the whole town knew exactly how very much in L-U-V they were when, on different locations shooting different movies, they told their friends they still slept together all night every night . . . by putting their phones on their pillows . . . calling each other and keeping the line open all night so they could hear each other breathing.

CHAPTER 19

It's a Wrap!

COLT
We're going to be zombies when we get to New York.

ANNE
Then you can do your zombie act. New York expects it of you.

COLT
All right, fuck me! Zombies we will be!

Hearts of Fire

Sharon Stone and Bill Macdonald were sitting across from each other at the little restaurant around the corner from Paramount and I saw how their eyes sparkled and how they laughed.

This was the first moment they'd spent any real time together—they'd seen each other on the set and said a few words . . . but even this lunch had happened almost accidentally.

Bill had come to the set with me and Sharon said, "Do you want to eat?" I said "Sure" and she'd glanced at Bill and said, "He can come."

After lunch, back in his office, he said, "God is she incredible! She is *awesome!*"

I said, "Do you want to pop her? She can probably be had."

He looked at me aghast. I knew Bill tended to prudery, still very much the good Catholic boy trained by the Jesuits at Bellarmine. He would run from the room when a tampon commercial came on TV and he had lectured me often about my extramarital flings and one-night stands.

"Gerri is your *anchor*," he would say.

We'd been out together at night, both of us married now—he had recently, finally, married Naomi after ten years—and I'd never seen him make the slightest move toward another woman. He blanched when he saw me flirt with a girl in a bar or a club . . . and he was horrified and nearly evangelistic the morning after he'd pretended to sleep on the couch while that young woman and I were making love on the living room floor beneath him.

I told him in his office that Sharon didn't have much going on in her romantic life. She had an alleged "boyfriend," Charlie Peters, producer Jon Peters's wealthy young son, but Charlie didn't look like any serious obstacle to me.

Sharon had told me of the time she'd seen a red dress in a store window while driving by on Melrose, called Charlie on her cell phone, said, "I just drove by this red dress I've got to have," and young Charlie had driven right down and bought it for her.

Jon Peters, meanwhile, even as his son was seeing Sharon, was telling me about a wild weekend he'd spent with Sharon in a New York hotel many years ago . . . a sexual extravaganza which Sharon said was "a great big ugly lie" designed to one-up his own son.

"So," I said to Bill, "she's popable."

"Will you please stop it?" he said.

He came to see me the next day to say that he had just visited her on the set. He was glowing . . . flying.

"I haven't felt like this about a girl since I was thirteen years old," he said. "I think I'm in love with her."

I laughed. "How can you be in love with her? You don't know anything about her. You haven't spent any time with her."

"I don't know, but that's what I feel."

I saw Sharon on the set and she said, "Tell me everything about him."

"Who?"

"You *know* who."

"Well," I said, grinning, "what do you want to know?"

She seemed to be as cranked up as Bill was when I had seen him.

"How long have you known him?"

I told her and she said, "Tell me what you think of him. Don't fuck around."

"You know what I think of him," I said. "You've seen us together. He's my friend."

"Are you going to start this Renegade company with him?"

"We're talking about it. I love the logo. We've got a dark screen—"

"I love it, too. The bullet shatters the screen. He told me all about it."

She smiled to herself. She was thinking.

When Sharon thinks, it is a *dramatic* think. You can see the wheels *clanking* on-screen.

"Sharon," I said, "he's married. He just got married a few months ago."

"So are you," she said, a knowing smile on her face.

"He's different. He takes his Catholic upbringing seriously."

She thought about that and she said, "Well, he's not married to *me*, is he?"

I said, "No he's not, *Catherine*."

"What's she like? What's her name?"

"Naomi. She's smart as a whip and she's beautiful."

"How beautiful?"

"With a wife like that," I said, "I wouldn't give you a second look."

"You're horrible." She smiled. "Why did *you* have to create me? Why couldn't someone nicer create me?"

Guy called me that night and said, "What's going on between Macdonald and Madam Stone?"

"I'm not sure what the hell's going on. What do you hear?"

"True love," Guy said.

"He doesn't even know her. He hasn't even spent any time with her. You know how Bill is. I'm sure as hell he hasn't slept with her."

"They were lovers in a past life," Guy said.

I said, "You've *got* to be shitting me!"

"That's what Madam Stone says."

I suddenly got the giggles. I knew where that "lovers in a past life" stuff was coming from. Sharon had just read my script *Original Sin,* which was about two people who'd been lovers in a past life.

Sharon was talking about starring in it for her next movie.

She was, I thought, prematurely getting into the part.

Evans called next—as always, direct.

"Is Bill fucking Stone?"

"Not a chance," I said. "You know Bill."

"There are rumors all over the set. They're goony over each other."

"That part of it's possible."

"Did you introduce them?"

"Yes."

"That was brilliant, my boy. Do you think he can talk to her for me about this dog collar stuff?"

"Ask *him*, Bob. He works for *you*."

"If she's goony over him, maybe she'll listen."

Then Evans added, "Why would she be goony over the fuckin' *putz*. I don't get it."

Bill and I went shopping for Valentine's Day at Maxfield's on Melrose.

I bought Sharon a silver Chrome Hearts hash pipe.

Bill bought Sharon a silver signet ring.

I bought Bill a silver Chrome Hearts watch which I was going to surprise him with later.

Bill said that was all he was going to buy.

I said, "You've gotta buy Naomi something."

He said he didn't have any more money.

I paid for Naomi's gift from Bill. I even selected it: a silver broken heart on a leather cord.

I bought Gerri Eszterhas nothing.

The next day was the *Sliver* wrap party, to be held at the Roxbury, a Sunset Strip club. Bill met me at my hotel late in the afternoon. He was almost *eating* cigarettes and knocked down a triple vodka as soon as he came in.

"I'm in love with her," Bill said. He was upset, pacing the floor.

"Jesus Christ, man," I said, "you just married Naomi."

"I know it. She's coming to the wrap party."

"Of course she's coming to the wrap party. She's the star of the movie."

"No," he said, "Nomer."

"You're bringing Naomi to the wrap party? With Sharon there? With everybody on the set talking about you and Sharon? Are you out of your mind? Do you want to humiliate your wife?"

"I couldn't do anything about it. I tried to dissuade Nomer from coming, but she really wanted to come."

"Well, call her and tell her she can't come. Make up something."

"It's too late," he said, looking at his watch. "She's on her way from the Marina. She's meeting us here."

I said. "You can't let Naomi come to this party. Do you want to blow your own marriage?"

"Jesus, I know it," he said. "You're right. What the hell can I do?"

He slugged another vodka and sat down on the couch, his head in his hands.

So I thought up a cockeyed story about the threat of a lawsuit from MGM as a result of rumors about the formation of Renegade.

"Go downstairs," I said. "Wait for Naomi. Meet her when she comes in. Tell her this suit thing just came up and it's an emergency. Tell her we probably won't make it to the party either because we have to have a meeting at Guy's house."

"You're pretty good at this," he said as he left to go downstairs.

"I've had a lot of practice lying to my wife."

I watched them from the window of my suite as Bill gave Naomi the silver broken heart which I had selected and paid for.

I watched as Bill kissed her goodbye and as she drove away in her vintage Mercedes.

"God she looked beautiful," Bill said after he came back up. "I can't believe how beautiful she looked."

I agreed with him.

When I saw Sharon and Bill at the wrap party, I was happy I'd stopped him from bringing Naomi. They were all over each other, laughing, flirting, wrapped up in a little world of their own far away from everyone else.

"Lovebirds," Evans said, watching them. "Goony birds. She goes for *him* and she thinks *I'm* de Sade."

He was shaking his head in wonderment, finally permitted to be in Sharon's eyesight now that the shoot was over.

At that wrap party, Robert Evans went up to the woman who'd banned him from his own set and presented Sharon with a gleaming silver cross.

As he handed it to her, he denied once again keeping her model friend on a dog collar at his house and said he would pay Sharon $300,000 if she could prove that he had done it.

Sharon took the cross, but never answered Evans, turning all of her attentions on Bill.

As she walked away with Bill, Evans watched her sadly and said, "The cunt won't even talk to me!"

"Thank you," Sharon said to me while Bill was getting her a Perrier.

"For what?"

"For introducing us. You *knew* this would happen, didn't you?"

"How can anyone have known this was going to happen?"

"You *knew*." She smiled. She looked radiant. *"You created me."*

At that moment Bill came back with her Perrier and Sharon said, looking at him, "You created *us*."

Bill called me the next morning and said we had to talk. I was going back to Marin that afternoon. We met at the Four Seasons bar. He looked like he hadn't slept. His hands trembled as he lifted the vodka to his lips.

"I'm leaving Nomer," he told me.

I shook my head. "This is crazy."

"I'm getting a divorce."

"You've lost your mind," I said.

He smiled a little. "I know it," he said.

"You think you're in love with Sharon?" I said. "Fine. Have an affair with her, give it some time, see where it leads. But you don't have to leave your wife and get a divorce to do that."

"I can't just have an affair with her," he said.

"What do you mean you can't have an affair with her? That's the way it's done. People don't have lunch with somebody and then *five days later* say they're getting a divorce!"

"She won't sleep with me until I leave Nomer."

"What is that? One of the Ten Commandments?"

"She says it's her rule."

"Bill," I said, "she is an *actress*. She *acts*. That's what she does. She loves drama. She loves *scenes*."

"She's in love with me," he said. "I can't believe this. Sharon Stone is in love with me. *Me.* Bill Macdonald."

"She's in love with you but she won't sleep with you unless you dump your wife. What's Naomi? Some kind of sacrificial offering that has to be dropped at Sharon's feet before Sharon opens her legs?"

"*Come on.*" He was hurt. "Don't talk about her like that. You know how much Sharon likes you."

We sat without saying anything for a long moment.

"She's going to get me off cigarettes and booze," Bill said. "She's got an organic and healing approach to life. We were lovers in a past life, you know."

I couldn't help laughing. "I told you, she's an *actress*. She's reading you bad lines out of some New Age paperback one of her girlfriends bought her."

"I know you don't believe in past life stuff," Bill said, "but I do."

I shook my head and ordered another Bloody Mary.

"She'd be perfect for Renegade," Bill suddenly threw in.

"Bill," I said, "if I would have wanted to go into a business partnership with Sharon, don't you think I would've asked her?"

"Think about the headlines," he said. "Stone, Eszterhas, and Macdonald—in one production company. I've talked to her about it. She wants in."

"Well I don't want her in."

"She'd be terrific," Bill said. "You should hear her ideas about *Atlas Shrugged*."

Listening to Sharon Stone pontificating about Ayn Rand seemed like a vision of hell to me. I worried that Bill really had lost his mind. Maybe, I thought, whatever was wrong with Evans was communicable.

I looked at Bill. *This* was the guy I was going to go into a business partnership with?

"When are you going to tell Naomi?"

"I don't know," he said. "Today, tomorrow, the next day. Whenever I get my courage up."

"Jesus," I said, "you've been married *five months*, and *five days* after you have lunch with Sharon you leave your wife."

"The only reason I married Nomer," Bill Macdonald said, "is because our dog died in a fire."

The Sheriff

His dad was a big macho TV star, always playing cowboys, cops, or soldiers, living it in his personal life, too: the big ranch, the horses, the gun collection, the vintage pickup trucks, Mexican spurs, silver-inlaid saddles.

He was his father's first child and idolized him, although it was mostly the image of his father he idolized since he saw his father more on television than in real life. His dad was on his fourth marriage now and the father of little kids and he sometimes felt very out of place at his father's house on Thanksgiving or at Christmas, a big, hulking twenty-seven-year-old playing on the floor with kids who were young enough to be his and not his father's children.

He worried what his father thought about him. He was still taking acting lessons but wasn't really getting any real parts, even with his dad's agent's help. He vaguely had his father's looks but lacked his father's swagger, his "Don't fuck with me 'cause if you do I'm gonna fuck you up bad" style.

The only thing about himself, he knew, that really pleased his dad was that he had gotten a job as a part-time, mostly weekend, sheriff's deputy in the Valley. He could tell that when his dad looked at him wearing his yellow slicker with Sheriff's Department on the back, or when his dad saw him in his sheriff's uniform wearing his gun, his dad was really proud of him.

"My kid's a sheriff's deputy," he could imagine his father bragging to one of his old drinking buddies, usually stuntmen or the Teamsters who drove him to his sets, "nobody fucks with him."

He didn't tell his dad that the reason he had gotten the sheriff's job was that the *personnel people had recognized his father's name. He didn't tell his dad that he wasn't allowed out of the office; he sat there on weekends in his uniform, wearing his weapon on his hip, in front of a computer all day, while the other guys in the office asked him questions about his dad, his dad's TV shows, his dad's wives, and the women his dad had dated.*

CHAPTER 20

[Naomi's Journal]

Industry Dirt

TEDDY
You played me. You played me so well.

JACK
No!

TEDDY
You set me up from the very beginning.

Jagged Edge

April 6, 1993

How do I begin to explain the events which have brought me to this point? I'm on a plane bound for Hawaii with Joe and Gerri Eszterhas, friends who have reached in and pulled me from the burning structure that has become my life.

I will begin with February 17, the anniversary of my mother's death, the day a part of me died.

The day before Bill had come home anxious and depressed. He said it was because of this vicious and awful movie business. I tried to encourage him but he went to sleep without saying very much. He looked so disturbed.

As I waited for him to come home on February 17, I felt a great sadness. My mother's memory was with me all that day and her absence was so pervasive.

Bill was late as he had been all week and I called him in the Jeep. He said he'd had a horrible day.

"Is it Renegade?" I asked. He said no.

Finally, in tears, he said, "It's us."

He said, "I'm in love with someone else."

I said, "Sharon Stone?"

"Yes," he said. "She went to a psychic who told her we were lovers in a previous life. She broke up with Charlie Peters for me."

I said, "I thought you were happy the day we got married."

He said, "It was the happiest day of my life."

He said he was confused, that he needed time, that he couldn't live without me in his life, that it was the saddest day of his life. He asked me if I would give him two months to sort his feelings out.

I asked if he had slept with Sharon.

He said he hadn't because he didn't want to "dishonor" me.

He said that Joe and Gerri had known for days that he was in love with Sharon.

The next day I told my older brother Bernie I was going to fly back to Ohio. I didn't tell him why.

As I waited for Bill to come home from the office, I decided that we would not spend this night in tears. I cooked a beautiful dinner, dressed beautifully, and tried to put on a bright face.

Just before Bill came home, I called Gerri Eszterhas.

What I learned from Gerri is that, in fact, Sharon had given him an ultimatum: "You can't touch me until either she or you are out of the house."

I learned that Guy McElwaine, whom I'd never met, and Joe had tried to talk Bill out of walking away from a ten-year relationship for a woman he hardly knew and had never slept with.

When Bill got home I told him what I'd learned. He denied that Sharon had given him an ultimatum. I *wanted* to believe him but I knew that Gerri had told me the truth.

In the morning, as the reality sank in, I said, "I'm scared."

And he said, "Me too."

He asked that I please give him the two months to sort out his feelings and I named one condition.

"I'll give you the two months if you promise me you won't see her for just ten days. Soul-search for ten days. Give me some consideration. Think everything over for ten days before you see her."

His eyes filled with tears and he hugged me hard. "I promise," he said.

I held up my chin and headed to Ohio.

That was a Friday morning. What I learned subsequently was that after I left, Bill told everyone, including and especially Sharon, that I had moved to Ohio, that we were getting a divorce, and that we were over.

He told friends that the night before I left—the night I dressed up and made a special dinner—I had mixed up a bunch of barbiturates in a cocktail and was threatening to drink it. He said I was suicidal.

When I left that morning, he had promised me the ten days I had asked him for.

What I learned later is that that same night he took Sharon to see a movie we had planned to see and he took her in my car, not his . . . my old vintage Mercedes.

I couldn't pick up a magazine in Ohio without seeing Sharon Stone on the cover. My brother Bernie and his wife, Joyce, tried to keep my spirits up.

"Nobody has a successful marriage in Hollywood," Bernie said.

I said, "My friends Joe and Gerri Eszterhas do."

And then I found out why I was having such severe cramps. While Bernie and Joyce were at work, I took a cab to a nearby clinic. There I discovered I was experiencing a "precarious pregnancy." I was four weeks pregnant.

I asked, "Could you please put that in writing?"

And the doctor said, "For insurance purposes?"

And I said, "No. For my husband."

I told no one. I told Bernie I was going home. I prayed. I got on a plane and arrived in L.A. on a Wednesday night.

Bill wasn't there. I knew where he was.

I sent the dog sitter home and spent the night curled up next to our dog, Jake.

The next morning I called Bill in his Jeep. As I

guessed, he was on his way to work at the Robert Evans Company.

I told him I was back in L.A. and it was urgent that I speak to him.

When he walked in the door I said, "I asked you to give me ten days to think of me and what I meant to you. I gave you ten years, I asked for ten days, and you didn't even give me ten minutes."

He said nothing and looked down at his feet.

Then I showed him the note from the doctor.

He paced back and forth, talking to himself.

"I've got to call Sharon," he suddenly said.

When he came out of the bedroom I said, "What did Sharon say?"

"She said, 'Well, this certainly adds a whole new twist to things.' "

The next twenty-four hours were grueling. He said he knew he was destroying me and destroying himself. He said he was probably destroying his career, too, all for a woman "who probably doesn't give a shit about me."

He crawled around on the floor, putting his head in his hands, telling me he never wanted to hurt me and that he'd rather be dead.

Yet he kept talking to Sharon. She would call or he would call her.

She wanted to know why he hadn't packed his things and left.

At one point, I sat in cramped pain by the fireplace in the living room while he spent nearly forty minutes in the bedroom on the phone.

When he came out I asked, "What did she say?"

And he said, "She said, 'Are *you* the only person she can talk to about this? Doesn't she have any friends she can call?' "

I realized that, besides cramping badly, I must also have managed to catch my little nephew's strep throat in Ohio.

In between the bouts of tears, I felt my throat closing. I welcomed the physical pain. It was a throbbing distraction from my emotional hurt.

Bill told me he adored me. He told me I was beautiful. He told me he was still very physically attracted to me.

He told me *I* was his soul mate, that he couldn't live without me.

And he told me he couldn't stay with me.

"The reality is, Nomer," he said, "I don't deserve you."

At some point during this endless evening, something in me began to protect *me*. I heard these awful hurtful things yet I no longer felt them.

I asked him—"What are you saying—that I should get rid of the baby?"

And he said, "Maybe that would be best."

I saw his lips move, but what came out . . . . crushed me.

He finally said, "I can't take this anymore, I have to leave," and he walked out and went to Sharon's house.

I was cramping badly and my throat ached and my heart was broken.

I called Jeremy, my little brother, who worked in L.A. in public relations.

I hadn't told him anything was wrong with my marriage.

I asked him to come and get me.

"Jeremy," I said, "Bill is in love with Sharon Stone. He's leaving."

He didn't know what to say.

He was there very quickly.

As he drove I told my little brother in a numb monotone of the events that had transpired.

As I told him, I remembered one of the most hurtful things Bill had said to me that night, *"Don't I deserve to love someone as much as you love me?"*

Jeremy took me to a clinic the next day. My throat was nearly closed and my stomach cramps were worse. I discovered that I had strep throat. And I discovered that I had lost the baby.

I went back to stay at Jeremy's apartment and Carl, a friend of Bill's, came to see me. He was very upset about what had happened. He had known both of us for a long time.

He said that Bill was sitting calmly by our fireplace amidst the boxes I had packed and he said, "You know, Carl,

this is very Machiavellian. I have Joe Eszterhas in my
pocket, I have Sharon Stone, I *own* Paramount."

Then Bill said, "But, you know, I'm really worried.
Nomer worked so hard to clear up my credit rating, and now
all these bills are coming in and no one's keeping the books
and I'm afraid my credit is going to get screwed up again."

The day after I returned to our apartment, a friend called.
She is an actress and always privy to "industry dirt."

She said, "I heard."

I said, "About Sharon and Bill?"

And she said, "Last Saturday a friend of mine went to a
huge party in L.A. and she told me Sharon Stone was there
with her new boyfriend. She said he was married but was
dumping his wife for Sharon. When I asked her his name, she
said 'Bill Macdonald' and I almost fainted. Since then I've
heard that you're pregnant and that you've tried to kill
yourself."

One morning after about a week at home, Carl called. He
said, "Bill called me and asked me if you were spreading
rumors about town."

I said, "Me? Why would I say I'm suicidal? That's the
only rumor I've heard."

Carl said, "He's such a coward. He wanted me to ask you
about it, but I told him he'd have to call you himself."

An hour later Bill called.

He said, "Are you going to be home later? I want to come
over and talk to you about all these rumors I've been hearing. They're not true."

He arrived promptly. He gave me a very awkward hug and
said, "That's a nice top."

"I bought it for the *Sliver* wrap party."

He said, "You look really pretty. Your teeth are so
white."

I said, "My teeth have always been white."

He said, "I want to talk about these rumors."

"Good. I've been hearing I'm threatening to drink barbiturate cocktails."

"That's ridiculous," he said. "We don't have anything in
the house stronger than aspirin."

. . .

He handed me some papers.

I asked, "What's this?"

"They're dissolution of marriage papers that my attorneys drafted."

He asked me to take my time over the weekend and read them.

"I won't cheat you, Nomer," he said.

Then he said, "We have to get our story straight to the press."

"What do you mean?"

"We have to decide what story we want to tell publicly."

"Why don't we just tell the truth?" I said. "So many people already know the truth."

"Yes, but people only believe what they read."

I said, "What story would you like me to tell?"

"Why don't we say that you decided you didn't like the movie business, that I was never home and you were unhappy and you left me."

"*I* left *you*?" I said.

He said, "It's just that Sharon is afraid that this will hurt her career. And I don't want to end up looking like Mr. Stone."

I said, "I'm not going to lie to protect Sharon Stone."

He asked me to please think about changing my story—to protect *myself.* He told me I should sign the dissolution papers—to protect *myself.*

"Protect *myself?*" I said, "I haven't done anything."

He said, "Can you imagine if it gets out that I'm living with Sharon and you don't even have a formal separation? It'll be embarrassing."

"I'm willing to endure the humiliation," I said. "I have so far."

He shrugged and said, "Chances are the press won't call *you* anyway."

He said he'd call me on Sunday to see what I'd decided. As he walked to the door, he paused and asked, "What are you doing tonight? Do you have plans?"

I said yes.

"Where are you going?"

I said I was going to an art show.

He asked if I was going with this person . . . or this person . . . or that person.

I said, "What does it matter, Bill?"

He put his head down and said, "Okay."

Then he walked to the elevator and turned and said, "Who are you going with? *Tell me.*"

I didn't want to tell him I was going alone.

"I guess I can't ask you that anymore, can I?" he said.

"No."

He looked lost. He lingered still as he held the elevator door open and then as I closed my door, he quickly ducked into the elevator.

A few days later, I was home alone, fixing myself a sandwich. I couldn't remember the last time that I'd eaten.

Just as I finished making it, the phone rang. It was a woman from the Paramount Pictures publicity department.

She said, "We've just learned that Sharon is going to announce her engagement to Bill on the Barbara Walters special after the Academy Awards.

"Since we're handling Sharon's publicity, we thought we might be able to handle any media calls for you."

I hung up and gave Jake the sandwich.

Bill was on the Barbara Walters special. He was introduced as Sharon Stone's new fiancé.

He didn't even know who she was the first time I mentioned her. After we saw *Total Recall* I said to him, "That woman is going to be a big star." He said, "Who?" I said, "Sharon Stone." He said, "Which one was she?"

Then she did a black-and-white nude pictorial in *Playboy,* which Bill never reads and I subscribe to. I showed him the pictures. "Remember her? From *Total Recall*?" He barely glanced at them. "Yeah, I guess," he said.

Then she was the lead in *Basic Instinct.* Bill wasn't interested in seeing it, so I went without him. Afterward I told him, "You should see it." He said he would see it when it came out on video.

Next came her *Playboy* interview. I was reading it in bed and kept reading parts of it aloud to Bill. I saved the interview for him. I put it on his nightstand, but he never picked it up.

After she was cast as the lead in *Sliver,* I said, "Hey— maybe you'll get to meet Sharon Stone . . ."

One day he came home and said, "I finally met Sharon."

I said, "What's she like?"

He said, "I think she liked my tie."

I went out and bought him some new Hermès ties.

And now she's his fiancée and I'm his wife.

Clash of the Super-Studs

Renata was the girl who got away, the girl Evans didn't like to talk about.
She was a German model. She was one of Evans's girls, staying in Evans's house, which was where, at a party, she met Eddie Fisher.

This was years back, when neither Evans nor Eddie were golden agers.

Eddie met Renata and lightning struck. True love. Roomsful of roses. The whole Hollywood schmeer.

Evans was pissed. He was a legendary Hollywood super-stud and he wasn't going to let Eddie, this other legendary Hollywood super-stud, take her.

Evans proposed a duel on his tennis court at dawn. A real, old-time cinematic duel. With real guns!

Eddie was game, but Renata, even though she was German, didn't like violence.

And: she suddenly decided she was in love with Evans, not Eddie. Lightning struck again. Roomfuls of roses. The whole Hollywood schmeer.

Evans flew her to New York and away from Eddie. Evans flew her two dogs, which Eddie had given her, to New York, too. Evans even flew her blind cat, which she had found wandering around Beverly Hills, to New York.

But . . . away from Eddie . . . Renata missed him.

And: Renata suddenly decided she was in love with Eddie, not Evans. Lightning struck again. Blah blah blah.

Eddie flew her to Vegas and away from Evans. Eddie flew her two dogs and her blind cat and blah blah blah blah blah.

Renata started to gamble in Vegas. She couldn't lose. She won thousands of dollars.

And: she decided she was in love with neither Eddie nor Evans.

She flew back to Hamburg with her two dogs and her blind cat. She built her mother a beautiful house.

And: away from both Evans and Eddie, Renata was happy.

CHAPTER 21

Tabloids and Flailing Scissors

FRANK

You're fucking my wife?

JEREMY

Of course I am.

FRANK

I'm gonna kill you!

JEREMY

Frank, Frank—this kinda stuff happens, okay?

Male Pattern Baldness, unproduced

When I went back to Marin from L.A. and told Gerri that Bill was divorcing Naomi, she got hysterically upset. She called Sharon a witch and a demon and said Sharon had wrapped both Bill and me around her little finger.

I knew how close Gerri felt to Naomi, but I knew, as she carried on, that it was more than just that.

My relationship with Gerri had been strained for some time. We had grown apart as Steve and Suzi had grown up. As I watched my wife of twenty-four years now, she was raging, it seemed to me, not just about Bill's betrayal of Naomi but of her own husband's intimate betrayals that played themselves out in one-night stands and painful morning-afters (never discussed, never mentioned).

When Gerri flailed at me with a pair of scissors, just missing my face, I saw the shape she was in. Gerri was a strong woman, not prone to hysterics. I suggested professional help and she snapped at me that she didn't need it. She'd frightened me with the scissors. I didn't know what to do to try to calm her down. I finally booked a suite for the two of us, without the kids, at the Kahala Hilton on Oahu, where we'd spent so many happy times as a family.

Our second day there, over breakfast, Gerri suddenly said, "You're screwing around on me, aren't you, Joseph?"

I looked at her. Her eyes were red. She looked like she'd been crying all night. It was the one question she'd never asked me in twenty-four years.

"Please don't ask me that," I said. "I'm not going to lie to you. The answer to that question doesn't have anything to do with my affection for you or with our marriage."

She told me that she knew. She told me that she'd had a vision "beamed to her from L.A." by Sharon Stone.

She saw me making love in this vision to a woman with short blond hair. Then, Gerri said, the woman turned so she could see her face. It was Sharon.

"My God, Gerri," I said. "Sharon and I are friends."

"You're lying to me, Joseph," she said. "She's a demon. You took her body and she took your soul."

We went back to Marin County and Gerri kept it up about demons and witches and Sharon. She bought a collection of books about witchcraft and spent long hours underlining them.

I remembered my mother ranting at my father and me when I was a boy, calling us *"Ördögök!"*—Devils!

As I watched Gerri alternate between tears and rage . . . we somehow kept it from Steve and Suzi, now eighteen and sixteen, busy with their teenage social lives . . . I realized that my personal life had turned into a nightmare.

On any intimate level, my marriage had been dead for a very long time. Whatever brief solace I had found with women in bars and clubs was illusory and meaningless.

Wanting to escape and think, I flew down to L.A., where there were problems with *Sliver*, which was still in the editing room.

Phillip Noyce's cut of my script, a word-for-word shoot, had been tested by the market research people and found to be lacking.

The studio had decreed a rewrite and reshoots. Noyce, who believed in the script, was aghast at the studio's "suggestions."

But he agreed to make the studio's changes. Evans viewed the market research failure of the movie as his personal triumph. He was working around-the-clock on his *own* cut as well as his *own* musical score (*Love Story*–like).

Evans was going to be the hero now. Evans was going to "*save*" *Sliver*.

Stanley Jaffe was the head of the studio at Paramount and his son, Bobby, a nice young man, was a vice president of production.

Bobby was going to London on business and he wanted to get laid there so Stanley Jaffe asked Evans to set it up for him.

Evans called me, nearly crying. "This is what my life has come to," he said, "getting the boss's son laid."

What was he going to do? I asked.

No problem, said Evans. He had called his friend Heidi Fleiss, the famous madam, who had called her friend the financier Bernie Cornfield in London and Bobby Jaffe was all set.

"In like Flynn," Evans said.

The studio was aswirl with stories of Sharon and Bill. They were tabloid fodder now. Bill had moved in with Sharon and was accompanying her everywhere. He looked trapped in the headlights to me—in Paris, in Rome, in Vegas.

A friend had sat next to them at an exhibitors convention in Vegas. "Bill came in a little late. Sharon looked at him and said, '*Change that tie*.' He didn't say a word, just went upstairs and reappeared with a new tie."

At the same time, Sharon was telling the *Star:* "He is square, square, square. I love it. He's really macho with a deep voice. It gives me such a thrill that he's so square after all these really hip guys with their waist-length hair and their mellow artistic temperaments. Give me my macho, old-fashioned square boyfriend who says 'Come here' and I do—because it'll be good when I get there. Last weekend my boyfriend just said, 'You're done working weekends. You're not doing more than two pictures a year.' The point is, he can take charge. There's a bit of tension there, and I like that. At this point in my life, no one is going to take control of me. The point is finding somebody over whom I don't have *complete* control."

While Sharon was talking to the *Star,* Bill's seventy-five-year-old mother, Jane, who lived north of Los Angeles in Ojai, was talking to the *National Enquirer*. The *Enquirer* ran the story under a headline that said: "SHARON STONE IS A SLUT WHO COULD GIVE MY BOY AIDS."

I went back to Marin. Gerri called Naomi in L.A. and asked her to come up and "hide out" at our house if she wanted to.

Naomi was being besieged by paparazzi. One of them had even tried to pay her dog sitter off for a photograph.

Gerri handed me the phone and I urged Naomi to come up to see us. She sounded devastated. I knew, though, that she had a great sense of humor and I thought I detected it when she mock-berated me.

"I blame you for all of this," Naomi said. "She never would've been in *Sliver* had you not written *Basic*. This is all your fault."

I knew that Gerri and Naomi had become good friends and hoped that her presence would brighten Gerri a bit. And then there was the bottom line: life in our house these days, with problems out in the open now between Gerri and me, was bleak.

I liked being around Naomi. She made me smile.

As Naomi and Gerri spent their days together, I tried to work on the rewrite the studio was insisting upon.

Evans sent me a case of scented candles for inspiration.

I kept thinking about how Ira Levin, a writer I admired, would feel when he saw the movie . . . he had called to praise and thank me when he'd read my first draft, now about to be obliterated.

Naomi and I, always in Gerri's company, were seeing a lot of each other.

Gerri, I thought, was lightening up a little. She even started laughing at herself one day when she was reading aloud from a witchcraft book and drawing analogies to Sharon.

I told Naomi I gave the relationship between Sharon and Bill six months. We were already hearing stories, through Guy, still Sharon's agent, of divalike hotel rampages and smashed table lamps.

When Sharon discovered, I said, that Bill owned no Texas ranch, that there was no offshore fortune, that General Douglas MacArthur was not in the family, that Bill's old-money Armani and Bohemian Grove act . . . was an *act* . . . it would be the final curtain.

One day while Naomi was staying in Tiburon with us, Gerri and I drove her out to a fisherman's restaurant called the Tides on the coast in Bodega Bay.

Naomi and I smoked a joint in the car on the way back . . . and Gerri offered to drive while the two of us giggled at nothing like loons.

There was a Beatles tape on in the car and we heard the song called "Don't Let Me Down."

"Play that—" I said, and Naomi hit the button again before I even finished the sentence.

We played that song over and over again until we got to Tiburon.

Gerri said, "I don't know why you guys like that song so much."

On another night in Tiburon, all three of us had smoked a joint and Naomi told us how, after Bill had met Sharon, Naomi had given Bill a nice new tie for Bill's next meeting with her.

"Freud would say," I began, "that you wanted Bill to look nice for Sharon, that you subconsciously wanted out of your relationship with Bill and wanted to palm him off on Sharon."

"*Oh, Freud!*" Gerri suddenly said. "I'm so tired hearing about Freud from you! Fuck Freud! That's what I say! *Fuck Freud!*"

Naomi and I, sky-high, started to laugh and couldn't stop as Gerri went into a full rant:

"Joseph and his Freud! You have no idea how tired I am of hearing about him! *What would Freud say?* Who cares? Nobody cares! *Nobody cares,* Joseph! Fuck Freud!"

After a while Gerri started to laugh, too, and soon she was laughing harder than we were. Suzi came down from her room and saw us laughing like idiots.

"You guys are sure having fun!" Suzi said, and she started to laugh, too.

Gerri and I and Steve and Suzi and two of their friends had a spring vacation trip planned to Maui in a week and Gerri asked me if we could invite Naomi along.

We were both enjoying her presence. She was lightening the gravity of our marital problems, the kids liked her very much, so I agreed.

Naomi didn't want to come.

I knew what she meant. We were having *too much fun* together, even though it was always in Gerri's company.

We had too much to talk about, we had too many things in common . . . Ohio and reading and music and ethnic backgrounds . . . and even Evans.

For all those reasons, Naomi didn't want to come . . . but I convinced her.

Gerri, meanwhile, was confiding in Naomi like she'd never confided in any other friend. She told her how unhappy she had been in our marriage for a long time. She told her how she should have stayed in Lorain, the small Ohio town where she grew up. And she talked over and over again about Sharon Stone being a demon.

Naomi told her Sharon Stone was not a demon . . . just a woman who happened to have fallen in love with Naomi's husband. And she told Gerri that *I* was *her* husband and that Gerri should stop railing at me about infidelities real or imagined.

I felt Gerri was feeling much better (and so, I thought, was Naomi) and I went back down to L.A. to have what turned out to be my final meetings over *Sliver*.

Evans, looking reborn, racing around in a White House cap given to him by Marlin Fitzwater, was trumpeting his own cut.

Noyce, unshaven and haggard, looked like he'd eaten some poisonous mushrooms.

Stanley Jaffe, the head of the studio, perhaps sensing that his days at Paramount were numbered, looked like he needed an IV of Maalox.

Tom Berenger, awaiting the reshoot, was taking swigs off a bottle of vodka in his trailer.

And Sharon and Bill were off somewhere in Tabloid Nirvana, paparazzi in hot pursuit.

I told Evans and Noyce and the studio that I was going to Maui. Lots of luck on the reshoot, guys, but I was gone.

Phillip Noyce, a hangdog and forlorn sadness in his eyes, said, "You, too, mate. You have abandoned me, too."

Bill Macdonald appeared in Guy McElwaine's office.

"Evans," Bill said, "will have Sharon killed if she doesn't support Evans's cut of the movie over Noyce's."

Bill told Guy that he knew for a fact that Evans had already had three people murdered.

Guy knew it was bullshit. Everyone who knew Evans knew that Evans was the devil, but everyone also knew that he was incapable of ordering the murder of anyone. Evans was the devil with a heart: Lucifer Sweet.

"If what you're saying is true," Guy said to Bill, "put your allegations into writing. Then I can present it to the FBI and the powers at Paramount."

Bill, of course, never put it into writing.

But Sharon walked into studio head Stanley Jaffe's office and told him what Bill had told Guy . . . and added that she was afraid for her life.

Stanley Jaffe knew, too, that Evans wasn't a murderer . . . knew better than anyone probably because Bob was the godfather of one of his children.

But Stanley called Bob in to tell him what Sharon had said Bill had told her about him.

Evans collapsed and was rushed to Cedars Sinai. It seemed at first to be a massive coronary, but it wasn't . . . only Bob's blood pressure, sky-high, out of control.

Naomi, meanwhile, started talking to the press. She talked about how she had lost her baby. She talked about how Sharon had gone to a psychic to learn that she and Bill were lovers in a past life . . . about how Sharon had given Bill the ultimatum about not sleeping with him until they had broken up . . . about Bill asking her to "get their stories straight" for the press so Sharon wouldn't be embarrassed.

The tabloids went bonkers, her story blew up around the world, and Sharon Stone was an international home wrecker.

The headlines said, "SHARON STONE STOLE MY HUBBY . . . HEART OF STONE . . . STONE-COLD . . . JILTED BRIDE CASTS A STONE . . . ANGUISH OF BRIDE JILTED FOR SEX SIREN." The *Boston Herald* headlined, "NEWLYWED SAYS SHE MISCARRIED AFTER STONE STOLE HUBBY" and *USA Today* said, "FIANCE'S EX ON THE HEART OF STONE." The *London Sun* used an old nude photo of Sharon on her hands and knees on the front page and bannered: "SHARON STONE COST ME MY BABY!"

. . .

I was in my last *Sliver* meeting at Paramount with a roomful of executives and they were talking about the new ending to the movie.

Someone suggested that the villain go down in a bloody hail of bullets and then someone mentioned Naomi and the potential damage of Sharon being known worldwide as a "home wrecker."

"That's it," Stanley Jaffe said sardonically. "We've got our new ending. Sharon's career is over anyway. We shoot the bitch."

Word of the film's problems had leaked to the press, as evidenced by a Richard Johnson column from the *New York Daily News*. Talking about her interview with Barbara Walters, Johnson wrote: "Stone talks about her affair with Macdonald in the interview she taped for the Oscar night special. Why would she go public? Word in Hollywood is that *Sliver* isn't doing too well with test audiences and that the decision was made to help it out with *even this* kind of publicity."

When I got back to Tiburon, only a few days away from leaving for Maui, I saw that my hope that Gerri's condition was improving was false.

I was sitting in my downstairs den, reading. Gerri had gone out for a walk. She came bursting through the door, sweated and hysterical, and threw the car keys at me.

She was yelling . . . she was sorry she'd ever met me . . . I'd ruined her life . . . she had nothing in her life, I had all the friends and all the glory. She hated . . . California . . . Hollywood . . . herself . . . me.

She started knocking things off desks and counters, taking books off shelves and throwing them at me. She was crying, in a blind and furious rage. I tried to calm her down. I talked about Steve and Suzi, our two beautiful kids (who, luckily, were out of the house), about the good times we had shared in our twenty-four years of marriage.

I was crying now, too, trying to calm her, but nothing worked. She was laying waste to the den, which contained the mementos of thirty years of writing.

As she was going through the bookshelves, ripping and tearing at the books I had collected and loved so much, I ran upstairs to find Naomi, who was somewhere in the house.

I asked her if she could try to help Gerri and ran to the phone to call a doctor friend. He was at the house ten minutes later and found Gerri sobbing and hysterical, holding on to Naomi.

He forced Gerri to take two Valiums and she drifted off to sleep in the den.

I went up to the kitchen, poured myself a stiff drink, and sat at our hammered wooden monk's table, not able to stop my tears.

Naomi came up after a while, poured herself a drink, too, and I noticed she was also crying.

We sat there for a long time sipping our drinks, not saying anything. She asked me if I was hungry and she made fried bologna sandwiches with pickles and mayonnaise, the kind I used to eat when I was a kid growing up in Cleveland.

We ate our sandwiches in silence and I suddenly turned and looked at her and said, "Do you want to come to Mars with me and play?"

She smiled at me and I put my hand on hers. She took my hand and held it. It was the first time that I'd touched her.

We didn't look at each other; we stared out the big picture window at the bay.

We sipped another drink, holding hands in the kitchen, saying nothing to each other.

She got up and went upstairs and I sat at the kitchen table, staring out the window.

I knew my marriage was over. It had been over for a long time and Gerri and I had swept its death under the rug for the sake of Steve and Suzi. We had dodged the truth for too many years, but Steve and Suzi were grown now, leading their own lives, mostly gone from the house. Gerri and I were left there, alone, with the death of our relationship between us.

Gerri came up from the den as I sat at the kitchen table. She was still crying, but they were tears of heart-wrenching sadness, no longer tears of rage.

"I'm so sorry," she kept saying, "I'm so sorry, Joseph. It's my fault. I know it's my fault. I'm so sorry."

"It's not," I said as I held her. "It's not, Gerri. It's my fault, forgive me."

That night, as we were falling asleep, Gerri said to me, "Naomi's the perfect woman for you. She's the one you should have married."

I said, "Please stop this," then I put my arm around her, pulled Gerri close to me, and kissed her forehead.

She turned away from me.

I turned the other way and fell asleep listening to my wife crying.

The Girlie Girl

Michi was twenty-two years old. I met her at Bob Evans's house in Beverly Hills. She lived either at Bob's or at an apartment she sometimes shared with her mother in West Hollywood. She was an "actress-model."

I knew it was going to be such a good day. Bob was at the Carlyle in New York talking to Liz Smith and there wasn't anybody in the house except for Ali, who was in the guesthouse sleeping in.

Mom called and said Ferdy was giving her the limo. Ferdy was another big mucky-muck producer. Mom said she was going to take me out to lunch at the Grille so I did some girlie things and painted myself up for the longest time and by the time Mom showed up in Ferdy's big white stretch I was ready. I had that little red skirt on that Bob got me from Fred Heyman's for my birthday with the sparklers on it. Nothing tacky, not Vegas or even Palm Springs sparklers, just little ones. Cool. Retro.

We went to the Grille but first we stopped off on Melrose because Mom wanted to get Alan an old tie. Alan is the maître d' there and he always gives Mom and me a great table and he collects old ties.

Mom looked great. Honest to God, you can't tell she's forty—you can't even tell she's my mom, a lot of people think she's my older sister. She was wearing a little nothing of a sunflower dress from Chanel and she had the Chanel backpack that Ferdy gave her for Christmas and the Cellini Rolex that was inside the backpack when she got it.

She was in a great mood. She said Ferdy was going to take her to the Hôtel du Cap for a month because he was down in the dumps and had to get away. David's suicide really got to Ferdy, the way David did it and all, just checking into the Century Plaza and doing it. The Century Plaza! Not even a bungalow at the Beverly Hills or the Chateau Marmont, the

Chateau would have been the really cool place for it, but the Century Plaza with all those Japanese tourists—tacky!

We had the steak tartare at the Grille with their cucumber salad and three margaritas. The only other place I'd ever have the tartare is at Le Dome, but the one at the Grille is spicier, I think they use more mustard. Alan loved his tie and we saw a bunch of people. Don Johnson was there with this amazing tan and smoking a big cigar and he gave me the eye and a wink when he was leaving. Anytime! Any-old-time! Mom saw him wink but didn't say anything, probably because there was no doubt he was winking at me. I wish Bob would have Don over to the house instead of the old guys, but Warren would probably have a coronary. Don looks way too good.

Mike Ovitz was there. I've never met him and neither has Mom but I think he's pretty cool. People sort of stop talking when he walks by and watch him. He'll never come over to the house, though, that's for sure. I hear he's not like that . . . the word gets out sooner or later on everybody . . . and he doesn't like Bob, at least that's what Bob says.

It has something to do with some money that Bob owes him on a commission that Bob didn't pay him a long time ago. Last year Bob got all nervous about Mike Ovitz not liking him so he sent him a letter apologizing for not having paid him . . . with the money he owed him enclosed in the letter. Mike Ovitz sent the check back torn up in little pieces. Bob was sitting there in the screening room with this torn-up check in his hand, bawling like a baby. I sort of think on the one hand it's cool to send a check back torn up like that, but on the other hand Bob has enough problems without having Mike Ovitz do him like that.

Pretty soon Mom got a little high on the margaritas and started crying about how she could have been a really good actress—not crying with her eyes, she wouldn't ever want to ruin her makeup, but crying with her mouth—and that led her into crying about how Ferdy was never going to marry her. She was afraid she was going to find him dead in bed next to her one morning or out on the bathroom floor wearing his glasses like Don Simpson. And she was afraid she'd kill him in bed, although I know they don't hardly ever do anything directly together. If that happened, Mom said, we'd be back living at the Sunset Hyatt like we did after we got here from England.

I said to Mom that wasn't so bad . . . I remember the Sunset Hyatt and all the speed . . . I was thirteen then . . . and she said it wasn't so bad for you because it was so bad for me. I said what does that mean? And she said well, because it was so bad for me made it possible for it not to be so bad for you. And I said—Oh, you mean that record company guy you were seeing who was always putting his hands on me? She said—He was just one aspect of it.

That made me laugh. Mom sometimes has this English accent she picked up from the time we were in England after we left Crete and the way she said "Ass-pect" was funny.

She asked me about how the party was with Helmut. Ferdy decided at the last minute that he wasn't strong enough for it so poor Mom couldn't come. I told her Helmut took some more pictures of me and Mom said— Like what? And I said—You know. Mom didn't like that. She didn't say anything for a while and then she said what I should do is see Ferdy's attorney, she could fix it up for me, and see if I can get a piece of the money Helmut makes off the pictures.

If he gets a piece of you, at least you should get a piece of him, Mom said and I said—All he does is take my picture.

Sometimes I think about Helmut's pictures of me, though, and I think—Jeez, some guy somewhere is using up a lot of Kleenex and getting off on me big time and I'm not getting off and I'm not getting paid for it, I'm just ordering more candles for Bob's bedroom or doing the other stuff Bob likes me to do.

We were both starting to get a little down from talking like that, blue, or at least chartreuse, so it was either sitting there slugging more marga- ritas or doing something so we decided to do something and get our hair done. The limo took us down the block to Christophe—José Eber was closer, but nobody goes there anymore—and we were lucky, Cici squeezed us in and made poor Joanna Pacula wait. (That's all she's doing these days anyway, waiting, she even waits around at Bob's house a lot.)

Cici is so great! Both Mom and I got more highlights, but the thing that's greatest about Cici is that she doesn't use that tinfoil stuff that takes hours and makes you feel like a geek. She's an artist, Cici, she paints you the way a famous painter would with these little brushes and when you leave you look like you've just spent a week on Maui.

Cici is so cute, I just love her! She's got a friend who's dating one of the guys in Mötley Crüe and her friend met Pamela Lee and Cici says Pamela Lee gave her friend a pair of plastic pants that are unreal and Mom and I went "Plastic pants!" And we all decided we've got to get some. Cici knows everybody and she said Keanu was in the other day for a trim with Barret and Cici said the way Keanu was looking at her she was sure that all that Geffen stuff was shit.

Mom and I walked out of there feeling great! I just love my hair when I've been out in the sun and Mom told the driver to take us over to Neiman's because she wanted to get a surprise for me. She took me over to

Kieselstein-Cord inside and picked out this amazing cross in black gold that is so cool. It's a regular cross, but it's got all these like African or Egyptian women on it instead of any bleeding body. She bought herself one, too, and gave the guy Ferdy's platinum card.

She wanted me to go over with her to say hi to Ferdy and I didn't want to for the usual reason but she said nothing was going to happen and Ferdy was asking about me and maybe I could cheer him up a little. I said—Oh, God, Mom . . . but we'd had such a great day and it was such a cool cross that I said okay.

When we got to Ferdy's I had my cross on but Mom had hers in her purse and said she'd put it on later. Ferdy was sitting in the living room with about six monstro lines of coke laid out in front of him and wearing his pajamas. He looked terrible, the way he always does—fat, pale, sweaty, his hair gone, jowls gray and like sunken down.

Jennifer was sitting there doing the lines with him. I could see right away how Mom was pissed off when she saw Jennifer there with him. Jennifer is younger than Mom but I don't think she's as pretty.

Ferdy is trying to be cool with the whole thing—"Michelle, sweetheart! Aren't you looking beautiful!" And his usual jive. All Jennifer does is wet her lips with her tongue and sniffle her nose. I've never liked Jennifer. Every time she comes to Bob's all she wants are downers and she acts so high and mighty hippity hop. Give me a break! She used to be in Khashoggi's harem turning tricks with Arabs. She may be married now but her husband is a phony and a loser, he hasn't produced a movie in five years and even then all he was was associate producer.

Pretty soon Mom and I do some of the lines and pretty soon Ferdy starts what he always starts but I'm not into it, I'm certainly not into it with Jennifer, which is what Ferdy's got in mind. But we snort a couple more lines and Ferdy pops a bottle of Dom and Jennifer is telling me how much she likes my cross and I start to go with it a little but then I think . . . I just can't.

Ferdy's a little pissed off at me but he's too high to be really pissed off, besides that Mom is here with Jennifer so it won't be a total loss for him. I give Ferdy a hug and I let him cop his usual feel and I give Jennifer a hug—she looks disappointed, she really does.

I give Mom a big kiss and I thank her for the day and I tell her how much I love my cross.

I head out for the limo and Mom goes over and sits down close to Jennifer.

CHAPTER 22

[Flashback]

I Live with Priests

GUS

It must be something, being a writer, making stuff up all the time.

CATHERINE

It teaches you to lie.

GUS

How's that?

CATHERINE

You make it up, but it has to be believable. They call it suspension of disbelief.

Basic Instinct

My mother decided that she was going to speak French. She went down to the library, brought home Berlitz recordings, and listened to them. "Why are you learning French, Nana," I asked her, "and not English?"

She said, "That's my business."

"Why is she learning French and not English?" I asked my father.

My father said, "Be thankful it's not Russian."

Jack Russell was the city's political boss, the president of the City Council. He was Hungarian. He had come from Hungary as a boy at the turn of the century. He had been a junkman in the city's East Side Hungarian community, working the alleys with a horse and buggy. One day he realized he knew just about every Hungarian on the East Side and decided to run for the council.

He was a fat man with a pale complexion and slicked-back, greasy hair. He smoked a big cigar.

"What do we need an interview for?" he said in Hungarian to my father. "I already sent the check for the ad. I send the check, you give me the endorsement—that's the way it works, isn't it? The priest I talked to didn't say anything about any interview. You've got the money, so don't waste my time."

My father said, "Fein, Mr. Rusnyak," and we started heading back out. He thought Rusnyak was Russell's real name.

"Russell," Jack Russell said. "Don't give me any of that old-country bullshit."

Many years later, when I was a reporter for the Plain Dealer, *I wrote a story about Jack Russell that characterized him as an old-style Tammany boss, not much different from Jake Arvey, the Hungarian in Chicago who had engineered the Kelly and Daley machines. Jack Russell was offended by my story and asked me to come see him at his Buckeye Road office.*

He was a sick old man then, the weight hanging off of him, pale as a frog's belly, the cigar unlighted in his mouth, his eyes so bad he had to wear sunglasses all the time.

He had recently been deposed as the president of the City Council but he was still a councilman. He of course didn't remember the sixteen-year-old Hungarian boy he had met with his father. He spoke to me in English.

"You can call me a fuckin' political hack or whatever other names you wanna call me in your paper," Jack Russell said, "but remember this. When I first ran for council, they pissed on us Hungarians. The Union Club assholes and the Shaker Heights crowd. We were the niggers then.

"And it was guys like me and Arvey in Chicago that changed all that. Because we looked these high-class phonies in the eye and said—'No more!' You play ball with us—you give me what I need for my people . . . a community hall, street repairs, cops that don't shake you down . . . or I'm gonna make sure you don't get what you need for your *people!*

"We didn't go to school like they did, like you did. We barely spoke the language. But the fact that Hungarians don't get screwed over no more, all those Hungarians who came out here or Chicago to work in the factories, is thanks to guys like me and Jake Arvey in Chicago."

I said, "Maybe I'll write an article one day about that, too, Mr. Russell."

"I don't give a shit what you write," Jack Russell said. "I just wanted to look you in the eye and tell you so you can't pretend to yourself you didn't know it."

I told him then about the visit my father and I had made to him when I was sixteen.

"That's what I've been tryin' to tell you," he said. "I took care of your old man with the money and he took care of me with the paper. The Hungarians took care of

me at the ballot box and I took care of their streets, their neighborhoods. That's the way this great country works. And maybe one day the day will come when you won't stick your nose so goddamn high and mighty in the air about it."

"Was there any politician you endorsed who didn't buy ads in the paper?" I asked my father.

"Just one," he smiled. "Kennedy. Nixon bought many ads but I couldn't bring myself to endorse him."

"Did the Franciscans give you any of the money they got for the endorsements?"

"The Franciscans?" He laughed. "Those swine! You've got to be kidding."

A Hungarian ball was held at the St. Patrick's Church hall, just a couple of blocks from us on Bridge Avenue.

"I think we should go," my father said to my mother. "It will be a big Hungarian event. As the editor of the paper, I should be there."

"You go," my mother said, "I'm not going."

She changed her mind. She found a long black dress at one of the rummage shops on Detroit Avenue and told my father the morning of the ball that she was going. He was happy and hugged her. Even I was going. I had agreed to work in the kitchen and wash dishes with other Hungarian kids for a dollar an hour.

I watched them from the kitchen when they arrived. He wore his favorite suit—a white flannel one from St. Vincent DePaul's. Her new used dress looked good on her—a little tight maybe. She'd gained weight again. She wore lipstick and makeup, which she rarely did.

As the ball began, I saw them sitting with other Hungarians, talking, enjoying the waltzes. I saw my father dance with other women. I knew how shy my mother was and how much she hated to dance.

I was washing dishes in the kitchen when my father came in.

"Have you seen your mother?" he said.

I went out into the hall with him but we couldn't find her anywhere. No one had seen her.

"Maybe she went home," my father said. "We should go."

We left, walking quickly down Bridge Avenue toward our apartment. It was late and very dark. We came up 41st from Bridge and hurried down Lorain Avenue.

As we passed Nick's Diner, I saw her out of the corner of my eye. She was inside, sitting at the counter. Neither my father nor I could believe our eyes. My mother never went inside American bars or diners or restaurants.

I stared at her a moment. She was wearing her long black rummage store dress, a cup of coffee in front of her, a cigarette in her hand. Her head was down. She seemed to be examining the counter. The place was nearly empty.

We went inside.

"What are you doing, Mária?" my father asked, his voice shaken.

Next to my mother on the counter I saw, neatly placed on a napkin, her new false teeth.

"I'm drinking a cup of coffee," she said, her voice even. "My teeth hurt. The hot coffee feels good on my gums."

My father said, "Let's go home, Mária."

My mother said to him, "When did you stop loving me? Did you ever love me?"

My father said, "Mária, please, don't act like this. Let's go home. I love you. Jozsi loves you."

She looked up at him and smiled. "No," she said, "you don't."

It was like I wasn't there. She never looked at me.

"I am not going home," my mother said, "you go home with the boy."

She sipped her coffee and calmly lit up another cigarette.

"Jozsi," my father said, "go home. We'll be there in a little while."

He saw me staring at her and asked, "Please Jozsi, let me talk to your mother alone!"

I was lying down on my couch when they came in about an hour later. They thought I was asleep and said not a word as they went into their bedroom. They didn't talk or whisper in there, either, and I fell asleep.

Sometime in the night, I felt her lips brush my face but I pretended to be asleep. She hadn't kissed me in a long time. In the morning, when I woke up, I thought maybe I'd dreamed it.

I saw her in the kitchen and said, "Good morning, Nana," but she didn't respond. It was one of those days when she said nothing. A few days later, I saw that she had thrown her new used black dress into a garbage can.

My father was asked to go to a meeting with other fathers at Cathedral Latin. He took the buses and the rapid transit just like I did every morning; something was wrong with our new used Ford.

When he came home late at night I saw he wasn't in a talkative mood but I pressed him anyway.

"What did they talk to you about, Papa?"

"Money," he said. "They want money for new classrooms."

"What did you say to them?"

"I told them I'm a poor man and I can't give them money."

"What did they say?"

He didn't answer the question for a moment and then he said, "Nothing. And then this priest laughed at me. And then the other fathers laughed at me."

I said, "I'm sorry, Papa."

He smiled. "Perhaps they thought I was making a bad joke."

The United States Marine Corps was staging an amphibious landing on Lake Erie. It was in the *Plain Dealer* and on the radio and the TV. Everybody was talking about it. A hundred thousand Clevelanders would watch it from specially constructed bleachers at Edgewater Park.

My father told me we were going to see the marines land.

He took me to an office downtown and he explained in his broken English that he was the editor of the *Catholic Hungarians' Sunday* and I was his newspaper's American correspondent. They took our photographs and put them inside plastic tags that said "Press."

On the day of the mock Marine Corps invasion, as the other Clevelanders sat in the bleachers, my father and I were allowed on the ships and on the landing crafts and on the beach as the marines charged ashore.

"Are you having fun?" he asked me as armed vehicles roared by us.

I was wide-eyed and excited.

"Yes," I said, "this is great!"

"You see?" he laughed. "Your hunkie DP greenhorn father is a powerful man, isn't he?"

The Cleveland Indians had a player I liked as much as the now departed Rocky Colavito. His name was Walter Bond. He was 6-7, 235 pounds. He was a towering home run hitter. Casey Stengel said, "Everything he hits is in the trees."

He was exciting to watch. The *Sporting News* compared him to Hank Aaron. He was traded. And then he died. Of leukemia.

Big news!

The Franciscans were moving the *Catholic Hungarians' Sunday* to Youngstown, about eighty miles southeast of Cleveland. They had already bought a monastery there. We would move, too. They would buy us a house there!

There was one wrinkle: the move wouldn't take place until next March, but my junior year of high school was beginning next month. I couldn't switch from Cathedral Latin to a new school mid-year, so I would have to go to Youngstown next month and come back to see my parents on the weekends.

Where would I live while I was alone in Youngstown?

With the Franciscans . . . *at the monastery!*

I was overjoyed that I could leave Cathedral Latin, but I was sick that I would be living with the Franciscans.

I loved my parents and would miss them. But I wouldn't miss seeing my mother cementing windows, going mute, or laughing her hyena laugh.

The Franciscans enrolled me at Ursuline High School in Youngstown and we drove down to their new monastery. It was a castle, with its own wooded park grounds and was bigger than Louis Bromfield's Malabar Farm. The Franciscans even had servants and maids.

"The newspaper, I see, is doing very very well," my father said ruefully as he looked at their new monastery.

He was responsible for the newspaper's success. It was thanks to him that the Franciscans were able to buy their new castle and pay their servants and maids . . . while we lived in our cramped, dank apartment on Lorain Avenue and they paid him $100 a month.

It was decided that I would live in a room above the monastery garage. I would eat with the Franciscans. One of them would drop me off at school in the morning on his way to saying Mass at a parish downtown.

My father gave me a present before they drove back to Cleveland: a transistor radio small enough to fit into my shirt pocket.

From my room above the garage, I watched my father and mother drive away in our green Ford. I missed Lorain Avenue already. I missed the cussing, foul-mouthed voices in the street. And I missed my blazing neon Papp's Bar sign.

Father Peter was in Youngstown. So was Father Gottfried, whom I'd hailed with my chunk of lead . . . and Father Ákos, still grilling his rats.

There were other Franciscans I hadn't met on Lorain Avenue, including Father Steve, a second-generation American Hungarian who spoke better English than Hungarian.

At dinner, the priests were mostly silent, eating heaping platters of sausage and dumplings prepared by the Hungarian cooks. When they spoke, they spoke angrily about the presidential election only a month away. They hated the Catholic candidate, these Catholic priests. "Kennedy is surrounded by Jews," they said. "He is a Jew-lover. He is just like the Jew president, Rosenfeld."

I had two joyous moments my first few months living at the monastery in Youngstown. When Bill Mazeroski of the Pittsburgh Pirates hit a home run in the World Series and beat the hated New York Yankees. And when John F. Kennedy was elected president of the United States.

One of the Franciscans I hadn't met on Lorain Avenue, Father László, offered to drop me off at Ursuline my first day of school. He had come to America after the freedom fight.

He was in his thirties, grossly overweight, and bald. When we got into his car, he reached into the back seat and put a white cowboy hat on. He had a tape recorder hooked up to his radio and switched it on. It blasted Elvész and Paul Anka and Frankie Avalon.

When we stopped at traffic lights, he reached over and picked a microphone up. If a girl or an attractive young woman was crossing the street, he whistled or said "*Gimme litta puszi puszi.*" He had a loudspeaker under the hood of his car.

Puszi, in Hungarian, means "a kiss."

(Really.)

I noticed the girls first, naturally, at Ursuline High School. There were so many girls here in so many shapes and sizes! And they were friendly and chatty and smiling. So were the boys. So were the nuns.

My first day, the new kid in school, I was asked by three different people— boys and girls—to sit with them at lunch.

I was overwhelmed at first. At Cathedral Latin, I had put myself into an aggressive mode on the way to school each morning. I had keyed myself up— ready for hostility, ready to return a punch or a shove. But there were no shoves or punches here. I didn't need to feel aggressive.

It took me a while to figure out why the atmosphere was so different at Ursuline. *One:* it wasn't a rich kids' school. Youngstown was a steel town and the kids came from all class levels to Ursuline. *Two:* there were *girls* here and their very presence softened and scented the air.

When the priests dropped me downtown on the way to their seven o'clock Mass, I had two hours to kill before school began. I spent those hours sitting on a stool at a diner filled with workers from the steel mills, drinking coffee, smoking cigarettes, playing the jukebox, and reading. I could have all the coffee I wanted for a dime and when I got hungry, I'd order myself some toast.

I read a book at the diner that would change my life. I had taken it out from the school library. It was called *The Diary of Anne Frank.* I cried when I finished it and the waitress said, "Are you okay, honey?"

Well, no, I wasn't, really. I wasn't okay at all.

The kids in school viewed me as an exotic figure. I was living alone—without my parents. And I was living in a monastery that looked like a castle most of them had read about in the *Youngstown Vindicator.* And I had spent my early years in refugee camps! For the first time in my life, I was popular. Even the nuns liked me. For the first time in my life, I really studied, getting all As and Bs. And everyone—kids, nuns—pronounced my name right.

The Franciscans, I discovered, couldn't care less *when* I got back from school. They ignored me.

If I wasn't there at dinner, no one said anything. I arranged with one of their servants to leave me a glass of milk and a sandwich each night.

Father Ákos, the rat-griller, captured a deer in the woods and kept it in a fenced-off area of the park. He was fattening it. He said we would soon eat Transylvanian Venison Stew with garlic and paprika.

On the way to school one morning, wearing his cowboy hat, Elvész blasting on his tape recorder, Father László asked me: "Have you kissed any girls yet?"

"No, Father."

"You haven't?"

"No."

I was embarrassed.

"Have you put your tongue in their mouth?" the priest asked.

"No, Father."

"Have you sucked on their breasts?"

"No, Father!"

I laughed louder, more embarrassed.

"Have you spread their legs apart?" His face was red.

I looked away and shook my head.

"Have you put your fingers into their behinds?"

I said nothing, looked out the window of the car.

"Have you stuck your *pimpli* into their hole?" His voice was hoarse.

We stopped at a red light.

"I've gotta meet somebody," I said, opened the door, and jumped out of the car.

I was walking away from the car. I heard his laughter, amplified and guttural. He had the loudspeaker under the hood turned on.

Father László moved from the main house of the monastery to the room next to mine above the garage. I could hear his tape recorder blasting rock and roll all the time.

He'd come into my room unexpectedly sometimes. Once he said he'd taped a new song I had to hear. Once he came in wearing nothing but his underwear. Once he came in while I was getting dressed.

My door didn't have a lock on it.

On the way to school one morning with Father Steve, the American Hungarian Franciscan, I told him about Father László and how he'd come into my room wearing his underwear and the questions he'd ask me about girls.

Father Steve put a lock on my door.

From then on, only Father Steve drove me to school in the morning.

On a pretty moonlit night, I sneaked into the woods and freed the deer from its fenced-in yard.

Father Lászlo moved back into the monastery and out of the garage.

I went home every other weekend on the Greyhound, happy to be seeing my parents but afraid each time of what I would see. My mother was back in the printing shop, working the linotype machine, breathing the lead in.

She was alone in the apartment a lot of the time now; my father was often away making speeches to chapters of the Committee for Hungarian Liberation in other parts of America. I asked him how she was doing and he looked away for a moment, his eyes weary.

"I have come to the conclusion," my father said, "that there is great wisdom in saying *fein* to everything. How is your mother? Your mother is *fein*." His smile was a sad one.

They weren't speaking much, he said. For years, he said, they had been putting $10 a month away and hiding it in a book on the shelf. It was money they were going to send me to college with.

One morning he discovered that the money—more than $400—was gone. My mother admitted that she'd taken it. She had sent it to her stepmother in Hungary, the former prostitute her father had found with his ads in the Budapest newspaper.

"To that *kurva*," my father said, "whom she has always hated. I asked her why and she said, 'They're poor.' "

My father smiled. "What are *we*, millionaires?"

They moved down to Youngstown a few months later. The Franciscans had bought us a house on a quiet suburban street only a block away from the new printing shop.

Compared to our apartment on Lorain Avenue, the house was a mansion— two stories, three bedrooms upstairs, with a yard in front and back. For the first time in a long time, I saw joy in my mother's eyes. "This is so beautiful!" she said. "*Oh*, this is *so* beautiful!"

Kay Jeffries had freckles and green eyes and thick auburn hair. She came to school from nearby Sharon, Pennsylvania, each morning on the bus and she sat next to me in French class.

I asked if I could walk her downtown after school to the bus station, and she said sure. Pretty soon I was walking her every day and we were having lunch together in the cafeteria every day, too. I bought her ice cream cones and cups of coffee after school and we were kissing on street corners and holding hands in the school hallways.

When I wasn't with her, I thought about her all the time. Not just about the way her breasts felt when I pulled her up against me, but about her smile, her throaty laugh, the way her eyes sparkled and the way the wind tousled her hair. We even had our very own love song: "Daddy's Home" by Shep and the Limelites.

I was in love and, for the first time in my life, really happy.

My father was waiting for me in the living room of our beautiful house when I got home.

"Jozsi," he said, "I'm sorry. I know you're happy here, but at the end of your school year we're going to have to move back to Cleveland."

I couldn't believe what he was telling me. "*Why?*" I said. "You just got here. We've only been in this house for six weeks."

"You will be going to college in a couple of years," he said. "I asked the Franciscans for a raise, but they refused to give it to me. I found another job at a Hungarian life insurance company on the East Side in Cleveland. I will do that job and I will also still do the newspaper job from Cleveland. I will send my articles down here to Youngstown by mail."

"But where will we live?" I asked.

"We will find an apartment in the Hungarian neighborhood on the East Side," he said, "on Buckeye Road. That's where the insurance office is."

"Where will I go to school?"

"You will finish your last year at Cathedral Latin," he said.

"No!" I said. "I don't want to go back to Cathedral Latin! I hate Cathedral Latin! I don't want to leave here!"

I started to cry.

"Jozsi," my father said, "I'm sorry, but we have no choice. You have to go back to Latin. How would it look if you went to *three* different schools in high school? We will be living closer to Latin. We'll be on the East Side. It will be easier for you to get there."

I was crushed.

My mother was in the backyard of our house on Portland Avenue in Youngstown, looking at the roses she had planted, the roses she would never see bloom. She was crying soundlessly, the tears on her cheeks.

"He misses his friends," my mother said, "he misses the applause. There aren't enough Hungarians here to make speeches to. There aren't enough Hungarians to come into his office to tell him he is a great man. It doesn't have anything to do with your going to college, it has to do with *him,* with the silly stickers he sticks in his books. *Ex Libris!* He knows that what he is doing by taking us back to Cleveland is terrible. *He is using you as his alibi.*"

"Stop it," I said. "Nana, please, stop it." I felt myself starting to tremble.

"He doesn't love you," she said. "He doesn't love me. He is not capable of loving anyone else. He loves himself."

I turned and ran from her into the house.

I was reading a book about Auschwitz in my bedroom. My father came into the room.

"Auschwitz," he said, "a terrible thing."

"Tell me about Mauthausen," I said. "This book mentions Mauthausen."

"I can't tell you much," he said.

"But you told me we were there. When I was little."

"No," he said, "we were not exactly at Mauthausen. Not at Mauthausen itself. We were at an adjunct of Mauthausen called Perg."

"But you said we ate the same food that the Jews did."

"Yes," he said, "but we were removed from them."

"Did you know that at least five hundred thousand Hungarian Jews were taken to Auschwitz?" I asked.

"By the Germans," he said. "They invaded our country. Their troops occupied Hungary just like the Russians occupy it now."

"Did you know that the Jews were taken down to the Danube in Budapest and murdered?"

"We all heard rumors," he said. "But that's all they were. *We didn't see anything firsthand.* We didn't know."

"What would you have done," I asked my father, "if you would have seen it yourself? Would you have tried to stop it?"

My father looked at me a long moment.

"I could tell you that I would have," he said. "It would be easy for me to say that to you. I could look like a big hero in my boy's eyes. But it was a feverish and insane time. The Nyilas [Hungarian Nazis, the Arrow Cross] were terrorizing everyone. I don't know what I would have done if I would have seen it myself. But I hope I would have done the right thing."

He thought about that a moment and handed the book back to me. He smiled.

"Why are you engaged in such depressing reading?" he asked.

"Shouldn't I be reading it?"

"Of course you should," my father said. "The more you know about history, the better. We must learn not to make the mistakes of the past."

[Close-up]

The Auteur

The script he had written was from the heart. Not only did all the studios bid on it, but one of them asked him to direct it. It was all a dream. Millions of dollars and his first directing gig. His career was guaranteed.

And then, on top of everything else, Bruce Willis agreed to play the lead. Millions of dollars . . . control . . . and the biggest box office star in the world (except for Tom Cruise)!

In the first week of the shoot, he gave Bruce Willis an acting suggestion and Bruce said, "Are you an actor?" He sheepishly said, "Well, no, but—" And Bruce said, "Okay then."

He gave Bruce no more acting suggestions. When he saw the rough cut, he felt that while Bruce was sometimes over-the-top, the movie still worked. But Bruce didn't think so. Bruce thought his performance was completely over-the-top.

The studio didn't blame Bruce; the studio blamed him. He was the director, wasn't he?

Then Bruce demanded to recut the picture.

The director went to the studio head to complain and the studio head said, "Are you kidding me? This is Bruce Willis! He can do anything he wants!"

Bruce recut the picture but Bruce still didn't like his performance so he said he'd do no publicity for it. The studio then decided to cut the ad budget for the movie in half.

The movie was released but failed miserably. Most critics blamed the director for Bruce's performance. The studio not only blamed the director but also his screenplay, saying that while it "read well" it obviously didn't "play." Word spread among the other studios that the director "couldn't work with actors."

Bruce went on to make $20 million for his next movie. The director wrote another script but no one bought it. Many of those who passed said the script didn't have "a commercial touch."

The last I heard the director was no longer writing but still directing—episodic television.

CHAPTER 23

[Naomi's Journal]

Please Take Care of Joseph

CARLY

Did you and Naomi sleep together?

ZEKE

I hardly knew her.

CARLY

She told someone you had an affair with her.

ZEKE

It never happened. Maybe she fantasized. She did have an affair
with your friend.

CARLY

What friend?

ZEKE

Your writer friend.

Sliver

April 30, 1993

 The day after I last saw Bill, Gerri Eszterhas called me
from Marin and asked me to go up there and get away from
everything.

 "It'll do you good," she said, "we'll have fun."

 And then Joe got on the line, telling me to "get the hell
up here."

 They both stayed on the phone and we started to talk.

And the more we talked, the more we discovered that Bill had lied to us on so many recent occasions.

The night I went to all that effort and made that wonderful dinner and got all dressed up—Bill trashed that night the very next day. He called Joe and said, "It was awful. Last night Naomi was hysterical and then the roof started leaking and Jake got loose on the beach and when I finally caught him, I came back in and Naomi was threatening to drink a barbiturate cocktail." I was *stunned*.

As much as I trust Joe, I don't think I would have believed something this heinous—that Bill was spreading *this* about me—except for the details. Because it was Bill's favorite excuse, the one he used all the time when someone was trying to reach him from the office, the one he had told me to tell people. That "*the roof was leaking and Jake had gotten loose on the beach*" and he'd had to come home to help.

Gerri met me at the airport when I arrived in San Francisco. It was wonderful to see her. I had lost nearly fifteen pounds in the past two weeks but I felt good in my jeans and boots and hugged her as I tossed my bag into the trunk.

Joe greeted us at the door of the house. He had thrown his back out—a chronic ailment—and was stooped over and walking with a cane. The first thing he said was "You look great!" and that meant so much to me since I felt I'd been through hell and back since he last saw me. They both made me feel so welcome. Suzi and Steve came down the stairs with shy smiles hiding their sadness about what had happened to me.

Gerri fixed an elaborate dinner and after the kids excused themselves and went about their high school ways, Joe, Gerri, and I began to talk.

We compared notes. They told me that shortly after Bill dropped his bomb, they went off to Hawaii together, largely because Gerri was so undone by the events.

While in Hawaii, Gerri had what she called "a vision." It was very strange. She said she woke up cheerful. Then she went for a walk. When she returned, she sat down to take off her shoes and looked out the window. Her vision blurred to a white screen. She saw Joe in a passionate embrace with another woman. She even described the woman's hair, since she was facing Joe and visible only from the back.

She said Joe appeared to be in a state of great excitement, and when her vision cleared, she felt she had to ask Joe if he'd been unfaithful to her. As strange as this story seemed, Gerri would repeat it again and again and again. She felt that Sharon Stone was "a demon" who had "beamed" her the vision from L.A.

She even went so far as to elaborate that whenever Sharon had called the house, after an initial hello, her voice would deepen to become "the voice of the beast."

She believed Sharon Stone was a demonic being who had cast a spell on Bill and had, she believed, also seduced her husband, though Joe vehemently and repeatedly denied it.

Gerri told how, after her vision, she confronted Joe and asked him if he had been with other women. Gerri said she fled to the bathroom to rip off her wedding and engagement rings, running her hands under the water to try and force the rings off her fingers.

One day in Tiburon Suzi, Gerri, and I went shopping. While Gerri went into a store, Suzi and I decided to wait for her in the car. At sixteen, Suzi has never been in love.

She suddenly said, "You know, Naomi, I just don't understand caring about someone so much that it would make any difference to me if they left. I'm really independent. I mean—if some guy wanted to go, I'd just say 'Fine. Go!'"

I considered for a long moment and said, "Well, I guess it's like if your dad left. And you knew from that day on, everything would change. Your life as you've known it for so many years would never be the same again."

Her eyes widened for a moment and then she said, "Ohhhhhh."

I talked to Gerri about how much I love books. How, in any situation, I've always taken comfort in a book.

She said, "You're just like Joseph. He loves his books. I've never liked reading much."

I said, "I've read since I was a child. I can't imagine not reading."

"You know," she said, "you and Joseph have so much in common. You're the woman he should have married."

I said the usual things about how important she is to Joe; how she shouldn't always underrate herself. But truthfully I find this dynamic between the three of us more and more strange.

A Current Affair called wanting to interview me. One night when Joe talked to Gerri from L.A., he asked her to give me the phone.

"Are you going to do *A Current Affair*?" he asked.

I said, "I don't know. I've always stood up for myself and I hate what I'm reading about the breakup, but I'm not sure I want to talk about it. What do you think I should do?"

He said, "I can't answer that for you. Only you know the answer to that."

So I said, "What would *you* do in my place?"

And he laughed. He thought about it and said, "You know what I think? I think Sharon and Bill think they can take this hick from Ohio and say anything they want about her, create any story that suits their needs, and she won't do a thing about it, she'll just roll over."

I said, "I'm doing *A Current Affair*."

Last night on the way home Gerri started to confide in me about her lack of an intimate relationship with Joe. I have never felt comfortable discussing other people's intimate lives, but she just seems so desperate to talk and I don't want to hurt her feelings.

She said, "Sometimes I just get in the car and drive around and cry."

The other night at dinner we were talking about children. I was describing my childhood in the country, which was ideal, and Joe said, "It was a Norman Rockwell existence."

I said, "Someone once asked Bill what he would want for his children, should he ever have them. And Bill said, 'I want them to go to the finest private schools in the world. I want them to speak several languages. I want them to see the world.' "

Then they asked me.

I said, "I want them to know the complete unbridled joy, the absolutely exhilarating freedom of bolting out the front

door barefoot, running outside, and not hearing the screen
door slam until you're halfway down the driveway."

Joe and Gerri were both completely silent. Joe looked at
me intently.

Then he said, "That's really wonderful."

I think Joe is the first person I've ever told that to who
actually understands it. He looked at me until I looked
down.

Yesterday Gerri took both of my hands and said, "If anything
ever happens to me, please take care of Joseph."

I said, "Oh, Gerri, nothing is going to happen to you."

But she just stared.

My heart is breaking for them all. Gerri asked me to go
to Hawaii with them and I said I'd go but my conscience says
I should go home and start my life.

The day my interview on *A Current Affair* was set to air, I
was a nervous wreck. I had misgivings about doing the interview, which had been difficult, and now had just as much
apprehension about it airing.

Joe was in L.A. that day and Gerri and I were going to
watch it together. Then we realized it wouldn't be airing in
Tiburon due to a baseball playoff game.

Gerri said, "We're going to San Jose to see it!"

I was unsure I wanted to see it at all, but she was
determined and so we did. We booked a room in a hotel and
drove down to San Jose and watched the segment.

When it ended I felt great relief that the whole ordeal
was over. I got up on the bed and began to jump—really
high—and was laughing and yelling and bouncing to the ceiling. Gerri stood in the middle of the floor smiling up at me.

Then she said, "You're just like Joseph. You have a
tremendous life force."

I took it as a great compliment. A few minutes later she
called Joe, who'd been watching in L.A.

After a moment she said, "He wants to talk to you."

I took the phone and, as Gerri sat smiling at me, I heard
Joe say, "You were great! I'm really proud of you." And at
that moment I realized my heartache had stopped.

I felt only happiness.

. . .

Bill called Joe here in Tiburon and said very cheerily, "Hey, how you doin'?"

And Joe said, "I don't want to talk to you. I don't want to see you. Renegade is off. As far as our personal relationship goes, we'll let time tell."

Bill said one word—"Okay"—and hung up.

A few hours later Sharon called.

She said, "Joe, Bill is here. He's crying, I'm so sorry."

And Joe said, "I'll tell you the same thing I told Bill. I don't want to talk to you, I don't want to see you. As far as our personal relationship goes, we'll let time tell."

She said, "But, Joe—" and he said goodbye and hung up.

That night Guy McElwaine called and said, "Sharon called me crying. She said: 'If I would've known Joe would act this way, I would have picked *him*.' "

Guy said to her, "You couldn't have had him, Sharon, he's happily married."

Sharon said, "He fools around all the time."

Guy said to Sharon, "But he doesn't leave his wife."

I told Joe and Gerri that I was having tortured dreams.

Last night I dreamed about Joe. I'm not going to go into details, but when I saw him in the morning, I couldn't look him in the eyes.

I was reading in the living room and he walked in. I'm convinced he reads my thoughts.

He said, "Good morning! So what did you dream about last night?"

I just kept looking at my book and said, "As a matter of fact, you were in it."

He said, "What did I do?"

I said, "You were the good guy."

"It doesn't sound like me," he said.

He laughed. I kept reading.

CHAPTER 24

[*Flashback*]

Howdy Doody Triumphant

DINEY

Do you really want to be a writer?

KARCHY

I wanna be somethin', that's the truth.

Telling Lies in America

My father found a downstairs apartment in a duplex off Buckeye Road, the Hungarian neighborhood's main drag, on East 122nd Street. It was owned by two Slovak sisters in their sixties, the Zniks.

The apartment was bigger than the one on Lorain Avenue had been but a third of the size of the house we'd lived in in Youngstown. There was no yard.

The neighborhood was residential, like the one in Youngstown, but it was at war. Black people were moving into the neighboring streets and the Hungarians had formed a vigilante committee to keep the neighborhood free from crime. Signs on the Hungarian butcher shops selling kolbász and paprikaed bacon said "Soul Food."

I missed Kay Jeffries and spent my time daydreaming about her and calling her on the phone. We didn't have much to say except that we missed each other and loved each other very much. If parents were in the room when we were on the phone, we didn't say, "I love you, too," we said "*Me too!*"

When the phone bill for the month arrived, my father told me I had to get a summer job to pay him back.

I owed him $123.76.

I got a job moving office furniture with a Hungarian moving company. Office furniture is heavy and when I got home each night, muscles were cramping that I didn't even know existed in my body.

I earned $170, then had to quit because school was starting at Cathedral Latin. I repaid my father what I owed him.

I had three days left until school started and I spent them talking to Kay on the phone again and listening to Gary U.S. Bonds singing "Quarter to Three" on my mother's record player. I turned the volume up as high as it would go and played the song over and over again. Upstairs, the Znik sisters stomped the floor. They didn't like Gary U.S. Bonds.

The Znik sisters told us we had till the end of the month to get out. My father asked them why they were throwing us out and one of the Zniks pointed at me and said, "*He is the devil!*"

The Zniks thought that, of course, because they considered rock and roll to be "the devil's music" and because they thought I was trying to drive them out of their minds with "Quarter to Three."

And maybe I *was* trying to drive them out of their minds—as payback for always snooping on us.

Sometimes when I saw them I made ugly faces and stuck my tongue out at them lasciviously. And sometimes, when no one was looking, I'd greet them in the American way with my middle finger!

We moved to an upstairs duplex apartment on East 117th Street even nearer to Buckeye Road. The place was small and cramped but I had my own tiny bedroom. Directly across the street from us was the back of St. Margaret of Hungary Church.

The landlord, an old partially deaf second-generation Hungarian, lived downstairs. I could play Gary U.S. Bonds here as loud and as much as I wanted and the landlord wouldn't mind.

When he rented us the apartment, he said, "You don't have to worry. There are no *boobocks* on this street."

Boobock is what Hungarians called black people.

The word has no meaning in Hungarian, although Hungarians also call blacks *rigos* (crows) and négers, which translates not to "nigger" but to "Negro."

Our new landlord's son, an American-Hungarian man in his forties, offered to sell my father a gun for $20.

"For the *boobocks*," the landlord's son said. It was a .22 Beretta. My father bought it and kept it in his pocket.

"For the Komchis," my father said to me.

· · ·

I was back at Cathedral Latin with the classmates and priests and brothers I loathed, but it was different somehow.

Maybe, I realized, *I* was different. Maybe I wasn't intimidated anymore. Maybe it didn't matter much to me that these kids were rich, that their clothes were better than mine, that they wouldn't pronounce my name right. I had seen the real America at Youngstown Ursuline. I saw that I fit into the real America just fine. And I had been kissed many times by the beautiful Kay Jeffries!

I stopped calling Kay—finally understanding that it *was* too expensive—and she stopped calling me.

She skipped some letters and I skipped some letters and slowly, painfully, I started trying to forget her. The disc jockeys stopped playing Shep and the Limelites and I heard a new song that I loved: "*He's a rebel and he'll never be any good. He's a rebel 'cause he never ever does what he should!*"

My mother and father spent their days in a small storefront office just off Buckeye Road on East 116th Street: the American Hungarian Catholic Society Life Insurance Company.

Old Hungarians who lived in this, the city's largest Hungarian neighborhood, dropped by to make their monthly payments, usually in cash taken from the stash they still kept under the mattress.

My mother went into the office with my father every day, even though she wasn't paid, to do the bookkeeping. She was the one who worked there, really, even though her headaches were so bad that she kept an icepack on her head in the office.

My father spent all day in the insurance company office writing his articles for the newspaper.

They left the office at six o'clock at night, walked across the schoolyard of the St. Margaret of Hungary Church, up some steps, and they were on East 117th, directly across the street from our apartment.

We ate our dinner quickly and my father continued working on his articles. At nine o'clock, or at 9:15 at the latest, he and I jumped into the Ford and drove downtown—a forty-minute drive—to the main post office.

My father waited in the car and I ran inside and threw the envelope into the Special Delivery slot—the last pickup was at ten o'clock.

Then we drove back to the apartment the same way we had come—up Carnegie and then Woodland Avenue, through the heart of the city's black neighborhood.

Going both to and back from downtown, my father clutched the Beretta in his pocket.

We did that five days a week.

. . .

Johnny Holliday was the hot new disc jockey in town at WHK. He had a slightly Southern twang and a fast, slurry style delivered in a sleepy kind of voice. Everyone at Latin listened to him. Every high school kid in Cleveland listened to him.

The most popular part of his daily show was "The WHK High School Hall of Fame." Kids were supposed to mail postcards to him nominating their most popular classmate in school.

I bought a bunch of postcards, signed my classmates' names to them, and nominated myself to be in the WHK High School Hall of Fame.

About a week later, on my way to the bus taking me to school, my transistor radio in my pocket, I heard Johnny Holliday say "In the WHK High School Hall of Fame today, from Cathedral Latin High School, *Joe Eszterhas!*" The station played Johnny Holliday saying that every hour for the next twenty-four hours. *He'd even pronounced my name right!*

By the time I got to school, I saw by the sneering looks on my classmates' faces that the news had spread. Some of them even glared at me. But a couple kids who'd hardly spoken to me in the past said "Congratulations" and "Nice goin'!"

After school, I went to the American Hungarian Catholic Society office and put my transistor radio on for my parents.

We waited until we heard Johnny Holliday's voice placing me in his High School Hall of Fame.

"This is fantastic!" my father said. "It is *fantastic!*"

"*Kon-gra-tu-lay-shon,*" my mother said in English.

They asked me how I had been selected for this very public honor.

"The teachers at each school," I explained, "pick out the student they think has the most potential for success."

My father turned to my mother: "You see, Mária, all the work we do for the boy, all our sacrifices for him, they are worth it!"

He was calling me "Joe" now, even when he spoke to me in Hungarian, not "Jozsi." And I was calling him "Pop" when I spoke to him in Hungarian and not "Papa."

It had begun as a joke. I teasingly called him "Pop" a few times and he teased me back by calling me "Joe" and then we started doing it for real.

I was scratching my groin with my hand in my pocket one day as we were walking down Buckeye Road.

"What are you doing, Joe?" he asked me.

"My *pimpli* itches," I said.

"You don't have a *pimpli* anymore." He laughed. "It's too big to be a *pimpli,* I'm sure. Now you have a *fasz.*"

I liked that.

No Hungarian, after all, ever said "*Lo pimpli a seggedbe!*"

"How do you say *fasz* in English?" he asked.

"Dick," I said.

He thought about it.

"Dick! Dick!" he said, and started to laugh. "*Dick Nixon!*"

Now that I was a senior, I was allowed to join the staff of the school newspaper, the *Latineer*, and I convinced the editor, Stanley Osenar, that the *Latineer* should run some article that the students would actually read instead of the holy-holy religious BS the *Latineer* was usually filled with.

What was it that almost every student at Latin had in common? That almost every student was passionately interested in? *Besides* sex? Rock and roll!

Ricky Nelson was coming to town. He was at the height of his fame with hits like "Travelin' Man" and "Hello Mary Lou."

"Let's do an interview with Ricky Nelson," I told Stanley Osenar.

"The brothers would shit!" he said. "Rock and roll? In the *Latineer*? Oh boy." But Stanley went for it.

I got on the phone, called the radio station sponsoring the concert, and identified myself as a reporter for the Cathedral Latin *Latineer*. He referred me to Ricky Nelson's publicist in Hollywood, a man named Jerry Folidaire, who told me to call him at the Cleveland Hotel when he got into town. I did and he told me Ricky was too tired to talk now but did I want to have breakfast with him in his suite tomorrow morning? And did I want a backstage pass for the show tonight?

Yes, I did!

In the dressing room that night I met Joey Dee and Cozy Cole and the next morning I had breakfast with "Rick" and Jerry Folidaire. I asked one question dumber than the other, but they were both nice to me, even when I said, "I noticed last night in the dressing room that Joey Dee and his guys all had guns in their pockets or suitcases. Do you carry a gun, too, when you travel?"

Ricky looked at Jerry Folidaire not knowing what to say and Jerry Folidaire said, "No, you know, it's those New York guys, it's part of their tradition."

"I'm from California." Ricky smiled and laughed.

I laughed, too, but I was hardly paying attention. *Here I was having breakfast at the city's most famous hotel, a place I'd never been, in a suite, a thing I'd never seen, with one of my all-time rock and roll heroes, who was being very nice and friendly to me!*

An awestruck *Latineer* photographer took our picture as Rick and I came out of the Cleveland Hotel together and, in the next issue of the *Latineer*, there was the story bannered across the top of the front page—"Rocker Rick Nelson Voices Views on Talent." And next to it was a big picture of me shaking hands with and looking buddy-buddy with Ricky Nelson!

I enjoyed watching my classmates and the priests and brothers, who hated me, as they looked at my picture across the top of the front page!

The priests and brothers went crazy. No more rock and roll stories, they told Stanley Osenar. But my father was impressed. There was my picture across the top of the front page of the *Latineer!* This after I had already been picked for the WHK High School Hall of Fame!

Stanley now let me do a regular column. My photograph would be next to the column in each issue. The column would be entitled "A Touch of Ease." (*Ouch!*)

For my first one, I wrote a review of Tennessee Williams's *Night of the Iguana,* praising the play and underlining the fact that the main character was a whiskey priest who had lost his faith in God.

It was my last column.

Stanley Osenar almost got fired.

Letter sweaters were awarded by the priests and brothers for distinction in activities like sports, journalism, or speech and debate. Even though I had written more articles for the *Latineer* than anyone else and was now the features editor, the brothers didn't award me a letter.

I admired the sweaters—Stanley Osenar had one and I saw how the girls were drawn to him at record hops.

Stanley told me that even though he had been awarded it, he still had to pay his own money to buy it at the school bookstore.

"How do they know at the bookstore that you're eligible to have one?" I asked. "Do you have to have a note or something?"

"They *don't* know. They just sell it to you."

Then Stan looked at me and said, "Don't even think about it! They'll throw you out of school!"

I immediately went down to the bookstore and bought my letter sweater. I wore it to the hops where the priests and brothers never came. I explained to my parents that being awarded a letter like this was a great honor.

First the WHK High School Hall of Fame! Then the big photograph with Ricky Nelson! Now a letter sweater! My parents were beginning to view me as an American success story.

And many years later I wrote a movie about me and the WHK High School Hall of Fame called Telling Lies in America.

It got the best reviews of any I'd written.

Newsweek *even said that with the lies I told in the movie called* Telling Lies in America, *I'd redeemed myself.*

And when I was a successful American screenwriter, Stanley Osenar sent me his Cathedral Latin letter with a note that said, "I think you've earned a real one!"

. . .

Our green Ford was rusting out and we needed a new car. Now that I had a temporary driver's license, my father said I could help pick it out.

We drove from one East Side used car lot to the other. The moment I saw it, I was in love with it. It was a 1956 red-and-white Ford convertible with red leather seats.

"This is the stupidest car we could possibly buy," my father said. "Look at it. The floor is already rusted. This car got wet too many times. The seats are cracking. Look, this crack here—it has been glued together. The top is difficult to put on and take down. It will break. What will we do in the winter? Cold air will come right through the top and the sides. We will freeze, that's what we will do."

I thought it was the most beautiful used car I'd ever seen. I imagined myself driving it—my hair slicked back, the radio blasting, sunglasses shielding my eyes, a gorgeous girl cuddled up against me . . . parking it at a lovers lane spot around Shaker Lakes.

We looked at five or six other used car lots but I saw nothing that I liked. I couldn't stop fantasizing about the red-and-white Ford convertible. We went back again to see it.

"I would look like an idiot driving this car," my father said. "I am fifty-five years old. I have a belly. I wear thick glasses. I am almost bald. I wear a beret. This car is not meant for a man who looks like me. Anyone seeing me driving this car would laugh. This car would make me look like a joke. Don't you agree?"

"No," I said, "you could drive this car—"

"The truth, the truth," my father said. "Don't you agree?"

"I don't know," I said. "Okay, maybe, if you look at it that way."

"Maybe?" He laughed. "No maybe. Absolutely, positively, certainly one hundred percent without doubt!"

My father bought the car.

I saw him driving our Ford convertible one day in the winter. The top had broken and was half down. It was snowing. My father wore his trench coat, a scarf, gloves. My father wore thick glasses and a beret. That moment I loved my father very much.

The very day we drove our new used convertible home from the dealer, I bought a red Ban-Lon shirt and a pair of Ray-Ban sunglasses.

I pulled the convertible's top down and turned the radio up full blast: "*Come on, baby, let's do the twist! Come on, bay-bee, let's do the twist!*"

I cruised up and down Buckeye Road for hours. The old Hungarians stared at me, the *Elvész Prezli* of Buckeye Road!

The next week I put three coats of wax on it and shined it for days. Then I drove it down one morning to Cathedral Latin. A group of my classmates stood nearby, staring, slack-jawed.

I put the top up, locked it, said "Hey, how ya doin'?" and *bopped* by them.

I went to Mass with my parents each Sunday at St. Margaret of Hungary but one day after Mass I told my father: "I'm not going to go to church anymore with you, Pop."

"What do you mean you're not going to go to church anymore?" he said. "We go every Sunday."

"It doesn't mean anything to me," I said.

"What doesn't?"

"The church. The priests. Their sermons. Confession. Communion. Praying. All of it. I don't believe any of it."

My father seemed more hurt than angry.

"The priests are human," he said. "They don't really have anything to do with God. We go to church to talk to God."

"I can talk to God anytime, anywhere," I said. "I don't have to go to church to do it."

"You're angry," he said. "Are you angry at God?"

"No," I said, "I'm not. Really. I've thought about it. But I'm not angry. I just don't care about God. Any more than I think God or his priests care about me."

"This is my fault," my father said. "I think that, through me, you have met too many bad priests."

"I know there are good priests," I said. "I remember how much Father John helped me."

"You're going to break your mother's heart with this," he said. "You couldn't cause her greater pain than this."

"What should I do, Pop?" I asked him. "Should I go each Sunday and sit and kneel there with you pretending to pray? Pretending to receive Communion? Lying? Being a hypocrite just to make Nana happy? Is that what I should do? Turn God into a pill for my mother?"

"God *is* a pill for your mother," he said, almost smiling slightly.

"God is a pill for everybody," I said.

"I hope that one day you will feel differently," my father said, "or that at least you will understand that God is a good and necessary pill for everybody."

"Maybe one day I will," I said, "but I have to work it out for myself, don't I?"

He said, "Let *me* tell your mother about church, Joe."

She never said anything to me about it, but she ignored me for a couple of weeks.

"What did she say?" I finally asked my father.

"It doesn't matter what she said."

"Come on, Pop. Please. Tell me."

"She says it's all *my* fault," he said. "For bringing us to America, a godless place. For leaving Hungary. For letting you become American. For not making you go to the Hungarian Boy Scouts. For not praying with you at night when you were little. For letting you listen to your radio. For letting you drive a car, any car, but especially this stupid red car."

He was smiling to himself sadly.

"*I* took you away from God," he muttered.

I said, "I'm sorry, Pop."

"Please," my father said, "you and I both know too well that to take your mother seriously is to break our hearts. We mustn't do that, must we?"

Maybe because I got him into so much trouble, Stanley Osenar, the editor of the *Latineer,* and I became friends.

We hung out after school in the coffee shops and diners around East 105th Street and Euclid, smoking, drinking coffee, playing "Fingertips" and "Please Mr. Postman" on the jukebox, and talking, talking, talking. Stanley was as much of a reader as I and we talked about Allen Ginsberg and Jack Kerouac and Gregory Corso. We talked, too, about politics and Communism.

Communism was a noble experiment, Stanley Osenar believed, but Stalinism had caused it to fail. Marx and Lenin, he said, fought for the rights of the working man and the poor. Countries like Hungary and his native Yugoslavia had been repressed by a feudal, slaveholding system which had brutalized the poor and the working class until Communism came along.

"You're full of shit," I said, and reminded him of the twenty million people Stalin had killed, of the massacre of the revolutionaries in Hungary in 1956.

"I'm not defending Stalin," Stanley said, "I'm defending the theory of Communism as opposed to Communism in practice, although I'll argue that Communism in practice gives the poor basic services which they never have in a feudal society."

Was it possible, I asked myself, that there were *good* Komchis?

On the way home from one of those arty, highfalutin after-school conversations with Stanley Osenar, on the way to the bus stop at East 105th and Euclid, I heard a woman singing.

The sound was coming from a bar with its door open. I went up to the door and stood there, transfixed by her voice. A sign on the door advertised a young unknown rhythm and blues singer.

Appearing that night: Aretha Franklin.

I joined speech and debate again and, at a weekend tournament, saw a girl with bright red hair and green eyes. Her name was Peggy Carney. She was sixteen, tall, well built, a sophomore at Beaumont, a private girls school on the East Side. I forgot Kay Jeffries completely the first time I saw her.

I saw her again at another tournament the next weekend and asked if I could drive her home in the red-and-white convertible that I'd waxed and polished the day before with just this in mind. She agreed and we stopped off at Howard Johnson's where I bought her a burger and a milkshake. We talked about rock and roll and our reading. She, too, loved Ginsberg and the Beats. I drove her home to an expensive suburban house and she asked me to meet her parents.

We went out to a record hop the following Friday. I wore my self-awarded letter sweater and she wore a tight blouse and skirt. We did the twist on the dance floor and I saw the other guys from Cathedral Latin watching me enviously. When I took her home, she kissed me with her tongue in my mouth and put my hands on her breasts. Her breasts were the size of oranges.

"Do you want to do something tomorrow?" she asked.

I said sure.

"Well," she said, "my parents won't be home. Why don't you just come over and wake me up in the morning and we'll figure out something to do."

When I got there the next morning, the front door was open and I said, "Peggy?" There was no answer. The house was quiet. I went upstairs and saw an open door. I walked in and saw her. She was in bed, asleep. Naked.

I went to the bed and kissed her and she put her arms around me dreamily and pulled me onto the bed. Her eyes were closed as though she were sleeping. Her skin was snowy white, a tangle of bright red hair was between her legs. I had never seen anything so beautiful. She kept kissing me, her tongue in my mouth, her eyes closed.

I took my clothes off and moved on top of her, my *fasz* huge. When I entered her, she smiled and moaned but kept her eyes closed. She moved in rhythm with me and kept smiling and moaning but never opened her eyes. We came at almost the same time and, afterward, I lay at her side, devouring her body with my eyes. She was as asleep as she had been while making love to me.

When Peggy "awoke," she said, "Hmm, that was a nice cuddle, wasn't it? Don't you just love *cuddling?*" She got up shyly and put her clothes on.

I felt like jumping up and shouting it to the whole world:

I did it! I did it! I did it!

After all those years of dreaming and fantasizing and just about ripping my *pimpli* and my *fasz* out of myself. I did it! The real thing! With a real, flesh-and-blood beautiful girl who couldn't wait to stick her tongue in my mouth! With a girl built like a *brick shithouse!* With a girl who had big *tits!* With a girl who had an *ass* to die for! And it was everything I had dreamed and fantasized it to be! Magical! Fantastic! Divine!

Howdy Doody triumphant!

I couldn't get enough of Peggy and, it seemed, Peggy couldn't get enough of me. In the car. In her bedroom. On the couch in her basement. But each time she was "asleep" as we made love. And she never addressed the fact that we had made love; she talked about how she loved to "cuddle" with me.

"I hope you don't get pregnant," I said to her.

She snapped at me, her eyes huge. "*Pregnant?* How could I get pregnant? We haven't *done* anything. *Silly!*"

"Who is she?" my father said to me one day.

"Who?"

"I don't know who," he said, "that's what I'm asking you. But *you* do. So please tell me her name."

I laughed. "How do you know there is anyone?"

"Because you're acting like a moonstruck cow," he said. "You're either in love or you're losing your mind like your mother and maybe I should start worrying about the radio cords again."

I told him about Peggy Carney then—about her red hair and green eyes and her sense of humor and how much fun it was being with her.

"You're making love to her, aren't you?" He smiled.

I felt myself blushing and nodded.

"Life can be quite wonderful at times, can't it?" my father said.

The great Puskás Öcsi was in town, the greatest soccer player in Hungarian history, a man some said had been the greatest soccer player in the world.

"He's an old friend," my father said. "He called and said he'll be in town and wants to see me. Do you want to come?"

We met the great Puskás at a football field on the East Side where he was doing a coaching exhibition for young players. He was a bear of a man, his face red-veined, spare tires around his middle, his hair graying. He was a coach in Madrid now.

He and my father hugged each other when they met, laughing about how they'd aged.

"I'll tell you a story about your father," the great Puskás said. "We grew up in the same neighborhood in Kispest. We belonged to the same gang. We would have battles each day with the other gangs from other neighborhoods. We threw beer bottles at each other. Your father couldn't run because of his limp. So he constructed a wooden shield for himself that he put on his back like armor. All the beer bottles bounced off his back.

"But one day a kid nailed him in the jaw with a bottle, dislocating it. We rolled him through the neighborhood on a wagon, yelling "*Meghalt a Pisti*"— Steve has died! When we got him home and his mother heard us yelling that he had died, she ran to the wagon sobbing, hysterical. Your father said, 'I'm not dead, Mama,' and smiled. 'See, I'm alive, Mama!' And his mother hit him so hard that his jaw snapped right back into place."

I watched the two of them laugh at the memory.

"Limp or no limp," the great Puskás said, "your father was one of the toughest kids I've ever met."

There was one other Hungarian kid at Cathedral Latin. He stopped by my table and ate his lunch with me. His name was George Árpád. He told me that his father read my father's articles in the *Catholic Hungarians' Sunday* and hated my father.

"He says your father is a Jew-lover," George told me. "My father keeps a book called *The Protocols of the Elders of Zion* on his nightstand. It explains how Jews run the world."

"What is it with these idiot Hungarians always hating Jews?" I asked.

"What do you mean?" George said. "My father's right. The Jews *do* run the world. You must be a Jew-lover like your father."

I said, "You must be as dumb as *your* father."

He never stopped by for lunch again.

Peggy had to do a book report on John D. Rockefeller, Cleveland's famous billionaire. She wanted to see the cemetery he was buried in.

On a hot summer day, we drove out to Lakeview Cemetery. There was no one else there. John D. Rockefeller had a big vault and tomb which was closed. We were sweated out and lay down in the cool grass.

I started to kiss her and she fell "asleep."

And I felt *as rich as Rockefeller*!

My father watched me warily as I read books from the library about the Russian Revolution and Marx and Engels and Lenin and Trotsky and Stalin. One night I said to him, "Why didn't you tell me there were some good Communists, Pop?"

"Like who?" he said.

"Like Lenin, for example."

"Lenin?" he said, his voice rising. "Lenin was a cold, heartless revolutionary who believed that the ends justified the means."

"He cared about the Russian people," I said, "about the poor, about the oppression of the czars.

"What about Imre Nagy?" I asked. "Wasn't he a good man?" Imre Nagy, a lifelong Communist, had led Hungary against the Soviet Union in the 1956 freedom fight.

"At the end he was. But only at the end. His hands were just as bloody as the others until then. And look what happened to him. The Soviets captured him and executed him."

"But he became a Communist in Hungary," I said, "because he saw how his parents, poor parents, were oppressed in a feudal system that used peasants as slaves. He had to become a Communist if he wanted to change that system."

"*My* parents were poor people," my father said. He was getting angry, his face flushed. "*I* didn't become a Communist!"

"Why didn't you?" I said. "You were poor. Your father worked in a canning factory. I bet he was paid and treated like a slave."

"I don't want to hear this in my house!" he said. My father was yelling at me now. "What is this . . . this *szar*—shit—you are telling me?"

I had hardly ever heard him use the word—it sounded odd coming from his mouth.

"You are swallowing all this propaganda you are reading. The Komchis are very good at propaganda!"

"Why are you yelling at me?" I said calmly. "I'm just trying to have a discussion with you."

"Because it's *shit!*" he yelled. "It's the same shit I've been fighting my entire life! I never thought I'd hear you, my son, saying this Komchi *shit* to me!"

"I don't have to agree with you politically," I said. "I can have my own political opinions, can't I? Can't we disagree politically?"

"Disagree . . . about the Komchis?" he said in disbelief. "You're going to take the Komchis' side? You call that a *disagreement*? How can you love me if you take the Komchis' side?"

"What are you saying?" I said.

My own voice was raised now.

"That if I love you I can't disagree with you? I can't have my own opinions?"

"About the Komchis?" he yelled. "Yes. That's exactly what I'm saying. You can't disagree with me about the Komchis!"

"That's not fair," I yelled.

"*Fair?*" he yelled back. "Is it fair to piss on what I've done with my whole life? Why do you think I left Hungary and started all over again and chose to be dirt poor? So *you* wouldn't live and be raised under Communism! So *you* would be free! And now you are taking the side of those that I freed you from? *I did it for you* and now *you're* making a mockery of what I did? *Is that fair?*"

"I was just trying to have a discussion with you about Communism," I said, "and you turn it into an argument about love. How can we discuss anything intelligently if you turn it into something so emotional?"

"*Emotional?*" he yelled. "Don't you understand? My whole life has been ruined by Communism! *Ruined!* I am not back in Budapest living in a big house writing my novels! I am here in this dump of an apartment working two jobs to have enough money to send you to school! *You* are the one thing that I have to live for! And if I keep hearing Komchi propaganda coming from your lips, I will have nothing to live for!"

I got home from seeing Peggy one Friday night and saw my father sitting at his desk with the English-Hungarian dictionary in front of him and another thin volume.

"What are you doing up so late, Pop?" I asked.

He showed me the book. It was my copy of Allen Ginsberg's *Howl.* My eyes almost popped out. Here was my father, the Catholic anti-Communist editor of the *Catholic Hungarians' Sunday* reading Ginsberg, the radical Communist homosexual poet!

"Who is this man?" my father asked.

"He is an American poet," I said.

"A *bitnik,*" he said. "I read about the bitniks in the *Plan Diler.*" He laughed. "Avant garde. When I was a young man in Hungary, it was the Dadaists. Tristan Tzara, a crazier Romanian than other Romanians, put a bunch of words into a hat, pulled them out individually, and wrote them down one after the other. He called it a poem. Now it's the bitniks."

"So," I said, "Pop—tell me. How do you like Allen Ginsberg?" I was trying to hide my smile.

"He is crazy," my father said, "but that is good. All poets and pharmacists are crazy. This 'angel-head' business he writes about, is *insane.* He thinks it's metaphysics. I think it must be delirium tremens from drunkenness. An 'angel-head' pink elephant maybe, but exciting, I grant you! The kind of stuff that races your pulse, but the kind of stuff that I am not sure, in the end, says very much, at least to me. Who is this Ginsberg? What kind of person is he? He writes like he expects to die tomorrow morning. Or is that just the poet's usual professional hysterics? Novelists, you see, can't afford to be hysterical. Novels take too long to write."

"Who is he?" I said. "A Jew, a Communist, a homosexual. A brilliant poet."

"Really?" he said, looking a little stunned. "All three?"

"Really," I said casually. "All four. A brilliant poet, too."

"It figures," he said, almost applaudingly. "Jews, Communists, homosexuals, they are usually educated people. They read. You see? You must read, as I always say to you."

· · ·

The speech and debate city-wide finals were coming up and I wrote an essay for the original oratory finals called "Jesus Was a Bum." Obviously influenced by Allen Ginsberg, it was the story of a hobo reviled by society until society realizes he is Christ come back. I was proud of my essay and thought I had a chance of winning.

The finals were in three rounds. There were twenty contestants and the score was tallied at the end of each round. I got two first places my first two rounds.

Peggy was with me, as excited as I was. The whole tournament was buzzing about the piece of original oratory called "Jesus Was a Bum."

My third-round judge was a Jesuit priest from St. Ignatius, the high school which was just down the street from the apartment where I'd grown up on Lorain Avenue. The priest heard my recitation without any expression on his face and then posted his score: Number twenty, last place.

That would make sure that I didn't have a chance to win any awards, let alone first place.

When I saw the score he'd given me, I confronted him.

"How can you give me a last place when the two other judges gave me first places?" I said.

"What you write is blasphemy," the priest said. "It shouldn't have been allowed into the tournament. I'm sorry the other kids here were exposed to it. I'm notifying your principal at Cathedral Latin Monday morning."

I felt tears coming to my eyes.

"Well fuck you," I told the priest, "and the dumb fucking *ass* you rode in on."

The priest blanched. "You're going to regret this, Mr."—he glanced at my entry card—"Esterhaze."

My father and I were sitting in the principal's office at Cathedral Latin. The principal was a priest in his sixties. He was reading my essay "Jesus Was a Bum."

"This is garbage," the priest said. "You represent Cathedral Latin at a speech tournament with this garbage?"

"You *critic?*" my father asked in his thick Hungarian accent.

The priest seemed taken aback by his question.

"You priest," my father said. "You pray. *Critic* write."

"He swore at a priest!" the principal said to my father. "That's a sin and a sacrilege!"

"Yes!" my father said, his voice rising now, too. "He swore at priest because priest stupid . . . not fair priest! Joe lose temper! Now Joe *calma*, no more temper . . . but priest he *still stupid priest!*"

"You are suspended from Cathedral Latin!" the principal yelled, pointing his finger at me.

"You stupid priest like other!" my father said calmly to him. "You suspend from school—I sue! This free country! America no *cenzura!* Stupid priest no censor! Boy write true! Jézus come back like bum, everybody piss him. Stupid priest like you piss him! What boy write strong, original. This *my* opinion. *I* writer, not *you,* stupid priest! *My* opinion educate. *You* opinion stupid priest opinion! *Ohkay, fein,* you want sue, I sue! City Klevland know what stupid priest you! What boy write . . . *Plan Diler* write, too . . . cos I sue. *Ohkay, fein.* Whole City Klevland read what boy write. That you want? *Ohkay, fein.*"

I wasn't suspended after all from Cathedral Latin.

I was allowed to graduate.

My father and mother came to graduation night, where I got my diploma.

Afterward, my father said, "I was embarrassed. All those other students went up to that stage for this and that honor. You went up only for your diploma. No honors for speech and debate. No honors for the newspaper."

I said, "Well, none of those other kids were picked for the WHK High School Hall of Fame. What's better, Pop? To get another piece of paper on graduation night or do something that the whole city can hear about on the radio?"

My father thought about it.

"You have a point," he said.

When the Cathedral Latin school yearbook came out, I noticed that my senior picture wasn't in it. I was there in the group pictures of speech and debate and *Latineer* members, but my individual yearbook photograph wasn't included. Pictures of the other graduates were there, but not mine.

I went to the brother who was the yearbook adviser and asked him why my picture wasn't there.

"It's not there?" the brother said, and paged through the book.

"I'm sorry," he said. "It must have been lost somehow—at the printer maybe. But look—I saw your picture in the *Latineer* so often this year that I'm sure it more than makes up for this mistake, Mr. Esterhose."

My mother didn't say much to me anymore. She didn't ask me why I didn't go to church anymore. She didn't ask what I was reading. She didn't ask me about school. She cooked. She complained of her headaches. She smoked. And she went to the office every day with my father.

Once, as we were eating Hungarian bacon together, I asked her, "Nana, remember the times we'd stay up till midnight on Friday and you'd make bacon soldiers on bread?"

"Yes," she said.

She didn't smile. She didn't look at me.

The Negotiator

A negotiator with the studios representing some of the top talent in the world, the lawyer had a reputation as a ballbuster. The studios hated negotiating with him. He made the lives of their executives a living nightmare.

His clients, naturally, adored him.

His clients didn't know that he padded his income about a million dollars a year by writing screenplays under a pseudonym . . . and selling them to the same studios he was negotiating with on behalf of his clients.

The studios bought his scripts, never made them into movies, and paid him the money in the hope that it would give them the slightest edge in negotiations with him involving his clients.

But he kept busting their balls, having figured out there was no reason to compromise his integrity just because they were so willing to compromise theirs.

CHAPTER 25

Love Hurts

MILANO

He's gonna remember, huh?

DOYLE

He don't forget. He's a hundred percent.

MILANO

Nobody's a hundred percent.

F.I.S.T.

G erri was happy we were going to Maui, especially so because Naomi was coming with us along with Steve and Suzi and two of their friends.

"I don't want to argue anymore," my wife said. "Let's just have fun. I want to sit and watch a lot of sunsets."

From Naomi's journal, April 6, 1993:

We left for Hawaii this morning. There's so much energy in the house when Joe is there. It's a whole different dynamic. As we were getting ready to leave, Steve said, "My dad wants to see you in his office."

I love Joe's office. It's full of books and leather furniture. It smells heavenly. I go down when he's not there sometimes just to read.

I headed down and Joe was holding an armload of books, scanning the shelves for more. "Here," he said, "this should keep you busy." He gave me Larry McMurtry and Joyce Carol Oates and Anne Tyler and Updike—a treasure trove. It's so strange. No one else in the house reads. It's like speaking

a language with him no one else understands. I thanked him
and headed upstairs.

As we all prepared to pile into the limo, it was cold. I
have so few clothes—only the ones I brought when I first
came here.

Joe said, "Are you cold?"

I said, "No, I'm fine. I'll be fine in the car."

He said, "Grab my jean jacket behind you."

I argued but he insisted. So I took it. As I put it on, I
felt Gerri, Steve, and Suzi all watching me. I was self-
conscious.

It was just a moment, but it felt a little strained.
Maybe I'm imagining it, I don't know. But I loved wearing
his coat.

As the kids partied, Gerri, Naomi, and I spent most of our time together on the
beach in the blazing sun, sipping Seabreezes and Mai-Tais.

Gerri slept much of the time and Naomi and I talked about the roads that
led us here. My life in the refugee camps . . . her gawky high school years . . . my
years at *Rolling Stone* magazine . . . her years working on Wall Street, at Warner
Communications and American Express. I felt such an electric undercurrent
between us that I almost jolted when my arm brushed against her as we played
backgammon. Except for those few moments in my kitchen when she had held
my hand, we'd never touched each other.

While we were out there on the beach, we kept playing the Beatles's "Don't
Let Me Down" over and over again.

From Naomi's journal:

Each day, Joe and Gerri and I sit down on the beach and
watch the sunset. It's my favorite part of the day. The
weird thing is almost invariably Gerri falls asleep.

Suzi and I were in the pool this afternoon. She is so
excited about a rave that's going on this weekend on Maui. I
guess Steve and his friend Tommy are going, but Suzi's
afraid her dad won't let her and Dana go.

She said, "Naomi, can you talk to my dad and ask him if
we can go?"

I said, "Why don't you ask your mom?"

She said, "She'll just tell me to ask him. It's always
his decision."

I said I'd see what I could do.

Then she said, "I want to thank you for being such a good friend to my mom. You've really helped her." Suzi is very protective of her mom. It's almost like their roles are reversed. She worries about Gerri like a little mother.

That night at dinner I chose my moment and leaned over to Joe and said, "You know, there's this rave tonight and Steve and Tommy are going."

He said, "I know."

I said, "Well, maybe, if Suzi and Dana stick with them and come home with them, they could go, too? They go to raves at home all the time . . ."

He thought a minute and then said, "Hey Steve, take your sister and Dana to the rave tonight, okay?"

Steve about died. Suddenly he was going to have his sister tagging along. But he just said, "Okay, Dad." Suzi and Dana were overjoyed.

After a few minutes Joe leaned over and said quietly, "My daughter thinks you have influence over me . . ."

I said, "Well, she's going . . . isn't she?"

Gerri was in the pool when two little children flitted by us on the beach. They were almost silhouettes in the setting sun.

Suddenly Joe said, "Do you want to have children?"

And I said, "I've always wanted children."

It was quiet for a moment.

Then Joe said, "Me too. I'd love to have more children someday." He was looking out at the sunset, so I couldn't see his eyes.

I thought—Is he talking to me? Because certainly Gerri can't have more children. Or is he just wishing something he knows won't be? Or is he telling me something?

Last night I tried to excuse myself from drinks on the terrace, but both Joe and Gerri said, "Why?" and seemed disappointed. Almost a little hurt. It was after dinner and I said it was late, and they said, "Just one drink." Truthfully I wasn't tired, I just thought they might like to have a little time by themselves.

But more and more I find I'm not in control. I'm just

going with the flow. And it's getting very strange. We smoked
a joint this time, and Joe said something outrageous, I
don't even remember what it was.

I said, "You know, you're really insane. You should commit yourself."

He laughed.

Gerri looked at me and said, "If he's insane, what are
you?"

She said it with a smile, but I felt very uncomfortable.
I said, "I don't know, what am I?"

And she said, "You're . . . scandalous."

We all laughed, since I had been tabloid fodder in the
past month. But an uneasiness was clearly there.

Then she said, "And what am I?"

I didn't answer. We all sat for a few seconds.

Then Joe said, "I know. You're responsible, Gerri.
You've always been very responsible."

She smiled. I smiled. We all smiled.

Maybe I should go home.

I love Hawaii and Joe and Gerri are great company, but this
trip is becoming more and more strange each day. I feel like
I'm in some twisted play that never ends. The kids have
brought their friends, so they aren't around much of the
time. Which leaves the three of us.

Gerri and I go down to the pool and Joe says he will be
down to join us. If I sit next to Gerri on the end she says,
"Oh no! Sit next to Joseph."

I'll say, "But I want to sit next to you."

She says, "Then sit in the middle."

When we go out for dinner in the van, she says, "Sit up
front next to Joseph, I'll sit in back." If I argue, she just
gets in and smiles and says she wants to sit with the kids.

So there I am, up front with Joe. It makes me self-
conscious. I love to talk to Joe, but it's weird to be riding in front with him. Maybe I'm being paranoid or petty but
this is just becoming more disconcerting for me.

At the pool yesterday Joe, Gerri, and I were all lounging in
the sun. I don't remember what we were talking about but I
said something to the effect that sometimes nothing seems to

make sense anymore. Maybe not quite that esoteric but something in that vein.

And Joe was lying there with his sunglasses (he always wears sunglasses, so you never know where he's looking or what's going on inside). He said, "Well, I've lived forty-eight years and I would say I have learned one thing for sure: Life is strange."

Yesterday Gerri wanted to go shopping. I don't much like shopping to begin with, let alone on Maui where I'd rather just lounge by the pool or read a book. But I always go or she'll have to go alone and I'd feel terrible.

So we're in a sort of barren department store and I see this little red dress. I don't think I've ever owned a red dress but it was on sale and caught my eye and I bought it. She wanted to buy it for me but I said, "Please, Gerri, let me treat myself."

Then she came over to me with a black lace bed jacket. She loves lingerie.

She said, "Oh, let me get this for you."

I said, "Gerri. I'll never wear it."

She said, "But Joseph would love it on you. You can wear it for cocktails."

I should explain that each night after the sun sets, we come up and put our robes on and have a drink before dinner on either my balcony or Joe and Gerri's. (We are in adjoining rooms.) But these are big, bulky terry cloth hotel robes—not lacy underwear.

I said, "Gerri. I won't wear it—please."

She walked away, but again I think I hurt her feelings.

I really looked at her when she said Joe would like it. I thought—Maybe she's being sarcastic or testing me. But she just seems guileless. I have never been in a stranger situation.

When we were alone, Gerri told me how much fun she was having. "Isn't this the greatest vacation?" she said. "Naomi and the kids are having a lot of fun, too, aren't they?"

I saw, though, that she had a stack of books about witchcraft and demonology and was still reading them as I fell asleep each night.

. . .

The day before Guy McElwaine was supposed to arrive,
Gerri decided to go with Suzi and her friend for a long
hike.

Joe and I sat in the sun, had lunch, and talked. He
always makes me laugh, really laugh. He said, "We think
alike, you know," and I knew what he meant immediately. We
always seem to have some level of communication that's
beneath the surface. Here we are having conversations with
his entire family around, but it sometimes seems to me we're
the only two people in the room.

The hikers weren't due back until dinnertime. At around
four o'clock Joe said, "Let's have a beer at the Hyatt. It's
a beautiful bar." So we did. I have not had so much fun in
years.

As the sun set, I thought, I would love to just climb in his
lap and stay there forever. He feels like home. I don't know
if my feelings are because he has rescued me at a time when
I have felt so alone, or because I'm falling in love with
him. All I know is that no matter who's in the room anymore,
I only see him.

Just then he looked at me and said, "I think I'm falling in
love with you."

I was stunned. Joe never says or does anything
carelessly.

He said, "I'd love to spend my life with you, just like
this. I'd love to have children with you."

It was the first time I'd ever seen him nervous. He
looked like an awkward boy. I wanted to hug him.

I said, "I think I might be falling in love with you,
too."

And then he smiled. So beautifully. He took my hand and
squeezed it. I felt like an electric current ran up my arm.
I thought—I don't know what this is but I've never felt it
before.

We said nothing more, but when we walked back to our
hotel he held my hand. It was so wonderful. Bill would never
hold my hand. I realized the last person who had held my
hand like that was my mother.

We had dinner that night but as I listened to Gerri's and
Suzi's account of their hike, the words felt like they were
coming through a haze. I felt guilty and I felt overjoyed.
But I felt warm, and so different than I ever had felt in my
life.

After dinner, Gerri, Naomi, and I smoked some dope on the patio of our suite.
Gerri nodded off after a while and fell asleep in her chair.

Naomi and I went inside to pour some more wine and I kissed her, more
and more passionately. Naomi said, "We can't do this."

I picked her up and carried her into her own bedroom and locked the con-
necting door to the suite.

I kept kissing her and we were on the bed now, our clothes off, making love;
the intensity of the feeling that had built up between us suddenly exploding.

I was smoking a cigarette and we were lying there quietly in each other's arms
when we heard a loud pounding on the door to the suite. It was Gerri. Her voice
was stoned and slurred.

"Joseph!" she yelled. "I know you're in there, Joseph."

She started throwing fruit from the complimentary fruit basket at the door.
Apples, oranges, and pineapples smashed on the door.

"You've got to get out of here," Naomi whispered to me.

I kissed her quickly, put my shirt and shorts on, and ducked out a door
which led to the stairway, then ran seven floors down to the lobby.

An hour later, I reappeared in the suite. Gerri was sitting quietly on the patio,
staring off. Pulped fruit was everywhere on the rug around the door leading to
Naomi's door.

"Jesus," I said to Gerri, "what did you do?"

She said, "I thought you were in there with Naomi."

I said, "What? You thought *what*?"

She said, "Where were you?"

"I got stoned out on the patio and went down to the beach to straighten
out."

She said, "Where's Naomi?"

"I don't know," I said, "she's probably asleep in her room."

I looked at the pulped fruit on the rug again and said, "Gerri, you've gotta
stop this. You're flipping out."

Gerri looked at me, tears in her eyes, and said, "I know. I'm sorry."

I held her and said. "It's okay. It must've been the dope. This Maui stuff is so
strong it can make you paranoid."

. . .

Guy came over from the Big Island, from his beloved Mauna Kea Hotel, to spend a few days with us. He had never met Naomi Macdonald, he didn't even know we were good friends.

I told him that Naomi was here with us and that I thought I was falling in love with her.

He seemed shattered. He knew me well. He knew I had a *reverence* for my family. He knew, too, that I was lonely . . . he knew about the other girls and the "research" trips in different cities. He also knew and liked Gerri.

And, of course, he was still Sharon's agent, unofficially representing Bill Macdonald now, too, who was talking about forming a production company with Sharon and was trying to find scripts for her to star in (including *Atlas Shrugged*).

"What are you going to do?" he asked.

"I don't know."

"Does Naomi love you?"

"I don't know. I think she does. I feel that she does."

"She's a train wreck," Guy said. "Her husband leaves her for Sharon Stone after five months of marriage and two months later you, her husband's best friend, fall in love with her. She's gotta be reeling."

Joe said to me, "I'm going to meet Guy for a drink before you and Gerri come down. I'm going to tell him that I think I'm in love with you."

I panicked. "But I've never met him. What is he going to think of me?"

Joe said, "Trust me."

When I was ready to go downstairs, I knocked on Gerri's door. She said to come in, but she had just come out of the shower and wasn't ready.

"You go on down," she said, "I'll meet you."

"That's okay," I said, "I'll wait."

She insisted. "Go on, I'll be down soon."

And so I went. I'll never forget how they both looked as I walked in. Guy was smiling, but his eyes were sweeping all over me curiously. Joe was beaming. They both stood up when I walked up to the table. I was wearing my little red dress, the one Gerri wanted to buy for me.

. . .

Joe, as he always did, told me how pretty I looked. As we began to talk, I felt at ease. We were laughing and talking about nothing at all and I was so happy.

Guy said, "You know even Stevie Wonder would see what's going on here."

Then Gerri arrived. She seemed almost giddy. And as the evening wore on, and she had more to drink, her eyes were bright and she was increasingly bubbly.

And I thought—*She knows*.

We went to eat at Avalon in Lahaina, with Guy, Steve and Suzi and their friends. We had a lot to drink and when we came out of the restaurant we walked up the stairs to Lahaina's only live-music rock club, Moose McGillycuddy's.

It was a meat market, it was packed. Gerri went outside to talk to the kids, to see what their plan for the evening was. Joe walked up to the dance floor, where many people stand and watch the band. I was left with Guy, who was slowly sipping a drink.

I glanced back at the table and saw Naomi sitting with Guy as, one after another, the guys in the place went up and asked her to dance. I saw her shaking her head. Gerri wasn't there.

I thought—I know what Joe's doing. The tension is thick. He's catching his breath for a minute.

I wanted to dance with her. That's all I felt. I wanted to hold her in my arms.

As I looked at him, I thought—I want to be near him. I don't want to sit here with Guy. I said, "Guy, I'm going to talk to Joe. Will you watch my purse?"

He looked at me long and hard. Then he just reached out his hand and took my purse.

I watched her come toward me from the table. As she came up, I saw Gerri back at the table, standing there, her eyes on me.

The band was called the Missionaries. They were playing rock and roll. When Joe saw me, he was silent for a minute. Then he said, "You want to dance?" He said it so calmly.

I said, "Yes."
So he put his drink down and took my hand.

I felt Gerri's eyes burning at us, laserlike, across the room.

Just as we walked to the floor, the song ended. We stood
there a few seconds. Then the band began to play a slow,
throbbing love song. The floor cleared. For a moment I
thought he would say, "Let's wait for the next one." But he
didn't.

I danced with her. We melted into each other out there alone on that dance
floor, holding on to each other as though each of us was a lifeline. We were both
trembling.

He took me in his arms and in that moment the club disappeared for me. I only felt him, smelled him, saw him. I
wanted never to let go.

Guy was there suddenly.
He said, "You don't want to do this."
I said, "Leave me alone."
He said, "You don't want to do this like this—come on, go back to the table,
let me dance with Naomi."
I said, "If you touch Naomi, I'm gonna break your fuckin' neck."

Joe gave him one of those looks that can stop a wild boar in
its tracks. My heart was pounding. Guy went back to the
table.

Gerri was out on the dance floor.
"Do you want me to go, Joseph?" she said.
She wasn't crying. She almost whispered the words, her eyes almost blank
now.
I said, "It's up to you."
She stood there a moment as I held Naomi, watching us, and then she went
back to sit down with Guy.

We finished the dance. We quickly left the club. Gerri had
given the kids the van, so we took a cab back to the Four
Seasons. I rode up front with the driver, the girl in the

little red dress. Joe sat with Guy and Gerri in the back. It
was forty minutes of utter dead silence.

I remembered on that taxi back to Lahaina what I had said to Bill Macdonald to
stop him from letting Naomi come to the *Sliver* wrap party: "*Do you want to
humiliate your wife?*" I knew that I had just humiliated mine.

When we got to the hotel Gerri quickly got out and hurried into the lobby ahead
of us.

Guy said an awkward good night. He had tears in his eyes.

I took out another room in a different wing of the hotel under a false name.
Naomi and I went up to the room and I took Naomi's red dress off with my
teeth.

She left at four in the morning and went back to her own room. I ordered a
pot of coffee and sat out on the patio watching the sunrise and trying to sort out
what I was going to do with my life.

The next morning at eight Joe called me in my room. "What's
going on next door?" he said. I hadn't heard anything yet.
I said, "I'm going to go over."
He said, "I'm on my way up, do you want to wait?"
I said, "No, I'll meet you there."
Gerri had a right to confront me alone, to say what she
wanted, without me walking in under Joe's protection.

I went up to Guy's room first. He hadn't slept all night.
"What are you going to do?" he said.
"I'm going to tell Gerri."
"You can't do that," he said. "Not now. Not here. Not on a vacation with
your kids here."
"There's nothing left to tell her, Guy," I said. "She saw everything last night."
"People have too much to drink," he said. "Things happen. Gerri wants an
excuse not to believe what she saw."
"She knows I didn't spend the night with her last night. What does she think
I was doing?"
"You went down to the beach," Guy said. "You fell asleep on the beach. I
found you there this morning. We'll go in together. Get in my shower and get a
little wet, then we'll go up."
"Guy," I said, "I'm tired of all the lying and all the stories. It's gone on too
long."

"Fine," he said, "but you don't have to end it here, with your kids here—before you have a chance to think out what you really want to do."

"I know what I really want to do," I said. "I want to be with Naomi."

I knocked on her door and said, "Gerri?" She said, "Come in." She was sitting on the couch with her elbows on her knees, wearing the hotel robe. She turned and looked at me with raw hatred.

"You were my friend!" she said. *"I told you everything!"* Her words hung and I just stood there. Then she looked back down at the floor. I closed the door and went to sit in the chair next to the couch.

"I'm sorry," I said. "I am so desperately sorry. I don't know what happened. I lost control. I am so strongly attracted to him I can't even think straight. I'm sorry. I don't know what else to say. It was awful and I'm sorry."

She was sneering. Her eyes were coal-black. "I told you all my secrets," she said, "and you used them against me. You told him everything I said and then turned him against me."

"I never told him anything," I said. "I was trying to help you and then, I don't know what happened, I am just so drawn to him."

"What are you telling me?" she said. "That you're in love with my husband?"

I thought for a moment. Should I lie? What will Joe say to her? And I thought—I've been honest with her until now. I won't lie.

I said, "I don't know, Gerri. I guess I am."

She said, "Is he in love with you?"

And I said, "I don't know. You'll have to ask him that."

She looked at the floor and then, as it bubbled up inside her, she raged. She said I was evil. She said I had planned the whole thing. She said I had "poisoned" Joe.

I listened for a while and then I said, "What did *you* do? Always insisting I sit beside him, leaving us alone together for hours and days, trying to buy me sexy lingerie because he'd like it. What was *that*? You were practically throwing him at me!"

She thought for a minute and looked down. We sat in silence for what must have been fifteen minutes. It seemed like hours.

. . .

I was standing in Guy's shower, wearing shorts and a T-shirt, getting wet but not too wet . . . just wet enough for having fallen asleep on the beach.

I felt like a schmuck. I was forty-eight years old and I was playing out the first part of an idiotic, absurd charade.

I got out of the shower and Guy looked me over and said, "*Perfect!*"—it was one of his favorite words and the title of one of the biggest failures he had green-lighted when he was the head of Columbia.

I said, "This is demeaning!"

"You'll thank me for this later," he said. "I know what I'm talking about. I've been in this situation." He shrugged. "Lots of times."

"I can't go through with this," I said.

"Sure you can. I didn't think I could go through something like this either," he said. "The first time."

There was a knock at the door, Gerri answered it. Before Joe could say anything, she said, "So here's the man who's in love with Naomi Macdonald!"

I said, "I didn't say that, Gerri. I said you should ask him yourself."

She was standing right in front of Joe.

She said, *"So are you?"*

I thought—Well, this is the moment. The moment when most men, at least the ones I've known in my life, say, "Now everybody calm down. Let's sort this out. Things are way out of control . . ." and somehow beg the question. Or deny it completely.

I said—Yes I am.

Guy just turned and headed for the door.

Gerri looked at me and said, "I want to speak to my husband alone!"

Joe said, "Guy, will you take Naomi and wait next door?"

Gerri said, "I want her out of the hotel!"

Joe said, "I want her next door."

Gerri started to cry, almost in a whimper, when they left the room.

The mother of my beautiful children, my wife of twenty-four years, a lovely woman with a gentle and big heart, and I started to cry, too.

We cried and talked for nearly three hours, discussing intimate and painful things we should have talked about many, many years ago. Our talk was hurtful, loving, draining . . . and too late.

She begged me not to leave her and she said that both Sharon and Naomi were demons. "*Sister beings*," she said. She said I was possessed by both of them.

I told her that I had never wanted to hurt her, but had been lonely for a long time.

"I'll change, Joseph," she said, "I promise you, but please don't do this."

I told her that we would call it a trial separation. I said I was taking Naomi to the Ritz-Carlton, on the other side of the island, and that I was going to come back tomorrow to tell the kids (who were camping).

"What will you tell them?" she said, almost in shock.

I told her I'd tell them the truth.

"How can you do this?" Gerri said. "How can you hurt your own children this way?"

"I don't know," I said. "I don't know how I can hurt them this way. I never thought I would."

I went into the bedroom and started packing my suitcase.

"What are you doing?" she said, horrified.

"I'm packing, Gerri. I told you. I'm going over to the Ritz-Carlton."

"But I always pack *for you*," she said.

I had to look away. I felt I was being choked by an overwhelming sadness.

"Aw, come on, Gerri," I said. "Please."

She went to the suitcase and started packing my things.

When we got to my room, Guy said, "I need a beer. Where's the key to your minibar?"

I said, "I don't use it. The only thing I ever drink is Diet Coke and I don't like to get it from the minibar because it's too expensive."

He looked at me like I was deranged.

"I'm going to my room to get a beer," he said. "I'll be right back."

When he came back, we sat out on the balcony in silence for a moment. I had only met him the day before and we'd just been through a lifelong twenty-four hours.

He took a long drag on his cigarette and said, "This is very serious. This marriage is in a worldful of hurt. Are you sure you love him?"

I thought long and hard. I could profess undying love, but I wanted to answer as honestly as possible.

"Well, I know what people are going to say. That I was in
love a month ago with somebody else. That I'm a trauma victim and that I don't know what I'm doing. That it's impossible to so quickly be over the ordeal I've been through. That
I cried because Sharon ruined my marriage and now I'm wreck-
ing Gerri's. And I understand that.

"All I know is that I always thought I was happy. But now
I don't think I ever knew what happiness was. I certainly
never felt like this. All I think about is him. When he's in
the room, I'm happy. Even if he's across the room talking to
someone else, I feel overjoyed to have him near.

"I can't focus on anything else. And I know that for a
long time, they weren't happy. Before either of them knew
me. And I just can't let the best thing that's ever happened
to me walk away just because Gerri is my friend, too. Or
because I will be ridiculed for the hypocrisy and the
immorality of it. It's bigger than all that. And that's the
best way I can explain it."

Guy thought about it and said, "Well, that sounds like
love to me."

I kissed Gerri on the cheek, asked her to forgive me, and said I'd be back the next day to talk to Steve and Suzi.

I went next door and saw Naomi sitting on the bed.

"How quickly can you pack?" I asked.

He looked like he'd aged five years in that other room. I
thought he was telling me that I was going back to L.A.

He said, "We're going over to the Ritz-Carlton."

Naomi held me. She went to get her suitcase and had trouble lifting it. I helped her. We were both shaking, overwhelmed by the moment.

We couldn't figure out why the suitcase was so heavy.

When we opened it, we found that Gerri had filled it with gift soaps and shampoos during our stay. Naomi held these things . . . that Gerri had planned as a surprise for her . . . and started to cry.

I went out on the patio and Guy looked at me and said, "How was it?"

"Awful."

"Did you tell her?"

I nodded.

"All of it?"

I nodded.

Guy took a long slug off his beer bottle. "I'll stick around for a couple days," Guy said, "give Gerri somebody to talk to, walk the beach with her."

"Thank you," I said.

I'd leave with Naomi . . . and my *agent* would stay behind to work the deal . . . and hold Gerri's hand.

It was such a Hollywood ending.

We drove across to the Ritz and as I held Naomi snuggled against me, I felt exhilarated and decimated.

I was in love like I'd never been in love before . . . and I was decimating a woman whose only crime was that she and I had grown in different ways and in different directions in the course of twenty-four years.

And I, who had always worked so hard to protect my children from hurt and harm, would now inflict upon them the greatest pain of their young lives.

On the way over to the Ritz-Carlton, as I held her against me, I told Naomi my greatest secret.

I told her about my father . . . about how much I had loved him and how, three years ago, in 1990, I had tried to stop loving him . . . the man who'd been the most important person in my life.

I cried sometimes as I told her. After a while Naomi cried with me. For me. For us. For everything.

CHAPTER 26

Sins of the Fathers

ANN
This Michael László must have lied when he got his citizenship.
He's accused of war crimes.

HER FATHER
What I know war crime? I don't do nothing *like that*. I not *like
that*.

ANN
Papa, it's not you. It's somebody else. They made a mistake. We'll
clear it up. Don't worry.

Music Box

Jane Fonda had never met Richard Marquand although, she was saying, she would have liked to. She said she had liked *Jagged Edge* very much.

"I should have done it," Jane said, "I made a mistake."

We were sitting at Don's Hideaway at the Beverly Wilshire in 1987 (Jane had called and asked to see me).

She said, "I have an idea that I would very much like you to do. I don't know what it is with the two of us—it never seems to work out—*Silkwood*, then *Jagged Edge*, maybe this one will."

She wanted to do a remake of *All About Eve*, set in the movie business. It was one of her favorite movies. She thought the story could be better told shifted to the world of film from Broadway.

I agreed with her. It was an exciting idea, but there was no way I would do it.

"Jane," I said, "I live in Marin County. I don't know the innards of this town. I try to stay away from it as much as possible to keep myself relatively sane. I don't want to hurl myself into this world."

We went back and forth and I finally convinced her.

"Well, damn," she said, stopping the waiter, "can I have a triple tequila please?" She was kidding. We all laughed.

I smiled. I very much wanted to work with this woman. Putting it at its simplest, I admired her.

"I've got another idea," I said. It was something that I'd been thinking about for a long time, even before I started writing screenplays. "How about a piece about an American lawyer of ethnic descent who discovers one day that her father, a man she adores, is being accused of having been a war criminal in the old country. She has to defend him."

Jane said, simply, "Yes. It puts chills down my back."

The next day her agent made a deal for United Artists and the story of the lawyer and her accused war criminal father was slotted into my new three-picture deal. I asked Irwin Winkler to produce it. He liked the idea as much as Jane did.

"What nationality will you make her?" Irwin asked.

"Well, she's American," I said, "she came to this country when she was very little."

"No," Irwin said, "I mean her father—what nationality will you make her father?"

"Hungarian," I said.

Irwin looked at me strangely for a moment and then he nodded.

The movie which I wrote, *Music Box,* is about a Hungarian immigrant named Mihály László who comes to America from the refugee camps and raises his children to be successful Americans. His daughter, Ann Talbot, becomes a respected criminal attorney in Chicago.

One day, out of the blue, the Justice Department's Office of Special Investigations announces it is prosecuting her father for war crimes allegedly committed in Hungary many years ago. Ann Talbot defends him.

Thanks to her efforts, her father is cleared of the charges. It is only then that she discovers he is guilty. Her father, the man she has loved most in her life, is a war criminal, a moral monster.

Costa-Gavras committed to direct my script the moment he finished reading it. Jane Fonda loved it, too. She had no suggestions, no notes, no changes. Jane said, "When do we shoot?"

She admired Costa, who was also a friend—she and her husband, Tom Hayden, had even taken Costa, the world-respected intellectual, to the Super Bowl. And Costa admired both Jane's acting and politics, but came to the conclusion that she was too old for the part. Irwin Winkler and I disagreed with him. We both thought Jane would be wonderful as Ann Talbot. I thought that Jane was so talented she could do anything she wanted to do.

Costa called Jane and told her he was suddenly having difficulties seeing her in the part, but didn't say why.

Jane called and asked me to help her. "I know he's got a problem," she said, "but I don't know what it is."

I respected Jane and told her the truth: "He thinks you're too old for the part."

"Shit," she said, "what can I do?"

"Convince him you're not," I said.

She *asked* to do a screen test. In a town where most stars considered even *reading* for a part to be demeaning, here was Jane Fonda, one of the biggest stars in the world, *asking* for a screen test. She changed her hairstyle, had a makeover, and called me to say, "I'm going to convince him I'm nineteen."

Irwin and I thought her test was sensational. Costa didn't. He thought Jane looked too old. She was heartbroken. Costa didn't budge.

She was paid $1.25 million "to go away."

"*Going Away Money*," I knew, was viewed as the kiss of death to a movie career. Costa cast Jessica Lange instead.

Marlon Brando was our first choice to play Jessica Lange's father, and Costa flew to the Fijian island where Brando was living. When he got back to L.A., Costa said he had met with Brando and had ruled him out, even though Brando said he was interested in the part.

I didn't get it: Brando was an icon; his presence in the movie would immediately have high-profiled it.

Costa was reluctant to tell me why he had ruled Brando out, but I pressed him.

"It is a problem of focus," Costa finally said.

"What do you mean?"

"Brando focus on other things," he said in his Franco-Greek accent. "Other thing than this script."

I said, "Like what?"

Costa smiled and shrugged.

I said, "I still don't get it."

Costa sighed and said, "Okay, I tell you. Brando, he has this . . . this . . . *collection* on his island. He want to talk about this collection more than the part he would play in script. He want me to add to collection."

I said, "What does he collect?"

Costa said, "Shit."

"*Shit?*"

"Shit. He collect shit from people go to visit him. He keep it in bottle, separate bottles for each person who give to collection."

I said, "You're right, Costa, he's not focused."

Costa finally cast the German actor Armin Mueller-Stahl, who, I thought, was too cerebral for the part, lacking a more elemental, Anthony Quinn–like temper, but the shoot went smoothly.

Costa embraced me the night before we began shooting and said, "Joe, I thank you for your script and your passion."

I loved the finished movie. While I still had some reservations about Armin's coldness, I thought Jessie's performance was genius.

I was proud of the film on a very personal level. I, who was Hungarian-born, had showed the world what the Hungarians themselves . . . not occupying Nazi forces but the *Hungarian people themselves* . . . had done to the Jews at the end of the war.

When the war was decided and over, when there was no more ammunition, Hungarians had taken those Jews not already sent to Auschwitz down to the Danube and strangled them with their bare hands. I took great pride in exposing the full magnitude of this Hungarian horror to the world.

The movie got some terrific reviews and did very little business. "Joe Eszterhas," the respected critic Michael Sragow wrote, "has written the ultimate feminist screenplay." Elie Wiesel praised it.

We weren't surprised the movie wasn't doing much business. We hadn't expected much—it was, at its core, a piece about a time in Hungarian history.

It very nearly wasn't made. When I finished the script, MGM-United Artists, which had financed the script, told us they were pulling out.

"No one's going to care what happened in Hungary at the end of the war," an MGM-UA executive said.

We sent the script to Universal and Tom Pollock, the head of the studio, said he'd make the movie if I changed the ending: If Ann Talbot got her father off *because he was innocent*. If, in other words, I changed it to the clichéd, everybody's happy Hollywood ending.

"I can't do that," I said. "If I changed it to that ending, the movie would become a rallying point for all those arguing that prosecution of war criminals fifty years after the fact is unfair. The Justice Department, and the Office of Special Investigations, would be villains."

"Yes," Tom Pollock said, "but with a happy ending—a daughter saving an unjustly accused father—you'll have a chance—still a long shot—at a hit movie."

Most producers in that situation do *anything* to a script to get it made, but Irwin Winkler was a very special producer. "We're not changing anything," he told Pollock. "We'll find somebody who'll make it our way."

Irwin did, too. He found Carolco, whose co-chairman, at the time, Andy Vajna, was Hungarian and Jewish and had lost relatives in the Holocaust.

When the movie won the Best Film award at the Berlin Film Festival, Irwin, Costa, and I weren't surprised. It was, after all, a very European movie. I was personally pleased to hear that it played for six sold-out months in Budapest.

And when Jessie was nominated for an Oscar, I was overjoyed for her and hoped she'd have better luck than Bob Loggia, who'd been nominated for *Jagged Edge*.

My father, eighty-three years old, saw the movie in Cleveland and said, "I've never been prouder of you than I am at this moment."

As the weeks went by, he told me the Hungarian émigré community in America was enraged. They were accusing me of humiliating Hungary in the eyes of the world and betraying my heritage. He sent me an editorial from an émigré Hungarian-language newspaper which called me a "traitor."

When he went to a Hungarian meeting, my father said, he was hissed and booed when he walked in.

About a year later, in November of 1990, while I was in L.A., Gerri called me early one morning to tell me my father was desperately trying to reach me.

"He sounds panicked," she said.

I called my father in Cleveland and he was so upset he could hardly speak. He had just received, by registered mail, a letter from the Department of Justice.

He read it to me over the phone. It informed him that he was the target of a war crimes investigation by the Office of Special Investigations. The letter announced dates for hearings to be held at the federal building in Cleveland.

I sat down as he read the letter. I was dumbstruck. *I remembered the scene . . . the scene I had written . . . in* Music Box *where Armin Mueller-Stahl tells Jessie about a letter just like this one, and Armin says, "It must be a different Mihály Lászlo."*

"What can this be about?" I asked my father.

"I don't know," he said, "I don't know."

I told him I'd be in Cleveland the next day and called my old friend Gerry Messerman, one of the city's top criminal lawyers, a nationally respected figure who had devoted much of his life to civil rights issues and causes, a lawyer so good that F. Lee Bailey once said that if he were in trouble, he'd want Gerry Messerman to defend him. He had a brilliant, razor-sharp analytical mind and great depth. He was, in my estimate, a wise and profoundly good man.

I told Gerry about the letter my father had received from the Justice Department. He was equally dumbstruck.

"You better get here as soon as you can," Gerry Messerman said finally. "This sounds very serious. Let me make some calls and see what I can find out."

When I saw him in Cleveland the next day, Gerry looked grave. "This is a full OSI investigation," he said. "They've been working on it for years. It has mainly to do with a book your father wrote in Hungary."

"What book?"

He looked at his notes and spelled it. N-E-M-Z-E-T P-O-L-I-T-I-K-A.

He saw the startled look in my eyes. It was the book—*National Policy*—which my father said he could never find, the *only* book of his that he could never find, *the book that I had promised as a child that I would find for him when I grew up.*

"There's other stuff, too," Gerry Messerman said. "He allegedly worked in the Propaganda Ministry during the war. He was allegedly in charge of anti-Semitic propaganda and he allegedly wrote anti-Semitic articles in newspapers."

It felt like the ground was shifting under me. My father had always told me he worked in the Hungarian Prime Ministry, as an assistant to the prime minister; he had never mentioned the Propaganda Ministry or anti-Semitic propaganda. I remembered the times as a child when I had seen him arguing with the Franciscans or other Hungarians who had said ugly things about Jews.

I *believed* in the Office of Special Investigations. I had just written a movie heroizing the office and its agents. I believed that prosecuting war criminals fifty years after the fact was a just and honorable endeavor.

Now the very people whom I'd heroized in a movie seen around the world, the very people who, I believed, were heroic doing what they were doing . . . were investigating *my* father!

"What's going to happen?" I asked Gerry Messerman.

"They'll hold hearings first and—depending on what happens in the hearings, they can move to prosecute him. If he's found guilty, he'll be deported to Hungary."

I said, "Jesus God."

"I have to ask you something," Gerry said. He kept his eyes, burning chunks of coal, on mine.

"You knew about this, didn't you?"

I said, "No. God no!"

"Then why did you write *Music Box?*"

"Because I hated what Hungarians did at the end of the war."

"How do you *know* what they did at the end of the war?"

"I read it. I've studied the subject since I was sixteen."

"Why did you study the subject?"

"Because I felt awful that *Hungarians* had done it."

"It didn't have anything to do with your father?"

"No!"

"Nobody will believe that," Gerry said. "Everybody will think you were writing about your father, exposing what he did. You felt guilty because of what he did and because he's your father, so you exposed him."

"Bullshit!" I said. "I didn't know any of it."

"Maybe not consciously," Gerry Messerman said, "but you had to know it."

When I saw my father that night at his little house in Cleveland Heights, the same house where my mother had died in 1967, I saw he was terrified. I told him what Gerry Messerman heard the OSI would allege.

He told me he hadn't read *Nemzet Politika* since 1934, the year he wrote it, but he was certain there was nothing anti-Semitic in it. He said categorically that he'd never written anti-Semitic propaganda and insisted the "little work" he'd done for the Hungarian government was in the Prime Ministry.

I sat in the darkness of my suite that night at the Ritz-Carlton watching the lights twinkling across the Cuyahoga River on the West Side streets where I'd grown up. I could see St. Emeric's church spire from my window.

I thought about those times I'd seen my father arguing with the Hungarian anti-Semites.

My father had taught me that all men are equal and I had spent my lifetime as a human being, as a journalist, as a screenwriter dedicated to that proposition . . .

. . . And I suddenly flashed on a line of dialogue in *Music Box:* "*You* are his best alibi," someone says to Ann Talbot about her father.

Was it possible that my father had instilled humanitarian values in me so that my public expression of those values in America would serve as an umbrella to hide sins he had committed in Hungary?

Was it possible that you could love your son and train and use him as your alibi at the same time? Because I had no doubt how much my father had loved me all of my life. He was, once my mother got sick, the *only* parent in my life . . .

. . . And I flashed to *Music Box* again: Why had I created a scenario in which Ann Talbot's mother *dies* when she is very young and her father becomes her *only* parent?

It took me back to Gerry Messerman's question: Why, with a worldful of other things to write about, did I write *this* particular story?

· · ·

My father met me the next day in Gerry's office. He looked haggard, the pouches under his eyes purple bruises. The OSI had Fed-Exed us a copy of *Nemzet Politika* and when I tore the envelope open I was shocked to discover that it was in English. I realized that the Justice Department had gone to the trouble and expense of translating *Nemzet Politika* in its entirety.

My father had always dreamed that one of his books would be translated into English. Now, thanks to the U.S. government, his dream had come true.

Gerry and I scanned through the pages hungrily as my father sat there calmly, staring out a window. It didn't take us long to find it, a section headed "The Question of the Jews."

My heart sank.

It read like the Hungarian version of *Mein Kampf.* Jews were "parasites" that "the body politic had to rid itself of." There were sentences like: "The iron fist of the law must be applied to this parasitic race."

The words blurred in front of me as tears filled my eyes. Gerry held his head in his hands as he read the pages. I couldn't even begin to fathom what he must have been feeling . . . this proud and strong Jewish man, my dear friend, who had lost so many family members in the Holocaust.

A government investigator had this opinion of *Nemzet Politika:*

"It slanders the democracies, most of all the United States, and insists that a dictatorship is the highest form of efficient government; it incites to murder against the Jews and advocates 'radical methods to silence the Jews forever.'"

A United States immigration affidavit that my father signed said:

"I have never advocated or assisted in the persecution of any person because of race, religion, or national origin."

My father was still staring out the window.

"Is it bad?" he asked me.

"It's bad," I said.

"I wrote it so long ago," he whispered.

"But you wrote it."

"I must have," he said. "If it's there. I didn't remember."

"I don't believe you," I said.

He looked at me, tears flooding his eyes too now, then he looked away.

I said, "It's filth. It's shit. You've smeared your whole life with this shit. You're smearing my life with this shit. How could you have written this filth?"

"I was young," he said. "I was so young I even forgot about it."

I said again, "I don't believe it!"

. . .

Gerry Messerman and I spent much of the next week questioning him in preparation for the hearings . . . grilling this old and sometimes feeble man who had raised me to be the man I was, who had supported me when I needed support, who had somehow made me believe in myself.

He kept denying that he'd been a part of the Propaganda Ministry, insisting, even, that his job with the Prime Ministry was so innocuous that he'd written his novels at the office while on the job.

Gerry and I both felt that he was lying over and over. He denied things or said he couldn't remember.

"I'm eighty-three years old," my father said. He waved his age like a flag.

At the end of our days grilling him, Gerry and I were depressed and badly shaken, as exhausted as my father.

As I drove him home one night, my father said, "You don't have to act so cold to me."

I didn't respond and he said, "You're my son. I've never loved anyone or anything in my life as much as you."

"Why did you write these horrible things?" I asked.

"I never hurt any Jews," he said. "I didn't hit anyone or kill anyone."

"But others may have struck them or killed them after reading the things you wrote."

"It was a different time," he said. "I was poor. I was ambitious. Everybody hated the Jews."

"So you wrote these things, this filth, for your career?"

"I never hated Jews," he said, "like so many did. I've never been a strong man. I've always been weak. I'm not like you."

"Don't!" I said. "Don't try to manipulate me! Please!"

"This wouldn't be happening," he said, "if we wouldn't have lost the war."

"*You,*" I said. "Not *we.* Not *me. You.* If *you* wouldn't have lost the war."

"Yes, *me!*" he said bitterly. "You don't know. What do you know? You, the American! My American son! What do you understand? You don't know what it was like in those days. *Everybody* was crazy then. Hitler on one side, Stalin on the other. We were such a small country. We were too small to survive alone. We *had* to go to one side or the other. We tried Communism with Béla Kun in 1919. There were dead people hanging off the lampposts everywhere. Nobody wanted to go through that again."

He said, "Good night, my American son!" when we got to his house, "I love you."

I watched him go slowly up the porch steps in his heavy overcoat and Hungarian peasant hat.

. . .

I went back to my hotel those nights and played a tortured game with myself. I tried to figure out what I had known as a child.

I realized my father must have been in constant fear in the forty years he'd by then lived in America. Fear of being uncovered. Fear of being deported.

Was that why he had stayed so close within his Hungarian world in America? Was that why he'd worked so long for paltry wages for the openly anti-Semitic Franciscans? Was that why the Franciscans had *chosen him* to edit their paper? Because they knew of his anti-Semitism?

Why then did I see him arguing with the Franciscans and other Hungarians who wanted to write anti-Semitic articles for the newspaper? Was that because he was afraid those articles would come to the attention of Americans who would then look into *his* background?

And I thought about my mother—my pious and religious mother. She must've known about his writings. Did she agree with that filth?

Did she, too, live in terror of being deported? How much did all that have to do with her illness and her paranoia?

Was her paranoia the result of her fear that my father's activities in Hungary would be uncovered?

I remembered some things my mother had said to my father when I was a child:

"You are still fighting your war. We lost it! We lost it!"

And: "I have always known the truth, haven't I?"

And: "Did you forget the bad things that you learned in Hungary?"

And: "Liar! Liar! I believe not a word anymore! I have heard all the lies! I have seen through all the lies! I know what you are!"

And: "A murderer! Your son! Like you!"

I knew, of course, that many of the things she had said were a manifestation of her schizoid madness. I knew my father wasn't a murderer or torturer, literally speaking. He didn't kill or torture Jews with his own hands.

But did the words he wrote and said cause those who read and heard them to murder and torture Jews?

The only honest answer to that, it became evident to me, was . . . Yes, that was possible.

I remembered what Father John Mundweil had said about my mother and father: "I know more than you know about your parents. They are good people. Human. Like you. Like me. But *good* people. Both of them."

I said to myself: Maybe Father John knew some things about them, but he didn't know *enough*.

. . .

"You're my friend," I said to Gerry Messerman one day. "But I would understand if you told me you don't want anything to do with this case."

"I've thought about it," he said. "I never imagined that *I* would defend anyone on these charges. And I know he doesn't deserve me defending him."

"Then don't," I said. "Please. You're right."

"I think your father is the most manipulative man I've met in all my years as an attorney and I've met some pretty manipulative people. I don't care about your father, but I care about you."

"You're going to defend him because of me?"

"That's right," he said. "Do you know what would happen if this case went to trial? Do you know what the media would do with this? You're the guy who wrote *Music Box,* about a war criminal and his child. You're Hollywood's most high-profile screenwriter. How would people out there feel in the future about paying millions of dollars to the son of an alleged or proven or deported war criminal? I'm going to do everything in my power not to let this go to trial and go to the press."

"It's more ironic than *Music Box,* Gerry," I said. "A dad commits war crimes. He raises a kid who abhors any kind of bigotry. The kid becomes good friends with a prominent Jewish attorney. When the dad's war crimes are discovered, the prominent Jewish attorney defends him against the war crimes—not because of the dad but because of the kid. The fact that the attorney is Jewish is key to helping the dad get away with what he did to other Jews. By raising a kid who loathes any kind of bigotry, the dad planted the seeds of his own escape."

"That's all occurred to me." Gerry nodded. "I'll trade you an irony. The dad has been a professional anti-Communist his whole life, partly to obscure the fact that he's pro-Nazi. Then one day Communism falls. That's the cause the dad has devoted his whole life to—the Fall of Communism. And *that's* what causes him to be uncovered. Because for the first time, the Justice Department has access to records *back there.* The dad never would have been uncovered had Communism not fallen."

I told my father that Gerry Messerman had agreed to represent him at the hearings.

"I will thank him," he said. "It is a wonderful thing to do for me."

"He's not doing it for you," I said. "He loathes what you did. He's doing it because of me."

My father seemed surprised.

"Oh," he said.

And then, after a moment, he said, "But it will be very good for me to have a Jew representing me in this situation, no?"

He saw the scorn in my eyes as I turned away from him. I heard him say, "But it's true, no? Why are you so angry?"

Gerry gave my father a list of questions to answer. Among them:

Q—Did you see the movie *Music Box*?

A—Yes I did.

Q—How did you respond to it?

A—I told Joe I am proud of him. I congratulate him. I told him the drama is a perfect literary piece.

Q—Do you have some feeling about the effect that the investigation of you might have upon Joe?

A—Yes I do. I am deeply sorry. Maybe those Hungarians planned this who were angry with *Music Box*. Maybe they went to Justice Department to get me to get Joe. And they accomplish maybe what they planned. I am sorry.

Q—What are your feelings?

A—I told one Hungarian who was complaining against Joe: I love Joe because he is my son. I respect Joe because he is a talented writer. That means that I respect my son and love what he is doing. The *Music Box* tells the truth.

Q—Did Joe read any of your books?

A—You have to ask that from Joe.

Q—Did you ask him to read your books?

A—We are both writers. Perhaps not in the same category—he is, thank God, greater than me. But anyway we are writers. And a writer never ask another writer if he has read his book.

Q—What are your feelings about any of Joe's work?

A—I am proud of Joe. His most important characteristic is the sense of justice. He hates crime against humanism, and he loves everybody and everything which is human. And that is the great gladness of my life after all the injustice I have seen.

I dreaded the start of the hearings. I was ashamed of what we already knew my father had done and was afraid, never mind his steadfast denials, of what else we'd find out.

Gerry had convinced the Office of Special Investigations not to hold the hearings in the federal building because of my high profile. They would be held, instead, in the conference room of his law office.

I told my agents in L.A. that I would have to be in Cleveland for an extended time because my father was ill.

I waited with my father in Gerry's office as the OSI people filed into the conference room and then the three of us went in.

Neal Sher, the head of the OSI, was there with his top man, Eli Rosenbaum.

I knew who these people were because I'd researched the OSI for *Music Box*, but I'd never met or spoken to them.

I admired their dedication to this cause and as I watched them, sitting there next to my father and Gerry Messerman, I thought to myself:

I'm sitting on the wrong side of the table.

With them was a Hungarian historian named Judith Schulmann. She had difficulty even looking at my father and I was sure she had lost relatives in the Holocaust.

I knew her aversion to my father's face wasn't directed at me, but *I* felt ashamed.

My instinct was to go to Judith Schulmann and *beg* for her forgiveness, even though I knew this was irrational: I'd done nothing wrong.

My father stared stonily at all of them.

Neal Sher questioned my father under oath:

Q—Mr. Eszterhás, you said earlier that you've come to believe, while in the United States, that what you wrote in the book about the Jews was bad and was wrong?

A—Yes.

Q—Precisely when or what event triggered you to rethink that?

A—Well, I have seen that I am wrong earlier, too. When they take out the Jews from Hungary.

Q—And that was in 1944?

A—I think so, yes.

Q—The Jews were put in a ghetto?

A—Yes.

Q—And they were deported to Auschwitz?

A—I have seen a march of old women they take to the station, railway station.

Q—And deported?

A—Yes.

Q—And that was very near the end of the war?

A—Yes.

Q—1944?

A—Yes.

Q—So at that point, when you saw what was happening to the Jews, it made you feel bad about what you had written in 1934?

A—Yes.

Q—And you have felt bad about it since?

A—Yes, it was always stronger and stronger.

Q—During the period you were in the refugee camps in Europe—before you came to the United States—you had a recollection of what was in your book; you knew generally that you were advocating—you had advocated the persecution of Jews, am I correct?

A—I know that—that I was an anti-Semitic and so I advocated. It was a general feeling that it was wrong and I was among the people who did wrong.

Q—So you knew then, while you were still in Europe, before you came to this country, that you had advocated anti-Semitism?

A—Yes.

It was one of the longest days of my life. They asked my father a question and he either denied something or said he couldn't remember. Then they provided documented evidence of what they were alleging.

I learned that . . . my father had indeed worked in the Propaganda Ministry . . . had written hundreds of vicious anti-Semitic editorials . . . had even edited government-funded anti-Semitic publications . . . and had even organized a book burning.

I sat there looking at the evidence, listening, my head down.

A book burning!

How could a *writer* be involved in a book burning?

How had he published all those novels in Hungary? By stopping other writers from being published? By banning and burning their books as an official in the Propaganda Ministry?

Almost as an aside at the end of that first day, I learned that my mother—*my shy, pious, religious mother!*—had been *a registered member* of Hungary's Arrow Cross Party, Hungarian Nazis openly dedicated to the extermination of Jews.

I felt too tired to talk at the end of that day, said a quick goodbye to Gerry Messerman, ignored my father, waiting to talk to me, and went back to the hotel.

There was no doubt about any of it now. *Even my mother* had joined the only party in Hungary openly espousing the extermination of Jews.

The Arrow Cross Party was the same heinous, sadistic, bestial party which Armin belongs to in *Music Box.*

How could my mother have done it?

What kind of guilt did she feel after the war—in the refugee camps and in Cleveland?

What did her guilt have to do with her mental illness?

. . .

I remembered the moment when I was a child and she had shrieked at my father, "*I know the man you are!*"

What had she really meant?

What had she really been saying?

I knew what her Arrow Cross Party card meant to me: she knew everything my father had done and approved of it.

Fervently so.

I was bombarded with a buzzsaw of childhood memories as I sat in the darkened living room of my hotel suite that night, slugging my Tanqueray . . . staring out the window across the river at the West Side where I had grown up.

I remembered my father screaming at that bitch, Margie, who ran that Hungarian diner in New York, screaming the words into her face: "*I am not a Nazi!*" and her response: "You're all Nazis, all you dirty DPs."

I remembered my mother telling me that the Zsidos had killed Jesus and my father telling her to "stop filling the boy with nonsense . . . Jesus was a Jew."

I remembered the Franciscans who wanted to run anti-Semitic articles in their newspaper and my father's shouted words to them: "Stop this madness! You can't say these things here! Didn't you learn your lesson?"

And I thought about the words which had shaped my whole life, words my father had said to me: "Remember this, Jozsi. Jews are people like any other people, some good, some not so good. Just like Hungarians. Some good, some not so good. *Never judge a man by his nationality or his color or his religion. Judge him by his character. Whether he is a good man or a not so good man.*"

I saw a hundred quick flashes, too, inside my head as I stared across the blackness of that river at the streets where I had grown up:

My father at that Indians game in his beret and trench coat, reading *Crime and Punishment* . . . Walking down Lorain Avenue with a bag of popcorn under his coat so it would stay warm for me . . . Telling me the world wasn't ending as my mother knelt on the floor and prayed . . . Playing his cheap, half-busted violin in the cabin in Cook Forest, tears in his eyes . . . Buying the red-and-white Ford convertible (for me) that he looked so ridiculous in . . . Urging me to read, to "*sitzfleisch,*" to make something of myself . . . Sitting on the bench at the library, telling me masturbating wouldn't make me blind . . . Paying a fortune for the neon sign at Papp's Bar that I had destroyed with my BB gun . . . Telling the priest off at Cathedral Latin after I had written the essay called "Jesus Was a Bum" . . . Being booed by his Hungarian friends because his son had written a movie called *Music Box.*

. . .

Eli Rosenbaum was the principal deputy director of the Office of Special Investigations.

He questioned my father under oath:

Q—Mr. Eszterhás, you have repeatedly characterized *Nemzet Politika* to us in this hearing as a bad book that you regret having written. Could you explain?

A—That's because the whole book is bad. The anti-Semitic attack in the book is not only ugly in the description but it's stupid and in the conclusion it's bad. It's bad, it's anti-Semitic, and I hate it today.

Q—When did you come to the conclusion that *Nemzet Politika* was a bad book?

A—When I got a copy of the book now. Because I did not know—I completely forgot what was in the book. And now that I read it I was shocked and ashamed, too, I have to say.

Q—I just want to ask you whether you agree that there is a great deal of inflammatory language about Jews in this book?

A—Yes, there is. I hate the book. I hate the book and everything that you say about the anti-Semitism in the book is true.

As the hearings continued, I felt like I was being buried by an avalanche of filth.

My father had lied on his immigration application, never mentioning his novels or his writings. He'd listed his occupation as "printer." It was obvious why: if he had said he was a writer, he ran the risk of someone finding what he had written.

The Nazi camp our family had gone to when we left Hungary, Perg, wasn't "a part" of Mauthausen, as my father had told me. It was *near* Mauthausen, but it wasn't a camp . . . it was a place of safe haven granted by the Germans to friendly government officials at a time when the Russians were invading Hungary.

I understood now the real import of a story I had been told as a child . . . my father had gone from refugee camp to refugee camp fleeing the Communists. But I knew now that he hadn't been fleeing Communists; he *had been fleeing Hungarian war criminal charges.*

I kept playing my nightmarish mental game with myself: matching stories I had been told as a child to what I was learning now.

I had been told that my mother, very pregnant with me, had left Budapest and gone to the town of Szombathely because of invading Russians. But that, I learned now, wasn't the whole truth. Szombathely had been designated by the Arrow Cross government as the place to which all dependents of government officials were to be evacuated.

The Arrow Cross! A foaming-at-the-mouth, murderous regime . . . and my father had been a part of its government!

There was even some evidence, not completely corroborated, that my father had either been a part of or in charge of the Arrow Cross's efforts to burn government documents as the Russians approached.

And there was the affidavit of a man who had worked with my father in the Propaganda Ministry who referred to him as "a rabid anti-Semitic ideologue."

I heard the names of his friends I remembered hearing about or meeting in my childhood . . . some of them the subjects, I now learned, of other OSI war crimes investigations.

I remembered all those stories I'd heard as a child about my father's trip to London as the guest of "Lord Razmeer" and Ward Price of the *London Daily Mail.*

I remembered because I heard now that Lord Rothermere and Ward Price, both English Nazis, had invited Europe's most fervent young Nazis to England—among them my father. Ward Price, I heard now, had even been charged with war crimes at Nuremberg.

And I remembered this scene from my childhood.

"Did you get a copy of Nemzet Politika *yet?" I asked him.*

"Why do you ask me about Nemzet Politika." *My father smiled. "You don't read my books anyway."*

"You said it will be the most difficult to find."

"No, I don't have a copy yet," my father said.

"When I grow up," I said, "I will find it for you."

"Thank you." He smiled. "Will you read it, too?"

"All right," I said. "I promise that if I find Nemzet Politika *I will read it."*

"Thank you," he said, his arm around me. "That means very much to me. I will hold you to your promise."

And I remembered the moment when I was a teenager in Youngstown and he found me reading a book about Auschwitz.

"Did you know that the Jews were taken down to the Danube in Budapest and murdered?" I asked my father.

"We all heard rumors," he said. "But that's all they were. We didn't see anything firsthand. We didn't know."

"What would you have done?" I asked my father, "if you would have seen it yourself. Would you have tried to stop it?"

My father looked at me a long moment.

"I could tell you that I would have," he said. "It would be easy for me to say that to you. I could look like a big hero in my boy's eyes. But it was a feverish and insane time. The Nyilas [the Arrow Cross] were terrorizing everyone. I don't know what I

would have done if I would have seen it myself. But I hope I would have done the right thing."

I knew now, though, that he was lying to me in Youngstown when he had said, "We all heard rumors. But that's all they were. *We didn't see anything firsthand. We didn't know.*"

In his testimony at this hearing, he admitted that he *had* seen it firsthand when he said to Neal Sher: "*I have seen a march of old women they take to the station, railway station.*"

Sher: "And deported?"

My father: "Yes."

And what had he done?

Had he, as I had so naively asked him when I was a teenager, "tried to stop it"?

No, he had worked for the government . . . for the Arrow Cross government, for the Nyilas . . . until the last moment before the Communists took control of Budapest.

As I watched my father deny everything or claim not to remember, I thought suddenly of his childhood friend, Puskás Öcsi, the internationally famous soccer star, and what he had said: "Your father was one of the toughest kids I've ever met."

"*Your father couldn't run because of his limp,*" Puskás Öcsi had said. "*So he constructed a wooden shield for himself that he put on his back like armor. All the beer bottles bounced off his back.*"

Whenever a new charge was made, my father either denied it or said he couldn't remember. And when the evidence was presented, he stared and blinked at the newspaper or affidavit or the internal memo with his signature on it and shrugged or shook his head.

At the end of a day of the hearings, the first Gulf War broke out and Saddam Hussein fired his rockets at Israel. As Gerry Messerman and my father and I were leaving the building, there were erroneous news reports that Tel Aviv had been hit with chemical weapons. We hurried to the car and put the radio on. My father asked me in Hungarian what was going on and I told him that Tel Aviv had been hit with chemical weapons.

And in English he said to Gerry, "Horrible. Why somebody do something so horrible to Israel?"

We dropped Gerry off and I went inside my father's house.

"You hate me," he said.

I said, "No, you're my father. I love you but I will hate what you did to the day I die."

"No," he said. "You hate me. I feel it."

I said, "Why did Nana join the Arrow Cross?"

"Everybody joined it."

"Not everybody," I said.

"Her friends were all joining it."

"Did she hate Jews?"

"How can you ask me such a thing?" He was offended. "You know how your mother was. She couldn't hate anybody."

"No," I said. "I don't know how my mother was. I thought I knew how *you* were, but I don't. I don't know how you could have done all these things."

"I did it for you and your mother," he said.

I said, "Stop. Don't try to blackmail me with your love. You wrote that book ten years before I was born!"

"Why did this have to happen to me?" he cried suddenly. "I don't care about these hearings! I don't care if they deport me! I'm eighty-three years old! All I care about is you. All I've ever cared—"

I said, "Please don't, Pop."

"Is *this* my punishment? That you hate me? My son hates me? Every damn thing in my life I lost. I lost my career, I lost my country, I lost my money, I lost my house, I lost my books, I lost my wife to her madness. Now I lose you? Is this what my fate is? To lose everything, finally and even—you?"

He was crying. "My God," he said. "I wish I wouldn't have lived this long for you to learn about all this shit."

I went over to Gerry Messerman's house and fell asleep on his couch while I waited for him to come back from dinner. He saw the shape I was in when he returned, saw how much I needed to talk.

"My dad sold used cars," Gerry said, "and one day I discovered he was playing with the odometers."

He let it hang there and he said, "Well, it ain't exactly the same thing!" and we both started to laugh.

It was classic Messerman. I knew that he was almost as broken up that night as I was, but he always managed to find a kernel of humanity or humor, even if by necessity the humor was dark.

"I wish I could say something to you to really make you feel better," he told me. "The things we heard today were awful. Neither of us will ever get over the things we heard in that room today and I suspect you'll spend a lifetime trying. But I do ask you as your friend to remember that your father was always *your* friend, he was always there when you needed him. His love for you wasn't and isn't fake. No matter how you feel now about his motivations, remember that."

On one of those hearing days during the Gulf War, Eli Rosenbaum told Gerry that his parents lived in Israel now.

It was obvious to us that Eli was concerned about his parents' safety and the dire hourly developments in Israel.

Gerry didn't have a television in his office, so I went out and bought one and set it up so Eli could catch up on the news during breaks in the hearings.

I watched Eli as he anxiously scanned the news . . . on the TV set bought by the son of an alleged war criminal . . . so he wouldn't worry about the fate of his Jewish parents in Israel.

On one of those days when my father was testifying, his voice had weakened and the microphone in front of him wasn't picking him up well. One of the court reporters propped the mike up so it was angled closer to him.

I stared at that prop underneath the microphone.

It was a tape of *Music Box* which Gerry and I had given to the OSI representatives.

The microphone picked up my father perfectly with *Music Box* underneath it . . . and my father continued with his denials and lies.

Gerry and I talked about the legal case itself. "They've got all the cards," he said. "They're good. They put together a very solid investigation. I'm impressed. They've got his naturalization application where he flat-out lied and said he was a printer. He entered the United States under false pretenses. On the basis of just that, they can deport him. If they do, he may face war crimes charges in Hungary."

The next day my father told Gerry and me that he would voluntarily go back to Hungary and in that way avoid a trial.

"I don't want to cause you trouble," my father said to me. "I don't want to cause you public embarrassment or hurt your career."

One night when I was driving him home, I said to my father: "Do you remember the cat that I had—the cat that would always piss on your manuscripts?"

He nodded and said nothing to me.

"The cat that ran away," he finally said.

"Nana said you killed it."

My father said nothing.

"I was looking for it for weeks in the alleys, but Nana said I was wasting my time because you killed it."

"Nana was sick," my father said.

I said, "You killed it, Pop, didn't you?"

He looked at me and then away and out the window.

"All these accusations," he said, "and now you're accusing me of killing your *cat*."

I said, "You *did*, didn't you?"

It hung there for a moment, and then my father turned to me and said, "No. I did not kill your cat."

He looked out the window again and said, "But I did take it down to the Animal Shelter. I couldn't tolerate it in the house anymore."

I said, "You took it down to the Animal Shelter and they killed my cat for you. You didn't have to kill it yourself."

"This is absurd," my father said. "What are you trying to do—draw analogies from this absurdity?"

I said nothing to him and he continued, "Look. You're a writer yourself. How would you feel if you had a cat who pissed on what you wrote as soon as it came out of your typewriter? Would *you* tolerate that?"

After a while I said, "No. I wouldn't. But I wouldn't lie about doing it."

"I had to lie!" my father said vehemently. "I had no choice. You would have hated me for getting rid of your cat. You didn't understand then. You were a child."

I said, "So your lie worked."

"*I had no choice!*" he said again. "I had to lie to you! You understand now because you're an adult and because you're a writer yourself. You're able to forgive me now."

I said, "I'm not sure I can forgive you now."

My father said, "You will. But it will take you some time."

Gerry and I spoke alone about the case that night.

"We've only got one card to play," Gerry said. "You."

"It's like *Music Box* again," I said. "I'm his alibi. *I* get him off the hook."

"That's right," Gerry said. "They can deport an eighty-three-year-old man and, in the process, publicly damage the career and life of his son, who stands for the things the OSI stands for. It's an unusual case only in the sense that *Music Box* would bring so much attention to it. Is it worth it for the OSI to send an old man back to Hungary and in the process to hurt you? I don't think so and I don't think they're going to do it. They're good and decent people. Let's just hope it doesn't leak into the press. Once this is out there, it's all over the world and our best argument to stop the OSI from doing it is gone."

. . .

At the end of the hearings, in an off-the-record session with the OSI, Gerry spoke to Neal Sher and Eli Rosenbaum and Judith Schulmann and pointed out how the publicity attendant to my father's deportation or trial would hurt me both personally and in Hollywood.

I had written three movies about racism and anti-Semitism: *Betrayed, Music Box,* and *Big Shots* . . . and one of the projects I wanted to do in the future, Gerry Messerman said, was about Father Charles Coughlin and the anti-Semitic isolationist forces rampant in America in the thirties and early forties.

The OSI decided to "continue the investigation" and my father was neither deported nor placed on trial.

I had gotten my father off—just as my character Ann Talbot had saved her father in *Music Box.*

But, like Ann Talbot, I felt like a piece of my heart had died. I'd lost my mother at thirteen, when her madness began, and now, at age forty-seven, I felt like I had lost my father as well.

My father promised me that he would write a book about the nature of anti-Semitism and describe what he had seen in Hungary and what he had experienced. It would be a confessional book.

"If you write that book," I said, "I will be proud of you. I didn't think I could ever be proud of you again."

He moved to hug me.

I moved away and remembered how my mother had often moved away from *me.*

After the hearings ended, I sat down and watched *Music Box* again . . . the movie I had written two years before I knew about the things my father was accused of.

I had seen the movie dozens of times, but never from this perspective.

It was the saddest movie I've ever seen.

I cried all the way through it.

These were some of its saddest moments for me:

The prosecutor: "You're an anti-Communist, Mr. László, swell, so was Hitler. But you can't hide behind it anymore. It's over."

Ann's ex-husband: "What if your father did it? Would it make any difference? He'd still be your *dad.* You'd still love him. Blood is thicker than spilled blood, that's the bottom line."

Michael László: "You my daughter. I got trouble, *you* help. You got trouble, *I* help."

Michael László, to his daughter: "You know everything about me. If you don't know me, then nobody know me."

Michael László, to his daughter: "It not me they talkin' about. They make mistake. It not me. I don't do nothin' wrong. That not you father."

Jack Burke, to Ann Talbot: "That's the perfect camouflage, isn't it? You raise some good, all-American kids, you avoid even any shadow of suspicion. *You're* his best alibi."

Michael László: "We come this country, everybody call us name. Greenhorn, dirty greenhorn. DP. Dirty DP. We *people* just like Jews. Jews no dirty. *Jews* people."

Michael László: "I live too long, that the trouble."

Michael László: "No! I did not do this! I am a father! I was a husband! I loved my wife. I could not do these things!"

Ann: "I don't care who says what. I don't care what it looks like. He's not a monster. I know that better than anyone."

Ann, to her father: "It makes me ashamed to be Hungarian, Papa."

Ann: "You make my skin crawl, Papa."

I will never watch *Music Box* again.

My advice to writers: Be careful what you write . . . what you write can break your own heart.

In the course of the next year, I rarely spoke to my father.

About five months after the hearings ended, I asked him if he was working on his book.

"What book?" he said.

"The book about anti-Semitism."

"Oh, that," he said. "I'm not writing it. I'm too old to write that book."

He called often and begged to come to California to visit his grandchildren. I told him I wasn't ready to see him yet.

"Let's let some time go by," I said.

"I'm eighty-three now," he said. "I don't have much time."

He asked me if I had told Steve and Suzi about the things he'd done in Hungary.

"No. Not yet," I said. "They're too young. I'll tell them when they're older."

"Tell them when I'm gone," my father said.

I finally let him come out to California to visit a year and a half after the hearings.

He'd lost weight and was pale. We were wary and strained around each other. I scheduled an L.A. trip to get away from him while he was around Steve and Suzi.

One night when I was in L.A., he woke up and couldn't breathe. Paramedics rushed him to Marin General Hospital. An angiogram determined that he needed a heart valve replacement, very serious and dicey surgery at age eighty-five.

"What do you want to do?" I asked him.

"What do *you* want to do?" my father asked me.

"It's up to you."

"They say if I don't do this I'll be dead in six months."

"Yes."

"I want to live," he said.

He looked at me. "Do you want me to live?"

I said, "Yes, Pop . . . if you want to live."

We scheduled the surgery and I saw him in a small basement room in the hospital after he'd been scrubbed and readied for surgery. He was sitting on a gurney, bare-chested and looking very frail. He had his head down and he was crying.

When he saw me he grabbed my hand—his hands were shaking—and he kissed it.

"Forgive me," he said. "Please. I beg you."

I wanted to hug him as he sat there but I couldn't bring myself to do it. I held his hands.

I wanted to say "I forgive you" but I couldn't form the words.

He survived the seven-hour surgery and, three days later, had to be operated on again for a circulatory breakdown in his intestines. He spent three *months* in intensive care.

I stood next to an ICU doctor one night watching him and the doctor said, "You know, I never believed in miracles until I saw your dad. He should have died six times. I've never seen a human being with this kind of will to live."

As I sat in my father's room with him sometimes, he hallucinated—a result, the doctor said, of the surgery and the medication. He whispered feverishly to me in Hungarian. He always thought I was his father.

"Papa," he whispered. "Are you here? I'm scared, Papa. I don't want to die. Please don't let me die, Papa."

Five months later, the doctors thought he was ready to fly back to his home in Cleveland Heights. The night before he was to leave, I went to his room to say goodbye.

I was startled to see he was watching *Music Box* on a cassette.

He took my hand and held it as he watched the movie and then he shut it off with his remote. He stared at the blank screen for a while and then, without looking at me, he said, "Tell me the truth. Do you still love me?"

"I love you, Pop," I said, "but I love you differently."

He said nothing as he held my hand and then he said, "That's not so bad, is it?"

I said, "It feels bad sometimes, but not all the time, not anymore."

He nodded. He said, "No man could have a better son."

I kissed his forehead and the next day a man who worked for me took him to the airport, stayed with him on the plane, and drove him home to Cleveland Heights.

I didn't do that myself.

I easily could have, but I didn't. I paid a stranger money to take my father home.

I saw my father only occasionally. His health prevented him from traveling anymore and I went to see him about once a year.

At each visit, he kept repeating three things.

"I never lied to you," he said.

And: "Everything I did, I did for *you*."

And: "I love you."

My friend Gerry Messerman said to me: "You have to forgive him."

I said, "I've tried. I can't."

Gerry Messerman said, "You have to try harder."

The first draft of my screenplay wasn't entitled *Music Box*.

It was entitled *Sins of the Fathers*.

I didn't change the title: Costa-Gavras did.

I remembered the dream my father had told me about so often.

I was a little boy and we were walking through a labyrinthine train station. He was holding my hand and he somehow let it go and suddenly . . . he had lost me.

He was sobbing, running up and down, yelling my name, trying to talk to people who didn't speak his language.

No one understood what he was trying to say . . . and I was gone, lost somewhere in this foreign world.

CHAPTER 27

Two for the Road

> BRAD
>
> This is the city of car-jackings and drive-bys, home invasions and holdups.
>
> MATT
>
> L.A.'s gonna kill her?
>
> BRAD
>
> You'll kill her. L.A. will take the fall.
>
> *The Perfect Crime*, unproduced

Our suite at the Ritz-Carlton had been Jerry Garcia's favorite. Suite 1729 overlooked the pineapple fields and the sea.

Naomi and I stayed in those rooms three days without leaving. We made love five and six times a day. We hardly ate, but I cleaned out the minibar completely.

I smoked up a storm, of course. There were so many post-climactic cigarettes to smoke . . . and we talked a lot, too.

I learned these crucially important things about Naomi:

She loved Mrs. Fields cookies and could eat a dozen at a time.

She loved Cole Porter and Hoagy Carmichael and Johnny Mercer.

She prayed each night to the Blessed Virgin Mary and kept a rosary in her purse.

She adored *Peanuts* and Charlie Brown.

She'd paid for her vintage Mercedes with her own money.

Gerri had told her that she loved me so much that when I walked into a room, Gerri felt like she couldn't breathe.

. . .

We left the suite and went downstairs to the bar.

We sat at the bar and I realized I liked nothing better in the world than sitting at a bar and drinking with Naomi, who, except for a rare wine spritzer, was a nondrinker.

"A thousand bar stools," I said to her.

"What?"

"Before it's over," I said. "Before it's over, we will have sat on a thousand bar stools."

The drinking helped me deal with what was happening at the Four Seasons, on the other side of the island.

Gerri, Guy told me over the phone, was destroyed . . . pulverized . . . riven . . . nearly hysterical.

"This is painful stuff," Guy said. "I'm not sure how much good I'm doing here. I walk the beach with her, but I'm crying as much as Gerri is."

I dreamed often about Gerri. She was always crying in my dreams. It was always the same dream, really.

I had hurt her terribly and I felt terribly guilty. She was young in my dreams—the Audrey Hepburn lookalike I'd fallen in love with.

I achingly wanted to stop her tears. But I knew I couldn't. *Because I knew I was causing them.*

"I love you, Joseph," she said in my dreams. "I've always loved you. I've always been your friend. You don't understand how much I love you. I will cry every day, Joseph, until the day I die."

Naomi comforted me when I awoke. She blamed herself for Gerri's pain.

I knew the truth: *I* was to blame. No one else. Gerri didn't deserve what I'd done to her.

Leaving her was the worst thing I'd ever done. And the best.

I drove over to the Four Seasons the next day and told Gerri I wanted to speak to Steve and Suzi alone.

I told them that I was in love with Naomi. I told them that they wouldn't see me very much for a while. I said I had to "straighten my head out."

They looked down at the table and said nothing. Not a word. *They didn't react.*

I told them that this was no one's fault—not their mother's, not Naomi's, not mine . . . and *certainly not theirs.*

They didn't react to that either.

I realized, as I looked at them, that they were in shock.

I had put the kids I loved so much into a state of shock.

. . .

Then I spoke to Gerri alone. She looked like she hadn't slept in days. Her eyes were red and badly swollen.

I told Gerri the same things I had told Steve and Suzi.

After a while Gerri put her hand on mine and softly started to cry.

"Please don't leave me, Joseph," she said. "Please don't do this to us."

Gerri kept saying, "Please don't, please, please," whispering the words to me.

"I'm sorry," I said, "I have to go."

She said, "Okay."

I saw her tears roll off her cheek and strike the table. She said, "But when will we see you?"

I said, "Tomorrow. I'll come over tomorrow."

She said, "Okay."

I went over to the Four Seasons to see them every day until they left.

Steve and Suzi still had hardly any reaction at all.

Gerri said, "You asked me the other day why I want the marriage to work. Sometimes the strain of all this makes it very hard to be really honest. I hate these guarded conversations we're having now. I'm so used to being honest with you. But it's very hard under the circumstances.

"I want this marriage to work because you are so deep inside me, so much a part of me. I'll never be free of you and I miss you a lot. And ultimately because I feel the good things far outweigh the bad and we've both lost sight of that now. And because I've always felt and still do that we are *Two for the Road* and that's a long, long time."

Another day Gerri said, "Just because I'm so angry with you doesn't mean I don't love you."

Naomi's journal:

    I feel like I'm wrestling with myself. On the one hand,
    I've never been so happy in my life. Everything looks dif-
    ferent. Trees are breathtaking, a sunset makes me want to
    weep; the wind feels like soft kisses. I feel like my heart
    is soaring.
        And then, when I think of Gerri and the kids, which hap-
    pens every few minutes, I feel heartsick and guilty. Joe's
    pain is so palpable. I try to be a comfort, but I know there
    is little I can do.
        The worst thing is, I miss them, especially Gerri. I
    wonder what she is doing; I wish I could talk to her. But I
    know she must loathe me now.

```
Joe keeps saying over and over, "You are not responsible
for the end of this marriage. It was over a long time ago."
     But I know that Gerri and Steve and Suzi don't think
that. And I will forever be the cause of their pain. My
happiness is creating their suffering.
```

Gerri left to go back to Tiburon with Steve and Suzi and their two friends.

She threw up all the way back.

I couldn't sleep.

I was throwing up in the middle of the night, too.

I couldn't get the image of Steve and Suzi out of my head, looking down at that table, at the Four Seasons, shell-shocked, almost like they'd been lobotomized.

Naomi and I were down on the beach at the Ritz-Carlton during the day and I suddenly noticed, fifty feet to the left, a guy taking a picture of us.

I got up to go after him and he started to run.

At that moment, I saw a guy about fifty feet away to the right taking pictures, too. Then *he* ran.

I called hotel security and they stopped the two guys in the parking lot . . . local stringers for the *National Enquirer.*

Guy called from L.A. to say that someone from the industry saw us at the hotel and word in Hollywood was out that I was with Naomi.

Guy said that Sharon, who was still his client, had walked off the set of *Intersection* for the day when she heard.

Guy was being bombarded with interview requests and suggested that we "get ahead of the press" by issuing a statement.

The statement which Guy issued in my name read:

> Joe Eszterhas and his wife of nearly twenty-five years are in the process of a trial separation.
>
> His great friendship with Naomi Macdonald has nothing to do with the marital problems that led to his separation.
>
> The only comment Eszterhas will make is: "Life is strange."

The premiere of *Sliver* was fast approaching.

Paramount sent me a publicity packet of articles that mentioned *Sliver.* Among them were:

The *Boston Herald:* "In a scandal that could rock Hollywood, a heartbroken bride said she tragically miscarried after Sharon Stone stole her husband. 'I think she's heartless,' said Naomi Macdonald."

New York Newsday: "If it were up to Naomi Macdonald, actress Sharon Stone would be stoned."

The *New York Post:* "Abandoned bride Naomi Macdonald says sex bomb actress Sharon Stone destroyed her marriage, stole her husband and played a key role in the death of her unborn child."

The *Washington Post:* "It's starting to sound as if Sharon Stone is playing out one of her vampy roles, what with all the lurid details dribbling out about her new romance."

The headlines were: "Newlywed Says She Miscarried After Stone Stole Hubby . . . Stone Hit for Rocky Marriage . . . Sharon Stone Stole My Hubby! . . . Heart of Sharon Stone."

Reading these stories Paramount publicity had proudly sent me, I told Naomi I thought Paramount was trying to sell *Sliver* by trashing Sharon.

I missed Steve and Suzi so much I couldn't stand it.

Naomi and I jumped on a plane and flew to San Francisco to see them.

We noticed the photographer as soon as we got out of the limo in front of the Huntington Hotel.

He took three pictures, waved good-naturedly, and was gone.

I took Steve and Suzi to the Mandarin, on San Francisco's wharf, for dinner. It had always been our favorite restaurant—but it had been our favorite *family* restaurant.

As soon as they sat down, I knew I'd made a mistake by picking this place.

They looked like they were still in shock, but they asked me questions:

Where are you going to live, Dad?

How long are you going to stay with her, Dad?

Did you tell Grandpa, Dad?

Do you know Mom cries all the time, Dad?

Then Steve said, "You and Mom aren't going to get divorced, are you, Dad?"

I said I didn't know the answer to that one yet.

Then Suzi said, "We miss you so much, Dad."

Steve said, "Promise me something, Dad. Promise me that if you divorce Mom, you won't do it for a year. Promise me that, Dad."

I did.

Then Suzi said, "I hope Naomi dies, Dad."

. . .

We were flying to Cleveland the next day to see my father and Naomi's father and her siblings.

We didn't want them to hear about this from the newspapers.

Naomi and I slept that night at the old Victorian that Gerri and I owned in Stinson Beach.

I had to drink a lot of Tanqueray and smoke a couple of joints to be able to fall asleep.

As soon as we left the next day, Gerri sent a workman to take the mattress Naomi and I had slept on.

He took it out on the beach and burned it . . . as Gerri had instructed.

In Lorain, Ohio, meanwhile, Gerri's brother, Bob, found an oil portrait of my mother, which Gerri and I had left in her family's house before we moved to California.

Bob took the oil portrait out into the backyard and burned that, too.

I hadn't seen my father in a long time. Even after everything he and I had been through, I was still nervous about telling him what I was going to tell him.

He had always been so fond of Gerri.

But Gerri, he said, had already been there. He already knew what I was going to tell him.

Gerri told him that I had lost my mind, that I was having a middle-aged identity crisis. She asked him to intervene and speak to me.

"What did you tell her?" I asked my father.

"I told her that you are my son," my father said. "But that she is not my daughter."

I remembered the line from *Music Box: Blood is thicker than spilled blood.*

I thought that my father's response to Gerri after all the years of affection between them had been cruel and insensitive.

Yet I knew I had no right to think that after what I had done to her . . . on that dance floor on Maui at Moose McGillycuddy's while I danced with Naomi . . . and at the hotel later that night when I left her to sleep with Naomi.

I had done these things to Gerri . . . *after all the years of affection between us.*

"When you were about thirteen years old," my father said to me, "I fell in love with a woman. I didn't let it go anywhere because we were Catholics and because of you. I've wondered all these years what my life would be like today if I had followed my heart back then."

I wondered: Huldah Kramer or Katherine Webster?

And did it mean that he really *didn't* love my mother—that she had been *right* all those times when she told me he didn't love her.

I was sorry he had told me.

And, of course, I noticed that he was using *me* again as his excuse.

He hadn't followed his heart *because of me*.

He had sacrificed his own life *for mine*.

"When will I see Noemi?" my father asked, pronouncing her name the Hungarian way.

"Tomorrow," I said.

"Remember what I said to you when you were a boy: Italian women are the most beautiful women in the world."

"This isn't going to be easy," I said to my father. "Many people will think less of me and less of Naomi for doing this, especially with two kids involved."

My father said, "Hold on to each other and shit on the world."

The coldness of his advice jarred me.

Yet it was exactly the advice I wanted to hear.

I knew he was purposely giving it to me to make me feel better.

And I knew he was purposely giving me this advice so that I would feel better about him.

I remembered Gerry Messerman telling me that of all his very many clients, my father was the most manipulative.

Naomi's journal:

I finally met Joe's dad. I keep feeling like being with Joe is like going back home, to the realness of Ohio. Walking into his dad's house was almost eerie in that it looked exactly like my grandparents' house had for so many years and my dad's house did now.

On the wall was a picture of the Blessed Virgin with an old yellowed palm (no doubt blessed) hanging behind it. There was an old chair by the door, and as I went to sit in it I dropped lower than my knees, since the springs were shot. The house smelled of mouthwatering ethnic cooking and was warm and cozy and inviting and all so familiar.

I knew when I walked into that house that the reason I am so completely in love with Joe, so immediately comfortable, is that we come from the same place. His father kissed my hand (which is a traditional Hungarian greeting).

I was nervous that he would resent me for the unrest in his son's life, but his eyes danced and he seemed genuinely happy. We sat at the table and I found I was ravenous. A home-cooked meal like so many in my past sat steaming on the little table.

We talked and ate and laughed and I couldn't believe how easy it felt to be there. Or like I'd been there before. I hoped meeting my family would be as wonderful for Joe.

My father said to me afterward, "She's beautiful and she's funny. She's everything I imagined she would be and more. You're a very lucky man. I envy you."

I smiled and said, "Thank you, Pop."

"Tell Gerri that she can speak to me anytime she wants. I think I can help her."

I said, "What will you say to her, Pop?"

My father said, "These things happen."

Naomi's journal:

That night we joined my brothers, Bernie and Bep, and their wives for dinner. I had already told Joe some specifics, "Bernie is white-collar right-wing conservative. Bep is a former Vietnam vet, blue-collar, staunch Democrat. They are both physically big . . . 6-2, 200 pounds . . ."

Joe said, "Should be interesting . . ." When we walked in they said, "You look beautiful. You haven't looked this happy in a long time."

Their eyes were wide. Joe is a lot to take in at first glance. We ordered drinks and proceeded to have such a wonderful time.

At one point Bep (who was in the National Guard) started talking about Kent State. He was going on about how he could understand how the guardsmen felt, how it happened that they fired on those students, as tragic as it was, etc., etc.

I knew Joe had written a book about Kent State, and certainly knew his sympathies did not lie with the guardsmen. So I held my breath. Finally, Bep paused. I was sitting in between the two.

Joe leaned over me and said, "Let me tell you something. You don't know what the fuck you're talking about."

The table froze. Everyone was uneasy except Bernie; he seemed to be loving it.

Finally Bep looked at Joe and said, "You know, you're probably right." It was hilarious.

The next day we visited St. Emeric's in Cleveland, where Joe went to elementary school. We even went to the basement where there was a little classroom. On the small chalkboard were children's names in Hungarian. Joe looked at it like he was a million miles away.

We went up to the church and tiptoed in. It felt so strange. A few months before, I hardly knew this man. Now I was visiting the deepest parts of his past; the most difficult parts of his life. I felt so grateful.

A church is such a familiar place for me. I spent the first thirteen years of my life going to church every morning six days a week. So, once again, I felt I had gone back home.

Joe suddenly leaned over and whispered in my ear, "I will love you forever. I promise you that." He said it with such earnestness and gravity, it was like a boy who makes a small cut on his finger, and then cuts yours, rubs your blood together with his and makes a vow for life.

I walked her from St. Emeric's over to the West Side Market, where I had spent so much time when I was a boy.

As we were walking through, an old Italian vendor spotted me. He had a huge grin on his face.

He yelled, "Here ya go, Joee!"

And he tossed me an apple . . . just like he had when I was a boy.

We went back to L.A. so I could do a week's publicity for *Sliver*. The interviewers, I quickly discovered, weren't interested in *Sliver* . . . or me . . . as much as they were interested in the story of Sharon and Bill and Joe and Naomi and Gerri.

The *New York Times*: "His girlfriend, Naomi Macdonald, is sitting next to Mr. Eszterhas, wearing a lace bustier, cutoff jeans, and matching brown leather boots. He has given her a few pounds' worth of silver necklaces and bracelets based on Apache designs that match his own. . . .

"As Guy McElwaine, his agent at International Creative Management, points out, Mr. Eszterhas's life has become as lurid a psychosexual drama as his scripts, with Ms. Stone taking a role in real life that could prompt some people to confuse her with Catherine Tramell, the man-eating, manipulative, hypnotic vixen of *Basic Instinct*. . . .

"Although it has been said that Mrs. Macdonald resembles Ms. Stone, the only resemblance is in coloring. Mrs. Macdonald has blond hair and blue eyes, but she is more the sweet Midwestern farm girl than Hollywood glamour boat."

People magazine: "Appearing on Fox's *A Current Affair* April 6, Naomi Macdonald claimed that Stone has brought a calculated end to what had been a blissful marriage, causing Naomi so much stress she'd suffered a miscarriage. 'What Sharon did was cruel,' Naomi charged, 'cold-blooded and heartless.'

"Naomi, however, was in no position to throw Stones. Just weeks after her teary TV appearance, she went from woman scorned to woman smitten. Her suitor: none other than Joe Eszterhas.

"Left out in the cold is Gerri, who, along with being Eszterhas's wife, used to be Naomi's best friend. 'Even by Hollywood standards,' says one Paramount executive, 'the whole thing's weird.' "

Guy suggested we sit down with Army Archerd, Hollywood's unofficial gossip historian.

We had a delightful lunch with Army at the Four Seasons in Beverly Hills and I told him that "Guy McElwaine kids me about setting this whole thing up, of introducing Bill and Sharon purposely so I could have Naomi for myself."

When Army's story came out, at the very top of his well-read column, it said, "Joe admits that he introduced Bill and Sharon so he could have Naomi for himself."

Everyone in town was suddenly talking about Army's story . . . about how the guy who wrote *Jagged Edge* and *Basic Instinct* was so manipulative and devious that he even manipulated his friend (Bill) to get his friend's wife (Naomi).

It reminded me of the time Army said that I had quit the Rolling Stones rock band to write the script called *F.I.S.T.*

There was a party at Evans's house for the cast and crew of *Sliver*.

Naomi and I decided to go.

We got a standing ovation from everyone when we walked in.

One of Bob's bimbos—the one who'd come over to my hotel with a note from Bob wearing nothing but a fur coat—said to me, with Naomi right beside me, "So why her and not me?"

Jon Peters, the fabled producer, and Mark Canton, the chairman of Sony, wanted to talk about *Gangland*, the script I had contracted to do for them . . . over dinner at the Grille in Beverly Hills.

I asked if I could bring Naomi but they said this was business only and I left Naomi in our suite at the Four Seasons.

We had a pleasant dinner during which it became obvious to me that Jon was the man in charge. Mark even referred to him several times as his "rabbi." Jon had a street-smart gravitas about him (in relative Hollywood terms), while Mark kept bobbing around him like Jon's own little jack-in-the-box.

I remembered the first time I had met Mark at Warner Brothers nearly twenty years ago, and Mark had shown up with a pair of bright red boxing gloves because he had heard I was a tough guy.

Nothing much had changed, I saw, in twenty years. I could imagine him with the shiny red boxing gloves at this dinner, too.

As dinner was winding down, two young women who just happened to have the booth right next to us came over to the table.

Jon and Mark knew them and introduced them to me. They were above-average Hollywood model-actresses carved by surgeons, puffed by chemicals.

Mark excused himself and said he had to go home. Jon asked the two young women to join us.

They sat down—one next to me, one next to Jon—and I said I had to go, too.

Jon said, "No you don't. Let's all go to my house and smoke some great dope and get to know each other better."

I looked at the two young women and I realized there was nothing better I would have liked—before I met Naomi.

"Jon," I said, "I'm just in the process of putting my ex-wife and kids through a terrible time and the woman who I'm doing that for is at the Four Seasons waiting for me."

I grinned and said, "I've gotta go, man," and got up.

"Hey," Jon said, "what she doesn't know won't hurt her."

I said, "It'll hurt me."

One of the young women put her hand on my arm and said, "That's so sweet!"

Jon said, "Putz."

But he was smiling as I left.

I knew he had good reason to think that kind of evening might appeal to me.

The first time I met Jon, about eight months before I met Naomi, I was supposed to see him for lunch at his house at 11:30.

I got there at 12:45.

He was pissed.

"Where the fuck were you?" he said.

I said, "I got delayed."

"You couldn't call me?"

"I don't have a cell phone."

"Time to get one," he said.

He said, "I make a deal with you for over three million dollars and you can't show up on time for our first meeting? What kind of shit is that?"

I decided the one chance I had here was to tell this pissed-off Hollywood animal the truth.

I had been with a young woman in my suite at the Four Seasons who'd been with me the night before . . . and we got up late and had a champagne room service breakfast . . . and one thing led to another . . . and I knew that if I went nosing and prowling around inside her . . . I'd be late for Jon . . . and I chose her over Jon.

"I'm really sorry I was late," I said as I concluded my story.

He glared at me—his eyes like flat rocks—and he said, "You've got a lot of balls to tell me that story."

I said, "From everything I hear about you—in that same situation—you would've made the same decision. You would've been late for lunch, too."

"Only when I was younger," Jon Peters said. "When I cared about pussy more than money."

He smiled a killer smile. "I'm older and wiser now."

Then he said, "Come on, I'll show you around," put his arm around me, and led me outside to show me his magnificent estate.

With tabloids all over the world writing about what they called "the Bob and Carol and Ted and Alice aspect" of our relationship, Guy convinced me that I needed a Hollywood PR man to "handle the situation."

I had just left my wife of twenty-four years for a much younger woman and my new press representative (or "rep") was nervous that my movie *Sliver* was being released "in this climate."

"I'm worried," my rep said. "You're too high-profile. The media's going to come down on you. 'Husband and Father Leaves Wife and Kids for Hot Blonde.' That's going to be their take. I need an angle."

"What kind of an angle?"

"Something you can talk about in the interviews before *Sliver* opens. Something that will neutralize the flak."

I knew his credentials were good. He represented big-name movie stars.

"Like what?" I said.

"Were you abused as a kid?"

I said, "What do you mean?"

"Anything from sex to being hit."

"My mom used to slap me a lot. My dad separated his shoulder hitting me once."

"He *separated his shoulder* hitting you? That's awful! I'm sorry."

I said, "Forget it. It hardly hurt. He was in really bad physical shape. Way overweight. It sounds worse than it was."

"What about your mother's slaps?" he said. "What kind of slaps were they—did they hurt?"

"Sure."

"Did they traumatize you?"

"Sure. She wanted to traumatize me. It got my attention."

"Do you want to talk about it publicly?"

"She did it for my own good. She was right. I deserved it."

"Come on"—he smiled—"get with the program here. We've got to find something."

"I loved my parents," I said. "My mom's life was hard. She was a schizophrenic."

"Voices?" he said. "Split personality? All that?"

"Yes."

"It couldn't have been easy."

"It wasn't."

"So you want to talk about it publicly?"

I said, "No thank you."

He laughed.

"Okay," he said, "how did you grow up?"

"Poor. Dirt poor. I got into trouble a lot."

"What kind of trouble?"

"Rolling drunks. Breaking and entering. Stealing cars. I almost killed a kid with a baseball bat."

"Jesus," he said, "you're kidding."

I said, "It wasn't as tough as the refugee camps."

"What refugee camps?"

I told him about the camps in Austria, about eating pine needle soup, about getting rickets, about watching the old lady who lay down on the railroad tracks in front of the train.

"*You saw that?*"

"I did."

"You ate that stuff—what was it? Tree leaf soup?"

"Pine needle soup. I ate it, yes."

"Fantastic," he said. "*Fantastic!*"

He booked me on TV shows and on radio. He even booked me into chat rooms on the Internet.

All before *Sliver* came out.

I talked about the pine needle soup, about the rickets, about the old lady on the railroad tracks.

It worked.

An old lady committing suicide on the railroad tracks is a much better story than just another wife dumped after twenty-four years of marriage.

Sharon was going to the *Sliver* premiere with Bill and I was going with Naomi. Paramount was nervous. Sharon, the diva, insisted that she and Bill arrive last so that she and Bill would be the stars of the paparazzi show.

I purposely delayed our driver and got there late, minutes before Sharon and Bill's scheduled arrival.

The paparazzi had never seen Naomi and me together and wanted hundreds of pictures. We smiled and posed for them.

A Paramount PR person came up to us. "You guys have to get inside," she said.

"We've got time," I said casually.

"No we don't. We've got to start on time. Sharon isn't here yet."

"She'd better hurry," I said.

Naomi and I started smooching for the photographers. The PR woman started to sort of jitter around in circles.

I glanced behind us and saw Sharon and Bill arriving. They couldn't wait any longer. The showing would start without them.

The paparazzi were still taking pictures of us smooching. Sharon and Bill were only a few feet away now.

A reporter yelled, "How do you spell Naomi's last name?"

I stopped and yelled, "M-A-C-D-O-N-A-L-D!"

Sharon and Bill were ten feet behind us. Bill looked stricken. Sharon looked like she could kill me.

I looked at Naomi. She was smiling radiantly.

Naomi's journal:

We went to the *Sliver* premiere Tuesday night. As we got out of the limo, Joe had his arm around me so tightly I could see white imprints on my shoulder from his fingers. I was overwhelmed by the whole scene. I've never even been to a premiere let alone the center of attention at one. Then we finally get inside in the dark and I'm so relieved.

When Joe wrote the script he had used my name in it for a peripheral character. Bill told me months ago, but I had forgotten. About fifteen minutes into the movie, Sharon says, "You slept with Naomi, didn't you?"

Joe laughed and I died. I felt like thirty pairs of eyes looked over at me. It was all so twisted.

```
    Then we went to the after-party. Joe had told me earlier
that his only concern for anything ugly happening was some
inordinately close girlfriend of Sharon's who reportedly was
seething from my Current Affair performance. I never saw her.
    Actually, I barely remember seeing anyone—it was all a
blur. But I heard later from Joe and others that she was
perched above on a balcony overlooking the room giving me
the evil eye.
```

It was the first time I'd seen the movie.

I hated it.

The final line of dialogue—"Get a life!"—was the final nail in the coffin . . . a line written, studio executives told me, by Sharon Stone, although the whole world thought I'd written it since I was the only writer listed.

The big mistake had been made by Stanley Jaffe, the studio head, who took the first focus group's dislike of the original ending so seriously that he forced Phillip Noyce (and me) to junk the script and reshoot the movie.

It made me wonder what would have happened if *Basic Instinct* had been focus-grouped. I was sure that a focus group would have hated that ending, too.

Stanley should have stuck to *Sliver*'s original ending and its rough cut . . . Sharon finds out Billy Baldwin is the killer and essentially says, "I don't care what he is, I love him and I know he loves me."

It would have been a daring and provocative movie instead of this mess.

Critics thought it was a mess, too, although audiences abroad put the movie above the $100 million mark.

Naomi and I and Evans and a bimbo took a limo across town the night *Sliver* opened and talked to the theatergoers who had just seen the movie.

"Hello," Evans said to a young black woman who had just come out of the theater. "Did you just see *Sliver?*"

"Yes."

"How did you like it?"

"It sucked. It was terrible. It was the worst. Don't waste your money on it."

"Really."

"Don't do it!"

"Well, all right, thank you."

"Hey, man," the young black woman said, "who *are* you?"

"I'm just a poor broken-down Jew."

"You're what?"

"I'm the most miserable Jew in the world," Evans said.

. . .

We limoed over to Palm Springs with Evans and one of his bimbos. He stayed at the Racquet Club, a famed Hollywood resort of the thirties and forties, now fallen on seedier times.

Naomi and I stayed at the Ritz-Carlton in Rancho Mirage; we didn't want to be around Bob *all the time.*

We were in Evans's bungalow one night and one of Bob's girls, now hooking in Palm Springs and Vegas, took out a Polaroid camera and started taking pictures of us.

"You take one more picture of us," I told her, "and I'll break the camera."

I didn't trust where a Polaroid taken by one of Evans's girls would wind up.

When we were headed back to L.A., Naomi and I picked Bob and his bimbo up at the Racquet Club. Bloody towels were everywhere around the pool. The bimbo liked to sunbathe in the nude and she was having her period.

The odd thing was that as sky-high, over-the-top in love as we were, I missed Bill and Naomi missed Gerri.

Bill and I had spoken every day for many months before he and Naomi broke up—we'd prowled the bars and clubs together, shared a thousand laughs.

And Naomi felt the same way about Gerri. She kept telling me stories about how much fun she and Gerri had had . . . before I broke up with Gerri.

Neither of us had a close friend that we loved around us anymore . . . and it made us sad.

Bob's brother, Charlie Evans, who had advanced me two million dollars to write *Showgirls,* was threatening to sue me.

I was a month late with the script and I hadn't even started writing it yet.

I liked Charlie and sat down to have a drink with him. He liked to drink almost as much as I did.

Charlie said, "I hear on pretty good information that you're never going to be able to write again, that your wife is the anchor in your life and without that anchor, you won't be able to write. I think you're going a little crazy."

I said, "Charlie, have you ever been crazy in love in your life?"

Warily he said, "Yes."

"Do I look like a man who's crazy in love to you or a man who's lost all his marbles?"

He looked at me, smiled, and said, "Okay. I hear you."

I said, "Who told you all this stuff about my wife being my anchor?"

"Bill Macdonald," Charlie said.

I told Charlie to hold off suing me for two months—which is when I promised I'd have the script.

. . .

We decided to go back to Maui, rent a house, and stay there while I wrote *Show-girls*.

We flew up to San Francisco so I could see Steve and Suzi and so I could tell them what we were going to do. They told me that Gerri wanted to see me this time.

Before I met Gerri at Sam's, an outdoor bar in Tiburon, Naomi and I had lunch at Scoma's on the wharf in San Francisco. I suddenly started to shake. I went to the bathroom, where I tried to take deep breaths. It didn't do any good. Now I was not only shaking but I felt like I couldn't breathe.

I went back to the table and lit a cigarette with dancing hands and told Naomi I thought I was having an anxiety attack.

I reached for my glass of wine, but I was shaking so badly I couldn't get it to my lips. She held the glass to my lips and I drank the wine.

Then I did that myself with two or three glasses and I was okay.

I got to Sam's early and had another three or four glasses of wine before Gerri got there. I was starting to shake again; my guilts kicking into overdrive.

I got up to hug Gerri when she came in but she backed away and sat down in the booth across from me. She looked pale and exhausted. We found it excruciatingly difficult to look at and talk to each other.

I asked how Steve and Suzi were doing.

She said they were okay—Suzi, she said, cried a lot; Steve had sunk more into himself.

"So, Joseph," Gerri said without looking at me, "are you happy with your whore?"

"Don't do that," I said. "It's beneath you to do that."

"I saw the pictures of the two of you kissing at the movie premiere," Gerri said. "Tell me something, Joseph? Why would you want to hurt me like that? Why would you want to hurt Steve and Suzi like that? Didn't you even consider the pain those pictures would cause us?"

I said, "You're right. I'm sorry. It just . . . happened."

Gerri said, "What's going to *happen* now, Joseph?"

"I don't know."

Gerri said, "Are you still in love with her?"

I said, "Yes. Completely."

She looked down at the table—as though she couldn't stand to look at me anymore. In a wounded little girl's voice, Gerri said, "What should I do, Joseph? Tell me what I should do to help myself. You've always been there to help. Tell me what I should do now, Joseph."

I put my hands on Gerri's. She intertwined her fingers with mine . . . a little girl, holding on and scared . . . and I said, "Get a good lawyer."

She looked at me with a worldful of hurt in her eyes. She said, "Have a nice life, Joseph," got up, and was gone.

I sat in the booth and ordered another glass of wine and then another and another.

I still had to see Steve and Suzi.

My children got there about an hour after their mother left.

Steve was inheld, monosyllabic. Suzi was pissed.

She said, "Do you have any idea how much I used to admire you, Dad? I used to think I had the best father in the world. Well I don't anymore, Dad!"

Suzi said, "I hate Naomi—I hate her! I hate her! I hate her!"

I said, "Naomi didn't cause this."

Suzi said, "That's bullshit, Dad! You and Mom never even argued. We never heard a single argument between you."

I said, "That's because your mother and I worked very hard not to upset you guys. Not to let you *hear* us argue. Believe me that we argued hundreds of times through the years. All the arguments ended with your mother crying and saying 'Please don't leave me, Joseph.' "

Suzi said, "I don't care how many times you argued. People argue, husbands and wives argue. But you didn't leave Mom until Naomi came into your life, did you, Dad?"

I said, "I started leaving your mother a long time ago in my heart."

Suzi said, "*Bullshit!* You're just trying to protect Naomi. You're just trying to deny her part in all this!"

We said nothing for a while and I finished another glass of white wine.

Steve said, without looking at me, "What are you going to do now?"

I said, "We're going back to Maui."

Suzi said, "You're just running away. Maui isn't the real world."

I said, "I can't argue that."

We rented a little house on Maui overlooking the golf course at the Kapalua Hotel behind iron security gates.

The island's most successful real estate agent found the place for us. Once we told him how much we loved the house, he said, "What kind of dope can I get for you?"

I quickly realized that Maui wasn't a bad place for a screenwriter to do his business.

Producers, directors, and studio executives flew over from L.A. to have meetings. They usually took a couple of hours and then they and their significant others stayed at the Ritz or the Kapalua for the next four or five days and charged it all to the studio.

They didn't argue much with me either about the script or the new deal we were discussing because they were relying on me to tell the studio that our meetings took four or five days and not a couple of hours.

On occasion they even relied on me to introduce them to my real estate agent who provided them with various island substances that made them more catatonic than they already were.

They flew back to L.A. and told their friends in the business how much they'd enjoyed their meetings with me and then their friends flew over . . . and my new deals to write more screenplays kept piling up.

My real estate agent was making so much money thanks to me that he was providing *my* weekly Baggie for free.

The Baggies started piling up and that may have been one of the problems with the script I wrote on Maui called *Showgirls.*

I started to write *Showgirls* and, as I sometimes do, I kept a diary.

Entry #1: I'm going to call her Nomi—Naomi's mom used to call her that and since I'm going to spend the rest of my life with her, I like it that the first script I write since we've been together will have her nickname as the central character . . . Nomi's young, nineteen, we're probably going to have trouble with casting, she's going to have to be a helluva dancer besides being able to act, but I'll let Paul Verhoeven worry about that—*thank God I don't direct.* Nomi Malone—the sound's nice and symbolic, a young woman alone in the world.

Entry #2: Spent a lot of the day out by the pool, trying to chart the rest of it . . . it feels like it's going to be long . . . a big story . . . but I have to take her from the lap-dancing, sleazy stuff to the big Vegas stage stuff—different worlds, have to show her progression from one world to the other—have to show the worlds themselves— that takes time and scenes. At the end, is the world of Vegas big stages actually sleazier, more corrupting than the world of the lap-dance clubs? Does Nomi make it and realize that she's lost it—internally, spiritually? I like the irony.

Is the world as full of irony as my own life is?

Entry #3: Cristal's in it now . . . the meeting between Cristal and Nomi . . . the beginning of the flirtation or battle or fight or sexual attraction maybe, although I'm

not sure where I'm going to take it. Does Cristal like
Nomi? Does she see Nomi as a kind of young, unformed image
of herself—the mirror reflection—is that good or bad? Does
that attract her or repel her? Does Cristal hate or love
herself or a gray between the two shades.

Cristal will be a hot part for somebody. *Sharon?* Can
Sharon dance? *Vertically?* Wouldn't that be the ultimate
irony—Sharon, after all this personal tangle, playing
Cristal. Paul would probably love it, though—we bring
Sharon back as a dancer.

Paul's waiting . . . Charlie Evans going batshit to get
the script—everything's backed-up like crazy thanks to the
craziness of my own life.

Entry #4: We're going to have ratings trouble, but there's
no honest way to describe what these clubs are like
without making them sleazy—they *are* sleazy—can't
cosmeticize it but the language itself could get us into
ratings trouble—more worries for Paul.

Entry #7: I like what I've got. I think it's working. It's
great to be writing again. It makes the pain with the kids
easier. With all the swimming I'm doing, too, I'm a little
bit more cooled out at night maybe. Sleep is easier and I
love Naomi—not the script's Nomi, but my Nomi—more than
I thought it possible to love anyone. Jesus, I waited
almost fifty years for her.

Entry #12: Debate taking the day off, but I'm too much
into it—the characters are speaking to me—up to page 55.
The audition scene—Tony. Tough scene, verbal rape,
simulated rape—in a way sleazier than the Zip City, lap-
dance club stuff. I like that the hotel-casino is supposed
to be a classy place and that she's violated there in a
simulated way . . . much worse than what she went through
at the lap-dance club.

How far will I push the bisexual thing with Cristal?
I'ts almost impossible to push the sexual stuff too far in
a movie about Vegas . . . People think Vegas is gambling
and money—that's only the top, visible layer ·. . .
underneath it's all sex.

Entry #17: I've stopped at page 73 and I'm retyping the
whole thing from page 1. I'm going to send the first chunk
to Verhoeven when I'm done with it. Paul is getting itchy

and I don't want to lose him. I think this piece is so out there on the edge that if Paul doesn't direct it, nobody else can or will.

It's completely Nomi's piece . . . if she doesn't work, we're dead—if she isn't cast right, we're dead. Is it possible to find a nineteen-year-old who can act *and* dance?

Why can't I ever do anything that's easy?

Entry #20: I wrote one of the dance sequences for the brothers and priests who'd taught me at Cathedral Latin:

BLISS

The set: a blazing neon cross is center stage. We see spotlights, the spinning red lights of police cars. Time: Night.

When we open, we see Cristal on the neon cross, crucified. She wears only a G-string and pasties. We see the stigmata on her body. A moment of silence as we see her on the neon cross, the others around the cross, barely clad . . . and then the music begins . . . and her limbs begin to move on the cross . . . and she dances off the cross.

On the ground now, the others dance around her, kneeling to her, beseeching her . . . the women are topless but they wear veils . . . not giving her any space. She tries to dance away . . . we see the blood from the stigmata on her body . . . but they block her, hem her in, with their prayers and their pleas.

She blesses them, dancing . . . she touches them . . . they reach out constantly to try to touch her . . . putting their fingers into the stigmata . . . smearing her blood on themselves . . . genuflecting.

And she constantly tries to dance away from them . . . but they surround her . . . swoop in on her in a group . . . force her to the ground . . . and converge on her . . . kissing her body, touching her . . . devouring her body and blood . . . until finally—

She breaks away from them. She dances back toward the cross, the others after her . . . she dances herself up the cross again . . . crucified again . . . her limbs moving again . . . and then she stops as the others on the ground beneath her dance their hallelujahs.

. . .

Entry #22: I took the 73 pages down to the Kapa Lua offices here and faxed them to Paul.

I'm on page 94.

With Nomi and Cristal, it's spiritual combat played out in sexual terms. Isn't that what we all do? It's so intertwined, their thing. Cristal's view of the entertainer as hooker and Nomi's refusal to be that . . . or to accept that . . . or to realize in the deepest part of her that she's *done* that . . . can you actually hook, actually do it, and protect yourself somehow from being tarnished, corrupted? Is that an amazing strength of character or is it self-delusion, fatuousness, naivete? Is Cristal purposely trying to corrupt Nomi—or *trying to force her to recognize and reject corruption?* Is she trying to hurt Nomi by doing that or is she trying to help her grow up? And, in the middle of this complicated tangle, Cristal wants to sleep with her.

Entry #27: Paul loves the pages—great news—meanwhile I'm to 112 script pages.

Cristal is on the offensive with Nomi—pushing and pushing her. It's sort of like it was with Gerri. Pushing and pushing me, pushing Naomi and me together. Subconsciously, she wanted the marriage over—she just didn't want to be the one to do it because of the kids. Subconsciously, Cristal wants out of being a star the same way Gerri wanted out of being my wife.

Entry #33: Done. Way too long, but I like it. A difficult script to write at a helluva difficult time, but maybe the fact that I called my lead "Nomi" and saw little pieces of Naomi in the woman I was creating helped. A kind of tribute to Naomi, though not quite a labor of love, considering Charlie Evans's lawsuit threats.

Entry #34: Retyping the final chunk—there was a big rainbow out there this morning.

Naomi will read it tonight, the first one to read it in toto and it's the first script of mine she'll have read.

Entry #35: Naomi didn't like it. She found it "dark and depressing."

I'm deeply disappointed in her reaction, of course, but I love her for her honesty.

I hope she's wrong.

. . .

While I was writing *Showgirls,* Naomi read an interview with Sharon in which Sharon spoke about Jake, who had been Naomi's dog . . . but who was now Sharon's.

Naomi told her lawyer to tell Bill's lawyer that she wanted Jakey back. Bill's lawyer said no way—Sharon liked Jakey.

It drove Naomi nuts that Sharon was now playing with her dog.

I called Bill, who was staying at Sharon's house off Mulholland overlooking the Valley.

Bill picked the phone up.

I said, "Listen, if you don't give Naomi the dog back, I'm going to squish you like a fucking bug."

Bill said nothing . . . but he held the phone for a few seconds . . . and then hung up.

Bill's lawyer called Naomi's lawyer shortly afterward to say that Naomi could have Jakey back.

We had to board him at a kennel until we got back from Maui.

Paul Verhoeven called to say that he was coming over to Maui to talk about the script. He was bringing his wife of nearly thirty years, Martine, with him.

At the same time, I read an interview with Paul in a film magazine.

"It was very personal to me," Paul said about *Basic Instinct.* "It was the relationship between me and Sharon that was not consummated in the bed. To have been involved with her would have been a disaster, but the movie was good because of my feelings. . . .

"I was not aroused by the lap dancers in Vegas. Ultimately, sex for the sake of sex is boring. I have never had a relationship in my life for one day. Even when I was married, I've always had relationships that were for years, never one-night stands. Why bother? I prefer to drink a cup of coffee."

As I read the interview with Paul, I remembered two moments during our *Showgirls* research trips to Vegas:

A dancer we were having drinks with said to Paul: "What's the most important thing to you?"

Paul said, "My work. I couldn't live without my work."

She turned to me and said, "What's the most important thing to you?"

I said, "Love."

The dancer smiled and said, "You're *so* bad."

Paul said, "He is! He is! You are exactly right! He is!"

I was smoking a joint in my suite with two dancers I had interviewed that day. I called Paul and asked him to come over.

He came but he wouldn't take a hit off the joint. He said he never put anything poisonous into his lungs.

He watched the three of us as we acted dumb and stoned and loose. He left suddenly.

One of the girls said, "Who was that masked man?"

The other girl said, "Did you see his wristwatch? It had Jesus' face on it."

Naomi's journal:

```
I'm holding my breath there won't be some meltdown that
ends with Paul flying out of here in a huff and the script in
limbo. He makes me nervous anyway.
    He's very likable, but there's always some push and pull
when he and Joe are together.
    Last night at dinner we were talking about marriage.
Paul suddenly said matter-of-factly, "I stopped being
faithful the day I stopped wearing my wedding ring." No one
said anything. It felt sad.
    Then on the way home in the limo, Paul sat facing back-
ward at one end and we sat facing him on the other. The song
"Take the Money and Run" came on the radio.
    Joe laughed and said, "Hey Paul! Listen! They're playing
my song!"
    And Paul said, "Ah yes. Who wins? Joe wins."
    The ride continued and Joe and I were sitting nearly on
top of each other, laughing and generally enjoying each
other as we always do.
    I looked up and could just barely see Paul in the dark-
ness. Staring at us.
```

Paul sketched every scene of the movie in his copy of the script. I looked at a page and saw a sketch of an odd-looking, octopus-like object.

"What's this?" I said to Paul.

"A pussy," Paul said.

Naomi's journal:

```
    I like Martine, but they do seem like an odd couple.
With both of their girls grown and moved away, she is into
her music and her dogs and Paul is never home.
    Last night they joined us for dinner outside on the
lanai at our house. We were talking and Joe said something
```

```
to the effect that, yes, he probably could have stayed mar-
ried and kept seeing me secretly, but that would have been
living a lie and he just didn't want to live that way. There
was a silence then.
     Martine looked at her wine glass.
     Then Paul said, "If I divorced Martine, she would take
every penny I have, wouldn't you, Martine?" He said it with
a smile, but there was such resentment in it.
     She smiled back and said, "Everything."
     We all laughed, but it was nervous laughter.
```

Naomi and I were blissfully happy, but I couldn't get Steve and Suzi out of my mind no matter how much I wrote or drank or how much weed I smoked.

My dreams were full of things that had happened to them in their child-hoods:

The time Suzi choked on a hot dog and I had to hold her upside-down by her ankles as she turned blue . . . The time Steve missed a curveball I threw him and it went smashing into his nose . . . The times they collaborated on home videos, "written by Suzi, directed by Steve" . . . The time Steve played barber and chopped out a big chunk of Suzi's hair . . . The time they scrawled "Zorro" all over the walls of the house.

I dreamed several times of a moment when we were living in San Rafael, on a street that was a cul-de-sac, and Steve, who was about six, was playing in the front yard . . . and a van without windows came down the street . . . and I suddenly didn't see Steve. I went running out into the street bare-chested, yelling his name, hearing no response, waiting for the van to come back down from the cul-de-sac . . . here it came . . . I got in front of it, then went around to the driver's front door, swung it open, grabbing the driver (a petrified teenage boy) by his shirt and swung him out of the van, yelling "Open the fucking back!" . . . when I suddenly heard Steve's voice from the side yard: "Dad? *Dad?*" . . . and hurled the teenage kid back into his van, saying, "Get the fuck outta here!"

And the poor kid flattened his gas pedal and went roaring away.

I dreamed of Suzi holding on to me, sitting on my shoulders watching fire-works on the Fourth of July . . . Suzi losing her dolly in London and how I'd moved hell and high water to get it back . . . and Steve, very sick with a virus, in the emergency room at Marin General Hospital saying, "Don't hurt you tummy, don't hurt you tummy."

I dreamed of the time Suzi wore a T-shirt to high school which said "Jesus" on the front and "Joker" on the back, and her school principal told her she'd be suspended from school if she wore it again . . . I said to him, "Do you really want to get into a war with me? Think about that. I don't think you do because if you get into a war with me, I'm going to turn your life into a legal nightmare."

Suzi was allowed to wear her Jesus T-shirt anytime she wanted.

I was a wild man when it came to defending my kids.

The wild man who'd always defended and protected them had turned his back on them now and was sitting in the lotus position with a joint in his hand on the island of Maui Wowee.

Suzi called, crying, late at night. She said she was sitting in the den in Tiburon with the lights out.

She said that's what my absence from the house was like: darkness.

"Like the sun in my life has been shut off."

That night I got up and threw up and when I came back to bed Naomi said, "I'm sorry."

I said nothing and she said, "Is all this pain we're causing to everybody worth it?" She was crying.

I held her and said, "I love you so much."

While Suzi at least talked to me . . . yelling or crying, angry or sad . . . Steve cut me out of his life.

He never called me and when I called him, he never wanted to talk long.

Once he said, "What's there to talk about, Pops? You made your choice. You're there and we're here."

Drinking and smoking too much, throwing up in the middle of the night, desperately missing Steve and Suzi, I started snapping at Naomi.

"What have *you* accomplished with *your* life?" I asked her during a dinner.

And: "What do you know about movies? You didn't even know Brando was a method actor."

Sometimes Naomi turned to me, out of the blue, with tears in her eyes, and said, "I'm sorry."

And at those moments I said, "I'm sorry, too."

Naomi said, "I messed up your wonderful life."

I said, "You've made my life wonderful."

I flew up to see Steve, who was in school at the University of Oregon in Eugene. Naomi came up with me, but stayed in the room while I waited for Steve in the lobby of our hotel.

He got there forty-five minutes late and was in an ugly mood.

I said, "What's the matter, Mano?"

He said, "I think maybe it'd be better if we didn't see each other for a while."

I suddenly started to shake. I got up and said, "I left something in the room, I'll be right back."

Every breath I took seemed a struggle. Every step felt like I was wearing cement boots.

I got back to the room and Naomi said, "Oh my God! What's the matter? You're snow-white." Then she saw how badly I was shaking and said, "Lie down."

I lay down flat on the floor and lit up a cigarette and Naomi poured me a glass of wine. I glugged three or four glasses and felt okay enough to hurry back to Steve.

He was still sitting in the lobby, staring at nothing.

"Come on, Mano," I said to him. "I flew all the way up here—at least have a drink with me."

He came into the bar with me and after a couple drinks, Steve loosened up a little.

He took me down to his quad and showed me the room he lived in—it was a hovel.

He made a point of telling me that one of his neighbors had recently OD'd on smack.

We flew back to Maui.

But I was hurting so much that as the weeks went by on Maui, I couldn't face thinking about Steve's or Suzi's or Gerri's pain.

Because if I thought of their pain, it would make *my* pain unbearable. I'd start to shake or throw up or I'd reach for another joint or another glass of Tanqueray or white wine.

I missed my house, too, the Tara-like dream home atop a hill in Tiburon that overlooked the bay.

I had decorated every room, had selected every African mask and every painting and every vintage, turn-of-the-century Tiffany lamp. I had designed even the crystal in the kitchen door and the tulips in the kitchen tile.

I missed driving my big black Mercedes on a foggy day over the hill to my other house in Stinson Beach, which I had decorated with a Hungarian motif, even finding a cabinet carved in the 1870s with the figures of hussars all over it.

And I missed my dogs: Macko, the hard-headed husky who listened only to my directions . . . Bookshi, the ugliest dog in the world, a Chihuahua I'd bought at a flea market for ten dollars . . . Cigi, our lab, the Mexican army dog who ran away at the first sign of trouble.

I missed my *home*.

. . .

I went back to Tiburon with Naomi for Steve's high school graduation. I sat next to Gerri at the ceremony while Naomi stayed at the Huntington hotel.

I hugged Steve as he came down the aisle with the other graduates.

He looked away from me when I hugged him.

I had a drink with Gerri afterward and told her I couldn't handle the pain of this anymore. I told her I was coming back home.

When we got to the house, Suzi was there. I told her that I was coming back home and Suzi held me and cried.

I looked at Suzi in her pretty purple dress and realized that my little girl had grown up.

I also realized that Naomi had bought her . . . what seemed like such a long time ago . . . the pretty dress Suzi was wearing.

I went inside, called Naomi at the hotel, and told her. I was crying when I said the words, "I'm going back to Gerri and the kids."

Naomi said, "Is someone desperately ill?"

I said, "No. You should go back to L.A."

Naomi said, "Can I see you before I go?"

I said, "No."

Gerri and I sat and drank and I asked where Suzi was. Gerri said Suzi had gone to an all-night graduation party and would be back the next day.

What about Steve? Where was Steve? Steve didn't even know I was home.

Steve was at an all-night graduation party, too.

I was exhausted and I went to bed and after a while I heard Gerri come in and go to her bed.

I pretended to be asleep.

When I got up the next morning, Gerri was already downstairs. I sat on the side of the bed, looked out on the bay, and started to cry.

I went downstairs and Gerri was on the phone telling everyone that I was back.

I tried to call Naomi at the hotel. She had checked out.

A messenger arrived with a letter from her.

I was reading her letter and crying when Gerri came running down the stairs to my office yelling, "*I won! I won!*"

She took one look at me reading Naomi's letter and froze. She knew from the look on my face who the letter was from.

"I need some time to think this out," I said.

Gerri glared at me, her jaw set.

She went running up the stairs.

· · ·

Naomi's letter:

June 17, 1993

And yet another irony, Bill announced he was leaving me on the 17th.

You just called and I suppose it's safe to say that I'm in shock. Or at least I must be, because I'm unable to feel anything.

I do know several things which I will try to articulate:

1. I will miss you deeply. I love you deeply.

2. I will pine for you and the beautiful home we created (or at least began to create) on Maui. Our Jeep. Our spiders. Our life.

3. I will never understand why you wouldn't (or couldn't) do me the courtesy of telling me in person. You're certainly not one to shirk those sorts of responsibilities. Such an abrupt dismissal seems unnecessarily cruel, but perhaps you think I don't deserve more.

4. I will always grieve for the loss of our future children, "our barbarians." They would have been extraordinary people.

5. I'm sorry if you felt I didn't love you enough. I loved you with every ounce of my being, but perhaps there wasn't enough of me left.

6. I will miss what you called me: "the Little Guinea." You discovered her, and her crooked smile, and her clodhoppers, and her declaiming manners, and her mongoose temper, and I guess it means that I now have to say goodbye to yet another piece of me. No wonder I feel like a shell. "I should have been a pair of ragged claws . . ."

7. I can't hate you. You gave me too much. I hope you don't go back to your lonely ways; you deserve so much more.

8. (I must keep writing. I've been left so totally alone and I'm afraid to stop.) I'm sorry I wasn't able to say more over the phone. I was (and am) in shock. I was waiting in my white dress to throw myself in your arms, tell you how much I missed you, and glow . . . while you told me how pretty I looked. The scenario that ensued is so dreadful that I can't even express the pain. If I open that door, I think I may not even come back.

What do you suppose I have done in my life to warrant such sadness? Have I looked at the world through rose-colored glasses for so long that I must now see a harsh, cruel reality? Am I never to see the bright side again? I wish I could talk to you. Was it something you felt I did? I can assure you, I never lied to you. I was only honest. What a sadness. We are a human tragedy, aren't we? At least I certainly am. I never betrayed your love.

I am grateful that we had such a lovely last night and last day together. I loved you immensely today. I felt that perhaps the sadness and pain was

*truly behind me and that, as you said only yesterday, great joy would
make me forget all the past heartache. But instead I find I'm in for more.
How will I endure without you? And so you've left me, sitting alone in this
room, surrounded by your things. I suppose I understand what has happened, but what I don't understand, and probably never will, is, once
again, the way it was executed. Maybe someday you will, as my great
friend, be able to explain it to me.*

I love you,
Naomi

P.S.

*Thank you for everything you've given me. I just wish I weren't left here
alone with no one even to hold my hand or offer some hope. I love you,
Joe. I guess I just didn't show it to you enough. I would have been a great
friend, and even greater partner. But thank you for giving me the past
three months. A final kiss—X.*

*P.P.S. When we went to St. Emeric's, you told me you'd love me forever.
You told my dad you would never hurt me. I still love you anyway.*

I sat there for hours, thinking, crying, rereading Naomi's letter. I got on the
phone and tried to reach her in L.A.

Gerri came downstairs and I asked her to forgive me. I couldn't do it. I loved
Naomi too much. *I was leaving again.*

Gerri started to cry and said, "Joseph, how can you do this to us?"

Gerri's psychiatrist arrived. She had called him. He sat in my office and told me
that I was "addicted to Naomi." He said this was going to be as difficult to break
as any other addiction, but he was sure he could help.

He wanted to put me into a hospital under sedation for three or four days,
then do some psychological testing, then put me into another hospital for about
a month.

I said no thanks, watched him walk out and get into his car.

His license plate read "Go-For-It."

I took his license plate's advice. I reached Naomi in L.A., told her how much I
loved her, and told her to get back to the Huntington as soon as she could.

Steve and Suzi got back from their parties around dinnertime. We sat down
in the dining room and I told them I was leaving again.

We were all crying.

I begged them to try somehow to forgive me.

Suzi said, "Fuck you! I hate you, Dad!" and left the house.

Steve said, "My dad is a real asshole," and left, too.

. . .

I went to the phone to call a cab.

"I'll drive you into the city," Gerri said.

I said, "No, please, it's better if I take a cab."

"Let me drive you in, Joseph," Gerri said.

I couldn't stop crying as she drove the big Mercedes.

Gerri said, "What have you done to yourself, Joseph?"

When Naomi got to the Huntington a few hours later, I was still crying. We were both crying as we fell asleep in each other's arms, after the moments when we conceived our first child. The next day we flew back to Maui.

I felt that Steve and Suzi were too far away from me on Maui.

I wanted to go back to Marin with Naomi, but my kids argued against it, saying that Gerri would freak if I went back there with Naomi.

We decided to rent a place in L.A., although as far away from L.A. as we could be—in Malibu, on the sea, where we could pretend we were still on Maui.

We rented a furnished house in the fabled Malibu Colony, where our neighbors would be John McEnroe and Kate Jackson and Brian Keith and Paul Reiser.

Flying from Maui to the mainland, as Naomi and I were dozing off in the darkly lighted cabin . . .

A man wearing a baseball cap and sunglasses startled us awake.

He stuck a mini tape recorder in my face.

Speaking very quickly, he said, "I'm Bob Blanchard from the *Enquirer*—can you tell us about this tawdry romance you're involved in."

I put my arm up and pushed him and said, "Back the fuck up a minute, okay?"

And at that moment I recognized him. It was my producer friend Don Simpson, whom I hadn't seen in years.

I introduced him to Naomi and asked him what he was doing and he said he was trying to lose some weight—he'd been at a fat farm on Maui, was stopping at home in L.A. for a week, and was then headed for a fat farm in Arizona.

Naomi went back to sleep and Simpson and I sat down together in some empty seats and talked for hours, catching up on each other's lives.

After a while I went back and sat with Naomi and when the plane landed in L.A., Naomi and I were the first to get off so I could race to the bathroom for a cigarette.

A valet who was a film student at USC met us at the gate to handle our carry-ons.

I suddenly realized I hadn't said goodbye to Simpson and said to Naomi, "Wait a minute, I want to give Don a hug."

I left Naomi with the valet and went back to the gate.

Simpson came out the door and saw me there waiting for him.

The film-student-valet said to Naomi, "This is a historic moment here. There's Don Simpson and Joe Eszterhas."

I gave him a hug and Don hugged me around the waist and picked me up high in the air . . . and as he held me, he started to topple backward.

The film-school-valet said to Naomi, "There's Don Simpson and Joe Eszterhas falling down."

I fell right on top of Simpson, who was on his back, his legs apart, while I lay between his legs.

"Get off me!" Simpson barked.

I knew what the position we were in must be doing to Don's hyper-extended sense of macho.

The film-student-valet said to Naomi, "There's Joe Eszterhas between Don Simpson's legs."

"*Get off me!*" Simpson yelled.

I started to move my hips atop him and mock-kissed him on the lips.

The film-student-valet said, "There's Joe Eszterhas humping and kissing Don Simpson."

Simpson pushed me off of him in a huff and got up.

Simpson, red-faced, said, "That's not funny, goddamnit!"

My knees were bruised from the fall and since I wore shorts in the summer to all my meetings, I explained to everyone that Don Simpson had given me rug burns.

We rented our house in the Colony from a producer who had had one hit nearly thirty years ago and was now living in a tiny apartment in Studio City . . . and living off the rental of the house he still owned in the Colony.

The house had been added on to so many times that all the floors were uneven—each room higher or lower than the other.

I kept falling, stumbling, or twisting my ankle as I went from one room to the other.

It was a dump of a little house with its own Hollywood history. Previous renters included Bette Midler and Tim Hutton and Woody Harrelson, who'd left behind the teepee he built on the lawn next to the house.

After about a month there, I started thinking I really was losing my mind.

I kept losing things. First some underwear, then some tank tops, then some sun-bleached navy Polo shorts I'd worn for years.

Naomi was laughing at me and I had to admit that I couldn't conceive why anyone would want to steal my somewhat frayed size 38 Fruit of the Loom jockey shorts.

We were over in the Valley, sitting in a coffee shop one day when my producer-landlord walked in with some of his friends.

We chitchatted about how much we liked living in his house and about the movies I was working on and then I told him how much I liked the sun-bleached navy Polo shorts he was wearing and he told me that he'd worn them for years.

There were no paparazzi at the Colony. The security guards at the only entrance made sure of that.

And our new neighbors, who'd read every headline of the Sharon/Bill/Naomi/Joe tabloid extravaganza, were nice to us and protective of us.

Naomi was becoming more obviously pregnant each day and Jon Peters, who lived across the street from us, sent his maid over with specially prepared pastas. Once he and his girlfriend, Vendela, even sent her roses.

Early one morning, I saw someone nosing around our new Land Rover and I went out there and found that it was John McEnroe.

"Sorry." He grinned. "Great wheels."

We had to fly back to Ohio for a family member's funeral and when we put the TV on in our hotel room in Cleveland, we saw that Malibu was burning.

The news said the massive fire was approaching the Colony. We couldn't get through by phone to see if we'd lost the few belongings that we had.

The next morning, as we hurried through the Cleveland airport to catch a flight home, the TV news told us, just as we were getting on the plane, that the Malibu Colony had burned to the ground.

The gods, I thought to myself, were angry at us (probably justifiably).

The house Naomi had shared in Venice Beach with Bill Macdonald had burned to the ground and now this . . .

Naomi's journal:

On the way to the funeral home, his father told Joe he wanted to come to California to live with us.

Joe told him, "No, Pop, you're better off here."

When we got to the funeral home, we sat in the first row—Joe's dad, then Joe, then me.

Joe leans over and says, "I'm going out to have a cigarette. Can you please move over next to my dad when I leave?"

So I do. His father turns and stares at me. Right in the eyes, a long hard stare. It said everything.

It said, "*You. You* could have made it possible for me to come to California. If *you* wanted me to come, he would let me. And *you* sold me out. A lot of good *you* did."

And then he snorted, and turned back to look straight ahead, as if to say, "I don't need you to sit next to me."

So I leaned over and said, "Well, at least I'm better looking than Joe is . . ." knowing full well that, in any circumstance, Joe's dad always loves to sit next to a young woman.

He never looked at me, he just laughed one big "*Haw!*" out loud.

Then he said, "Zis is true."

The Pacific Coast Highway to Malibu was closed, but the cops finally let us through when we convinced them we were residents.

The air was filled with ash. Hillsides were still blazing. We drove inch by inch through a brown-hazed war zone. Burning embers and tree branches were all over the road.

It took us almost three hours to get to the Colony. Hundreds of fire trucks were lined up in a wall guarding it, spraying the fields in front of the Colony walls.

Much of the rest of Malibu had burned, but this panzer division of fire trucks had kept the Colony safe.

Of course, I thought to myself.

Jerry Perenchio was one of our Colony neighbors. Jerry, a television magnate, was one of Governor Pete Wilson's biggest contributors.

The gods may have been angry at us . . . but our neighbors had *juice.*

We got Naomi's golden retriever, Jake, back from the ranch where he'd been temporarily staying and now Jake was with us in our house at the Colony.

There was one problem, I quickly noted. Jake wasn't just Naomi's dog . . . he was also Bill Macdonald's.

Jake hated me. He snarled and barked at me.

Every afternoon, as I did my laps in the pool, Jake waited for me and . . . at just the right moment . . . Jake hurled himself onto the middle of my back, trying to drown me.

Naomi went for a walk on the Colony beach with Jake.

Jake started going after a piece of driftwood in the water. Naomi called for him but he wouldn't come. The tide was coming in quickly. Jake went farther out in the water. Naomi kept calling for him but he wouldn't come. The tide was getting higher.

Naomi had to run for the steps that lead from the beach. She barely made it before the water covered the steps. And here came Jake swimming for the ladder!

He made it.

Naomi was petrified and soaking wet when she got back to the house.

I got the .45 out of my nightstand, put it to Jake's head, and blew Bill Macdonald's dog's brains out.

(Just kidding.)

Jake shat the rug constantly, but only on my side of the bed.

Jake was history.

Naomi gave Bill Macdonald's dog away to a nice couple far away who owned a big ranch.

I kept missing Steve and Suzi. They were in their first year of college—Steve in Oregon, Suzi in Colorado—and I saw them rarely, though I spoke to them almost every day.

They wanted to have nothing to do with Naomi.

When they came down to visit, they refused to stay with us and stayed at the Malibu Beach Inn down the Pacific Coast Highway.

When they came to the house, they refused to speak to her. I spent the days out in the streets with them when they visited—on Melrose, on the Santa Monica Promenade, on Venice Beach, trying to do things together on days filled with long silences.

Suzi and a girlfriend were at our house once and they were eating Chinese food and Naomi told me Suzi picked up a carton and then put it down.

"Why aren't you having any?" her girlfriend asked her.

"Because she ate from it," Suzi said, pointing at Naomi.

Naomi left the room.

All I could hope for was that with the passage of time, Steve and Suzi would forgive me for leaving their mother, that as they got older they'd understand the complexities of love and the vagaries of the heart.

I didn't have much hope that this would happen soon or even in the near future.

All I could hope was that my kids would remember all the time I'd spent with them in their childhood: the Little League games, the animal rights meetings and protests, the hugs, the laughs, the barbecues, the Gang Up On Dad Dunk'ems in so many swimming pools.

One day maybe they'd realize that my breakup with their mother had nothing to do with them . . . that the marriage had lasted as long as it did *because of them.*

The day before Christmas Eve, Naomi and I went down to Rodeo Drive to feel Christmas in the air. We were looking for carolers and Salvation Army Santas and steaming hot mugs of Irish coffee and maybe some Dickensian fog.

There were no carolers, no Salvation Army Santas, and no Dickensian fog. It was 92 degrees. We were drenched in sweat. We drank ice-cold beers in an air-conditioned place as Mel Tormé sang "The Christmas Song" on the piped-in music.

When we came back out of the place, we finally saw Santa, but he was riding a camel down the middle of Rodeo Drive, sweat streaming down his face as he dispensed little bottles of tequila in a promotion giveaway.

We went back to Malibu, cranked the air conditioner up as high as it would go, pulled the drapes, put the Christmas tree lights on, built a fire, and watched a video of *A Christmas Carol.*

After a while it got so chilly we joyously put sweaters on.

As I sat in the predawn hours beating away at my Olivetti manual typewriter with the surf crashing behind me at the Malibu Colony, I thought to myself: *Man, what are you doing here?*

You don't even *like* L.A. You lived in Marin County all those years and commuted down here because you didn't want to get too close to this place. And now you're not only living in L.A., but in *Malibu,* behind gates at the fucking *Colony,* the holy of holies of Hollywood showbiz and glamour.

Oh, sure, you may be wearing your Cleveland Indians T-shirts and your Brotherhood of Teamsters jacket, but you're getting takeout pizzas from Wolfgang Puck's Granita and Jon Peters's model girlfriend, Vendela, is telling the world that you're her favorite writer.

You're *Vendela's favorite writer?*

You're living in Woody Harrelson's house and smoking weed in his teepee? *What the fuck?*

The road begins in the refugee camps of Austria and ends in the Malibu Colony? With the ghost of a nude Marilyn Monroe slinking in and out of the fog on rainy nights?

In an interview in *Us* magazine, Sharon Stone was asked: "Are you planning your wedding soon?"

"Bill and I love each other very much," she said, "and are committed to spending the rest of our lives together. Primarily, I feel and think how happy I am to have found such a beautiful love in my life and how grateful I am for the existence of that love. My life is full of joy. I'm in love and I'm really, really happy about it."

Robert Evans called to tell me he was going to remake *Breakfast at Tiffany's* and wondered whether I had any interest in writing it. I knew why he wanted to remake it.

Like so many other beautiful young girls from the Midwest, Rhonda somehow wound up staying at Bob's house. Bob was always nice to his girls and introduced them to his friends, who were nice to the girls, too. Barely out of her teens, soon Rhonda was going out with studio heads and celebrities she saw on TV.

Rhonda wanted to be an actress, of course, but meanwhile she kept going out with Bob's powerful friends and even got a part-time job in a real estate office in Beverly Hills.

One afternoon a man with a gun came into the real estate office and for some reason—was it a robbery? Did it have to do with one of Evans's powerful friends?—blew Rhonda's brains out.

Evans was devastated and spent many sorrowful hours thinking about her life and made a deal with the studio to remake *Breakfast at Tiffany's* with an edge, Beverly Hills–style . . . Rhonda as Holly Golightly . . . Rhonda, a studio exec said, go-blithely, Holly go-*dead*.

Sharon and Bill Macdonald broke up—she sent his "antique engagement ring" back to him by Federal Express.

She dove quickly into another love affair—with the assistant director of the movie she was shooting.

Bill, we heard, was living only a few miles from us in Malibu, above a garage.

I wrote a script called *Foreplay* about serial killers—a spooky, dark comedy, set in St. Petersburg, Florida, where Gerri, Steve, Suzi, and I had done so many of our summer beach crawls.

Guy McElwaine decided to auction it and a new production company named Savoy Pictures outbid six others.

The deal we structured gave me $1 million up front and another $4 million when the movie was made. But I was also guaranteed *two and a half cents for every dollar Savoy took in from all income, including video.* I was also guaranteed *one percent of soundtrack sales.*

"This is the big barrier we've wanted to cross for some time," Guy told me. "Even a lot of big-time actors don't have it. No writer with the possible exception of Neil Simon has ever gotten it, and if he did then he got it for adapting one of his stage plays to the screen."

The media covered the *Foreplay* deal as a landmark breakthrough.

A reporter named Jerry Carroll of the *San Francisco Chronicle* said to me: "Writers all over America are lighting joss sticks in your honor."

"Or they're out of their minds with jealousy," I said.

The man who made this landmark deal with me . . . who gave to a writer what a writer in Hollywood had never gotten before . . . was the head of Savoy, Frank Price.

Frank Price was the former head of Columbia, the man who'd insisted I change the ending of *Jagged Edge,* the man whose firing I had waited out before turning in my script.

Since I'd worked on my spec script *Foreplay* while I was also working on a picture, *Gangland,* for Columbia and Jon Peters . . . I thought it only fair to let Jon read the script before anybody else.

Guy agreed with me.

I called and told Jon that I had written a new spec and that he would be the first to read it.

He was overjoyed.

"You know what?" he said, "that's one of the nicest things anyone has ever done for me. You're good people. When can I read it?"

"Whenever you can come over here," I said. His house in the Colony was almost directly across the street from the one we were renting.

"I'll send somebody over to pick it up," Jon said.

"I can't do that," I said. "I can't let it out of my hands. You'll have to read it over here."

"I'm not going to let anybody else read it," he said. "I'm not going to show it to anybody else. I give you my word."

"I'm sorry," I said, "you've gotta read it here."

"You're not going to take my word?" Jon said. "My word isn't good enough for you?"

"Jon," I said, "I'm giving you a jump on the whole town. What are we arguing for?"

"You wanna get into a fight with me?" he yelled suddenly. "I'm not fuckin' Mike Ovitz fraternity boy! You don't want to get in a fight with me! Trust me!"

I said, "Listen, man, we're friends."

"Then give me the fucking script!" he yelled.

"I can't!" I yelled back. "You gotta read it here! You can't take it! I can't take the chance it'll get out somehow! For Christ's sake, don't you get it? I'm trying to do you a favor!"

Jon hung up on me.

· · ·

At ten o'clock the next morning, our gate bell at the Colony rang. I saw it was Jon and let him in. He was wearing a sport coat and tie. He looked sensational.

"All right," he said with a grin. "Where is this fucking script? It's probably a piece of shit anyway. I'll tell you what: if I wanna buy it, maybe I'll just give you my beach house for it and we can call it a deal."

I got the script and handed it to him.

"You can sit right in here," I said. "It'll be quiet in here."

"I'm just going to take it across the street to my house and read it there," Jon said.

I stared at him. *Was he serious?* After *everything* I had said to him last night? Very slowly I said, "I told you. You can't do that."

He stared back at me. Very quietly he said, "It's just across the street."

In a whisper, I said, "No."

Almost pleading, he said, "I'm not going to Xerox it or show it to anybody."

I said, "No. You're going to read it right here in this room and not take it anywhere."

He sat down on the couch and put the script in front of him on the big teak coffee table. His face, I saw, was a dark shade that was nearly purple.

He suddenly smashed the coffee table with his clenched fist—so hard that the table cracked.

He jumped up.

"*You cocksucker!*" he yelled into my face. "*You sonofabitch! You know what you are? You're a mean motherfucker!*"

He gave me an ugly look, brushed by me, and went out the door. When he got to the gate, he had trouble opening it.

The teak coffee table he cracked was a recent purchase Naomi and I had made at the Wirtz Brothers secondhand furniture store in Santa Monica.

It had belonged to the famous and respected producer David Wolper.

That fact made it a truly incestuous Hollywood moment: Jon Peters broke David Wolper's cocktail table because he got mad at Joe Eszterhas.

Guy told me that Jon showed up at Columbia the next day with his hand in a cast.

He was telling people, Guy said, that he'd had a "creative difference" with me . . . and had scaled my gate "like Batman" and had hurt his hand.

Two days after Savoy bought *Foreplay,* bootleg copies of the script were being sold at bookstores on Sunset and Hollywood Boulevard for $25 a Xerox copy.

Signs on the bookstore windows said "New Eszterhas Script Available Here."

· · ·

Years later I was having lunch with former Sony head Mark Canton at the Bel-Air Hotel and I told him about Jon, who was a friend of Mark's, and *Foreplay*.

"Jon's dyslexic," Mark said, "didn't you know that?"

"No," I said, "I didn't."

"Everybody in town knows that."

"Neither Guy nor anybody else at ICM said anything to me about it," I said.

"Jon doesn't read scripts himself," Mark said. "Either someone reads a script to him or he hires people who dramatize the script and put it on tape for him."

"I'm sorry," I said, "I didn't know that."

"Sure," Mark said. "Jon figures everybody knows that. So when you were going to make him sit there and read the script, he figured you were being a mean motherfucker . . . because you knew he couldn't do that due to his dyslexia."

"I swear to you I didn't know that," I said.

Mark said, "You'll never convince Jon."

The reason Mark Canton and I were having lunch was because I was working at the time with Wendy Finerman, an Oscar-winning producer who was soon about to become the ex–Mrs. Mark Canton.

That was because Wendy walked in one day on Mark and the director Luc Besson's secretary as they were getting to know each other atop Mark's desk.

I think Mark wanted to know what Wendy was saying about him behind his back . . . but *I* didn't tell.

Based on Mark's response to my script *Foreplay*, I was nervous about how Columbia was going to react to my script about John Gotti—*Gangland*, based on Howard Blum's best-seller. I wrote Mark Canton, then the studio chairman of Columbia, a letter:

> *Dear Mark,*
>
> *I wanted to express my concern and consternation to you concerning your response to* Foreplay.
>
> *The script, you told me, "had no plot . . . not many surprises . . . no sense of jeopardy . . . needed more plot twists." In addition, you thought it "nihilistic and dark" and said it needed "more savvy, James Bondian cops." You said it was "neither* Jagged Edge *nor* Basic Instinct *and dismissed the humor as a "series of one-liners."*
>
> *This was your response to a script that sold for the highest price in Hollywood history in a deal that calls for no rewrites but calls for only a director's polish.*
>
> *After having said all of those things to me—and after having heard*

Guy McElwaine's response on my behalf expressing my feeling that you
were totally out to sea—I was completely flabbergasted when I heard that
you offered a million dollars to buy Foreplay.

What concerns me is that I am deep into the Gotti script, which I will
deliver to you on June 30. I genuinely hope your response to Gangland *will*
not be as benighted as it was to Foreplay.

At the same time, I want to underline my oft-reiterated position that
John Gotti is not, as you once said to me, "a Robin Hood figure." He is a
man who, according to Howard Blum's book, once chain-sawed another
man with his own hands. He will be a villain in my piece—colorful,
larger-than-life, but a villain—as he deserves to be. I will have nothing to
do with sugarcoating him for public perception.

I bear no bad feeling, incidentally, for Jon Peters. While I have never
before had anyone come into my home, fracture his hand on my coffee
table, and spew forth a series of obscenities . . . I appreciate his passion for
Gangland.

> *Best,*
> *Joe*

Suzi was in town with a girlfriend from college. They were staying at the nearby Malibu Beach Inn. I'd been out to dinner with them and had then come home to Naomi and our house in the Colony.

At 4:30 in the morning, the house felt like a box being violently shaken up and down. I screamed "*Quake!*" The shaking continued.

Naomi was eight months pregnant. She froze. I lifted her off the bed. A bookcase collapsed and dumped books everywhere near us. I half carried Naomi outside. The water in the swimming pool was a storm-tossed sea. Car alarms were wailing.

I held on to Naomi, who was crying. I was shaking so badly I didn't think my knees would hold me up.

"We're okay," I kept saying. "We're okay."

Then it hit me: *Oh, God, Suzi was here* . . . three blocks away . . . on the top floor of a hotel with three floors.

Naomi grabbed a robe. We jumped into the Land Rover. The security guard at the Colony gate stopped me. He said it'd been the Big One. He said power was out and damage was heavy. Power lines were everywhere in the streets.

"You can't go out there," he said.

We drove out onto the Pacific Coast Highway. Fire trucks and police cars were screaming by in both directions.

I prayed that when we got to the Malibu Beach Inn I wouldn't find a pile of rubble.

It finally came into view and I saw the building was still standing. I raced into the lobby. Fallen plaster was everywhere. Suzi was there with her friend.

"I knew you'd be the first car here, Pops," Suzi said with a smile. She and her friend were shaken up and still shaking, but unhurt. They'd run down the stairway from their room, dodging the plaster falling all around them.

I told Suzi that Naomi was outside in the car. I told her we were going to go back to our house in the Colony—all four of us. Suzi said she wasn't coming. She said she wasn't going to get in the same car with Naomi, let alone the same house.

I yelled at her. I told her we'd just lived through the Big One. I told her the roads would be closed, food wouldn't be available, the aftershocks would start. Just then the first aftershock struck—a single, hard jolt as though the hotel had been kicked in the butt.

Suzi agreed to come to our house with her friend. They stayed with us for three days until the roads reopened. Suzi acted like Naomi wasn't there. She said not one word to her. She looked right through her. We kept running in and out of the house to the lawn during those three days whenever there was an aftershock.

When I drove Suzi and her friend to the airport, Suzi didn't want Naomi to come with us.

"Forget it," I said to her, "I'm not leaving the woman I love who is eight months pregnant with our child alone when there is an aftershock every couple of hours. If you want me to drive you, she's coming. If you don't, take a cab."

Naomi came to the airport with us, but Suzi didn't say a word all the way there.

The aftershocks continued after Suzi was gone. We weren't getting any sleep. I was worried about the effect on Naomi's pregnancy. We drove down to San Diego. We checked into our hotel room at six o'clock at night and were asleep by seven. We slept until eleven the next day.

Spago is a glitzy place. We walked in. The room froze. Everyone gaped. We were with Muhammad Ali!

Ali suffers from Parkinson's. Ali didn't say much. Ali's speech was slurred. Ali's wife spoke for him. Ali looked down at his plate. Ali ate his food. Ali kept his head down. Over dessert, Ali looked up. Ali stared straight ahead.

Bimbos, sluts, and starlets wiggled by, smiling at him.

Ali's face was set. Ali's eyes were glassy. Ali didn't react.

Ali's wife went to the bathroom.

Ali stared at nothing. Ali leaned over to me suddenly. Ali smiled. Ali whispered something. Ali's voice was clear.

"Man, they got some fine foxes in here, don't they?" Ali said.

. . .

We were having dinner at Morton's late in Naomi's pregnancy and, excited, she took the sonogram photo of the baby we had decided to call Joey . . . and passed it around the table to our friends.

We didn't know that a reporter from *Buzz* magazine was hovering around nearby.

Buzz wrote: "What is Joe pulling out of his pocket for all to see? Why it's the sonogram of the littlest Eszterhas, issue of his adulterous union.

"Now, sonograms passed around like snapshots are creepy enough . . . but here comes the truly frightening thing! While most sonograms look like blurry fish, in this one—and there was no mistaking it—the fetus looked . . . *exactly like Joe*."

I wrote *Buzz* magazine a letter.

"I know I'm a former journalist," I wrote. "I know I make a lot of money. I know some present-day journalists who don't make any money might have a very personal problem with that.

"But come on—some things should be sacred. To say that our beautiful baby boy looked like me when he was in his mother's womb is unfair to our baby boy . . . even the *National Enquirer* wouldn't lower itself to saying that.

"The only thing that gives me solace is knowing that your writer is doomed to a lifetime of penury, jealousy, and oblivion.

"Oh, well. Poor schmuck."

Naomi's journal:

I went for an ultrasound today. As the nurse was looking at the screen she said, "I'll go get the doctor . . ."

As soon as she left I got frantic. Joe said, "Be cool. This is nothing. Don't get hysterical. Everything's fine. Trust me."

He held my hand. The doctor came in, looked at the screen, and said, "Well, we can't get a measure of the size of the baby because it's off the screen. It's too big for this machine, which means it's well over nine pounds now. You can go over to Cedars and we'll use another machine, or we can end this and just induce labor. We can go tomorrow, or Thursday or Friday. What do you want to do?"

I thought to myself, tomorrow is just too scary. I need a day. Thursday is March 10, Sharon Stone's birthday . . .

I said "Friday."

We agreed I would go in Thursday night for delivery on Friday.

Joe drove me to the hospital about 8:00 P.M. I was terrified. I knew this baby was big, and I couldn't believe they were going to be able to get it out. Joe sang "Volare" all the way to the hospital while holding my hand. He knows it makes me laugh.

My fear proved justified. The first drug didn't work. No labor pains. So they had to do a second procedure (a torture test that I won't relive by writing it). As I lay there waiting to feel something, anything, I could hear a woman screaming, "Jesus God help me! God help me!" It went on all night.

For hours, as I inched closer to higher and higher levels of pain, I listened to her pleas. I asked a nurse about her. She said, "Oh, she's a lightweight . . ."

This was barbaric. By the next afternoon, after hours and hours of labor and no baby movement, they finally saw something on my heart monitor that caused them to do an emergency cesarean. They also felt the baby was in distress.

They made Joe leave the operating room as soon as he walked in. They said he looked like he was going to faint.

So I was alone. They couldn't get the baby out. They had to get two people to scrub up and come in and literally lay on my stomach to help push it out. I kept saying, "I can't breathe."

Finally I heard the doctor say, "Say hello to Son of Bigfoot! Somebody get me a scale! This is a big baby!"

He weighed ten and a half pounds. The doctor said he would have easily been eleven pounds or more if we'd left him in until he was ready. He became known in the nursery as "the Moose."

I couldn't even hold him or see him. My eyes were swollen shut (from the strain of trying to push him out myself for a day) and the drugs had given me uncontrollable shakes. I didn't hear him cry. I thought he was dead.

But then they held him close and I could vaguely see golden fuzz all over his head, and tiny ears. Joe had always teased me that our children would have bright red hair and big ears. I smiled. He wasn't Howdy Doody.

. . .

In her twenty-third hour of labor with Joey, Naomi was drenched in sweat, her face was purple, and her heartbeat was arrhythmic.

Our Ob-gyn, who was also Madonna's gynecologist, a former major league baseball player, was sitting right next to her, at the Hospital to the Stars, holding her hand.

"You worked with Jennifer Beals, didn't you?" he said to me. "She always looked to me like she'd be really hot. Was she?"

After Joey was born, Evans asked if he could have his foreskin. Evans said he was suffering from dire impotence and he was sure that Joey's foreskin would cure it.

I went down to a pet shop and got a dried pig's ear—the kind dogs chew on—and said it was Joey's foreskin. Evans was impressed by the size of it and had it framed, although he never told me whether it cured his impotence.

I realized that I loved Gerri, that I would always love Gerri—as a sister, not as a partner and a wife and a lover.

I decided I was filing for divorce.

When I told Suzi, she started to cry. When I told Steve, he said, "Are you sure, Pops? Are you absolutely sure?"

I said I was sure.

He said nothing and finally I said, "You know how much I love you, Mano."

"I know that, Pops," he said.

When I told Gerri, she said, "Fuck you, Joseph!" and hung up.

All my male friends and business associates—every single one of them—told me not to get divorced. Even those who'd been divorced themselves.

This was their argument:

Look, you've been married almost a quarter century. That's a very long time. You've got two beautiful grown kids—if you do this, you're going to lose all the money you've made.

Forget the fifty-fifty stuff in California . . . there's something called community goodwill, too . . . in a long marriage like yours, your wife will argue that she helped make your career.

You're going to lose your houses, your cars, everything. Is that worth it? To be broke again when you're *almost fifty years old?*

This happens all the time. A guy your age meets a woman Naomi's age and a guy your age loses his mind.

You've got a beautiful family! There's no need to destroy a family over this and lose all your money and hurt your kids.

All you have to do is keep Naomi on the side. *It happens all the time in this town.* Don't get a divorce. Support Naomi, support the kids you might have together. And hold on to everything you've got.

I couldn't quite believe that here I was telling all my Hollywood friends that I was getting a divorce . . . and my Hollywood friends were responding by telling me about *family values!*

The lawyer had come highly recommended to me. He was one of the top lawyers in Los Angeles.

He came to our house in the Colony but he didn't want to talk there. He asked if we could go for a walk on the beach.

He spoke softly as we talked—I could barely hear him above the crash of the waves.

"You're fucked," he said. "That's the truth. There's no way around it. You've been married twenty-four years. You have two grown kids. You're completely fucked."

"Is that why you wanted to come out here?" I asked him with a smile. "To tell me that I'm fucked? I don't need *you* to tell me that I'm fucked. I can tell if I'm fucked myself. I've been there before in my life."

He smiled back at me and said, "Not like this you haven't."

Then the smile stretched into a grin and he said, "You're a real *pistola,* aren't you?

"Your wife will go away," he whispered. "A hundred grand. Paid to me for legal services."

I thought I might have misunderstood. I said, "What?"

He kept grinning and said, "Come on, no bullshit. Yes or no."

I said, "Go away where?"

"I don't know where. I'm not sure how I feel about an afterlife."

"I can't do that," I said.

He said, "You're gonna lose every penny you've got."

When I stared at him, horrified, and shook my head, he said, "It's *your* funeral then."

I fired him, even though I hadn't really hired him.

Evans, I heard, was back in the fetal position.

Four hookers had written a book about their Hollywood adventures.

Evans was featured prominently in the book, greeting them in his screening room, feeding them booze, coke, and Quaaludes . . . then taking them into his bedroom and giving them directions: "Lisa, you lick Tiffany there . . . Tiffany, darling, put your finger in there!"

I always suspected Bob was a frustrated director.

This was the final Evans direction in the book: "*Tiffany, my dear, would you please pee on me?*"

This is how incestuous Hollywood is:

The head of the publishing company which published the hookers' book was Evans's *next-door neighbor!*

On our first visit to our pediatrician in Beverly Hills, I noted that his office was filled not with pictures of children but with signed movie posters.

At the end of our first visit our new pediatrician asked me if I could send him two signed posters of my movies, too.

On our next visit I noted that my posters were up on the wall, too—*Basic Instinct,* and *Showgirls*—centerpieces of a roomful of coughing and sneezing and crying little boys and girls.

Many a night at the Malibu Colony after Joey's birth, Naomi and I stayed up at night rocking him back to sleep.

We had the TV set on in the background and watched the chases as we rocked him. The TV stations in L.A. covered all police chases live. Most of them took place late at night, so we saw a lot of them.

We started rating them like movies. While the O.J. chase, years later, became the *Gone With the Wind* of chases, Naomi and I saw a lot of great B movie chases while we rocked Joey.

We saw one that began on the 405, the San Diego Freeway, cut over to the 10, the Santa Monica Freeway, then onto the streets of Santa Monica and onto the Pacific Coast Highway.

We stared as the chase came closer and closer on the PCH toward our house in the Colony.

We lowered the volume so we could hear the sirens pass us outside in real life and not on the TV.

On the 6th day of April, 1994, I asked Naomi to come for a walk with me.

We walked in the Colony—past Jerry Perenchio's house, past Irwin Winkler's, past where Burgess Meredith used to live. When we got to the actor Brian Keith's house, we walked across the back of his yard and jumped down to the beach. The sun was setting on a warm and rare Maui-like day.

I handed Naomi a little box and she looked at it and started to open it with trembling fingers and exactly at the moment when she opened it and saw the ring . . . I said, "Will you marry me, Guinea?"

She jumped into the air like a little girl and yelled, "*Yayyyyyyyyy!*"

And then she said, her teary face very close to mine, "You don't have to marry me."

· · ·

I remembered the moment I had asked Gerri to marry me a quarter century earlier . . . at night, at a romantic spot in a meadow near Shaker Lakes in Cleveland.

Gerri opened the box and took the ring out of it to put on her finger . . . and *I dropped it!* Into thick grass.

Gerri and I got down on the ground to find it . . . but we couldn't see.

Because exactly at that moment—Honest to God, this is true—there was an *eclipse of the moon!*

We had to wait fifteen minutes in the pitch-black before we could even begin the hunt for Gerri's engagement ring.

We found it, and as I put it on her finger, *I dropped it again!*

I told Steve and Suzi and Gerri that I had asked Naomi to marry me and it was one of the saddest phone calls of my life.

All three of them cried.

I told my lawyers and accountants that I was marrying Naomi and they didn't cry, but they certainly sounded sad.

When I told them there wouldn't even be a prenuptial agreement, I thought I heard at least one accountant start to sniffle.

These, according to the court's ruling, were the terms of my divorce based on "community goodwill" and the fact that Gerri and I had been married for twenty-four years:

Gerri got both houses, all four of the cars, and most of the cash.

I was to pay her $32,500 a month in alimony—after taxes. In other words, I had to earn $65,000 a month to pay her.

I was to pay for the kids' college educations.

I was broke, starting all over again, a refugee again, living in Los Angeles, a place that I hated.

I didn't care. Naomi was worth it.

Naomi said, "You threw everything away for me, your castles, your carriages. You're risking your relationships with your children for me. Your friends think you're crazy. I feel like Wallis Simpson."

I said, "From what I know about the Duke of Windsor, I don't want to feel like the Duke of Windsor."

Sharon Stone was telling the world that she'd been "tricked" into doing *that* scene by Paul Verhoeven.

I knew what Sharon was doing and she was doing it well. She didn't want to be forever known for showing the world her pubes; she considered herself, after all, a serious actress.

No one needed to know that, the morning she had shot *that* scene, she had handed her scented panties to Paul and said, "I won't be needing these today."

As part of her campaign to rehabilitate her image—post-pube redemption—she even engaged in a public fight with a studio head, telling him that under no circumstances would she do a nude scene.

I knew what she was doing and laughed when a limo driver in New York told the world that Sharon had yelled at him: "Don't you know who I am? *I'm the American Princess Di.*"

Sharon Stone as the American Princess Di? Well sure. It made sense. From a flash of cinematic beaver to American royalty.

After all, she had even dated Dodi Fayed . . . back before he'd met the other Princess Di . . . even before she'd handed Paul Verhoeven her scented panties.

April 6, 1994, the day I proposed to Naomi, was my father's birthday . . . his eighty-seventh birthday.

I thought about calling him to wish him a happy birthday.

I thought about telling him that I asked the love of my life to marry me on his birthday.

I thought about it . . . but I didn't make the call.

A Joint for Robert Mitchum

Not wanting to be bothered, Robert Mitchum was sitting at a table with his back to the bar on a dank Saturday afternoon at the Formosa Café, in L.A., where his photograph was up on the wall.

The photograph showed a sinisterly handsome young man with a smile that was a sneer and eyes that bespoke a certain nihilism of the soul.

The old man sitting with his back to the bar now and sipping his tequila had a face like cracked Moroccan leather and a body pouched and ravaged by time, cigarettes, the tequila, and a bad temper.

For many years he was one of the biggest movie stars in the world, separate from the others because of a wildness in his soul which the camera wouldn't hide no matter what the role. James Dean was a simpering poseur compared to him.

As a young man he spent time in a chain gang for smoking a joint. As a movie star, he resolved a contract dispute by defecating on the studio chief's white shag rug. As an older man, he countered a belligerent woman's request that he not smoke in the smoking section of an airliner by bending over and passing gas into her face.

I sat at the bar of the Formosa Café as he sat with his back to us not wanting to be seen or bothered. I didn't want to bother him but I couldn't resist.

I went over to his table and took the joint I had in my pocket and said, "Mr. Mitchum, I just wanted to tell you how much I admire your work," and handed him the joint.

Robert Mitchum took it, sniffed it, and grinned.

"Son," he said, "it'll be a helluva nice ride back to Santa Barbara."

CHAPTER 28

We're Hollywood Animals

CATHERINE
What happened, Nick? Did you get sucked into it? Did you like it
too much? Nicky got too close to the flame. Nicky liked it.

Basic Instinct

Madam Stone, as Guy always called Sharon, fired him.
I was the one who convinced her to hire him and I was sure I was
the reason she fired him.

It took her a while, but I knew after Guy came to the *Sliver* premiere with
Naomi and me . . . and not with Sharon and Bill . . . that his days were numbered.

Guy knew it, too, but came with us anyway.

I knew Sharon . . . and I knew she *especially* wanted Guy to be with them
and not with us . . . because I was with Naomi, who had called her a "home
wrecker" on TV.

When Guy came with *us*, Sharon felt betrayed.

Now that he no longer represented Sharon, I was Guy's only "star" client.

I had told Robert Evans about my outline for the movie to be called *Jade* while
we were working on *Sliver.*

I had sold it in the late eighties to the Weintraub Entertainment Group. It
was about the wife of a philandering husband who gets even with him by hooking on the side.

The outline, I told Evans, was lost in a morass of legal problems. The Weintraub Entertainment Group had gone into bankruptcy . . . the rights to the
outline somehow had to be pried loose from WEG's other bankruptcy assets.
Over many months, Bill Macdonald had worked heroically and had pried the
outline loose through truly Herculean and shrewd legal efforts.

. . .

Sherry Lansing, the new head of Paramount, made *Jade* her first big green-light announcement. And now, as we were living in the Malibu Colony, I finished the *Jade* script.

Naomi and I were in Palm Springs the weekend the studio executives read it, and we were suddenly bombarded with bottles of Cristal and tins of caviar.

Sherry called me and asked me to come in to talk to her as soon as I got back from the desert. The script, she said, was ready to go out to directors and she wanted to see who I had in mind.

I was flattered but I smelled what was coming. Sherry was married to Billy Friedkin, who desperately needed a hit movie—*The Exorcist* and *The French Connection* were so very many years ago.

The very first thing Sherry said at our meeting was "Billy just loves your script."

I nodded and didn't say anything, forcing her to say, "How do you feel about Billy directing it?"

I said, "Billy hasn't had a hit in over twenty years, Sherry. There are people in town who think the only reason Billy still works is because he's married to you."

Sherry said, "That's not true!"

"Nevertheless," I said, "some people think that."

She said, "He just loves this script. He thinks it's the perfect script. He wouldn't change a comma."

"He wouldn't?"

"Not a comma," Sherry said. "I promise you."

I said, "*You* promise me?"

Sherry said, "*I* promise you."

I had lunch with Billy Friedkin and he repeated that he wasn't going to change a comma.

"Music to my ears, Billy," I said.

"I mean it, Joe," Billy said. "It's the perfect script."

I liked Billy's gray-haired, gone-to-fat, street-kid style . . . I *loved* Billy's attitude about the script . . . and I sat back down with Sherry, who said she had a problem.

She was going to be criticized, Sherry said, for letting Billy direct *Jade* . . . and she wanted me to say it was my idea for Billy to direct *Jade,* not hers.

As I thought about it, Sherry said, "I'll owe you a favor, honey."

I smiled and simply said okay and Sherry said, "I love you, honey."

The headline in the Calendar section of the *Los Angeles Times* of April 18, 1994, read "FRIEDKIN SIGNING KEEPS 'JADE' IN LANSING FAMILY."

The subhead read: "Selection of Paramount Chief's Husband as Director Raises Eyebrows, Even in an Industry Known for Nepotism."

The article said:

"Eszterhas, also the film's executive producer, maintains that Friedkin had long been his first choice to direct *Jade*. He vehemently objects to the insinuation of nepotism . . .

"Said Eszterhas: 'What Friedkin brings to the party is a kind of spooky, dark energy which fits perfectly into *Jade*. He has a great sense of visual style. . . .'

"Eszterhas said he was also impressed when Friedkin 'told me he doesn't want to change a comma.'

"But more skeptical observers say that Friedkin would never have been given this opportunity if not for his marriage to Lansing."

My father called to tell me that one of the nurses who had taken care of him in Tiburon after his heart surgery visited him in Cleveland Heights.

"Amelia," he said, laughing.

I knew it had to be Amelia.

She was in her early forties—my father was eighty-five then—and she considered herself a poet and a painter. I didn't know that, of course, when I hired her to take care of my father; I thought I was hiring a nurse. She painted an oil portrait of my father while she was in Tiburon and one day she asked to speak to me. She told me she was in love with my father.

I spoke to my father and we agreed that I should fire her. And now, five years later, she had showed up at his house in Cleveland Heights.

"What did she want?" I asked.

"To move in," my father said.

He was laughing.

"What did you say to her?"

"I showed her my catheter. I asked if she knew how to clean it. Then I asked her if she was strong enough to support me to the bathroom."

"What did she say?"

"She didn't understand why we had to get rid of the nurses if she moved in. She said she had to visit another friend here and then she'd stop back. That was a week ago."

He was laughing again.

He said, "This catheter would scare anybody away."

We sent our friends this invitation from our son, Joey:

"Joseph Jeremiah Eszterhas invites you to celebrate the marriage of Joe Eszterhas and his great friend, Naomi Baka . . . at the Kumulani Chapel of the Ritz-Carlton Kapalua on the island of Maui."

At the bottom left-hand corner of the invitation were these words:
"*Life is strange.*"
"*Life is amazing.*"

Naomi's journal:

This afternoon I went to the Kapalua Ritz-Carlton salon
on Maui to have my nails done with my sister. The place was
buzzing with gossip about hotel guests who are there for my
wedding. It seems Guy's fiancée is having her hair and makeup
done for the big day. "You'd think *she* was getting
married . . ." one of the hairdressers griped. She came in
to have it done this morning on a trial basis so it looks
good for tomorrow. I'm just doing my own hair and makeup at
home in the morning.

The big buzz though was about Evans's "writers." He
brought two young girls with him to the hotel and said they
are writing the book he's working on. He introduces them as
"my writers."

One of the stylists said, in her New Orleans accent,
"Wa, I sweya, those girls can't be more en fifteen years old!
Do you know what one o' them told me? She said, 'We're so
excited! Evans says we can do anything we want—massages,
manicures, pedicures—he's payin' for everthin'!' They were
like two schoolgirls in here, ooooin' and ahhin' ova everthin' . . . and then they go upstaiyas to that old man."

The party last night was fun but a little weird. To mix
these people with my family and Dana, my childhood best
friend from Ohio (who showed up as a surprise), is like
seeing a screwball comedy. Evans is talking about how the
last time he was in Maui was on one of his honeymoons and
divorce followed soon after.

The strangest moment of the party was when Guy's fiancée
sat next to me. Looking into her eyes is like looking into
two blue marbles. She had an absolutely huge diamond on her
finger.

I said, "I love your ring." She said, "Oh, I'm taking it
back. It isn't at all what I wanted. For starters, the diamond's too small. I told Guy I wanted two baguettes on
either side of a pear-shaped diamond. This is just not what

I told him I wanted. He never listens. It's like his new
glasses. I told him I hated them and he still hasn't gotten
new ones."

I said, "But he picked the ring out for you, doesn't
that make it special?" (I couldn't resist.) She stared
blankly at me and said, "I told you, I don't like it."

I got up on the morning of July 30, 1994, the day I married the Great Love of My
Life, by answering the phone: "Last Chance Saloon."

I missed Steve and Suzi badly, but knew there was no chance they'd be here
for *this* party.

Naomi went over to the Ritz to get ready with her sister and her friends and
I sat in the sun and swam my laps and thought about my wedding with Gerri: it
was a solemn High Mass at St. Margaret of Hungary Church in Cleveland—
there were so many people there, police were needed to direct traffic.

I was afraid a former girlfriend—whose mother had threatened to commit
suicide when she heard I was marrying Gerri—would show up.

I had given the girlfriend's picture to the ushers and told them to escort her
as quietly as possible out of the church if she showed up.

I was twenty-three years old.

I had gone to a coffee shop that morning and had some donuts and played
the jukebox and thought:

Maybe you're a little too young to be doing this.

I'd been right.

And that, maybe more than anything else, was the main reason my marriage
to Gerri broke up nearly twenty-five years after that morning in the coffee shop.

After I finished my laps, I went back to the house we were renting to put my
white Armani suit on. I wore it with a black tank top and cowboy boots with
Naomi's silver bullets around one boot.

Guy was there and so was Gerry Messerman, who'd flown in from Cleveland along with Naomi's brothers.

We had a couple glasses of champagne, and headed over to the chapel at the
Ritz-Carlton.

When I saw Naomi, she looked so pretty I got tears in my eyes. In a few
moments, the world's most beautiful little devil barracuda gun moll would be
my wife.

Joey was there, screaming in his nanny's arms. The little bastard didn't seem
like he was happy about being legitimized.

Paul Verhoeven was there, taking pictures—our unofficial wedding photographer.

I sure wasn't twenty-three years old anymore.

. . .

Bernie, Naomi's brother, read a letter from Naomi's late mother to Naomi when she was in her early twenties urging her to "color every page" of her life.

Gerry Messerman read from Faulkner's Nobel Prize address.

Jeremy, Naomi's little brother, sang a song he had written for us called "Two People Together."

Our New Age nondenominational minister said a few New Aged words . . . we made our vows . . . and Naomi jumped up and yelled "*Yayyyyyyy!*"

Outside, in a meadow near the beach lighted by torches and the moon, we ate sashimi and filet mignon and lobster and drank Cristal.

Guy sang "I'll Remember You."

Evans made a toast, babbling once again about that past trip to Maui that had doomed one of his marriages. (Next to him stood one of his "writers" in a see-through dress.)

I made a toast and then Naomi and I, holding Joey between us, danced . . . to Rod Stewart and Leonard Cohen and most of all to the Beatles and "Don't Let Me Down."

The toast I made at my wedding was this: "I came to this country when I was six years old. I've felt like a loner all of my life. Naomi, I don't feel that way anymore. Thank you."

When I finished my toast, Naomi left her seat at our table, ran across the grass, and hugged me. I held her close. I smelled plumeria and Naomi and the sea.

Gerry Messerman told me that my father had written him a letter begging his forgiveness for the things he had done in Hungary.

Gerri Eszterhas went back to court and sued me for 50 percent of my writing income *for the rest of my life!*

Her argument was that I had come up with or may have been influenced to come up with . . . *ideas* . . . during the course of our marriage . . . which I might turn into scripts sometime later.

It would be a full-scale court proceeding in front of a judge in Marin County with expert witnesses testifying on both sides.

I had no choice but to fight it, of course.

I wrote a four-page outline for a script called *One Night Stand* about a man who falls in love at a corporate convention.

Guy loved the outline and showed it to Jeff Berg, the head of ICM, who showed it to Adrian Lyne, who had directed *Flashdance* and *Fatal Attraction* and

Indecent Proposal. Adrian loved the outline and said he'd direct the movie. ICM decided then not to wait for the script but to auction the four-page outline with Adrian attached to direct it.

Berg said that Adrian and I were so "hot" after having written and directed hit movies that the auction would be a "no-brainer." He was right. I sold the four-page outline for $4 million to New Line.

The sale made such big news that the *Today* show decided to do a series about *One Night Stand* from sale to release in the theaters.

On the first segment of the series, the reporter asked me how long it had taken me to write the outline.

I told him the truth: "About three or four hours."

A million dollars an hour!
   A million dollars a page!
   I wasn't broke anymore.
   Naomi and I had the money to buy a house.

When we bought our house in Point Dume, we made sure it was far from any fault lines. That's one of the reasons we picked Point Dume, which was in very northern Malibu.

Joey, eighteen months old, was sensitive to the slightest noise, coming screaming awake when a window rattled, sensitive to even the slightest jolts when he was being driven around in his baby carriage.

Two months after we moved into our Point Dume house, on a quiet Sunday afternoon, our new house was badly jolted three times. It felt like the house had been hit by a bulldozer.

I ran upstairs, grabbed Joey, and helped Naomi run down groggily from the bedroom. She had viral pneumonia.

We thought it was yet another accursed aftershock of the Northridge quake. It wasn't.

It was a brand-new quake on a brand-new, previously undetected fault line.

Its epicenter: Point Dume.

Naomi said, "Point Doom."

Our house stood next door to a shack, proof positive of Malibu's egalitarian spirit, evidenced, too, by the fact that Barbra, *the* Barbra, *that* Barbra, another one of our neighbors, lived near a successful and convicted dope dealer.

I could see into the shack next door to us. There were opened scripts all over the floor of the main room. A balding man with long gray hair in the back of his head crawled on his knees from one open script to another. He seemed to be reading each script—but only for a few moments, as though his concentration span couldn't afford each script more time.

I recognized the man. He was a producer who had won an Oscar for Best Picture twenty-some years ago.

A young woman knocked on our door one afternoon. She was frazzled, out of breath, and sweating—selling carpet cleaner door to door.

"What's the matter?" I asked. "You okay? Did someone hurt you? Should I call the cops?"

She held the carpet cleaner cans up. Her hands were shaking. She was having trouble speaking. There were tears in her eyes.

"I just sold two cans," she said. "To Bob Dylan! Can you believe it? To Bob Dylan himself! He opened the door himself."

I offered her a glass of water. She glugged it down and smiled. She looked at me.

She said, "You're not Joe Cocker, are you?"

"Come on, you guys have to come, it'll be fun!" the producer said, but Naomi and I were uncertain.

The producer always hugged Naomi a little too warmly, and his wife had tried to play footsie with me only days after I'd married Naomi.

We thought we understood the kind of extendedly familial trip to Vegas they had in mind, and we hadn't ever even met the man who would be our host, the producer's friend Dodi Fayed.

"We'll take Dodi's plane," the producer said. "He'll be there with his girl-friend. He's paying for the whole trip. Suites at the Mirage, dinner at Spago, we'll catch some shows, fly back in his plane. You'll love Dodi. Come on, you guys gotta come, it'll be fun."

But we decided not to join them and, a few days later, the producer's wife came over to our house and brought dozens of little packages of smoked salmon from Harrods with a card enclosed that said, "Compliments of Dodi Fayed."

"You guys missed the greatest time," the producer's wife said, but Naomi and I were happy we hadn't gone to Vegas and we very happily ate Dodi Fayed's delicious smoked salmon.

Costa-Gavras came to visit us in Malibu. I told him about Father Charles Coughlin and the isolationists of World War II who kept America from going to war—even when the American government knew about Auschwitz and Dachau.

I told Costa how Coughlin was the most popular commentator of his time—an anti-Semite who knew how to use the media (and the pulpit) to spread hatred. I showed Costa the big box of research I had amassed—though I didn't tell him why I was so impassioned to write this script . . . or how I thought about Neal Sher and Eli Rosenbaum and Judith Schulmann's faces as they sat in a theater in a few years watching this movie.

Costa thought it would be a powerful, important film and wanted to direct it.

Together, we went to meet with Phoenix Pictures and several of their executives, including Mike Medavoy, one of the smartest and most literate producers in town.

I outlined our story for the executives and one of them said, "But what kind of movie is this? Who will we have to root for?"

I said, "That's one of the stupidest remarks I've ever heard in twenty-five years of meetings like this."

The executive grabbed her Kleenex and fled the room.

I looked insufferable once again.

Phoenix Pictures passed on doing a movie about Father Charles Coughlin.

Peter Bart, the editor of *Variety,* was a smart and classy man who liked sticking the needle into Hollywood types.

Since I was now obviously a Hollywood type living in Malibu, Peter stuck his needle into me in two places: my obsession with making big script sales and my many appearances on television.

I replied quickly:

1. You're right about my obsession with big bucks. I was paid $275,000 to write Flashdance; *it made the studio over $300 million. I was paid $500,000 to write* Jagged Edge; *it made the studio more than $50 million. I was paid $3 million to write* Basic Instinct; *it made the studio more than $400 million. I was paid $1 million to write* Sliver; *it made the studio more than $100 million.*

If you put all those numbers together, I was paid $4,775,000.

The studio's take was $850 million.

They made $850 million and I made less than $5 million. They made about two hundred times more than I did.

At that rate of exchange, wouldn't you, too, get a little obsessed about making more, about evening things out . . . just a little bit?

2. You're right about all the TV exposure. I forgot for a second that screenwriters should be neither seen nor heard. They are at the bottom of the monkey-point food chain. They should live in obscurity, beset by melancholia and Styron-like depression. They should be victims, proud of their Victimhood. They should write books about their victimization and make money off their self-proclaimed misery, impotence, and humiliation.

*I promise, in the future, to try to act depressed, even though—since I'm
happier now than I've ever been in my life—it won't be easy. I'll take the
bullets off my cowboy boots and keep Bill Goldman's* Adventures in the
Screen Trade *on my nightstand next to Jimmy Carter's book of poetry.*

Naomi's journal:

We finally went on the set of *Showgirls*. Paul was asking
and asking and finally Joe said, "Okay, but don't film any of
the nude scenes on the day we go." Paul agreed.

We had heard that Paul was now living in a hotel with
Elizabeth Berkley, but we'd never met her. We know his wife,
Martine, quite well, so we were curious.

It was all arranged for Thursday at Paramount and I
asked Joe what I should wear. He said, "Why don't you wear
your new pearl necklace?" So I did. I chose a tiny jumper
with a white blouse underneath and the pearls. It was a
little snug because at three months of my second pregnancy,
I'm starting to show, but it passed.

When we got to the set I immediately noticed as we
entered that everyone was in jeans. I said, "I'm really
overdressed." Joe said, "You look beautiful." Then I overhear a guy say as I walk by, "Who's the prom queen?"

It gets worse. We enter and the set is a Vegas strip
joint. I've never been to Vegas, never been on a set, and
never been to a strip joint. It was hot, smoky, and loud. We
were there with Guy and Sam Fischer, Joe's lawyer.

As I look to my left, up on a stage, Elizabeth Berkley is
stark naked with three other women. They are humping a pole
with their legs spread and their tongues out. Elizabeth
licks the pole. She is supposed to kick her G-string panties
off her ankle, but they keep getting caught on her heel. So
they keep doing it again and again. From my angle it was
nearly gynecological.

Over the throbbing music Paul yells, "Joe, I saved this
scene for you!"

Guy is cool, Joe is amused, and Sam is overheating.

Gina Gershon comes over and starts to say how much she
admires Joe and how she knows he must have modeled Cristal
after Aphrodite or some such theory. I'm not really listening, but at least she's dressed.

Then Paul yells cut. All the women grab a robe, except
Elizabeth. She skips down the stairs and comes jiggling over
to us. She is so hot and so close to us I can smell her.
Heat is emanating from her. She has on shiny body glitter
and high heels. And that's all.

She says, "Hi Nomi! I'm Nomi!"

I say, "Well, it was a childhood nickname of mine but
the similarities end there." She tilts her head and laughs.

When you talk to someone in a crowded room who is naked (as
I discovered) you try to keep contact with their eyes. The
weird thing is that her eyes are two different colors. One
is green and one is brown. So even that is uncomfortable.

She shakes hands with Guy and Sam and Joe and then
starts gushing about how this character is her and how Joe
is like a god on the set.

Suddenly I feel extremely nauseous. Either morning sick-
ness, the smoke, or the conversation.

Anyway, I think, "I can't just bolt out of here. They'll
think the prom queen can't handle it." So I take deep
breaths.

Then Paul comes up behind Elizabeth and puts both arms
around her waist and his hands on her belly. And he smiles.

"At last you meet Nomi," he says to Joe. I'm looking for
an exit. Joe, who knows me so well, leans down and says,
"I'd like to go outside for a cigarette; join me."

When we get out there I can feel the wind cooling the
sweat on my upper lip. He looks at me and says, "Jesus
Christ," but that's as far as he gets, because out comes
"Nomi" and she's making a beeline for us.

She's now wearing a G-string and holding a top about the
size of a wet-wipe. She's talking and appearing to be trying
to untangle her top so she can put it on, but she's bouncing
up and down with her efforts.

She says as she's fumbling, "How did you like it?" And
Joe says, "Boy that was something . . ."

Then he says, "You know, Paul looks really happy . . ."
sort of fishing to see how she feels about Paul.

And she says, "Yeah, well, did you know that I sing? I
heard you have a script with a singer in it . . ." Joe looks
at me blankly.

I say, "*Foreplay.*"

He says, "Oh, yeah."

She goes on about how she would love to read it. She finally gets her top on and hooks her fingers into the arm-holes. It's a loose tank top. As she talks, she swings her hands back and forth in front of her so that her breasts pop in and out of the armholes.

I'm watching. Nipples. No nipples. Nipples. No nipples. I'm still feeling queasy.

Suddenly, Sam Fischer bolts out the door and races up to us. "I'm going to get water! You guys want any?" I say yes, Joe passes.

Seconds later Sam comes racing back with two Dixie cups splashing on his coat sleeves. As I watch him, I'm thinking, "He's coming undone . . ."

In the meantime, Elizabeth has brushed my hair back from my shoulder, Joe's hair back from his shoulder, and is say-ing how she'd love to get together. Mercifully, she is called back to the set to have her nipple rouge touched up for the next scene.

Joe says, "Let's go," and we head to the limo.

On the way there Paul comes out and he says, "Joe!" He looks like a maniac. His hair is hanging in damp hunks around his face and he's laughing. We all laugh.

Then Joe says, "So do you think we're going to get an R rating?"

And Paul says, "Considering what I've shot so far? No."

And Joe says, "Tomorrow is the last day of shooting."

And Paul says with a smile, "I know." When Joe and I finally get into the car we sit there for about thirty sec-onds in silence.

Then Joe says, "He cast a blow-up fuck doll as Nomi Malone."

Paul was always a little vague when asked how he'd cast Elizabeth Berkley as Nomi Malone.

He said that he'd seen her in an "open audition" and was immediately impressed.

But I knew the real story from Charlie Evans.

Charlie had auditioned Elizabeth in his New York hotel room and had called Paul after the successful audition. Charlie recommended her enthusiastically.

Paul yelled at Charlie. "*You* don't audition! *I* audition! Are you crazy? You're auditioning girls in your hotel room? Do you want to get us sued before we even roll any film?"

Charlie insisted that this young woman was very talented. "Please," he said to Paul, "just audition her!"

Paul said, "Forget it. I don't even want to know her name."

Paul told me it was "just a crazy coincidence" that Charlie had auditioned the star of *Showgirls* before he did.

Gina Gershon came to lunch today. The buzz on the movie is huge, but Joe and I are still reeling from the casting of Elizabeth Berkley. I wondered what Gina thought, so at lunch, I asked.

"What do you think of Elizabeth?"

She took a deep breath and said, "Well, she's not nineteen years old, I can tell you that . . ."

"How was it working with her?"

She hesitated and then said, "I'll level with you guys. She doesn't know what she's doing. She can't act. She would say 'Oh Gina, please help me with this scene!' and then, while I'm trying to get her into the moment and teach her stuff she already should know, she's telling me how she's going to suck Paul's cock that night . . ."

Billy Friedkin, the director of *Jade*, who had said he wouldn't "change a comma" of my script . . . sent me a memorandum full of changes he wanted to make.

I sent him a letter dated "Halloween, 1994":

Dear Billy,

The reason I was in support of you directing Jade *is that you said, repeatedly and publicly, that you "would not change a comma of the script." Considering your memo of the 25th of October, it is clear that you lied to me.*

The lie rankles, of course, not only on a creative level, but on a personal one. Considering the fact that the last time you had a hit movie was in the early seventies, you never would have gotten a chance to direct a script that was viewed as the hottest in town without my support. Considering the fact that Sherry is the head of the studio involved made the situation even more complicated. You needed my public support to avoid any charges of favoritism. You needed it and you got it. We even had a discussion outside Alice's in Malibu one day about how, thanks to my quotes in the L.A. Times, we had put the issue to rest.

As you know, I have listened to your ideas at great length and have incorporated some of them in my latest draft. I also, as you know, did an earlier draft for Sherry, gratis, as a favor, in our misguided effort to land Tom Cruise and Julia Roberts for the parts. I have done my best to work with both you and Sherry.

But your latest suggestions, outlined in your memo of the 25th of October, are so misguided we're not talking about changing commas anymore. We're talking about destroying the material, burning its fabric, vitiating its power. You're taking an original piece of work and turning it into clichéd, watered-down television. You're taking a very commercial piece and making it boring.

Since I view my scripts as my children, I will not do anything to hurt my children. Nor will I stand idly by while someone does one of my children harm. Unlike most screenwriters, I am willing to go to the wall in defense of my children, no matter what that means.

To address your points individually:

1. You say—"I feel it serves no purpose to suggest that Trina is a hooker."

The very basis of this piece, even in outline form, was exactly that this successful nationally respected clinical psychologist has a whole other life as a high-priced hooker. It is a startling notion dramatically and, I believe, commercially. It is also a daring, very un-television-like notion.

Your suggestion that she not be a hooker but be in search of "wild sex because she's not getting it from Matt" is the oldest cliché, one even that television has worn out. Men and women who cheat always cheat because they're having sexual problems with their mates—what is unique about that? What is dramatic? Are you seriously suggesting that we can get an audience's attention in the nineties by trying to feed them this old warm spit? They've seen it. They know it. There is nothing startling about it. Why in the world would they want to see a movie with this as its underlying theme—as opposed to a movie about a very successful, intelligent, classy woman who hooks on the side?

Your suggestion also diminishes Trina as a character and implies a sexism I want to avoid. Trina has a whole other life as a hooker because she likes it and because she has the balls to do it. She is very nineties. Her life knows no boundaries and she can carry it off. Now you want her to have sex with a bunch of guys because "Matt doesn't give her enough wild sex"? Come on—it's not sexual frustration that's fueling my Trina—it's an unlimited horizon. And it's anger at Matt for cheating on her.

2. You suggest that we "try and see a bit more of the public life of Matt and Trina."

This is a tightly knit murder mystery. You can show their public life by showing the existing scenes powerfully—the black-and-white ball, Trina making her speech at the convention, the Belvedere house and all its trappings. Introducing scenes that underline the fabric of the piece in a tight murder mystery will destroy the piece's pace and thrust.

I remind you that we've already added one unnecessary chase scene—the more unnecessary, irrelevant scenes you add, the more you affect the tightly wound spring.

3. You suggest that Matt only kill Medford and that the governor's men kill the others.

The fact that Matt kills all *of them is a central tenet of the piece. What is shocking . . . and must be shocking . . . to us at the end is that this moneyed, educated, sophisticated criminal attorney is capable of killing a lot of people as part of a deadly game aimed at his wife.*

By suggesting that the governor's men do all the killings except one, you destroy one of the most psychologically intriguing parts of the script. You also indulge in clichés left over from the sixties. I am so tired of movies where elected officials or government people are depicted as the bad guys. It is the kind of knee-jerk, simplistic liberalism that I loathe. We are in the nineties!

4. You suggest that we clarify the Porsche situation—who is driving which Porsche at which killing.

This movie is a mystery that I want people to think about. Yes, the business with the cars is complicated, but logical. Audiences can handle complicated plots—as Basic Instinct *shows. I want them to leave the theaters and figure things out afterward. It makes them think and talk and argue about the movie. Your suggestion that we clarify this "so that the idea of whose Porsche did what to whom doesn't have to be talked about so much" is dead wrong. Don't you get it? We want them to talk about it. We want to give them a movie that has some ambiguity and gray.*

5. You suggest that David "make two or three stops" after we know that his brakes have been cut.

Upon reflection, even though I made the change, I think showing the cutting of the brakes is wrong. It creates greater suspense not knowing whether anything was done to the brakes or whether David is getting paranoid about everything. We should never know if anything was done to the brakes—we should let the audience make up its own mind . . . and argue about it.

But to suggest that he make two or three stops afterward, after the brakes have been cut, is ludicrous. It's just bad television—a cheap device that I am convinced today's audiences are too smart for. This is and has to

be *a tight murder mystery—to glop cheap television stuff into it diminishes the piece's visceral power.*

*6. You suggest that David not kill Hargrove himself at the end but that
the others kill him in a "grassy knoll" scenario.*

*The point is . . . and it is a central point that you clearly don't under-
stand . . . that David gets so sucked into all this personally that at the end
he kills a man with his own hands . . . a man who, we realize at the end of
the picture, was innocent. Thematically, it is the final indication that
David's hands have become not only dirty, but bloody.*

*"Grassy Knoll Scenario"? This is not a political thriller. This is a psy-
cho-sexual murder mystery. You are taking a visceral, tightly wound piece
and turning it into some kind of half-assed political conspiracy movie left
over from the sixties.*

*I also want to address your last paragraph. "Were I to just shoot the first
draft without bringing my own sensibilities to it," you write, "the resulting
effort could turn out flat." What I want you to bring to it, Billy, is your
explosive visual power. I have enormous respect for your sense of visual,
explosive theater. I have little respect for your abilities as a writer. You
didn't hire on to write this piece, you hired on to direct it. Stick to your
turf, I have no intention of invading yours.*

*By trying to rewrite it, instead of directing it, you are your own worst
enemy. You are taking a script that would be a hit movie and turning it
into a failed movie. Why? Why do that to yourself? You need a hit movie
and you've got one in your hands.*

I signed the letter "Trick or treat."

I added this P.S.: "Paul Verhoeven shot the first draft, the white pages, of
Basic Instinct. He brought his own explosive visual power to it. The movie
grossed over $400 million."

After the executives read the finished script of *One Night Stand,* New Line was
knocked out. The script was 90 percent dialogue, guaranteeing that it could be
made for a small budget. Mike DeLuca, the head of production at New Line,
told me that people at the company liked it so much that they were going
around the office reciting lines of dialogue.

But Adrian Lyne, after reading the script, said he didn't want to direct it. He
was going to do a remake of *Lolita* instead. New Line was enraged and threatened to sue him but Adrian wouldn't budge.

The *Today* show wanted to do the second part of its series about the making
of *One Night Stand* and New Line and I were dodging them. They had paid me
$4 million for a script the director didn't want to shoot—we didn't think that
would sound very good to moviegoers.

. . .

Gerri gave Guy an expensive, gold ID bracelet for his birthday.

He showed it to me, obviously pleased with the gift.

"You accepted it?" I asked.

"What do you mean?" he said.

I said, "She didn't earn the money she bought it with; I did."

He said, "I'll send it back to her if you want."

I said, "She paid for it out of the $32,500 a month alimony the court said I have to pay her."

He looked fondly at the bracelet on his arm and said, "Okay, I'll send it back to her."

I could tell how much he liked it, so I said, "It's okay, don't worry about it. Pretend *I* gave it to you."

I was upset, though. I was fighting for my financial life and my friend and agent was accepting gold trinkets from what I considered my ex-wife's pirated stash.

Naomi and I were sitting at the bar in the Dume Room, our neighborhood beer joint, sipping our Negras and looking at Jan-Michael Vincent's framed photograph behind the bar. He was a young man in the picture, the embodiment of the golden boy Californian, blond, tanned, flashing perfect teeth, a bimbo on each arm.

It was taken a long time ago when I was a beginning screenwriter and when it looked for a while like Jan-Michael Vincent was going to be a big movie star. Then he got into booze and coke and became what we call "unemployable," a fate worse than death in L.A., part of the living dead. There was a messy divorce: his wife said that he wanted her to have sex with his friends while he watched. There was an automobile accident: he broke his neck.

I saw a picture of him in court recently: bloated, his face a roadmap of pain, his eyes unfocused and vacant.

But he was still up on the wall behind the bar at the Dume Room, grinning at us, full of life, the golden boy catching a wave, grabbing a piece, dreaming the dreams he was so certain would never die.

I was in a war with Columbia over my adaptation of Howard Blum's *Gangland* and appealed not to Mark Canton, the studio head, whom *Newsweek* once labeled "moronic," but to his boss, Mickey Schulhof, the head of Sony Corporation of America.

> *Dear Mr. Schulhof,*
> *I don't like to begin a letter by listing my credentials, but in this case I*
> *feel that I must. I have written eleven movies—my twelfth,* Showgirls,

directed by Paul Verhoeven, is filming now. My thirteenth, Jade, directed
by William Friedkin and starring David Caruso and Linda Fiorentino,
begins filming in January.

My movies have grossed more than a billion dollars at the box office—
among them are Basic Instinct, Jagged Edge, Flashdance, Sliver, Music
Box, and Betrayed.

In terms of my ability and willingness to be a part of a collaborative
process, I have worked with three directors—Paul Verhoeven, Costa-
Gavras, and Richard Marquand—twice. As I probably don't have to tell
you, it is not likely that a director of their stature will work with the same
writer twice . . . if that writer is not willing to be a part of a collaborative
process.

In 1993, I began working on Gangland for Columbia Pictures. We had
agreed from the beginning, as my quote in Daily Variety upon the
announcement of the project shows, that Gangland would be "an epic,
larger than life story" about John Gotti.

Mark Canton urged me to write a script with ambiguity and grays—so
that at the end of the picture, audiences would feel ambivalent about the
relative values of Gotti and the FBI. Since I have at other times in my
work dealt with ambiguities and processes of corruption, I not only agreed
with Mark's suggestion but felt it was one of the reasons I was picked for
the project.

Jon Peters, the producer, urged me to view it as an American epic.
Indeed, it was the way I viewed it. I felt that if we were to do yet another
Mafia story, the only way to do it fresh was to do it as a kind of raw, in-
your-face street epic.

I coordinated a massive research project so that we would have other
background sources besides Howard Blum's powerful book. I worked
closely with Howard at my home, picking his brain, trying to tap into the
wealth of knowledge he possesses about Gotti and the FBI.

In June of 1994, I turned in my script to the studio. It was more than
170 pages long. I felt it to be a blistering, powerful, emotionally moving
epic whose underlying theme was a corruption of the spirit on both
sides—the FBI side and the mob side.

The script was read by more than a dozen people who'd read my work
in the past and whom I respect, both industry and media people. Without
exception, they told me that it was the best script I had ever written. Some
of them said it was the best script they had ever read.

Since Paul Verhoeven and I had worked on Basic and Showgirls
together, I showed the script to Paul. Paul, of course, is one of the world's
premier directors, a man whose movies have grossed more than a billion
dollars at the box office, a man who, I thought, would be ideally suited to

direct Gangland. *Paul, a tough judge of material and at times in the past a sharp critic of my work, told me that he thought the script was "excellent" and the best script I had written. Then, to my great joy, he told me he would be "very interested" in directing the movie.*

Days after I'd turned in the script to Columbia, there was no response from the studio. A week later, two weeks later, three weeks later . . . there was still no response. Nobody even bothered to call me. It was like I had dropped the script into a vacuum. Finally, about a month after I delivered the script, my agent was informed that the studio had "notes." Neither my agent nor I heard what the studio thought of the script—we just heard that the studio had "notes."

I informed Columbia, through my agent, that Paul Verhoeven loved the script and was interested in directing it. I was flabbergasted to hear that, except for a cursory phone call to Paul's agent checking his availability, no effort was made to tie him into the project. No one met with Paul. No one called Paul. I didn't understand how a studio allegedly in the business of making money could treat a man of Paul's stature and track record this way. I began to wonder, frankly, if anybody was at home at Columbia—if the varied press accounts that I had read about the studio's failed movies, executive arrogance, executive indecision, were true.

Please understand what I felt at the time: I was the most successful screenwriter in Hollywood. I had managed to interest one of the most respected directors in the world in a script that I had written. It was a script that I was hugely proud of; a script that everyone who read it said was the best that I had done. And at the studio . . . there was nobody home; it was Looney Tunes/Daffy Duck time; some kind of private circle-jerk seemed to be in progress. I was coming to the conclusion that maybe the studio really was, as the Wall Street Journal *later headlined—"In a League of Its Own."*

And then the "notes" finally arrived. Pages and pages and pages of them, opinions hidden, of course, beneath the corporate umbrella, anonymous except for the Columbia logo and the majestic Columbia "We." The "notes" were moronic. They trashed the script that was there. They made the case for a bad television movie that had already been made. To agree with the notes, I felt, would be agreeing to destroy my own work, to kill my own baby, to turn what I was convinced would be a unique, $200 million movie into . . . warmed spit.

I disagreed vehemently with the "notes," both through my agent and also in direct conversation with both your studio executive Barry Josephson and Jon Peters, who finally called me a month after I'd turned the script in. Both Jon and Barry began to back away from the "notes." These weren't directives, they said, these were suggestions. Would I think about the suggestions—that's all, just think about them? Well, I said, as much as you could "think" about something "moronic," I'd "think" about them.

At the end of the summer, while in Maui, I got a phone call at seven o'clock one morning from Adrian Lyne. Adrian had directed Fatal Attraction, Indecent Proposal, *and* Flashdance, *among other things. Adrian was excited. His agent had sent him* Gangland. *He was calling from the South of France. He thought the script was brilliant. He thought it was one of the most amazing scripts he'd ever read. He was very interested in directing it.*

I was thrilled . . . and sick . . . at the same time.

Here was another world-caliber director . . . another director whose movies had grossed more than a billion dollars, another director who, I felt, made constantly exciting, visually dazzling movies . . . responding with great excitement to my work . . . the work which was being trashed by moronic "notes."

Would Adrian Lyne, I wondered, become another victim of the Looney Tunes/Daffy Duck circle-jerk?

Through my agent, I informed Columbia of Adrian's interest. The studio pretended to be excited. There would be a meeting with Adrian, I was told . . . as there would be a meeting with me.

In the fall of this year, I finally had my only meeting with the studio about my Gangland *script. More exactly, my meeting was with Jon Peters. Jon brought his new head of development with him to the lunch, then dismissed her a half hour later so we could talk alone. He made the following suggestions for the script: 1. Strengthen the part of Jed, the lead FBI agent; 2. Give the FBI agents working on the case more of a* Dirty Dozen *feel; 3. Write a scene where Jed, the lead FBI agent and Sammy "the Bull" Gravano are boxing and Jed beats Gravano up in the ring, causing Gravano to turn against Gotti.*

What about everything else in the pages and pages and pages of notes?—I asked Jon. He told me to forget everything else in the notes. He said that if I incorporated his suggestions into the script it would "neutralize the masses over at Columbia who were taking shots at it." He told me that if Columbia was not pleased with the changes he was suggesting, he would take the project in turnaround to Warner Brothers and we'd get the movie made there. Would Columbia agree to let him take it to Warner's?— I asked him. Jon said it wouldn't be a problem because once Mark left Columbia, he'd go back to Warner's and work with Jon.

At the same meeting, I urged Jon . . . in the strongest way . . . to make a holding deal with Adrian Lyne. He said he'd meet with Adrian and they'd make a holding deal with him. The meeting between Jon and Adrian did take place, but to my bewilderment . . . and to the complete bewilderment of Adrian's agent . . . no holding deal was made with Adrian and no attempt to make a holding deal with him was made, either.

It became clear to me that my fears were justified. Columbia seemed as interested in making Gangland with Adrian Lyne as they were in making Gangland with Paul Verhoeven. This was a studio that, for whatever reason, was not interested in working with two of the top directors in the world. This was a studio, I concluded, more interested in its masturbatory games than in making money at the box office with a unique and startling piece of material.

I began the rewrite, using Jon's suggestions . . . but only to a point where I felt they wouldn't hurt the script. I wrote new scenes strengthening Jed's part. I wrote a new scene emphasizing the Dirty Dozen aspects of the agents working the case. I did not write the scene between Gravano and Jed in the boxing ring because I felt it would be unrealistic and juvenile. Writing the boxing ring scene, I felt, would vitiate the power of Gravano's turn on Gotti as it existed in the script.

I turned the rewrite in two weeks ago. Adrian Lyne called me to tell me he thought it was terrific. Howard Blum, author of the book, called to tell me it was "brilliant." "We've got to move heaven and earth to get this made," Howard said.

To date . . . I have heard nothing from Columbia . . . nada . . . from anyone at Columbia . . . from Jon Peters.

I did hear, about a week ago, from an industry journalist. This is what he told me: "Columbia is going to sue you for breach of contract for not doing an adequate rewrite."

I am writing to you, Mr. Schulhof, as an appeal to some sort of reason, decency, and fairness. I wrote a 170-page script that has been praised by everyone who's read it—except the people at Columbia. My script attracted two of the premier directors in the world to the project. The author of the book feels that the script is brilliant. And I am being accused of breach of contract?

Forgive me, Mr. Schulhof, but something is very wrong at your studio. I don't know who is in charge. I don't know if anyone is in charge. I don't know what the agendas are, though I am convinced they have to be private and politically tangled ones. I do know that the agenda is not to make original and successful movies.

I don't even know, most depressingly, who at Columbia has even read my script. A conversation my agent had with an executive more than implied that neither Mark Canton nor Jon Peters had read the script and/or the rewrite.

You pay a man more than $3 million to write a script—that's what this total deal is—and then you don't read it? It's something out of Orwell or Kafka.

My appeal to you, Mr. Schulhof, is that you read my script and my rewrite . . . that you read it yourself . . . don't ask a "reader" to read it for you . . . don't read someone else's "coverage" . . . read it yourself . . . please.

I don't think it's too much to ask. I put my heart and soul, all of my creative innards, into Gangland. *I wrote something I am proud of. My words attracted two of the best directors in the world.*

My hope is that your reading will save my script. My hope is that you will stop the morons from doing their moronic pitiful dance at the cost of an original and successful movie. A few years ago, they danced with a script of mine called Pals, *which was transmogrified into an awful movie called* Nowhere to Run.

Perhaps, as part of your reading, you should check the grosses for Nowhere to Run.

P.S. Please forgive the vagaries of my manual typewriter. It does feel strange writing a letter to the chairman of Sony on a manual typewriter, but I'll make a deal with you. If you read my script, I'll do my best to learn to write on a computer.

Mickey Schulhof never responded to my letter, but Columbia didn't sue me, either. Many other screenwriters were brought into the project for rewrites. The movie, to this day, hasn't been made.

At the height of my battle with Columbia, Jon Peters took me out to lunch again and urged me yet again to make the changes I refused to make.

"Come on," he said, "this is *me* talking now. This is the guy who got them to pay you more than three million bucks. I stuck my neck out for you. Come on, make the fucking changes. As a personal favor to me."

I said, "I can't. The changes would destroy the script. The changes are stupid."

Jon said, "So what? *They're just words.*"

I said, "I'm a writer. They're not *just words.* Words are what I do."

Jon said, "I'm asking you as a favor to me—to your friend. Change the fucking words!"

I said, "I can't."

He said, "You can but you won't."

"All right," I said, "have it your way. I *won't.*"

Jon said, "You know what that means, you cocksucker, *it means we're not friends anymore!*"

"Jon," I said, "you don't get it."

"No!" he said. "*No!*" He stuck his finger at me like a gun.

"*You* don't get it!" he said, got up, threw his napkin down, and left the patio restaurant of the Bel Air Hotel.

They came right after the last fire, the one that took out much of Malibu east of the Pacific Coast Highway. They came in armies.

The big mucky-muck multi-zillionaires of Malibu were sitting on their glass-walled patios or watching the sun set in their wrought iron gazebos when they saw them traipsing across the lawn or scampering around the palm trees.

Squirrels? No, they weren't squirrels. They were Norwegian rats. They got under the houses and into the walls. They chewed holes through the screens and got into the kids' rooms. At night you could see them in the moonlight, seemingly getting fatter by the hour.

The big mucky-muck zillionaires of Malibu fled. Those who also had houses in Beverly Hills or Bel Air went there. Those who didn't went into Beverly Hills and got a suite at the Four Seasons or the Peninsula.

They paid fortunes for exterminators to come immediately and do whatever had to be done. The exterminators made them bid against each other, made some of them wait three days, even a week.

It became a status thing. If you were really powerful, if you really had money, you didn't have to wait.

I didn't have to wait at all, although I wasn't a big mucky-muck zillionaire. I was one of the first whose house was exterminated, whose walls were cleaned out, whose attic and crawl spaces were cleared.

Why was I one of the first? Why did I get faster, better service than Michael Eisner and Michael Ovitz and Jerry Perenchio and Irwin Winkler?

Because *my* exterminator wanted to be a screenwriter. He had some scripts he asked me to read. He wanted me to give him career advice after I'd read them.

I read his scripts quickly. I told him he had promise. I asked if he had others I could read.

Thank God he didn't.

I had heard rumblings from both Evans and Craig Baumgarten, *Jade*'s producers, that Billy had made some changes which I "might not like."

My interpretation of that was that the changes must have been so serious that neither Evans nor Baumgarten could tolerate them—though they would never say so (considering that Billy was married to the studio head).

I asked Billy to lunch in Malibu, looked him in the eye, and said, "When am I going to see the rough cut?"

Billy said, "In about a month."

I said, "Look. If you've changed things I don't know about, tell me now—so I can get used to the idea somewhat before I walk in there and get kicked in the gut."

Billy said, "Joe, Joe—I give you my word—I shot your script. I'm not stupid. I know how you are about your words. We're going to do a lot of other movies together. I'd tell you if I changed anything."

I was a little calmed by that but Billy's next sentence set off all my shit-detectors.

"I'm telling you, Joe," Billy said, "this movie that *you created* is really something."

I had never heard a director use that phrase to a screenwriter: *This movie that you created.*

And I was convinced that any director who used it was trying to cover up something truly awful that he had done.

I finished another spec script . . . this one about the soul singer Otis Redding that I called *Blaze of Glory.*

I'd been working on the script a long time and had secured the rights to Otis's music, and to the "life rights" of his best friend and manager, Phil Walden, and of Otis's wife, Zelma.

I'd always been drawn to Otis's music and was the last person to interview him in Cleveland before his plane crashed into a Wisconsin lake in the late sixties.

I felt that the script was more than just another script about a rock star. By focusing on the relationship between Phil Walden and Otis Redding, a white man and a black man in the sixties, I hoped I was telling a story that was a metaphor for the civil rights movement.

Guy and Jeff Berg read the script and loved it and so did my lawyers, who agreed with ICM that the script would sell for $5 million.

Boy, I thought to myself, that would keep Gerri Eszterhas's wolves away from our door for a long time.

We had a strategy session at my house. Guy said he was going to send the script out on Wednesday and set a Monday deadline for responses.

"By the way," he announced, "I'm leaving for Palm Springs Wednesday afternoon."

I was incredulous. He was sending the script out *Wednesday morning* and leaving for Palm Springs *Wednesday afternoon?*

"You're doing what?" I said.

"I'm in a golf tournament," he said. "Last year I won ten grand."

"You're going off to a golf tournament the same day you're sending my script out on auction?"

"It's okay," he said. "I can call people from there. They can reach me on my cellular."

I gaped at him.

When agents send a script out for auction, they call and schmooze the potential players, trying to get one to bid against the other. It is the moment when the agenting process turns into a Byzantine fine art, a political and manipulative game that has to be played subtly and intensely. It is a mammoth and time-consuming task, especially when you're sending the script to thirty some production entities—as we were doing with *Blaze of Glory*.

I couldn't believe what Guy was saying to me. He knew how to run a successful auction. He knew the focus which a successful auction requires.

He was going to do this auction from his golf course. He was literally going to *phone this one in*. On his cellular.

I felt my blood pressure rise.

"You can't go out of town when you're auctioning my script," I told him.

"It's okay," he said. "I'm telling you. We'll be fine."

"What if somebody just loves it and wants to preempt everybody else and buy it immediately? How are you gonna make a deal?"

"On the phone," Guy said.

"From the fucking golf course in Palm Springs?"

He shrugged and lit a cigarette.

"It's too late to move the auction back," he said. "I've already let most of them know it's coming on Wednesday."

"It's not too late for you not to go to your golf tournament."

"I won ten grand last year," he repeated.

"Guy," I said, "I'm not asking you not to go. I'm *telling* you."

He looked down and flicked the ash of his cigarette into the ashtray with his thumb.

He said, "Okay."

The script went out, no one bid, and I fired Guy McElwaine, my close friend of so many years, the man I'd defied Michael Ovitz for.

Not because he couldn't sell *Blaze of Glory*—I had written several other spec scripts through the years that went unsold.

I fired Guy because he had let me down at a crucial time in my life . . . when I literally couldn't afford to be let down. I fired him because he *knew* what a crucial time in my life this was.

I fired him because he wanted to play golf when my new family's welfare was on the line.

I fired him because of the way he had flicked the ash into the ashtray and said, "Okay."

I fired him because I had risked *everything* for him with Michael Ovitz and now, five years later, he didn't want to give up a golf tournament and a possible ten grand for me.

"Remember this," Guy had said to me a long time ago, "there is no heart as black as the black heart of an agent."

I remembered.

I told him I was firing him at lunch at a Malibu restaurant. We both sat there with tears in our eyes.

Guy said, "I hate this town."

I said, "So do I."

Guy said, "We had fun, didn't we?"

I said, "We sure did."

No longer my agent (still my friend?) he started advising me on which agent I should switch to.

"Whatever you do, don't go to Rifkin," Guy said.

Arnold Rifkin had revitalized the somnolent William Morris Agency and was ICM's biggest competitor.

"I won't," I said.

I felt sick about firing Guy. I remembered too many moments through so many years and so many drinks. I remembered Guy saying to me, through so many crises, "Well, I'm back in the bunker again—*incoming! incoming!*—waiting for the next plane to Paraguay."

I didn't know then what I would learn with the passage of time: firing Guy McElwaine was the biggest mistake I ever made in Hollywood. I never had as much fun again. His heart wasn't black; he loved me like a brother. I had fired my own brother the way Johnny Kovak had killed his own brother in my original draft of *F.I.S.T.*, the first screenplay I'd written.

By firing Guy, I had become a Hollywood animal. I had bought into the whole *ethos* of the town—an *ethos* I had resisted for so long: Guy screwed up, so *Fuck Guy!* He had to pay the price. *Fuck Guy!* I would *make him pay the price!* He would never work in this town (substitute: for me) again.

I should have forgiven him, of course. I should have understood that he was human, too, that he was coping with the wolves at his own door and with his own divorce. He needed the ten grand he might have won in Palm Springs.

And there was the gold bracelet Gerri had bought him with my money. Did

I feel that he'd betrayed me . . . by accepting the bracelet . . . while I *hadn't* betrayed him . . . by leaving Ovitz? Was it my star-sized ego that he had wounded by accepting that bracelet and by wanting to go to that golf tournament? Was I making him pay the price by starlike behavior?

Ultimately, I hurt myself by firing him. An unlikely pair, the Golden Beef and the Refugee from Cleveland, we had jousted at all the windmills and had had uproarious fun . . . until I pushed him from his saddle and left him trampled on the side of the road.

Fuck me!

On the playing field of deal-making and strategy, I was alone now without my mentor and swordsman ("two Iagos," the director Phillip Noyce had called us) . . . just another Hollywood animal scuttling from Morton's to the Ivy to Spago . . . just another hotshot *player* who remembered too well the wild and exhilarating joy of jousting at windmills with the brother he'd left behind on a mean and bloody road.

When I got home from lunch with Guy, I immediately called Arnold Rifkin.

The William Morris Agency released a press release when I became a client.

Arnold Rifkin was quoted as saying, "Joe Eszterhas has redefined the status of the screenwriter in Hollywood. His movies have grossed more than a billion dollars. His name brings people to the theaters. We are thrilled to be representing him."

I was quoted as saying, "My decision to leave ICM has nothing to do with my close and continuing friendship with Guy McElwaine."

Those words had an echo of the statement Guy had released for me when I broke up with Gerri Eszterhas: "His great friendship with Naomi Macdonald has nothing to do with the marital problems that led to his separation."

I liked Arnold Rifkin. He had come out of the fur business, had once sold Frye boots even . . . he was full of a lot of New Age malarkey his friend Tony Robbins pumped into him . . . he butchered the English language extraordinarily in a town filled with masterful butchers of the English language . . . and he bragged all the time about his low body-fat count . . . but I *liked* him.

Arnold Rifkin was human and real and he had a heart unlike the black hearts of other agents.

He went to work for me immediately. I asked him to sell *Blaze of Glory,* the script about Otis Redding.

What I was asking wasn't easy. *Blaze* had failed at auction—which meant every production entity in town had read it and passed. Now the script was damaged goods—now it had the clap—and I was asking Arnold Rifkin to pimp it . . . when everyone in town knew failure was infectious.

Arnold devised a smart plan. He got the script to the director Jon Avnet, who liked it and said he'd be "interested" in directing it. He wasn't "committing" to direct it—he was just saying he was "interested."

Knowing that Universal liked Jon Avnet and wanted to work with him, Arnold went to Universal with *Blaze of Glory*. He also knew that Universal wanted to be very nice to him . . . to Arnold Rifkin . . . because one of his top clients had just starred in a movie there and Universal was hopeful that the star would do a lot of publicity for the movie.

Universal read my script . . . and because the executives there wanted to work with Jon Avnet and wanted the star to publicize their movie . . . Universal bought *Blaze of Glory* for $1.25 million.

Before they paid me the money, though, they wanted to have a "creative meeting" with me.

I told Arnold I wanted to have the "creative meeting" *after* I was paid, not before. I wanted to tell them what they could do with the imbecilic suggestions I was sure they'd have . . . *after* I already had their money in my bank.

The Universal executives, no fools, knew about my reputation and insisted the meeting be held *before* I was paid.

Arnold Rifkin then informed them that unless I was paid the $1.25 million *immediately* . . . *before* any meeting . . . his star client would do *no* publicity for his Universal movie.

I got the $1.25 million check that afternoon.

Universal said there was no reason now to have a "creative meeting."

I worked on a rewrite with Jon Avnet, who then withdrew from the project saying he didn't like my rewrite.

Universal put *Blaze of Glory* on its shelf and the movie was never made.

The star did a lot of publicity for his Universal picture.

The publicity did no good; the movie failed.

I admired how Arnold had engineered all of it, especially admired the fact that he was willing to use one of his most powerful clients as a weapon on behalf of a much lesser client, me.

It was a violation of Hollywood agenting's cardinal rule: Care about only the biggest fish—all the other fish are part of the food chain.

On Christmas Eve, my new agent, Arnold Rifkin, called me from Africa, where he was on safari in the Serengeti.

He called to wish me a Merry Christmas and to tell me he was happy to "have you in my life."

I said then to Arnold Rifkin the same phrase which he had so often said to me . . . the same phrase which Sean Penn had said to me . . . the same phrase which Cuba Gooding, Jr., had said to me . . . the same phrase which was sweeping through Hollywood:

I said, "*Right back at ya!*"

About a week later, Arnold Rifkin sent me a note. It said: "I love having you in my life!"

I sent him a note in response.

It said: "*Right back at ya!*"

Now it was in writing.

Naomi's journal:

We have a new housekeeper. She's from the Philippines. I told her during the interview that this was a hard job.

After one week she said, "This job is easy. At my last job they would wake me up at two in the morning and tell me to pack for Hawaii, and then after packing all night they would say they changed their mind and I had to put everything all back in the morning."

I said, "They would wake you in the middle of the night?"

She said, "Yes, sometimes just to take a dirty glass to the kitchen from their bed."

She said, "I even had to give the lady a sample of my urine every week, because her husband was having her tested for drugs."

I said, "She used your *urine?*"

She smiled and said, "Yes. But they pay good money."

The big black limo was waiting in the driveway, some chilled bottles of white wine and an ice basket of Beck's beer in the back.

We were on our way to the Paramount lot to see the rough cut of *Jade.* Steve, who was visiting from Oregon, was coming with us.

Steve and Naomi were ahead of me as I went running out the front door of our house. We were late. I was wearing shorts, sandals, and a Hawaiian shirt.

As I hurried out the front door, I twisted an ankle and went straight down on the ground. Dazed by the fall, I was flat on my back.

Steve, ashen-faced, was above me.

"Is it your heart, Dad?" he asked.

Naomi was panicked. "I'll call an ambulance!"

"No," I said, "it's my foot."

They helped me up. My foot hurt like hell. I couldn't put any weight on it.

I asked Steve to grab a cane from the house.

"You can't walk," Naomi said, "we can't go."

"Are you kidding me?" I said, "I'm not going to miss the rough cut of my movie!"

Steve said, "This is really dumb, Pops! How are you going to walk?"

"If I can't walk, Mano," I said to him, "I'm going to ask you to carry me in. If you can't carry me in, I'm going to crawl in. Okay?"

I hobbled to the limo with my cane and got in. I stretched out and Steve took the sandal off my left foot. It was red and already swollen.

We could see a *huge lump sticking out of the left side of my foot.*

Naomi said, "We've got to go to a hospital."

Steve said, "Pops, look at that bone."

I said, "I'm seeing my movie."

Naomi said, "You're crazy."

I said, "It's *my* fucking foot, okay?"

I got one of the chilled bottles of white wine and poured myself a glass. I felt better. I poured another glass. Better yet. One more. My foot hardly hurt.

I stuck the CD which I had brought with me into the stereo. The Stones. I found the song I wanted—the song I'd played more and more lately to pump me up before meetings or divorce-related court appearances.

I poured another glass of wine and listened to the song and felt almost good.

"Sympathy for the Devil"!

We got to the small screening room. Billy Friedkin wasn't there, but Arnold Rifkin was. I'd asked him to come and give me his "take."

I knew that even though Billy wasn't there, one of his spies would be—not to watch the film but my reaction to it.

I came into the screening room hobbling and carrying my cane and a Coke container filled to the brim with white wine. Arnold took one look at my naked foot, swollen with the bone sticking out of it, and ran to get a bag of ice.

I put the foot up on the seat in front of me, Arnold placed the icebag on it, and *Jade* started rolling.

I stared in disbelief. I watched entire plot points and scenes and red herrings that weren't in my script. I heard dialogue that not only wasn't mine but was terrible to boot.

Friedkin, the coward, had lied to me again: *"I shot your script. I'm not stupid. I know how you are about your words. We're going to do a lot of other movies together."*

. . .

This movie that you created.

This movie I was watching was awful—it was without dramatic tension; it was heavy-handed and over-the-top—but, more important, *it wasn't my movie.*

I got nauseous and my foot started to throb.

I told them to stop the film—I had to go to the bathroom.

Steve helped me as I hobbled into the bathroom with my cane.

I leaned over a toilet, threw up, and started to shake.

I lit up a cigarette with some difficulty, slugged what was left of the white wine in the Coke container, and threw up again.

I stood there deep breathing.

"Jesus, Pops," Steve said, watching me. "Fuck this. Nothin's worth this. You gotta get out of this town."

I felt better and Steve helped me hobble out of the bathroom.

They started to roll *Jade* again. It was still awful.

I glanced at Arnold—he gave me the thumbs-down and shook his head.

Naomi rolled her eyes.

Steve just glared at the screen like he wanted to punch it out.

The film suddenly stopped and the lights came on.

What now? I thought.

Billy Friedkin's secretary came down the aisle and stopped next to me. "There's an emergency phone call for you," she said.

Naomi and I looked at each other in panic: *Oh, God, please no—something terrible must have happened at home.*

Billy's secretary said, "Your father's calling."

I said, "My father?"

She said, "From Cleveland."

I said, "I know where he lives."

Here I was at a rough cut screening of my movie. The movie stunk and wasn't even mine. My foot was broken and had a bone sticking out of it. I had just thrown up. I was out of wine (though there was more in the car).

And the father whom I loved and loathed had reached me at exactly this moment!

I hobbled with my cane and Naomi and Steve and Arnold over to Billy Friedkin's office to take the call.

Thankfully, Billy wasn't there. I would have caned him to death if he had been.

"I slipped in the shower," my father said.

I said, "You did what?"

"I slipped in the shower."

"Why are you calling me to tell me this?" I said.

"I'm frightened."

"Of what?"

"I bumped my head when I fell. I'm a little dizzy."

"So am I."

He said, "What?"

"Never mind. Call an ambulance."

"We did already."

"Then why are you calling me?"

"I just wanted to tell you."

I said, "How did you get this number?"

"Your housekeeper. I told her it's an emergency. Are you angry with me for calling you?"

I said, "No, Pop, it's okay."

He said, "Should I call you after I get to the hospital?"

"I'm in a meeting," I said. "I'll call you when I get home."

"Do you promise?"

"I promise."

He said, "How are you?"

"I'm fine," I said.

"*Fein fein fein*," he said, "like all the other Americans." I had to smile. I could tell he was smiling, too.

I said, "That's right."

"You hardly call me anymore."

"I'm busy."

"What are you so busy with?"

I said, "Writing the movies that pay for all your nursing care."

He laughed and said, "Thank you. Stay busy."

"I have to go, Pop."

My father said, "*See-ya, see-ya, see-ya,*" and hung up.

Steve said, "Is he okay, Pops?"

I said, "He'll never die."

I hobbled back to the screening room with Naomi and Steve and Arnold. When the movie was over, we talked outside.

"That's a really bad movie," Arnold said.

"That's not your script," Naomi said.

"It's not the script I read," Steve said.

I opened another bottle of the white wine and Arnold and I came up with a plan right there in that Paramount parking lot to get even.

. . .

As they say in Hollywood, just 'cause you get fucked doesn't mean you've gotta kiss anybody.

I called Sherry from the limo, screamed at her and told her she'd used me and her husband had used me to get a job . . . and had then lied to me about not changing my script.

I told Sherry I wanted my name off the movie and was going to tell the media how she'd asked me to say Billy was my idea to direct my script so it would seem like there was no nepotism involved.

"You can't do that, honey, please," she said, and I hung up on her.

Arnold called Sherry to tell her I was out of control and wanted my name off the movie.

I called Evans and screamed at him. I told him he was a whore who'd allowed his own movie to be fucked by the studio head's husband for fear he'd lose his own deal with the studio.

I called Billy and screamed at him. I told him he was a liar and a coward and he said, "I didn't change anything, Joe! I swear to you! What did I change? Write me a memo. *I'll change it back!*"

My father called from the Cleveland Clinic to tell me he was being sent home. There was nothing wrong with him.

I said I was happy to hear it.

Sherry and Arnold spoke the next day and she asked him what it would take "to make Joe happy."

Daily Variety announced my new deal with Paramount on the front page: "A blind script commitment . . . that insiders said will pay the scribe two million dollars against four million dollars."

Sherry Lansing was quoted as saying, "I have enjoyed our relationship with Joe through the making of *Jade* and we look forward to continuing it."

I was quoted as saying, "I'm flattered that Paramount has such faith in my work."

Right back at ya!

I sent Billy Friedkin a three-page memo detailing the changes which I thought were necessary to save *Jade*.

My memo ended: "The reason *Basic Instinct* and *Jagged Edge* stunned audiences is because the filmmakers and the studio had the courage to do something daring that people told each other about. With *Sliver*, all they told each other about was probably the worst last line—'Get a life!'—in the past decade. Let's not make that mistake again."

I got no response to my memo.

. . .

Naomi's journal:

Last weekend we spent an entire day at a *Showgirls* press junket at the Four Seasons. What an ordeal. After a grueling morning session we headed back to our room. I lay down on the floor, since I'm due in two weeks and this monstrosity I'm carrying was breaking my back. As I lay like a great mound on the floor Joe was sitting in the chair. We were talking about how *Showgirls*, which was rated NC-17, would be unavailable to teenagers.

Suddenly he said, "You know what? Most teenagers I know have fake IDs. You know what I'm going to do? When I go back in there I'm going to start telling all the teenagers to use their fake IDs to get into *Showgirls*."

I just lay there for a moment. Contemplating the repercussions. After years of being in the PR business myself, the words "damage control" have taken on a whole new meaning since I've been married to Joe.

"Oh God, Joe," I said. "Why?"

He smiled down at me and said simply, "Because I can . . ."

When we went back in he immediately used his idea in his first interview. There was a sudden scurrying in the next room. The PR guy came hustling in and said nervously in my ear, "You know, the MGM people are spastic. Joe has to stop saying the stuff about the IDs immediately."

I said, "If you tell him to stop because MGM is panicked, he'll just do it more."

He said, "Well, I have to say something . . ."

I said, "Fine, you tell him. But right now he's doing it about every third interview. If you provoke him, it could get worse."

He whispered to Joe and Joe whispered back. Red-faced, the PR guy left.

From that moment on, Joe used the ID line in every interview.

At the press junket, Gina Gershon explained to reporters what *Showgirls* was about: "This movie really represents the Aphrodite-Psyche myth dead-on. Aphrodite is the goddess of love and beauty, and she hears about some mortal chick who all of a sudden people are treating like a goddess, and this does not sit well with her. So she sends her lover/son Cupid down to destroy Psyche. Now, Cupid would kind of be Kyle MacLachlan's character, and Nomi is Psyche, and I'm Aphrodite. And instead of killing Psyche, Cupid recognizes her beauty and potential and falls for her."

United Artists announced it had no problem with the film's NC-17 rating. NC-17 for "Nudity, exotic sexuality throughout, graphic language and sexual violence." "We're accepting the rating because we believe the rating is proper," studio head Frank Mancuso said.

Verhoeven said: "It's really exciting to be able to release the movie in the United States as I shot it. I think the American people are strong enough."

Michael Medved, host of the PBS series *Sneak Previews,* said: "The NC-17 is the kiss of death."

"*I created her character,*" Paul Verhoeven said in an interview about Nomi Malone, played by Elizabeth Berkley, "with elements from two or three people. I was even thinking about my mother. She could suddenly explode in an outrageous situation that was based on nothing. I am not a big fan of Freud, I have always rejected him because he's right, he knew too well about me. Let's reduce it to that, it's all about my mother."

He *created the character* based on his mother . . . from the script which I wrote based on Naomi, the love of my life.

So Nomi, to Paul, was his mother . . . and Nomi, to me, was my lover . . . and Paul was popping Berkley during the shoot, who was playing his mother and my lover . . . and maybe that's why Paul, the motherfucker, got sort of confused with . . . *his creation.*

Naomi's journal:

We went to the *Jade* focus group screening last night. It was at a theater in the Valley. All the things they had discussed, all the changes that were supposed to happen, the ending that was going to be changed back to the original one Joe wrote, weren't there.

It was the same movie we saw at Paramount. The same stupid ending. I could tell Joe was inflamed. The answers coming from the test audience were dismal. It was a nightmare.

When it was over, we walked out and I could tell this wasn't one of those times where Joe was going to think it over. He wasn't going to go home and then write a note or call the next day.

He walked up to Jonathan Dolgen, the head of Paramount, and said something I didn't hear, but judging from Dolgen's face, it was memorable.

Then he turned to Sherry and said, "Your husband ruined it. He ruined the fucking movie."

He grabbed my hand and I was nearly running to keep up with him. We got in the limo and he said, "Go."

As we drove away I heard Sherry Lansing yelling, "Joe! Wait! Please!"

I looked back and she was running. Running after the limo in her high heels and Armani suit. I felt sorry for her.

Naomi's journal:

He's here. Nicholas Pompeo Eszterhas.

As Joe held him, he was so quiet and inquisitive. Not frightened at all by the bright lights and the noise. He looked all around and kept sticking his tongue out, as though he didn't quite know what to do with it. "A Mick Jagger tongue," Joe said.

They took him to the nursery and took me to my room.

Joe held my hand. Above him, the TV set was on. Joe was telling teenagers to "use your fake IDs" to see *Showgirls*.

CHAPTER 29

Everybody's Pissed Off

DICK

He's a demagogue. A grandstander. He's a loose cannon. A wild
hair. He'll do anything!

FEIGHAN

One fucking lunatic—that's all that it takes—one twisted wacko
and the whole world goes gaga!

City Hall, unproduced

Showgirls was released by MGM on September 22, 1995, and was met with
eviscerating reviews. While its box office numbers for the first weekend
were good enough to put it into the number two position, it plummeted
headfirst in its second weekend of release.

Jade was released by Paramount three weeks later, on October 13. Its reviews
were equally deadly and commercially it was dead when it opened.

The abysmal failure of the two movies together, three weeks apart, was an
unparalleled disaster in the history of Hollywood. Imagine two *Heaven's Gate*s
or two Oliver Stone or Alfred Hitchcock movies failing cataclysmically three
weeks apart.

The reviews were blistering and often personal. Sometimes it seemed that
the money I was making was getting reviewed as much as the two movies.

Typical of the *Showgirls* reviews:

- "*Showgirls* is your basic sleazathon du jour. Slicked up with glossy
  visuals and a driving beat, it will, if nothing else, bring people together. It'll bring women's rights advocates to their feet in
  anger, and bring the conservative right to its knees in gratitude
  for new ammunition against Hollywood Babylon . . . a big silicone
  implant . . . *Trashdance.*"—*Boston Globe*

- "Eszterhas is the highest-paid screenwriter in Hollywood history. . . . What seems to turn Eszterhas on are women with knives (a switchblade appears in the first sixty seconds), lesbianism, sex for cash and violence. . . . His insights into human nature come from pulp fiction, and a fear of women palpitates in all his best work (they'll kill you—but if you're lucky they'll have sex with you first, and maybe put on a lesbian show)."—Roger Ebert
- "*Showgirls* manages to make nudity exquisitely boring."—*Los Angeles Times*
- "*Showgirls* author Joe Eszterhas is the highest-paid screenwriter in Hollywood, which is only appropriate since he knows the most clichés."—*Charleston Gazette* (West Virginia)
- "A prurient no-brainer, the work of the overpaid hack Joe Eszterhas."—*Manville News* (New Jersey)
- "An abominable movie."—*Washington Times*
- "As a screenwriter, Eszterhas is colossally inept."—*The Pantagraph* (Bloomington, Illinois)
- "Verhoeven literally strips his women naked for long stretches and exploits them in a way that makes every other contemporary film that has demeaned and humiliated women look positively constructive and healthy."—*Sacramento Bee*
- "*Showgirls* is a porno flick that is being shown in mainstream theaters. . . . If *Showgirls* is a financial success, Hollywood will make similar films. Do you want it to stop? . . . Show more opposition to people like Joe Eszterhas, who ought to keep his porno flicks in the bad neighborhoods."—syndicated columnist Cal Thomas

And a sampling of the *Jade* reviews:

- "Please, what have we done to deserve another Joe Eszterhas movie? Okay, we acquitted O.J."—*Baltimore Sun*
- "With a salary of $2 to $4 million per script, Eszterhas is a very wealthy case of arrested development . . . sleaze-monger Eszterhas reverts to his *Jagged Edge* mode of mock-clever plot twists."—*Seattle Times*
- "It is a little frightening to think that Joe Eszterhas, the highest-paid screenwriter in history, and one of the sickest, may be sitting in front of his computer at this very moment coughing up something I will one day be obliged to look at in a theater."—*Newsday*
- "If there were any justice in the world, *Jade*, scripted by the infamous Joe Eszterhas, would be remembered as the laughable sleazy bomb it is. Instead, it was overshadowed by Eszterhas's even more egregious *Showgirls*."—*The News & Advance* (Lynchburg, Virginia)
- "I can't wait for Joe Eszterhas to write a comedy about a leper colony

that becomes a nudist camp for serial killers. He's on the way there, although his latest, *Jade,* gnaws its rather bloody bones in a cave somewhat higher up the valley from *Showgirls.*"—*San Diego Union Tribune*

- "*Jade* is the thriller for which screenwriter Joe Eszterhas was paid $2.5 million. Eszterhas's most likely comment on the matter: "S-s-s-s-s-uckers!"—*Tampa Tribune*
- "Just another lame, confusing, noisy template in the Joe Eszterhas formula."—*Monroe Enquirer-Journal* (North Carolina)
- "William Friedkin does the best he can with what appears to be screenwriter Joe Eszterhas's atonement for *Showgirls*—the men are the crude, duplicitous sexual predators here."—*St. Petersburg Times* (Florida)
- "We feel we know Joe's tastes by now: he likes chicks, chicks who dig chicks, chicks who turn tricks, and chicks with ice picks."—*London Daily Telegraph*

"Round up the posse. Load the shotguns. We're going after Joe Eszterhas," the *St. Louis Post-Dispatch*'s Ray Mark Rinaldi wrote.

"The fact that this writer was paid a reported $2.5 million for his *Jade* screenplay is downright criminal, and if Hollywood won't take him out, it's time for good movie-going citizens to take things into their own hands."

Posses? Loaded shotguns?

Take me out?

Citizens taking things into their own hands?

All because of *a screenplay that I wrote*?

Some people were mighty pissed off at me.

In Philadelphia, *Inquirer* film critic Carrie Rickey went to the shrinks to try to explain *Showgirls* . . . and me.

"What kind of male screenwriter creates women who are *only* sexual?" Rickey asked.

James M. Pedigo, chief psychiatrist at Philadelphia's Joseph Jay Peters Institute, "which deals with sexual offenders and their victims," answered Rickey's question this way: "A man with ideas that sex is not something that brings people closer together but is a powerful tool to be used by women, probably grew up in a house where he saw that and where he did not see parental tenderness, where Mother might have let Father know if he didn't take out the trash, there wouldn't be sex tonight."

I tried to imagine my Catholic, painfully shy, old-world mother telling my father that if he didn't take the garbage out, she wouldn't . . .

To get that opinion of me, critic Carrie Rickey had gone to a shrink who dealt "*with sexual offenders and their victims*"?

I was a *sexual offender* now? Because of something I had *written?*

Dolores Barclay, the arts editor of the Associated Press, began her review this way: "Early on in *Jade,* there's a scene in which an assistant district attorney finds a cuff link at a murder scene. He immediately recognizes it and suppresses it as evidence—a move that's totally out of character and pretty dumb."

When I read the review I got nauseous.

Because I agreed with Dolores Barclay.

It was one of the scenes that was not in my script, that Billy Friedkin had inserted.

It was one of the scenes that made me throw up when I saw the rough cut.

As more reviews savaged the screenplay of *Jade,* Billy Friedkin called to offer me support.

He had destroyed my script . . . he had butchered the movie . . . he had mostly avoided the critical beating I was taking . . . and here he was offering to support me through the battering . . . *he had caused.*

"Don't lose heart, Joe," Billy said. "Think about Gustav Mahler. He was a genius, a creative maestro, and he never got one good review in his life."

Bill Macdonald showed up at *Jade*'s premiere, held in the Paramount lot. He had a date with him neither Naomi nor I knew.

A few feet from us at times, he kept his eyes down and never looked up. When his producer credit appeared on-screen, one person in the theater applauded.

He and his date left before the lights came up at the end of the movie.

No longer my agent but still my friend, Guy McElwaine called me.

"There's one thing you've got to remember," Guy said to me. "You're a star. There's never been a screenwriter who was a star. You're a big, burly guy who knows how to play to the cameras and the public. You didn't have to end your letter to Ovitz the way you did, with that *Fuck you, Mike* stuff, but you knew how it'd play in public. And you didn't have to kiss Naomi for all the photographers at the *Sliver* premiere, but you knew that if you did, you would upstage Sharon and Bill. You can't sit in a restaurant or stand in a theater line without getting asked for an autograph. Imagine how some pissant little failed screenwriter who's doing reviews for some newspaper or magazine must hate you! *Why you and not him or her?* If I were one of those assholes I'd hate you, too.

"We live in a town," Guy McElwaine said to me, "where you don't root for your friends to fail. You root for your friends to die."

I wrote the *Los Angeles Times* this letter—a response to the barrage of criticism:

> *In his review of* Jade, *critic Kenneth Turan wrote: "And despite the writer's recent protestations that his women are strong masters of their own fate, he once again hasn't been able to come up with female protagonists who aren't victims or hookers or, more likely, both."*
>
> *Every critic, of course, is entitled to his or her own opinion, although the opinions about my last two movies,* Showgirls *and* Jade, *have been . . . um, personal. Most critics have begun their reviews by analyzing my income as though deputized by the IRS. Then they go on to loftier things. A sampling:*
>
> *"He is a troll-like man who wants to be Ernest Hemingway" . . . "He is an ape of a screenwriter" . . . "He is the Overwriter—overpaid and overweight" . . . According to Liz Smith, an upcoming episode of* Roseanne *will have a character say: "Every Joe Eszterhas film is his revenge against some girl who ignored him in high school. Having seen him, I'm sure he has a thousand more in him." And Roger Ebert, who wrote* Beyond the Valley of the Dolls, *wagged his finger at me on television and said, "He is afraid of women!"*
>
> *Well . . . golly . . .*
>
> *I do have long hair, although I've always considered Ernest Hemingway an insensitive boor who destroyed the lives of the people who loved him. I have always been fond of apes, especially silverback gorillas. Maybe I am overweight, but I'm trying to swim more. Some girls did ignore me in high school (and college), but others didn't. I have seen myself in the mirror, and I don't consider what I see pretty. And as far as being afraid of women—sure, some powerful women, like some powerful men, have scared the bejesus out of me—but it seems to me that if you are only afraid of men and not women—that* is *misogynistic.*
>
> *There is, however, a thematic echo (besides the dollar amounts) to some of the criticism that I feel compelled to address: it is Turan's point that I write women who are either hookers or victims or both and that, parenthetically, my writing is misogynistic.*
>
> *The central tenet of* Jade *is that a wife whose husband cheats on her decides to cheat on him. She doesn't want to fall in love with anyone, so she cheats with a series of men, once with each man.*
>
> *The central tenet of* Showgirls *is that a young woman turns her back on stardom rather than be spiritually destroyed by the corruption of the*

male-dominated world that she is in. She turns her back on the money, the glamour, the ambition—and goes back out on the road. Alone.

In both movies, the women, Trina and Nomi, take action as a result of what men have done to them: Trina's husband betrays her; Nomi's male-oriented Vegas world betrays her. They refuse to be victimized and, strong women, they do what they have to do to control their destinies.

It is a theme I've explored in other movies: In Jagged Edge, *Glenn Close kills the man who manipulates her. In* Betrayed, *Debra Winger kills the man who wants to corrupt his own children. In* Music Box, *Jessica Lange turns in the father she loves to save the child she loves. In each case, it's a woman who refuses to be victimized by a man who is using her. Indeed, the critic Michael Sragow called my script for* Music Box *the "ultimate feminist screenplay." Jessica Lange was nominated for an Academy Award.*

I find it ironic that while one critic calls something I've written "the ultimate feminist screenplay," other critics accuse me of misogyny, of writing of "hookers and victims." The fact that I've had some of the best actresses of my generation—Close, Winger, and Lange—playing my characters (when they were submitted almost every other script in Hollywood) is viewed by the critics as not relevant. The fact that Flashdance *was the inspiration for a generation of young women to pursue their own dreams and ambitions is also irrelevant.*

As far as writing women who are hookers is concerned, the point in Showgirls *is exactly that while Nomi has hooked in the past to survive, she will not sell her soul and become part of the Vegas machinery. She has preserved a part of herself that is inviolate and pure no matter what she's been through. When Cristal tells her that she is a whore, she not only denies it but the action she takes at the end of the movie denies it. In* Jade, *Trina doesn't simply hook, she gets even with a man who betrayed her—in the exact same way that he betrayed her—with a series of one-night stands.*

What I fear happening, as a writer in the nineties, is this: if you depict women who are being abused and manipulated, you are accused of being an accomplice to that manipulation and abuse. Never mind the societal reality—never mind that in Vegas, for example, women auditioning to be dancers are put through exactly the kind of nightmare the movie shows. The audition scene in the movie was based, literally, down to some of the dialogue, on research. Never mind the societal reality that there are women in the world who, discovering that their husbands have betrayed them, decide to cheat themselves, to get even.

Which leads to another point that the critics have made. It is a kind of satellite argument to the misogyny I am charged with: that the women I write are "angry."

Considering the things that have been done and are being done to women in our society, shouldn't women be angry? Shouldn't men who care about women be just as angry? Of course Trina is angry in Jade that the man she loves betrayed her. Of course Nomi is angry about the way she is treated in Vegas and the way she has been treated in the past. Her anger explodes in a rage directed at the man who raped her best friend. But he is only a symbol of the Vegas world and, indirectly, of the male world. The violence she does to him is cathartic and freeing and justified.

Writing angry women, writing a woman who carries a switchblade, does not mean that you find women threatening. It means that you share their anger, that you think there is a need for a woman moving in a certain part of the world to carry a switchblade. It means you don't see them as victims but as people who will defend themselves and fight for themselves.

Without movies showing women who refuse to be victimized, who confront and fight the forces trying to victimize them, we will be left with movies about women that are touchy-feely, Hallmark Moments filled with speeches about sisterhood and close-ups of hands holding.

That may be what the critics want, that may be the view of a roseate, politically correct, nonconfrontational, Prozac-driven generation. But as many women will tell you, that's not the real world. Pretending that it is the real world in the hope of creating role models doesn't have to do with writing or with drama. It has to do with public relations and politics.

Things are not rosy and feel-good out there and if we find reality as it is . . . in Vegas and in the privacy of the bedroom . . . hurtful, sleazy, and ugly, then we should work to change the reality instead of pretending it's not out there.

The critics can blast away at the messenger all they want, but sticking our heads in the sand will never make the world a better place.

Responding to the criticism of *Showgirls*, Paul Verhoeven said: "I don't think that the religious moralists or right-wing feminists are heartless or cynical, but I think that they are similarly misguided in their attacks on sex in movies. Fundamentally, they both argue that a woman showing her tits is being degraded, is being exploited, is being humiliated, and that the act of showing her tits contributes to the downfall of civilization.

"I don't think that's true. What that woman is doing is demonstrating our strong human instinct for procreation. Most heterosexual or bisexual men like to see tits and ass because those sights stimulate our sexual drives, our natural desire to fuck and create babies. Most women like to show off their bodies in skirts that reveal their legs or blouses that emphasize their breasts because they like to use their sexual power—they know that dressing this way will attract men who will ultimately give them babies. (Of course this is not a conscious process.) That's the simple biology lesson of it all. We need to accept that we are just animals who are running around doing one thing rather effectively, which is to procreate."

Well . . . Elizabeth Berkley had clearly sucked Paul's brains out.

Showgirls, Paul Verhoeven told the media, was influenced by *Flashdance,* the movie I co-wrote in 1983.

What Paul didn't know is that before I wrote the *Flashdance* script, the director, Adrian Lyne, asked me to watch a Dutch movie he had just seen called *Spetters,* about a group of kids who dream about being motorcycle racers.

I saw *Spetters* and liked it and I'm sure it influenced the script of *Flashdance,* which then influenced the script of *Showgirls.*

Spetters was directed by Paul Verhoeven.

It was fair to say then that Paul Verhoeven was the *original* original inspiration for *Showgirls.*

Heh heh heh.

In a review of Susanna Moore's novel *In the Cut,* Nancy Pate of the *Orlando Sentinel* wrote: "I can't help but think that because Moore is a woman who writes highly polished prose, people are calling *In the Cut* 'daring' and 'provocative.' Whereas, if Joe Eszterhas, say, were the author, those adjectives would be 'sick' and 'exploitative.' "

The *Los Angeles Business Journal* did a front-page story asking industry people what they thought would happen to my career:

An anonymous executive: "He's a member of the club. He's a tacky and repulsive man, but if he writes a good script we'd love to have a chance at it."

Steve Cesinger, an entertainment specialist at a Los Angeles–based investment bank: "Nobody knows if a movie is going to be a hit until it's released. When you have a name writer attached to a film, it's like an insurance policy. It eliminates one of the biggest risk factors. You don't want an untested, no-name writer."

Jerry Bruckheimer, producer: "Joe is a conceptual guy who understands big entertainment. As an ex-journalist, he understands deadlines and stories that are very dramatic and easily understood. We all go through peaks and valleys. He is an enormous talent."

Frank Price, producer: "Joe is a tremendously talented writer who has great originality. He takes chances. Remember, Babe Ruth was the home run king who also had the strikeout record."

Anonymous producer: "The secret is out. The bloom is off the rose. He keeps repeating himself."

Anonymous screenwriter: "At the root of the Eszterhas phenomenon is titillation. There is a sense of danger about him, violence. For a lot of movie executives, who have no life experience, he's exciting, exotic. They get a sense of danger by being in business with him."

Bob Berney, producer: "Everybody wants to shoot down the top guy. He is a wild guy who has led a flamboyant life. He likes to get into trouble. He can be his own worst enemy."

Jeff Berg didn't renew Guy's contract at ICM, putting Guy out of the agency business.

Had I not fired him, I'm sure Jeff would have picked up Guy's contract.

I never would have fired Guy, though, had I not risked my career for him when I fired Michael Ovitz as my agent.

In that sense, Guy was yet another casualty of the Ovitz fallout . . . in addition to Irwin Winkler and Barry Hirsch.

My friend Don Simpson died. I smoked a couple of joints and did a double-bubble dose of Cristal in his honor.

I wasn't as close to Don as some, I didn't hang out with him as much as some others, but I loved the guy. I knew I could call him at four o'clock in the morning for help of any kind and he'd be there for me; I think he knew I'd be there for him if he called, too.

Don wasn't really a producer; he was a rock and roll star. He was a fat, smart little kid from Alaska who, like Bill Clinton, a fat smart little kid from Arkansas . . . and so many others of us . . . grew up wanting to be a rock and roll star.

Don Simpson started in the music business, then took his outlaw rock and roll ethic into film—that's probably what he was best at with all of his movies. He selected the music himself; the music was perfect for and perfectly drove each movie. On a personal level, he remade himself: the fat little kid was gone; he even redid the planes and contours of his face.

Sex, drugs, rock and roll: Don did as many drugs as Elvis and died Elvis's death: collapsing to the floor from the toilet while reading a book . . . wearing the reading glasses he (and Elvis) never wore in public . . . Elvis's book was about the Shroud of Turin, Don's was about wannabe rock and roller Oliver Stone.

I have two poignant memories of him though the two are really one. It is a scene I'm sure Don played out hundreds of times; I just happened to be witness to it in two places, years apart.

In both, we are with slutty women we have met only hours ago—once in New York, once in Vegas—and both times Don is pouring his heart out to the bimbos he has just met, telling them about his strict Baptist upbringing and his strict parents.

The bimbos are listening, their smiles glazed, their lips puffed, their eyes even welling with icy tears. They are thinking about the part this big-shot producer will give them if they play their cards right.

Don is thinking, as he mumbles soulfully about his upbringing, about the body parts the bimbos will give him in exchange for the heartbreaking stories he is telling them.

What he doesn't know, though—or won't admit to himself—is that he doesn't have to tell his Dickensian stories . . . he doesn't have to betray his parents to these bimbos . . . he doesn't even have to *talk* to them at all . . . they'll give him their body parts just to get the parts he can cast them in.

So Don treats them not like bimbos but as young ladies . . . pretending he needs to seduce them . . . pretending he has to break their hearts with his stories.

The bimbos pretend that they *have* hearts and Don can pretend to kiss them as he grabs hold of their proffered body parts.

Relations between Sherry Lansing and me were—understandably so—somewhat strained until she called me one day and asked me for a favor.

"This woman is doing a photo book on famous directors," Sherry said, "and Billy needs a writer to do a short essay on him praising his work. He's too embarrassed to ask you himself, but do you think, honey, as a favor to *me*, you can write some nice things about Billy for the book?"

I wrote the essay for her.

Right back at me!

I told you I was a Hollywood animal, didn't I?

I was sitting at a table with a group of people at an old-time Hollywood kind of place with leather booths and twinkling little lights near the Burbank Studios.

I glanced around and saw Guy sitting with his back to me on the other side of the room. He was reading a script.

I went over to him and we hugged and he asked me to sit down. We hadn't spoken in a long time. He looked tired.

He was trying to make a production deal with a studio, he told me, but wasn't having any success. The house in Beverly Hills was gone; he was living in an apartment on Wilshire.

He asked about Naomi and the boys and I told him to come over and see us sometime. He nodded.

I asked him for his phone number and as he gave it to me he said, "You won't call me."

I said of course I would call him.

"We had a helluva run, didn't we?" Guy said and we hugged again and he walked out with his script under his arm.

I didn't call him.

In Marin County, Gerry Eszterhas had me back in court, trying to get an equal share of all my *future* earnings (the premise being that she had inspired me as a writer, so my output was really due to her).

She presented her expert witnesses: screenwriting professors, mostly from UCLA, who took Gerri's money (mine really) and parroted her point of view on the stand:

That the *idea* is what's important, not the screenplay. That I was being paid these astronomical amounts of money not because my scripts were good, but because the ideas were.

I hated these smug academic whores up there on the stand, all of them failed screenwriters or failed television writers who then turned to teaching kids what they themselves didn't know and couldn't do. There they were, pontificating—and not able to look at me, like Gerri—because they knew what they were doing here was an obscenity. They were being paid to try to damage someone who had succeeded at what they had failed at.

The only part of it I enjoyed was my lawyer's reiterated question to each one: "What screenplays or teleplays have you written?"

They responded by haltingly listing unproduced scripts or low-level TV productions from thirty years back or collaborations without credit on someone else's screenplay.

I smiled during these moments as their faces turned red or as they set their dewlapped jaws.

I laughed out loud once as a "professor" shamefacedly mentioned his paltry credits and then reached for his glass of water with a trembly hand.

We flew back to L.A. together—Naomi, my lawyer, Gerri's lawyer, and me. Gerri's lawyer was across the aisle from us.

I couldn't stop myself, of course, and started talking loudly about odd plane crashes where only one side of the plane . . . the one Gerri's lawyer was on . . . suffered fatalities.

At LAX, I was standing outside, smoking a cigarette, waiting for Naomi, when Gerri's lawyer passed me.

"Merry Christmas," he said and smiled.

I smiled, too. And said, "Fuck you!"

The lawyer actually looked hurt . . . like he didn't understand why I'd say something like that to him.

As Christmas approached, a mutual friend called to tell me that Guy wasn't in very good shape, not even coming over to his house for the Sunday football games.

He was going to ask Guy over for Christmas but had decided to go out of town instead and wondered if *I* could invite Guy over to my house.

I hadn't seen Guy in a while but called and invited him. He seemed choked up and accepted the invitation.

When he was an hour late on Christmas Day, I called him but got no answer. We waited another hour but the kids were hungry and the turkey was already overdone, so we ate without him.

He never showed up.

In its overview of the 1995 year in film, the *New York Times*'s big headline read "FROM AUSTEN TO ESZTERHAS."

Janet Maslin castigated "nasty, irresponsibly super-violent, sleaze-filled exploitation films (here's the moment to mention Joe Eszterhas) that Bob Dole had no trouble making a campaign issue out of."

A screenwriter of my acquaintance who hangs out at the Rose Café in Venice made a list of three hundred hit movies. He put each movie on an index card, mixed the cards together, and put the cards into a hat.

He pulled the individual cards out of a hat and matched them into twos indiscriminately. These are some of the combinations he came up with: *Rocky* and *The Turning Point; Cliffhanger* and *Clueless; Top Gun* and *Ace Ventura; Network* and *The Fight Club; Midnight Cowboy* and *As Good as It Gets; The Sixth Sense* and *Flashdance; The Usual Suspects* and *Star Wars; Jerry Maguire* and *Deliverance; The Towering Inferno* and *Dressed to Kill; The Godfather* and *The Blair Witch Project; Pulp Fiction* and *All About Eve.*

He pondered his combinations for several days at the Rose Café and picked three: *Jerry Maguire* and *Deliverance* (a young agent with a wife and child finds himself on vacation in the Carolinas, where he has to defend his family from a backwoods madman), *The Towering Inferno* and *Dressed to Kill* (a homicidal maniac sets a fire in a high-rise, trapping the victims he picks off one by one),

Pulp Fiction and *All About Eve* (a blue-collar girl who is a street hood schemes to become the star of her high school play).

He pitched all three to different studios and sold all of them for a total of $1.7 million. All three went into studio development but none of the three has so far been made.

My father kept calling us at three and four o'clock in the morning.

My heart almost stopped every time the phone rang at that time for fear that something had happened to Steve or Suzi.

He claimed to have forgotten the time difference each time.

I said, "Pop, there are babies in this house. You wake them up and you scare the hell out of me."

"Oh," he said, "I'm sorry, but this is very important" . . . and would then tell me some absurdity involving his nurses. They were stealing his cans of Coke or nibbling at his dried Hungarian sausage or purposely giving him the wrong medication.

The middle-of-the-night phone calls kept happening—but he would hang up when I picked up. I knew it was him because we had caller ID.

I called him back each time he hung up on me and he denied that he'd called.

"Pop," I said, "I know it was you. I have this thing on the phone that tells me."

"It must be malfunctioning," he said.

"Please stop calling me at these times," I said.

"It wasn't me," he said.

We finally got an answering service. My father was checkmated now. The service picked up at three and four in the morning. We weren't bothered.

He even conned the service once or twice into putting him through, telling them that it was an emergency and that we had just called him.

I had to leave instructions with the service: Even if my father said it was an emergency, they couldn't put him through. At least one operator, I knew, considered me heartless.

Then he started calling eight or ten times a day and leaving messages with the service. Sometimes I'd call him back two or three days after the first call—and there'd be thirty messages from him in total.

He was angry when I finally called him.

"Why don't you call me back? You're my son!"

"I do call you back, Pop, but sometimes I get busy."

"Too busy to call your own father back?"

"All right," I said, "sometimes I'm not busy. Sometimes I just don't feel like calling you back. What is it? Why did you call me, Pop? What do you want?"

He said, "I wanted to hear the sound of my son's voice."

I said, "Well I don't want to hear the sound of *your* voice right now."

"Then you won't hear it," he said, and hung up.

The screenwriters sip their cappuccinos at the Rose Café in Venice, their brows knit, their laptops overheating, as they wait for their muses to unearth box office gold.

They are there in the mornings but never after dark, when the kids from the projects two blocks away come by with their Uzis and perform Sam Peckinpah drive-bys.

But in the mornings, when the gangstas are still asleep, the screenwriters create and kibitz and dish and crank themselves high with dreams and caffeine. Sometimes they even ask each other to read and criticize a scene and engage in lengthy dialogue about the relative merits of dialogue and spine.

But oh, if they'd only stick around until the gangstas came by or if they'd only see the blood in Venice's streets, oh the stories these screenwriters would be able to tell! Though they also know they'd be stories they wouldn't be able to sell.

Endings don't end happily in Venice after dark.

Young, hip, no dummies, by mid-afternoon the screenwriters get the hell out of there.

I wrote a script called *Male Pattern Baldness* about a man in Cleveland who literally winds up going to war against the forces of political correctness.

It was a dark, satiric comedy and my gut told me it had potential to be a hit movie.

I called Arnold Rifkin and told him I had written a new spec and how excited I was about it and he said, "Send it over right away."

Then he said, "Hold on a minute," and put me on hold.

He came back and he said, "I've checked my calendar. I'll read it on"—and he gave me a date.

The date he gave me was two weeks away.

I didn't think I'd heard him right.

"That's the earliest date I've got to read anything," he said.

I wanted to say: It takes about an hour to read a script—you don't have an hour in your day for two weeks?

I wanted to say: Do you move your lips when you read, Arnold?

I didn't say those things and Arnold Rifkin said, "Gotta go. Congratulations. Send it over. I look forward to reading it."

I thought: Way, way forward.

Two weeks forward!

. . .

I sat in my den and thought:

I was the highest-paid screenwriter in town. I'd been paid astronomical, record prices for my scripts. Every spec script I wrote turned into an event. The last one, *Blaze of Glory,* wound up on the front page of the Calendar section of the *L.A. Times* for . . . *not* selling.

Half the producers in town would have made trips to Malibu to read the script if I had let them.

And yet my own agent wouldn't read it for two weeks.

Because he was too busy.

Too busy *for two weeks* to read something *for an hour.*

I was hurt.

He loved having me in his life, huh?

Would he have been too busy to see Bruce Willis's dailies?

Too busy *for two weeks* to see Bruce Willis's dailies?

I fired Arnold Rifkin.

Not in person. (I was too busy.)

Not by phone. (I was too busy.)

By fax.

Right back at ya!

My fax to Arnold Rifkin said:

> *Dear Arnold,*
>   *It has, unfortunately, become painfully clear to me that due to your other responsibilities and obligations I am not receiving the kind of representation I deserve. I have, as a result, decided to leave the William Morris Agency. I wish you the best, both personally and professionally.*
> *Sincerely,*
> *Joe*

I didn't know then what I would learn with the passage of time: *Firing Arnold Rifkin was a mistake, too.* Certainly not a grave mistake like firing Guy McElwaine, but big enough that over the years I came to regret it.

Arnold wasn't my brother, *but he was a goodhearted friend.* He got too busy sometimes, that's all . . . and it took him too long to read a script.

I needed an agent and I thought about my old friend Bob Bookman. Bookie was one of the few people in town who read. He loved Proust and Flaubert and spent as much time as he could out of town . . . preferably in France.

The only problem was that Bookie's agency was CAA and it was still headed by Michael Ovitz.

It had been nearly ten years since our bust-up but I remembered Wolfgang Puck's advice—"Ovitz never forgets"—and was wary.

I had lunch with Bookie at my house and asked him to sniff out how Ovitz would feel if Bookie represented me.

Bookie called back quickly and said Ovitz had no problem with it.

I said I'd do it only if we sent out a joint press release which I'd co-write.

Bookie called back and said Ovitz agreed.

We went back and forth on the press release. Everything was fine until I added this sentence. *"Ovitz said, 'I have always admired Eszterhas's talent.'"*

When Michael Ovitz read that sentence, Bob Bookman said Ovitz felt "a surge of animosity" and the deal was off.

I went back to Jeff Berg and Jim Wiatt at ICM. I had been back and forth with those two so often through the years that Jeff had even written me a letter once (after I fired him) telling me he looked forward to the next time I hired him.

"Changing agents," Sean Penn said, "is like changing deck chairs on the *Titanic.*"

Jeff and Jimmy came out to Malibu on a Friday afternoon and read *Male Pattern Baldness.* They thought it was very commercial and thought we could sell it to someone for as much as $4 million.

They went back to the office to devise a game plan. They said they'd get back to me by the end of the day Monday.

After they left, I picked up the phone and called the director I thought would be ideal for this script.

Betty Thomas had done comedy much of her life, had directed *The Brady Bunch Movie,* and was working on *Doctor Dolittle.* More important, she was every studio's directorial flavor of the month.

I told her what I'd written and she wanted to read it right away. I said I'd get the script to her house in the Valley the next day—Saturday.

She read it Saturday and committed to direct it.

Since she owed Paramount a movie, she got the script to Sherry Lansing on Sunday.

Monday morning Sherry called Jeff Berg and bought *Male Pattern Baldness* for $4 million—two now and two upon commencement of principal photography.

The script was *sold* and *green-lighted* with *a director attached* before Berg and Wiatt even had a chance to call me with their sales plan.

ICM took 10 percent—for what I guessed was a ten-minute phone call.

Movieline magazine picked "the 100 dumbest things the folks in Hollywood have done lately:

"#40—Elizabeth Berkley remarked about *Showgirls:* 'I'm really proud of this performance and this movie.'

"#41—Joe Eszterhas named the unprincipled nude dancer in *Showgirls* 'Nomi' after his own wife, Naomi.

"#42—Joe Eszterhas claimed that he thinks *Showgirls* star Gina Gershon is 'The Anna Magnani of the '90s.'

"#43—Joe Eszterhas stated in his trade ad defending *Showgirls*—'It is my operating principle as a writer that society will never change if we stick our heads in the sand and pretend that abuses to women, blacks, Jews and gay people aren't happening every day.'

"#44—Joe Eszterhas claimed that *Showgirls* was 'a deeply religious message on a very personal level.'

"#49—David Caruso said, 'You'll see. *Jade* will be rediscovered by audiences in the future. In fact, I will make a prediction that this film will have a resurgence.' "

Discussing *Showgirls*'s failure during an interview, Paul Verhoeven said, "There was a perception problem. It was hyped as the kind of sexy, pornographic movie that would go through the boundaries. That was wrong. Audiences went looking for thrills and emerged unaroused and that made them hate the film. Beyond that, *there were problems with the script.*"

In other words—*Fuck me!*—it was *my* fault.

Finally . . . about *Showgirls.*

Naomi was right.

"Dark and depressing" was what she had said when she read it in its first draft on Maui.

Most of the critics expressed some variation of that same theme after seeing the movie.

My father had been calling and leaving messages for two days but I hadn't yet called him back. Steve was visiting us and I'd been hanging out with him.

On this particular afternoon, I was writing and Steve was off doing something in Melrose.

Our gate bell rang.

I picked up and a voice said, "Is this Mr. Eszterhas?"

I said yes.

He said, "This is Deputy Miller of the Los Angeles Sheriff's Department. I have an emergency message to give you."

I felt the chills go down my back. My heart started to beat like a jackhammer.

He said, "I have to give it to you personally."

At that moment, I knew that Steve was dead—that he'd had an accident on the way to Melrose.

I said, "I'll be right out."

I knew I was going to have a heart attack before I walked by the swimming pool and the guesthouse and the garage and got to the gate. My heart now felt like it was going to burst out of my chest. I was shaking.

I opened the gate and saw the uniformed cop standing there next to his Sheriff's Department cruiser. He looked grim.

And exactly then I saw Steve's car driving down the street toward the house.

Steve was alive.

But what about Suzi?

The cop said, "Are you all right?"

"No," I said, "what's your emergency message? Is it my daughter?"

The cop said, "Your daughter?"

I said, "She's in school in Boulder."

The cop said, "No, sir. Your father called us from Ohio. He said he's been calling your house for days and not getting an answer. He was worried something was wrong. He asked us to come out to the house to make sure everything was okay here. That's why I had to see you in person."

I said, "Everything's fine. My father's ninety-three years old. He's got Alzheimer's disease."

The cop said, "I'm sorry, sir. My uncle's got Alzheimer's, too. I know what it's like. We won't be bothering you again."

He got back into his car and Steve said, "Is everything okay, Pops?"

I said, "Grandpa called the cops."

Steve said, "I heard what you said. Why didn't you tell me Grandpa's got Alzheimer's."

I started to laugh as we walked back to the house. I said, "He doesn't, Mano."

I thought about Gerry Messerman's contention that my father was the most manipulative man he'd ever met.

My father had managed, at the age of ninety-three, with a broken English accent, to con the L.A. Sheriff's Department into thinking we'd been robbed or home-invaded or murdered and to send a deputy to our house.

I was convinced it was his revenge for me not calling him back . . . and for hiring the answering service that he had to deal with each time he called us.

My father was saying—You may have the money to wall yourself off from me . . . but you still aren't beyond my reach.

I called him and read him the riot act. I told him that Steve was visiting and that he had almost given me a heart attack with his call to the cops. I told him I had told the cops he had Alzheimer's so they wouldn't listen to him if he called them again. And I told him that if he kept harassing me with his phone calls, I'd make sure the nurses took his phone away from him. *

My father said he was terribly sorry and swore that it would never, ever happen again.

Then he said, "What you said about the Alzheimer's, that was pretty fast thinking," and laughed.

Still angry, I called a Hungarian man who was my father's closest friend in Cleveland and told him what my father had done . . . but he knew all about it already . . . even knew that I told the cop my father had Alzheimer's.

He had just gotten off the phone with my father.

"Your father said, 'Oh, I really got Joe mad this time.' Your father laughed so hard I was worried about his heart."

I said, "He thought it was funny?"

He said, "Not what happened, but how angry you were."

Naomi's dad, who'd smoked cigarettes all of his life, was sick with lung failure. I bought him a hospital chair and a big screen TV. We went back to visit him in Mansfield and I trimmed his hair and beard and nails and toenails.

He wasn't eating or drinking much, but we smoked a couple of cigarettes together and told a couple of dirty jokes. We buried him at the cemetery in Mansfield, about a month later.

I loved Barney Baka, a man who had built houses with his own hands, an ornery old Polack who was known as "Ebeneezer" to his children and grandchildren. Maybe because we were both ethnics who shared a lifelong love of the Cleveland Indians—but it was as though we recognized each other when we met. Sometimes, sitting in cars next to each other, I even held the old man's hand.

His funeral was held on a glorious spring day. Butterflies were everywhere; squirrels scampered in the trees. As we prayed over Barney's casket and I looked at Naomi and her brothers and sister, the family that I, an only child, had never had, I thought:

You did good, Ebeneezer, raising these decent, good kids, even though you did it in your crotchety, old-timer way.

And I thought to myself:

Would I be able to raise my boys to be good and decent people in Malibu, on the bluff where Sean Penn and Charlie Sheen and Emilio Estevez had grown up? Above the beach where the honking of sound trucks and star trailers mixed in with the crashing surf and the seals' cries?

. . .

Cleveland mayor Michael White and I held a joint press conference to announce the filming of *Male Pattern Baldness*.

Mayor White said: "Cleveland's stardom as an urban success story in the nineties has been followed by local, national, and international news media. We've shed our rust-belt image to reveal a new American city that will be revealed to the world on Hollywood's silver screen. I'd like to first commend Joe Eszterhas for returning to his hometown to make this spectacular announcement and secondly to thank him for the economic impact this movie will garner for Cleveland and its citizens."

I said: "Cleveland is the only real hometown I've ever had—and I'm glad that I can give something back to the people and the town that treated me with great feeling and affection when I was growing up here."

The press release mentioned that Betty Thomas, who'd direct the film, "was born in Willoughby, Ohio, attended South High School, and began her career as a student teacher in the Willoughby area."

I was even presented with the flag of the city of Cleveland.

In Marin County Court my lawyer, Patricia Glaser, made a brilliant case against Gerri's position, hammering away at the unfairness of putting a man into creative servitude for the rest of his life—and then tried what she described as "a very long shot."

Without calling any expert witnesses, without a detailed presentation of our side and our case—she asked the judge to dismiss *their* case. To throw it out of court. Because an idea, according to the law, is not property.

A month later, the judge did exactly that.

The story ran across the top of the front page of the *Marin Independent Journal*.

Gerri, Suzi said, was "humiliated."

I was free . . . if you could call payments of $32,500 a month and giving up millions of dollars, two houses, and four cars . . . *freedom*.

Richard Dreyfuss came to our house for lunch, carrying an Evian bottle that had a piece of elastic tape on its side that said "RICHARD DREYFUSS."

He left it behind and our housekeeper, starstruck, asked if she could have it.

She kept it next to her bed in the guest bedroom and, about six months later, when Naomi's older brother Bep visited from Ohio, he stayed in the guest bedroom, got thirsty in the middle of the night, and slugged the water from the bottle next to the bed.

Our housekeeper let out a shriek when Bep left and she realized her Richard Dreyfuss water was gone.

She grieved for days.

I offered to call Richard to ask him to send over another bottle of his Evian water, but the housekeeper said it wouldn't be the same thing as the bottle she'd had.

We called Bep and told him he'd guzzled Richard Dreyfuss's six-month-old water and all Bep said was "*Yuck!*"

Naomi and I were never apart. We had lunch and dinner together every day—Naomi cooked or I grilled and we listened to Billie Holiday and Renzo Arbore and his orchestra a lot. We were also having one baby after another. On September 27, 1997, our third son, John Law Eszterhas, was born.

Sometimes we left the kids with their nanny and drove over to Palm Springs or down to Laguna . . . and put more babies in the oven.

The only nights we were ever apart were when Naomi was readying to ease another baby *out* of the oven.

We were so close that our only separations were caused by our lovemaking.

My father sent me a document headlined "STATEMENT" and witnessed and also signed by his housekeeper.

Written in Hungarian, it said, "My book *Nemzet Politika* (National Policy) is anti-Semitic. Its assumptions, conclusions, and observations are faulty and wrong. I find it necessary therefore to withdraw and deny the faulty and wrong assumptions, conclusions, and observations in my book.

"Historical events after the publication of this book proved my anti-Semitic assumptions, conclusions, and observations to be shameful.

"I forbid any future publication of a new edition of this book."

My father called to tell me that Father Miklos Dengl, the Franciscan priest who fired him from the *Catholic Hungarians' Sunday,* visited him.

"He's dying of heart disease," my father said. "He asked me to forgive him for firing me. He said he knows now that what he did was cruel and unjust."

"Did you forgive him?"

"I threw him out of the house," my father said.

I said, "What did he do?"

"Cried," my father said, "the same way I cry sometimes because you won't forgive me."

He laughed.

I didn't think it was funny.

I said, "Maybe I've forgiven you."

My father said, "Don't tell me any of your Hollywood lies."

I thought that *was* funny so I laughed.

My father laughed with me.

For a brief moment, we shared our laugh.

When Michael Ovitz left CAA and became an executive at Disney, I wrote him a public note in *Los Angeles Magazine*:

Dear Michael,

Kevin's gone, Sly's gone, Barbra's gone, even Seagal's gone. The new CAA president, Richard Lovett, has allowed some folks to take a picture of his ass. Sweet Jesus, Michael, all these years after our Incident at Rashomon, they have asked me—Me!—what I'd do if I ran CAA. It's as screwy as asking Bob Dole what he'd do if he ran the country!

This is what I would do, Michael. I would do anything to convince you to come back. I would buy the CAA building and give it to you. I would buy the Peninsula Hotel across the street and give it to you. I would buy Wilson's House of Leather and give it to you. Hell, I'd go down Wilshire and buy the ICM building and give it to you. I'd buy Roy Lichtenstein and give him to you.

Forget about the hobnobbing you're doing with Mickey Mouse and Donald Duck, forget about the NFL franchise the papers say you're work-ing on—(What for? Does anybody really miss the Rams?). The town is not the same without you. It is like the Yankees without Ruth, boxing without Ali, the Tonight Show without Carson, the Kremlin without Stalin.

It's so boring that I don't even give the CAA building the finger any-more. Now I wave. I had fun giving it the finger. I feel middle-aged waving.

Nobody gets inscribed copies of The Art of War anymore. Nobody gets Japanese techno-gadget birthday presents. (Remember the wake-up clock and the watch you gave me?) Nobody gets the kind of expert medical care you used to provide. (Remember the acupuncturist you were going to send up to Marin County when I hurt my back in Santa Fe?)

When you were around, there was this mad, amok buzz all the time about the skullduggery that was either going on, thought to be going on, or hoped to be going on. It must have been the kind of power breakfast gossip that went on around the Borgias—deals and conspiracies and turnarounds and buyouts and princes in favor or out of favor. Michael Ovitz couldn't even take a trip out of town without the hall mice and the wannabe hall mice, the sycophants and the guileful, spinning their red-sky-at-sunset theories: His assistant says he's in Tokyo, but that must mean that he's not in Tokyo, otherwise the assistant wouldn't have said he's in Tokyo.

Michael, I saw a producer who barely knew you call Jimmy's, the Grille, and the Palm one mid-morning to try to find out if you were having lunch there that day. I saw the man reduced to near hysterical desperation when he couldn't get a straight answer. Do you know what he did? He went from one place to the other, hoping to find you, and when he didn't, he went over to the Hamburger Hamlet and disconsolately scarfed down a pound of cheesy meat.

About a month ago, a friend of mine saw you eating in the executive dining room at Disney. You were having lunch with Cruise. My friend said Cruise looked great, with that extraordinary sparkle the man has. And he said you looked . . . bored.

I've worked with Michael Eisner, I like Michael Eisner, although I think he makes too much money. (I know, I know, people in glass houses, etc. etc. etc.) But conspiring with Michael Eisner can't have the same jolt as conspiring with Ronnie at CAA. You and Ronnie Meyer went after the world. You and Michael Eisner are going after the cash.

You are in an Elba of your own creation, Michael.

Come on, man, gather the foot soldiers and grab the guns. I miss the sound of gunfire in the night. I miss the smoke in the air. Wilshire Boulevard has become a demilitarized zone. If things go like this, one of these days someone will graffiti the CAA building.

Come back and kick ass, Michael. Send out the copies of The Art of War *again.*

That's the difference. You kicked it. Richard Lovett shows it.

Betty Thomas had changed her mind about directing *Male Pattern Baldness.*

Paramount, naturally, was upset.

The studio had made a $4 million deal with me with Betty attached to direct it. They wouldn't have made a deal that lucrative with me without a hot director like Betty attached.

Jeff Berg and Jim Wiatt were even more upset.

This was the second time this had happened.

New Line had paid me $4 million for *One Night Stand,* with Adrian Lyne attached to direct it.

The next time we went out with a spec script, Jeff and Jimmy feared correctly . . . *with a director attached* . . . every studio would remember what had happened with Betty and Adrian.

I had lunch with Betty at the Bel-Air Hotel to try to find out why she didn't want to direct *Male Pattern* anymore.

She told me that she had lost faith in the script. She had organized a "reading" with some actor friends and the script, she said, "just didn't play."

She was also questioning who would go to see the movie.

A contemporary hit comedy, Betty said, was "laughs and liberal inserts"—whereas my script was an assault on liberal political correctness.

"Maybe the fly-over people will see it," Betty said. "But they don't go to movies. Hit movies are made by the two coasts and I don't think the coast people will like this attack on political correctness . . . because they're too politically correct."

Betty said she feared the movie would fall "between the pews."

I told her I'd heard a rumor that she didn't want to do her next movie for Paramount and was making a case against the script so she could get out of her commitment.

Betty Thomas looked at me, smiled, and said, "Esty, I just can't believe you sometimes."

Sherry Lansing told me she had the hottest young director in town signed up to Paramount and he wanted to direct *Male Pattern Baldness*.

Mark Illsley had just directed *Happy, Texas,* a Sundance Film Festival hit that Harvey Weinstein had bought for Miramax for $10 million. The movie hadn't been released yet but everyone knew, Sherry said, that it would be a big critical and commercial hit.

I asked to see it and both Naomi and I thought it was nothing special. We couldn't believe it would be a hit and couldn't believe Harvey had paid $10 million for it.

Mark Illsley, a pleasant young man, came to the house and told me how much he loved my script and how little he wanted to change it.

He gave me his suggestions and I responded by saying his suggestions would change the script not "a little" but "a whole lot."

His response was to shrug and tell us that on the day Naomi and Bill Macdonald's house burned down in Venice . . . Mark had been hanging around Evans's office, heard about the fire, and drove out to Venice to see if he could help. He had carried some of Naomi's and Bill's scorched possessions out of the house.

Mark Illsley was clearly a nice, good-natured, and sympathetic young man. I liked him.

His suggestions were sophomoric, idiotic, and asinine.

I considered his suggestions for a while and finally wrote Sherry Lansing a letter:

Dear Sherry,

I have grappled for months now trying to do the rewrite with Mark Illsley on Male Pattern Baldness. *After trying several drafts, I've concluded that I've involved myself in a process which is, simply, a mistake. It isn't just that Mark's vision of the third act is sophomoric . . . that Frank not kill himself, that the movie end with shit (literally) flying from sewers and faucet taps and fountains . . . it is a catastrophic diminishment and trivialization of what my script is about.*

The title of the movie is <u>Male</u> Pattern Baldness. It is a comedic and metaphoric examination of what is happening to many men in our society today. Men are being made to feel isolated, alienated from the ethics and values which they grew up with. They are, in Susan Faludi's terms, "stiffed." More and more men are angry and more and more men are responding in the classic primal male way—by getting a gun and going to war with the world. It is happening over and over again—two days ago in Honolulu, yesterday in Seattle.

It is that explosive male rage which this script taps into. But you can't tap into something by removing the "something." By removing the rampage and the suicide at the end of the third act, we would be castrating the script at its core. The script is timelier than ever—indeed, tragically, it seems to become timelier each day. By removing the rampage and the suicide, we are removing its very timeliness. If the script is filmed without compromise, the movie can be a shark that bites deeply into the national psyche. By removing the rampage and the suicide, the movie will be a tranquilized shark without teeth and will swim by audiences who won't even notice its presence in the water.

We have a script that could become a movie that forces America to pay attention. The news is our greatest ally. You say you want to make a movie about male rage and the part you want to leave out is the rage. I don't get it.

Sherry Lansing didn't respond to my letter, but *Happy, Texas* was released and bombed both critically and commercially.

Mark Illsley was off *Male Pattern Baldness.*

My script went up on the shelf and is still unproduced.

A couple months after Mark's departure from *Male Pattern,* I considered writing Sherry a note suggesting that Billy Friedkin would be perfect for it—but I started to laugh so hard thinking about it that I didn't do it.

There was still a chasm between us and Steve and Suzi, but it wasn't as wide as it had been.

When they came to visit, they slept in our house and we ate together, although they still had little to say to Naomi.

Now Naomi also came with us on our day-long jaunts and ate lunch with us.

What gave me great hope for the future was that when Steve and Suzi visited separately or with a friend they were significantly warmer to Naomi than when they visited us together.

I thought I understood that: together, they wanted to show each other that they were being loyal to Gerri's hatred of Naomi, but separately, they couldn't help showing that they had always, before the breakup, liked Naomi very much.

When Mark Canton was fired as the head of Sony, I applied for his job. I wrote a letter to Mr. Nobuyuki Idei, the president of the Sony Corporation. It appeared in *Daily Variety*. It was headlined "I Want Mark's Job."

> *Dear Sir:*
>
> *In your honor I am writing this not on my manual typewriter but on a computer.*
>
> *Since you seem to be having some difficulty replacing Mark Canton, I thought I'd tell you why I am perfect for the job.*
>
> *I realize this situation is so grave that everyone is losing hair over it. Here are my qualifications:*
>
> - *I have more hair than Jon Peters and Peter Guber combined. Theirs is thinning—Jon's more than Peter's.*
> - *I once called Mark Canton "benighted." It has taken you some time to agree, but we clearly think alike.*
> - *I have recently produced only male offspring.*
> - *Women, the most important moviegoers, discuss my films endlessly.*
> - *I have won three major industry awards—one Sour Apple, two Razzies.*
> - *I smoke heavily. So does most of our country.*
> - *I stayed at the Kahala Hilton at the same time as Mr. Morita. We swam in the same ocean.*
> - *The media loves me. My wife and I were both picked as two of the scariest people in Hollywood. If I get this gig, we will entertain!*
> - *I don't speak Japanese, but I do speak Hungarian. I used to speak broken English; the critics say I write it. We can communicate.*
> - *Pat Buchanan once attacked me in a column for being a "foreigner." Solidarity, Mr. Idei.*
> - *I refused to rewrite Gangland for your studio because the notes were dumb. I did it for you, Mr. Idei. You would have been embarrassed. Now you can thank me honorably.*
> - *I gave your company $2 million back when I refused to do that rewrite. You have already profited off of me.*

- *I drive a Toyota Land Cruiser, listen to a Sony Discman, and watch a big-screen Mitsubishi.*
- *The* Los Angeles Times *says Michael Ovitz has been giving you advice. He has given me advice in the past, too.*
- *Michael Ovitz sent me* The Art of War. *I read it. I learned from it. I sent him a letter.*
- *Sharon Stone and my wife and I have an intimate connection. So we wouldn't have to pay Sharon $20 million per movie.*
- *My wife refers to herself as my "faithful concubine." That's got a historical ring to it, doesn't it?*
- *I know Jack Valenti. He always asks about my health.*
- *I know Jerry Bruckheimer intimately. We interviewed strippers together.*
- *I would make a three-picture deal with myself. That* would *cost you $20 million.*
- *I wouldn't publicize the deal, but it would leak. I would publicize* nothing, but *everything* would *leak.*
- *I would convince Paul Verhoeven to turn* Starship Troopers *into the first NC-17 bug movie with a spiritual message.*
- *Kevin Bacon is a friend of mine. All roads lead to Kevin Bacon. (It'll help with casting.)*
- *I tried to reflect the Japanese point of view in* Showgirls . . . "In America, everyone is a gynecologist."
- *I'm a writer. Studio executives want to be writers. They're crazy. I want to be a studio executive. I'm not crazy.*
- *You fired Jon Peters. But my coffee table broke his hand. (You're welcome.)*

My father called the day after his birthday and said, "You didn't call me to wish me a happy birthday."

I said, "You haven't called *me* for years."

"So you punish me by not calling me on mine?"

"Is treating you the same way that you treat me punishment?" I said.

He laughed and said, "*Touché.*"

I said, "Why don't you call me on my birthday anymore?"

"I don't know," he said, "maybe I have Alzheimer's."

"You don't have Alzheimer's."

"I know," he said, "but can't we pretend I do so you'll feel sorry for me and forget me not calling you on your birthdays?"

He laughed.

"By the way," he said, "happy birthday."

I said, "It's not my birthday."

My father said, "I know, but store my best wishes away for when I don't call you next year."

I said, "Happy birthday to you, too."

He said, "Thank you. That's why I called you. To hear you say it. And now you did."

He hung up.

I told Evans that my son Nick was always finding things outside at his preschool, stones, coins.

"Putz," Evans told me, "don't you get it? The kid's a born producer."

I told Evans I worried that Nick was maybe stealing some of this stuff.

"Like I said," Evans said, "he's a born producer."

I wrote a best-selling book about politics and Hollywood called *American Rhapsody*. It was published in 2000.

A split second of its 432 pages mentioned that, at a party in Pacific Palisades, Farrah Fawcett had pooped the front lawn.

It was the same kind of split-second revelation as Sharon's in *Basic Instinct*.

I was in the restroom at Dulles Airport outside Washington, D.C., washing my hands.

A guy next to me said, "Hey, I just read *American Rhapsody*. I loved it."

I said, "Thank you."

And at that moment, a guy inside the locked toilet stall behind me yelled, "Is that Joe Eszterhas?"

The stall door burst open.

He had his hand out to shake mine. His pants weren't on all the way. His belt wasn't buckled.

I shook his hand . . . a bit warily . . . and he said, "Congratulations." I said thank you and he said, "Did Farrah really shit that lawn?"

I left the restroom and Naomi and I got on our plane.

A stewardess came over as we were settling in and said, "Mr. Eszterhas, the captain would like to speak to you for a moment."

She was smiling, so I figured Naomi and I probably weren't in any kind of trouble.

I went up to the cockpit and the captain shook my hand.

"I saw you on the *Today* show," the captain said. "And I bought your book. I read parts of it out loud to my wife. But I gotta ask you—did Farrah Fawcett do what you said she did at that party?"

. . .

Cathedral Latin's alumni association wrote asking me to be their guest of honor at an alumni event.

Naomi wrote the president of the alumni association back.

> *We received your recent correspondence and I would like to reply by informing you that my husband does not remember you. As a matter of fact, the only memories he does have of Cathedral Latin School are painful ones he would rather forget.... While I certainly can't hold you responsible for the treatment my husband was subjected to at your school, I strongly encourage you never to write to him again. Also, please communicate to other members of the alumni association that Joe Eszterhas wants nothing to do with your organization nor any of the people who may have attended school with him. Do not send him your newsletter nor solicit him for donations. Do not invite him to attend any other events.*
>
> *My husband has always loved Cleveland and has spoken many times publicly and privately of his deep affection for the people there. Unfortunately, those feelings do not extend to Cathedral Latin. Please do not continue to assume they do.*

I did the *Today* show with a Mormon video store owner from Utah who was editing sex, violence, and profanity out of the videos he was renting out. He even edited out Rhett Butler saying he didn't give a damn in *Gone With the Wind*.

I said, "You have no right to do these things. You're a vandal and you should be viewed as a vandal."

He said, "And you're a pornographer."

I said, "You're a terrorist."

That night we met again on *The News with Brian Williams*.

He called me a pornographer again.

I said, "Mormon is only one letter away from moron."

My kindergartner, Joey, came home one day all excited. One of his classmates had brought his daddy's Oscar to class on "Share" day.

Joey had held the Oscar, had felt it, had liked the feel of it.

Joey wanted to see *my* Oscar, too.

I told him I didn't have one.

Joey said, "How come?"

Those of us who lived in Point Dume had the bejesus scared out of us one night when it felt like the world was suddenly exploding. Car alarms rang, dogs howled, babies screamed while the adults ran around trying to figure out what had happened. It wasn't an earthquake. It was louder than a sonic boom. It couldn't have been fireworks since it wasn't the Fourth of July.

We rocked the babies, shushed the dogs, turned off the car alarms, and called the cops. The cops told us there was nothing to fear. Brad and Jennifer were getting married down near the beach and their ceremony had gotten delayed and they had imported some super-megaton fireworks from Bali.

We forgave Brad and Jennifer. It was obviously an industry event and they were the new golden couple and we forgave them just like we forgave the helicopters and the sound trucks which were always down there below us on Westward Beach filming, keeping us awake.

We all fed off the Industry tit, so how could we complain about Brad and Jennifer or Jerry Bruckheimer re-creating Pearl Harbor right outside our bedroom balconies?

Two weeks later, though . . .

Boom! Boom! Boom!

Holy Jesus, the babies were screaming and the dogs going nuts and the car alarms screeching and the cops told us it was another wedding.

Two nobodies had read about Brad and Jennifer's wedding, and decided to copycat it right down to the imported fireworks from Bali. Two people who didn't work in the industry. Two civilians.

Two *civilians*? Waking us up? Making our babies cry and our dogs howl and our car batteries run down? The Malibu City Council passed a resolution the next week. All weddings with fireworks would have to be approved on an individual case-by-case basis by the City Council.

Naomi's journal:

Our housekeeper, Aurora, whom I adore, was talking about her hair yesterday. It's black, but the ends of it are red. She said she wished it were all one color.

"Why did you dye it? Did you want a change?" I asked.

She said, "Oh no. This lady I work for in Beverly Hills, she ask me to."

I asked why.

She said "She tole me her cats are afraid of dark-hair peoples. She say if I dye it, she pay for it. So I did. Why not? Is free!" She smiled.

I said I couldn't believe anyone would actually say that.

Then she told me about the time she used to have to sweep the Pacific Coast Highway. The woman she worked for didn't like the sand that stirred up every time a car went by, so

Aurora would wait for a lull in traffic, run out, and sweep as much as she could from the road in front of the house.

"I did that every day, for one year, and then one day she told me I was too fat, so I go."

CAA, the agency formerly headed by Michael Ovitz, asked me to participate in a fifteen-minute comedy film that premiered at the agency's annual company retreat.

"As you would probably expect," said the agency's letter to me, "the scene would make an allusion to the 'foot soldiers' incident that took place several years ago."

I played myself.

I said, on camera, to a Michael Ovitz–type agent, "My foot soldiers who go up and down Zuma Beach will blow your brains out."

The scene, I heard, was a big hit at the CAA company retreat.

Guy still couldn't get the production deal he was looking for.

"You gotta know when to get off the stage," our mutual friend Frank Price had told him, but Guy couldn't *afford* to get off the damn stage, he had too many ex-wives and children.

Two young screenwriters he'd represented formed a television production company and they gave Guy an office and a salary.

He had been a titan in Hollywood, the head of three studios, an agent with superstar clients like Yul Brynner and Peter Sellers and Steve McQueen and Burt Reynolds and Jackie Bisset—all of whom, as far as Hollywood was concerned, were dead.

Here he was, in a little office in a building where he couldn't even smoke for Christ's sake.

He had to go down and stand *on the street* every couple of hours and hope that the two young screenwriters wouldn't get upset that he was out of the office again.

Naomi's journal:

We went to the Grille for lunch today. I love going there. We always sit at the bar. As we finished our meal I spotted Mark Canton coming toward us.

Someone from a booth stopped him so I said to Joe, "It's Mark Canton! He's seen us! And you've said all those nasty things about him in public!"

Joe says, "Be cool."

I say, "But you've called him a *moron!* More than once!"

Joe says, "He won't stop. He's just heading out."

I turn around and look in the mirror behind the bar. I can see him behind us. Sure enough, he looks up at us and heads right over.

He puts his hand out and says, "Joe! Good to see you!"

Joe shakes his hand and says, "Mark, you remember my wife, Naomi." He says, "Nice to see you." Then he says softly, "Hey, Joe, listen, I just want to thank you for all the kind words . . ."

He was totally guileless. He *wasn't kidding*. No *hint* of sarcasm.

Joe says, "You're welcome. Good to see you Mark," and Mark says, "Great to see you, too. Take care," with a big smile and walks out.

Steve gave Joey a shark tooth for his birthday that Steve had worn as a child.

Joey wore his shark tooth proudly everywhere he went.

Naomi and I had our fourth son, Luke. I could hear Carrie Rickey of the *Philadelphia Inquirer* saying, "He is so misogynistic that he impregnates his gun moll only with boys."

Naomi's journal:

I took the boys Christmas shopping in Beverly Hills. It was hovering at 90 degrees and we all had on shorts, but I tried to make it feel like Christmas.

We walked by a display window on Rodeo Drive. They had little pieces of Styrofoam blowing out of a snow-blower, amid woolly caps and gloves and coats. Joey screamed, "Snow! Snow!" And they all pressed their noses against the glass, marveling at something they'd never seen, but heard so much about.

Sometimes I ache that they won't share my wonderful childhood memories. I try to tell them about it. But how can you explain how it feels to live in the seasons? To be buried in a mound of multicolored leaves? How the excited voices of the children burying you grow fainter and fainter as more handfuls are piled on, until you're left with only the intoxicating smell of autumn leaves and a deafening, crunching wall of sound.

Or how it sounds to walk in the snow. Sort of squeaky.

And sometimes, when it's really, really cold, you can walk
on top of it when you're little. And once in a while it
caves in and your heart leaps to your throat if it's really
deep. And the absolute rapture of rolling over in your bed
as your mom says, "No school today, guys. Too much snow. Go
back to sleep." Or hearing the crickets and tree frogs
announce spring, after the absolute silence and stillness of
winter. Or how it feels to catch a lightning bug at dusk in
early summer, and watch it glow in your cupped hands. Then
set it free again by blowing on it until it flies blinking
off into the night. Or massive thunderstorms that nearly
rock and roll you out of bed.

Sometimes I feel like they live in a gilded cage. The
ocean is there, but Point Dume is so treacherous they can't
even go in. The view is spectacular, but you can't take off
on your bike behind a gated wall. They know beauty, but they
don't know freedom.

As I watched them celebrate the snow I said, "That's
Styrofoam, guys. It's not real snow." They didn't care. It
was close enough.

I told Steve and Suzi about the things their grandfather had done in Hungary.

It didn't matter to them. They remembered how he had played and drawn
and colored with them while they were children.

They loved their grandfather.

Blood is thicker than spilled blood.

The Poet Laureate
to the Stars

The best Hollywood poet I've ever met doesn't write poems. He collects things. Independently wealthy, he spends vast amounts of money to purchase the objects which are the stanzas of his magnum opus. His house in the Hollywood Hills, not far from the Hollywood sign, is the volume within which he displays his genius. His collection includes:

Humphrey Bogart's last half-smoked cigarette.
Shirley MacLaine's Tibetan prayer beads.
Clara Bow's USC Trojans pennant.
A video of Orson Welles's last Paul Masson commercial.
A handwritten death threat from Hunter S. Thompson to Bill Murray.
Marlon Brando's Polynesian muumuu.
Devine Brown's dental dam.
Joan Crawford's coat hangers.
An envelope inscribed from Owsley Stanley to Dennis Hopper containing three tabs of LSD.
John Belushi's syringe.
Sylvester Stallone's Roget's Thesaurus.
Robert Downey, Jr.'s, nose-dropper.
Bobby Darin's mitral valve.
A handwritten death threat from Hunter S. Thompson to director/producer Art Linson.
Mae West's gold-studded girdle.
The crumpled front fender of James Dean's Porsche.
Marilyn Monroe's copy of Arthur Miller's screenplay of The Misfits, inscribed to her by John Huston.

Rock Hudson's butt plugs.

John Travolta's size 42 bikini shorts.

Audie Murphy's Medal of Honor.

A used condom once worn by Warren Beatty.

Sal Mineo's handcuffs.

Sissy Spacek's culottes.

A movie theater ticket stub purchased from Pee Wee Herman.

A .45 automatic with registry papers showing it belonged to John J. Stompanato.

Tony Curtis's toga.

Linda Lovelace's mouthwash.

A handwritten death threat from Hunter S. Thompson to director Alex Cox.

Elizabeth Taylor's stuffed Pekingese.

Jack Nicholson's black silk Hermès blindfold.

Tallulah Bankhead's oxygen mask.

Tori Spelling's chastity belt.

Kevin Costner's wedding ring.

A pair of gold-plated brass knuckles engraved—"To Jilly—always, Frank."

Madonna's vibrator.

Erich von Stroheim's riding crop.

A wooden, leather-padded "exercise bar" purchased from Peter Bogdanovich.

The satin shorts John Garfield died in.

A love letter from Bob Dylan to Elizabeth Taylor.

Sean Young's James Woods voodoo doll.

Elvis's adult diaper.

Valentino's eyelashes.

A Polaroid, possibly taken by Robert Evans, of Henry Kissinger naked.

Bela Lugosi's teeth.

Gary Cooper's dentures.

Sharon Stone's Chrome Hearts hash pipe.

A piece of Jayne Mansfield's head.

A handwritten death threat from Hunter S. Thompson to director Terry Gilliam.

Howard Hughes's toenails.

CHAPTER 30

I Redeem Myself

RIZZO
Nobody hustles like a screenwriter hustles. Forget Sammy Glick.
But remember that Sammy was *created* by a screenwriter.

An Alan Smithee Film: Burn Hollywood Burn

I wrote *Magic Man* in the early eighties, twenty years after I left high school, to get even with all those snobs and elitist idiots who had made life so miserable when I was at Cathedral Latin.

The script was about a sixteen-year-old Hungarian kid named Karchy Jonas who lived on Cleveland's West Side and went to Cleveland Cathedral High School, where he was bullied by a bunch of snobbish elitist idiots.

It was about how Karchy got into the WHK High School Hall of Fame by sending in a bunch of postcards forged with his classmates' names. It was about how Karchy dreamed of becoming an American writer and about his relationship with a disc jockey named Billy Magic and a young, working-class woman who worked at the West Side Market named Diney.

When no one wanted to buy the script, I knew that getting even for high school humiliations wasn't the most lofty and literary reason to write something.

One day, years after Guy McElwaine had tried and failed to sell the script, I got a call from a producer named Carol Baum who ran Dolly Parton's production company.

She—and Dolly—had read and been moved by *Magic Man* and wanted to produce it.

It didn't mean that they were financing it. It meant that they would look for a financing entity as well as a director and stars . . . in return I would authorize them to produce the movie.

I said, "Does this mean I'm going to be meeting Dolly?"

Carol said, "Probably."

It wasn't true. I never met Dolly.

But I did meet their first choice to direct it—the successful director of many "hot" MTV videos.

We had dinner at Morton's and the video director started telling me how I should rewrite the script. I listened until he was finished and then said, "You've never directed a movie, have you?"

He said no but went into a rap about how each MTV video was "a movie in miniature" with its own "dramatic arc."

"Do I tell you how to make your MTV videos?" I asked him.

He smiled and said no.

"No," I said. "I don't tell you because I've never done an MTV video and I would feel like an asshole if I started telling you how to do one. Yet you—you've never done a movie, but you don't feel like an asshole telling me how to write one. How come?"

He looked at Carol Baum for help. Carol smiled at me. She wasn't going to help him.

"I've got it," I said. "*I know how come!* You're an asshole but you don't feel like you're an asshole because you don't know you're an asshole. Just like most directors. But I'm telling you: You're an asshole."

He didn't know what to say. He tried to laugh it off and left shortly afterward.

Joe Roth was the next would-be director of *Magic Man.* He had just directed a movie with an immigrant theme, *Streets of Gold,* written by Richard Price, and said that while he hadn't intended to do "another immigrant story," he'd been "charmed" by my script.

Joe and Carol and Dolly tried to get financing for it but weren't getting anywhere and one day Joe Roth asked to meet me in the bar of the Beverly Wilshire Hotel and told me he was moving on to another project: *Revenge of the Nerds II.*

I was disappointed, but I liked his honesty. In a town where no one ever does anything for the money, Joe Roth said, "I need the paycheck."

Chris Cain was a down-to-earth, folksy man who was most interested not in Karchy, the kid, but in Billy Magic, the disc jockey. He had just directed Jim Belushi in *The Principal* (a moderate hit) and the two were interested in working together again.

Chris sent the script to Jim, who wanted to play Magic, and Chris and Jim and Carol and Dolly went out looking for financing again.

Everybody passed again.

The Principal, I was told, hadn't been a *big enough* hit to justify financing *Magic Man.*

Even though it had been a hit, that didn't mean Jim Belushi was a star.

After my very public conflict with Michael Ovitz in 1989, Carol Baum and Dolly Parton faded away from *Magic Man.*

Carol stopped calling me.

I wasn't surprised.

Dolly, I knew, was represented by CAA and Ovitz. Not that I suspected Ovitz of saying to them: "I don't want you working with Eszterhas." I knew that in Hollywood people were so afraid of Ovitz that they wouldn't take the chance of giving him apoplexy by working with me.

A couple of months after the newspapers wrote about my letter to Ovitz, I was at dinner at Wolfgang Puck's Eureka in Santa Monica with Gerri and Steve and Suzi.

Sitting at the next table with a group of people was Dolly Parton.

She kept staring at me all night. It looked like she was studying me, like she was trying to answer for herself this question: Why isn't that suicidal lunatic sitting over there wearing a straitjacket?

For a while I tried to ignore her awestruck and awful stares but then I gave up.

When Gerri wasn't looking, I winked at her.

Dolly saw the wink and looked for a terrifying moment like she was going to spit her food across the tables at me.

But Dolly stopped staring.

At about the same time, I ran into Joe Roth, who had chosen to direct *Revenge of the Nerds II* instead of *Magic Man.*

I was sitting at the bar of the Ritz-Carlton Hotel in New York. Joe came in the bar door and looked right at me. I was only a few feet away from him.

I grinned and waved. He turned right around and went back out the door.

I thought we were friends. He had even introduced me to his father-in-law, the zany impresario Samuel Z. Arkoff, a man who wore a hat with a propeller on top of his head.

Post-Ovitz, it seemed, Joe wasn't my friend anymore.

Fran Kuzui had directed *Tokyo Pop,* an international film festival smash, and Guy McElwaine sent her *Magic Man.*

She wanted to direct it and was certain that, after *Tokyo Pop*'s critical success, she could get the financing for it. She was considering making it with Burt Reynolds.

Six months later, she was still looking for the financing.

A year later, she admitted defeat.

Sam Goldwyn, Jr., who ran his own production company, got the script from Guy and asked us to a meeting at the Friars Club. Sam loved *Magic Man*. He wanted to buy it. He was willing to pay $750,000 for it.

But I'd have to make one change.

Just one.

I'd have to make it a contemporary piece instead of a piece that took place in the sixties. And, in keeping with making it contemporary, Karchy Jonas would have to be a Latino kid in L.A. instead of a Hungarian kid in Cleveland.

In other words, Karchy Jonas couldn't be *me* anymore.

I said no soap.

Seven hundred fifty thousand dollars wasn't enough money to make me forget about getting even with those idiots at Cathedral Latin.

I didn't say *that* to Sam Goldwyn, of course.

I said I couldn't make the changes because the script was "too close to my heart and my roots."

That was a noble reason and not a petty and vindictive one.

Sam Goldwyn even said he admired me.

"I don't know a lot of writers who'd turn this kind of money down because of their hearts," he said.

He didn't know how angry I still was at Cathedral Latin, either.

Guy gave the script to his client John Candy, who asked me to meet him at his office, which I was amazed to see was a bar. His *own* bar! A fully stocked and decorated barroom with stools, chairs, tables, neon decorations, and a jukebox.

John was the bartender, standing behind the bar as I sat on a stool in front of him.

I thought I was a heavy smoker but I was a baby compared to John Candy. A cigarette was *never* out of his hand. Once he had two of them lighted up at the same time . . . and smoked them both . . . *at the same time.*

I thought I could drink, but I was a teetotaler compared to John Candy. I drank five bottles of Heineken while we were in his bar. He drank thirteen rum and Cokes.

(Guy had warned me: "John and I were in Monte Carlo. He was doing publicity. I came back to L.A.—he was supposed to be back the next day. A week later, he called me. He was still in Monte Carlo, still partying.")

We went from his bar to dinner a few blocks away on San Vincente. I drove. At dinner I had two more beers. John had eight more rum and Cokes.

"I'm begging to do this movie," John said. "Please. You've got to promise me you'll let me do it."

He said he was trying to change his image from the goofball funnyman to a real actor. He'd starred in several movies that had tanked recently.

"You've got it," I said. "I promise you."

He hugged me. He didn't just have tears in his eyes. He was nearly sobbing.

I was sure he was drunk.

I knew *I* was.

A couple of weeks later, as we were trying to get financing for *Magic Man* with John Candy attached to it, John fired Guy as his agent. He went to CAA.

I knew right away that John's next step was to bail out of *Magic Man*.

I was right.

Ronnie Meyer, his new agent at CAA, informed Guy that John didn't want to do *Magic Man* anymore.

I was furious. I called John and, to my amazement, he took my call. Standard Hollywood behavior in such cases is to pretend the telephone has not yet been invented.

"How can you do this to me?" I screamed at him. "You gave me your word—I gave you mine! I *lived up to* mine!"

He started to cry.

"Call Ronnie Meyer," he said. "He's the one who told me I can't do it!" John was *blubbering* now. "He said it would hurt my career. Call Ronnie. Talk to him. Maybe you'll change his mind. I hope you do. I want to do *Magic Man*. I want to be Billy Magic. It's a great script. Call him!"

I called Ronnie Meyer at CAA, never thinking it even possible that he'd take my call. I knew how close (then) Ronnie and Michael Ovitz were.

But I got right through.

I screamed at him, too. "You tell Candy that it would hurt his career if he did *Magic Man*?" I said. "Bullshit. You don't want him to do it because it's *my* script! Because of me! Because of what happened with me and Ovitz!"

Ronnie started screaming right back at me. "You hurt CAA! *You hurt my business!* You expect me to help you after you hurt my business? Fuck you!"

He hung up. Here he was, years later, *admitting* that CAA was still after me because of my letter to Ovitz.

Ronnie Meyer was a tough, no-bullshit ex-Marine. I had forgotten his reputation for always telling the truth . . . in a town where, at best, truth was ambiguous.

Nearly ten years went by.

Magic Man was as dead as Burt Reynolds's career . . . as Wolfgang Puck's Eureka . . . as Cathedral Latin High School, razed and the site of a parking lot . . . as dead as my marriage to Gerri . . . as dead as John Candy.

· · · ·

Naomi asked to read all the scripts I'd written.

Her favorite was *Magic Man*.

"It's sweet," she said. "It's moving. It doesn't have any violence. Even the sex is gently done."

She had a suggestion.

"I'd like to see more of the boy's father," she said. "He's too much in the background for me."

I rewrote the script, focusing on Karchy's father, who was somewhat—but only somewhat—patterned after my father.

Naomi loved the rewrite: "I think you can get four really strong actors into this now," she said. "For Karchy, Billy Magic, Diney, and now the dad."

She also loved the new title I came up with for the script: *Telling Lies in America*.

I changed the title not because I didn't like *Magic Man* but to make it appear that this was a brand-new script.

It had been around for so long that there had been a change of generations at the top studio levels.

Many of today's executives wouldn't remember a script called *Magic Man* but if they went to their computers, they'd find it, along with readers' reports, which would or wouldn't be friendly.

By changing the title, I made sure that no studio readers' reports would be uncovered.

At about the same time, Fran Kuzui, the director of *Tokyo Pop*, whom I hadn't seen in all this time, was having lunch with a friend: a young director named Guy Ferland.

Guy told her he was working on a coming-of-age piece that he hoped to get financed and direct. Fran told him about the best coming-of-age piece she'd ever read: *Magic Man*.

Guy was incredulous. The author of *Basic Instinct* and *Sliver* and *Showgirls* had done a coming-of-age piece that Fran thought was the best she'd ever read?

"I'll send it to you, read it," Fran said.

Guy read it and called her. "*This* is the piece I want to direct," Guy said.

Fran said, "I'll call Joe."

Guy Ferland and I met and I told him about the new draft I'd done called *Telling Lies in America*. He read it and was very excited. I was, too. I liked Guy's sensitive approach to the piece.

He agreed with Naomi: he thought it possible that we could get four top-notch actors.

Financing wouldn't be easy, but Guy thought he could do the movie on a bare-bones budget and shoot it on location in Cleveland.

Fran Kuzui (my angel) and her husband had a production company of their own and Fran thought they could provide some of the financing.

Guy Ferland took the script to some friends of his at a new company called Banner Entertainment and they agreed to provide the bulk of the financing—*if* we would all agree to take very little money for our efforts.

I agreed to take $100,000 for the script.

I insisted, however, that since my rewrite was Naomi's idea, Naomi be made executive producer (at no fee, but with her own director's chair).

Casting came together quickly.

Brad Renfro, only fourteen years old but already an actor of enormous talent and potential, agreed to play Karchy Jonas.

Kevin Bacon, a superb actor who had somehow never been nominated for an Oscar, agreed to play Billy Magic.

Calista Flockhart was Guy Ferland's discovery. A relative unknown when Guy cast her as Diney, she was on the cover of magazines only a few years later as Ally McBeal.

Maximilian Schell agreed to play Karchy Jonas's father after a conversation with me. I had enormous respect for Max—both as an actor and as a human being. His courageous anti-Nazi stands in Europe had made him a hero to many Europeans.

"Where are you right now, Max?" I asked him over the phone.

"I am at a little farmhouse in Austria," he said. "I can see the Hungarian border from where I am. Where are you?"

"I am on the island of Maui," I said. "I can see a rainbow over the sea from where I am."

"But *you* are Hungarian," Max said. "You should be *here* looking at your border and I should be *there* sitting in the sun and looking at the rainbow."

I laughed and Max said, "Ach! There is never justice in the world!"

"Yes," I said. "On occasion there is!"

Max thought that was funny.

Max wanted $100,000 to do the movie.

The Banner executives explained to his agents that we were doing this on an extremely low budget . . . and that Max's part was the *fourth* lead. On a low-budget film, $100,000 for the *fourth* lead is astronomical excess.

Max's agents said they'd speak to him and when they called back they said Max was firm about the money. His part may have been the fourth lead, his agents said, but Max would have to come to Cleveland, Ohio.

That, his agents added, was a long way from Austria. It was also not exactly New York or L.A. or London or Rome or Paris.

The price of having to go to Cleveland, Ohio, was $100,000.

His agents also said Max had instructed them to ask this question:

How much was Joe Eszterhas being paid?

We had another actor begging us to play the part, but Guy Ferland felt it sounded too much like "stunt casting."

Charles Bronson was in his seventies now but he related to the story thanks to his own immigrant roots.

It made me smile, though.

A choice between Maximilian Schell and Charles Bronson. How many parts were there which attracted both of *those* men?

I said to the Banner executives: Okay, give Max *my* $100,000.

I was now being paid nothing to effect my revenge on my high school enemies at Cathedral Latin.

But I was happy to pay the anti-Nazi crusader Maximilian Schell $100,000 of my own money . . . to effect a very personal revenge on my anti-Semitic father . . . whom Max would play in the movie.

Kevin was doing the movie almost for free. He loved the part.

"Billy Magic is a very sexual character," he said. "Sex and music are the essence of what's flowing through his veins."

He and Brad Renfro had worked together in *Sleepers,* where Kevin played a prison guard who raped Brad. Now he was playing a role model who was corrupting him.

Brad was the oldest fourteen-year-old I had ever met. He played a mean blues guitar and liked beer. The bartenders at the hotel where he was staying obliged him and he spent some nights playing his guitar on the small bar's stage.

Girls surrounded him, driven to the hotel by their mothers, who waited in the car while Brad busied himself entertaining them.

At fourteen, he was already a chain-smoker. He fell in love with the Vietnam souvenir lighter that I carried. It said, "Vietnam—66–67 Phu Rieng." Underneath that, it said, "Water. Never touch the stuff. Fish fuck in it, you know."

I gave Brad the lighter and he was overjoyed.

I had others at home that said: "Ours is not to do or die, ours is to smoke and stay high."

And: "Being in the army is like a rubber. It gives you a feeling of security while you're getting fucked."

And: "There is no gravity. The world sucks."

. . .

I gave a small speaking part to my brother-in-law Joe Baka, a steelworker from Mansfield, Ohio, who had never had any acting experience and who did it as a hoot.

Bep thinned down, got into character, and was so good that agents began trying to sign him up. After the movie's release, while on a flight to visit us in Malibu, the stewardess *recognized* him.

Tempted to become an actor, Joe Baka, no dummy, hurried back to his steel plant in Ohio.

I was standing in the parking lot of the Num Num Potato Chip factory, where I had played ball as a kid, being interviewed by an NBC camera crew.

I told them about playing ball right here in the Num Num Potato Chip factory parking lot and as I was speaking, an old lady came over and handed me something. It was a free dinner coupon for two at . . . Nick's Diner, where my father had yelled "Frankfoorter! Frankfoorter!" at the top of his lungs and where my mother had fled alone after the Hungarian ball.

After the interview was over Naomi and I walked down to Nick's Diner to have a cup of coffee at the counter.

I felt tears in my eyes but forced myself to stop them and forced myself to smile.

The NBC cameras were outside, shooting us at the counter through the window.

Dick Jacobs, the owner of my revered Cleveland Indians, asked some of us from the movie to his private loge at Jacobs Field. I had long admired Jacobs, a grand old man in his seventies who had done more to revitalize Cleveland than maybe anyone else.

Brad Renfro was there, sneaking sips of beer that he thought no one noticed and dragging on a cigarette in the no-smoking seats.

"This is really amazing; what you've done with this ballpark," Brad said to Dick Jacobs. "It's beautiful."

"Aw," Dick Jacobs smiled, "don't flatter me."

"I'm not fucking flattering you," Brad Renfro said. "I wouldn't fucking flatter you. I'm serious."

Dick Jacobs's face turned red and his hands started to tremble. "You have very bad manners, young man," he said and walked away.

Naomi walked after him. "Dick, please," she said. "He's a kid. He didn't mean anything. He's only fourteen years old."

"At this rate," Dick Jacobs said, "he won't see twenty."

. . .

I wanted Maximilian Schell to be happy. When he arrived from Europe (with his daughter and her nanny), I took him to one of Cleveland's best restaurants, Johnny's Downtown. Max was tired and he had a cold and all he wanted was a bowl of vichyssoise.

Johnny's didn't have vichyssoise.

Maximilian Schell didn't want anything else.

I had a few words with the maître d', who sent someone scurrying to a nearby supermarket, and Maximilian Schell had a bowl of vichyssoise in front of him within ten minutes.

"I think this may be the best vichyssoise I've ever had," Maximilian Schell said. "Who would have thought I'd have the best vichyssoise of my life in Cleveland?"

When Max Schell found out that the character he was playing was based on my father, he asked if he could visit him.

I drove him out to my father's house and Max asked him if he could take some articles of my father's clothing to wear in the film and "get into character."

I knew that Max usually kept all the clothes he wore in films and wore them in real life. I told my father that and my father gave up his beret and one of his Hungarian peasant hats.

I knew that Maximilian Schell had devoted his life, at great personal cost, to fighting the Nazis and I wondered how he would feel if he knew that the beret and peasant hat he wore had once been worn by . . . an alleged war criminal.

And I thought: who could have imagined, back there on Lorain Avenue, that one day Maximilian Schell, the world-famous actor, would someday be wearing my father's beret?

Thinking back to those early days on Lorain Avenue from now on, I wondered: Would I see Maximilian Schell in that beret instead of my father?

During his visit to my father's house, Max asked if he had any tapes so Max could study my father's accent.

My father said there was a tape of a Hungarian television interview in his bookcase. Naomi went to get it and popped it into the VCR while Max kept talking to my father.

When I saw what came up on the screen, I motioned quickly to Naomi to turn it off.

It was a tape of a Hungarian movie from the forties filled with Nazi anti-Semitic harangues about the Zsidos.

"Wrong tape," I said to Max, who, busy talking to my father, hadn't seen it.

· · ·

The movie was finished and we were looking for a distributor to put it into theaters.

Our best shot was Miramax. The head of Miramax, Harvey Weinstein, and his wife came to see a rough cut in Beverly Hills on a Saturday afternoon. Harvey was restless during the screening and wandered around getting himself something to drink. But his wife was crying as she watched it.

"It's a terrific picture," Harvey said afterward. "But I gotta think about it."

"I loved it," his wife said. "I was moved."

Harvey Weinstein wrote me a note saying that he'd liked *Telling Lies* very much but that after great deliberation and against his wife's advice, he had decided not to distribute it.

I wrote him this note:

> *"I take no shit from nobody,"* Karchy Jonas says in Telling Lies. *I've lived my life that way and the first time I saw you, many years ago, taking the room over at the Ivy, I recognized a kindred spirit.*
>
> *This movie might find a distributor, but it will not find a home. You are its home.*
>
> *I ask you this . . . and it's something I have learned in only the past three years: listen, please, to your wife, as I listen to mine. It was Naomi who made the suggestions about* Telling Lies *that made me rewrite it. Women, I've learned, are smarter than we are. And I think, incidentally, women will love this movie—if they get a real chance to see it. Which brings me back to you. You would give people that "real chance."*
>
> *I have the feeling that your involvement with this is the difference between a hit movie and a barely remembered one.*
>
> *Maybe it's because I sense that you and I, in different ways, from different backgrounds, are both Karchy Jonas.*
>
> *At any rate, I ask you to reconsider your decision.*

Harvey thought about it some more and stuck to his decision: Miramax would not distribute *Telling Lies in America*.

While we were looking for a distributor, I called Joe Roth and asked him to see the movie. He was once going to direct it; now he was one of the studio heads at Disney.

Joe saw it and called me back quickly.

"It didn't do much for me," he said. "*I* wouldn't have done it that way."

We still didn't have a distributor, but we were getting rave reviews. Even *I* was getting rave reviews!

"Here's a surprise," wrote David Ansen in *Newsweek*. "Joe Eszterhas, the writer who inflicted *Showgirls* and *Basic Instinct* upon the world, redeems himself with this autobiographical tale."

"I loved this movie," said Roger Ebert. "This is one of the very best performances Kevin Bacon has ever given. The movie is so wonderful in terms of the relationship between the broken-down disc jockey and this young kid. And the disc jockey himself, what a rich character! This is really one of Eszterhas's best pieces of writing."

"Little that Joe Eszterhas has done for the screen would deem him likely to write something like *Telling Lies in America*. . . . There's a sweetness and an integrity here that seem completely out of character for this writer," wrote Marshall Fine for the Gannett Newspapers.

"The movie proves that Mr. Eszterhas still possesses sharp dramatic instincts," wrote the *New York Times*.

The Nation wrote, "Add this to the list of cinema's small but lasting pleasures: the sight of young Brad Renfro, in the role of the Hungarian immigrant Karchy Jonas, learning to pronounce 'the' in *Telling Lies in America*. . . . Yes, there's a movie now in the theaters in which a character faces a moral crisis. . . . But the most remarkable aspect of *Telling Lies in America* is unquestionably the identity of its screenwriter—the man responsible for the scripts of *Basic Instinct* and *Showgirls*. Until now, he has hardly made himself known as a framer of moral dilemmas, his characters' thoughts having tended, shall we say, toward the pudential. . . . Eszterhas once had a reason to write: every part of the world around him was scary and beautiful."

Not that *Telling Lies* won all the critics over. Carrie Rickey of the *Philadelphia Inquirer*, who trotted out the shrinks to analyze my parents' sex life after *Showgirls*, called *Telling Lies* "as cynical as its villain (Billy Magic) . . . as contemptuous and contemptible a piece of work as has ever been made."

Jay Carr of the *Boston Globe* was touting Kevin Bacon for an Oscar . . .

Telling Lies was picked to be shown at the prestigious New York Film Festival . . .

But the movie never found a distributor.

Banner Entertainment valiantly tried to release it itself, but *Telling Lies* failed commercially.

Everyone involved with the movie looked forward to attending the New York Film Festival. The movie's inclusion was truly an honor (the only American film selected besides Robert Duvall's *The Apostle*) and the media coverage would be celebratory and huge. But two weeks before the festival screening,

Naomi gave birth to John Law Eszterhas in Santa Monica. She developed a staph infection.

If Naomi couldn't go to New York, I decided, I wouldn't go either. The rewrite which made the movie work had been her idea.

The night of the festival screening in New York, I grilled hot dogs and burgers in Malibu.

Telling Lies opened the Cleveland Film Festival as well and, after the showing, I was signing autographs and having my picture taken when a man my age stopped me and said, "Joe, you probably don't remember me, but would you mind if I have a picture taken with you?"

I recognized him immediately. He was one of the kids at Cathedral Latin who had been ugly to me.

"I remember you, Marty," I said.

"You do?" he said with a sheepish half smile.

"I'm sorry," I said, "I don't take pictures with others," and turned away . . . to a man named George Gund, who is one of Cleveland's wealthiest and most famous men . . . and who was standing there asking if I would have a picture taken with him.

I put my arm around George Gund and smiled as he put an arm around me . . . as Marty from Cathedral Latin stood there staring at the two of us.

Weeks after *Telling Lies in America* was selected by the New York Film Festival, I got a letter from its director asking me for money.

I didn't know if this was the way film festivals worked: first they flatter you; then they ask you for money.

The letter explained that they wanted to use my money so that André De Toth, my fellow Hungarian, could attend a festival tribute in his honor.

Bandi Toth was in his nineties now and couldn't afford the travel fare. He had directed *Ramrod* and *Tanganyika,* movies which the critics said were "noted for their casual attitude toward violence and treachery"—things which had been said about my own movies as well.

A penniless old Hungarian director of violent films would be on his way to a fancy New York tribute if I paid his way.

But there was no way I was paying it.

I disliked Bandi Toth intensely.

Bandi had single-handedly driven the divine Veronica Lake, one of my all-time cinematic loves, off the screen. By marrying her.

Bandi ruined her sex life. "Whoever made up that line, wham-bam-thank-you-ma'am, must have had Bandi in mind," Veronica Lake said. When she left him, she had to spend three months alone on a mountain to cool out. And when she came off the mountaintop, Veronica Lake said, "Fuck you, Hollywood, you're one giant self-contained orgy farm with every male in the movie business on the make."

She never made another movie. She moved to New York and washed dishes in a restaurant. The only time she ever came back to L.A. was to pick up the papers of her divorce from Bandi Toth.

I was grateful that the New York Film Festival had selected *Telling Lies* ... but I wasn't giving a penny to the Hungarian who'd retired Veronica Lake.

The producer Don Simpson told me the best high school revenge story I've ever heard: "I was a complete nerd when I was in high school," Don said, "a fat little kid with his nose always stuck in a book. Never mind getting any pussy, I couldn't even get a date. I took a lot of shit from a lot of kids. Cut to me as a big-time, star Hollywood producer and it's time for my twentieth high school reunion. In Anchorage, Alaska. I hired a helicopter and two Penthouse Pets. We choppered onto the football field where the reunion was being held. I got off the chopper with the Pets. I looked skinny and sensational. I hadn't eaten any solid food for three weeks. I wore a white suit. Man, their jaws dropped. I mean—they shit themselves. I stayed about thirty minutes and then with a Pet on each arm, I got back on the chopper and they watched as I disappeared into the sky. *Motherfucker!* The best moment of my life!"

CHAPTER 31

I Burn Hollywood

JOHNNY BOY

I'm smarter than most. And I'm more vicious. I'm past all the boundaries. Listen to me closely. *Don't fuck with me!* Please. This is good advice. *Don't fuck with me!*

Gangland, unproduced

I felt like writing something different. I sat down on the Friday before a holiday and finished it Monday night. I wrote it for myself—as a goof.

The original title was *Amok,* although I changed it to *An Alan Smithee Film* before I was finished with the first draft.

It was a Hollywood satire. It incorporated many of the anecdotes and incidents which I had either heard, experienced, or suffered in the course of more than two decades of screenwriting. The style was that of a mock-documentary: talking heads telling their stories to the camera.

It used the names of real Hollywood players and the script called for three industry superstars—Schwarzenegger, Bruce Willis, and Sly Stallone to play themselves.

The Directors Guild's official pseudonym was "Alan Smithee." It meant that if any director felt that his movie had been ruined by a producer or studio, he could put the name "Alan Smithee" on the credits instead of his own. The credit "Alan Smithee" on a film was an immediate signal to critics and the public that the director felt that the movie had been botched.

While "Alan Smithee" was the Directors Guild's official pseudonym, the Guild had not bothered to copyright the name.

It meant that any troublemaking screenwriter could kidnap "Alan Smithee" and use him for his own twisted, perhaps even malicious ends.

. . .

We were sitting in the William Morris Agency's fanciest conference room and Arnold Rifkin—I'd not yet fired him—my agent and the head of the agency, said: "Put this script in a drawer, forget you wrote it. It's going to hurt your career and mine. It's bad for the industry."

"What are you?" Naomi said to him. "The poster boy for the industry?"

I took the Dogon fighting stick which I sometimes carried and slammed it into the ornate conference table, leaving a big dent.

Arnold Rifkin started waving his arms about, flashing the red and orange Masai bracelet which he had bought on his most recent safari.

We both stormed out of the room. Naomi ran to me and then ran to Arnold and we all went back to the conference room.

"Damage control," Naomi said to Rifkin, "is what I do."

Rifkin felt the dent I had left on the table with both hands and said that even though he didn't believe in the script, he'd try his best to see that someone bought it and made it.

And, since he represented Bruce Willis, he'd send the script to Bruce and to Bruce's *body double* in the hope that one of them would agree to be in it.

I decided to *Samizdat* the script like Solzhenitsyn.

A friend of mine and I Xeroxed it and sent it all over town. To anyone and everyone. I had to get people to read it. I had to get around my own agent's fear of it.

The script made its way around town.

The Hollywood trades wrote about it.

Arnold Schwarzenegger got very angry, Arnold's brother-in-law told me. Arnold didn't like reading about being in a movie whose script he hadn't even read.

I wrote Arnold Schwarzenegger a letter:

> *Dear Arnold,*
>
> *You are Austrian. I am Hungarian. There was once an Austro-Hungarian Empire. In 1848, the Hungarians revolted against the Austrians. We lost.*
>
> *The Austrians were very gracious to the Hungarians after the Hungarians made such fools of themselves in 1848. I guess history repeats itself. Can we get together and discuss changing the course of history?*

I signed the letter with my name, and in parentheses put the word "*Forehead.*"

It was Arnold's personal term, his brother-in-law told me, for people he considered fools—as in "Vat ees wrong vit that focking forehead Hungarian?"

Arnold Schwarzenegger wasn't amused by my letter or by my foolish "*Forehead*" witticism.

He didn't answer me.

Sly Stallone got the script through a mutual friend in Miami.

Sly thought the script was hilarious and said he'd do it. "If I can't laugh at myself after all the good things that have happened to me in this business," he said, "who can?"

On a personal note, he added, "You've certainly gotten crazier through the years."

Bruce Willis, Arnold Rifkin told me, was "a pass."

As the script made its way around town in the Solzhenitsyn manner, it started getting positive response from studio heads, producers, and directors.

Steven Spielberg wrote, "I had a chance to read *An Alan Smithee Film* over the weekend and I liked it a lot. It's funny and very wicked. . . . For your information, about sixteen years ago I developed a movie with Gary David Goldberg called *Reel to Reel* which was somewhat similar in tone to your film. Sixteen years later, I obviously have not made the movie, so perhaps I'm just a little over-cautious about telling a show business story which I'm too close to."

Arthur Hiller, in his seventies now but the director of *The Americanization of Emily* and *Love Story*, wrote: "Joe's done it again. This is an original, brilliant, and tricky satire on our industry . . . if Joe doesn't change anything, it's not to complain. It's a very clever parody, with wonderful characters and needless to say an original concept. Hollywood at its truest and funniest."

Bruce Willis's *body double*, Arnold Rifkin told me, was also "a pass."

Whoopi Goldberg hadn't read the script but she read *about* it in the trades.

She called Arnold Rifkin, also her agent, and said, "If I'm not in this movie by the end of the day, you're fired."

Knowing what Whoopi said to him . . . and remembering the dent I'd had to leave in the William Morris conference room table . . . I made Arnold beg me to put Whoopi into the movie.

I finally agreed to cast her—but only, I said to Arnold, "as a favor to you."

I told the press Whoopi was replacing Schwarzenegger, who, of course, hadn't even read the script let alone agreed to be in the movie.

"Whoopi," I said, "will be much better than Arnold Schwarzenegger."

Arnold's brother-in-law called to tell me that Arnold was now "very angry."

I said, "He was very angry before, wasn't he?"

"No," the brother-in-law said, "he was angry before. Now he's *very* angry."

My fellow Hungarian Andy Vajna at Cinergi told Arnold Rifkin that he would make the movie on a $10 million budget—my fee would be $250,000—if we were able to find three superstars who would play themselves.

Vajna said he was happy about Sly and Whoopi but disappointed about Arnold and Bruce. (He didn't mention Bruce's body double.)

Arnold Rifkin, perhaps feeling a little guilty about his earlier trepidations, promised Andy Vajna that he would personally find the third superstar.

Vajna took Arnold's word for it.

We had a deal.

We also had a go-movie.

The director I wanted to make it with was Milcho Manchevski. He had directed the critically acclaimed *Before the Rain* and done some visually startling MTV videos.

The choice was fine with Andy Vajna and Milcho started budgeting the script.

After wrangling over the budget with Cinergi, Milcho decided he couldn't make the movie on a $10 million budget and withdrew.

He also withdrew because I wouldn't let him dress Whoopi in the nun's habit she had worn in *Sister Act*. An internationally acclaimed auteur director, Milcho wasn't used to any screenwriter telling him what to do.

I told Milcho that I wasn't telling him what to do as the *screenwriter* . . . I was telling him what to do as a *producer*.

Milcho didn't buy it and, as his agent at William Morris said, was "a Pass-adena!"

I sent the script to Bob Rafelson, who came to my house and told me he wanted to direct it.

He wanted to make one change. He wanted to change Smithee, the screwed-over director, to Smithee, the screwed-over screenwriter.

I told Bob that I was tired of hearing about screwed-over screenwriters and that the more screenwriters heard about being screwed over, the more likely it was that they would volunteer to be screwed over in the future.

I said to Bob, "So why should I make this change?"

Bob said, "Because if you make the change, then I will direct the movie."

I said to Bob, "You're not worth it."

· · ·

About a year later I saw Bob at the outdoor patio of the Peninsula Hotel. He saw me and got up from his table and suddenly stopped and said, "I'm only coming halfway."

I got up from my table and went to where he was standing and we hugged . . . halfway.

I realized as I was hugging him that, a quarter century earlier, he was the first director I'd ever worked with.

He had been fired by United Artists before he'd ever been hired for *F.I.S.T.*, my first movie.

As I hugged him now, I said, "You wanna do the sequel to *F.I.S.T.*?"

Bob laughed.

I told the press that this $10 million production would be "the most expensive home movie in Hollywood history."

Andy Vajna got angry at me.

"I'm paying ten million dollars for a home movie?" he somewhat heatedly asked me. "How does that make me look?"

I remembered the letter Arthur Hiller had written. I liked Arthur enormously. I called and asked him if he wanted to direct *Smithee*.

He called me back the next day with a yes.

Both Cinergi and I were happy.

I loved the irony of the president of the Academy of Motion Picture Arts and Sciences directing a movie that made "very wicked" (Spielberg's words) fun of Hollywood.

Arthur Hiller had directed not only *The Americanization of Emily* for Paddy Chayefsky, he had also directed *The Hospital* for him.

I figured if Arthur was good enough twice for Paddy Chayefsky, he was good enough for me!

We had our third superstar. Jackie Chan would play himself, replacing Bruce Willis and/or his body double.

As I retailored the script for Jackie (not easy: he couldn't speak English), Arthur started casting the movie.

Naomi suggested Ryan O'Neal, producer Ben Myron suggested Chuck D. and Coolio, I suggested Sandra Bernhard, and Arthur handled the rest of it. He picked Eric Idle over Mick Jagger and Michael York, Richard Jeni over David Paymer, and Ryan O'Neal over Mickey Rourke.

Ryan O'Neal came over to our house and fawned over my script for two hours.

His fawning didn't surprise me. I knew that he knew that I knew that he was pretty much unemployable in Hollywood.

We drank two bottles of red wine.

When he left, he hugged me and then he *really* hugged Naomi.

The heroes of the piece, two street-smart and very cool black filmmakers, were based on Allen and Albert Hughes, who were originally going to play themselves.

The Hughes brothers, two of my Hollywood heroes, directors of *Menace II Society* and *Dead Presidents,* had even worked on their dialogue with me. But at the last minute, they decided they weren't comfortable playing themselves.

"Naw, man," Allen said. "Come on, dude. We're not *actors.*"

The Hughes brothers became the fictional "Brothers Brothers."

The character Sam Rizzo, a fictional private eye, was based on the real-life Hollywood private eye Anthony Pellicano.

In the original draft, Sam Rizzo's name was even Anthony Pellicano and Tony was going to play himself.

When Sylvester Stallone agreed to play himself and discovered that Anthony Pellicano was going to be in *Smithee,* Sly threatened to back out of the movie. He and Pellicano had been on opposite sides in a lawsuit.

I had to inform Tony that I had to fire him (from playing himself) because of Sly.

"Then who's gonna play me?" he asked.

"I don't know yet."

"Jesus," he said, "you write a part that's me, you have me playing me and using my own name, and now it's *all gone?*"

I called him back a couple of weeks later and told him that the head of Miramax, Harvey Weinstein, had volunteered to play the part.

"You're going to cast Harvey Weinstein as me?" Tony said in disbelief. "*Harvey Weinstein?* You take my persona, you take my name, and now you're going to turn me into Harvey Weinstein? I didn't do anything to deserve this!"

I changed the character's name from Anthony Pellicano to Sam Rizzo.

We needed to find an interesting-looking bartender for a scene.

I suggested Michael Ovitz to Arthur Hiller.

I thought Michael would make a sensational bartender.

Arthur thought it was a great idea and got in touch with him. Michael thanked Arthur but said he was busy.

Michael said he had also turned Albert Brooks down on another film.

Sly Stallone came out to our Malibu house a few days before the shoot began.

It was an adventure getting him there. Sly hadn't driven for a long time—his L.A. driver was having a family emergency. He was so nervous driving himself through L.A. traffic that he kept his agent, Arnold Rifkin, on the car phone speaker all the way from Beverly Hills to Malibu.

Arnold made sure Sly didn't have an anxiety attack or get lost.

When he arrived at our house, Sly was out of breath.

I wasn't sure what Sly wanted, although Arnold warned me that Sly hadn't yet signed his *Smithee* deal.

What Sly wanted, I quickly discovered in my living room, was for me to write a script for him where he could play a televangelist.

Since he hadn't signed his *Smithee* deal yet, I said I would . . . if he could get a deal from a studio.

Sly and I went to see Ronnie Meyer and a roomful of executives at Universal a few days later and tried to talk him into financing a script where Sly would play a televangelist.

Ronnie Meyer was Sly's former agent, but he fell asleep during the meeting.

Shortly after I tried to talk Universal into letting me write the script for Sly, Sly signed his *Smithee* deal.

On the way over to that Universal meeting, Sly and I had a heart-to-heart about writing.

He hadn't written a script for a long time and wondered why.

"Probably because you've had your head in pussy for the past thirty years," I said.

Sly laughed and said, "You know what? You're probably right."

Sly only had one day to shoot.

He hadn't memorized any of his scenes, it turned out.

He improvised all of it—every line of every scene.

More than twenty years ago, I had threatened to punch him out for changing my script in *F.I.S.T.*

Now, he and I were pals and he was changing my script of *Smithee.*

Chuck D. asked me to introduce him to Jackie Chan, who was his hero.

Chuck asked Jackie for his autograph.

I introduced Chuck to Whoopi Goldberg, too.

Whoopi's daughter was there and she asked Chuck for his autograph. He was *her* hero.

Bob Shapiro, my friend and lawyer and now, thanks to O. J. Simpson, one of the most famous men in the world, was on the set and asked me to introduce him to Sly.

Sly saw us coming toward him, got up, and started walking away.

I hurried after him.

"Hey, Sly," I said, "I wanted to introduce you to—"

"Get that motherfucker away from me!" Sly said. "I don't even want to look at him."

Bob Shapiro overheard him and turned away.

I went after him and said, "I'm sorry, Bob."

"Forget it," Bob Shapiro said. There were tears in his eyes.

Robert Evans had a love scene with the young and sultry Leslie Stefanson in Bob's pool.

He asked me for Leslie's phone number afterward.

I refused to give it to him.

Evans said, "You cocksucker, you're just a screenwriter, remember?"

Ryan O'Neal met Leslie Stefanson on the set, dumped Farrah Fawcett, his long-time love, and began living with Leslie.

Now Evans was really angry.

Ryan O'Neal had "stolen" the young woman whose phone number I wouldn't give him.

Evans and Ryan had "history together" as they say in Hollywood. While Evans was married to Ali MacGraw, Ali had an affair with Ryan.

So this was the second time Ryan had "robbed" Bob.

Deep into the shoot, Fred Leopold, the former mayor of Beverly Hills, an esteemed and venerable libel lawyer hired by Cinergi, raised objections to some lines in the script.

I wrote him a letter:

> *Dear Mr. Leopold:*
>
> *You have told me to remove the reference "In love with Michael Sovitz" on the fictional character Gary Samuels's card. Gary Samuels is an agent and I don't see any reason why he couldn't be in love with the fictional character Michael Sovitz. We changed the name Janet Maslin to Sheila Maslin to Sheila Caslin at your mandate. If the change Caslin for Maslin satisfied you, I don't understand why the change Sovitz for Ovitz doesn't.*
>
> *You have told me to remove the reference to the different fictional Saudi princes as well as to Hugh Grant. In a previous memo, you told me your-self that there are no such living Saudi Arabian princes and that the names themselves are unlike names that Saudi princes or Arabs anywhere*

would use. Then what is the problem? Your suggestion that I replace the names with the phrase "various Saudi princes" isn't funny. Please let me be the judge of what's funny and what isn't—I suspect I may have a better sense of humor than you do.

As far as removing Hugh Grant's name—let me remind you. Hugh Grant was arrested for hiring a hooker to blow him. The blow job became one of the most celebrated blow jobs in history. Hugh Grant copped—I purposely chose the word—to being blown on every talk show in the country. The blow job became a standing joke on Letterman, Leno, and Saturday Night Live. Are you really trying to tell me that to say that a woman with a checkered personal history like the fictional Aloe Vera has a lust for Hugh Grant is a libel or slander upon Hugh Grant's character?

You have told me to remove the reference to Sean Penn. It is a Sly Stallone improvised line: "If you don't get that camera out of my face, I'm gonna Sean Penn your ass!" Sean Penn has a lengthy and public history of beating up photographers. He even went to jail for it. His proclivity for beating up photographers has, once again, been the butt of jokes on every comedy show out there. What's the problem? Are you a friend of his? (I am.) Do you represent him?

I hope that I will hear from you soon and that you will end all this silliness.

The esteemed and venerable Leopold, who didn't represent Sean, probably tired of dealing with me, backed off.

As the shoot ended, Arthur Hiller and I couldn't have been happier.

But the first screening of the movie didn't go well.

It was my fault, not Arthur's. Arthur had shot every word of my script—a mock, all-talk documentary.

And the research screening audience drowned in all the words.

The only solution, I felt, was to cut the film drastically and add humorous, counterpointing music (the only music in Arthur's cut was "Hooray for Hollywood").

At Cinergi's request, I did my own cut of the movie.

I cut twenty-two minutes of my own words.

I put together a temporary musical score using well-known rock music.

Even though he disapproved of my cuts and disapproved of me cutting "his" movie, Arthur, in a heroic act of kindness, sat next to me in the editing room and helped me to do it.

. . .

Cinergi liked my cut and not Arthur's and made a decision to release mine in theaters.

Arthur felt he wasn't being given a fair shake by Cinergi. His rough cut wasn't a director's cut, he said, but only a "rough assembly." He felt he was owed further cuts and screenings.

But Cinergi's decision was firm: my cut would go into the theaters.

After a successful screening of my cut, I said, "Arthur, you should kiss my ass in Times Square for putting all this work into the cut."

The next day, at a meeting at Cinergi, Arthur agreed to go out into theaters with my cut and said, "I've already called Mayor Giuliani to make reservations for Times Square."

We laughed and hugged.

The following afternoon, without explanation, by fax, Arthur Hiller resigned from the film.

An Alan Smithee Film was now an Alan Smithee film.

The credits would say "Written by Joe Eszterhas, directed by Alan Smithee."

The press was all over Arthur and me.

The whole world thought the two of us had conspired in a gigantic publicity stunt.

The day after Arthur resigned, I was sitting in an editing room in Hollywood with a migraine headache.

I was finishing the cut of a movie—something I had never done before.

Cinergi, which had serious financial problems, informed me there was no more money:

A. To continue the editing process.

B. For the temporary music I was using for screenings.

C. For any music at all.

I agreed to waive my $250,000 fee so we could continue the editing process. But I had no idea how we'd be able to get any money to have any music in the movie. As I sat there, holding my head, Arthur, who had just resigned, walked in with a smile on his face.

"Well," he said, "I just thought you might need some help. If you do, I'm here."

I was getting up at four in the morning in Malibu to be in an editing room in Burbank by seven.

I finished at seven at night, got home at nine, and got up the next morning at four.

I did this for three months.

I hardly saw Naomi and the babies.

And I wasn't being paid a penny for any of it.

At a certain point, God spoke to me.

"*Putz*," God said. "*This is what* directors *do. It's time you finally realized that. You'd better be very nice to every director you work with in the future.*"

I promised God on the lives of my children that I would be.

Richard Jeni, the young comedian who played the studio head in the movie, wrote me a note: "I have to say it was an honor to be in your film. I have to say that because I got paid scale and I'd feel really stupid if it wasn't an honor. Thanks again for your support and encouraging words. If I had to sum up the experience in one word, that word would be: Fuckingreat!"

I was finally finished editing the film and now it was time to edit the music, which I thought the movie badly needed to relieve the unending stream of words and talking heads.

But Andy Vajna reiterated it: No more money. Not a cent more.

Desperate, I placed an ad in the trades begging unsigned talent for free music. A songwriters' organization published an ad attacking me. Editorialists accused me of "ripping off" unsigned talent.

But I received 9,200 entries from all over the world. I sat down in my den from seven in the morning till seven at night listening to it all myself. It took about a month.

Andrew Shack, the head of Priority Records, who'd seen my ads, asked to see the rough cut of the movie. He enjoyed the movie, listened to some of the music that was coming in from everywhere, and made an album tie-in deal with us.

The artists whose "free music" would be in the movie would be paid and paid again if their songs wound up on the Priority CD.

No one was getting ripped off and I had miraculously gotten music for my movie.

We didn't have film titles, though. Every movie had to have film titles. We didn't and, I was so tired of hearing it . . . *there was no more money!*

What was I going to do now? Put an ad in the trades for free titles at the beginning and at the end of the movie?

I decided to seek out some of the best graffiti artists in Los Angeles. I told them I needed titles for my movie. I showed them the rough cut. They said they were "down" with it. They painted some striking, beautiful sketches.

I paid them out of my own pocket.

I had my titles.

· · ·

I wanted to place a card at the end of the film, before final credits, which said, "Special thanks to Arthur Hiller."

I told Arthur what I wanted to do, he thanked me and said it was fine with him, but thought I should check with the Directors Guild.

I called the Guild.

The Guild voice, very sternly, said I would not be allowed to thank Arthur Hiller.

"*This is an Alan Smithee film!*" the voice said, almost spitting the words.

I turned the finished print over to Cinergi, who turned it over to Disney, who by contract with Cinergi had to distribute the movie.

By then I was in a war with Disney.

During my war with Disney, I changed the title of the film to: *An Alan Smithee Film: Burn Hollywood Burn.*

> TO: MICHAEL EISNER
> From: Joe Eszterhas
> Date: January 15, 1998
> Re: The Scenario for An Alan Smithee Film: Burn Hollywood Burn
>
> Dear Michael,
>   You and I collaborated on a screenplay once—Flashdance—that was pretty good. Try this one on for size; this one's pretty bad. Here it is:
>   In late October, the chairman of the Walt Disney Motion Pictures Group, Dick Cook, charming and friendly, sits down to lunch with producer Ben Myron and me. He bemoans his baseball injury, talks about the glory years of the Dodgers, and tells us that, while Burn Hollywood Burn will not get any TV ads, it "will get plenty of print—don't worry." He says he will be the point man of the project, asks me to speak to him directly, and says I will be receiving a marketing plan "next week." Liking him, happy about his attitude, I give him a hug as he departs.
>   In early November, Senior Vice President of Publicity Terry Curtin has lunch with my wife, Naomi, and me at the Bel-Air Hotel. She is full of ideas to publicize the movie, takes copious notes, and says, "Trust me. You have an ally. Dick Cook is a coward," she says. "If you get him on the phone, he'll say yes, but you'll never get him on the phone."
>   She tells us that "Corporate Disney is a weird place to work, like a sect. I'm still trying to get used to it." She tells us that "The reason Ovitz didn't last at Disney is that Eisner didn't support him and Ovitz floundered." Naomi says, "I thought I noticed that on Larry King." Curtin says, "Exactly. Eisner left him out there hanging." She tells us that one of her predecessors at Disney was fired for having an affair with a top-level Disney executive

(Curtin named them). Curtin says, "These old guys who pat you on the ass and give you a wink, so what? How does that hurt your career?"

She says that Disney is so disorganized at times that "We forgot to run an ad for Washington Square *on opening day in one of the major markets." She talks about how Whoopi Goldberg and her agent, Arnold Rifkin, "terrorized" Disney into giving Whoopi a $250,000 Picasso. "Whoopi got pissed off at a marketing meeting and said she wouldn't publicize the movie. Rifkin called and said the only way to smooth her feathers was to buy her this Picasso at a New York gallery. We had to have the money there by the end of the day or she wouldn't publicize the picture. Afterward, I called Rifkin and said, 'Just tell me you know this was wrong.' Rifkin said, 'I don't see anything inappropriate here.' "*

Curtin brags about her closeness to the press, singling out Claudia Eller of the Los Angeles Times *and Sharon Waxman of the* Washington Post— *"I've got them in my pocket," she says. "I talked to Claudia this morning," she says, "I told her I was having lunch with you and she said, "What are you having lunch with* him *for?" Curtin continues, "I got Sharon Waxman to kill a critical story about Disney the other day. She just had a baby, too. I said to her—'C'mon, give me a break. I'm sitting here with a breast pump on.' "*

Curtin finally gets back to Burn Hollywood Burn. *"When we screened it at Disney internally," she says, "everybody in the room was laughing. Afterward I went up to people outside the room and said, 'What did you think?' Everyone was afraid to admit how much fun it was. This movie is going to become one of Hollywood's greatest guilty pleasures."*

Terry repeats her mantra—"Trust me, I'm your ally." She says, interestingly, near the end of our lunch: "We're probably going to be enemies when this is over." To which Naomi responds, "I hope not. We're tired of fighting." Liking Terry, happy about her attitude toward the movie, we send her a bouquet of flowers after the meeting.

Days and weeks go by. No marketing plan and no return calls from my "point man" Dick Cook. No return calls from Terry Curtin either. On November 24, hearing nothing from anyone at Disney, getting no return calls, I write a memo to Dick Cook (with carbons to Curtin and your exec Phil Barlow) which is a marketing plan. The plan includes things either Cook or Curtin talked about. I get no response to the memo from anyone at Disney, though Curtin tells my publicist she is "happy" about my memo—"Joe made our job easy for us."

· · ·

I hear nothing from Disney—nothing at all relating either to my memo about marketing or about Disney's alleged marketing plan until shortly before Christmas when Terry Curtin comes to my home for lunch. She is brimming with excitement about the Tommy Lee/Pamela video, the size of Tommy Lee's penis, and notes that "Pamela Lee has a lubrication problem."

She turns to your exec Oren Aviv, who has accompanied her, and says, "Did you notice Pamela's lubrication problem?"

Oren looks down and clears his throat.

Curtin: "Don't tell me you didn't notice."

Oren: "I did, but I'm too much of a gentleman to comment on it."

She talks about Tommy Lee's "beautiful face" and says she and her husband saw the video the night before.

"My husband said, 'I don't understand how a guy like this can get both Heather Locklear and Pamela Anderson.'

"I said to him, 'Well, you're no Tommy Lee.' He said, 'You're no Pamela Anderson.'"

Curtin talks about how, at Fox's publicity department, she and her colleagues had a "P File." The "P File" consisted of full-frontal nude photos of actors, taken off the outtakes of the films they were in.

"You should see Willem Dafoe's," she says. "He wins the prize. His is really something."

She talks about feeling sorry for Macaulay Culkin. "We were doing interviews in this suite. He was in the living room. We could all hear his father and mother in the next room having sex."

She doesn't mention Burn Hollywood *until I ask her, once again, what marketing plans Disney has. Then she turns to Oren Aviv, who shows us two one-sheets—one of a naked girl whose breasts are covered with cans of film and the tagline "Good movie. Great cans." I am told, thankfully—this movie is not* Showgirls—*that we are not using this one-sheet, though Dick Cook has had it in his office, "considering it" for a week.*

Terry and Oren leave, but two hours later a Disney messenger arrives. Inside the big Disney package we find, not a marketing plan, but Beauty and the Beast: The Enchanted Christmas, Mary Poppins, *and the porn video of Tommy Lee and Pamela.*

Terry calls back later that afternoon, "Tell Naomi to call me after she sees it. I want to know what she thinks about Tommy's penis."

I tell Terry that we never talked about marketing at our lunch. She says the plan is on Dick Cook's desk, "You'll have it tomorrow."

· · ·

Tomorrow comes. No marketing plan . . . and no call to Terry from Naomi, who is horrified by the tape. Terry calls, though. She wants to know what Naomi thought of the size of Tommy's organ. I tell her Naomi didn't think much of the tape.

"She's so sweet," Terry says.

"The marketing plan," she adds, "is on the way."

At the end of December, two months after Dick Cook promised a marketing plan . . . five weeks after my marketing memo to Cook . . . two months *before* the February 27 release of the movie, I still *haven't heard anything from anyone at Disney. By now, we have* missed *long-lead press deadlines. I inform Rogers & Cowan that, since I'm getting no cooperation and no response from Disney, I will hire the firm at my own expense to publicize the movie.*

Meanwhile, adding to my frustration, even though very few media people have seen the movie, we're getting positive response:

"It's an A+," writes Harry Knowles's Ain't It Cool Network, which gets 160,000 Internet hits a day. "The movie rocked . . . I can't wait to take my girlfriend to see it."

Martin Grove writes in the Hollywood Reporter, *"One of the funniest movies to turn up in ages . . . what's nice is that the movie is really not mean-spirited. With media coverage of Hollywood behind the scenes so widespread these days, a lot of what might be considered inside humor is going to get laughs from paying audiences."*

Charles Fleming writes in the L.A. Weekly: *"The movie is hilarious . . . a far more savage look at Hollywood than* The Player . . . *unrelenting in its viciousness."*

In post-screening reactions: Anne Kolson of the New York Times *says: "I thought it was great. Very funny in many places."*

Stephen Farber of Movieline *says he "really enjoyed it" and will write a positive review.*

Karen Shapiro of Entertainment Tonight *says, "Very twisted and funny. I definitely laughed."*

Trish Becker of GQ *magazine says, "I really enjoyed it. I enjoyed the premise."*

Stephanie Tuck of In Style *magazine says, "I liked it. It was very clever. I thought it was great how it came together."*

Melissa Parvel of Access Hollywood *says, "I really liked it. I thought it was pretty slick and funny."*

Mimi James of VH1 *says, "I liked it. It was so cheesy."*

Robert Eli of Entertainment Asylum *says, "I thought there were some very funny moments. Stallone, Whoopi, and Chan could generate a whole new following."*

My publicist calls Disney to demand a meeting with Disney. Other film-makers don't have to demand such a meeting; it is routinely scheduled with them.

Disney grants the meeting and it is held January 9 in the Roy Disney Building's third-floor conference room. It is attended by—from Disney: John Cywinski, Geoff Ammer, Terry Curtin, Kristy Frudenfeld, Gina Ross, Brett Dicker, Chuck Viane, Chris Edwards, and Oren Aviv.

Also attending are: Andrew Shack, president of Priority Records, Dana Mason, head of Priority marketing, Alan Nierob, Christine Lamont, and Sandy Rice of Rogers & Cowan . . . and producer Ben Myron.

I begin the meeting, according to our transcript, this way: "As most of you already know, I am not comfortable with the idea of Disney distributing and publicizing this movie. As a result, at my own expense, I have retained Rogers & Cowan . . ."

Naomi cuts in: "Can I please say something before we begin the meeting?"

Joe: "Sure."

Naomi: "Thank you. I want to address my comments to Terry Curtin, since she is the only representative of Disney I have worked with. Terry, you sent a fax to us yesterday asking why we are angry. Well, I'd like to explain why. When we first met back in November for a four-hour meeting, I began by saying that the reason Joe and I were angry was because we felt we were being ignored by Disney. My experience in this town is that nobody ever wants to give bad news, and so instead they hide. I said that we had heard no response from Disney for weeks and we did not yet even have a distribution date.

"You said, 'Well, Dick Cook is a coward. If you get him on the phone the answer will always be yes, but you will never get him on the phone.' "

Terry: "I never said he was a coward."

Naomi: "You said he was a coward and that if you get him on the phone the answer will be yes, but you will never get him on the phone. But you said 'I'm not like that. I will deal straight with you' . . . Then you came to lunch with Oren. It was a three-hour lunch. You arrive and I can see again that you are really excited. You were very excited. You were coming out of your seat with excitement. But what you were excited about was the Tommy Lee/Pamela video and the size of Tommy Lee's organ, which you kept talking about. And then you digressed to the penis file at Fox and about how you've got all these photos of all these guys' penises and

*how big they are and I'm thinking, 'You know, you have a meeting with
Joe Eszterhas. You're having a lunch. What's your agenda. Oh, I know!
Maybe if I talk about penises and sex for two hours, it will distract him.'"*

Naomi concludes this way: *"I don't know about Disney. I have never
met any of these people. All I know about Disney is that growing up I
watched* The Wonderful World of Disney *on Sunday nights. Now I have
a peek inside at the people making the magic, and, to me, it's like lifting up
a big rock. All the little bugs immediately scuttle off to the side and you're
left with a big fat worm in the middle doing nothing. And the experience
has been disillusioning at best and insulting at worst."*

I then say, *"Let's cut the shit here today, okay? My shit detector has
really gone off. I've never really felt you people were allies. I think that I
have done this movie myself and will continue to. But for God's sake, let's
cut the shit. Get your hands off my dick, all of you. Let's just finally tell
the truth."*

*The bottom line of the meeting is that the entire advertising budget—all
print—is $300,000. ("You'll get plenty of print," Dick Cook had said in
October, "don't worry.") Three hundred thousand dollars for a nine-city
opening! Three hundred thousand dollars for a $10 million budget movie!
Three hundred thousand dollars—only $50,000 more than I myself was
asked to invest (and* did *invest) in the movie and $50,000 more than
Whoopi's new Picasso.*

*This is the advertising we have: The only full-page ads we have in the
nine markets are in the* Los Angeles Times *and the* New York Times *the
Sunday before opening and the day of opening.*

We have a two-line ad running at the bottom of page one of the New
York Times *which costs $400 a line (my idea). We have no press junket.
We have no TV ads. We have no radio buys. We have no magazine
advertising. We have an L.A. premiere, but we don't have one in New
York. We have no opinion-maker screenings. We have no plans for any
of the movie's stars to do a press tour. In the nine cities, we have one
single billboard—in L.A., on Crescent Heights, partially obscured by a gas
station sign.*

*On January 12, Terry Curtin, writing under Buena Vista Pictures letter-
head, expresses umbrage at my wife's remarks. She calls Naomi's remarks
"vicious and misdirected." (*Misdirected *is, I think, a telling word—What
it says to me is that Naomi's remarks were warranted, but not addressed to
Curtin. Equally telling is that she doesn't deny the* veracity *of my wife's
remarks at the meeting in her letter.)*

Curtin goes on to express "pity" for our "beautiful young children."

In disbelief that an executive of a public company is writing these words about my children, I don't even respond to her comments about them.

But her remarks about "having cared" about the movie and "working so hard to convince my co-workers to treat . . . this project with respect" make me question, once again, why she had to work so hard to convince co-workers if Disney had good-faith intent to distribute the film.

In the late afternoon of January 12, Dick Cook speaks to my agent, Jeff Berg, and says Curtin's letter to my wife was "out of line."

Cook tells Berg he's upping the ad budget to $500,000. Maybe, Berg and I think, we're making the tiniest, incremental progress here. On the 14th of January, Geoff Ammer, senior vice president of Buena Vista Pictures Marketing, tells producer Ben Myron that the $500,000 figure represents no additional advertising to what we discussed at the meeting of January 9. We've made, Jeff Berg and I realize, no progress at all: Cook's "up to $500,000" was a mirage. When Myron asks to see the marketing plan budget, Ammer tells him, "It's none of your business."

I am being asked then, after months of dodging, obfuscation, and disingenuousness, to take Disney's word for it: A) About the marketing plan itself, B) Its cost and budget, and C) About the alleged additional allotment in the budget allegedly being consumed by the ads already agreed to at the meeting of the 9th.

Am I really to expect that with this kind of attitude and with open and documented animosity from a high-level Disney executive, Disney is not doing everything it can to put this movie into the ground? Aw, come on, Michael. This is bad stuff, unfair and wrong. I killed myself for this movie. I sold the screenplay for $250,000 instead of my usual $4 million fee, believing in the movie's commercial potential. I cut it, rounded up the music, did the music edit, supervised the soundstage—without any pay. And then I put my $250,000 writing fee back into it, believing it was all worth it, believing I'd get a fair shake when it was distributed.

What I am left with in this scenario is a Tommy Lee/Pamela porn video messengered by Disney . . . a naked girl one-sheet on my bathroom wall designed by Disney . . . a Buena Vista Pictures letter expressing "pity" for my children . . . and a marketing plan budget which I am told is "none of my business."

This, Michael, is your Disney?

. . .

I never got an answer from Michael Eisner.

Paranoid that Disney wouldn't release the movie, I asked the production people to strike me my own print.

I knew that I had now committed a crime, but I had visions of myself, film cans in hand, invading the projection booths of neighborhood theaters for mysterious underground midnight showings.

We put the film cans in a closet behind the baby's bassinet.

I had a frightening thought:

Was I becoming Alan Smithee, who first steals his own film and then burns it? Was this the mad Smithee's cackling revenge upon me for having created him?

Ryan O'Neal needed a ride to a research screening of the movie in Beverly Hills.

He lived a few miles down the Pacific Coast Highway from us and we picked him up in our limo.

He was telling Naomi and me how happy he was living with Leslie Stefanson and as he spoke he put his hand on Naomi's bare knee and felt her leg.

I said, "If you touch her again, I'll break your fucking hand."

He took his hand off Naomi's knee.

At the screening, Ryan put his shades on and asked to be whisked into the theater just before the lights went down so no one would recognize him.

He was whisked in a little early. The lights were still on. People saw a pudgy middle-aged guy with shades.

From what I could tell, no one recognized him.

After the screening, when our limo pulled up, Ryan was suddenly there.

"I'm sorry," I said to him, "Naomi and I are going out to dinner."

"Can I come?" he said.

I laughed and said no.

"But I don't have a ride home," Ryan said.

I said, "Take a cab."

"I don't take cabs," Ryan said.

I smiled and said, "Yes, you do."

Disney ran its first ad for the film on the front page of the *New York Times* on January 16, 1998.

There it was, right at the very bottom of the front page, left-hand corner. Two lines: "BURN HOLLYWOOD BURN—'I'M A PRODUCER NOT A PIMP.' "

If you had a very strong magnifying glass, you could read it.

. . .

I submitted seventy-two one-liners from the movie to Disney to be used in the *New York Times* magnifying-glass ad campaign.

Disney sent my list back to me with the following one-liners crossed out:

PAGING DR. OVITZ! DR. OVITZ WHERE ARE YOU?
HOW DO YOU LIKE OUR TRUCK? SPIELBERG'S GOT ONE,
    GEFFEN'S GOT ONE, KEANU'S GETTING ONE.
HE SAID ONLY ROBERT EVANS COULD HELP HIM. ROBERT
    EVANS TRANSCENDED SEX AND DRUGS.
THEY PROMISED TO GET REDFORD INTO MY NEXT MOVIE.
    WHEN THEY REALLY WANT SOMETHING, THEY USE CRUISE
    AS THEIR BAIT. STILL, REDFORD IS ONE STEP UP FROM
    HOFFMAN.
MICHAEL OVITZ IS GONE, THAT'S WHAT'S WRONG.
HE WAS BIGGER ON THE RUSH LIMBAUGH CIRCUIT THAN
    HUGH GRANT AND HEIDI HAD BEEN.
WE HAD TWO PEOPLE FROM TOKYO IN THAT CONFERENCE
    ROOM. THEY UNDERSTOOD EVERY THIRD WORD, BUT
    STILL . . .

During the holidays, Arthur Hiller and I sat down at a small pub in Santa Monica with a fireplace crackling near us. He had just seen the final cut at a nearby screening room.

"I liked it," Arthur said. "It's very funny, but it's different than the movie I signed on to make. You know I wish you the best of luck with it."

We talked about the new projects we were working on.

"I'd like to work with you again," Arthur said, "but with certain rules."

"I'd love to work with you again, too," I told him.

We sat there for a moment, looking at the logs in the fireplace, and I put my hand over his.

I suggested taking the film to Slamdance, a film festival not to be confused with Sundance, its politically correct big brother.

Jeff Berg called a Slamdance director and set up a screening of the film for them. The director called back and said Slamdance would love to show *Smithee*—for a payment of $30,000 which would go, of course, to "developing young talents."

"Blow me," Jeff Berg said and hung up.

I introduced the movie at its premiere in Westwood.

"Good evening, ladies and gentlemen," I said, "I am the maniac responsible."

I began by saying, "First and foremost, with the greatest affection and respect, I want to thank Arthur Hiller, who directed this movie beautifully. I miss you here tonight, Arthur."

The critics hated it.

The *Wall Street Journal* wrote, "Somewhere along the way, *Smithee* became a movie about itself. The production was riddled with feuds and finger-pointing, egos and manipulation. The final product was rejected for this year's New York Film Festival; critics who have seen early screenings have savaged it."

In that same article, the *Wall Street Journal* described me as "a big, bombastic man with long blond hair" who "chews gum and smokes feverishly, frequently embellishing his tale with expletives" sitting in a room "littered with African art, movie artifacts, and lots of ashtrays."

Paul Verhoeven, I heard, was not amused at this bit of dialogue from the movie.

> SMITHEE
> If we believe in film—and we do—don't we have a responsi-
> bility to protect the world from bad ones?

> ONE OF THE BROTHERS BROTHERS
> Is the movie really that bad?

> SMITHEE
> It's fucking horrible. It's worse than *Showgirls*.

I was sorry Paul wasn't amused.
I put that line in there just for him.

I ran an ad in the trades after the movie's critical and commercial failure that said:

> In what he called "an act of abject cowardice," screenwriter Joe Eszter-
> has canceled his appearance this week at the U.S. Comedy Arts Festival
> in Aspen, Colorado.
> Eszterhas was scheduled to speak there after a benefit showing of
> his movie, *An Alan Smithee Film: Burn Hollywood Burn.*
> "Even Hungarians don't beat bleeding horses," Eszterhas said,
> explaining his cancellation.
> This was Eszterhas's reaction to the opening of *Burn Hollywood
> Burn* over the weekend:
> 1. I guess I pushed some people's buttons.
> 2. I extended a middle finger and the critics returned the gesture.
> 3. My redemption thanks to *Telling Lies in America* was brief.

4. The critical response to *Burn Hollywood Burn* redeemed *Show-girls*. I'm happy about that.
5. I hope Janet Maslin of the *New York Times* forgives me for her depiction in the film.
6. I am making plans to kiss Arthur Hiller's posterior in Times Square.
7. I will resist Kenneth Starr's subpoena of my White House script *Sacred Cows*.
8. I accept the Razzies and the Sour Apple awards in advance and will appear in person to accept them.
9. I am taking Jack Valenti's advice and will seek immediate medical attention on Maui.
10. I still think it's a funny movie.

Perhaps carried away by my promise to accept the award in person, Razzies officials nominated *Smithee* in a slew of categories, although my favorite nomination came not from the Razzies but from its competitor, the annual Stinkers Award.

I received a Stinkers nomination for . . . *worst on-screen hairstyle*.

Sharon Stone was nominated in the same category for *Sphere*.

The Directors Guild deliberated that the name "Alan Smithee" would no longer be its official pseudonym when a director wanted his name off the credits.

For some reason, the *Los Angeles Times* asked *me* for a comment. My comment was:

"Who says writers have no power in Hollywood?"

The Daddy

Art was seventy years old. I met him on a sunny Sunday afternoon in the Malibu Colony. He was a longtime and legendary Hollywood publicist:

My old man was in Minneapolis, working for a paper. He wrote sob sister stuff. Purple prose, that's what they used to call it. He always drank hard. He was a big guy, half German, half Irish. Tom Mix came into town, promoting something. He was the biggest thing in the world then. He and my old man drank. They liked each other and my old man said fuck Minneapolis and came to Hollywood.

He became Tom's publicist and Tom introduced him around and he became one of the biggest publicists in town. I was born in Culver City. We were living in a motel then. We were always living in one motel or another. My mom drank as hard as he did.

When I was a little kid he'd take me with him when he went to a star's house. He wanted me to see things. He was representing Crawford and Power and Clark Gable. The biggest names. He took me with him but there was one rule. I couldn't talk. I wasn't allowed to talk. My old man was a big guy. I never wanted to piss him off.

I got into the business through him. He died soon after I started. The bottle killed him. It killed my mom, too. They died six months apart.

When I was starting out, just a kid really, I met Ginger Rogers. She was more than twenty years older. She liked me. I was with her for about a year. She taught me everything about everything. What did I know? I was a kid from Culver City who grew up in motels. She taught me how to eat in a fine restaurant, how to tip the maître d', the kind of wine to order. She taught me a lot of things I could never adequately thank her for.

My favorite client was Judy Garland. She was in Vegas once and she called me in L.A. and said "I want you at the show tonight." It was like four in the afternoon and she was going on at nine. I said—Christ, Judy, I'm not sure I can make it. She said—"If you're not here when the show starts, I'm firing your ass." I about killed myself getting there and I got there late. She was already onstage. I was about pissing my pants. She saw me come in. I had this seat waiting in the front row.

She stopped the show. She said—Art, get up here! She looked pissed off. I didn't know if she was loaded or not. I went up there. She said—"Happy Birthday, Art," and Judy Garland sang "Happy Birthday" for me up onstage in Vegas. I had forgotten it was my birthday. It was probably the greatest moment of my life.

I've never had luck with women. No, that's not true, I've had a lot of luck with women, you know, that way, but I guess with what you'd call relationships, no go.

It's probably the zipper that's the biggest problem. I know it's not funny, but I just can't keep the damn thing zipped. I talked to Milton Berle about it once. Miltie just laughed at me.

The biggest love of my life was . . . well, I'm not going to tell you her name. You know the name. Everybody knows the name. She was a big star in the sixties. I still can't get her out of my head. I'm out at the Riviera or I'm out at the point at the Kahala and I think about her. She's been dead twenty years.

I met her in between her marriages. She'd been married and then after she and I broke up she remarried. She was the funniest woman I ever knew, the sexiest, too, but she hid it. It wasn't about a pair of tits in a tight sweater. She was classy. She was a trouper. She was my pal. She was a dame.

Good Christ we had fun. We'd go down to the beach and walk around by the Colony. Or we'd spend a weekend at Peter Lawford's house in Santa Monica. One night we closed this joint down. We were drinking tequila. The jukebox kept playing Frank all night. Everybody was gone finally. They knew me there—they gave me the key and said lock the door on the way out. I made love to her on top of a pool table in the back. You know something? I never . . . fucked her. I made love to her a lot.

But I fucked her sister. That's what killed it. She had a sister who was younger. Hot. The pair of tits in the tight sweater. She was always around us. So one night I fucked her. She got pregnant. I took her down to Mexico for an abortion. And she found out about it. That was it. I was such a jerk.

Almost the same thing happened with my fourth wife, but I think I got set up there. My fourth wife was an actress. You know who she was, you saw her on TV. Things were going a little rocky between us.

Anyway, my wife had a house guest. She's a writer. You see her on TV a lot these days, Sunday morning political kind of stuff. She writes columns in the paper. She's very political now but she wasn't then. She's French. Almost matronly now, very Santa Barbara, you know, but she wasn't then. She'd walk around the house in her nightgown. The nightgown wasn't Santa Barbara, if you know what I mean.

So my wife goes out of town to do a show in New York. That leaves me alone in the house with the Frenchie. It's not funny considering what it wound up costing me but I can't help laughing. Middle of the night, here comes the Frenchie. No nightgown, no nothing.

My wife comes back from New York, the Frenchie tells her what happened, and my wife sues me for divorce. I get wiped out and the Frenchie becomes the famous political socialite. And I have to see her on TV Sunday morning before the maid's even had a chance to make the Bloody Marys.

My fifth wife was a hooker, if you want to know the truth. I didn't give a rat's ass about that. Everybody in town knew she was a hooker but it never stopped me from taking her to the screenings and the openings and the parties and the banquets. I saw the way some guys looked at her, saw that smirk of recognition, but I pretended that I didn't. I liked Christy a lot and maybe . . . well, maybe if it hadn't ended the way it did . . . maybe I'd say that I loved her.

I met her in New York. I was in town promoting a new picture for Twentieth and I had a suite at the Pierre. I called a friend and said I needed a girl and Christy met me at the bar at the Sherry. She wasn't what I expected. She had a fresh, scrubbed quality about her, a lot of Doris Day and a little of Kim Novak. She wore a simple black dress and pearls. She was built, sure, my eyes are still okay, but it was all . . . held in.

She was modeling, she said. Yeah, I know, but not that kind of modeling. She was doing department store modeling for the ads in the papers, some lingerie, sure, but mostly dresses. She liked champagne, so we killed a bottle of Cristal at the bar and then went over to the Pierre and ordered another in my suite. Christ, her body. Christy had the most beautiful breasts of any woman I've ever seen.

We talked and she told me the truth, nothing fancy, no frills. She grew up in San Francisco, wanted to be an actress. That didn't work out—surprise!—so she drifted to modeling. That didn't pay enough so she did some hooking on the side, but only through friends. She had a very select client list. A lot of people in L.A. knew her, she said. She'd spent some time at Bob's house and Evans had taken her down to Acapulco a couple of times. Once, she said, she was walking around the beach there with her top off and she brought all the beach traffic to a stop. She laughed. She laughed a lot. I liked the way she laughed.

When I got back out here from New York, I missed her. Couple weeks later, I called her and flew her out, met her at the airport in a limo with some flowers, a bottle of Cristal on ice in the back, the whole thing. She stayed at the house with me. I still had the house from my last divorce but most everything in it was gone thanks to the damn lawyers. Even the paintings were gone.

We had fun together. She'd watch the games with me on Sundays and sip her champagne. We closed a lot of bars, saw a few friends of mine, went to some parties, went to Spago a lot, went to Vegas, went to Catalina, stayed at the Ritz in Laguna Niguel. We had a lot of breakfasts in bed.

Evans said to me at a party when she was in the loo, "God, isn't she some hank of pussy?" When he met her, Bob said, she was flying back and forth from L.A. to New York in first class trying to find someone to marry her. She'd somehow gotten ahold of a bunch of stolen airline tickets. I told Evans I didn't want to hear that kind of shit and Bob apologized. He's always been a gentleman.

We went to the Princeville on Kauai for a couple weeks and when we got back I bought her an engagement ring. It was a nice diamond. She said it was the biggest diamond she'd ever seen and cried when I asked her to marry me. "You know what I am," she said, and me—dumb fuck—I said it didn't matter, I didn't care. All that mattered was how we felt about each other. She said she loved me.

We had a great two years—come on, two years is eternity in this town—and then I noticed that she was drinking more champagne than ever before and asked her what was wrong. She was lonely, she said. She felt unfulfilled. She wanted a baby. She said she loved me.

I told her I didn't want any more kids. Besides, I'd had a vasectomy before my last marriage. She cried. As the months went by and I kept seeing a sadness in her eyes, I said fuck it—I didn't want her to be unhappy, it hurt me to see her unhappy, we'd adopt a child.

We adopted a beautiful six-month-old boy we named Art Jr. I hadn't named any of my kids after me—besides, naming him Art Jr. was her idea. God did we have a lot of fun with him. I never expected to spend as much time with Art Jr. as I did. I hadn't spent that much time with any of my other kids, so it surprised me how great it was being around him. He was a sweet, gentle kid who never cried. Christy was a terrific mother. Oh, she spoiled him, sure, but she couldn't help herself. She wasn't drinking much champagne anymore.

Everything seemed to be okay to me. I convinced her to come to the Cannes Film Festival with me without Art Jr. and we had a lot of fun in Cannes. A producer friend of mine had a yacht and we all got nice tans— you know, not the Evans kind of tan, but healthy ones—and we drank a lot of champagne. Hell, we were in Cannes, what were we supposed to do, drink water?

We decided to take the QE2 back. The studio was picking up the tab. Mel Gibson was in the suite across from us and we got to know each other and had a lot of laughs and drank more champagne. Christ, the champagne and caviar were complimentary, were we supposed to turn it down?

One night mid-passage I woke up and Christy wasn't there next to me in bed. I heard some voices and got up and followed the voices out into the corridor. Christy was out there buck naked trying to convince Mel to let her into his suite. Mel was grinning and saying he didn't think it was a good idea.

I dragged her back into our suite. She was crazy drunk and said a lot of ugly things. One of the things she said was that she'd been sleeping with an old boyfriend every time she visited her mother in San Francisco. Another thing she said was that she didn't love me and didn't think she'd ever loved me.

We got back and saw the damn lawyers and worked it out amicably, which means she got most everything I had left.

Art Jr. is eight years old now and he's with me three times a week. I take him to see the Dodgers and I take him to Pink's for a chili dog. Three times a week I drive him to school in the morning. He's a great kid and I can't tell you how happy I am that we adopted him.

CHAPTER 32

The King of Cleveland

BILLY MAGIC
Mistake on the lake.

OLD MAN
What'd you say?

BILLY MAGIC
"Mistake on the lake"—that's what they call this place, ain't it?

OLD MAN
Hell no! Where'd you hear that? They call this "The Best Location in the Nation."

Telling Lies in America

There was always some damn movie being filmed at night on the beach below us in Malibu keeping us awake.

And Joey found a used hypodermic to play with on the local playground.

And we were forced to buy what we called our "Brinks Mailbox" because one of our neighbors, starstruck, was stealing our mail.

And an Alaska Airlines jet crashed a few miles out at sea and the beach beneath us was awash for weeks with body tissue and suitcases.

And we'd fired one of our nannies because L.A. sheriff's deputies had caught her threatening and stalking the television actor Robert Conrad.

And yet, that wasn't really what was wrong. Something was very wrong, I felt, but none of those things, added together, summed up the problem.

I was the problem. Something was wrong *with me.*

· · ·

In some deep part of me, I didn't want to be here anymore. I didn't want to go to the wall and fight the battles . . . and do the seductive, empty chitchat at Morton's. I still wanted to write screenplays, but I didn't want the rest of the package: the fights with directors, the paparazzi at the premieres, the limos, the best table at Spago, the weekends in Palm Springs or Laguna.

I felt like I'd befouled myself somehow, like I had turned into something I didn't want to be: the screenwriter as Hollywood Animal . . . not as victim and servant and peon and whore . . . but as the Hollywood Animal, the gun in my hand.

An ancient Hollywood equation says that in the beginning of a project, the screenwriter has the gun and when his script is finished he hands the gun off to the director . . . and when the director's cut is finished, the director hands the gun off to the studio . . . and when the studio has the gun . . . the studio fires the gun and kills the screenwriter and the director with it.

Well, not me! I had the gun and kept it and could even aim it at studio heads and get them to throw their hands up and give me what I wanted!

Hollywood animal behavior. Another symptom of the same disease that had caused a producer friend of mine to slap his maid bloody for not moving fast enough at a dinner party, or another producer friend who viciously beat up his fiancée two weeks before their wedding date—a date he kept, but with another woman.

You'll never work in this town again was blackmail and extortion, because there was always an "if" attached to that time-worn sentence . . . "If you leave CAA," Michael Ovitz had said to me, talking about his foot soldiers who'd blow my brains out.

And now I was engaging in the same sort of blackmail and extortion. I was a Hollywood animal, I feared, just as much as Ovitz, pulling the same gangster tactics on the town that he'd pulled on me. I had become what I detested.

"So do whatever you want to do," I'd written to Ovitz, "and fuck you," more than implying that he was trash, Hollywood scum, and I didn't want to have anything to do with him. Now I was off my high horse, muscling and browbeating the other players in the gutter.

I felt like I should send myself the same letter I'd sent to Ovitz. There was no doubt in my mind that the Ovitz jacket I saw myself wearing fit to a tee: Michael had even turned on Ron Meyer, his best friend, the way I'd turned on Guy McElwaine.

I found myself reconsidering and reevaluating my whole battle with Ovitz. Was it really wanting Guy back in my life that made me resist Ovitz eleven years ago? Or was it me saying: *You're candy, frat boy. Welcome to Lorain Avenue. You don't have a chance. I'm gonna hit you in the fuckin' head with a baseball bat . . .*

because I'm the real Hollywood animal, asshole, I'm the real Thousand-Pound Gorilla!"

The longer I'd lived in this town the worse I'd become . . . until I was out of control, amok in Malibu. *Wildlife.* A barbarian hanging scalps and check stubs off his figurative dick. There was something about this cursed and glitzy town that infected you and fired you with delusions. Living here was like functioning on low-desert meth cut with just a crust of PCP.

L.A. was a separate *nation,* not a state within the United States . . . but a separate nation between the United States and Mexico whose Twin Towers was the Industry. It was impossible to imagine this separate nation without the Industry because the Industry was its big, beeping, buzzing, glowing sacred heart.

Everyone wanted to be a part of the Industry . . . as a screenwriter, actor, producer, gofer, gaffer, whatever—*it didn't matter.* As long as they could be a part of it and suck off its glamorous, poisonous, siliconed, corrupt tit.

Jeremy, Naomi's forty-year-old little brother, made a lucrative salary. He was a brilliant PR man, a talented singer and songwriter. Yet one day, out of the blue, he suddenly decided to write screenplays with a friend. Why? Because if Ben Affleck and Matt Damon could do it . . .

Jeremy read the trades too, tried to get invited to "industry events." He kept a list in his office of movie stars he and his co-workers had glimpsed in the outdoor cafés of the Sunset Strip.

A *screenwriter!* He was a screenwriter now! *Boom! Just like that! Out of the blue!* Even though he'd never written anything but songs and PR releases before. Even though he got so jittery sitting in one place for twenty minutes that he had to get up and pace around the room.

Naomi and I loved Jeremy and we feared this deadly suckhole of a town was sucking him in, too. He drove a hot car. He went to the gym each day. He was on his cellular all the time. He didn't check his at-home mail for a week, but he checked his e-mail at his office every hour.

The truth was that in the Nation of L.A. you . . . *didn't matter* . . . if you weren't sucking off the Industry tit. You were nothing even if it seemed that you were something.

A producer friend was introduced to Richard Riordan, who at the time was the mayor of Los Angeles, at a cocktail party.

The mayor took my friend aside and said there was something important he wanted to discuss with him.

My friend, a politically active man with a bubbling-over social conscience, was excited. Would the mayor ask him to be a part of some cultural commission? Would he ask him to be part of the board of directors of the Los Angeles Fine Arts Outreach program?

Mayor Riordan took my producer friend out on the lawn next to a gazebo and looked around to make sure no one could overhear him. Satisfied, the mayor *pitched the plot of a screenplay he was writing.*

This was the mayor of the Nation of L.A. acting this way, wanting to be a screenwriter instead of the mayor . . . a powerful man eager, his politician's mouth wide open, to suck on the tit . . . so eager that he was willing *to transmogrify himself into a powerless screenwriter . . .* just to get a taste of the tit.

Or maybe he, like Bono of U2, just wanted to grow up to be Joe Eszterhas`. . .` at the same time that Joe Eszterhas was looking into the mirror and trying to avert his eyes from Frankenstein's monster he had willed himself to become.

On a day when the beach beneath us was awash with detritus from the Alaska Airlines crash, I turned to Naomi and said, "You know, we've really got to get out of here."

I wasn't one of those Malibu New Agers anyway . . . standing on my cliff with Sharper Image or Hammacher Schlemmer binocs pressed to my eyes watching spouting whales. No, hell no, I didn't plop myself in the sand at sunset watching the smog-painted setting sun. Nor did I play Gregorian chants or Nusrat Fateh Ali Khan on my back-deck speaker, setting off dog howls as far north as Palos Verdes.

I was an aging street kid who prided himself on having come from Cleveland, a steel city, a rust belt pit, where the flame above the mills burned all night and bars stayed open after hours serving boilermakers and Cleveland martinis: a shot of Southern Comfort and a cold Bud.

Spouting whales? Nusrat Fateh Ali Khan? I preferred a honkytonk with a choking haze of viscous cigarette smoke, Jerry Lee Lewis, the Killer, stomping away on the jukebox, telling that little red-lipsticked high-ass sweetie to move it around just a little bit.

No New Age spirituality for me, thank you—even if Kenny G himself lived around the corner from our playground and scared my little boys shitless with the studio-quality special effects at his annual neighborhood Halloween party.

New Age spiritualism be damned! I still believed that iodine was more effective than Mercurochrome because iodine hurt. I understood Mike Tyson when he said he bit Holyfield because Holy kept butting him. I preferred the Stones to the Beatles; Howling Wolf to Yanni; Canseco to McGwire; Bukowski to Grisham; David Alan Coe to Toby Keith; Kinky Friedman to Robert Parker.

Sean Penn was another reason we began making plans to leave Malibu . . . for someplace.

He was over at our house chain-smoking and waiting for the steak I was grilling him and he told us that he had grown up right on this bluff and this beach.

He looked at the riptide surf outside our wall-high window and he glanced at Joey and Nick playing together, their hair long and bleached almost yellow by the sun.

It wasn't the Malibu sun—we had recently spent a month in Maui to warm up and get away from Malibu.

Sean asked, "They learn to surf yet?"

Naomi and I looked at each other and then at Sean like he was some kind of freak.

Sean saw the look and laughed.

"Let me tell you guys something," Sean said. "You guys may not go down to the Viper Room. You guys may not even know where the Viper Room is, but in a couple years Joey and his brother will."

That night before we fell asleep, Naomi said, "You're right. We're getting out of here!"

A couple of months later, Sean Penn's wife, Robin Wright, and Sean's kids got carjacked in Santa Monica.

Sean got out of L.A. fast with his wife and kids. He moved to the village of Ross, in yuppified Marin County, where I'd lived for twenty-two years.

We were having lunch on the patio at a little Italian place in the Cross Creek Center in Malibu . . . Steve was visiting us from Oregon . . . and word swept by the tables like a firestorm that Pamela Anderson Lee was down at the playground by the swings.

Steve, who was twenty-four, excused himself and went down to the playground. A mop-haired friend of Joey's from kindergarten came by our table and said to Joey, "*Dude! Pamela Anderson!*"

Joey, who was six, went down to the playground to join Steve.

We could see the two of them from our table, trying to look cool like the hundred other men and boys down there, watching Pamela Anderson in a cowboy hat and tight jeans and a T-shirt as she played with a baby on a swing.

"Oh boy," I said, "oh boy oh boy oh boy oh boy!"

"I know," Naomi said.

There were times when Naomi and I contemplated a life away from movie sets and television interviews, from the chitchat at the local market about how poor Pierce Brosnan's son got hurt in that wreck over the weekend. Times when we didn't want Johnny Carson or Cher or Barbra as our neighbors anymore. When we didn't want our boys trick or treating at Kenny G's or Gary Busey's house.

Sometimes we didn't even want to hear the surf crashing outside our windows anymore. The surf made us uneasy as we watched our boys watching it or skipping through it.

We kept thinking about what Sean had said about the Viper Room.

We didn't want them anywhere near the Viper Room.

She was a beautiful little girl with baby blue eyes. Her parents, friends of ours, dressed her in clothes special-ordered from Milan, strolled her down Rodeo in a gleaming English pram, backpacked her up and down the Santa Monica Promenade.

Her dad was an agent who showed up at all the charity dinners. Her mom was active in the Free Clinic, the Rape-Crisis Center, the Breast Cancer Foundation. Their friends were so happy for them. After eight years of trying to have a baby, after three miscarriages, they'd adopted this little angel.

When she was two years old, she started throwing up and falling down, screaming all the time, holding her beautiful blond little head. Her parents flew her to a pediatric hospital in Boston where it was determined that she had a congenital degenerative brain disease that would only get worse.

Her parents were heartbroken but resolved they wouldn't allow this to ruin their lives.

They have a beautiful little dark-haired angel with twinkling brown eyes now. The adoption agency was happy to make the exchange, happy to avoid costly litigation.

I was tired—more tired than I'd ever been in my life. My divorce from Gerri had drained me, as had the critical evisceration that had greeted *Showgirls* and *Jade*.

I was doing things now like giving speeches at the Hollywood Women's Press Association and at a roast for Peter Bart, the editor of *Variety*. I was autographing hundreds of Xerox copies of my scripts for sale at charity auctions across America. I was making highfalutin *pronouncements* at screenwriting seminars and doing interviews with publications like *People* and *Us* about things like my diet plan.

I was doing all those things instead of doing what I was telling young screenwriters to do in my pronouncements: sitting on my butt at my desk—*sitzfleisch*—and writing scripts.

And I had allowed myself, on my last movie, *An Alan Smithee Film: Burn Hollywood Burn,* to become the whacko filmmaker I had created in my screenplay.

Like Alan Smithee, I got into a hellacious pissfight with a production company.

Like Alan Smithee, I actually stole a negative of the film, intending to screen it myself if I had to.

My fatigue probably made me feel my mortality for the first time in my life—*one* reason, but not *the* reason, we were looking at houses in Cleveland, the only hometown the refugee kid who'd grown into a Hollywood animal had ever known.

"Remember, it's only a movie," the producer Irwin Winkler had said to me over and over again, trying to teach me how to stay human in Hollywood.

I had tried passing that lesson on to my director friend Richard Marquand when he was heartbroken that our film, *Hearts of Fire*, didn't work. But he didn't listen to me . . . and died.

And I had tried passing that lesson on to my screenwriter friend and colleague Jim Morgan, who'd written a script with me called *City Hall* and who was devastated that the studio wouldn't green-light it.

"Remember, it's only a movie, Jim," I told him, but he didn't listen to me . . . and died.

I was saying it to myself a lot these days.

"Remember, it's only a movie, Joe." But I wasn't sure I was listening.

I knew I was drinking too much.

I started drinking when I was fourteen years old—a shot of vodka in the morning in the Eastern European tradition—and there were very few days in the forty-two years since then that I hadn't had *something* alcoholic to drink.

I was never drunk. I never wobbled or slurred. I was never pulled over, never arrested. I never got mean or hostile due to alcohol.

I had an amazing tolerance for alcohol and loved the whole romantic malarkey that tied booze to writers and writing. When I was a kid, all the writers I admired—Faulkner, Steinbeck, Hemingway, Fitzgerald—were boozers.

And as I grew older, I fell in love with bars. The best bars were holy places where I was a participant in a sacred ritual, a kind of sacrilegious, alcoholic Mass where the bartender was the priest, the jukebox the choir, and the shelves full of bottled Eucharist.

I didn't, naturally, view myself as an alcoholic. Booze had a different effect on my system, I thought, than on that of others. Booze was my fuel, it gave me my energy. I sipped gin or cognac while I wrote (and smoked), and I had at least one glass of white wine before any major interview, including the *Today* show at four in the morning California time.

In the past year, I knew, but told no one, including Naomi, that I was drinking more than ever: a secret shot of gin in the morning, three or four glasses of wine with lunch, a couple of tall icy glasses of gin or Jack Daniel's before dinner, then a couple of bottles of wine.

I was never hung over, my energy was unflagging, but I'd put weight on and I hated to see myself on television or in photographs: my bloated face reminded me of Elvis's as he was about to set off on the last tour.

Truth to tell, I had stopped enjoying movies, too. It was almost common for those of us who worked in film not to enjoy seeing them anymore, but it was something I had sworn would never happen to me.

Seeing a movie, I remembered, used to be a magical experience, but not anymore. I knew too much now about the sausage factory grinding out the magic . . . about vacuous stars who were megalomaniacal monsters . . . about directors who did *anything* to keep working . . . about screenwriters who did thirty drafts of the same script so they could get a credit and keep collecting their Guild medical benefits.

I, like so many of my colleagues, didn't want to go to the movies anymore. I, like so many of my colleagues, rooted for every movie I *had* to see . . . to be awful . . . to fail spectacularly.

The only time I'll root for anybody to be a success," an Oscar-winning producer said to me, "is if he or she has cancer and I know for certain that the cancer is terminal."

I had gotten some death threats and the security people we'd hired had instructed us not to open any suspicious packages.

A package arrived in the mail from Neiman Marcus. It somehow looked suspicious to me, although it had a proper-looking Neiman Marcus return address. Naomi said she hadn't ordered anything from Neiman Marcus.

I got a kitchen knife and took the box out onto the lawn as far from our house as I could get.

Naomi was screaming that I'd lost my mind. She pointed out none too calmly that I was going to open a box that I suspected had a bomb in it with a kitchen knife. I thought Naomi had a good point there.

I told her to go back inside the house and stop bothering me. She started calling me ugly but not inaccurate names.

I opened the box very gingerly with the kitchen knife. There was another box inside it. The other box showed a photograph of a Sony video camera on its top. We didn't have a video camera. We *needed* a video camera.

I yelled to Naomi that it was a video camera. Naomi yelled back that she hadn't ordered a video camera and called me more ugly names.

I opened the video camera box very gingerly with the kitchen knife. It was filled with bubble wrap. On the bottom of the bubble wrap was a manila envelope with a Paramount Pictures return address.

I didn't think it was a bomb anymore. I started to rip the envelope open and Naomi ran out of the house and started screaming at me about letter bombs.

So I opened the envelope gingerly. Inside was a small white envelope and a script.

I opened the small white envelope (yes, gingerly, gingerly). It was a letter from a man in San Francisco. He said he was blind. He said he had five children, one of whom had brain damage. He wanted me to read his enclosed screenplay and pass it on to an agent so the agent could sell it for a lot of money. He enclosed photographs that showed a blind man in his forties and a child around ten who looked cross-eyed.

I certainly admired his chutzpah. He had gotten ahold of a Neiman Marcus box, a Sony video camera container, and a Paramount return address.

But it *could've* been a bomb . . . and I *would've* been dead by now and . . . blind or not, brain-damaged or not . . . I didn't read his script.

I thought of the seventeen years I'd spent writing screenplays while living with Gerri, Steve, and Suzi in Marin County, away from L.A.

I had enjoyed going to see movies in those days. I'd never gone to Hollywood parties. I'd never dispensed diet advice. I'd never made pronouncements at writers' seminars. I'd never spoken to the *Today* show at four in the morning. And I hadn't been drinking nearly as much, either.

My life in Marin had been focused on my family—especially Steve and Suzi. I attended Steve's Little League games and Suzi's animal rights protests. Guy used to say about me in Hollywood: "Joe's got the flu this month. His kid's in Little League. He'll be down here next month."

I had four little boys now and a wife I adored and I wanted to spend as much valuable time with them as I had spent with my first family.

I was burning out in L.A., tired enough to consider fleeing back to my old, weatherworn bag lady of a hometown . . . the place I had fled for California thirty years ago.

Maybe, I thought, I was doomed to be a displaced person, a DP, a refugee, all my life. Maybe that term "DP"—the first epithet ever hurled at me—would wind up defining my life.

I had sought refuge in Cleveland at age six.

I had sought refuge in California at age twenty-seven.

Now, at age fifty-six, I was thinking of going back to Cleveland.

I was tired of not living normally.

I hadn't been inside a bank in twenty-five years. I didn't know how to use an ATM machine. My finances were handled by accountants who went to the bank for me. When we needed cash, a bank messenger brought the money in plastic bags.

I didn't even see the checks I was getting; the amounts showed up on my weekly cash balances. I asked for a Xerox copy of a million-dollar check once just to see what one looked like.

I rarely drove one of our three cars. I had drivers who drove me in limos in L.A. and New York and San Francisco and Cleveland.

When we flew somewhere, a VIP representative met us at curbside as we were getting out of the limo, walked us to the VIP lounge, and then to the gate when the flight was taking off. Needless to say, we got on the plane before anyone else did.

We even had to be careful about what we got in the mail. I wasn't allowed by my lawyers to read any script sent to me for fear that someone would sue me, claiming I'd stolen an idea from them.

A store clerk at a kids' shop in Malibu introduced us to a producer's wife by saying, "She's one of us, too."

One of us.

Even our telephone answering service was incestuous: we often got Denzel Washington's messages.

The most I saw of "real people" was when they waved to the darkened window of the limo as we passed them on the freeway.

The housekeeper or one of the nannies shopped for food and liquor. I hadn't been in a grocery store since Steve and Suzi were kids and, as a special treat, I stopped at a grocery store to buy them some candy. I didn't know on that trip how to use my credit card at the checkout counter but, luckily, I had cash.

We didn't even leave the house to get our hair cut, styled, teased, and high-lighted . . . somebody from Cristophe—Lori, Lisa, Matteo—drove out to Malibu to "do" us at home.

Occasionally, when she happened to be in Beverly Hills, Naomi stopped by the Cristophe studio for a quick touch-up, noting how Lori, Lisa, Matteo, or Olivier would stop "doing" whomever they were "doing" . . . just to talk to Naomi and "get her started."

Naomi understood, consequently, when she was in the chair one day and Lori stopped "doing" her . . . and walked abruptly away from her chair . . . and got Steven Spielberg's wife, Kate Capshaw, "started" as Naomi sat there staring at herself in the mirror.

For Naomi, going to the doctor in Beverly Hills was always an educational experience.

Her dermatologist was also Michael Jackson's dermatologist and, during an office visit one day, Naomi learned that Michael had been prescribed a cream that bleached his skin . . . but that he had applied it to his genitals and burned himself there.

Her dentist was also Sharon Stone's dentist and, during an office visit one day, Naomi learned that Sharon had porcelain inlays.

Bill Macdonald and I (and the dentist) told Naomi that she had much nicer teeth than Sharon.

The fact that we were even thinking about Cleveland was, funnily enough, thanks to Chicago.

Naomi and I had always talked casually about getting out of Malibu and L.A. when the kids got older. And Joey was now in kindergarten. But we'd talked of places like Maui or Florida or Santa Fe or Tucson or Sonoma County or Santa Barbara, eliminating those places only after research and discussion.

The medical care on Maui was so bad people in trouble had to be helicoptered to Oahu. Santa Fe had a booming crime rate. Tucson was hell in the summer; Sonoma was too close to Gerri Eszterhas's house in Tiburon; Santa Barbara was as Hollywood as Malibu, Michael Douglas its pampered prince.

We were in Chicago on an extensive book tour and had some time to kill. It was a springlike summer day and I asked Naomi if she'd ever been in the neighborhoods here. She hadn't and I asked our driver to recommend a great Polish restaurant to us and we drove down there for lunch.

It was a neighborhood very much like the ones I'd lived in in Cleveland. The restaurant, which looked like a diner (linoleum and Formica tabletops), served world-class kielbasa and huge drafts of ice-cold beer. We sat there and had more fun for a few hours than anyplace else we'd been on the tour.

We drove through some of the other neighborhoods and then up to Winnetka and back to the Four Seasons, with its sweeping view of the lake.

"We could be happy here," Naomi said, "we'd have fun raising the boys here."

"You're right," I said."

"Let's do it," she suddenly said.

I wasn't surprised. She's Italian and *spontaneous*.

"Are you serious?"

"I'm very serious. It would be fun."

"Not a chance," I told her.

"Why not?"

"Because I hate this town."

"You do not!" she said. "I saw how much fun you had today."

"I hate Chicago," I said, "loathe it."

She smiled. "Why?"

"Because after the Cleveland Indians lost the World Series in 1954, they traded half the team to the Chicago White Sox, including knuckleball king Early Wynn, and the White Sox kept beating on the Indians after that. I've hated Chicago ever since, that's why."

"You're certifiable," Naomi said.

"I don't care about the White Sox," Naomi said.

"I don't either," I said, "but I care about the Indians. If you want to live in Chicago, we can live in Cleveland, instead."

She said, "*Great!*"

If we moved to Cleveland, I figured, we wouldn't even have to miss our great and devilish friend Evans. Because anyone who's ever been to Cleveland can tell you that Bob Evans in Cleveland, Ohio, is as big as the other Bob Evans in Hollywood.

Bob Evans's sausages are a staple of Cleveland's haute cuisine, almost as good as the chicken sausages Bob Evans *always* serves to his friends in Beverly Hills.

Evans would never be out of our minds in Cleveland . . . big billboard signs proclaiming Bob Evans's Restaurants are everywhere in Cleveland, all over the town, all over the state of Ohio!

The Cleveland that I loved and had grown up in was a shot-and-a-beer town where the locals wore T-shirts that said, "CLEVELAND—YOU GOTTA BE TOUGH!"

It was, as Huey Lewis sang, "The Heart of Rock and Roll" and boasted some of the best early rock and roll disc jockeys in the world: Alan Freed and Bill Randle and Pete (Mad Daddy) Myers.

Cleveland was the home of such great smash-mouth rock and roll artists as Bocky Boo and the Visions, the James Gang, Joey Walsh, Sonny Geraci, Eric Carmen, Pere Ubu, and Michael Stanley. It was the home of WMMS, which *Rolling Stone* magazine for many years called "the best rock and roll radio station in America."

Yeah, but you had to be tough all right: 10 below in winter, 100 in the summer, three bars on most city blocks, and a whole buncha smoke in the air all the time!

"The boys would learn about the Cleveland Indians and wear Chief Wahoo on their hearts and chests," I said.

"And they'd get their hearts broken by the Cleveland Browns and learn what it feels like to lose most games in the final thirty seconds," Naomi said.

. . .

I loved that you could smoke in the bars and restaurants in Cleveland.

I contemplated what bliss it would be: to be sitting at a great bar in front of a fireplace with the snow falling outside and the jukebox playing Elvis's "Merry Christmas, Baby" . . . a double shot of Cuervo in front of me . . . a cigarette in my ashtray next to the Cuervo . . . smoke snaking blue/white into the air . . . as I kissed Naomi, watching perfect, six-pointed snowflakes.

"Tell me some great things about Cleveland," Naomi said.

I told her the things I thought would impress her.

Cleveland had been named an all-American city five times, more than any other city in America. Some people called it "*Cleanland.*"

Its major export was salt. It had the biggest bowling alleys in Ohio. There were Picassos at the Cleveland Art Institute, sculptures by Oldenburg and Noguchi. There were buildings designed by Philip Johnson, Buckminster Fuller, and I. M. Pei, who had also designed Mike Ovitz's CAA building. There was a cinemathèque and a poets league and even a ballet for those in wheelchairs. There was even a rain forest at the Cleveland Zoo!

Restaurants? Bill Clinton had stopped twice at Parma Pierogi, JFK had dinner at Helriegel's, and Mussolini had said that his favorite chef in the whole world was Cleveland's own Chef Boyardee!

Celebrities had always *flocked* to Cleveland! Buffalo Bill Cody lived there. So did Bob Hope, Paul Newman, Debra Winger, Swingin' Sammy Kaye, Arsenio Hall, John D. Rockefeller, Drew Carey, Roger Penske, Halle Berry, Jack Paar, Wes Craven, Phil Donahue, Bone Thugs-N-Harmony, and Joel Grey.

Howard Stern partied there in the parking lot of a strip club called Tiffany's. Doonesbury's B.D. was based on former St. Ignatius High School quarterback Brian Dowling. Martina Navratilova and Bjorn Borg played for the Cleveland Nets. George Burns and Gracie Allen got married there.

Literary Cleveland was like the Paris of the Midwest. Hart Crane, Artemus Ward, Toni Morrison, Langston Hughes, Harlan Ellison, Bruce Catton, Jerry Siegel (the creator of Superman), were all Clevelanders at one time or another.

But most impressive to me: Elvis's favorite football team, whose games the King watched by special cable as he munched his fried banana and peanut butter sandwiches . . . the Cleveland Browns!

In the late eighties, trying to talk him into starring in my movie *Checking Out,* I visited Jeff Daniels at his big white house on a small lake not far from Ann Arbor, Michigan.

We went out on Jeff's paddleboat and talked about the script. It was a glorious summer day and as I watched Jeff's little kids splashing around in the water,

I thought: What a smart man you are, Jeff, to be away from L.A. and to be here, raising your children.

When we were done on the paddleboat, we drove into a nearby small town and had lunch in the town's best restaurant. We had two bratwurst sandwiches each and two ice-cold beers. Everyone in town knew Jeff, I soon realized, but they didn't know him as a Hollywood celebrity. They talked about his kids' Little League teams and the skunk problem under the bridge leading into town and the Fourth of July ox roast.

"We didn't want to raise our kids in Hollywood," Jeff Daniels had said to me during our script meeting in his paddleboat.

"Everybody's famous, and our friends, probably more often than not, would have been people in the Industry or famous people in the Industry. And I just wanted our kids to be away from that. There's a fantasy world there that can mix with reality, and I just didn't want them to be confused about that."

I wasn't sure I'd ever envied anyone more in my life than I did Jeff Daniels at that moment, when I shook his hand goodbye and drove over the bridge that smelled of skunk.

Naomi and I were going to drive over to Palm Springs with Evans and his new young girlfriend. At the last minute, Evans's girlfriend couldn't make it.

"Her stupid parents are taking her to Disneyland for the weekend," Evans said.

There was nothing to eat in Malibu, except sushi. Oh, not really, of course, but certainly metaphorically.

After seven years of living there, I decided that I was starved. I didn't want any more holy or saintly food. And I didn't want to see any more waiters who acted like I'd insulted their genealogy when I asked for the salt and pepper.

Damn it, I wanted a juicy, blood-dripping prime rib! I wanted golden-crusted, breaded fried fish! I wanted Wiener schnitzel and the food of my Magyar forefathers! Burnt pork chops and chicken paprikás drenched with sour cream and big, buttered, and garlic-stuffed baked potatoes, not those shavings of organically grown designer potatoes they served here.

I couldn't even find a decent loaf of bread in Malibu. Bread was unhealthy, bread put fat on you—I knew all the Malibu wisdom about bread—but I loved bread. I loved bread with butter on it, with anchovy paste on it, even, may the Good Lord forgive me, with deviled ham spread thick on it! But the bread they sold in Malibu was either so doughy it felt like you'd filled your stomach with bricks, or it was filled with all this healthy, good-for-you, you'll-live-forever crap—raisins, bananas, olives, figs, blueberries.

I didn't want it to be good for me! I just wanted to eat a crusty, light, and un-strawberry-douched loaf of bread that I could spread my deviled ham on or stuff my sausage into.

We had to drive forty minutes into Santa Monica to find the bread that I liked and, when I asked for the can of deviled ham at my Malibu grocery, the clerk tried to talk me into raspberry yogurt instead.

For those of us who felt that living in Malibu or Carbon Beach or Broad Beach provided a safe shelter from the violent hurly-burly of life in L.A. . . . . there were occasional nasty reminders that we weren't even safe out here.

Three chopped-up bodies were found in a park in Topanga Canyon, just off the Pacific Coast Highway.

And on a sunny Sunday afternoon, a man went up to a group of sunbathers on the beach, took out a nine-millimeter, and started firing bullets which sprayed the surf and sand. A group of men chased the gunman across the sand and up to the PCH and over it to the other side of the road into the hills as he shot at them and they shot at him.

Gangbangers, the police said, who'd come all the way from Compton to get a little sun on the beach just down the winding lane from Michael Eisner's estate.

We were bored, too, with our friends. Almost all of them were Industry Friends and, while we weren't big partygoers, we had them over for dinner or holidays. They had nothing to talk about, we painfully realized, except the Industry.

What movie Brad was doing next and why there was going to be no *Titanic* sequel and why Ovitz would fail with his management company.

It was like being around people who lived twenty-four hours a day inside a house wallpapered with *Daily Variety,* the *Hollywood Reporter,* and the *National Enquirer.* Discussions of even specific movies were not in terms of their artistic qualities but in terms of their budgets. Even those couples who had kids talked not about the kids but about the clothes at Baby Gap vs. the clothes at Fred Segal.

We couldn't discuss books with them because our friends didn't read books; they read scripts or, more likely, readers' reports of scripts. Many of them were nice people, but there just wasn't a whole lot of "there" there.

Many of them, too, didn't seem to project a personality. They listened, they asked questions, they smiled: it was as though they were *afraid* to talk about themselves, *afraid* to reveal things about themselves, hiding themselves within cool and possibly Prozac-ed cocoons while they "interviewed" Naomi and me.

They were the extended family equation of the agent who calls you three times a week and says, "I'm just checking in," and has absolutely nothing else to say. ("Don't check in," I said to such an agent once. "I'm a human being, not a hotel," and he was so shook up by what I said that I had to fire him soon afterward.)

To have a stimulating political conversation with our friends was nearly impossible. They believed in the Enlightened Political Positions, but that was exactly the problem. They were all Liberal Democrats imbued with a Social Conscience. It was like we were all Moonies who'd had the same programming.

Voicing a different opinion about a combustible political issue was sacrilege, met not with rebuttal but with shock. I startled a roomful of friends by making a case against Bill Clinton and they thought I was kidding, Joe doing his quirky court jester–dancing bear act again, Joe the provocateur trying to get a rise out of them.

Certain of our friendships broke up for other reasons: a producer who *did* read books and did offer opinions and revelations decided to retire, took Berlitz courses, and was in Italy much of the time . . . an agent who knew the history of the business lost his job and was so humiliated he didn't come out of his Westwood condo much anymore.

We started to realize that the only time we were at all stimulated by our friends was when they came in from out of town and were not Industry—or when they were family—especially Naomi's three brothers: Bernie and Bep, both in the steel business in Ohio, and Jeremy, the successful non-Industry public relations man in Los Angeles.

Bernie and Bep weren't interested in movie budgets and shooting schedules. They weren't afraid to say, "Boy, what a piece of shit that movie was!" as opposed to our Industry friends who, when they felt that way about a movie, said, "I haven't seen it yet."

Bernie and Bep spoke honestly, with real human emotion, about their kids' failures and successes. They weren't afraid to make off-color cracks or politically incorrect remarks. They weren't afraid to call Bill Clinton a "dumb asshole."

I purposely held some things back from Naomi about Cleveland which I was afraid she might find disturbing.

- Buffalo Bill Cody hated Cleveland. He wrote in his memoirs that it was "like living in a sinkhole."
- Rodin's internationally renowned *The Thinker,* located outside the Cleveland Museum of Art, was the victim of an unsolved bomb blast in the seventies.
- Cleveland was mass murderer and cannibal Jeffrey Dahmer's favorite city, the place he always asked his dad to take him when he was a little boy.

- Ray Chapman of the Cleveland Indians was the only player ever to have died in major league baseball, the victim of a beanball.
- Cleveland Mayor Ralph J. Perk banned the Beatles from appearing in the city.
- Ralph Waldo Emerson was booed off the stage during an appearance in Cleveland.
- Cleveland Orchestra director George Szell ordered all members of his orchestra to shave their beards and mustaches.
- Abolitionist mass murderer John Brown was raised in a small town just outside Cleveland.
- Future presidential assassin John Wilkes Booth was the popular star of the Cleveland Academy of Music.
- Cleveland's most celebrated poet, Hart Crane, committed suicide.
- The guy who wrote *Leaving Las Vegas* was from Cleveland, too. He, too, committed suicide.
- Hart Crane's father, Cleveland confectioner Clarence Crane, invented Life Savers.
- Hart Crane ate a lot of Life Savers, but they obviously didn't save his life.

In many ways, even living in glamorous fastest-track Malibu, we were already poster children for Midwestern family values.

Our focus was our family; our obsession was our children.

I grilled burgers and hot dogs on the Weber. We made a big deal about the Carving of the Thanksgiving Turkey. We took the boys down to see Baby Jesus in the nativity crèche on the Pacific Coast Highway each Christmas, as we took them to sit on Santa's knee at the Broadway mall in Santa Monica.

I drove a pickup truck; Naomi drove a Chevy Suburban. Naomi said prayers with the boys each night before they fell asleep. We didn't cheat on each other, we didn't even flirt with others, we were devoted to our marriage.

We went searching for fresh corn in the summer. I liked buffets where they served country ham for Sunday brunch. We liked "real" country music: Willie and Ray Price and Ernest Tubb.

There was one other way we were Midwesterners, too: we'd had the four kids in only six years.

We'd created a very big family very fast and were still at it, thinking how wonderful it would be if we had a little girl . . . or how terrific it would be if we had our own basketball team . . . or *baseball* team.

None of this West Coast family planning nonsense for us! We didn't give a *fuck* about the world's overpopulation problem! My global consciousness was limited to certain globes of Naomi's body.

There wasn't a whole lot to do in the dead of winter in the Midwest. Sometimes it was even hard to leave the house and get out on the road, so people stayed inside and enjoyed indoor activities and had gigantic families. Not cool, California-style "extended" families, but the real, sweaty, intercourse-created thing.

We'd been staying inside and growing our family in the dead of winter in California even . . . the size family we could grow as Midwesterners *actually living in the Midwest* . . . seemed unlimited to us.

Within this intimate context, the fact that I was Hungarian-born was relevant, too. A Reuters wire story said, "Forget Latin lovers—horny Hungarians are now the most active between the sheets, leading a charge of Eastern Europeans in the global sex charts. Condom maker Durex's annual global sex survey showed that Hungarian lovers enjoy sex 152 times a year. The French—fiercely proud of their sexual prowess—only manage 144 performances a year. The Italians and Spanish lag even further with scores of 119 and 123 times a year, while American make love an average of 118 times a year, Germans 120 and Australians 125."

Naomi told me a story: "When I was a little girl we lived on Mifflin Lake and each year we waited for the ducks to come. They were the same ducks each year, led by a glorious-looking, strutting mallard. All the other ducks were always fluttering around the mallard, but he only had eyes for one scroungy-looking little duck, always after her, just her, always *loving her.* One day as he was loving her, a snapping turtle took one of her legs off. That didn't stop the mallard. He kept loving her, just *her.* One year the ducks came and the mallard was there but the scroungy little duck he loved wasn't. I knew that little duck was dead. And I knew that mallard had *loved her to death.*"

Yet even as Naomi and I talked about moving to Cleveland, we couldn't, as we said in the Industry, "pull the trigger on the deal."

Part of it was that both Naomi and I, growing up on Lorain Avenue and in Mansfield, had been desperate to get *out* of Ohio. There had been a narrowness and provincialism there that used to drive me nuts, a grayness of the spirit symbolized by the leadenness of the sky and a sun which seemed trapped behind an iron curtain of pollutants.

I was an adventurer as a young man, flouting and rebelling against the rules of church and state. I finally fled to California where a lot of Clevelanders felt I belonged . . . out there on the Left Coast among all those drug-addled and *nekid* hippies, living not far from Berserkeley, my hair shaggy and long. Good riddance! America, love it or leave it!

And as far as they were concerned, they were sure I'd left it. Because California wasn't a part of *their* America. California was what was wrong with this country—it was no wonder that I was a Californian.

And now, thirty years later, the father of six children (so far), divorced, happily remarried to another Ohio girl, as I was nearing age sixty, I was contemplating going back.

Home. The return of the prodigal son. To a nice, quiet place where it would be fun to love my wife, raise my kids, and write.

To my *hometown*, which I'd thought so narrow and provincial.

Cleveland? Forget all my previous "adventures" of so many years ago. What about my more recent "adventures" for which I'd been, in some quarters, on dubious moral grounds, *pilloried*?

Did you hear the news, boys and girls? The guy who wrote *Basic Instinct* and *Showgirls* and *Sliver* and *Jade* . . . the guy who, even in the *Plain Dealer*'s opinion, was perhaps "Satan's agent" . . . this guy was going to set up shop in Cleveland? In Ohio? In the *heartland*? In Ronald Reagan and George W. Bush country?

At certain moments it put chills down my spine just thinking about it.

Naomi found an interview which Kevin Bacon had done during the filming of *Telling Lies in America.*

In the interview, Kevin called me "the King of Cleveland."

"Are you really the King of Cleveland?" Naomi asked.

"Hell no," I said, "I'm just another shitass honky refugee from the West Side trying to make his way in the big world."

The school system in Malibu troubled us, too. John Law and Nick were in preschool; Joey was in kindergarten.

I resented the intrusion of the teachers in our home. We got phone calls announcing the teachers' visits. They were constantly inviting themselves to our home so they could see "the home environment" the boys were living in.

I wondered what they were thinking: they were checking out "home environment" for two *preschoolers* and a *kindergartner?* They knew that the boys were living in a very expensive Malibu neighborhood and they knew that their father was a millionaire screenwriter. What kind of "home environment" did they think the boys were living in? A hovel? A pigsty? A child-abusing torture chamber? The teachers came and strolled through our house like prospective buyers.

They asked questions like: How long did you research *Showgirls?* Do you *know* Sylvester Stallone? Is he nice? Is Jean-Claude Van Damme really short? They asked me to contribute signed *Basic* and *Showgirls* posters to the school auction. They took a cursory look at the boys' rooms (home environment) and invariably asked about the signed Beatles poster and the signed Muhammad Ali photograph. One of them was a former Vegas dancer who said, "My best friend is the girl in *Showgirls* who chipped her tooth on a Quaalude."

"Community Involvement" was another teacher mantra. Three times a week, "family homework" was assigned and Naomi and I started feeling like we were back in school. A teacher told us we either had to "volunteer" for school activities or, if we were too busy, we had to pay the school $1,000 a semester. Nannies and housekeepers, school policy said, couldn't substitute for parents.

"A thousand dollars is extortion," I told Naomi, "not volunteer work," but we paid the money anyway.

"Field trips," I soon deduced, were the biggest scam. A field trip once a week to all parts of L.A.—to the Planetarium, the Imax Theatre, the Farmers Market in Santa Monica. Pile all the kids into strangers' cars, zip them down the Pacific Coast Highway, the most dangerous and lethal road in the whole state of California, and onto the freeways, which weren't just a dodge 'em collision course but a place where hucksters in teams faked accidents each day to cheat insurance companies.

All this to see fresh vegetables being sold at the Farmers Market? Why? Because the teachers were bored and wanted to buy some fresh produce for the weekend? Meanwhile, Joey in kindergarten couldn't spell or read but was learning to do both *at home* with the $300 phonics set we had bought.

The topper for me was when Joey's favorite teacher, a New Age, post-hippie earth mother was suddenly fired by the school one day. We made some inquiries and discovered that she was gone because she'd been living homeless in her car and had a killer prescription drug habit. She went to Florida to join her two grown children—both of whom, naturally, were . . . surfers.

It seemed to me, while I was living in Malibu, that I heard from just about every Hungarian who lived in the L.A. Basin.

Thousands of Hungarians writing, calling, telegramming, e-mailing their fellow Hungarian—the famous Hungarian screenwriter—to suggest to him a collaboration on a screenplay about . . . always about, *invariably* about . . . Attila the Hun.

In November of the year 2000, in a doctor's office in Beverly Hills, I was diagnosed with two benign polyps on my vocal cords. I was what is known as a polyp "grower" and had had benign nasal polyps surgically removed three times.

The doctor who made the diagnosis was known as an "E-N-T Man to the Stars." His office was filled with gold and platinum records given to him by singers he'd treated.

There was no rush to do the surgery, the doctor said; those polyps had been growing for a long time. But it would eventually have to be done because, as they grew, the polyps would block my air path.

The surgery would be done on an outpatient basis at Cedars Sinai and I would be released a few hours after it was done.

"Nothing to it," the doctor said. "I do it all the time. I've done thousands of them."

But I was uneasy. I knew that Cedars had almost killed Lew Wasserman, one of their biggest financial benefactors, the venerable former head of MCA Universal, counselor to presidents from Kennedy to Reagan. A routine surgery and Lew Wasserman had almost *died*. I knew that the puppeteer Shari Lewis's estate was suing Cedars, claiming that Lewis, in their care, had died choking on her own vomit.

I also knew that Julie Andrews and former California governor Pete Wilson had had this kind of benign polyp surgery in L.A. and Julie Andrews couldn't sing anymore and Pete Wilson could hardly speak.

For some reason, I didn't like the presence of all those platinum and gold records on my doctor's walls, either. I wanted to be in the hands of a doctor who kept medical certificates on his walls.

The Cleveland Clinic, I knew, had an international reputation equal to the Mayo's. Saudi kings flew there to have their surgeries.

"I'm not going to have these polyps taken out here," I said to Naomi. "I certainly don't sing as well as Julie Andrews did. But I still like to sing in the shower."

"You sing horribly," Naomi said.

"Yeah, I know," I said, "but nobody can hear me in the shower. I don't want some guy doing this who's got gold records on his wall. There's got to be some kind of limit put on starfucking in this town."

"Fine," Naomi said, "we'll get it done in Cleveland."

We drove our little boys over to Woodland Hills in the Valley to see the neighborhood which turned into a Christmas festival each year . . . and found the street we loved aglow with Christmas lights and blocked off by police crime scene tape.

A man was lying on the sidewalk in a pool of blood under a home-built papier-mâché float of Santa and his elves, shot to death less than an hour before by his girlfriend's jealous husband.

To consider, too, as we contemplated moving to Cleveland, was the matter of my father.

He was ninety-three years old and living in the same house in Cleveland Heights which he'd bought with my mother in 1966. I'd supported him since 1978 and, since 1992, I'd hired around-the-clock nursing care for him as well as a Hungarian housekeeper.

He was bed-bound now, with a catheter, and was in and out, lucid one day and befogged the next. There was a time in my life, when I was a young man, when my father had been my best friend. That time had passed.

I loved my father but we were no longer best friends. I loved him, but I also loathed him.

When he was accused of war crimes by the Justice Department, I discovered a painful jigsaw of lies that went to the core of who I thought my father was. I started avoiding him and avoiding talking to him because I knew all I'd get were more lies.

I spoke to him periodically on behalf of the black nurses who worked so hard to take care of him. He'd screamed at them to serve him his meals, hiding cans of Coke from them under his bed. I spoke to him on their behalf but it did no good.

His nurses couldn't take care of him anymore: he was too heavy to lift and difficult even to turn over. The Hungarian housekeeper made daily gastronomic extravaganzas of chicken paprikás and stuffed cabbage and my father, on a catheter and without teeth, somehow kept eating it all and getting bigger.

It was time finally, I knew, for a nursing home—the decision I'd been dreading because I knew how much being *in his home* meant to him. My father had always been there for me when I was a kid and an adolescent and as much as my feelings for him had changed through the course of the past decade . . . *I didn't want to do this to him* . . . He still spoke the English language, after fifty years in America, with a thick, difficult-to-understand accent. To take him out of his home and to put him into an American setting where they'd have difficulty understanding him would probably not only be a death sentence but a sentence of torture.

It occurred to me that by forcing him out of his house, I'd be effecting the deportation which Gerry Messerman and I had stopped the Justice Department from doing.

But the nurses kept calling to tell me we had to do something. My father lay in bed staring off, vegetating, not even watching the big-screen TV I'd bought for him.

He had bedsores, the nurses said, which were getting worse. *We had to do something . . . we had to do something . . . we had to do something.*

Shortly after New Year's of 2001, I got a call from one of my father's nurses telling me that he was failing and that we had to do something quickly about getting him into a nursing home. Naomi and I decided to fly back to Cleveland immediately to see him.

His hospital bed was in the middle of the living room and a nurse was changing his diaper when we walked in. I hugged him and he started to cry, held him as she tried to roll him over. I saw bedsores all over his back and body.

Naomi and I sat next to the bed and we tried to talk to him. He couldn't hear very well. He refused to use the hearing aid which I'd bought him. I couldn't shout because of the polyps in my throat and tried not to strain my voice because the doctors told me if I strained it, I'd lose it.

And Naomi couldn't speak Hungarian, of course, and my father, even when he could hear, couldn't understand English very well.

Naomi and I tried, as people do at moments like this, to joke, to brighten his life for a few hours, to talk about his grandchildren, whose framed photographs were all over his walls . . . to make him smile and laugh, to blot momentarily the grimness of his daily life, his catheter, his bedsores.

"Pop," I said, "listen to this. Joey is my Arab son, always making deals to his benefit with his little brothers. Nick is my Italian son, flashing his temper, instantly ready to use his fists, John Law is my Hungarian son—he's inherited our triple chins—and Luke, he's my Russian son. He's very charming but all he does is drink."

My father laughed, as he was supposed to. Granting us our victory over his misery. He was happy. Smiling and laughing. And then he closed his eyes—eyes exactly the slate-blue color of Luke's . . . and started to cry.

I held his hand.

He said, "I've never lied to you" and, knowing that it was a lie, I kissed his hand and held it. I was crying, too, and so was Naomi. We cried quietly for a long time, saying nothing, not looking at each other.

"Are you tired, Pop?" I asked him in Hungarian.

He couldn't hear me. My voice, now that I'd been talking for a while, was much weaker.

There was a cruel kind of poetic irony at work here, I thought.

He couldn't hear. I couldn't speak. The only way we could communicate now was through Naomi.

I repeated the Hungarian words slowly to her. Naomi yelled them phonetically into my father's ears.

"I am tired to death," my father said.

"Are you bored?"

"There is nothing I can do," my father said. "I can't hear, I can't see, I can't get out of this bed. Some mornings I wake up and I can't speak for an hour or so. I can't read, I can't write, I can't watch the TV. My friends are all dead. You're in California."

I tried to joke again.

"Well," I said in Hungarian, "the good news is that you can still eat. Margit"—his housekeeper—"makes great chicken paprikás for you."

He couldn't hear me again.

I repeated the Hungarian words slowly to Naomi again and she yelled them phonetically into his ear, again.

My father smiled at her.

"Very good," he said. "You speak Hungarian perfect."

"Thank you, Steffen," Naomi said and held his hand.

My father's eyes were suddenly frantic, his eyes like Luke's when he woke up in the middle of the night and screamed for us.

"Isn't there some way to make this go faster?" he asked me. "Isn't there some way I can die faster?"

I shook my head. I noticed he wasn't crying now.

"How much longer will it take?" he asked.

"I don't know," I said. "Nobody knows."

He nodded and looked away and shook his head.

"Are you scared, Pop?" I asked him.

"No," he said, "I am ready for the next adventure."

He dozed off then as we were holding his hand. He startled awake as I was kissing his forehead, saying goodbye.

"You're going?" he said, panicked again.

"We'll be back tomorrow, Steffen," Naomi said.

"Ah." He smiled at her. "Good."

"My son," he said to her, "married a beautiful woman."

"Thank you, Steffen," Naomi said, kissing his forehead.

"My son," he said to Naomi, "was always a very good *bájgunár*."

"What is *bájgunár*?" Naomi asked me.

"Cocksman," I said.

"You, Steffen," Naomi said, "like your son, are a very bad man."

"Very true," my father said, and laughed. We laughed with him.

We had come here to cheer him, but the final joke, as we were almost out the door—*bájgunár!*—was my father's and meant to cheer *us*.

It was still snowing as we sat in a bar a few blocks from my father's house. I was drinking a double Tanqueray gin straight and Naomi, who hardly drinks, was on her second glass of wine.

"Well," I said, "we're in Cleveland. We don't have a whole lot of plans here except to see him. Do you want to look at some houses in Cleveland?"

"I wondered if we were coming back here," Naomi said, "partly to do this?"

I said, "Subconsciously, you mean?"

Naomi told me a story: "We were living in downtown Mansfield when I was little and the downtown area was changing. More crime. Fights. Cops patrolling. Fights at the bars down the street. My dad wanted to get his kids out of there. He found a lot of land near Mifflin Lake that had small summer homes and cabins.

It was part of the state conservancy. They told him that he could build a home out there, but only if he became the conservator and took care of the summer homes. So my dad built a home for us with his own hands on that plot of land on the shore of Mifflin Lake. It took him a year. We had no one to play with except from June to Labor Day when the summer home owners would come. We were out in the middle of nowhere, just our family, on the shore of an amazing lake that turned into our own ice-skating rink in the winter. Then, when my older brothers got married and had kids, my dad and my brothers built houses for *them* across the street. It was the greatest thing that my dad ever did for us. He took us away from the influences he feared would hurt us and built a fairy tale for us with his own hands."

That night I prayed for my father to die—he wanted to die; it was the best thing for him—and the next morning we went to a real estate office in Chagrin Falls, a picture postcard village outside Cleveland that I'd always loved.

The area around Chagrin Falls is hilly and tree-lined, horsey and woodsy country. The houses vary from Tudor to French Normandy to Colonial, with sizable acreage around them.

On this day, as we drove along the Chagrin River, the sun gleamed off the fallen snow and the air was brisk and crystalline. We looked at houses with indoor pools and ballrooms and racquetball courts, estates with guesthouses and stables and corrals. At each stop, the real estate agent got his snow shovel out of the trunk of the limo and made a path to the door.

We had lunch with the agent in the heart of Chagrin, right next to the falls—at a little place called Rick's, which served great cheeseburgers and where I could smoke. We looked at a couple more houses after lunch—one in a tiny township called Bainbridge—and called it a day.

Just outside Chagrin, we saw a place called the Coyote Moon Café and stopped for a drink. We were on the way to see my father again and we were cold, too.

This time I had a double tequila. We liked the feel of the place—a bar where you could drink and smoke, a bar which served great nachos . . . a friendly bar with a vintage jukebox where, when I sneezed hard, a guy on the barstool next to mine said, "Hey, pardner, I just wanna tell you if you need any help, I'm close by."

But as I sipped my tequila to get ready to see my father, Naomi said, "You're not thinking of coming back here because—" She couldn't finish the sentence. She was choked up.

"Because—"

I knew what she was thinking and finished it for her.

"Because when I'm gone, this will be a good place for you and the kids?"

"Yes," she said.

"No," I said, "I'm not thinking of that."

"Do you promise me?" Naomi said.

"I promise you," I said.

It's not easy to find a good place open for lunch on Sunday in Cleveland and we wound up at an Irish pub called the Harp on 44th and Detroit Avenue, just a few blocks from where I'd grown up on Lorain Avenue.

We sat there watching the snow fall outside, ate a great Irish bacon quiche, drank a Guinness, and listened to Van Morrison and the Chieftains. A blazing fireplace nearby warmed us.

Neither Naomi nor I had really talked about it yesterday, but it came up here now in this warm and cozy place with the fireplace crackling . . . the *house in Bainbridge Township*.

It was the last house we had looked at before our talk about death at the Coyote Moon. It was a white colonial with a porch and a screened indoor gazebo room. It was 8,900 square feet. Its basement ran the length of the house, perfect for four little boys to raise havoc in. Its skylighted attic ran the length of the house, too, a perfect room for writing. Six bedrooms, formal dining and living rooms, a large kitchen, and, best of all, five acres surrounded by woods, ponds, and a private lake with a large private dock. It was out in the country, but only ten minutes from the town of Chagrin Falls, only forty minutes from downtown Cleveland on the freeway.

As we talked about it, Naomi and I could hear screen doors slamming, inner tubes hitting the lake, crickets chirping. We could see little boys free to ride around the neighborhood cul-de-sacs on their bikes, free to jump into the lake, to explore the woods for treasures.

"Let's go back to see it again," Naomi said.

"I thought we'd decided against this."

"Let's go back and see it anyway."

We called the real estate agent, who very graciously canceled his plans, and we went to see the house again. It was everything that we had remembered from the day before and more (the lake was stocked with bass and the snow on the ground was covering two sweeping lawns that led to the lake and an outdoor, red-brick patio).

We thanked the agent when we were finished and told him we'd get back to him. My feeling was that he was beginning to think that we were lunatics, but liked us anyway. We were given photographs of the house in winter, summer, and fall and took them with us.

We talked about the house and the effect on our family if we moved here— until we got on the plane to California the next day.

What we kept getting back to, over and over again, was *the house itself*. We were housebound, home-oriented people. I wrote and read much of each day. Naomi loved to cook and I favored her cooking over Wolfgang Puck's. We hung out at home much of the time in the kitchen and this house had a stunning kitchen with its own breakfast nook overlooking the dock and the lake. We didn't go out much at night. After seven years of marriage, we were still crazy in love and wanted to spend nighttime with each other, not with others.

So the truth was that if we moved to Cleveland, we'd really be moving *to this house,* this cocoon, this fortress.

Our family would be our community. With four growing boys and with my two grown children and with work and with our love for each other, we wouldn't have much time for too much else.

That night I had a dream that I was jogging down a street that led through thick black woods. It was a bright, sun-kissed, clear day, and as I jogged I was exhilarated and happy.

When I woke from the dream, its memory made me smile: I didn't and couldn't jog. I even had trouble hurrying through an airport to catch a flight. Thanks, no doubt, to the four packs of Salems I smoked each day.

As we pulled into Cleveland Hopkins International Airport heading back to Malibu, the last thing we saw before we pulled into the terminal was a factory, its torch afire in a leaden, gray sky.

Looking at it in horror, I whispered, "No way we're moving here."

As we got on the plane, I was wearing a brown fur Hungarian peasant hat my father had given me before we left his house.

But in exchange for the hat, I reflected, my father had taken my voice. I had shouted into his ear so often during this visit, straining my polyped vocal cords so badly, that I couldn't speak at all.

Struck dumb in Cleveland by my own father!

As we pulled onto the Pacific Coast Highway and saw the sun glistening off the sea, I said, "We can't ever leave here!"

I noticed that Naomi had the photographs of the house in Bainbridge Township in her lap.

As we resumed our Malibu routine, we found that the house in Bainbridge Township had snaked its way into our brains. We kept thinking and talking about it.

"It's exactly like where I grew up," Naomi said, "the house on Mifflin Lake that my dad built. There's even a road you can see in the distance across the lake. The kitchen even faces the lake like my mother's kitchen did."

We talked about how happy our little boys would be there, fishing in the lake, sledding down the hill that led to it. Bainbridge Township, Ohio, we agreed, was the real America. High school football on Friday night, not a party at Kenny G's house. Burgers and hot dogs in the backyard on Sundays, not a walk down the bluff, boogie board in hand, to the beach. A wasp's nest on Show and Tell Day in kindergarten, not Dad's Oscar.

But . . . *Ohio* instead of *Malibu*? Thermal underwear instead of bikini shorts? Maple syrup instead of soy sauce? Pancakes at the high school gym instead of sushi at Nobu? Lake Erie perch and walleye instead of Santa Barbara mussels?

Moving to Bainbridge Township was madness . . . *no,* moving to Bainbridge Township was real life . . . *no,* it was an act of nostalgia and masochism . . . *no,* it was a selfless and loving gift to our boys . . . *no,* our boys would be better off as surfers than as redneck hicks . . . *no,* Ohioans were good, solid, decent people, not redneck hicks.

I went back and forth, back and forth, driving myself and Naomi nuts.

We didn't know what to do.

So we put our Point Dume house up for sale and left the move to Ohio in the hands of God.

If our house sold fast, we decided, we'd move.

But Malibu houses sometimes took years to sell at their full asking price. The sale, we thought, would be further complicated by the construction which had begun in the lot next door. Whoever bought our house would be harassed by construction noise for years.

We also put an absolutely top-of-the-line, stretched-to-the-max list price on the house, hundreds of thousands of dollars more than our real estate agent said would be a fair price.

We weren't interested in fair; we were testing God.

It's in Your hands, yes, but we have to be sure You'll be making the right decision.

Michael Huffington, the ex-Senate candidate, looked at our house and its exorbitant price and passed. So did the actress Catherine Oxenberg, who, for a heartbeat, had been married to my great friend Robert Evans. So did Jack Nicholson's daughter. So did pro basketball coach Larry Brown.

And then a young dot.com couple came and looked at it and bought it. *At full list price.*

Our house had been on the market for a week.

We had six weeks to get out.

We had left it in God's hands and God had made the decision for us.

Boychik, God said, go home!

Three days after we bought our house in Bainbridge Township, Ohio, we heard Brian Williams on *MSNBC Nightly News* say that Cleveland had been hit by a 3.7 earthquake, its epicenter just offshore in Lake Erie.

"If Steffen doesn't die before we move back there," Naomi said, "will you let him see the boys?"

"He'll die," I said, "he is ready to go any day."

"What if he doesn't?"

"Sure," I said, "they're his grandchildren. He can see them."

"Will you let them kiss him?"

"Of course I will. I kiss him myself."

"Steffen won't die," Naomi said, "until he sees the boys."

Naomi said, "Will you tell the boys what he did in Hungary?"

"Now?"

"You know what I mean. When they're older?"

"I think it's important to tell them. I told Steve and Suzi, too."

"Why? Because you can't forgive him and you want to destroy him in the boys' eyes?"

"No," I said, "because I think all my children have to know what their family members have done, good or bad."

"Why inflict that on them?" Naomi said. "They don't deserve it."

"So they spend the rest of their lives," I said, "trying to make up for what their grandfather did."

"They'll hate him for it when they're older," Naomi said.

"No they won't. Not if we raise them right. They'll understand that this particular horror can be orchestrated even by a benign-looking grandpa who loves his grandchildren."

We told the boys we were moving and showed them pictures of the house in Bainbridge Township. They ran around the room whooping and hollering at decibels even louder than their routine ear-shattering levels.

They would have their own lake! And they could fish and swim! And in the winter they could ice-skate! And sled! They could ride their bikes *on the street!* Their rec room was the length of the house! We would build snowmen! We could watch thunderstorms!

Joey yelled: "I don't have to go to this stupid school! I hate my stupid teacher!"

Nick yelled: "We're moving out of this stupid house!"

John Law yelled whatever Joey and Nick yelled.

Luke yelled, "Dada! Dada! Dada!"

And when they were falling asleep that night Nick said, "Thank you, Dada, for moving us out of this stupid house."

And Joey said, "I hope I don't have another stupid teacher."

I realized with a start that John Law and Luke would have no California memories at all. They would remember that life for them began in Cleveland.

I decided I wouldn't tell my father that we were moving back until we were actually there.

If I told him before, I feared, he'd have his nurses call us ten times a day and drive us even crazier than I knew we'd be during the next six weeks.

I knew he would be happy that we would be near him but I also knew he would be decimated. There was no way around it: his nurses kept calling to tell me they couldn't take care of him anymore. I would have to deport my father from the house that he loved and put him into a nursing home as soon as possible after I moved back.

I still hoped that he would die before we got there. But I also wondered if this would be God's final punishment for my father's sins:

You lost everything during the war, Steffen, your career, your money, your country. You lived in dire poverty from the moment you left Hungary. You lost your wife, and then in a different way, you lost your only son. Now, Steffen, you will even lose your little house. Your son will force you to leave it.

The moving company we picked was just planning another big move from Malibu.

"Darcy Hughes," the moving company's appraiser said to me. "Maybe you know her?"

I did, but when I had known her it was Darcy LaPier, soon to become Darcy Van Damme. She and Jean-Claude were visiting Gerri Eszterhas and me at our house in Tiburon for lunch and afterward we played pool in the game room.

Steve and several of his friends were there but as the game went on, I noticed they were starstruck not by Jean-Claude but by the sexy and voluptuous Darcy.

Then Darcy and Jean-Claude had gotten married and divorced—cocaine and multi-party sex games the alleged cause, according to Darcy—and Darcy met a guy named Mark Hughes, who was worth hundreds of millions of dollars.

Mark Hughes dropped dead three months later; Darcy inherited $30 million, and now Darcy was going to Portland, going home like me . . . just another Hollywood success story taking the fruit of her labors back to her hometown.

Darcy had her thirty mil and I had Naomi and the four boys, both of us getting home thanks to the same moving company, one-way from Malibu.

. . .

"Tell me some more great things about Cleveland," Naomi said to me.

"You scared?" I asked.

"Maybe," she said, "are you?"

"*Terrified*," I said.

"Good," she said, "me too."

"Well," I said, "it was settled accidentally. The original founder, Moses Cleaveland, was drunk and he thought he was someplace else."

I said, "Sylvester Stallone saw a fight in Cleveland. Muhammad Ali and a barroom brawler named Chuck Wepner. Sly got his idea for *Rocky* from that fight. The whole *Rocky* franchise, billions of dollars, all because of Cleveland!

"Bruce Springsteen owes his career to Cleveland. He kept playing a little club called the Agora when nobody knew who he was. It was the beginning of his reputation."

I said, "Listen! *Elvis* wouldn't have happened without Cleveland. A disc jockey named Bill Randle started playing him when nobody else was. Cleveland and Bill Randle *made* Elvis!"

Naomi said, "I don't care where we live as long as you're there."

I said, "I don't, either."

I said, "That's probably the best possible attitude with which to move to Cleveland."

I kissed her and said, "No bad dreams."

She said, "Are you kidding me? I won't sleep a wink."

No one knew their origin, although the rumor locally was that their leader, a bull mastiff the size of a small boar, had once been one of Bob Dylan's dogs, a runaway who'd tired of the rock and roll life and gone howling into the Malibu hills.

There were about eight to a dozen of them, mostly big dogs—the mastiff, a shepherd, a Newfie, two pit bulls—and they were occasionally spotted running as a pack through the rugged canyons and burned-out treelines.

Wolves and the rare mountain lion were their prey and one resident on a hilltop overlooking Calabasas came back from Kauai to discover that everything in his house had been torn to pieces, including the hand-tooled Santa Fe couches.

I heard them howling down on the beach beneath our house in the hours before dawn and saw them in the moonlight: from above in the darkness they looked like spectral beings, their sheer size astounding me as they roared headlong down the beach road.

They came to the bluffs around the beach mostly when a movie was being filmed down there at night. They spread out on the hillside, primordial sentries crouched down in the brush hundreds of feet from each other, watching the klieg lights and the spotlights and the sound trucks—howling, incessantly howling—themselves a part of the show now as movie stars on the beach below tried to spot them with their infrared binoculars.

. . .

The boys were upstairs. They had gotten up with the rising sun and Nick, our four-year-old, saw a splash of sunshine on the little table they ate their snacks on.

"Look, Nana, look how bewteeeful," he said, touching the sunspot.

"God is painting," Naomi said to him.

"I heard that voice again," Joey, our six-year-old, said. He had told us about a voice that he heard "in his heart." A voice that kept telling him what he said to us now.

"God is stupid," Joey said. He started to cry, ashamed that he had heard the voice he didn't want to hear again.

Naomi comforted him. "Don't cry," she said. "God is great and good and wise and kind. He isn't stupid."

"Yeah," our three-year-old, John Law, said to Joey. "*You're* stupid!"

"No I'm not!" Joey said to John Law. "*You're* stupid!"

"Uh-uh," John Law said. "*You!*"

And as they yelled at each other and Naomi tried to shush them, I saw Nick. He was still looking at the table, his hand still trying to hold on to the sunspot.

Suzi called me and said, "I forgive you, Dad. I know that you must still feel guilty about you and Mom, but really I forgive you and I think I am beginning to understand. I've been waiting for the right time—the right moment—to say that. I have accepted your new life. I love my little brothers with everything inside me.

Steve called me and said: "You've always been my best friend. But now—since you came up to Oregon—I consider you one of the homeboys. I love you, Pops."

Gerri Eszterhas was working with a group of handicapped kids in Marin County, teaching them to dance, dancing with them onstage during their special programs. She was sixty years old.

I remembered how proud she'd always been of appearing in various small-town productions of *Oklahoma!*

I remembered that when she'd been a young woman going to Ohio State, the fraternities had given her a trophy for having the nicest legs in school.

I imagined my ex-wife at sixty up onstage dancing with those kids and I found myself moved to tears by the image, happy for Gerri, happy for the kids.

Like my great-grandfather, the stagecoach robber and Wild West outlaw, I was going home.

Where spectral old hags in black babushkas could see me playing in the cellar . . .

Not with the devil but with my sons . . .

Playing Ping-Pong, not cards . . .

Playing not for my soul but for . . .
Fruit Roll Ups!

Louis Bromfield lived happily in Mansfield for fifteen years before he died, just another Ohioan in a straw hat drinking his coffee in the coffee shop on the courthouse square, expressing very strong opinions about his beloved Cleveland Indians.

Sometimes some stranger would approach him shyly and say, "Excuse me, aren't you Louis Bromfield, the famous writer?"

And Louis Bromfield would say, "I used to be," and walk on.

Naomi said, "What I want for the boys is catching fireflies at night . . . kissing their scrapes and bruises and mosquito bites . . . playing cops and robbers and cowboys and Indians . . . seeing them run until they're out of breath . . . pillow fights . . . seeing them laugh so hard that their stomachs hurt . . . hearing "Eeeny meeny minee mo" and "Olly olly oxen free" . . . and Yoo-hoo . . . and Marco Polo . . . telling them to stop jumping on the bed . . . hearing their bikes with baseball cards in the spokes . . . helping them build the street's biggest snowman . . . making gallons of Kool-Aid . . . More than anything else, I want them to know the feeling of not hearing the screen door slam until you're halfway down the drive."

The last thing I did before we left our house in Point Dume was to take the mezzuzah off the front door. It had been put there by the previous owner.

The house had been good to us. We had four beautiful, healthy children while we were living here. I wrote eight scripts and a book here. We cooked or grilled thousands of tasty meals. We clinked wine glasses or beer bottles to hundreds of dazzling sunsets and five spectacular and rare rainbows.

The chasm between Steve and Suzi and Naomi had been nearly bridged here. Steve and Suzi had begun to love their little brothers here. And Naomi and I had watched our love for each other deepen and grow and become the unbreakable foundation of our lives.

As the limo pulled out our front gate for the last time, the boys sitting quietly for once, I kissed Naomi's hand and waved Bob Dylan across the street goodbye.

I was going from Birdview Avenue in Malibu, California, to Island View Circle in Bainbridge Township, Ohio.

The son of an alleged war criminal, I was clutching a mezzuzah in my pocket.

CHAPTER 33

I Finally Meet Me!

CATHERINE
What happens to them?

NICK
They fuck like minks, raise rugrats, and live happily ever after.

Basic Instinct

We left Malibu on March 10 . . . Sharon Stone's forty-third birthday . . . and moved into our new house in Bainbridge Township on March 11 . . . Joey's seventh birthday.

We put the mezzuzah up on our front door.

We put the big ornate flag of the city of Cleveland . . . presented to me by Mayor White for *Male Pattern Baldness*, a movie never made, up on our garage wall, next to the Ohio State Buckeyes thermometer the old owners left behind.

As soon as we got to Cleveland, we moved my father into a Hungarian-speaking nursing home in Akron, not far from our new house in Bainbridge Township.

My voice was worse and I went to an ear, nose, and throat man at a Cleveland Clinic branch near us. Naomi came with me. I was tired of croaking, so I wanted to get my polyps taken out as soon as possible.

I said to the ear, nose, and throat man that I would need a good anesthesiologist for the surgery.

He said, "Why?"

I said, "Because I smoke four packs of Salems a day and drink way too much."

He said, "You don't need a good anesthesiologist, you need a good psychiatrist."

I laughed at that.

He snaked a tube down my nose with a camera at its end and got it all the way down to my throat so he could see the polyps.

I told him that the ear, nose, and throat Guys to the Stars in Beverly Hills had done the same test and told me that I had two benign polyps wrapped around my vocal cords. I told him about my long history of benign nasal polyps and that I was a "polyp grower."

He said nothing but looked at his screen and then looked at me.

"These aren't benign polyps," he said. "These aren't any kind of polyps. They're tumors. You have throat cancer."

The first thing I did, of course, after leaving his office, was light up a cigarette.

I reassured Naomi. I didn't believe this Cleveland Clinic ear, nose, and throat man. I chose to believe the hotshot ear, nose, and throat Guys to the Stars in Beverly Hills.

Two days later, I was in Dr. Marshall Strome's office at the Cleveland Clinic. He had been at Harvard Medical School for many years. He was an internationally renowned throat surgeon. Some people thought he was the best throat surgeon in the world. He had done the world's only larynx transplant. People flew from all over the world to see him.

Dr. Strome snaked another camera tube down my nose, looked at my throat, and said that, in his opinion, I had throat cancer and needed immediate surgery.

I called Steve and Suzi and told them. We cried together and they flew into Cleveland the next day.

Nervous, I drank more and kept chain-smoking.

To say that Naomi and I were in shock doesn't do it justice. We had just moved across the country. Our children, removed suddenly from the world they had known, were crying much of the time. Our new house, with furniture and boxes all over the place, was a disaster zone. We had just put my father into a nursing home. And now we were told that I had cancer.

My father, at the Hungarian nursing home, called to say that he didn't want to be there. He wanted to go back to his house. All the Hungarians there disliked him, he said, because his son was the man who'd betrayed Hungary by writing the movie *Music Box*.

I couldn't speak to my father because I had no voice left.

Naomi couldn't speak Hungarian and he couldn't hear or understand what she was saying in English.

She spoke in English to a nursing supervisor, who then spoke to my father in Hungarian.

Naomi told the nursing supervisor, who told my father that as soon as we were finished moving in, we'd go and visit him.

We didn't want my father to know anything about what the clinic doctors had said.

We were afraid that what they'd said might kill him.

After all, I didn't want to be responsible for killing my father.

Naomi told my father again through the nursing supervisor about my "benign polyps."

My father responded by saying that he would give me his larynx in a transplant.

We went to see the head of the Cleveland Clinic's radiology department. This doctor looked at the video Dr. Strome had taken of my throat and said that in his opinion I didn't have throat cancer . . . but had a pre-cancerous condition which a round of radiation would "zap."

As soon as I left his office and got outside, I lit up a cigarette.

I saw other people out there smoking, too, people who had what looked like burn marks around their throats.

They were people who'd just had radiation treatment for throat cancer.

I knew I was deeply in denial, but even I couldn't make myself believe what the "zapping" radiologist had said about my "pre-cancerous condition."

I called Dr. Strome. I told him I was ready to go ahead with the surgery and he scheduled an immediate biopsy as a first step.

Before he could do the biopsy, I had to have a pre-op physical at the clinic.

I flunked it.

My blood pressure was sky-high and my bloodstream was filled with alcohol.

The doctors asked me about my drinking habits and I told them that every day since I was fourteen years old, I'd had something alcoholic to drink. I told them I was drinking three or four bottles of white wine a day now plus some gin or tequila or bourbon plus maybe a couple of beers.

I couldn't deny that I was an alcoholic any longer.

I'd have to go through detox at the clinic before Dr. Strome could do the biopsy.

The doctors were afraid that if I went through surgery in this condition, they'd have to do an autopsy instead of a biopsy.

. . .

I'd done a CAT scan on the morning of the day before. The instructions said I could only drink "clear liquids" before the test.

I drank two shots of gin.

The technician was a young woman who'd asked me for an autograph.

"What are you in here for?" she'd asked.

"Too much rock and roll," I'd said.

I checked into the clinic with a pocketful of stones I had asked Naomi and Steve and Suzi and the boys to paint me . . . for luck.

I kept them in my pocket.

I began detox. I was in the Cleveland Clinic's VIP wing with a room that was more a luxury hotel suite than a hospital room.

Naomi stayed with me in the room while the nanny stayed at home with the boys.

My neighbor in the VIP wing was a Saudi prince who, when he found out who I was, invited us to go falcon hunting with him in Africa.

His personal physician, a Frenchman, told me he always wanted to be an actor and not a doctor.

The Saudi prince's nephew, a little boy of about six, saw me playing with my painted stones and came over to see them.

I let him play with them and then he showed them to the prince, who played with them for a while, too. The prince was there for a brain tumor.

I was drugged up much of the time but, even so, went into severe withdrawal.

I saw rats scurrying around on the floor in my peripheral vision.

My hands shook so badly that I couldn't find my nose.

I was still smoking—in the bathroom, in a special smoking room, and outside, hooked up to my IV cart.

Sometime during that week of detox, Naomi and I made love in the shower of my clinic suite.

It was therapeutic. I stopped shaking for a while and it routed the rats from my peripheral vision.

My father kept calling for me while I was going through detox.

He wanted to speak to me. Naomi told him I was in the hospital with my benign polyps.

My father kept saying "*Joe? Joe? Joe?*"

. . .

I finished detox.

The rats were out of my peripheral vision, my shaking had stopped, my bloodstream was alcohol-free for the first time in forty-two years.

I felt a leaden flatness and a deep depression I'd never felt before.

I was ready for my biopsy now. My blood pressure was normal.

I held Naomi's hand, I kissed Steve and Suzi, and I was wheeled away into the operating room.

When I woke up in the recovery room, I couldn't breathe. I was desperately trying to catch my breath and couldn't. I felt like I was drowning.

A nurse kept saying, "Please, Joe, breathe, breathe!"

I asked another nurse afterward why I hadn't been able to breathe in the recovery room and she said, "Do you smoke?" I nodded and so did she.

While Naomi and Steve and Suzi were in the relatives' waiting area, a woman waiting there for her husband's surgery to be over . . . collapsed and died.

When Dr. Strome went to the waiting room and told Naomi and Steve and Suzi that I definitely had throat cancer, Steve turned red, said "*Fuck!*" and went outside to smoke a cigarette.

They wheeled me back up to my suite. I read Naomi's and Steve's and Suzi's faces immediately. I had cancer, the biopsy had showed.

Dr. Strome told them I not only had to stop smoking immediately but had to stop drinking, too. My esophagus looked pre-cancerous.

When they told me what Marshall Strome had said—I said, "*Cocksucker!*"

They thought that was funny.

I thought to myself: I've had all these fights my whole life against various enemies and now my life's greatest enemy is inside me and wants to kill me.

I remembered what I had said to Naomi on Maui: "A thousand barstools. A thousand barstools before it's over."

Heh heh heh: it was over!

While we waited for Dr. Strome to come to the suite, we had the local TV news on.

We saw film of our new house in Bainbridge Township shot from a helicopter. The news said that I had moved from Malibu back to my hometown.

Our nanny called from home to say there were helicopters circling the house.

. . .

Dr. Strome came to my suite looking grave.

He said that he would probably have to take my whole larynx out . . . which meant I wouldn't be able to swallow . . . which meant I'd never be able to eat or drink anything . . . and would have to feed myself through tubes inserted into my stomach.

I told Dr. Strome that I didn't want to live that way.

Naomi said that if that was my decision, she understood it and supported it. Then she started to cry. So did Steve and Suzi. So did I.

A priest came by and asked if I wanted to pray with him and receive Holy Communion.

I told him no and asked the nurses to post a sign on my door like the Saudi prince had: "ABSOLUTELY NO VISITORS!"

I was desolate. I loved my wife and children but if I couldn't eat or drink, I knew I'd walk into the woods around my house and lie down.

I had done this to myself. I had poisoned myself. I had been so stupid and arrogant and full of shit to think that while everyone else paid the price for smoking . . . *I* wouldn't.

I thought about the boys growing up without me to guide them . . . Naomi moving into middle age without me to hold her hand . . . Steve and Suzi having children I would never see.

Dr. Strome came back and said he'd been thinking about it.

He'd try a surgery that he'd never done before. After removing the cancer from my larynx, he'd take muscles from the left side of my neck and attach them to what was left of my larynx.

If it worked, I'd be able to swallow . . . and eat . . . and drink.

"But you have to quit smoking and drinking," he said. "The only chance you have—and it's a long shot—is if you quit smoking and drinking."

I said, "I've already quit drinking. I promise you this. If you do this surgery successfully for me, if I'm able to swallow, I'll quit smoking, too. I promise you. I give you my word."

He looked at me a long time—sadly, I thought—and nodded.

It would be a lengthy and complicated surgery. I held Naomi, Steve, and Suzi and thanked them for what they had brought to my life.

I watched the Indians lose, got my shot of Ativan, and fell asleep early.

At 5:30 on the morning of my surgery, there was an electrical storm that flashed for an hour. I was awake, still high from last night's Ativan, enjoying every flash and crash.

Fitting, I thought, for this day . . . the day that I might die . . . having been born during a bombing.

And I woke up thinking: If this is the last day of my life, how fitting, too, that the Indians lost last night.

The last thing I remember before going under in the operating room was the Supremes blasting on WMMS-FM.

At the last moment, as I was being wheeled into the operating room, I panicked.

"Where's Mano?" I said.

Steve was there, right next to me. He leaned down, kissed me, and said, "I love you, Pops."

The surgery took eight hours and I was another fifteen hours in the recovery room before I woke up.

A man near me was crying out, "Oh, God, help me! It hurts. Please, God, help me!"

A nurse came over to me, handed me a pad and a pen, and said, "How do you feel?"

I tried to answer her but what came out of my mouth was a hot, gaslike hiss. I realized I had a hole in my neck where my throat was.

I took the pad and pen and wrote: "Hot . . . anxious . . . where is family?"

Dr. Strome came in, looked at me, and told me to swallow.

This was the moment of truth.

If I was able to swallow, then the surgery had been successful.

If not, then we'd have to do the full laryngectomy and put me on the feeding tubes.

Eighty percent of my larynx was gone.

I took a deep breath, lowered my head to my chest, and tried to swallow.

I swallowed perfectly.

It didn't even hurt.

Marshall Strome grinned.

"Congratulations," he said.

Naomi and Steve and Suzi were soon there and Naomi had a child's toy with her—a Fisher-Price Magna Doodle, a magnetic slate on which I could write and erase quickly.

I wrote: "Too bright. Sunglasses."

I was having difficulty keeping my eyes open with all the bright lights in the room.

She handed me her sunglasses and I put them on.

I saw myself in a nearby mirror. Tubes were everywhere around me, attached to me and to machines. A thick tube was pumping blood and what looked like mucus from around my neck. My long hair was piled atop my head like the John Belushi samurai on *Saturday Night Live.* And I had Naomi's shades on.

A young recovery room doctor came by, looked at me, and said, completely deadpan, "Rock and roll."

Equally deadpan, I held up my middle finger at him.

He didn't laugh or smile, but a nearby nurse did.

"I think you deserved that," she said to the doctor.

Then the doctor smiled at me.

They took me to a post-op "step-down room," filled with patients whose throats were being suctioned after surgery. A tube was put down the hole in our throats and was supposed to pump phlegm and secretions from there.

When the suction device hit me, I felt like I was drowning again. The suctioning was necessary to prevent infection, but the treatment was like medieval torture.

They shot me up with drugs in this step-down room, with OxyContin and Ativan and morphine, but the drugs didn't do anything for me . . . except to put me into a very cold and lonely place in my head.

I felt isolated from everyone, near dead.

A nurse, while putting a catheter back into me, asked me what movies I'd written. I listed my credits.

When I mentioned *Basic Instinct* and *Showgirls,* she did something with the catheter that caused sudden lacerating pain.

I said to her, "You really hurt me."

She didn't say she was sorry, but she looked to me like she was smiling.

I wondered later whether she was really smiling about the pain she had caused me . . . or whether the morphine had made me imagine it. Looking back on it now, I think she was really smiling.

She looked a bit like Carrie Rickey, the film critic for the *Philadelphia Inquirer.*

For whatever reason, maybe the morphine, I became fixated that the man across from me in the step-down ward . . . suctioning himself . . . feeding himself through the floppy tube sticking out of his nose . . . was Billy Friedkin.

I watched them torture a big black man named Mr. Wilson, who had long surgical scars running down his chest and back. They were suctioning Mr. Wilson, who was gasping for air and who, while gasping, was watching me and smiling and saying—I am sure I heard him right—"*Heh heh heh.*"

. . .

They moved me back to my private suite. The Saudi prince shared a Mideastern feast they were preparing for him with Naomi and Steve and Suzi.

The television set in my room, I noticed, even had Saudi cable.

I tried to watch an Indians game but fell asleep as the Indians were losing.

I looked at Naomi and thought: Is this what happens to a great love story? One of the lovers starts to rot?

A supervisor at my father's nursing home called Naomi to say my father was hardly eating and had started saying *"Joe? Joe? Joe?"* all the time now.

He stared ahead and said my name over and over again.

Every time I swallowed I had to bear down. I lifted my head, then lowered it close to my chest, and pushed down as I forced what was left of my larynx to function.

I had a feeding tube sticking out of my nose. Mashed food was placed into it and it traveled through my nose into my stomach.

I hated it. It was like I'd grown a new appendage on my face.

In the middle of the night, drugged out of my skull, I ripped the feeding tube out of my nose, tore the suction tube off my neck, and yanked all my IVs out.

Naomi awoke and saw me sitting on the bed naked, smiling at her, with blood and clotted blood all over the wall and the floor.

I looked at Naomi and Steve and Suzi sitting at my bedside.

Watching Naomi with me here constantly, I thought my kids finally understood . . . and couldn't deny . . . how much she loved me.

How much did she love me? Her babies had been yanked out of their familiar surroundings and whisked across the country into a new world and a new house and suddenly their mother and father were gone from their lives. John Law, the nanny told us, was inconsolable, crying all the time.

Yet Naomi stayed in the hospital with me and slept on a cot in my room every night, going home only occasionally during the day for a few hours.

Dr. Strome decided to take the feeding tube appendage hanging from my nose out . . . and put me on an IV diet.

The doctors were pleased with my progress, even though I was losing a lot of weight on my IV diet.

I was walking the halls with my IV cart for twenty minutes to a half hour each day.

Dr. Strome felt confident that he had gotten all of the cancer out—felt, at this point, that I wouldn't need radiation or chemotherapy.

Naomi started going home on more afternoons to see the boys and sometimes brought them in to visit me.

Steve and Suzi went back to Oregon and California.

My Fisher-Price Magna Doodle was my voice now. I got very good at scrawling and erasing quickly on it. I kept it in my lap as I fell asleep each night. The last thing I wrote on it each night was "I love you" and held it up for Naomi.

A doctor who hadn't examined me before looked at my tanned, bare chest and asked with great concern: "Have you been out in the sun lately?"

I wrote, "Yes, I've been in California for thirty years."

I refused to wear my hospital gown. I went bare-chested and wore shorts. It made me feel better somehow. Maybe I was trying to pretend I wasn't really sick. Maybe it was my ultimate act of denial.

I learned that if I could convince my nurse to shoot my Ativan directly into a vein rather than through my IV . . . *I could fly!*

I felt like someone with an iron grip had his fingers around my throat and neck.

They put a breathing tube in my throat which had to be taken out twice a day, cleaned, and put back into the hole. The nurses taught Naomi how to do it.

Every time the tube was taken out or put back in, it set off a coughing fit . . . but it was like the cough couldn't get out normally because so much of my larynx was gone.

Once I coughed the whole tube out right at Naomi. It flew out of my throat and hit her in the face.

This wasn't what she had signed on for, I knew. I remembered the beaches on Maui and the beaches in Malibu, the limos and the red-carpet premieres in L.A., the luxurious hotel suites and all the fancy meals in fancy places.

Well, we were still in a luxurious suite . . . at a hospital . . . and she was eating a fancy meal prepared by the private chefs to a Saudi prince, but . . .

I was spitting a phlegm-coated breathing tube into her face.

She didn't even complain. She cleaned it off, kissed me on the cheek, and put it back in as gently as she could so it wouldn't make me cough.

As I was walking with my IV cart, one hand holding on to the cart, the other holding on to my Fisher-Price Magna Doodle . . . in case I needed to converse with someone . . . a male nurse stopped me. He was holding some index cards and a felt tip pen.

While he held my Magna Doodle, I autographed all the cards for him. I signed about a dozen but I would have gladly signed a thousand: he was the nurse who brought me my shot of Ativan each night.

A nurse from another wing of the hospital ignored the "Absolutely No Visitors!" sign and walked into my suite. She recognized my name, she said, not from a movie or a book or a magazine, but from my father.

She had taken care of my father here after one of his strokes. "Your father is such a charming man," she said. "I just had to see what the son is like."

She asked me how my father was doing and I wrote *fein*, thank you, just *fein*.

They took me off my liquid IV diet and let me eat applesauce, cottage cheese, French fries, yogurt.

Every swallow was excruciatingly difficult, but successful.

It took me an hour to sip and swallow half a glass of water.

George Harrison, the Beatle, whose company had made *Checking Out*, was dead . . . of throat cancer. His cancer had metastasized from his throat to his brain . . . a common spot, along with the lungs, to which throat cancers travel.

Babe Ruth, my great hero, died of throat cancer, too. He was a libertine and a glutton and an alcoholic and he chain-smoked cigarettes and cigars. No wonder he was my hero. No wonder he died of throat cancer.

On the day that I was released from the Cleveland Clinic, Marshall Strome told me once again that if I smoked or drank, I would die.

For a while I would have to come back to the hospital once a week, he said, to be examined.

I'd have the tube in my throat for at least another month.

I had lost forty pounds since my surgery. I'd gone from a size 42 waist to a size 36.

Almost as soon as we walked out of the clinic, I began having severe nicotine and alcohol cravings. I was using the anti-smoking patch, but my cravings continued nevertheless.

I wish I could say that I was overjoyed to have survived and to be back home . . . but I was badly depressed and jangled. My nerve endings were raw.

I felt myself to be half asleep and acutely restless at the same time. My heart raced sometimes and at other times seemed to be skipping beats. I was nauseous sometimes and had occasional gastrointestinal cramps.

I looked at my beautiful boys and my lovely wife and it was almost as though my cravings were blocking them out . . . all I could think about was having a cigarette or a drink.

My hands shook and I sweated out at night and I saw myself in vivid detail going down to Medic Drugs and buying a pack of Salems . . . and then driving over to the Coyote Moon Café and having an ice-cold beer and a shot of tequila.

I spent my days in agony, still feeling like I was in acute withdrawal from my dual addictions.

I still got the shakes and the sweats and I was profoundly depressed, writing few messages for Naomi on my Fisher-Price Magna Doodle.

This was no kind of life for a vibrant and beautiful still-young woman.

Maybe everyone would be better off, I thought, if I just crawled into a bunch of leaves under a tree, and died.

Naomi turned to me one day with great affection and great concern in her eyes and said, "Please, my great friend, *don't let me down!*"

I got home from the clinic on a Monday and asked Naomi to call the nursing home . . . to ask them to tell my father that we would be visiting him on Friday.

I couldn't tell him myself, of course, because of my Fisher-Price Magna Doodle.

That Thursday the nursing home called us to say that István Eszterhás had died in the night.

On the morning I heard that my father was dead, I needed a drink and a cigarette more than I'd ever needed them in my whole life . . . and I couldn't have them.

My father's funeral was held at the Louis A. Bodnar Funeral Home, across the street from Nick's Diner, a block from where I'd grown up on Lorain Avenue.

The week before my throat cancer surgery, I'd left instructions with Gerry Messerman that if I didn't make it through the surgery, I wanted *my* services to be held at the Louis A. Bodnar Funeral Home.

I asked Louis Bodnar to take my father's wedding ring off his hand. He gave it to me and I put it on my finger, right above *my* wedding band.

. . .

Gerry Messerman came to my father's funeral, to the funeral of the man he'd represented on war crimes charges.

I even asked Gerry to be one of the pallbearers and Gerry even accepted.

Steve and Gerry and I (with some others) took my father to his grave.

A woman my age showed up at the funeral home and said I had slept with her one night when we were in college.

I hadn't seen or spoken to her since . . . almost forty years ago . . . but she said she'd seen my father's obit in the paper and wanted to come by to express her condolences.

Gerri sent a tiny bouquet of flowers to the funeral home with a note that said, only "From Steve and Suzi's mother."

I didn't exactly blame her. "Joe is my son," my father had told her, "but you are not my daughter."

Right back at ya . . . even in the grave.

My father had died alone, surrounded by strangers, not his family. I hadn't been there to hold his hand like I had held my mother's.

And, as it turned out, I had literally exacted Jessica Lange's *Music Box* punishment upon him: he had never met or seen Joey and Nick and John Law and Luke.

Costa-Gavras had said to me, while we were working on *Music Box,* that every son needed to kill his father . . . and if that was right, then maybe I'd finally killed István Eszterhás, author and Hungarian nationalist and alleged war criminal . . . killed him for what he had done and not done, killed him for loving me and lying to me.

I am exacting the final part of Jessica Lange's punishment upon my father right now . . . with *you,* as you read this book. I am exposing what my father did just as Jessica Lange exposed what her father did in *Music Box.*

What I am referring to as "Jessica Lange's punishment" is, of course, a literary conceit and a personal evasion.

I created Jessica Lange's character, Ann Talbot. *I* told Ann Talbot how to punish her father. Cutting him off from his grandchildren and exposing him to the world were my ideas . . . not Ann's.

If what Costa-Gavras said was true, if every son needed to kill his father, then it meant that I would be killed five times by five boys . . . and what they would do to me would hurt me five times as much as I had hurt my father.

If, that is, I lived long enough . . . *heh heh heh* . . . to see my little boys grow into men.

My father's housekeeper came up to me at the funeral home and handed me a piece of paper. It was a new will my father had made out in the past month with the housekeeper as his witness.

In this new will handed to me at his funeral, my father directed me not to bury him here . . . not to bury him in America . . . but to fly his body back to Hungary and bury him there.

It was the final giveaway, I thought, as to how he felt about America. He hated America, I was convinced, as much as I loved her. Because America had defeated his Hungary, his *Nazi* Hungary, in the war.

He had lived in America for more than fifty years . . . *hiding* all that time in his strudel ghetto among other Hungarians who were also hiding from deportation . . . and these were his final words to the nation that had given him shelter and his son success.

Even dead, he wanted nothing to do with America. Even dead, he wanted to go back to Hungary . . . like he'd always wanted to go back to Hungary.

He could finally do it safely now . . . *dead* . . . because the Hungarian government didn't prosecute dead people for their crimes.

He said nothing in this new will, I noted, about disinterring my mother and flying *her* body back to Hungary along with his. He wanted my mother's body left in Cleveland. He wanted to go back to Hungary *without her*.

It convinced me that my mother had been right: he hadn't loved her.

He wanted to be free of *her*, too, along with America, *back in Budapest, alone.*

I refused my father's final, dying request.

We buried him at Calvary Cemetery in Cleveland, right next to my mother . . . the wife he wanted to leave behind in death.

I viewed it as maybe my father's final punishment.

I hadn't let him meet or see his grandchildren and I was going to write a book exposing him . . . and now I was putting him into the ground of the America he hated.

There were about a hundred Hungarians at my father's funeral. I couldn't speak very well to any of them because of the tube in my throat.

The only time I cried was when they sang the Hungarian national anthem at the end of the ceremony.

I thought I could hear him accompanying them on his violin.

My father willed his violin to Steve and the violin that was mine when I was a boy to Suzi. Neither of them played the violin and they didn't know what to do with them. They took them to Gerri's house in Tiburon, where the violins are on a shelf in the basement.

Back at home after the funeral, I cursed myself for what I had done to myself. I had maimed myself. I felt like a freak when I tried to talk. I saw people's heads swivel my way when they heard my raspy croak. I saw little kids nudge each other and stare.

Once upon a time, I had had such a good voice that a lot of people told me I should go into broadcasting. Now, thanks to my own actions, I had cut my own throat as surely as Marshall Strome had cut it to save me.

I felt a constant, overwhelming physical craving for a cigarette . . . centered almost exactly at the spot in my throat where the surgery had been done.

I had an intense physical craving in my mostly gone larynx for mentholated smoke . . . for smoke hitting my larynx and then moving down into my lungs.

It felt like a nearly sexual need.

My long hair, down to the middle of my back, was driving me crazy. It kept getting into my trach or into the hole in my throat along with the bugs and mosquitoes.

"Above-the-title hair," the columnists Liz Smith and George Christy had called it.

But I went to a barbershop now in the town of Chagrin Falls and had it cut off. Short. Very short.

I stopped highlighting my hair, too. I turned grayer—in spots whiter, in spots snow-white.

Besides going to the barbershop, I was going to the grocery store and driving my pickup truck and going to the bank and, one spring day, with the trach still in my throat, I went to play baseball with my little boys.

It wasn't a smart thing to do. Joey hit a line drive back at me that was headed for my throat. It could have shattered my trach, but I snapped my head sharply out of the way.

I visualized a *Plain Dealer* headline on the second page of the metro section: "SCREENWRITER KILLED BY THE GAME HE LOVED." The subhead read: "SON'S LINE DRIVE KILLS DAD."

In an effort to ease my cigarette and alcohol cravings, I changed my diet completely:

I became a near-vegetarian and drank juices all day—carrot juice and grapefruit juice and cranberry juice.

I ate lots of green vegetables, fish, and very little meat.

Swallowing was still extremely difficult at times but I forced myself to drink quarts of the juices.

Dr. Strome also put me on a regimen of multivitamins and antioxidants.

I noticed that if I was really tired, my cravings weren't as bad . . . so I started purposely trying to tire myself.

I went on an hour walk in the morning and walked for another hour at night.

My leg and back muscles started to hurt.

I started reading every book I could find about cancer, smoking, and alcoholism.

I discovered that Hungarian men had the highest death rate from cancer in the world . . . Hungarian women ranked second among women worldwide.

I discovered that it would take me many years before I could say that I had beaten either of my addictions. I'd been smoking for forty-four years and drinking for forty-two—not one day had passed in all those years when I hadn't had something to smoke or something alcoholic to drink.

Now, suddenly, just like that, I had stopped both.

My books told me that there was no way anyone could do that without suffering . . . that I would have to *suffer* my way through this for a long time . . . that I would have to conquer my body's cravings with my mind.

I couldn't watch the television news at six o'clock each night because that time of night was tied in to cocktail hour for me.

It was the time of night I'd always had a couple of stiff gins or Jack Daniel's.

Instead of watching the news, we'd have dinner early at that hour. I'd eat as fast as possible and leave the table because sitting there made me crave a drink and a cigarette.

I couldn't even listen to my favorite music, I noticed, because my favorite music—Dylan, Bruce, the Stones, Cohen, Otis, Johnny Cash, Sinatra, Billie Holiday—was all soaked with booze and cigarette smoke.

All those years I'd spent listening to that music while I was smoking and drinking . . . and now, when I heard it, I desperately wanted to smoke and drink again.

I'd developed allergies as well. I'd never had them in Ohio before but now, suddenly, my eyes and nose were dripping, my wound of a throat filled with nasal drip as I tried to hawk the stuff up.

It felt like I was drowning in my own snot.

. . .

I read a book by Stephen King called *On Writing*, in which he wrote honestly about his own addictions: he chain-smoked and drank a case of beer a day and he had such a bad cocaine habit that when he looked down, blood dripped from his nose. And he'd beaten all three of his addictions.

I read the book three times. It helped me. *Thank you, Stephen.*

I wasn't able to completely focus on either my reading or a movie. I often drifted off. At other times I suddenly got so restless that I immediately had to walk around.

"*Sitzfleisch!*" my father had said so often to me.

"*Sitzfleisch!*" I'd said so often to young writers.

"*Sitzfleisch!*" I said to myself now . . . but I couldn't do it.

Hollywood was not the kind of place where people wanted to work with a cancer victim . . . so we didn't want anyone to know I was sick. Nor, if my cancer came back, did I want the press keeping a gossip column death watch.

So Naomi told everyone who called that I couldn't talk because I'd just had two benign polyps removed.

A friend at the *Plain Dealer* told me that the paper had learned I was being treated for throat cancer at the clinic . . . but had decided not to report it.

I had four little boys who were most of the time doing something that they shouldn't be doing . . . that they could hurt themselves doing . . . and I had no voice to yell at them with.

I saw them going too fast with their bikes and I couldn't yell at them to stop doing that. I saw them get too close to the lake and I couldn't tell them to back up. I saw them trying to retrieve a ball from the pond and I couldn't yell and tell them to forget the ball.

I cursed myself for robbing myself of my voice.

We went to a baseball game at Jacobs Field that featured all the old Indians stars of the past. I saw Bob Feller and Al Rosen and Herb Score and Steve Gromek and Rocky Colavito . . . and as I saw them limp and shuffle onto the field, I felt tears in my eyes. I knew I wasn't crying for them. I was crying for me.

I suddenly remembered the day my father took me to the Indians-Yankees game when I was a boy. I smiled through my tears as I saw my father in his trench coat and beret, sitting in the stands reading his book as I watched the game. When I remembered the book he was reading that long-ago day, I felt like laughing.

Crime and Punishment.
Of all books.

Naomi and I went to Cleveland Heights with some movers and cleaned my father's house out.

I took some of his coats and hats for myself and I took the chair that he'd bought from the Volunteers of America and that he sat on when he wrote all of his books and articles.

I am sitting on my father's chair now as I write this book that will reveal his sins to the world.

I kept all of my father's Hungarian novels that I found in his house. On the first page of each one was a green sheet that said, "EX LIBRIS—István Eszterhás" and a painting of the Hungarian flag with the Holy Crown of St. Stephen in the middle of it.

I thought about my father as I sorted through his faded and dusty things and I realized that the first script I wrote after his Justice Department hearings, *Original Sin,* was about how the past doomed two lovers . . . and the ending of the second script I wrote after the hearings, *Sliver,* showed a woman disregarding the fact that her lover was a murderer . . . because she loved him.

My father died, I reflected, like his hero Lajos Kossuth, the Hungarian patriot . . . old, half blind, poor, and alone—not in Turino, Italy, but in Cleveland, Ohio.

I found a small plastic statue of Jesus which Father John Mundweil had given me for my first Holy Communion. I gave it to Naomi, who put it on her nightstand.

I found an old *Playboy* magazine featuring a mostly nude Suzanne Somers, one of my father's favorite actresses. I took it. I don't know why. It is on the coffee table in my office now, atop an old *Time,* with its Man of the Year cover of the Hungarian freedom fighter.

I found an old passport belonging to my mother among my father's things . . . as well as my mother's Arrow Cross identification card, complete with swastika-like arrow and cross symbols.

I found his old trench coat. I kept the trench coat and put it in my closet. It hangs there not far from Bill Macdonald's Renegade jacket.

. . .

Sitting on the front porch with Naomi and sipping the cold lemonade she had made me, I said, "I'm sorry, Guinea. Forgive me. I love you more than anything in the world. I haven't been treating you right. I've been rude to you at times, cold, distracted. I just wanted to tell you how much I love you and that without you, I couldn't be doing any of this."

Naomi kissed me and said, "I forgive you."

She bought me a present for not smoking and drinking: a 1997 Cleveland Indians American League championship ring, given only to team members and Indians' executives.

I wore my Wahoo ring proudly.

Steve stopped smoking, too. He was already a two-pack-a-day smoker, and stopping was very difficult for him but he did it. Now we were cheering each other on.

I asked him how he quit and he said, "I told myself that if I quit, Pops, you'd live, and if I didn't, you'd die."

My neighbors . . . even strangers . . . were a blessing. They'd recognize me at a Giant Eagle or pumping gas and say "Welcome home!" or "You're not one of those Hollywood people anyway!" and "Are you writing?"

I wasn't writing . . . partly because I couldn't focus and partly because every time I sat down to write, my cigarette cravings became excruciating.

I remembered how I'd looked forward to moving here and eating all the ethnic meats and sausages that I loved so much.

I couldn't eat any of it because:

1. Meat made me crave cigarettes and alcohol more.
2. Ethnic meats were cancer-causing.

I remembered the dream I'd had before we moved here about jogging by the woods each day.

I wasn't jogging, but I was walking at a pretty fast clip and there was little doubt I was living out my dream.

Joey hit a *horun* in his Little League game and as he ran around the bases I heard myself trying to yell "*Attaboy, Joee!*" but it came out as a soft croak and nobody heard me but me.

On a hot summer day during my morning walk, I gave up and sat down on the curb and started to sob.

I was sweating like a pig. Bugs and mosquitoes were attacking the tube in my throat. I was having trouble breathing. My feet and legs ached and cramped. I was shaking. I felt like I was going to throw up. My heart felt like it was going to explode. Every centimeter of me craved—*desperately craved*—a cigarette and a cold beer, two cold beers, three cold beers and a shot of tequila and . . .

I sat there and sobbed, the tears hitting the pavement in front of me.

And suddenly, inside my own head, I heard myself saying, "Please, God, help me. I can't do this anymore without you."

I knew as I heard myself saying it that this was the first time I had spoken to God since I was a boy on Lorain Avenue.

As I sat there, I prayed, really *prayed* for God's help. I said the Our Father and the Hail Mary and a Glory Be and then I said them over and over, begging God to help me overcome my addictions.

I begged God to keep me alive so I could help my little boys grow up. And I made God a promise. I promised Him that if He helped me through my misery, I would do everything in the time remaining to me to help others to stop smoking.

I sat there staring at the ground and praying a long time that day and when I got up I felt a renewal of strength.

I wasn't shaking anymore. My heart beat normally. The bugs and mosquitoes had eased off my trach.

I still craved the cigarette and the cold beers and the shot of tequila . . . but I'd asked for God's help, not a miracle.

We started going to church regularly. We picked the parish nearest us—Holy Angels—and took all the boys with us each Sunday.

I still couldn't speak, of course, and I could tell from their looks that our fellow parishioners knew who I was.

I knew how oddly it must have struck some of them: the author of *Basic Instinct* and *Showgirls* holding hands with his children and *praying* each Sunday. Wasn't this the same guy who'd told teenagers to sneak into that X-rated movie?

Naomi went to Holy Communion each Sunday but I didn't.

I viewed God as a newfound friend. I didn't want to be presumptuous. I didn't want Him to think I was trying to suck up to Him.

On my walks—I was walking three miles a day now—I was praying throughout, asking God to show me the way, asking for His help.

I started doing what I'd heard Johnny Cash did to begin each day.

First I said, "Good morning, God."

Then I said, "Praise the Lord!"

At home, we taught the boys catechism and prayed with them before they fell asleep.

One Sunday in church, as Naomi went to Holy Communion with Luke in her arms, I got up behind her and went to Holy Communion, too . . . the first time since I was a schoolboy at St. Emeric's.

"Body of Christ, Joe," Father Bob Stec said, giving me the Host, and I put the Host in my mouth and swallowed it with my ravaged throat.

I felt an inner glow all of that day and I felt God's love surrounding me.

A dark and deeply cynical voice from a cold and dark place inside me said, "Now that you've found God in Cleveland, will you find *Elvész Prezli* alive here, too?"

Marshall Strome took my trach out and my new voice sounded weaker and higher and thinner than Brando's in *The Godfather.*

If we got lucky, Dr. Strome said, my voice would sound louder and lower over time.

The bar I'd liked so much, the Coyote Moon Café, the place where Naomi and I had discussed death and dying before we'd moved here . . . burned to the ground.

I was sure God had burned it down just for me.

Dr. Strome had been looking at my throat every week. Everything had looked good to him.

Suddenly, three months after the surgery, he saw something in my throat he didn't like. He thought it was another growth.

I needed to have surgery again immediately.

I was at peace this time. I hugged and kissed the boys the night before and made love with Naomi.

I prayed and felt at peace, my fate in God's hands.

I told Steve and Suzi not to fly out again . . . but to lead their lives.

As I was wheeled into the operating room, I heard the Supremes blasting again.

It made me smile. I'd never much liked the Supremes.

I fell asleep saying the Our Father and thinking about making love on the beach on Maui with Naomi.

It wasn't a new cancerous growth. It wasn't a growth at all. It was granulated tissue from the previous surgery.

I was *fein.* Marshall Strome didn't even have to tell me. I knew the moment I saw his face.

I was cancer-free.

· · ·

"You're not smoking or drinking, are you?" Dr. Strome said.

"No, sir," I said. "If you remember, I made you a promise."

"I remember very well." He smiled.

This occurred to me: Was it possible that I had conjured God because an after-life had suddenly become a very important concern to me? Was my ego too large to make peace with an afterlife of rot and worms? Was I the nearly satiric evidence of "foxhole religion"?

I had the feeling that I didn't know this sober, clear-eyed, and lucid person that I had become.

I had the feeling that I had to get to know myself again.

I had this thought, too:

I started flooding my brain with nicotine and tobacco when I was twelve . . . and I started flooding my brain with alcohol when I was fourteen . . .

Was it possible that I had *never* gotten to know the *real* me?

Was it possible that I had hidden the real me from myself with nicotine and tobacco and alcohol?

Was I now, finally, pushing sixty, meeting the real me for the first time?

Sometimes . . . in the middle of a five-mile walk . . .

I had the odd feeling that I had died and that I was now living someone else's life.

A friend that I hadn't seen for years bumped into me on the street and looked right through me.

I realized he didn't recognize me. I'd cut my hair and lost almost fifty pounds and I was wearing an Indians Chief Wahoo baseball cap like everybody else in Cleveland, even bank robbers caught on videotape.

I thought to myself: If you don't look like you and talk like you and smoke like you and drink like you . . . then *who are you?*

While we were no longer in Hollywood, we saw that some people here in Bainbridge took movies as *seriously* as some people in Hollywood.

After the first screening of the new *Star Wars* movie at Chagrin Cinemas, police were called because a group of filmgoers gathered in the parking lot and staged a mini-protest. They thought the movie was so bad that they wanted their money back.

· · ·

We drove down to Mansfield one day and visited Looey Bromfield's Malabar Farm. The boys were bored and wanted to hurry and get a sub *sangwich* at Mansfield's "world-famous" Leaning Tower.

But I lingered over Looey's old Royal typewriter, the one he'd written all those books and scripts on. It still looked in fine shape, I reflected bitterly to myself, much better shape than all the new Olivetti Lettera manual typewriters I had in my closet.

I said to Naomi, "Where's Oh Jesus Hill?"

Naomi smiled and said, "Oh, Jesus, I don't know."

The Indians traded or got rid of the good players who had made them pennant contenders for so many years. Now that I was back home, the Indians stunk again just like they'd stunk through all the years when I'd lived here and lived and died by them.

I found a new bar that became my favorite—out on a two-lane blacktop road in Amish country . . . nothing but a neon sign that said "Skip's" on a vacant lot. The building had been razed.

The grip around my throat was still there—but it didn't feel like iron anymore . . . it was rubber.

We found a beach spot on Lake Erie that we liked a lot and that was pollution-free.

I sat there on the sand bare-chested in a bathing suit, watching my boys frolic in the water with Naomi. I felt old.

I thought of the carefree life we had led on Maui . . . before we had the responsibility of children and before I had cancer . . . when we jumped the riptides together and I couldn't wait to get back to the beach to sit at the little bar with the attached roof where I could smoke a cigarette and have a frozen Seabreeze.

Lake Erie wasn't Maui. There were no riptides here and no thatched roofs and no cigarettes and near-frozen Seabreezes.

But Naomi was still here, playing with the little boys I loved so much, and when they came back from the water with the shells and stones they'd collected for me . . . that made me feel younger.

My voice was better. It had come off its high perch into down-low registers. I thought that on my good days I sounded like Louis Armstrong on his bad ones.

Naomi said I sometimes sounded like Kristofferson, sometimes maybe even Bogart.

Still, my official medical condition was "day to day."

I was, "for the moment," cancer-free. I hadn't even reached my two-years-without-recurrence mark—viewed by cancer survivors as reaching first base.

Marshall Strome also said, "This is a horrible disease. You can have a lump appear on your neck tomorrow and in six months you'll be dead."

I dreamed I was smoking again. It tasted and felt sensational. Cigarette in hand, I was asking where I could buy a bottle of Porfidio tequila.

But I was feeling somewhat better and had relatively fewer addiction attacks.

Sometimes I'd pass a bar and feel deep pangs and once when that happened, on a snowy day, watching a fireplace inside and a group of people with drinks in their hands . . . I felt tears in my eyes.

Walking through a smoking area at Jacobs Field, I was first struck by the wretchedness of the stink . . . but then, almost against my will, I took a big breath and breathed all the smoke in and it felt . . . *orgasmic.*

I walked five miles now even in the dead of Ohio winter, when the wind-chill was eight below. I walked bundled up in many layers, in heavy hiking boots. I carried the walking stick Naomi had made for me on Maui so I wouldn't slip in the ice and snow.

I looked like the Abominable Snowman. I never missed a day.

In church one Sunday, Father Stec stopped next to me on his way from the altar and said, "Do you know what this means? This means that the best is yet to come. The best part of your life is still ahead of you!"

He said it out of the blue, as though we'd been having a conversation . . . but *he and I* hadn't . . . unless he'd somehow overheard a part of my ongoing conversation with God.

We put four flags up in front of our house for the Fourth of July.

We counted three hundred flags on the houses in a one-mile proximity to us.

I told Naomi we were real Americans now in the real America. We didn't smoke or drink. We went to church. We prayed with our kids each night. We had Old Glory in front of our house. And we lived and died by the Cleveland Indians and by Little League baseball.

On the night of the Fourth, we went to Solon High School's football field and watched the fireworks from our lawn chairs. We took our ball caps off as we sang the national anthem. We were wearing Old Navy Old Glory T-shirts. On the way back home we stopped at *McDonhole* and bought the boys Happy Meals.

. . .

Every night after dinner, I took Naomi and the boys down to Dairy Queen for vanilla cones with jimmies on them.

No, it wasn't as good as a little cognac or amaretto after dinner.

But it was . . . pretty damn good!

And it was a lot of fun, sitting there with ice cream all over us, laughing, enjoying the summer night. If we got lucky, we saw some heat lightning on the way home.

We bought our vegetables from a farmer down the street who put his fresh corn and squash and eggplant and tomatoes and peppers into a shed . . . and we stuffed the cost into an envelope that went into a box.

It was definitely not a Hollywood way to do business: the honor system.

I dreamed that Father John Mundweil and I were at the Debrecen Hungarian Restaurant on Lorain Avenue, almost across the street from where I had grown up.

We were both adults. We were sitting at a table laughing, smoking, and drinking glasses of red Hungarian bull's blood wine.

Father John knocked the cigarette out of my mouth and the glass of bull's blood out of my hand and he said angrily:

"What's the matter with you? Didn't you get the message that God gave me to give to Father Stec to give you?"

Sometimes Naomi and I went on adventures to the many antique stores near us.

I found a tin container from the Num Num Potato Chip factory.

Naomi found a dolly just like the dolly she had when she was a little girl.

I found an old Rocky Colavito card.

Naomi found a crystal Blessed Virgin Mary statue.

I found a souvenir knife from Niagara Falls, the same kind of souvenir knife with a Mountie on it that my father bought me when we visited Niagara Falls.

Except for Gerry Messerman and his wife, Gale, and Naomi's family, we saw few people. I couldn't talk very well. I couldn't handle being in a setting where people smoked and drank. My life, I realized, bored people. Nobody wanted to hear about cancer. Nobody wanted to go through the nightmares of withdrawal. Nobody wanted to hear about God.

On the local Bainbridge radio station run by golden agers and high school kids, I heard "I'll Remember You" and remembered Guy singing it at our wedding. I suddenly missed Guy McElwaine's presence in my life so painfully that it was as though I'd cut into a wound.

George W. Bush was quoted as saying he believed in "prayer and exercise."

A lifelong liberal Democrat, I agreed with President Bush wholeheartedly. I, too, believed in prayer and exercise.

I had a new line now to replace the old one I had used whenever something went wrong: Hey, it ain't the refugee camps!

Hey, it ain't cancer!

John Law fell off the top of a shopping cart onto the hard cement of a parking lot . . . smashing his head on the pavement with a sickening "thunk" which Naomi and I will never forget. We rushed him to a hospital only a block away. He was *fein*.

Joey fell headfirst off his bicycle onto the blacktop at the end of our driveway without a helmet. His eyes were black and blue and so was much of his body. We took him to the hospital. He was *fein*.

Steve fell between first and second base during a softball game in Portland, Oregon. He suffered a badly broken leg, needed major surgery, and screws put into a bone. For a while he was in a wheelchair and then on crutches and then he limped . . . and then he was *fein*.

Suzi was sideswiped by a speeding driver in Mill Valley, California. She was seriously hurt. She had to go through extensive physical therapy . . . and she was *fein*.

God is good!

It seemed sort of perfect that Bainbridge Township, where we lived, was part of a village called Chagrin Falls . . . a place where chagrin *fell* . . . so very far away now from Point Doom.

I dreamed I was smoking again. I felt horrible in my dream. I felt like I'd betrayed myself and Naomi and the boys and Steve and Suzi.

Eighteen months after my surgery, keeping my promise to God, I wrote an article for the Op-Ed section of the *New York Times* revealing that I had throat cancer and begging Hollywood not to make movies showing smoking on-screen.

I took the blame for the many smoking scenes I had written in my movies.

I did the *Today* show and CNN's Paula Zahn and, later, *Hardball with Chris*

Matthews talking about Hollywood's moral responsibility not to show smoking on-screen.

That interview I did for the *Today* show was the first interview I'd ever done stone-cold sober.

I said a prayer before I went on—instead of slugging from an Evian bottle filled with gin.

The prayer worked. I felt calm and articulate.

While I was speaking to Paula Zahn, a crawl at the bottom of the screen said, "Has throat cancer . . . speaks with difficulty" so people wouldn't think there was something wrong with their TV sets.

"Smoking was an integral part of many of my screenplays because I was a militant smoker," I wrote in the *New York Times*. "I have been an accomplice to the murders of untold numbers of human beings. . . .

So I say to my colleagues in Hollywood: What we are doing by showing larger-than-life movie stars smoking on-screen is glamorizing smoking. What we are doing by glamorizing smoking is unconscionable.

Hollywood films have long championed civil rights and gay rights and commonly call for an end to racism and intolerance. Hollywood films espouse a belief in goodness and redemption. Yet we are the advertising agency and sales force for an industry that kills nearly ten thousand people daily.

A cigarette in the hands of a Hollywood star on-screen is a gun aimed at a twelve- or fourteen-year old. The gun will go off when that kid is an adult.

We in Hollywood know the gun will go off, yet we hide behind the smoke screen of phrases like "creative freedom" and "artistic expression." Those lofty words are lies designed, at best, to obscure laziness.

I know. I have told those lies. The truth is that there are a thousand better and more original ways to reveal a character's personality.

Screenwriters know, too, that some movie stars are more likely to play a part if they can smoke—because they are so addicted to smoking that they have difficulty stopping even during the shooting of a scene. The screenwriter writing smoking scenes for the smoking star is part of a vicious and deadly circle.

My hands are bloody; so are Hollywood's. My cancer has caused me

to attempt to cleanse mine. I don't wish my fate upon anyone in
Hollywood, but I beg that Hollywood stop imposing it upon millions
of others.

The *Plain Dealer* reprinted my *New York Times* article and a lot of people
came up to me in church and whispered, "I'm praying for you."
I thanked them all and told them I needed their prayers.

While I got many phone calls from friends in L.A. concerned about my health,
collective Hollywood met my proposal to ban smoking on-screen with resound-
ing silence.

Naomi and I went out to L.A. for the first time since we'd left and I asked
studio executives and producers why the studios kept showing smoking on-
screen when statistics indicated, for example, that more and more young women
were smoking while the cancer rate for women smokers was skyrocketing.

The big reason, I discovered, was movie stars. Many movie stars smoked.
Many of them were so addicted that they wanted to smoke on-screen. They
didn't care about influencing kids to smoke. They cared about satisfying their
cravings.

The studios all wanted to work with movie stars. They weren't about to tell
stars they couldn't smoke on-screen for fear the stars would do other movies for
other studios.

I saw Guy McElwaine on that trip. I asked him to forgive me for firing him. I
told him it was the biggest mistake I'd made in Hollywood.

Guy said, "You know I'll always love ya."

Straight men in Hollywood who love each other always say it that way:
"*ya*" . . . never "you."

Guy was back in a big office at a big, successful production company called Morgan Creek, where he was the number two man. He looked sensational. He was
nearing seventy and still a *player,*, defying all the clichés about Hollywood being
a young person's town. Guy was reading scripts now with Brad and Leo and
Cruise in mind . . . as he had once read them with Yul and Sellers and Burt in
mind. He wore a gold ring emblazoned with the Sinatra family crest, given by the
Sinatra family only to family members and their closest friends. Frank was dead,
but inside Guy's heart Frank (and a golden era in Hollywood) would never die.

I saw Irwin Winkler, too, and we agreed to work together on an idea he had: a
movie based on the Mariah Carey–Tommy Mottola relationship based on the
old classic movie written by Emeric Pressburger called *The Red Shoes.*

I loved seeing Irwin but when I got home I lost interest in writing the script. I was fighting cancer and cigarettes and alcohol . . . and I just couldn't stay interested in Mariah Carey and Tommy Mottola.

Naomi and I saw Billy Friedkin and Sherry Lansing for dinner at a place where they bought us $150 plates of white truffle pasta.

I was telling Sherry what I'd been through . . . about hallucinating that Billy was in the step-down room at the clinic getting his throat suctioned . . . and Mike Myers was suddenly at our table and Sherry was introducing me to him not as a screenwriter but as a cancer survivor.

Mike went into his Austin Powers shtick and everybody laughed . . . except the cancer survivor, who was watching Billy Friedkin, the man who'd lied into his face and whose lies had cost Paramount millions of dollars.

Watching him, the cancer survivor suddenly imagined that Billy Friedkin was wearing a toupee. The cancer survivor laughed then, too, but not at Mike Myers as Austin Powers.

There were lots of hugs and kisses between Billy and Sherry and Naomi and me as we got into our cars.

Sherry said, "Call us when you come into town, honey. Let's do it again!"

Billy looked at me and said, "You know, I'm not at all sure I like the new you."

I said, "You never liked the *old* me, either," and Billy Friedkin laughed.

I called Arnold Rifkin. I wanted to see him to tell him personally that I had treated him badly and that I regretted it.

His secretary, very friendly, said she'd put him right on. Then she came back after a long wait and said Arnold would have to call me back.

But Arnold never did.

Right back at me, even after he knew I had cancer.

We went to see Evans at his house. Maybe he looked a little more frail, but nothing else had changed. The same bimbos were there. Evans and Naomi and I laughed and hugged each other.

As we talked, Evans noted that he and I sounded alike now.

"You're the only man in the world who sounds like me," Evans said.

I think he meant it as a great compliment.

"Bob," I said, "the cancer wards are filled with guys who sound like us."

I could tell by the look on his face that he thought I was making a bad joke.

"Bob," I said, "they had to *cut my throat* to get me to sound like you."

Evans stared at me a moment and then he said, "*Heh heh heh.*"

Evans reenacted the strokes he'd suffered—he actually *fell to the floor*—

literally *fell*—twice. He wanted me to write a book with him about improving vocabulary by using five new words each day.

We kept hugging before we left. We didn't want to let each other go.

As we were getting into our car, Evans ran back into the house to get something. He handed me a bunch of bumper stickers.

We hugged again and then Evans and I kissed. Like devils. On the lips.

And then we cackled.

Naomi and I went back home to Bainbridge Township, happy to be home, happy to have been *visiting* L.A.

When we got home, the Writers Guild's monthly magazine was waiting for me in the mail. On its cover was a screenwriter smoking a cigarette.

Not much later, the *New York Times*, in its coverage of the Sundance Film Festival, noted that what most of the films had in common was that many of the actors in them were smoking.

When we got home to Bainbridge Township, I took the bumper stickers Evans had given me and put them on our pickup and Suburban.

Each bumper sticker had a picture of Evans and each bumper sticker said something different:

"OMISSION ISN'T LYING."

"ONCE BRANDED, ALWAYS BRANDED."

BEWARE . . . I'M DANGEROUS."

"PARTING IS SUCH GREAT JOY."

"I BRAKE FOR ROBERT EVANS."

I had another dream: Naomi and I were back in the house on Birdview Avenue in Malibu and I was drinking and smoking. We were listening to Renzo Arbore and his orchestra on our boom box.

I was enjoying myself and telling her about an awful nightmare I'd had. I dreamed that we'd moved to Cleveland and that I had cancer of the throat.

I got sixteen letters from people who'd read my *New York Times* piece and were writing to tell me they'd stopped smoking as a result.

My *New York Times* piece and my TV appearances didn't appear to have achieved anything.

But I had made a promise to God. So, a month later, in *Daily Variety*, I wrote a piece attacking movie stars for their irresponsibility and hubris.

That didn't achieve anything either. Maybe I was wasting my breath. But I knew I'd never stop. How can you renege on a promise to God?

. . .

A producer flew from L.A. to talk to me about a script. I took him down to Jacobs Field. He sat there with his cellular ringing and his headset on, watching the Indians lose. He hurried back to L.A.

I wrote two anti-smoking public service messages I would appear in. We needed a director to film it.

Somebody mentioned Paul Verhoeven.

I laughed.

Sure: the perfect way for Paul and me to follow *Basic Instinct* and *Showgirls:* my croaky voice talking about cancer.

One public service message said:

"I used to think smoking was so cool, so hip, so rock and roll. Then I got throat cancer. Cancer isn't cool, hip, or rock and roll. Cancer hurts. Cancer makes you cry. And then it kills you. Please—don't smoke."

The other public service message said:

"Hello. My name is Joe Eszterhas. I'm a screenwriter. I always glamorized smoking in my movies. I thought smoking was cool. Then I got throat cancer. Maybe that's my punishment. Please—don't let Hollywood sucker you into smoking. Please—don't let people like me kill you. Don't smoke."

Looking at my throat during the next exam, Marshall Strome said: "Your tissue can't possibly look better and be healthier than it is. Now I'll say it officially. I've never seen this in all my years of practice. This is a triumph of lifestyle . . . or *something* . . . over cancer. It's *miraculous!*"

I was finally able to listen to my old favorite music again. It happened with Bruce Springsteen. As I stood listening to his new CD, I didn't feel like having a drink or a cigarette. I felt like a jolt of oxygen was coursing through me.

I saw an old whistle at a flea market and bought it, polished it up, and put it around my neck.

Now I could yell at my kids again, yell not to go too close to the lake and the pond, not to go too fast on their bikes. My old whistle did the yelling for me.

I hardly took my old whistle off . . . just in case my whistle and I had to yell at one of the boys.

For some reason, I got a big kick out of driving to Bob Evans's Restaurant for lunch in Solon, Ohio . . . in a pickup truck with a bumper sticker that said, "I BRAKE FOR ROBERT EVANS."

. . .

At a Little League game, another father stopped me and said, "Excuse me, aren't you the famous writer?"

I heard Looey Bromfield saying "I used to be" and saw him walking away.

But I said, "I'm the writer all right."

The other father grinned and said, "What are you writing?"

I told him I'd been sick.

"I heard that," he said. "But you gotta keep writing, okay? Keep writing, cause . . . we like that stuff, you know?"

He winked at me and walked away.

I laughed.

Here in the heartland. At a Little League field, the tabernacle of family values. And they . . . *like that stuff,* you know? Wink wink.

I made a button game for the boys like the one my father had made me.

And Joey and Nick and I played soccer with the buttons on the big green board every night.

Joey got good enough to beat me pretty soon, just like I'd gotten good enough to beat my father pretty soon after I'd started playing with him.

The boys liked the game so much that six months later they were still begging me to play it with them each night.

I realized that while I had kept them from meeting my father . . . my father had indirectly given them the best gift they'd ever gotten.

The hard rubber grip around my throat loosened to elastic.

Naomi and I were walking together one day and an airliner on its way to the airport flew low over us.

I stopped and waved at the plane.

"We have become my audience," I told Naomi. "We are the fly-over people."

Naomi and I started going to movies. I wasn't consumed now with the cigarette I was going to have as soon as the movie ended. My Evian bottle wasn't half full with gin. I ate popcorn and sometimes even Raisinettes and I drank pink lemonade.

And I realized that I was having fun going to the movies again.

Sometimes somebody from my Hollywood life would come to Cleveland for an appearance—Whoopi or Jon Bon Jovi or Richard Jeni or Spike Lee or Richard Dreyfuss or Jeff Daniels—and I'd think about calling them to say—"Hey, you're here, let's have lunch and catch up."

But then I'd think—catch up on what? Traches? Feeding tubes? Antioxidants? Regenerating tissue?

Over drinks maybe at Johnny's Downtown?
In the smoking section?

I woke up one night and something told me that I should say a prayer for Gerri.
I included her after that night in my daily prayers.

I was reading a lot about the real, historical Jesus. I knew that Paul Verhoeven
was a member of the biblical and historical study group called the Jesus Seminar
and attended its meetings every year.

I knew that Paul was fascinated by Jesus.

And I had this thought: What if, with my new interest in Jesus, Paul and I collaborated on a film about the historical Jesus? What a way to follow *Basic Instinct*
and *Showgirls*! I suddenly wondered what rating our Jesus movie would be.

Sometime in the future, I resolved, when I felt stronger, I'd talk to Paul
about it.

Shortly after *Showgirls*, Gloria Steinem and I had had a meeting about doing a
movie about the young Marilyn Monroe.

I took the idea to Paul and he'd turned it down.

The media had a lot of fun with it, though: Gloria Steinem producing a
movie done by the *Showgirls* guys.

This, of course, would be even more sensational news: *Jesus* in the hands of
the *Showgirls* guys.

I never went anywhere without a cross. I noticed, though, that Ozzy Osbourne
wore a cross all the time, as did fellow Clevelander, boxing promoter, and former numbers king . . . Don King. Most gangsta rappers and Hollywood starlets
wore crosses, too.

I remembered one of those bimbos in Vegas pointing out to me that Paul Verhoeven was wearing a watch with Jesus' likeness on its face.

Now I was sometimes wearing a ring with a crucifix on it.

Although, at times, I wore a ring that was a black heart on my other hand.

I kept my black heart ring on my left hand. Underneath it was my wedding
band, inscribed "Naomi." Above it was my father's wedding band, inscribed
"Mária."

Naomi had a matching black heart ring which I'd bought her.

The Ladies' Auxiliary at Holy Angels Church made me a get-well prayer quilt
which I framed and put up on the wall, not far from my *Basic Instinct* and *Showgirls* posters.

. . .

Steve hadn't had a cigarette in more than two years. He'd devised a system for himself that worked: he ate spicy food to ease his cravings and chewed ice gum a lot.

If my son didn't smoke another cigarette for the rest of his life, then my entire travail had been worth it.

Even though I hadn't smoked a cigarette or had a drink in nearly two years, I didn't believe that I had beaten either addiction.

I was fully aware of the inestimable power of alcohol and nicotine and tobacco. I was a recovering smoker and a recovering alcoholic and prayed that I would be that until my dying day.

I had become obsessed by my five-mile walks. I needed the little buzzing high at the end of them. I needed to feel the rush of air through my maimed larynx and my lungs. I needed it as badly as I'd needed a cigarette or a drink in the past.

And I got it . . . I gave it to myself every day, without fail, when it was 97 degrees and when it was eight below zero.

I sucked that air in and breathed it as deeply as I could and experienced the profound joy of being alive.

I dreaded getting a cold. Phlegm piled up in my throat and bronchial area. I'd have to work until I was exhausted each morning to cough everything up so I could breathe normally.

With 80 percent of my larynx gone, coughing is heavy labor.

I was still as addicted as I was before, but to different things: to fresh air, freshly made carrot juice, ruby red grapefruit juice, organic cranberry juice, lime yogurt, fresh cauliflower and broccoflower, fresh corn, Roma tomatoes, watermelon, cantaloupe, pomegranate, and bananas . . . to life, no longer to death.

On the first day of spring, I watched Joey, Nick, and John Law burst barefoot out the front door to ride their bikes. The screen door didn't slam until they were halfway down the driveway.

On the second anniversary of my surgery, I called Marshall Strome to tell him that I wanted to raise a tall glass of cranberry juice in his honor.

"Thank you," he said, "but raise it in yours. I can tell you now that when you told us you'd stop smoking and drinking, none of us believed you."

. . .

I rubbed Naomi's feet and sang "Volare" for her. I sounded like a punk rocker imitating a karaoke-bar drunk imitating Johnny Cash. I sounded like the Creature from the Black Lagoon. I sounded like Robert Evans!

To celebrate my second anniversary, we took the boys to an Amish restaurant where we ate country-fried chicken, drank lemonade, and watched the horse-and-buggies go by.

I watched an old Amish man in a straw hat walking to his buggy and when he got there he turned and looked right at me and smiled.

He looked just like my father.

I froze and he got into the buggy.

I turned away and there was Luke smiling and looking at me with my father's slate-blue eyes.

I smiled back at Luke, ruffled his hair, and kissed his eyes.

"Why is Dada crying?" Joey asked.

"Allergies," Naomi said.

We all went to the cemetery a week later, stood at my father's and mother's graves, and said the Lord's Prayer. Even Luke jibber-jabbered along.

Then we stood there quietly for a long moment and I said in Hungarian to my father: "I love you, Pop."

And: "Thanks for everything, Pop."

And: "I forgive you, Pop."

And: "I *think*."

Driving away from the cemetery, I thought: You don't belong here anyway, Pop, in the America that I love. You belong in that Jew-hating old country that you loved so much.

The next day I called the consulate of Hungary and asked them what it took to disinter a body here and send it to Hungary for reburial.

The fact that I was going to send my father's body back to Hungary and doing what he wanted me to do . . . didn't mean that *blood is thicker than spilled blood.*

But maybe it meant that love is more powerful than hate.

In my head I heard Father John Mundweil say to me: "You're doing it because you love him and because you finally forgave him. Enough already! Forget about ambiguity! This isn't one of your unsatisfying movie endings!"

Wherever my father was, he'd be with us in Luke's slate-blue eyes. At the age of two, Luke was squat—with a fleshy torso and a bowling ball head. Naomi called him "Steffen" sometimes and he loved *hoadog.*

. . .

Good morning, God. Praise the Lord!

And hearing me say that, some will agree with Mark Twain that God is the last refuge of scoundrels.

My response is that many critics referred to Twain as "the devil's apprentice" and "the devil's disciple."

And what can the devil possibly know about God?

Or was Twain, too, talking about himself?

Ke sera sera, vatever vill be vill be! my father sang to himself sometimes.

Life is strange! . . . our wedding invitation said . . . *Life is amazing!*

ALSO BY JOE ESZTERHAS

*"Part tell-all, part fiction, part rant, part history. It's all
wicked and witty and hard to ignore."*
—The Denver Post

AMERICAN RHAPSODY

If the Watergate scandal was a previous generation's National
Nightmare, then maybe the Clinton scandal was our National
Wet Dream, and who better to narrate it than the screenwriter
Joe Eszterhas, whose credits include *Basic Instinct* and *Showgirls*,
and *Charlie Simpson's Apocalypse*, which was nominated for the
National Book Award. Taking full advantage of his considerable
journalistic and storytelling talents, Eszterhas gives us every fact,
rumor, and innuendo surrounding the president's foibles in the
context of late-century American politics and entertainment.
Here Washington and Hollywood do more than just flirt with
each other; they share the same bed. From scandalmongers Matt
Drudge (who began as a Hollywood gossip) and Ken Starr, to
would-be presidential paramours Sharon Stone and Barbara
Streisand, to his final unimpeachable witness, Willard—none
other than President Clinton's talking penis—Eszterhas gives us
the goods on the story that nobody could stop talking about and,
thanks to *American Rhapsody* , will be impossible to think about
the same way again.

Current Affairs/0-375-72554-7

VINTAGE BOOKS
Available at your local bookstore, or call toll-free to order:
1-800-793-2665 (credit cards only)